John Warwick Montgomery

Christ As Centre and Circumference

Christliche Philosophie heute
Christian Philosophy Today
Quomodo Philosophia Christianorum Hodie Estimatur
Band 13

Band 1
John Warwick Montgomery
Tractatus Logico-Theologicus

Band 2
John W. Montgomery
Hat die Weltgeschichte einen Sinn? Geschichtsphilosophien auf dem Prüfstand

Band 3
John W. Montgomery
Jésus: La raison rejoint l'histoire

Band 4
Horst Waldemar Beck
Marken dieses Äons: Wissenschaftskritische und theologische Diagnosen

Band 5
Ross Clifford
John Warwick Montgomery's Legal Apologetic: An Apologetic for All Seasons

Band 6
Thomas K. Johnson
Natural Law Ethics: An Evangelical Proposal

Band 7
Lydia Jaeger
Wissenschaft ohne Gott? Zum Verhältnis zwischen christlichem Glauben und Wissenschaft

Band 8
Thomas K. Johnson und Ron Kubsch
Herman Bavinck. Christliche Weltanschauung

Band 9
John Warwick Montgomery
La Mort De Dieu

Band 10
David Andersen
Martin Luther: The Problem of Faith and Reason A Reexamination in Light of the Epistemological and Christological Issues

Band 11
Wim Rietkerk
In dubio: Handbuch für Zweifler

Band 12
Patrick Werder
Wenig niedriger als Gott: Der Mensch als Person von der Antike bis zur Gegenwart

John Warwick Montgomery

CHRIST AS CENTRE AND CIRCUMFERENCE

Essays Theological, Cultural and Polemic

Christliche Philosophie heute

Christian Philosophy Today

Quomodo Philosophia
Christianorum Hodie Estimatur

Band 13

WIPF & STOCK · Eugene, Oregon

CHRIST AS CENTRE AND CIRCUMFERENCE
Essays Theological, Cultural, and Polemic

Copyright © 2012 John Warwick Montgomery. All rights reserved. Except for brief quotations in critical publications or reviews, no part of this book may be reproduced in any manner without prior written permission from the publisher. Write: Permissions, Wipf and Stock Publishers, 199 W. 8th Ave., Eugene, OR 97401.

This edition published by Wipf and Stock Publishers by arrangement with Verlag für Kultur und Wissenschaft.

Wipf & Stock
An imprint of Wipf and Stock Publishers
199 W. 8th Avenue, Suite 3
Eugene OR, 97401
www.wipfandstock.com

ISBN 13: 978-1-62032-519-3

Manufactured in the U.S.A.

A

Lanalee, Jean-Marie, Laurence, Sarah et
William Warwick Montgomery

Une famille nonpareille dont le chef est Christ

"We have redemption through his [Christ's] blood, even the forgiveness of sins: who is the image of the invisible God, the firstborn of every creature: for by him were all things created, that are in heaven, and that are in earth, visible and invisible, whether they be thrones, or dominions, or principalities, or powers: all things were created by him, and for him: and he is before all things, and by him all things consist."

—Colossians 1:14-17 (*A.V.*)

"Aller Dinge Grund und Ende ist sein eingeborner Sohn: daß sich alles zu ihm wende!"

—J. S. Bach, chorale *Die Himmel erzählen die Ehre Gottes* (BWV 76), based on Psalm 19

"Jésus-Christ est l'objet de tout et le centre où tout tend. Qui le connaît connaît la raison de toutes choses."

—Pascal, *Pensées*, No. 449

Do not separate your life from created reality

There are rare thinkers who exhibit such intellectual vitality that they do not merely add to the thought of an age but radically transform it. John Warwick Montgomery is such a thinker. By the middle of the twentieth century, theological liberalism and scientific materialism had become so entrenched among Western intellectuals that a robust Christian theism no longer seemed tenable. Serious Christian thinkers saw themselves as needing to accommodate secular thought at every turn. Yet rather than preserve faith, this strategy of accommodation led to its steady erosion. By the 1960s, one would be hard-pressed to find a theologian at a mainstream seminary or divinity school who did not hide behind metaphor to deny the biblical miracles or invoke advances in philosophy to question core Christian doctrines. Intellectual integrity seemed to require abandoning Christian orthodoxy.

Enter John Warwick Montgomery. Bursting on the intellectual scene of the 1960s like a meteor, he was a theologian with an attitude. Christian orthodoxy was for him not just true. Nor was it merely defensible, as though it were but one among many credible intellectual options. For Montgomery, Christian orthodoxy could be and needed to be vindicated. And with unstoppable energy he was going to make that happen. Not only did he begin a furious publication schedule but he also took his assault on secularism as well as the vindication of Christian orthodoxy right into the belly of the beast—to the highest levels of an academy that had spurned Christianity.

In our day, when debates in academic venues between evangelical Christians and secular thinkers are common fare, to characterize Montgomery's engagement of secularism in such revolutionary terms may sound overblown. But if we think that, we forget that such debates are now common fare precisely because of Montgomery. He blazed the trail. Things only seem easy in retrospect. It took Montgomery to get in there and mix it up with the theologians who proclaimed that God is dead or with the philosophers who embraced situation ethics and its underlying moral relativism.

Montgomery, as a Lutheran theologian, enjoys the plain speaking of Martin Luther. In debating situation ethics, for instance, he could analyze its philosophical problems as well as anyone. But in debating situation ethicists before a live audience, he would also point out that situation ethics places no premium on truth, with the result that situation ethicists are "morally obligated" to lie to their audience if the situation demands it. So why should the audience trust anything his interlocutor was saying at this moment?

Such in-your-face challenges by Montgomery did not endear him to the academy's wine-and-cheese intellectuals who prefer collegiality to honesty and respectability to honor. But Montgomery decided early in his career that Dale Carnegie's approach to winning friends and influencing people was inadequate for handling the theological disarray of his time. Stronger medicine was required. Notwithstanding, anyone who knows Montgomery recognizes in him a lover of life and people. If he stepped on toes, it's because toes needed stepping on. If people got angry with him, it's because they were covering up things that he was rightly exposing. Montgomery epitomizes Terence's dictum Homo sum humani a me nihil alienum puto (Nothing human is alien to me). Moreover, for Montgomery, Christianity is the key to humanity's full flowering. Thus, when people saw the tough side of Montgomery in vindicating Christianity, it was because he saw false ideologies as suffocating the human spirit and needing to be debunked. We might say that Montgomery's apologetics consisted of opening windows in stuffy deoxygenated rooms.

Thus we find that Montgomery is a world-renowned man of law and practices at some of the highest courts in the world. At the same time, he has a longstanding ministry of research, academic teaching, and writing. It's hard to believe that one and the same man could achieve in two worlds what others typically do not reach in one. After having published four of Professor Montgomery's books in German, English and French, representing but a sampling of his academic breadth and productivity, the Verlag für Kultur und Wissenschaft is gratified that with this book we may make a considerable number of Montgomery's really important essays and articles available, especially since many of these have never have been published or are difficult to access.

As for the volume in hand, it is a truly remarkable collection, the only overlap with the author's first such collection (The Suicide of Christian Theology) being the seminal essay in Part Two, "The Theologian's Craft"—a treatise deserving to be read by every generation of serious theologians and students of classical Christian theology. The present work contains a considerable number of original, biblically faithful arguments for the truth of the faith once delivered to the saints, several of which involve sophisticated legal reasoning (Parts One, Three, and Four); analyses of central topics in dogmatics and the social application of the gospel (Parts Five and Eight); fascinating excursions into Reformation history (Part Six); discussions of vital literary and aesthetic issues (Part Seven)—and, if this were not enough, numerous short treatments of contemporary problem areas (Part Nine), together with a concluding mini-encyclopedia of theological, legal, and cultural subjects. In a word, this book contains something for everyone. The reader can take it up and put it down as time permits, but the likelihood is that he or she will be drawn like a moth to a beneficent flame so as to find it almost impossible to set aside. Seldom has a collection of Christian essays been of greater importance.

Thomas Schirrmacher

Contents

Introduction 13
Acknowledgments 14

Part One: **A General Perspective** 17
Speculation vs. Factuality: An Analysis of
Modern Unbelief and a Suggested Corrective 18

Part Two: **Science and the Faith** 39
1. The Theologian's Craft: A Discussion of
   Theory Formation and Theory Testing in Theology 40
2. Computer Origins and the Defense of the Faith 78
3. God at University College Dublin 104
4. Dawkins' Irrationality 110

Part Three: **Apologetics Per Se** 113
1. A Short History of Apologetics 114
2. Apologetics for the 21st Century 126
3. The Holy Spirit and the Defence of the Faith 138
4. Christian Apologetics in the Light
   of the Lutheran Confessions 147
5. Pain in Theological Perspective 164

Part Four: **Legal Evidence,
Resurrection and Human Rights** 173
1. Legal Evidence for the Truth of the Faith 174
2. A New Approach to the Apologetic for Christ's Resurrection
   by way of Wigmore's Juridical Analysis of Evidence 182
3. The Need for Epistemological Sophistication
   in Human Rights Teaching 194
4. The Rights of Unborn Children 210

Part Five: **A Bit of Systematic Theology** 243
1. Did Christ Die for E.T. as well as for *Homo Sapiens?*................................. 244
2. The Freewill Issue in Theological Perspective 270
3. Some Remarks on Punishment and Freewill
   in Legal Theory & Classical Christian Theology 278
4. Legal Hermeneutics and the Interpretation of Scripture....................... 286

Part Six: **Reformation Heritage**..297
1. The Celebration of the Lord's Supper according to
   Calvin: A Study of His Genevan Rite of 1542 (etc.)....................................298
2. The Life of Paul Luther, Physician..314
3. John Gerhard: Theology and Devotion 328
4. Chemnitz on the Council of Trent: An Evaluation
   of Chemnitz's *Examen Concilii Tridentini* 352
5. An Historical Study of the *"Dignus Est Agnus"* Canticle...........................373
6. Robert Preus (1924-1995) 383

Part Seven: **Literature and the
Aesthetic in Christ's Service**...387
1. Chesterton the Apologist 388
2. Tolkien: Lord of the Occult?...393
3. Christianity and Rosicrucianism 400
4. Transcendental Gastronomy 415

Part Eight: **The Impact of the Gospel**.. 419
1. Slavery, Human Dignity and Human Rights..420
2. C. T. Studd... 440
3. Life Can Be Difficult If You Are Bessarabian Orthodox 457

Part Nine: **Letters from Europe** 497
1. The Strange Decline of American Evangelicalism...................................498
2. Eugen Drewermann's Trivialization of Theology 501
3. The Bishop and the Muslims..503
4. A New Archbishop of Canterbury..505

5. Trust Me?..507
6. Anglican Priestesses..509
7. Can a Scientist Pray?..511
8. Did Jesus Exist?..513
9. When Is a Jew Not a Jew?..516
10. Feminism and Theology 518
11. New Light on the Abortion Controversy? 520
12. Fido in Heaven? 523
13. Lessons from the Amish 525
14. The Virgin Birth: A Problem?..528
15. Je*sus in the Dic*tion*ar*y 530
16. So Much for Hell and the Second Coming 533
17. Dracula or Jesus?..535
18. On the Reliability of the Four Gospels 537
19. Philosophy Revisited 540
20. Back to the Sixties 543
21. The Religion of Doctor Johnson...545
22. The Famous in France: Why They Believe............................547
23. The Idea of Empire and a Christian Renaissance..................550
24. Jesus and the Bell Curve 552
25. Will the True Biblical Scholar Please Stand Up? 555
26. On Becoming a French *Avocat*..557
27. Passion Play Problems...562
28. Religious "Irrationality" and Civil Liberties...........................565
29. Christianity's Unique Intellectual Opportunity 568

Part Ten: **A Mini-Encyclopedia** 571
1. Law..572
2. Human Rights...585
3. Blasphemy 595
4. Canon Law..596
5. Capital Punishment..599

6. Divorce 600
7. Euthanasia 602
8. Existentialist Theology 604
9. Inerrancy of the Bible 605
10. Kenosis 607
11. Llull, Ramon 608
12. Natural Theology 609
13. Neo-Orthodox Theology 610
14. Oberammergau 612
15. Process Theology 613
16. Prophecy 615
17. Schweitzer, Albert 617
18. Trinity 619
19. Truth 622
20. Vaughan Williams, Ralph 623

Index of Names 625

Introduction

The Worshipful Company of Scriveners is one of the City of London's Livery Companies (gilds founded in the Middle Ages). Their Grace before Meat begins:

> God bless this food upon our board
> And may Thy name be aye adored.
> We thank Thee for Thy gifts assured
> By death and resurrection of our Lord.

As a liveryman of the Scriveners', I recently attended a lunch for the Lord Mayor of London at the Mansion House, and was seated next to the Head of International Investment Banking for Goldman Sachs. This gentleman had received his undergraduate degree and his Ph.D. in economics at Harvard University and we naturally got onto the subject of the predictive value of economic theories. I expressed the opinion that the area was roughly equivalent to an occult science. He agreed one hundred per cent and said that for this reason he had gone into banking rather than into theoretical economics. (Considering Goldman Sachs' recent difficulties, one might wonder if this was in fact the wisest possible decision, but that is another matter!)

Unlike economic theory, classic Christian theology is solidly based in fact —historical fact, empirical reality, and the kind of evidences that stand up in courts of law. The essays and articles collected in the present volume all attest to this. They also endeavour to show how relevant the faith once delivered to the saints is to issues of contemporary life and thought.

Forty years ago (*tempus* does indeed *fugit*!), I prepared a similar collection under the title, *The Suicide of Christian Theology*. The liberal theologies critiqued in that volume have, typically, gone the way of all flesh, and the Christianity of the historic creeds remains as vital as ever. The present book should provide further ground for affirming that Jesus Christ is indeed the same "yesterday, today and forever"—and that the Holy Scriptures still "cannot be broken."

John Warwick Montgomery
Strasbourg, France
The Feast of Pentecost, 2010

Acknowledgments

A third of the essays in this book are being published here for the first time; the rest have appeared in journals, encyclopedias, or Festschriften and are thus not readily accessible. Many of the inclusions were presented at scholarly conferences around the globe and under the auspices of a variety of sponsoring organisations; information on those presentations appears with the articles themselves. Here we give only the bibliographical data on those articles which have been published previously, and we thank those publishers for their willingness to allow a wider impact for the material contained in them. Some essays have undergone minor revision for their appearance in this volume.

"Speculation vs. Factuality": *Bibliotheca Sacra*, January-March, 2011.

"The Theologian's Craft": *Concordia Theological Monthly*, February, 1966; *Journal of the American Scientific Affiliation*, September, 1966; *The Suicide of Christian Theology* (Minneapolis: Bethany, 1970), pp. 267-313. (N.B. This classic article has been pirated on the web on several occasions, but, interestingly enough, without the key diagram in the final section of the article—the absence of which renders the article almost incomprehensible.)

"Computer Origins and the Defense of the Faith": *Perspectives on Science and Christian Faith: Journal of the American Scientific Affiliation*, September, 2004.

"God at University College Dublin": *Modern Reformation*, January-February, 2009.

"Dawkins' Irrationality": *Global Journal of Classical Theology*, October, 2006.

"Apologetics for the 21st Century": *Reasons for Faith: A Survey of Contemporary Christian Issues and Evidences*, ed. C. Meister and N. Geisler (Wheaton, IL: Crossway, 2007).

"The Holy Spirit and the Defense of the Faith": *Bibliotheca Sacra*, October-December, 1997.

"The Apologetic Thrust of Lutheran Theology": *Lutheran Synod Quarterly*, Fall, 1970; *Ditt Ord är Sanning: En handbok om Bibeln*, ed. S. Erlandsson (Uppsala: Stiftelsen Biblicum, 1971) [in Swedish]; *Modern Reformation*, January/February, 1998 [abridged]; *Theologia et Apologia*, ed. A. S. Francisco, K. D. Maas, and S. P. Mueller (Eugene: OR: Wipf & Stock, 2007).

"Christian Apologetics in the Light of the Lutheran Confessions": *Concordia Theological Quarterly*, July, 1978.

"Pain in Theological Perspective": *Faith and Thought Bulletin* [Victoria Institute, U.K.], October, 2007.

"Legal Evidence for the Truth of the Faith": Revised version and conflation of *Law and Gospel: A Study Integrating Faith and Practice* (2^d ed.; Calgary, Alberta, Canada: Canadian Institute for Law, Theology and Public Policy, 1994), chap. 16 (in article form in *Modern Reformation*, March/April, 2006), and "Witnesses, Criteria for," *New Dictionary of Christian Apologetics*, ed. C. Campbell-Jack and G. J. McGrath (Leicester, England: Inter-Varsity Press, 2006). A shorter version of this article appeared in *Border Crossings: Festschrift for Irving Hexham*, ed. Ulrich van der Heyden and Andreas Feldtkeller (Stuttgart, Germany: Franz Steiner Verlag, 2008).

"The Rights of Unborn Children": *Simon Greenleaf Law Review*, Vol. 5 (1985-1986).

"Did Christ Die for E.T. as well as for *Homo Sapiens*?": *Faith and Thought Bulletin* [Victoria Institute, U.K.], October, 2004.

"The Freewill Issue in Theological Perspective" and "Some Remarks on Punishment and Freewill in Legal Theory & Classical Christian Theology": *Free Will in Criminal Law and Procedure: Proceedings of the 23rd and 24th IVR World Congress Kraków 2007 and Beijing 2009*, ed. Friedrich Toepel (Stuttgart, Germany: Franz Steiner Verlag, 2010).

"Legal Hermeneutics and the Interpretation of Scripture": *Evangelical Hermeneutics: Selected Essays from the 1994 Evangelical Theological Society Convention*, ed. M. Bauman and D. Hall (Camp Hill, PA: Christian Publications, 1995).

"The Life of Paul Luther, Physician": *Lutheran Forum*, Fall, 2004.

"John Gerhard: Theology and Devotion": *Not Omitting the Weightier Matters*; *Festschrift for Dr Robert Rodgers,* ed. K. Mathews (Belfast, Northern Ireland: Ambassador Publications, 2002).

"An Examination of Chemnitz's *Examen*": *Soli Deo Gloria: Essays in Reformed Theology*, ed. R. C. Sproul (Nutley, NJ: Presbyterian & Reformed, 1976).

"An Historical Study of the *Dignus Est Agnus* Canticle": *Concordia Theological Quarterly*, April, 2004.

"Robert Preus (1924-1995)": *Christian News*, December 12, 2005.

"Chesterton As Apologist": *Christian History*, Fall, 2002 [abridged and badly edited]; *Global Journal of Classical Theology*, June, 2003.

"Tolkien: Lord of the Occult?": *Light Beyond All Shadows: Religious Experience in the Work of J. R. R. Tolkien*, ed. Paul Kerry (Madison, NJ: Fairleigh Dickinson University Press, 2010).

"Transcendental Gastronomy": *Christianity Today*, November 22, 1974.

"Slavery, Human Dignity and Human Rights": *Evangelical Quarterly*, April, 2007; *Law & Justice: The Christian Law Review*, No. 158 (Hilary/Easter, 2007); *Human Rights—A Global Agenda*, ed. V. B. Malleswari (Punjagutta, Hyderabad, India: Icfai University Press/Amicus Books, 2007).

"Life Can Be Difficult If You Are Bessarabian Orthodox": *Law & Justice: The Christian Law Review*, No. 151 (Trinity/Michaelmas, 2003).

"Letters from Europe": contributions to the *New Oxford Review*, September, 1992-March, 1995; except for the articles "Anglican Priestesses" (*Christian News*, February 1, 1993), "Will the True Biblical Scholar Please Stand Up? (*Christian News*, March 27, 1995), "On Becoming a French *Avocat*" (*Amicus Curiae: Journal of the Society for Advanced Legal Studies* [U.K.], Winter, 2009), "Passion Play Problems" (*Christian News*, August 16, 2010, and "Religious 'Irrationality' and Civil Liberties" (*Amicus Curiae*, Summer, 2010).

"A Mini-Encyclopedia": contributions to the *Encyclopedia of Christian Civilization*, ed. G. T. Kurian (Oxford: Blackwell, 2011)—except for the first article ("Law"), included in *Omnibus 4: The Ancient World*, ed. Gene Edward Veith, et al. (Lancaster, PA: Veritas Press, 2009).

Part One
A General Perspective

Speculation vs. Factuality:
An Analysis of Modern Unbelief
and a Suggested Corrective*

"Any mental activity is easy if it need not take reality into account."
— Marcel Proust (*The Faber Book of Aphorisms*, ed. W. H. Auden)

We begin—and we shall end—with Sherlock Holmes: "Facts, facts, facts" insisted the Great Detective. "It is a capital mistake to theorize in advance of the facts."[1] "I can discover facts, but I cannot change them."[2] The theme of the present essay is remarkably simple, even though the arguments and illustrations supporting it are occasionally complex and difficult. It is this: modern unbelief departs from factual reality in favour of unsupportable speculation, leaving its advocates in a never-never land without hope either in this world or in the next.

Our examination of this theme will be restricted to the modern secular era—since the rise of modern secularism in the so-called 18th-century "Enlightenment." But speculation substituted for factuality did not begin there. An example: in the greatest debate among Protestant leaders during the Reformation period, the Marburg colloquy between Luther and Zwingli, the Swiss reformer argued that the whole Christ could not be present in the Eucharist, the Lord's Supper. Why? because (argued Zwingli) bodies can have only one location, and Christ had ascended into heaven, so that his body was located at the right hand of God. To this metaphysical speculation as to what Christ's body could or could not do, Luther responded simply by writing again and again in chalk on the table, *"Hoc est corpus meum"*—Christ's declaration as to the bread at the Last Supper, "This is my body."[3] In his writings, Luther was prone to assert that "metaphor is the Devil's tool."[4]

It is our contention (whether or not one agrees with Luther's Eucharistic position) that speculation has indeed been one of the Enemy's chief instruments in modern times. We shall survey the major areas of modern thought illustrating

---

* The Patrick Henry College Faith & Reason Lecture, Fall, 2010.
[1] From: *The Second Stain*. Cf. also Holmes's remarks in *A Scandal in Bohemia, A Study in Scarlet, The Copper Beaches,* and *Shoscombe Old Place*. In general, see John Warwick Montgomery, *The Transcendent Holmes* (Ashcroft, B.C., Canada: Calabash Press, 2000), p. 126.
[2] *The Problem of Thor Bridge*.
[3] See the scholarly reconstruction of the Marburg Colloquy by Herman Sasse: *This Is My Body* (Minneapolis: Augsburg, 1959).
[4] Cf. Montgomery, *Crisis in Lutheran Theology* (rev. ed.; Minneapolis: Bethany, 1973), I, 66-70.

this fact—the fields of philosophy, science, theology, literature, the arts, legal culture and society—and then endeavour to determine why speculation rules and what can be done to counteract it.

Areas of Modern Misery

Philosophy

Our first area for analysis is, naturally, that of philosophical thought—since it purports to be the most general and all-embracing field of scholarship.[5]

At the centre of what Thomas Paine termed the "Age of Reason" was the Deistic conviction that God, having created a perfect world, would never intervene to perform miracles, much less undergo an incarnation. David Hume asserted that it is always more probable that one reporting a miracle is a deceiver or mistaken than that the miracle actually occur—so it is a waste of time to investigate any miracle claim. What trumps miracle evidence is "uniform experience against the miraculous." Wrote Hume: "It is no miracle that a man, seemingly in good health, should die on a sudden. ... But it is a miracle, that a dead man should come to life; because that has never been observed in any age or country."[6] The problem with this speculative argument, to be sure, is the brute fact that at least one dead man returned to life has indeed been observed—in Palestine, during the days of the Roman Empire.[7] It will be noted that in the Humean argument speculative Reason is permitted—indeed, encouraged—to replace factual investigation.

The history of 19th-century German idealistic philosophy is the story of metaphysical speculation gone wild. Hegel is the most egregious example. He held that the *Weltgeist*—the immanent World Spirit of Reason—is moving humanity to higher and higher levels and would eventually produce a state of

---

[5] But what about library science? It also operates with maximal generality and is not subject to the criticisms which follow! See my essay, "Luther and Libraries," in my *In Defense of Martin Luther* (Milwaukee: Northwestern Publishing House, 1970).

[6] Hume, *Enquiries concerning the Human Understanding*, ed. L. A. Selby-Bigge (2d ed.; Oxford: Clarendon Press, 1902), sec. X ("Of Miracles"), pt. 1, p. 115. Cf. J. Earman, *Hume's Abject Failure: The Argument Against Miracles* (New York: Oxford University Press, 2000); David Johnson, *Hume, Holism, and Miracles* (Ithaca, NY: Cornell University Press, 1999).

[7] Not to mention the raising of Lazarus and a few remarkable dead coming back to life as mentioned in passing in the Book of Acts.

perfect freedom.[8] Kierkegaard rightly observed that such confidence in knowing the "essence" of the universe constitutes mere *hubris*, for no human being has the perspective to see the cosmic process in its totality. There is no way factually to justify such a viewpoint.

F. H. Bradley, the English Hegelian idealist, spoke along the same lines. Proclaimed Bradley: "The Absolute enters into, but is itself incapable of, evolution and progress."[9] How, precisely, could such a claim be justified? One is reminded of Woody Allen's comment in his hilarious essay, "My Philosophy": "Can we actually 'know' the universe? My God, it's hard enough finding your way around in Chinatown."[10]

Twentieth-century atheistic existentialism is often regarded as a corrective to German idealism. Epistemologically, however, it commits the same overarching fallacy of speculating without concern for evidential support. Heidegger: "What is to be investigated is being only and—*nothing else*. ... *Does the Nothing exist only because the Not, i.e., the Negation, exists? Or is it the other way around? ... What about this Nothing?—The Nothing itself nothings.*"[11]

We are told that we are entering a time of "metaphysical recovery" as a result of linguistic philosophy. If this means that cosmic speculation has been rehabilitated, that claim is very doubtful. The central issue remains: Does *ontology* (one's worldview) determine *epistemology* (the search for truth), or is it the reverse? In one sense, ontology is fundamental, since when one commits to a method of investigating the universe, one starts with the unprovable assumptions that the world exists, that I exist as an investigator, and that the inferential functions of the human mind (deduction, induction, abduction) are valid. But those who start with substantive metaphysical views as to the nature of the universe (Deistic "Reason," the Hegelian "World Spirit," existential "Angst," etc., etc.) are setting forth mutually incompatible and unprovable pictures of the universe.

Only if we start on a level playing field with others in an effort to discover what the universe is all about can we hope to arrive at truth. Facts need to determine the legitimacy or non-legitimacy of worldviews, not the reverse. The story

---

[8] See my *Where Is History Going? Essays in Support of the Historical Truth of Christian Revelation* (Minneapolis: Bethany, 1969), pp. 18-19; and my *The Shape of the Past: A Christian Response to Secular Philosophies of History* (2^d ed.; Minneapolis: Bethany, 1975), pp. 70-72.
[9] See my *Crisis in Lutheran Theology* (*op. cit*), I, 26-27.
[10] *The New Yorker*, December 17, 1969, pp. 25-26. See also Allen's recent and parallel masterpiece, "Thus Ate Zarathustra," *The New Yorker*, July 3, 2006.
[11] Cf. Rudolf Carnap's decimation of this argument in his "The Elimination of Metaphysics through Logical Analysis of Language," in *Logical Positivism*, ed. A. J. Ayer (Glencoe, IL: Free Press, 1959), pp. 69-73; the original German text was published in Vol. II of *Erkenntnis* (1932).

is told of Hegel that when a student objected, "But the facts disagree with your view," Hegel replied, "Then the facts be hanged!" The story is doubtless apocryphal (it is also told of Kant), but it well describes the staggering consequences of allowing metaphysics to swallow up an epistemological determination of the factual nature of things.[12]

Science

Close to philosophy lies the domain of cosmology. When at University College Dublin I debated atheistic cosmologist Sean Carroll, and Carroll was confronted by the implication of the Second Law of Thermodynamics that the universe must be finite (and must thus have been created), he responded that he was working on a repeal of the Second Law![13] This reminded me of T. S. Eliot's Macavity the Mystery Cat: "Macavity, Macavity, there's no one like Macavity, /He's broken every human law, he breaks the law of gravity." The fact of entropy did not compel Carroll, as it certainly should have done, to find a more satisfactory route than the eternal existence of the universe; he preferred utterly unsupported speculation.

Non-Christian cosmologists have also appealed to the notion of "multiverses"—arguing that our universe may be only one of many and that other universes may obey totally different laws (and thus, presumably, not be subject to the Second Law or the equivalent, and so not need a creator). However, multiverses are pure speculation. Even if such universes existed (for which there is not a shed of evidence), their "laws" would either be the same as ours, or, if not, we would be incapable of comprehending them anyway. And there would need to be a "multiverse generator" to account for all of them—which, again, would need to be governed by our physical laws or, if not, be entirely incomprehensible to us and therefore a nonsensical subject of discussion.[14] Atheist-turned-deist

---

[12] But can language represent the real nature of things? Willard van Orman Quine apparently did not think so (*Word & Object* [Cambridge, MA: M.I.T. Press, 1960], pp. 29 ff.): if a translator hears a native cry *"Gavagai!"* as a rabbit appears, this could mean the physical rabbit—but it could also mean "a rabbit is here momentarily"—or even just "the quality of rabbitness." So, allegedly, there is no inherent correlation between things and signification or between language and reality (cf. *Philosophie Magazine*, November, 2009, p. 75). But it should be obvious that such an argument does not eliminate factuality or objectivity: (1) what appears is a rabbit and not a hippopotamus; (2) the range of meaning of *"Gavagai!"* does not extend beyond rabbithood; (3) no one is questioning the factual existence of the rabbit, the native, or the translator.

[13] See my write-up of the debate: "God at University College Dublin," *Modern Reformation*, XVIII/1 (January-February 2009), 32-34, 43, and reprinted in the present volume.

[14] Cf. Jeff Zweerink, *Who's Afraid of the Multiverse?* (Glendora, CA: Reasons to Believe, 2009), *passim*. Sadly, Stephen Hawking has succumbed to multiverse illogic, recently claiming that since

Antony Flew put it this way: the multiverse speculations are little more than "escape routes ... to preserve the nontheist status quo."[15] One is reminded of what physicist Wolfgang Pauli wrote in the margin of a colleague's paper: "This isn't right; it isn't even wrong."

And then we come to secular endeavours to deep-six intelligent design—in spite of the impressive scientific evidence marshaled in its behalf. Orthodox evolutionism admits that there is no such thing as a single missing link and that there is no way ever to provide such. And full-blown evolutionary theory depends on unlimited time periods for the required developments and transitions to occur—yet time is not a causal concept: mere passage of time cannot bring about event x rather than events y or z. Given infinite time, anything can theoretically occur—including proof of the falsity of Dawkins' *Blind Watchmaker* scenario! "Huxley's notion that monkeys typing at random long enough will eventually produce literature ('the works of Shakespeare') has been tested at Plymouth University, England: over time, the monkeys (1) attacked the computer, (2) urinated on it, and (3) failed to produce a single word (AP dispatch, 9 May 2003)."[16]

Another stimulating example of the pervasiveness of speculation versus factuality lies in recent attempts to understand computers as "minds." John Searle, in his celebrated Chinese Room Argument, argues against what he calls "strong Artificial Intelligence"—the claim that an appropriately programmed computer has cognitive states such as understanding and is therefore necessarily a mind. The strong AI advocate counters that even if at the present computers do not appear to have arrived at the point of mind, all that is needed is to add something to them to achieve this: "one needs only find out what necessary additional properties come with what sorts of programs, and then on the basis of that knowledge design the Right Program that could not be run without producing mental states." Searle quite rightly replies to this idea of brain simulation that "our current knowledge of the brain does not give us any clue as to what to simulate, and the hypothetical future knowledge might turn out to exclude the possibility of computational simulation." This response is right-on-the-money, since the entire strong AI position is based on nothing but pure speculation. Searle's own position of biological naturalism seems in ten-

---

there are a vast number of possible universes, some (including ours) would simply by chance have the properties needed for the existence of life. Indeed, "spontaneous creation is the reason there is something rather than nothing, why the universe exists, why we exist. It is not necessary to invoke God to light the blue touch paper and set the universe going" (Stephen Hawking and Leonard Miodinow, *The Grand Design* (New York: Bantam, 2010), p. 180.
[15] Antony Flew and R. A. Varghese, *There Is a God* (New York: HarperOne, 2008), p. 137.
[16] Montgomery, *Tractatus Logico-Theologicus* (4th ed.; Bonn, Germany: Verlag für Kultur und Wissenschaft, 2009), para. 3.86111.

sion with his eminently sound assertion that "anything else that caused minds would have to have causal powers at least equivalent to those of the brain."[17] Following this factual route, one would appear to arrive at a rational Source of human rationality, i.e., an Intelligent Designer.

So far does modern thinking move from the realm of factuality that attempts have even been made to argue that scientific activity is really not the product of factual investigation of the nature of things but the result of the metaphysical presuppositions, commitments, and *Weltanschauung* of the scientist. The most prominent example of this is the celebrated "Kuhn thesis": Thomas Kuhn's argument[18] that one major scientific paradigm replaces another because of a shift in metaphysical orientation — not because increased factual knowledge leads to a better understanding of things. Now, one grants that changes in the ideological climate may contribute to movements in scientific theory, and questionable scientific notions can arise or succeed due to the *Zeitgeist* (evolutionary theory was readily accepted because of the 19th century myth of inevitable Progress). But good science moves from one paradigm to another as a result of "crucial experiments" — as Einstein's special theory of relativity, which reduced Newtonian physics to a special case within relativity theory, was ultimately accepted when the Michelson-Morley experiment put paid to the belief in an "ether" as a universal medium for the transmission of electromagnetic waves.

Where the subject-object distinction is discarded or weakened, meaningful scientific investigation disappears. "Bohr has emphasized the fact that the observer and his instruments must be presupposed in any investigation, so that the instruments are not part of the phenomenon described but are used."[19] One thinks of humorist Robert Benchley's story of his (anything but scientific) experience in his college biology course: he spent the term carefully drawing the image of his own eyelash as it fell across the microscopic field. And one recalls the suspicion that Italian astronomer Schiaparelli's Martian *"canali"* were in part the result of incipient cataract in his own eye.

Pace some philosophers of science, the Heisenberg Indeterminacy Principle does not break the subject-object distinction, since any possibility of the validity of that Principle requires presupposing the subject-object distinction. Were

---

[17] See the valuable discussion in Josef Moural, "The Chinese Room Argument": *John Searle*, ed. Barry Smith (Cambridge: Cambridge University Press, 2003), pp. 214-60.
[18] Thomas Kuhn, *The Structure of Scientific Revolutions* (3d ed.; Chicago: University of Chicago Press, 1996). The literature on the Kuhn thesis and its difficulties is considerable.
[19] Victor F. Lenzen, *Procedures of Empirical Science* ("International Encyclopedia of Unified Science," I/5; Chicago: University of Chicago Press, 1938), p. 28.

Heisenberg himself interlocked with his data, his formulation of the Principle would not necessarily reflect physical reality but rather Heisenberg's personal perspective on the world.

Polanyi's position in this regard is not entirely clear, but his notion of "personal knowledge" does not, as some have suggested, "overcome the subjective-objective divide."[20] True, as Polanyi says, the scientist is "passionately interested in the outcome of the procedure," but Polanyi is equally correct when he observes that the scientist functions "as detective, policeman, judge, and jury all rolled into one. He apprehends certain clues as suspect, formulates the charge and examines the evidence both for an against it, admitting or rejecting such parts of it as he thinks fit, and finally pronounces judgment."[21]

Theology

Liberal theology since the onset of modern secularism has offered a series of truly wild speculations on which ecclesiastical edifices can supposedly be built.

Starting from 18th-century suggestions (Jean Astruc) that the early books of the Bible might be later, editorial compilations, German 19th-century "higher criticism" (Graf, Kuenen, Wellhausen) speculated that the Pentateuch—the first five books of the Bible—attributed to Moses by Jesus himself, were actually a 10th-century B.C. paste-up of four sources: J (using "Jehovah/Yahweh" as the word for God), E (using "Elohim" as the word for God), P (the priestly, or sacrificial, material), and D (the legal material). No such subdocuments have ever been found. The theory is based entirely on the assumption that literary variations in style and vocabulary prove multiple authorship. By the time I was a theological seminary student (mid-20th-century), the number of alleged sources had multiplied: Morgenstern of Hebrew Union College was dividing the hypothetical K source into K proper and K_1. A "Polycrome Bible," projected to display these sources by diverse coloured typefaces, was never published—the reason being that the critics could not agree on the sources or where one started and another left off.

By the 20th century, the higher (or redaction or *Formgeschichtliche Methode*) critics had moved on to employ this same approach to the New Testament. The four Gospels were said not to have been written as unified documents by their traditional authors, but were held to be compilations of earlier source material.

---

[20] Mark T. Mitchell, *Michael Polanyi: The Art of Knowing* ("Library of Modern Thinkers"; Wilmington, DE: ISI Books, 2006), pp. 90 ff. Cf. Priyan Dias, "Is Science Very Different from Religion? A Polanyian Perspective," 22/1 *Science and Christian Belief* (April, 2010), 43-55.
[21] Michael Polanyi, *Science, Faith and Society* (new ed.; Chicago: University of Chicago Press, 1964), p. 38. Cf. Montgomery, *Tractatus Logico-Theologicus* (*op. cit.*), para. 2.72-2.722.

The early Christian communities were supposed to have done the editing—in a manner to convey their diverse "faith experiences" through the pictures of Jesus they created. Again: no subdocuments have ever been found to confirm such a thesis, and the earliest post-biblical Christian writers say just the opposite: they maintain that their teachings represent a fixed apostolic tradition deriving from the actual words and deeds of the historical Jesus.

Rudolf Bultmann, one of the most influential of all the higher critics of the New Testament, asserted that the historical details of Jesus' life were of no consequence anyway, since our personal, existential experience of Jesus is all that counts theologically. What is needed biblically is just the *Dass*—the "thatness" of Jesus—that someone of the name existed. The contemporary Jesus Seminar now votes regularly on the historical value of the Gospel materials, using coloured balls to represent the varied materials, ranging from what the early church superadded (virtually everything) to what can in fact be attributed to Jesus (very, very little).[22]

These conclusions are entirely the product of stylistic judgment and the identification of supposed inconsistencies in the Gospel accounts. None of the dismemberments or dehistoricisings by the liberal biblical critics depends upon actual manuscript sources preceding the New Testament documents. Indeed, as already noted, the very existence of such materials is entirely speculative.

Interestingly, these critical methods have been found wanting in classical scholarship (Homeric criticism), in parallel Near Eastern studies (Ugaritic literature), and even in the study of the English ballad tradition. C. S. Lewis pointed out that when reviewers tried to use the same kind of subjective, stylistic analysis to uncover the true sources of his Narnian stories, they never succeeded—and they were operating in Lewis's own time, in his own language. How then, asked Lewis, do the biblical critics think that they can succeed on a similar basis with biblical materials preceding them by two thousand years and deriving from cultures and languages alien to their own?[23]

Once the biblical documents have been dismissed as unhistorical, theological doctrine inevitably becomes a matter of speculation as well. Karl Barth, des-

---

[22] The Jesus Seminar, noting that the non-publication of the "Polycrome Bible" was due to a hopeless lack of scholarly unanimity on the critics' part, has managed, by employing the Seminar's voting system, to publish a colour-coded edition of the Gospels (including the Gnostic "Gospel of Thomas"): Robert W. Funk, Roy W. Hoover, and the Jesus Seminar, *The Five Gospels: The Search for the Authentic Words of Jesus* (New York: Macmillan, 1993). Their conclusions as to the historical accuracy (better, inaccuracy) of Jesus' sayings and deeds are based, not on any existing documents preceding the canonical Gospels, but solely on their personal speculations concerning the literary aspects—style, etc.—of the canonical material.

[23] C. S. Lewis, "Biblical Criticism," in his *Christian Reflections,* ed. Walter Hooper (Grand Rapids, MI: Eerdmans, 1994).

perately wanting to hold to the gospel of Christ's death for our sins and resurrection for our justification, but also accepting the so-called "assured results of modern biblical criticism," hit upon Martin Kähler's distinction between "ordinary history" (*Historie*) and "supra-history" or "salvation history" (*Geschichte*): the miraculous events recorded of Jesus, such as the resurrection, happened not in ordinary, verifiable history, but in the realm of supra-history, accessible only to faith.[24] To this, Bultmann countered—and with good reason—"Then why regard such events as historical at all?" Thus were the saving events of Christ's life walled off from historical criticism—but at the expense of no longer being part of normal history. A Pyrrhic victory, indeed.

Paul Tillich stated early in his career that he was attempting to find a basis for Christian theology that could stand even if the very existence of the historical Jesus became improbable.[25] Tillich's solution was to try to lay a foundation for theology in "Being Itself"—in Schelling's philosophical ontology. But did this mean that God is coterminous with the world (i.e. a pantheistic Deity) or just that God is the "Ground of All Being" (in which case his existence would still need factual support)? Tillich never tells us. Christ becomes the source of the "New Being"—but without any necessary biblical or historical foundation. The "Protestant Principle" is set forth: every theological idea must be subject to criticism, else it become idolatrous. But would this not mean that Tillich's own ontological theology can be subjected to the same critical negation? The death-of-God theologians of the 1960s (especially Thomas Altizer) thought so, and thus within the framework of mainline liberal theology God himself died.[26]

Literature and the Arts

Post-modern literary interpretation, as exemplified by Jacques Derrida, maintains that the meaning of a literary work resides in the interpreter. Works of literature, therefore, are not to be understood as having an objective, factual meaning residing within them, capable of being discovered by careful exegesis. Rather, they are open to creative deconstruction by the sensitive critic.

Literary scholar Frederick C. Crews, in his marvelous little book, *The Pooh Perplex*, "analyzed" A. A. Milne's perennial children's classic, *Winnie the Pooh*, through assuming the guise of "several academicians of varying critical

---

[24] See Montgomery, "Karl Barth and Contemporary Philosophy of History," in his *Where Is History Going?* (Minneapolis: Bethany, 1969), pp. 100-117.
[25] See Montgomery, "Tillich's Philosophy of History," *ibid.*, pp. 118-40.
[26] Montgomery, *The Suicide of Christian Theology* (Minneapolis: Bethany, 1970), pp. 76-173. Also, his *La Mort de Dieu* (2^d ed.; Bonn, Germany: Verlag für Kultur und Wissenschaft, 2009).

persuasions."[27] Here we have a series of hilarious examples of what invariably happens when interpreters allow themselves total personal latitude in the handling of their texts. "Harvey C. Window," author of a dehistoricising casebook titled, *What Happened at Bethlehem,* writes on the "paradoxical" in Pooh; for him "all great literature is more complex than the naive reader can suspect," the literal meaning is to give way to "multivalent symbolism," and when the events of the book do not fit his paradoxical categories, they are reinterpreted until they do so.

"P. R. Honeycomb," a poetical contributor to the "little magazines" who engages in "intensely personal criticism," brings his existential stance to bear on the text: "In wondering what I shall set down next in these notations, I am reminded of Heisenberg's Uncertainty Principle. The only thing that is certain is that I am uncertain what to set down next, and in this I typify the whole modern age and the collision of elementary particles in particular, a fact I find peculiarly comforting." "Myron Masterson," a distinguished "angry young man" for the past 20 years, writes on "Poisoned Paradise: The Underside of Pooh," employing as his guides Karl Marx, St. John of the Cross, Friedrich Nietzsche, Sacco and Vanzetti, Sigmund Freud, and C. G. Jung; he rejects those finicky "experts" who have said that "there exist differences of opinion among these thinkers," for, after all, "each of them has helped to shape my literary and moral consciousness."

"Woodbine Meadowlark," a perpetual graduate student romantically overwhelmed by the Angst of existence, paints a poohological picture in exact conformity with his worldview:

> The most perfect emblem of ignorance is contained in the "Woozle" scene, which gives us Pooh and Piglet (ethereal, pure-hearted Piglet, the real hero of the book) wandering helplessly in circles, following their own darling little tracks and misconceiving their goal ever more thoroughly as they proceed. Is this not the very essence of modern man, aching with existential nausée and losing himself more deeply in despair as his longing for certainty waxes?

"Simon Lacerous," editor of the feared quarterly, *Thumbscrew,* describes Pooh as "Another Book to Cross Off Your List" and terminates his acid analysis by completely losing the subject-object distinction between the book and himself: "The more I think about it, the more convinced I become that Christopher Robin not only hates everything I stand for, he hates me personally." Finally, "Smedley Force," a spokesman for "responsible criticism," completely submerg-

---

[27] Frederick C. Crews, *The Pooh Perplex* (New York: Dutton Paperbacks, 1965).

es the text by his interest in literary antecedents, conjectural emendations, and the "discovery" of errors and inconsistencies in the book. Such endeavours, he is convinced, place us "on the threshold of the Golden Age of POOH!"[28]

The point of Crews's volume is simply that, if interpreters are allowed this kind of existential, Post-modern latitude, all meaningful interpretation collapses and no one will understand the meaning of any text under analysis.

Fortunately, the desire to avoid just such a "golden age of Pooh" has led more and more responsible literary critics to reject the so-called "Hermeneutical Circle"—the claim that the interpreter and the object of interpretation are inextricably locked together so that not only does the object influence the interpreter but also the interpreter colours what he or she interprets, thus making objective interpretation impossible in principle. The path out of the "Pooh perplex" is exemplified by Elder Olson's "Hamlet and the Hermeneutics of Drama,"[29] where Olson defines a perfect interpretation as "one which is absolutely commensurate in its basic, inferential, and evaluative propositions with the data, the implications, and the values contained within the work." But to follow that route would, of course, mean a return to a world where literary works had a factual meaning of their own, apart from the speculations of their critics.

And literature is not by any means the only cultural area in the modern secular world where factual reality is ignored. One thinks immediately of Magritte's celebrated painting, which declares both that reality has no objective meaning and that language and reality are entirely disconnected:

---

[28] With considerable difficulty, I have restrained myself from giving a sampling of Marxist and psychoanalytic interpretations of Pooh from Crews's book.
[29] Elder Olson, "Hamlet and the Hermeneutics of Drama," *Modern Philology*, LXI (February, 1964), 225-37.

The fields of music and photography are likewise not exempt from the secular effort to make imaginative creation the only reality.

> No longer bound by the traditional rules, composers were forced to create their own. Schoenberg, Webern, and Berg explored serialism, Cage threw out the bathwater (and some would say the baby), continuing with the chaos of his own imagination. …
>
> So too with photography: through the discipline's history, artistic photographers have been limited by images in the physical world—even with burgeoning manipulations, they have depended on existing images as starting points. No longer. Today, photographers are almost completely free of the rules imposed by the real world.[30]

Conservative Roman Catholic essayist and novelist Georges Bernanos, whilst properly condemning the evils of 20th-century materialism and technocracy, went much too far when he declared: *"On ne comprend absolument rien à la civilization moderne si l'on n'admet pas d'abord qu'elle est une conspiration universelle contre toute espèce de vie intérieure."*[31] In point of fact, one understands absolutely nothing about modern civilization unless one starts by admitting that it is a global conspiracy against every sort of *extrinsic, objective factuality*—and an idolization of the subjective, inner life.

Law and Society

It would seem fairly obvious that the legal treatment of constitutions, statutes, judicial decisions, contracts, wills, and the like should follow standard interpretive canons. And this has indeed been the case through the history of the Anglo-American and the European civil law traditions. Such rules of "construction" as the so-called "literal rule" have been sacrosanct: words are to be given "their ordinary and literal meaning."[32] Lord Bacon put it aphoristically: *"Non est interpretatio, sed divinatio, quae recedit a litera"* ("Interpretation that departs from the letter of the text is not interpretation but divination").[33] One

---

[30] Garth Sundem, *The Geeks' Guide to World Domination* (New York: Three Rivers Press, 2009), p. 151. The consistently high quality of our scholarly citations will be particularly evidenced by this reference.

[31] Georges Bernanos, *La France contre les robots* (Bordeaux: Castor Astral, 2009). Bernanos (1888-1948) is of course best known for his *Journal d'un curé de campagne* ("The Diary of a Country Priest").

[32] Cf. Lord Esher MR, in *R v Judge of the City of London Court* (1892), 1 QB 273.

[33] See Montgomery, *Law and Gospel: A Study in Jurisprudence* (2^d ed.; Calgary, Alberta: Canadian Institute for Law, Theology and Public Policy, 1995), pp. 24 ff.; also, Montgomery, "Legal Hermeneutics and the Interpretation of Scripture," in Michael Bauman and David Hall (eds.), *Evangelical Hermeneutics* (Camp Hill, PA: Christian Publications, 1995), pp. 15-29.

only employs other canons of interpretation, such as the "mischief rule" (finding the purpose of the enactment, decision, or text) when literal construction would lead to absurdity.

But in contemporary American jurisprudence, another, very different approach has come on the scene: the so-called Critical Legal Studies movement.[34] CLS, as it is popularly known, appeared on the American law-school scene in the 1970s; it has since become an important influence in British legal education as well. The two most noteworthy advocates of the position are Roberto Unger and Duncan Kennedy, whose emphases and concerns, while differing in certain respects, are fundamentally the same.[35] These thinkers build upon the pragmatic, social orientation of American legal realism, and carry to a far greater extreme Llewellyn's view that formal legal judgments are little more than rationalisations of social practice. For CLS, the law is to be viewed from the standpoint of radical skepticism: all legal judgment is a matter of choosing one set of values over another. That being so, the purpose of legal activity is not a search for principles of justice embedded in and developed by the legal tradition, but the conscious advancement of a political vision. The law is inherently indeterminate; its literature has no single and objective meaning, being capable of virtually any interpretation; legal principles are contradictory; indeed, the law, in the final analysis, is but a tool generally serving the interests of the powerful and the maintenance of the status quo.

It will be observed that this approach subordinates the meaning of legal texts to the interests (political, social) of the interpreter, and thus has strong affinities with the deconstructionist literary schools treated earlier. Even though American judges would not generally want to be identified as adherents of CLS, they quite regularly handle their cases in a pragmatic, sociological fashion. The most egregious—and tragic—example is surely the 1973 U.S. Supreme Court abortion decision in *Roe v. Wade*, where the Court refused to be influenced by the objective fact that the entire genetic-chromosomal pattern of the human person is created at the moment of conception, and instead let pragmatic, instrumentalist issues determine the legal outcome.[36] Here untrammeled speculation and legal theorizing in the face of scientific fact have led to the loss of millions of human lives.[37]

---

[34] This movement, mercifully, has had practically no influence on European philosophy of law.
[35] On CLS, see the citations in Montgomery, "Modern Theology and Contemporary Legal Theory," in his *Christ Our Advocate* (Bonn, Germany: Verlag für Kultur und Wissenschaft, 2002), pp. 32-33.
[36] See Montgomery, *Slaughter of the Innocents* (Westchester, IL: Crossway, 1981).
[37] In diametric contrast to CLS, Matthew H. Kramer, Professor of Legal and Political Philosophy at Cambridge University, argues *in extenso* that "objectivity ... is integral to every system of legal governance" (*Objectivity and the Rule of Law* [Cambridge: Cambridge University Press, 2007],

And, on the social scene, one encounters a remarkably similar phenomenon: the substitution of a personally constructed reality for the world as it actually is. A perceptive recent analysis—albeit touched by some outmoded leftist ideas—is Barbara Ehrenreich's aptly titled book, *Bright-Sided: How the Relentless Pursuit of Positive Thinking Has Undermined America*.[38] Speaking of the current economic turndown and the sub-prime catastrophe, she says: "American corporate culture had long since abandoned the dreary rationality of professional management for the emotional thrills of mysticism, charisma, and sudden intuitions." The root problem? One reviewer describes her argument in the following terms:

> She begins with a look at where positive thinking originated, from its founding parents in the New Thought Movement (inventors of the law of attraction, recently made famous in books such as "The Secret") through mid-20th century practitioners like Norman Vincent Peale and Dale Carnegie, to current disciples ranging from Oprah Winfrey to the preachers of the prosperity gospel. We're not talking here about garden-variety hopefulness or genuine happiness, but rather the philosophy that individuals create—rather than encounter—their own circumstances .... Positive thinking, in Ehrenreich's view, has become a kind of national religion.[39]

Here, reality disappears: through "positive psychology," the individual and the nation can make of the status quo an illusory ideal—or newly construct it in any fashion whatsoever, since all is plastic and open to re-creation.

A Suggested Corrective

The manifold problems just discussed have a common denominator: disregard of fact and the substitution of speculation for reality. We shall conclude by suggesting a way out of this morass—offering as well a very short analysis of why our culture entered this quagmire in the first place.

---

p. 232).
[38] Barbara Ehrenreich, *Bright-Sided* (New York: Henry Holt/Metropolitan Books, 2009). And see Hanna Rosin's parallel treatment of the prosperity gospel in her trenchant article, "Did Christianity Cause the Crash?," *The Atlantic*, December, 2009, pp. 38-48. (This is, to be sure, the Hanna Rosin whose book, *God's Harvard: A Christian College on a Mission to Save America*, put Patrick Henry College on the national and international map—for better, not for worse, in this writer's opinion.)
[39] Kate Tuttle, "The Downside of Cheering Up," *Washington Post*, November 15, 2009.

The Proposal

The formal error in secularist speculation is epistemological: it relates to how one arrives at truth. If one believes that truth depends in the final analysis on one's own stance, the problems we have described here will follow as the night the day. Philosophically, one needs to distinguish the real world from one's encounter with it. The subject-object distinction is the beginning of epistemological wisdom. As Sigmund Freud—of all people—put it: "If there were no such things as knowledge distinguished from our opinions by corresponding to reality, we might build bridges just as well out of cardboard as out of stone."[40]

No one seriously questions that interpreters are capable of regarding the object of interpretation in an almost infinite number of ways, depending on the interpreter's background, prejudices, and interests. The question is: *Ought one to do so?* Are there objective limits to interpretation, created by the factual nature of what one is interpreting, that should restrain the interpreter?

This question has long been raised in the field of constitutional interpretation. Does the American Federal Constitution, for example, have an inherent meaning which should bind future generations of legal interpreters and judges, or is it a document capable of infinite re-understandings by each subsequent generation, according to present interests and needs? If the latter, does not the Constitution lose all normative force? That is the judgment of those thinkers who argue (as did Chief Justice John Marshall) that texts must be understood in their original sense, not twisted to fit the interpreter's agenda. Robert Bork

---

[40] Sigmund Freud, *New Introductory Lectures on Psychoanalysis*, ed. and trans. James Strachey (New York: Penguin Books, 1973), pp. 212-13.

admits to the difficulty of psychoanalysing the Founding Fathers to discover what they really "intended" in framing the American Constitution (the dilemma thrown up by liberal constitutionalists such as Laurence Tribe), and so prefers the expression "original understanding" to the more common phrase "original intent": "What we're really talking about [is] not what the authors of the Bill of Rights had in the backs of their minds, but what people who voted for this thing understood themselves to be voting for."[41]

If, however, trying to determine the "original intent" of the author over and above his text poses extreme problems (Sibelius, for example, was hopeless in explaining the true intent and significance of his *Finlandia*!), the same dilemma attaches to the original audience of the text: they, too, may have misunderstood it—for any number of personal, societal or cultural reasons.

Thus the most sophisticated academic analysis of legal interpretation—or of interpretation in general—is surely the Wittgenstein-Popper approach: the analogy of the shoe and the foot. Interpretation is like a shoe and the text like the foot. One endeavours to find the interpretation that best fits the text (allowing the text itself to determine this). Here, "intent" or "understanding" is decided by the text itself.[42]

Such an approach is another way of stating the principle that "the text must be allowed to interpret itself"—in the sense that when different or contradictory interpretations of it are offered, each will be brought to the bar of the text to see which fits best. Interpretations therefore function like scientific theories that are arbitrated by the facts they endeavour to explain: the facts ultimately decide the value of our attempts to understand them.[43]

In the Wittgenstein-Popper model, the interpreter of course brings his prejudices (aprioris, presuppositions, biases) to the text, but it is the text that judges them also. And the meaning of the text is not to be established by extrinsic considerations, such as the background, prejudices, or stance of the interpreter, for that would yield an infinite regress. If the given fact or text has no inherent meaning and one must appeal beyond it to the interpreter for its true significa-

---

[41] Robert Bork, interview in "Bork v. Tribe on Natural Law, the Ninth Amendment, the Role of the Court," *Life* (Fall Special, 1991), pp. 96-99. For his position in detail, see Bork, "Neutral Principles and Some First Amendment Problems," 47/1 *Indiana Law Journal* (Fall, 1971); Bork, *The Tempting of America* (New York: The Free Press, 1990); and cf. Ethan Bronner, *Battle for Justice: How the Bork Nomination Shook America* (New York: W.W. Norton, 1989).

[42] Though Karl Popper developed this analogy in dependence upon Ludwig Wittgenstein's philosophical insights, the two were very uncomfortable with each other. See the brilliant treatment by David Edmonds and John Eidinow, *Wittgenstein's Poker* (London: Faber and Faber, 2001).

[43] Cf. Montgomery, "The Theologian's Craft," in his *The Suicide of Christian Theology* (*op. cit.*), pp. 267-313.

tion, then that must also be true of the extrinsic facts to which one appeals: "Bigger bugs have littler bugs upon their backs to bite them/And littler bugs have littler bugs/And so—*ad infinitum*."

The Wittgenstein-Popper approach to texts has direct application to the investigation of the world in general. We are to seek the best explanations of what we encounter, whether in literature, science, religion, history, law, or everyday life—i.e., the explanations that best "fit the facts."

One may notice a certain affinity here with the so-called "Scottish common-sense philosophy" of the late 18th and early 19th centuries (Thomas Reid, *et al.*), often regarded as simplistic.[44] And yet the principle of Occam's razor is applicable also to epistemology: the simpler solution is, all things being equal, better than a complex solution. If it looks like a duck, walks like a duck, and quacks like a duck, chances are that it is not a platypus.[45]

If what we are here suggesting seems rather childish, perhaps we should recall Jesus' rebuke to his disciples who wanted to send children away from him: "Suffer the little children to come to me, for of such is the kingdom of heaven." The acceptance of factual reality as it is should be a goal for adults seeking truth, not just a description of how children view the world.

But does not our approach militate against "faith"? Did not Augustine teach us, *"Credo ut intellegam"*—that we must first believe in order to understand? If Christians take this Augustinian axiom to mean that truth can only be found through our personal stance, then we fall into exactly the same pit as the secularists we have been examining—and whom, presumably, we are trying to bring to a better understanding and to the historical, factual Cross of Christ.

There are two ways of regarding Augustine's statement and they must be clearly distinguished. First, the phrase can mean "all truth begins with prior faith"—or, in modern parlance, every worldview commences with unprovable assumptions. This is true enough, but we regularly overlook the fact that although all unprovable assumptions are equal, some are more equal than others! That is to say, it is vital to start with (admittedly undemonstrable) methods of

---

[44] One should not forget that this epistemology was fundamental to the solid biblical theology and apologetics of Old Princeton (Archibald Alexander, Charles Hodge, B. B. Warfield); of their "Christian Baconianism" a careful scholar of the subject has declared: "The Princeton Theology ... with its historical pillars resting squarely upon the Baconian Philosophy of facts, is an important bridge across which influences continue to stream from antebellum to present-day American religion" (Theodore Dwight Bozeman, *Protestants in an Age of Science* [Chapel Hill: University of North Carolina Press, 1977], p. 173).

[45] And, *pace* Christian philosopher Nicholas Wolterstorff, Reid's common sense epistemology in no sense requires the rejection of classical foundationalism or one's being left only with the issue of interpreting reality (hermeneutics).

investigation—deduction stemming from the law of non-contradiction, induction, retroductive inference—rather than with full-blown worldviews, none of which can be confirmed or disconfirmed if there is no commonly accepted methodology for distinguishing fact from non-fact.

Secondly, Augustine's phrase can mean "belief is the foundation of true understanding"—and that also is quite correct. Until one enters into a personal belief relationship with the object of one's search for truth, one understands only from the outside. Interiorising fact is the only way to comprehend it fully. Understanding marriage theoretically is a far cry from comprehending it from the inside, when one actually marries. The classical theologians rightly insisted that faith entails not just *notitia* (factual knowledge), but also public commitment to it (*fides*), and, most important, *fiducia* (a personal, living relationship with the Author of gospel truth).

But it is still of absolute importance to *believe in what is indeed genuine factual knowledge!* In religion, the object of belief is paramount. "The magic of believing" can be dark magic. Belief *per se* saves no one. If one believes in a false god or false faith-system, one will indeed "understand" it in the deepest way—but that will entail damnation rather than eternal life. So, as the Scripture says, we must "test the spirits," not naively assume that any kind of belief is sufficient for the proper understanding of things. And non-Christians need to be helped factually to see that only Jesus is (as he himself proclaimed) "the Way, the Truth, and the Life," and therefore the only proper object of religious faith.

We must all therefore start by investigating the world so as to arrive at factual truth. In religion, this will mean investigating the case for the Word—both Christ the living Word and the Holy Scriptures the written Word—and follow the positive results of that search with a personal commitment to Christ as Lord. When Christ said, "I am the Truth," he was telling those who had seen him heal the sick and raise the dead that they needed not only to accept those evidences of his Deity but also to enter into a personal relationship with him for time and for eternity.[46]

---

[46] Cf., as but a single example, Jesus' response to the disciples of John the Baptist, who enquired of Jesus whether he was indeed the Messiah whom John had proclaimed: "Now when John had heard in the prison the works of Christ, he sent two of his disciples, and said unto him, Art thou he that should come, or do we look for another? Jesus answered and said unto them, Go and shew John again those things which ye do hear and see: the blind receive their sight, and the lame walk, the lepers are cleansed, and the deaf hear, the dead are raised up, and the poor have the gospel preached to them. And blessed is he, whosoever shall not be offended in me" (Matthew 11:2-6).

Why Do Secularists Prefer Speculation to Fact?

And now, at the end of our journey, we ask: Why have so many areas of modern life fallen under the sway of secular speculation rather than adjusting to the factual nature of things? Why would anyone prefer unfounded speculation to factual reality?

One explanation frequently heard in the history of ideas places the burden essentially on the social conservatism of traditional Christianity. Until the French Revolution, theology was comfortable absolutising the political and social *status quo*. The "Great Chain of Being,"[47] as classically formulated in early medieval times by Pseudo-Dionysius the Areopagite, related the "Ecclesiastical Hierarchies" (the structures of church organization on earth) to the "Heavenly Hierarchies" (the graduated tiers of angelic and demonic beings).[48] When combined with a notion of the Divine Right of Kings, human social organization appeared to be an unalterable fact to which everyone must bow.[49] Thus, once revolutionary thinking recognized quite rightly that given social structures were but human constructs, not divine orders,[50] this placed a question mark over all accepted beliefs. Modern man then asked himself if perhaps the whole world was inherently pliable — open to speculation and manipulation in all respects.

There is certainly a point to the claim that professing Christians contributed, if inadvertently, to the secular move from fact to speculation. Indeed, whenever Christians have identified political and social conservatism with the will of God, great harm has been done: legitimate critics of the *status quo* have been led to believe that Christianity supports entrenched injustice.[51] But the reason why today's secularist prefers speculation to factuality goes much deeper than historical considerations.

---

[47] Cf. Arthur Lovejoy, *The Great Chain of Being: A Study of the History of an Idea* (Cambridge, MA: Harvard University Press, 1957).

[48] See Preudo-Dionysius, *The Complete Works,* ed. Paul Rorem, *et al.* (Mahwah, NJ: Paulist Press, 1987).

[49] Cf. John Neville Figgis, *The Divine Right of Kings,* intro. G. R. Elton (reprint ed.; New York: Harper Torchbooks, 1965); and Roland Mousnier, *Les Institutions de France sous la monarchie absolue, 1598-1789* (Paris: Presses Universitaires de France, 2005), Pt. I, chap. 15.

[50] Note that even though any given socio-political order is not revelationally derivable or divinely inspired, this does not say that political order *in general* is purely a human creation. The Reformers were quite right in holding to *Schöpfungsordnungen* — "Orders of Creation" — imbedded in a fallen world by God to keep sinners from destroying themselves. See Emil Brunner, *The Divine Imperative,* and Werner Elert, *The Christian Ethos*: discussed in Montgomery, *The Shape of the Past* (Minneapolis: Bethany, 1975), pp. 358-74.

[51] Montgomery, "Evangelical Social Responsibility in Theological Perspective," in Gary Collins (ed.), *Our Society in Turmoil* (Carol Stream, IL: Creation House, 1970); reprinted in *Christians in the Public Square* and *The Church: Blessing or Curse?* (both published by the Canadian Institute for

The trouble with facts is that one has to subordinate oneself to them—to succumb to them. The world is no longer plastic, able to be adjusted to fit one's personal desires and interests. The attractive thing about speculation is that it places the speculator at centre: the world can be readjusted as he or she wishes. Speculation and autonomous self-centredness go hand in hand.

Luther criticized Erasmus for treating the Bible as a "waxed nose" which he could twist in any direction he wished.[52] The secularist—the man without God—wants to create his own universe, untrammeled by anything. Someone has rightly said, "First God created us in his image, and ever since we have been returning the compliment." The secularist wants to become his or her own god, creating a world that will be maximally satisfying and personally undemanding.

This move seems particularly evident in the arts. Parallel with the speculative operations we have described earlier, the contemporary secular artist has eschewed attempts to represent the world or to plumb its depths, as did Michelangelo and Rembrandt, and has preferred, in post-impressionism, cubism and dada, to give vent to personal expressions which leave the meaning of artistic works to the vagaries of each individual observer. One thinks of Marcel Duchamp's "Nude Descending a Staircase" (which could as equally represent an elephant ascending a staircase).[53] Some years ago, a painting was carelessly hung upside down in the Metropolitan Museum of Art in New York City; no one realized this until, months later, the artist complained bitterly of the mistake.

As Dostoyevsky recognized in *The Brothers Karamazov*, "If God doesn't exist, then everything is permitted." If there is no transcendent God who has revealed his will for us, then it follows inexorably that "anything goes"—and thus that any and all speculations are possible. From here it is a very short step to the most bizarre explanations, such as Francis Crick's naturalistic proposal for explaining the origins of life on earth that the basic genetic structure of bacterial DNA was seeded from outer space—a theory without a modicum of empirical support.[54]

Facts are a serious impediment to unbelief. The factual case for intelligent design is far better than the case for a godless, irrational universe. The evidence

---

Law, Theology and Public Policy, Calgary, Alberta: http://www.ciltpp.com).
[52] Cf. Montgomery, *In Defense of Martin Luther* (*op. cit*), pp. 70-75.
[53] Reproduced, for the delectation of the reader, in Montgomery, *The Suicide of Christian Theology* (*op. cit.*), p. 24.
[54] Francis Crick, *Life Itself: Its Origin and Nature* (New York: Simon & Schuster Touchstone Books, 1982).

for the resurrection of Jesus Christ from the dead, and thus the soundness of his claim to Deity, is far better than the speculative truth-claims of other religions and the sects.[55]

The speculator is like the builders of the Tower of Babel. Without a fragment of evidence, and against all reason, they attempted to erect a building that would reach to heaven. All they received for their Herculean efforts was a confusion of languages: the loss of meaningful discourse. And that is precisely the case with the modern world. Example: John Lennon of The Beatles, and his lyric, "Imagine":

> Imagine there's no heaven
> It's easy if you try
> No hell below us
> Above us only sky
> Imagine all the people
> Living for today
>
> Imagine there's no countries
> It isn't hard to do
> Nothing to kill or die for
> And no religion too …

Yes, speculation "isn't hard to do." But what we need is more, not less factuality. As Saint Paul says to the Stoic philosopher Seneca in a recent French dramatic production: "It's not a question of believing or not believing: it's enough to open one's eyes!"[56] We need to open our eyes to God's facts, as embedded in the creation. We need to open our eyes to the facts of Christ, as manifested, "by many infallible proofs,"[57] in his historical life, death, and resurrection. We need to open our eyes to the factual presence of the Holy Spirit, promised by Christ himself, as he convicts the world of sin, righteousness, and judgment.

We began with the Great Detective. We conclude with him: "We are suffering from a plethora of surmise, conjecture, and hypothesis. The difficulty is to detach the framework of fact—of absolute undeniable fact—from the embellishments of theorists."[58]

---

[55] See Montgomery, *Tractatus Logico-Theologicus* (4th ed.; Bonn, Germany: Verlag für Kultur und Wissenschaft, 2009), *passim*.
[56] "Il n'est pas question de croire ou de ne pas croire, il suffit d'ouvrir les yeux!"—Xavier Jaillard, *Après l'incendie: Saint Paul et Sénèque; pièce en 8 tableaux* (Levallois-Perret: Editions ACTE, 2007), p. 11. First presented at the Petit-Hébertot theatre, Paris, on 8 October 2009. Paul and Seneca were contemporaries, though there is no historical record of their actually having met.
[57] Acts 1:3.
[58] From: *Silver Blaze*. Cf. my essay, "How Many Holmeses? How Many Watsons?," *The Baker Street Journal*, Summer, 2002, pp. 26-30.

Part Two

Science and the Faith

1. The Theologian's Craft: A Discussion of Theory Formation and Theory Testing in Theology*

Synopsis

What is it to "do theology"? Numerous conflicting and inadequate answers (e.g., Bultmannian existentialism, the post-Bultmannian "New Hermeneutic") hold the field today; these have in common a basic misunderstanding as to the relation of theological theorizing to theory construction in other fields of knowledge, and a fundamental misconception in regard to the proper way of confirming or disconfirming theological judgments. In this essay, a detailed comparison between scientific and theological methodologies is set forth, and the artistic and sacred dimensions of theological theorizing are explicated by way of an original structural model suggested by Wittgensteinian philosophical and linguistic analysis.

Scientists are generally at a loss to know precisely what theologians do. Mailmen deliver letters; bartenders serve numerous varieties of firewater; otorhinolaryngologists concern themselves with ears, noses, and throats: but what exactly do theologians endeavor to accomplish? The aura of mystery surrounding theological activity troubles not merely the scientist, who generally has a clear-eyed view of his own professional function, but also the so-called "average man," who, though his awareness of his own role in life may be exceedingly vague, is even more troubled by the peculiarities of "religious" vocations. The wry comment of the parishioner, "We take care of pastor in this life and he takes care of us in the next," well illustrates the gulf that, in general, seems to separate theological activity from the meaningful work of the world.

A theologian of course theologizes, i.e., he does theology. But the tautological character of this statement requires us to press on: What is it to "do theology"? Etymologically, as everyone knows, "theology" involves a "speaking-of-God," and this expression should be regarded very carefully, for its double meaning suggests the source of difficulty in understanding the theologian's craft: theology speaks *about* God (the objective genitive of the grammarians), but only because of "God's speaking" to man (the subjective genitive); it is the active presence of the Numinous in the work of theology that renders its task so strange to those who look upon it from the outside. But leaving aside (for the moment only!) the active numinosity in theological endeavor, and concentrating on the object of theological research, we can say very simply that the theologian[1] is one who engages in forming and testing theories concerning the Divine.

Our task in this paper is thus the clarification of what it properly means to form and to test theological theories; and it is hoped that the result will aid both the non-theologian (particularly the scientist) to understand and to appreciate better the nature of theological endeavor, and the theologian himself to keep his methodological sights correctly focused. The center of attention will be neither the historical circumstances attending theological theorizing[2] nor the psychological factors relating to theological discovery[3] — interesting as these subjects are. We shall hold ourselves quite closely to the fundamental realm of theological prolegomena, and seek to discover the nature of the operations that make theology theology. As the reader enters the rarified air of this domain, he is warned to prepare himself for innovation and groundbreaking; it is the writer's conviction that precisely here lie the basic sources of error in much contemporary theological thinking, as well as the relatively untapped resources for theological recovery in our time.

Through a Welter of Confusion

Any attempt to get at the nature of theological theorizing runs the immediate danger of being bogged down in a morass of conflicting interpretations of theological activity. On the one hand, the student of the subject is faced with dogmatically simplistic and pejorative definitions, such as that of Princeton philosopher Walter Kaufmann:

---

[*] An invitational paper presented August 24, 1965, at the 20th Annual Convention of the American Scientific Affiliation, convened at The King's College, Rriarcliff Manor, New York.

[1] It will be observed that in this essay the term "theologian" is being used in the strict sense of "systematic theologian" or "dogmatician," not in the more general and perfectly legitimate sense of "professor on the theological faculty" (a category including exegetes ["biblical theologians"], church historians, homileticians, etc., etc.).

[2] Fascinating studies of this nature are suggested by Etienne Gilson's *History of Christian Philosophy in the Middle Ages* (New York: Random House, 1955). Much needs to be done in the historical study of classical Protestant theological methodologies — e.g., the "analytic" and "synthetic" methods employed by dogmaticians of the 16th and 17th centuries.

[3] A work along the lines of Rosamond E. M. Harding's *An Anatomy of Inspiration and an Essay on the Creative Mood* (3d ed.; Cambridge, England: W. Heffer, 1948) would be an exceedingly valuable addition to the literature of theology.

First, theology is of necessity denominational. Second, theology is essentially a defensive maneuver. Third, it is almost always time-bound and dated quickly. Theology is the systematic attempt to pour the newest wine into the old skins of a denomination.[4]

To which it may be replied: First, even if all theologians were members of denominations (which is not the case), this would not make theology "denominational" any more than the (fallacious) assumption that all physicians are members of state medical societies would make medicine political. Secondly, the defense of the faith (technically: apologetics) is but one of the tasks of systematic theology, not the whole or even the center of it. Thirdly, one needs a firm criterion of obsolescence in order to assert that theology is "time-bound"—but the secularist is, *ex hypothesi*, in the worst possible position to establish such a criterion. Finally: to define theological theorizing à la Kaufmann one must gratuitously assume that its content (wine) is forever new and changing, that its interpretative categories (skins) are old and denominational, and that the theorizing process (the pouring) requires no special examination. None of these assumptions, however, is credible enough to warrant pursuing.

Alongside of simplistically objective definitions of theological activity, one encounters existentially subjective descriptions of the theologian's work. In his Cambridge University Stanton Lectures on "Theological Explanation," G. F. Woods asserts, in partial dependence on Tillich:

> The first sense of theological explanation is the ultimate personal being which is the real ground of the world. The second sense is the act of seeking an explanation of what is ultimate, both through our own efforts to make it plain and through its own endeavours to make itself plain to us. The third sense is the act of using ultimate personal being as an explanation of the world in which we live. These manifold acts of explanation take place on particular occasions and are markedly influenced by the circumstances of the day, particularly by the methods of explanation which happen to be dominant at the time. But, throughout the confused series of particular acts of explanation, there is the perpetual trend towards the use of explanatory terms derived from our own being. What we are is the source of all our methods of seeking to explain the actual world.[5]

Here one must unkindly lay stress on the author's phrase "the confused series of particular acts of explanation," for confusion does indeed reign in any

---

[4] Walter Kaufmann, *Critique of Religion and Philosophy* (Garden City, New York: Doubleday Anchor Books, 1961), p. 221 (para. 57).
[5] G. F. Woods, *Theological Explanation: A Study of the Meaning and Means of Explaining in Science, History, and Theology, Based upon the Stanton Lectures Delivered in the University of Cambridge, 1953-1956* (Digswell Place, Welwyn: James Nisbet, 1958), p. 151.

theological enterprise where "our own (existential-ontological) being," constitutes the center of the stage. As Carnap showed the analytical nonsensicality of Heidegger's "non-being," so A. C. Garnett has pointed up the unverifiable nonsense involved in "being"-assertions as theological starting-points.[6]

A third major variety of metatheological explanation is illustrated in William Hordern's book, *Speaking of God*, which endeavors to create a bridge between current "ordinary-language philosophy" and theology. Here Hordern, by an exceedingly unfortunate substitution of the later Wittgenstein for the earlier Wittgenstein, leaves the fundamental problem of theological verification aside and attempts to describe theology as a unique, *sui generis* "language game":

> Instead of thinking of theology as the queen of the sciences, can we think of it as the Olympic Games? ... The Olympic Committee does not legislate the rules of ice hockey, and much less does it train a hockey player how to play hockey. But ice hockey takes its place within the total pattern of the Olympics, and its players must meet the Olympic standard. ...
>
> By analogy, natural science and other language games are separate and independent, with their own questions, rules, methods of verification, and ways of giving answers. ... [The} Christian faith cannot answer scientific questions any more than the Olympic Committee can tell a hockey player how to shoot the puck. ...
>
> Theology, as the Olympics of life ... does not pretend to be a superscientific system with answers to all questions left unanswered by science. It is concerned with another kind of question than is science. It does not offer a systematic explanation of the universe; it is a means whereby man is enabled to live his life with a sense of purpose, direction, and integrity.[7]

Such an approach places theology in a mystical cloud of unknowing, and lifts the Mt. Olympus of theology off of the earth entirely.[8] Since theology, in Hordern's view, "cannot answer scientific questions," its axiological ship passes in the night the cognitive vessel of the scientific disciplines, and neither can communicate with the other. Moreover, and most important, the theological "language game" is without external verification, so its theories do not have to be accepted as "Olympic rules" by anyone who is not theologically inclined. It

---

[6] Cf. John Macquarrie, *Twentieth-Century Religious Thought: the Frontiers of Philosophy and Theology, 1900-1960* (London: SCM Press, 1963), pp. 274-75. Unhappily, Macquarrie does not personally take Garnett's critique to heart—or he would modify his own existentially-orientated theology!
[7] William Hordern, *Speaking of God: the Nature and Purpose of Theological Language* (New York: Macmillan, 1964), pp. 86-89.
[8] The Christian "Mt. Olympus," as Wittgenstein's student O. K. Bouwsma has well shown in his unpublished essay, "Adventure in Verification," is firmly embedded in the earth, and is indeed subjected to verifiability tests.

is too bad that Hordern did not see the point behind Wittgenstein's concern that his *Tractatus Logico-Philosophicus* be published along with his *Philosophical Investigations:* the latter, without the former, provides no answer whatever to the fundamental question: how do you know if a "language game" (e.g., theological theorizing) represents reality at all?[9]

In light of fallaciously objectivistic, existentially subjectivistic, and etherially olympian descriptions of theological activity, is it any wonder that tongue-in-cheek humor not infrequently captures the special-pleading character of contemporary theological theorizing? The January 15, 1965, issue of *Christianity Today* carries Lawing's cartoon of Moses' return from Mt. Sinai with the Commandments; a sly Israelite meets him with the suggestion, "Aaron said perhaps you'd let us condense them to 'act responsibly in love.'" Here Bishop Robinson's theological theory as to the "real" meaning of the Commandments is lampooned: the sick humor lies in the fact that the Israelite (probably) and Robinson (certainly) lack awareness of the degree to which cultural conformity and personal preference dictate the content of their theological constructions.

How can we gain clarity in this vital area? Let us, for the moment, step outside of the theological realm and examine the essential nature of theories by way of the discipline in which they have been most thoroughly discussed: the field of science. Here we can gain our bearings and find an immediate and meaningful entrée to the larger question of theological theory formation and testing.

Theory Construction in Science

Though there have been many theories as to the exact nature of scientific theories, a general convergence and agreement among them is not hard to find. Popper uses Wittgenstein's analogy of the Net: "Theories are nets cast to catch what we call 'the world': to rationalize, to explain, and to master it. We endeavor to make the mesh ever finer and finer."[10] Comments Leonard Nash of Harvard:

---

[9] Cf. C. B. Daly, "New Light on Wittgenstein," *Philosophical Studies* [St. Patrick's College, Maynooth, Ireland], X (1960), 46-49.

[10] Karl R. Popper, *The Logic of Scientific Discovery* (2^d ed.; London: Hutchinson, 1959), p. 59. For Wittgenstein's presentation of the "net" analogy, see his *Tractatus Logico-Philosophicus*, 6.341-6.35. My former professor Max Black, in his exceedingly valuable work, A *Companion to Wittgenstein's 'Tractatus'* (Ithaca, New York: Cornell University Press, 1964), pp. 347-61, finds difficulties in the network analogy, but concludes: "According to the view I have been presenting the principles of mechanics are neither empirical generalizations, nor *a priori* truths. Taken together, they constitute an abstract scheme of explanation, within whose framework specific laws of *predetermined* form can be formulated and tested. If I am correct, Wittgenstein's central idea in his discussion of the philosophy of science has thus been vindicated." On Popper's approach to scientific theoriz-

"He who realizes the existence of such a conceptual fabric, and is capable of lifting it, carries with it all its cords, all the colligative relations it accommodates."[11] The use of an image (the net) to illustrate the nature of scientific theory construction points to an especially vital element in such theories: the employment of "models"—representations that carry "epistemological vividness."[12] So, in speaking of the discovery that "light travels in straight lines," Stephen Toulmin notes that "a vital part of the discovery is the very possibility of drawing 'pictures' of the optical state-of-affairs to be expected in given circumstances—or rather, the possibility of drawing them in a way that *fits the facts*."[13]

To concretize these abstract remarks on scientific theorizing, let us consider a dramatic and very recent case of successful theory-building: the 1962 Nobel Prize discovery, by James Watson and Francis Crick, of the molecular structure of DNA (the nucleic acid bearing the blueprint of heredity).

> Watson was convinced by reasons based upon genetics that [the] structure could only be built around two spirals arranged "in a certain way." The answer lay in this "certain way."
>
> The only way of representing the three-dimensional structure of an invisible molecule is to replace atoms or groups of atoms by spheres and then build a model of the molecule.
>
> This is exactly what Crick and Watson did, tirelessly attempting to arrange the two spirals. To quote the expression used by one of them, all of their models were "frightful," and quite inadequate to cope with DNA's known qualities ("You couldn't hang anything on these spirals"). ...

---

ing, see Thomas H. Leith's unpublished Boston University Ph.D. dissertation, "Popper's Views of Theory Formation Compared with the Development of Post-Relativistic Cosmological Models," and Leith's article, "Some Presuppositions in the Philosophy of Science," *Journal of the American Scientific Affiliation*, XVII (March, 1965), 8-15.

[11] Leonard K. Nash, *The Nature of the Natural Sciences* (Boston: Little, Brown, 1963), p. 61. Cf. Commissioner Tarquin's philosophy of scientific crime detection: "The trick is to surround it [the total crime situation] and then pull it all together" (Sébastien Japrisot, *Compartiment Tueurs* [Paris: Editions Denoel, 1962], chap. i).

[12] The expression is Frederick Ferré's; see his article, "Mapping the Logic of Models in Science and Theology," *The Christian Scholar*, XLVI (Spring, 1963), 12-15. I am not happy with certain interpretations in this article (e.g., the author's distinction between theories and models: his belief that scientific theories, unlike theological theories, can exist without models), but in general the article deserves the highest commendation for its incisive wrestling with an exceedingly important methodological issue.

[13] Stephen Toulmin, *The Philosophy of Science* (London: Hutchinson University Library, 1953), p. 28 (Toulmin's italics). Cf. also Toulmin's more recent work, *Foresight and Understanding: An Enquiry into the Aims of Science* (Bloomington: Indiana University Press, 1961), *passim*; and Max Black's *Models and Metaphors: Studies in Language and Philosophy* (Ithaca, New York: Cornell University Press, 1962), *passim*.

Then came the famous "spiral night." Crick was working late in a laboratory upstairs. On the ground floor, Watson also was going over a list of possible solutions. That night Crick had a revelation, a solution whispered to him by his intuition: there were only two spirals, they were symmetrical, and they coiled in opposite directions, one from "top to bottom" and the other from "bottom to top" (this hypothesis also reflected certain laws of crystallography).

Crick raced downstairs—it was a spiral staircase—and enthusiastically explained his theory to Watson. Watson received it calmly: it sounded simple to him, much too simple. Then, mentally, he built a spiral form based on this idea, and all the various chemical, biological and physical requirements he put forward were met by it. Now he too was excited; he paced up and down the laboratory, repeating: "It must be true, it must be true."[14]

This lively description of the key point[15] in the discovery of DNA's molecular structure drives home several basic truths about scientific theorizing—truths expressed formally in the definitions previously cited. First, theories do not create facts; rather, they attempt to relate existent facts properly. The DNA molecular model is a "net" thrown to catch the "world" of "chemical, biological and physical requirements" demanded by empirical facticity. The theory maker must never suppose that he is building reality; his task is the fascinating but more humble one of shaping a "conceptual fabric" that, with "epistemological vividness," will correctly mirror the world of substantive reality.[16]

The DNA discovery illustrates, moreover, that theories in science are not formed "either by deductive argument from the experimental data alone, or by the type of logic-book 'induction' on which philosophers have so often concentrated, or indeed by any method for which formal rules could be given."[17] Writers such as Braithwaite have effectively argued the case for the indispen-

---

[14] Roger Louis, "A Team of Experimenters: The Men Who Discovered DNA," *Réalités*, No. 154 (September, 1963), 45-46.
[15] The process of discovery in the case of DNA can be traced back directly to Max Perutz's labors as early as 1936, and the Watson-Crick theory took several years to be collaterally confirmed by Maurice Wilkins, Perutz, and John Kendrew. All five were joint recipients of Nobel prizes (chemistry and medicine) in 1962. For a recent technical overview of the state of research in the DNA area, see Duane T. Gish, "DNA, RNA and Protein Biosynthesis and Implications for Evolutionary Theory," *Journal of the American Scientific Affiliation*, XVII (March, 1965), 2-7.
[16] Cf. the basic distinction made by Wittgenstein between "objects" or "things" ("Der Gegenstand ist einfach" — *Tractatus Logico-Philosophicus*, 2.02) and "facts" ("Was der Fall ist, die Tatsache, ist das Bestehen von Sachverhalten. Der Sachverhalt ist eine Verbindung von Gegenständen [Sachen, Dingen]"—2.0, 2.01). Of course, theories can themselves become the substantive grist for the mill of higher level theory, but this in no way lessens the need to distinguish sharply between that which is to be explained *(explicandum)* and that which does the explaining *(explicans)*.
[17] Toulmin, *The Philosophy of Science*, p. 43.

sable role of deductive reasoning in scientific explanation; but Braithwaite's concluding paragraphs stress the inductivist side of the coin: "Man proposes a system of hypotheses: Nature disposes of its truth or falsity. Man invents a scientific system, and then discovers whether or not it accords with observed fact."[18] G. H. von Wright has logically demonstrated that "if we wish to call reasoned policies better than not-reasoned ones, it follows ... that induction is of necessity the best way";[19] yet the appealing ghost of Francis Bacon's pure inductivism in science has been laid by such philosophers of science as Joseph Agassi,[20] and as the history of scientific discovery shows beyond question, the great advances in theory have not arisen through static, formalistic induction.[21] Rather than making invidious comparisons between deduction and induction in scientific theory formation, we should see these operations as complementary.[22] Instead of seeking monolithic explanation of scientific method, let us, with Max Black, "think of science as a concrescence, a growing together of variable, interacting, mutually reinforcing factors contributing to a development organic in character."[23] Nash provides the following helpful diagram, illustrating how scientific knowledge is generated by endless cyclical renewal:[24]

---

[18] R. B. Braithwaite, *Scientific Explanation: A Study of the Function of Theory, Probability and Law in Science* (Cambridge: Cambridge University Press, 1955), p. 368. Braithwaite, it should be noted, is a much more helpful guide in the realm of scientific explanation than he is in the field of theological analysis; in his book, *An Empiricist View of the Nature of Religious Belief* (Cambridge: Cambridge University Press, 1955), he argues the position, grossly inapplicable to the Christian faith, that religious affirmations are meaningful only ethically, not cognitively.

[19] Georg Henrik von Wright, *The Logical Problem of Induction* (2^d ed.; Oxford: Blackwell, 1957), p. 174.

[20] Joseph Agassi, *Towards an Historiography of Science* ("History and Theory Beihefte." 2; The Hague: Mouton, 1963).

[21] Kepler's discovery of Mars' orbit is a particularly good illustration. On the influence of Kepler's Reformation theology upon his scientific labors, see my essay, "Cross, Constellation, and Crucible: Lutheran Astrology and Alchemy in the Age of the Reformation," *Transactions of the Royal Society of Canada*, 4th ser., I (1963), 251-70 (also published in the British periodical *Ambix, the Journal of the Society for the Study of Alchemy and Early Chemistry*, XI [June, 1963]; 65-86; in French in *Revue d'Histoire el de Philosophie Religieuses*, No. 4 [1966] 323-45; and in my *In Defense of Martin Luther* [Milwaukee: Northwestern, 1970]). Cf. W. Pauli, "The Influence of Archetypal Ideas on the Scientific Theories of Kepler," in C. G. Jung and W. Pauli's *The Interpretation of Nature and the Psyche*, trans. Hull and Silz ("Bollingen Series," 51; New York: Pantheon Books, 1955), pp. 147 ff.

[22] See Arthur Pap's chapter on "Deductive & Inductive Inference" in his posthumously published work, *An Introduction to the Philosophy of Science*, with an Epilogue by Brand Blanshard (Glencoe, Ill.: Free Press, 1962), pp. 139-80.

[23] Max Black, "The Definition of Scientific Method," in his *Problems of Analysis: Philosophical Essays* (London: Routledge & Kegan Paul, 1954), p. 23.

[24] Nash, *op. cit.*, p. 324.

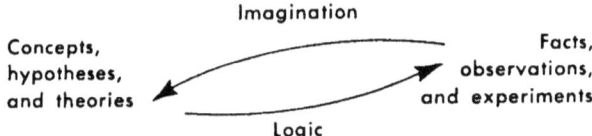

The essential place of "imagination" in scientific theorizing has been greatly stressed by Einstein; and its role can perhaps best be seen by introducing, alongside induction and deduction—as, in fact, the connecting link between them—Peirce's concept of "retroduction" or "abduction," based upon Aristotle's ἀπαγωγή type inference.[25] "Abduction," writes Peirce, "consists in studying facts and devising a theory to explain them. ... Deduction proves that something *must* be; Induction shows that something *actually is* operative; Abduction merely suggests that something *may be*."[26] N. R. Hanson has well illustrated the centrality of such "retroductive" reasoning to scientific theorizing; consider Hanson's ambiguous "bird-antelope":

> Were this flashed on to a screen I might say "It has four feathers." I may be wrong: that number of wiggly lines on the figure is other than four is a conceptual possibility. "It has four feathers" is thus falsifiable, empirical. It is an observation statement. To determine its truth we need only put the figure on the screen again and count the lines.
>
> The statement that the figure is of a bird, however, is not falsifiable in the same sense. Its negation does not represent the same conceptual possibility, for it concerns not an observational detail but the very pattern which makes those details intelligible. One could not even say "It has four feathers" and be wrong about it, if it was not a feathered object. I can show you your error if you say "four feathers." But I cannot thus disclose your "error" in saying of the bird-antelope that it is a bird (instead of an antelope).

---

[25] Aristotle, *Prior Analytics*, ii. 25; cf. *Posterior Analytics*, ii. 19.
[26] C. S. Peirce, *Collected Papers*, ed. Charles Hartshorne and Paul Weiss (Cambridge: Harvard University Press, 1931-1958), V, para. 146, 171. It should go without saying that acceptance of the Peirce-Aristotle-retroduction concept in no way commits one to Peirce's pragmatic philosophy; I myself have argued strongly against pragmatic epistemologies in my book, *The Shape of the Past: An Introduction to Philosophical Historiography* (Minneapolis: Bethany, 1975), pp. 320-29.

Pattern statements are different from detail statements. They are not inductive summaries of detail statements. Still the statement, "It's a bird" is truly empirical. Had birds been different, or had the bird-antelope been drawn differently, "It's a bird" might not have been true. In some sense it is true. If the detail statements are empirical, the pattern statements which give them sense are also empirical—though not in the same way. To deny a detail statement is to do something within the pattern. To deny a pattern statement is to attack the conceptual framework itself, and this denial cannot function in the same way. ...

Physical theories provide patterns within which data appear intelligible. They constitute a "conceptual Gestalt." A theory is not pieced together from observed phenomena; it is rather what makes it possible to observe phenomena as being of a certain sort, and as related to other phenomena. Theories put phenomena into systems. They are built up in "reverse"—retroductively. A theory is a cluster of conclusions in search of a premise. From the observed properties of phenomena the physicist reasons his way towards a keystone idea from which the properties are explicable as a matter of course.[27]

Watson and Crick's discovery of the molecular structure of DNA clearly displays the centrality of retroductive inference in scientific theory formation: they sought a "conceptual Gestalt" which would render intelligible the genetic and crystallographic data; and their resultant theory of two symmetrical spirals was successful precisely because it constituted a "keystone idea" from which the various physical, chemical, and biological characteristics of the molecule were "explicable as a matter of course."

It is particularly important to note that the validity of a scientific theory depends squarely upon its applicability as a "conceptual Gestalt"; experimental confirmation through predictive success is of secondary importance and is often, of necessity, dispensed with entirely. In paleobiology, for example, experimental prediction is ruled out by the very nature of the subject matter; and in astrophysics and cosmological theory predictive experiments are seldom able to be formulated. Watson could say of the DNA spiral theory, "It must be true," though several years would elapse before X-ray diffraction patterns of the molecule would become available, for his theory provided a full-scale ordering of the relevant data.

---

[27] N. R. Hanson, *Patterns of Discovery: An Inquiry into the Conceptual Foundations of Science* (Cambridge: Cambridge University Press, 1958), pp. 87-90; Hanson, following Peirce, illustrates retroductive inference by the classic case of Kepler's theorizing to an elliptical orbit for Mars. With the "bird-antelope," cf. Wittgenstein's detailed philosophical analysis of the psychologist Jastrow's ambiguous "duck-rabbit" (*Philosophical Investigations,* ed. Anscombe and Rhees [New York: Macmillan, 1953], II. xi. 194 ff).

Galileo knew he had succeeded when the constant acceleration hypothesis patterned the diverse phenomena he had encountered for thirty years. His reasoned advance from insight to insight culminated in an ultimate physical *explicans*. Further deductions were merely confirmatory; he could have left them to any of his students—Viviani or Toricelli. Even had verification of these further predictions eluded seventeenth-century science, this would not have prevented Galileo from embracing the constant acceleration hypothesis, any more than Copernicus and Kepler were prevented from embracing heliocentrism by the lack of a telescope with which to observe Venus' phases. Kepler needed no new observations to realize that the ellipse covered all observed positions. Newton required no predictions from his gravitation hypothesis to be confident that this really did explain Kepler's three laws and a variety of other given data.[28]

The Scientific Level in Theological Theorizing

We have found that scientific theories are conceptual Gestalts, built up retroductively through imaginative attempts to render phenomena intelligible. What relevance does this have for understanding the theologian's labors? Can any application be made to the field of theology? Is not theology a unique realm of the "spirit," unscientific by its very nature? To bring Tertullian's famous question up to date: "What has the Institute of Advanced Study to do with Jerusalem, the Laboratory with the Church?"

The answer to this last question is not "Nothing," but "Everything." Though theology is evidently something *more* than science (precisely what the "more" consists of, we shall see later), it is certainly not anything *less*. I say this, let it be noted, not simply in reference to the fact that any theology can be an object of descriptive, scientific study by specialists in the history, philosophy, or psychology of religion.[29] This is of course true in the case of all the world religions; but Christianity is unique in claiming intrinsic, not merely extrinsic, connection with the empirical reality which is the subject of scientific investigation. Christianity is a *historical* religion—historical in the very special sense that its entire

---

[28] Hanson, *op. cit.*, pp. 89-90. Readers of the present essay who wish to delve further into the nature of scientific theorizing are encouraged to consult J. O. Wisdom's bibliographical article, "The Methodology of Natural Science: Publications in English," *La Philosophie au milieu du vingtième siècle*, ed. Raymond Klibansky (4 vols.; 2ᵈ ed.; Firenze: La Nuova Italia Editrice, 1961-1962), I, 164-83.

[29] It is John A. Hutchison's great mistake that he stops here in analyzing the scientific aspect of Christian theology, thereby leaving his reader with the impression that the Christian religion is no more capable of objective validation than are any of the other competing world faiths (*Language and Faith: Studies in Sign Symbol, and Meaning* [Philadelphia: Westminster Press, 1963], especially pp. 244-47, 293).

revelational content is wedded to historical manifestations of Divine power. The pivot of Christian theology is the biblical affirmation that ὁ λόγος σὰρξ ἐγένετο (John 1:14): God Himself came to earth—entered man's empirical sphere—in Jesus Christ, the revelation of God in the history of Israel served as a pointer to Messiah's coming, and His revelation in the Apostolic community displayed the power of Christ's Spirit.[30] From the first verse of the Bible to the last God's *contact* with man's world is affirmed. And throughout Scripture human testimony to objective, empirical encounter with God is presented in the strongest terms.[31] Christian theology thus has no fear of scientific, empirical investigation;[32] quite the contrary, the historical nature of the Christian faith—as distinguished from the subjective, existential character of the other world religions[33]—demands objective, scientific theologizing.

Hence we should expect, Barth notwithstanding,[34] that theological theories, whatever suprascientific characteristics they may have, will most definitely

---

[30] I made this point *in extenso* in the apologetic lectures I delivered at the University of British Columbia on January 29 and 30, 1963; these have been published in a slightly abridged version as a series of four articles under the general title "History and Christianity," in *His*, December, 1964—March, 1965; the lectures are now available in original form in my *Where Is History Going?* (Grand Rapids, Mich.: Zondervan, 1969), chaps, ii-iii.

[31] See, for example, the accounts of Gideon and the fleece (Judges 6), Elijah on Mount Carmel (I Kings 18), and the primary-source testimonies to empirical contact with the risen Christ (Luke 24:36-43; John 20:25-28; cf. I John 1:1-4).

[32] To King Agrippa Paul thus defended the empirical facticity of Christ's fulfilment of prophecy and resurrection: "I am speaking the sober truth. For the king knows about these things, and to him I speak freely; for I am persuaded that none of these things has escaped his notice, for this was not done in a corner" (Acts 26:25-26). Peter's Pentecost sermon contains the significant lines: "Men of Israel, hear these words: Jesus of Nazareth, a man attested to you by God with mighty works and wonders and signs which God did through him in your midst, as you yourselves know ..." (Acts 2:22; cf. F. F. Bruce, *The New Testament Documents: Are They Reliable?* [5th ed.; London: InterVarsity Fellowship, 1960], pp. 45-46).

[33] It might seem that such a general statement would not apply in Islam; however, see my article, "The Apologetic Approach of Muhammed Ali and Its Implications for Christian Apologetics," *Muslim World*, LI (April, 1961), 111-22 (see author's "Corrigendum" in the July, 1961 *Muslim World*). No world religion other than Christianity stakes its life on the objective historical facticity of its claims; only the Christian faith dares to make such an assertion as Paul's: "If Christ has not been raised, then our preaching is in vain and your faith is in vain" (I Cor. 15:14).

[34] At the outset of his *Kirchliche Dogmatik*, Barth argues: "If theology allows itself to be called or calls itself a science, it cannot at the same time take over the obligation to submit to measurement by the canons valid for other sciences" (I/1, chap. i. sec. 1). This unwarranted opposition between theology and science directly relates to Barth's scripturally illegitimate distinction between "salvation history" (*Heilsgeschichte*) and ordinary history (*Historie*), to his unqualified rejection of natural revelation, and to the church-directed, anti-apologetic thrust of his entire theology. I have maintained elsewhere that Barth's fundamental difficulties here stem from his over-reaction to Protestant modernism and to his fear of subjecting the Christian faith to the secular examination

display the full range of properties of scientific theories. The theological theorist, like his scientific counterpart, will endeavor to formulate conceptual Gestalts—"networks" of ideas capable of rendering his data intelligible. He will employ "models" to achieve epistemological vividness. He will utilize all three types of inference (inductive, deductive, retroductive) in his theory making, but, again like the scientist, he will find himself most usually dependent upon the imaginative operation of retroduction.

Little more than superficial naiveté lies at the basis of the popular opinion that science and theology are in methodological conflict because the former "employs inductive reasoning" while the latter "operates deductively"! In point of fact, both generally proceed retroductively, and neither is less concerned than the other about the concrete verification of its inferences.

And how does verification take place? In science we have seen that the success of a theory depends upon its ability, as Toulmin says, to "fit the facts." The same is true in theology. Ian Ramsey—though he does not see that theology exactly parallels science here—introduces a valuable analogy when he writes that "the theological model works ... like the fitting of a boot or a shoe."

> In other words, we have a particular doctrine which, like a preferred and selected shoe, starts by appearing to meet our empirical needs. But on closer fitting to the phenomena the shoe may pinch. When tested against future slush and rain it may be proven to be not altogether watertight or it may be comfortable—yet it must not be too comfortable. In this way, the test of a shoe is measured by its ability to match a wide range of phenomena, by its overall success in meeting a variety of needs. Here is what I might call the method of empirical fit which is displayed by theological theorizing.[35]

This is precisely the verifying test that we have encountered in our discussion of scientific theories; the Watson-Crick spiral theory was just such a "shoe" whose adequacy depended squarely upon its ability to "fit" the relevant physical, chemical, and biological characteristics of the DNA molecule. Neither Watson and Crick, nor the great scientific theorists of past ages (we have already referred

---

for which John 1:14 constitutes a specific mandate ("Karl Barth and Contemporary Theology of History," *Bulletin of the Evangelical Theological Society*, VI [May, 1963], 39-49; reprinted in *Where Is History Going?* [*op. cit.* in n. 30], chap. v). Gordon H. Clark, in his excellent work, *Karl Barth's Theological Method* (Philadelphia: Presbyterian and Reformed Publishing Co., 1963), chap. iii, points up Barth's irrationalistic tendencies, and correctly notes that in citing and arguing against Heinrich Scholz's six scientific norms (*K.D., loc. cit.*), Barth is in actuality opposing the straw man of nineteenth-century Scientism (Scientific Positivism), not genuine scientific method. Unfortunately, Barth has never cared for science (Henri Bouillard, in his *Genèse et Evolution*, reports that even as a boy Barth disliked physics and mathematics); and his *Church Dogmatics* suffers for it on almost every page.

[35] Ian T. Ramsey, *Models and Mystery* (London: Oxford University Press 1964), p. 17.

to Galileo, Copernicus, Kepler, and Newton) achieved their primary success in theory construction through the predictive character of their formulations: both in science and in theology, it is "fit," not "future," that lies at the heart of successful theorizing.[36]

But clearly scientific and theological theories are not identical! Where do the differences lie? One important difference (we leave others until later) is pointed up by Ramsey's "shoe" analogy. This analogy immediately raises two basic questions about theorizing: first and most obvious, How do you make the shoe (the theory or model)? but second, and even more fundamental, What foot (data) do you try to fit? In science, the "foot"—the irreducible stuff which theorizing attempts to grasp in its net—is the natural world, and this includes every phenomenal manifestation in the universe. Science knows no investigative boundaries: its limits are imposed not by the stuff with which it is permitted to deal, but by the manner in which it can treat its data. *Ex hypothesi*, science is methodologically capable of studying the world in an *objective* manner only: it can examine anything that touches human experience, but it can never, *qua* science, "get inside" its subject matter; it always stands outside and describes. This is, of course, both the glory and the pathos of science: it can analyze everything, but it is prevented from experiencing the heart of anything.

On the objective, scientific level, however, theology has no greater advantage; it likewise stands outside its data and analyzes. But what precisely does it analyze? What are the *Gegenstände* of theological theorizing—the "simples" that the theologian attempts to render intelligible through his conceptual Gestalts? In general, for Christian theology, the "foot to be shod" is revelational experience. Theological theories endeavor to "fit the facts" of such experience; theology on this level is thus one segment of scientific activity as a whole—that segment concerned with revelational, as opposed to non-revelational, phenomena. Jean Racette, in dependence upon the great contemporary Jesuit philosopher-theologian Bernard Lonergan, puts it succinctly and well:

> La théologie n'est pas une science ou une sagesse quelconque. Elle est la science du sacré et du révélé. Elle est une démarche de l'intelligence éclairée par la foi. Elle est une réflexion systématique sur un donné reconnu et accepté comme révélé, et donc comme vrai.[37]

However, the expression "revelational experience" is manifestly ambiguous. What does it signify? This question, without a doubt, is of paramount importance for the entire theological task, since a false step here will tragically weaken

---

[36] Ramsey (*ibid.*) perpetuates a common fallacy when he asserts that theological models differ from scientific models in that the latter must generate experimentally verifiable deductions.

[37] Jean Racette, "La Méthode en théologie: Le cours du P. Lonergan au 'Theology Institute' de Toronto" (*Sciences Ecclésiastiques*, XV (mai-septembre 1963), 293.

the entire process of theological theorizing—either by emasculation (if one excludes from purview genuine revelational data), or by adulteration (if one mixes non-revelational considerations with the truly revelational subject matter). And, ironically, it is exactly at this point that Christian theology has all too often trumpeted forth an uncertain sound—or, worse, a positive discord! To change the metaphor, the theologian has not infrequently played the role of a blind cobbler, trying to make shoes without knowing what kind of foot he is shoeing; at other times, he appears as a bungling apprentice, busily preparing what should be dainty slippers for Queen Revelation when in fact he is putting together clod-hoppers to fit Lumberjack U. (for Unregenerate) Religiosity!

Through Christian history, the "revelational experience" which yields the proper data for theological theorizing has been understood as having either a *single* source or *multiple* sources. Traditional multiple source positions include Roman Catholicism, Greek Orthodoxy, and Anglo-Catholicism (all holding that the Bible and church tradition constitute valid revelational sources), and various sects having sacred books which they use alongside of the Bible as sources of data for theologizing (e.g., Mormonism, with its *Book of Mormon*; Christian Science, with Mrs. Eddy's *Science and Health*). Multiple source approaches also constitute the epistemological core of most avant-garde mainline Protestant theological positions today: a combination of biblical insight, church teaching, and personal religious experience is supposed to provide the fund from which systematic theology should draw its data for doctrinal theorizing. For Paul Tillich, the "survey of the sources of systematic theology has shown their almost unlimited richness: Bible, church history, history of religion and culture."[38] For advocates of the post-Bultmannian "New Hermeneutic" (such as Ernst Fuchs and Gerhard Ebeling), systematic theology has as its subject matter "the word event itself, in which the reality of man comes true," and by "word event" is meant "the event of interpretation";[39] thus theology has its source in a polar dialectic of biblical text and situational interpretation. Heinrich Ott, for all his differences with Fuchs, expresses essentially the same dual-source, dialectic approach when he finds the subject matter of theology in "the Christ event, the reality of revelation and of believing"[40] and proposes that "dogmatics

---

[38] Paul Tillich, *Systematic Theology* (2 vols.; Chicago: University of Chicago Press, 1951), I, 40.

[39] Gerhard Ebeling, *Theologie und Verkündigung; Ein Gesprach mit Rudolf Bultmann* ("Hermeneutische Untersuchungen zur Theologie," 1; Tübingen: J. C. B. Mohr, 1962), pp. 14-15. Cf. James M. Robinson and John B. Cobb, Jr. (eds.), *The New Hermeneutic* ("New Frontiers in Theology," 2; New York: Harper, 1964), *passim*.

[40] Heinrich Ott, "Was ist systematische Theologie?," *Zeitschrift für Theologie und Kirche*, Beiheft 2 (1961), pp. 19-46, sec. iii. Ott simultaneously regards "the gospel of Christ" as the subject matter of theology, and here also the dialectic operates: "The Christ event encounters us through the gospel of Christ, but the gospel is encountered through the Gospels and witnesses that are not yet

is simply to unfold thoughtfully without presupposing any philosophical schema the meaning-content experienced in believing from within the experience itself";[41] systematic theology thus serves as a "hermeneutical arch that reaches from the text to the contemporary sermon."[42]

All multiple-source views of the subject matter of theology are, however, unstable. They tend to give preference to one source rather than to another, or to seek some single, more fundamental source lying behind the multiple sources already accepted. Among the sects, the Bible has been virtually swallowed up by whatever special "sacred book" has been put alongside of it;[43] tradition has been more determinative than biblical teaching in the theological development of Greek Orthodoxy and Roman Catholicism; and the "New Hermeneutic" seems incapable of withstanding the old Bultmannian gravitational pull away from the biblical text toward the other dialectic pole of contemporary existential interpretation. In the "New Shape" Roman Catholicism of Karl Rahner, Küng, *et al.*, a conscious attempt is being made to get behind the dualism of Scripture and tradition through affirming a unity of "Holy Writ *and* Holy Church";[44] yet such a dialectic, like that of the Protestant "New Hermeneutic," does not escape the charge of question-begging. This is the essential, insurmountable difficulty in all multiple-source approaches to theological theorizing. They leave unanswered the question of *final* authority. What do we do as Roman Catholics when Holy Writ and Holy Church *disagree*? What do we do as Tillichians when church history, the Bible and the history of culture are not in accord? Obviously, one must either frankly admit that one source is final, or establish a criterion of judgment over all previously accepted sources—which criterion becomes, *ex hypothesi*, the final source! Multiple source approaches to the subject matter of theology thus logically—whether one likes it or not—reduce to single source interpretations.[45]

---

and never will be the gospel itself. What is actually spoken is only the gospel *according to* ... , the gospel according to Matthew, according to Mark, according to Luke, according to John, but also according to Paul, and why not also, dependent on those and secondarily, the gospel according to Martin Luther, Calvin, Rudolf Bultmann, or Karl Barth?"

[41] *Ibid.*, sec. v.

[42] *Ibid.*, sec. iii. Cf. James M. Robinson and John B. Cobb, Jr. (eds.), *The Later Heidegger and Theology* ("New Frontiers in Theology," 1; New York: Harper, 1963), *passim*.

[43] A point brought out with particular force in J. K. Van Baalen's fine work, *The Chaos of the Cults* (Grand Rapids, Mich.: Eerdmans, 1955), which has gone through a number of editions.

[44] On this trend, see especially George H. Tavard, who argues that "the authority of the Church's tradition and that of Scripture are not two, but one" *(Holy Writ or Holy Church* [New York: Harper, 1959], p. 244).

[45] Cf. W. N. Clarke's critique of philosopher Paul Weiss' *Modes of Being*, which conceives the universe as having four ultimate dimensions of being: the Weissian system "leaves untouched the ... fundamental and, for a metaphysician, unavoidable problem of the ultimate origin or source of ex-

If theology must ultimately admit that there is but a single "foot" which its doctrinal theories are to fit, the question becomes one of identifying that foot. The numerous identifications through Christian history contract upon examination, to four: Reason, the Church, Christian Experience, and Scriptural Revelation. During the eighteenth-century "Enlightenment" it was contended that the "natural light of Reason," not any alleged sacred writing or "special revelation," constitutes the final source of valid theological data.[46] Unhappily, however, pure reason (i.e., formal logic) is tautologous and cannot impart any factual data about existent things, whether theological or otherwise;[47] and "reason" understood as "nature" can yield atheistic ideologies almost as easily as deistic theologies.[48] In Romanism, the Church becomes the court of last resort for determining what are or what are not genuine data for theologizing. But the argument that this is necessary because even an infallible Bible requires an infallible interpreter suffers from the fallacy of infinite regress; one can always ask, Then how can the Church itself function without a higher-level interpreter? Moreover, no Divine mandate can be produced to justify the authority of the Church as interpreter of Scripture.[49]

Christian Experience is the most widely accepted Protestant answer to the question of the source of data for theological theorizing. For the unreconstructed Modernism of the Schleiermacher-Ritschl-Fosdick era, "constructive (i.e., subjective) religious empiricism" was expected to yield doctrinal reconstructions in accord with the needs of contemporary man. As a matter of fact, however, such a methodology yielded only the results permitted by the experiential aprioris of the particular theological investigator.[50] Bultmannian existentialism and the post-Bultmannian theologies stemming from his paramount concern with "existential self-understanding"[51] are actually "experience" theologies also:

---

istence and the ultimate principle of unity of this whole with its four irreducible modes" (*Yale Review*, September, 1958). Cf. my review of Weiss' *History: Written and Lived* in *Christianity Today*, VII (July 19, 1963), 43-44; reprinted in *Where Is History Going?* [*op. cit.* in n. 30], appendix E.

[46] See, for the most influential American example of this approach, Thomas Paine's *Age of Reason*, especially Pt. 2.

[47] Whitehead and Russell, in their great *Principia Mathematica*, showed that this is the case both for formal logic and for mathematics—and that the latter is a special case of the former.

[48] Joseph Lewis' *The Tyranny of God* (New York: The Freethought Press Association, 1921) is a popular example of an atheism built on the natural evils in the world; here the "Nature" which pointed Paine unmistakably (he thought) to a beneficent Creator points Lewis to a universe having no God at all.

[49] See my essay, "The Petrine Theory Evaluated by Philology and Logic," in my *Shape of the Past* (*op. cit.* in n. 26), pp. 351-57.

[50] I have demonstrated this in detail in my essay, "Constructive Religious Empiricism: An Analysis and Criticism," *ibid.*, pp. 257-311.

[51] See especially Bultmann's essay, "The Task and the History of New Testament Theology," in-

for them the current situation of the theologian, not an objectively unchanging biblical message, is the determinative factor in theological activity. In the same general class fall many of the recent attempts to interrelate theology and "ordinary language philosophy": Ramsey's concern with theological theories in relation to "our empirical needs";[52] Hick's interpretation of theological dogmas as "the basic convictions which directly transcribe Christian experience";[53] etc.

The absolutizing of religious experience commits the "naturalistic fallacy" (sometimes unkindly called the "sociologist's fallacy"): it assumes that the "is-ness" of the believer's "existential encounter" constitutes an "ought-ness." No answer whatever is given to the vital question: How is one to know that the divine and not the demonic is operating in the given experience? Paul Tillich argues with irrefutable cogency that "insight into the human situation destroys every theology which makes experience an independent source instead of a dependent medium of systematic theology."[54] Surely the psychoanalytic discoveries of the twentieth century should give us pause before we commit ourselves to the transparent purity of man's existential life!

> The analogy from human "encounters" suggests that at least some of the experiences which are held to be "encounter with God" really are subjectively produced; can the mere claim that the experiences are "self-verifying" rule out the uncomfortable suspicion that, when dissociated from any empirical personality, they all may be only illusion?[55]

---

cluded as an Epilogue to his *Theology of the New Testament*, trans. Kendrick Grobel (2 vols.; London: SCM Press, 1955), II, 241.

[52] See above, the quotation corresponding to n. 35. I suspect that Ramsey's overstress on religious experience, combined with relatively little emphasis on biblical authority, is an underlying factor in his defense of F. D. Maurice's uncertainty about the doctrine of eternal punishment (see Ramsey's *On Being Sure in Religion* [London: University of London-Athlone Press. 1963], especially chap. i).

[53] John Hick. *Faith and Knowledge* (Ithaca, New York: Cornell University Press, 1957), p. 198. For Hick, the "catalyst of faith"—the means of theological structuring the "apperceiving mass" of experience is "the person of Jesus Christ" (p. 196). But this Christ is not seen in the context of a fully reliable biblical revelation. Thus, in his article "Theology and Verification," Hick can make the amazing statement: "I will only express my personal opinion that the logic of the New Testament as a whole, though admittedly not always its explicit content, leads to a belief in ultimate universal salvation" (*Theology Today*, XVII [April, 1960]. 31). In regard to the existence of God, Hick holds the experiential view that "the important question is not whether the existence of God can be demonstrated but whether ... faith-awareness of God is a mode of cognition which can properly be trusted and in terms of which it is rational to live" (*The Existence of God*, ed. John Hick [New York: Macmillan, 1964], p. 19).

[54] For his full-scale treatment of this issue, see Tillich, *op. cit.*, I, 40-46.

[55] Frederick Ferré, *Language, Logic and God* (New York: Harper, 1961), p. 104; Ferré's entire chapter on "The Logic of Encounter" (pp. 94-104) is a masterly critique of much of the wooly "I-Thou," existential-encounter theology popular today.

What is clearly needed is an objective check on existential experience—in other words, a source of theological data outside of it, by which to judge it.[56]

Thus we arrive at the Bible[57]—the source by which Reason, Church, and Religious Experience can and must be evaluated theologically. We reach this point not simply by process of elimination, but more especially because only Scripture can be validated as a genuine source of theological truth.[58] It is the biblical message alone that provides the irreducible *Gegenstände* for theological theorizing—the "foot" which all theological theories must "fit." In the words of the Reformation axiom, "Quod non est biblicum, non est theologicum." The Christian theologian, like the scientist, faces a "given": he endeavors, not to create his data, but to provide conceptual Gestalts for rendering them intelligible and interrelating them properly. What Nature is to the scientific theorizer, the Bible is to the theologian. Franz Pieper astutely argued this parallel as follows:

> If we would escape the deceptions which are involved in the attempts to construct a human system of theology, we must ever bear in mind that in theology we deal with given and unalterable facts, which human reasoning and the alleged needs of the "system" cannot change in the least. There is, as has been pointed out, an analogy here between natural history and theology. Natural history studies the observable data in the realm of nature; its business is to observe the facts. All human knowledge of natural phenomena extends only so far as man's observation and experience of the given facts

---

[56] The foregoing criticisms, it is well to point out, also apply to those theologies which attempt to make a "living Christ" (as distinct from the Christ of Scripture) the source of theological theorizing. Such a "living Christ," if He is not known through Scripture, is necessarily known through extra-biblical experience. But, in the latter case, how can one be sure that one's "Christ of experience" is the *real* Christ and not a projection of personal or corporate religious needs and desires? The dangers of idolatry here are overwhelming.

[57] Limitations of space prevent us from dealing with the question of extra-biblical scriptures which claim to provide the ultimate interpretation of the Bible or revelational data superior to it (e.g., the *Book of Mormon*). Interested readers are referred to Van Baalen (*op. cit.* in n. 43), where the unverifiable nature of these claims is made patent, and where specific refutation of many of them is given.

[58] In my *Shape of the Past* (*op. cit.* in n. 26, pp. 138-39), I have summarized what I believe to be the crux validation: "1. On the basis of accepted principles of textual and historical analysis, the Gospel records are found to be trustworthy historical documents—primary source evidence for the life of Christ. 2. In these records, Jesus exercises divine prerogatives and claims to be God in human flesh; and He rests His claims on His forthcoming resurrection. 3. In all four Gospels, Christ's bodily resurrection is described in minute detail; Christ's resurrection evidences His deity. 4. The fact of the resurrection cannot be discounted on *a priori*, philosophical grounds; miracles are impossible only if one so defines them—but such definition rules out proper historical investigation. 5. If Christ is God, then He speaks the truth concerning the absolute divine authority of the Old Testament and of the soon-to-be-written New Testament."

extends. The true scientist does not determine the nature and characteristics of plants and animals according to a preconceived and hypothetical system.
...

This matter has been aptly illustrated by contrasting railroad systems and mountain systems. A railroad system is conceived in the mind of the builders before it exists; its construction follows the blueprint drawn up by the engineers. The mountain system, on the other hand, does not follow our blueprints. We can only report our findings regarding its characteristics, the relation of the different mountain ranges to each other, etc., as we find them. The theologian is dealing with a fixed and unchangeable fact, the Word of God which Christ gave His Church through His Apostles and Prophets.[59]

To be sure, the affirmation that Holy Scripture is the sole source of data for theological theorizing poses questions requiring serious attention. Specifically: (1) Is the Bible an inerrantly reliable source of revelational data? (2) Is the Bible self-interpreting? (3) Does the Bible provide the norms as well as the subject matter for theological theory construction? We cannot hope to discuss any one of these questions fully here, but we can indicate the central considerations which demand affirmative answers in each case.

Elsewhere[60] I have attempted to show that any view of biblical inspiration that rejects the inerrancy of Scripture is not merely incorrect, but in fact *meaningless* from the standpoint both of philosophical and of theological analysis. Anti-inerrancy inspiration positions are based upon dualistic and existentialistic presuppositions that are incapable of being confirmed or disconfirmed (thus their analytically meaningless character), and they fly directly in the face of the scriptural epistemology itself, which firmly joins "spiritual" truth to historical, empirical facticity and regards *all* words spoken by inspiration of God as carrying their Author's guarantee of veracity. Moreover, if in some sense Scripture were not unqualifiedly a reliable source of theological truth, what criteria could possibly distinguish the wheat from the chaff? Not the Scripture itself (by definition), and not anything outside of it (for the "outside" factors would then become revelation, and we have already seen that extra-biblical revelation-claims are incapable of validation)!

This latter point also applies to the question of the self-interpreting nature of the Bible: Were the Scripture not self-interpreting, then a "higher" revelation

---

[59] Franz Pieper, *Christian Dogmatics*, trans. and ed. T. Engelder, J. T. Mueller, and W. W. F. Albrecht (4 vols.; St. Louis, Mo.: Concordia, 1950-1957), I, 142-43.
[60] John Warwick Montgomery, "Inspiration and Inerrancy: A New Departure," *Bulletin of the Evangelical Theological Society*, VIII (Spring, 1965); reprinted in my *Crisis in Lutheran Theology* (2 vols., 2ᵈ ed.; Minneapolis: Bethany, 1973), I, chap i, and in my *Suicide of Christian Theology* (Minneapolis: Bethany, 1970), pp. 314-55.

would be needed to provide interpretative canons for it; but such a Bible-to-the-second-power cannot be shown to exist. And, indeed, there is no reason to feel that one should exist. If God inspired the Scripture, then its self-interpreting perspicuity is established. The Reformers soundly argued that "the clarity of Scripture is demanded by its inspiration. God is able to speak clearly, for He is the master of language and words."[61] True, "there are many impenetrable mysteries in Scripture which are unclear in that they cannot be grasped by human intellect, but these mysteries have not been recorded in Scripture in obscure or ambiguous language."[62] Present-day specialists in biblical hermeneutics who have been trained in general literary interpretation make every effort to impress upon their students and readers that the Bible must be approached objectively and allowed to interpret itself. Thus Robert Traina writes in the Introduction to his superlative manual, *Methodical Bible Study: A New Approach to Hermeneutics*:

> Now the Scriptures are distinct from the interpreter and are not an integral part of him. If the truths of the Bible already resided in man, there would be no need for the Bible and this manual would be superfluous. But the fact is that *the Bible is an objective body of literature* which exists because man needs to know certain truths which he himself cannot know and which must come to him from without. Consequently, if he is to discover the truths which reside in this objective body of literature, he must utilize an approach which corresponds in nature with it, that is, an *objective* approach.[63]

Such an hermeneutic approach has been explicitly adopted by the great systematic theologians, past[64] and present,[65] and *must* be presupposed in theologi-

---

[61] Robert Preus, *The Inspiration of Scripture: A Study of the Theology of the Seventeenth Century Lutheran Dogmaticians* (Edinburgh: Oliver and Boyd, 1957), p. 159.
[62] *Ibid.*, p. 157.
[63] Introduction, sec. C. 2. a. (p. 7); Traina's italics. This book was first published in 1952 and is available from the Biblical Seminary in New York. Serious application of its principles offers perhaps the best counteractive to such absurdly superficial judgments as Kaufmann's remark on "the overt ambiguity of the Scriptures" (*op. cit.* in n. 4, p. 227): "In no case can a theology really do justice to the Scriptures because it refuses to take into account their heterogeneity and their deep differences."
[64] E.g., the classical Lutheran dogmatician Johann Gerhard (1582-1637), in his *Loci Theologici*, ed. Preuss-Frank, I, 237-40.
[65] E.g., my esteemed colleague, J. Oliver Buswell, Jr., in his epochal work, *A Systematic Theology of the Christian Religion* (2 vols.; Grand Rapids, Mich.: Zondervan, 1962-1963), I, 24-25. Edward John Carnell has rightly praised Buswell for his "repeated insistence that a univocal meaning unites the mind of God with the mind of a Christian. The defense of univocal meaning implies a forthright rejection of all species of theology, ancient or modern, that either openly assert or tacitly consent to the hypothesis that truth signifies one thing for God (because he is almighty) and another for a Christian (because he is merely human)" (*Christianity Today*, IX, [February 26, 1965], 40).

cal theorizing if one is to avoid exegeting and systematizing one's own subjective opinions and desires instead of God's Word. The "circularity principle" of Bultmann and his former disciples[66] gives carte blanche to this latter error and invariably destroys the possibility of sound theological theorizing; as I have written elsewhere:

> When Bultmann argues that not only historical method but also existential "life-relation" must be presupposed in exegesis, he blurs the aim of objectivity which is essential to all proper literary and historical study. Following Dilthey as well as the general stream of philosophical existentialism, Bultmann attempts to "cut under the subject-object distinction"; he claims that "for historical understanding, the schema of subject and object that has validity for natural science is invalid." But in fact the subject-object distinction is of crucial importance in history as well as in natural science, and only by aiming to discover the objective concern of the text (rather than blending it with the subjective concern of the exegete) can successful exegesis take place.[67]

But does the Bible *per se* yield the norms, or only the subject matter, for theological theorizing? Not only from existentially orientated Bultmannians and post-Bultmannian advocates of the "New Hermeneutic," but also from Paul Tillich, who has valiantly endeavored to stiffen theological existentialism by means of ontology, we receive the negative reply that Scripture cannot in itself supply absolute norms for theological construction. After noting the variety of norms employed through church history for imparting significance levels to biblical data, Tillich asserts: "The Bible as such has never been the norm of systematic theology. The norm has been a principle derived from the Bible in an encounter between Bible and church."[68] Now we readily grant that church history presents a number of different normative approaches to Holy Writ: the early Greek church's stress on the Logos as the light shining in the darkness of man's mortality,[69] the sacramental Christology of the Western church in the Middle Ages, the Reformation emphasis on God's gracious forgiveness of sin, Protestant Modernism's concern with social amelioration, Tillich's own con-

---

[66] Heinrich Ott defends the "hermeneutical circle" as strongly as does Bultmann; see Ott's "Was ist systematische Theologie?" (*op. cit.*), sec. ii. The "hermeneutical circle" approach is, of course, an outgrowth and corollary of Heideggerian existentialism.

[67] John Warwick Montgomery, "The Fourth Gospel Yesterday and Today," *Concordia Theological Monthly*, XXXIV [April, 1963], 204; reprinted in the author's *Suicide of Christian Theology, op. cit.*, p. 435.

[68] Tillich, *op. cit.*, pp. 50-51.

[69] Cf. Jaroslav Pelikan's *The Light of the World: A Basic Image in Early Christian Thought* (New York: Harper, 1962), and *The Shape of Death: Life, Death, and Immortality in the Early Fathers* (New York: Abingdon, 1961).

centration on Christ as the New Being, etc. But are we, à la Tillich, to commit the naturalistic fallacy and assume that because varied judgments on the norm of biblical theology *have* existed, they *should* have existed? or that the various historical judgments on the norm have been equally valid, simply because they have met the needs of the time? or that Scripture does not in fact provide its own absolute norms for unifying its content? Tillich's dialectic "encounter between Bible and church" as the source of norms inevitably degenerates to historical relativism, leaving his own norm without justification along with the others.

In point of fact, one can readily detect unsound theological norms (e.g., Modernism's "social gospel") by virtue of their inability to give biblical force to central scriptural teachings, and by their unwarranted elevation of secondary (or even unbiblical) emphases to primary position. In other words, Scripture *does* very definitely supply "weighting factors" for its own teachings. Moreover, the majority of norms displayed in the history of orthodox theology have not really been as divergent as Tillich's discussion implies: most often they have displayed complementary facets of the overarching biblical message that "God was in Christ, reconciling the world unto Himself." Scripture itself makes this Christocentric teaching primary and ranges its other teachings in objective relation to it; and a sinful church learns the fact not through its historical "encounters" (which are always tainted), but from the perspicuous text of Holy Writ. Only Scripture is capable of truly interpreting Scripture; and only Scripture is able to provide the norm-structure for its interpretation and for the construction of theological doctrine based upon its inerrantly inspired content.

Terminating, then, our discussion of the scientific level of theological theorizing, we must reaffirm the fundamental thesis for which proof has been marshalled *in extenso:* science and theology form and test their respective theories in the same way; the scientific theorizer attempts objectively to formulate conceptual Gestalts (hypotheses, theories, laws) capable of rendering Nature intelligible, and the theologian endeavors to provide conceptual Gestalts (doctrines, dogmas)[70] which will "fit the facts" and properly reflect the norms of

---

[70] Hick (*Faith and Knowledge*, pp. 198 ff.) distinguishes between "dogmas" and "doctrines": the former "define the religion in question by pointing to the area of primary religious experiences from which it has arisen" (example: The Apostles' Creed), while the latter are "the propositions officially accepted as interpreting [the religion's] dogmas and as relating them together in a coherent system of thought." This is a useful distinction in practice, but Hick errs at several points in developing it: (1) Not "religious experiences" but the Holy Scriptures are the proper source of data from which Christian dogmas are developed (see text above at n. 53). (2) Doctrinal systems are not to be built upon "dogmatic foundations"; doctrines, no less than dogmas, are Gestalts that conceptualize *biblical* data. (3) The difference between dogmas and doctrines does not lie in the "fixed and unchangeable" character of the former as contrasted with the variable nature of the latter (*both* are

Holy Scripture. A tabular summary will perhaps offer the best conclusion to the rather involved discussion preceding it, as well as the best background for what is to follow.

---

theoretically alterable for only Scripture is inerrant), nor in the fact that dogmas are formulated by "a descriptive and empirical process" while the construction of doctrines is "speculative in method," involving "philosophical thinking" (*both* are Wittgensteinian "nets" to catch Scripture—not descriptive assertions or philosophical speculations). In actuality, the distinction between dogmas and doctrines is *quantitative*: the former are more stable because they are based on a greater wealth of biblical evidence, whereas the latter express theological convictions for which less scriptural support can be adduced. It follows that no strict or absolute line can be drawn between dogmas and doctrines, or between heresy (the rejection of orthodox dogma) and heterodoxy (the rejection of orthodox doctrine). Christian churches, in formulating tests of fellowship, should proceed with great care so as to avoid twin errors of laxity (stemming from an insufficiently defined or enforced dogmatic-doctrinal position) and bigotry (the bruising of consciences through required subscription to biblically doubtful doctrines). Thomas Campbell's rule remains the best guide: "Where the Scriptures speak, we speak; where the Scriptures are silent, we are silent."

[71] Absolute certainty, both in science and in theology, rests only with the data (for the former, natural phenomena; for the latter, scriptural affirmations). All conceptualizations on the basis of these data lack ultimate certainty (in science the Einsteinian revolution helped to make this clear), but some formulations are so well attested by the data that they acquire a practically (though not a theoretically) "certain" status; in science we call such Gestalts "laws," in theology, "creeds" and "confessions." Just as a denial of scientific laws removes one from the scientific community (cf. modern alchemists such as Tiffereau and Jullivet-Castelot), so denial of creeds and confessions results in one's separation from ecclesiastical circles. Scientific hypotheses and theological proposals, however, are never proper tests of "fellowship," for they lie, by definition, in the realm of open questions—which, hopefully, more investigation will either raise to a higher status or cause to be discarded. Scientific "theories" (in the narrow sense) and theological systems occupy an intermediate position between laws/creeds-confessions and hypotheses/theological proposals; thus although they are not generally made the basis of *formal* tests of fellowship they often have that function on an informal (social or psychological) level (cf. the negative reception in scientific circles of Immanuel Velikovsky's catastrophism). It is, of course, possible to develop a more extensive classification of conceptual Gestalts in science and theology (since only *quantitative* differences exist among the respective levels), but the above scheme appears to be the most generally useful; in Roman Catholic dogmatics, at least ten "theological grades of certainty" are distinguished, from "immediately revealed truths" to "tolerated opinion" (see Ludwig Ott, *Fundamentals of Catholic Dogma*, trans. Patrick Lynch and ed. James Bastible [2[d] ed.; St. Louis, Mo.: Herder, 1958], pp. 9-10, para. 8).

	SCIENCE	THEOLOGY
THE DATA (Epistemological certainty presupposed)	Nature	The Bible
CONCEPTUAL GESTALTS	Laws	Ecumenical Creeds (e.g., the Apostles' Creed) and historic Confessions (e.g., the Augsburg Confession)
(In order of decreasing certainty)[71]	Theories	Theological systems (e.g., Calvin's *Institutes*)
	Hypotheses	Theological proposals (e.g., Gustaf Aulén's *Christus Victor*)[72]

The Artistic and Sacral Levels in Theological Theorizing

A recent article describing the sorry Spiritualist phase at the end of Sir Arthur Conan Doyle's distinguished career concludes with this thought-provoking evaluation:

> He was ill suited by personal temperament and life experience to become a religious philosopher. His natural sympathies were located in the outer rather than the inner life of man, as seen in his power to describe actions in his literature and his failure to portray character. Thus he was continually drawn towards the appearance of an event, its overt significance, but denied the ability to perceive its inner meaning.[73]

Leaving aside the disputable point (to which no addict of Sherlock Holmes could possibly agree!) that Doyle was a poor delineator of character, one finds here an exceedingly important reminder that the theological realm requires

---

[72] On the "Christus Victor" atonement motif, set forth in historical context in Aulén's book of that title (English translation by A. G. Hebert, published by Macmillan of New York in 1956), see the Appendix to my *Chytraeus on Sacrifice: A Reformation Treatise in Biblical Theology* (reprint ed.; Malone, Tx.: Repristination Press, 2000), pp. 139-46, where I compare the Aulén approach with Anselm's "Latin doctrine" of the atonement and with Abelard's "subjective view."

[73] Sherman Yellen, "Sir Arthur Conan Doyle: Sherlock Holmes in Spiritland," *International Journal of Parapsychology*, VII (Winter, 1965), 54.

something more of investigators than scientific objectivity alone: it demands "the ability to perceive inner meaning." What is involved in this "inner meaning," and what connection does it have with theological theorizing?

A powerful hint toward an answer is provided in Luther's description of his theological method, which he characteristically drew from Scripture itself:

> Let me show you a right method for studying theology, the one that I have used. If you adopt it, you will become so learned that if it were necessary, you yourself would be qualified to produce books just as good as those of the Fathers and the church councils. Even as I dare to be so bold in God as to pride myself, without arrogance or lying, as not being greatly behind some of the Fathers in the matter of making books; as to my life, I am far from being their equal. This method is the one which the pious king David teaches in the 119th Psalm and which, no doubt, was practiced by all the Patriarchs and Prophets. In the 119th Psalm you will find three rules which are abundantly expounded throughout the entire Psalm. They are called: *Oratio, Meditatio, Tentatio*.[74]

By *Meditatio*, Luther meant the reading, study, and contemplation of the Bible (i.e., very much what we have spoken of in our foregoing discussion of the objective aspect of theological methodology); by *Tentatio*, he meant internal and external temptation—what we today would doubtless call subjective, experiential involvement; and by *Oratio* ("prayer"), the vertical contact with the Holy One, without which all theologizing is ultimately futile. Much the same threefold approach to theology is suggested by the treatment of the concept of faith in classical Protestant orthodoxy: faith involves *Notitia* ("knowledge"—the objective, scientific element), *Assensus* ("assent"—the subjective element), and *Fiducia* ("trust/confidence"—the vertical, regenerating relation with the Living God).[75] Quenstedt grounds this analysis of faith in John 14:10-12. He notes that "heretics can have the first, the second the orthodox alone, the third the regenerate; and therefore the latter always includes the former, but this order cannot be reversed."[76] Theology, like the faith to which it gives

---

[74] This passage appears in the Preface to the German section of the first edition of Luther's collected writings (Wittenberg, 1539). For an excellent discussion of it, see Pieper, *op. cit.*, I, 186-90.

[75] A particularly attractive presentation of this threefold conception of faith is given by Johann Gerhard (*op. cit.* in n. 64), III, 354 ff. A similar treatment can be found in Martin Chemnitz's *Loci Theologici* II, 270.

[76] Johann Andreas Quenstedt (1617-1688), *Theologia didactico-polemica*, IV, 282. For Quenstedt, as for many of the other classical Protestant dogmaticians, both *Notitia* and *Assensus* pertain to the intellect, and *Fiducia* to the will; however, *Assensus* is better regarded as bridging the gap between intellect and will, for, as Chemnitz correctly asserts, it involves "not merely a general assent, but that by which each one determines with firm persuasion, which Paul calls assurance (πληροφορία, Heb. 10:22), that the universal promise belongs privately, individually, and spe-

systematic expression, has objective, subjective, and divine levels, no one of which can be disregarded. Having discussed the scientific base in theological theorizing, let us now focus attention on the second, or artistic, level of theological activity.

The Theologian As Artist. John Ciardi, in his excellent introduction to literary criticism, *How Does a Poem Mean?*, quotes the following passage from Dickens' *Hard Times*:

> "Bitzer," said Thomas Gradgrind, "your definition of a horse."
> "Quadruped. Gramnivorous. Forty teeth, namely twenty-four grinders, four eye-teeth, and twelve incisive. Sheds coat in the spring; in marshy countries sheds hoofs too. Hoofs hard, but requiring to be shod with iron. Age known by marks in mouth." Thus (and much more) Bitzer.
> "Now, girl number twenty," said Mr. Gradgrind, "you know what a horse is."

Ciardi quite rightly points out that, after having heard this learned description, "girl number twenty" knew "what a horse is" only in a very special and limited way: she knew horses in a formal, objective, scientific manner, but not at all in a personal, experiential way—not in the way in which a poet or an artist endeavors to convey knowledge. In the same vein, Peter Winch argues for the legitimate, and indeed necessary, inclusion of subjective involvement in the work of the social scientist; over against psychological behaviorism he asks the rhetorical question: "Would it be intelligent to try to explain how Romeo's love for Juliet enters into his behaviour in the same terms as we might want to apply to the rat whose sexual excitement makes him run across an electrically charged grid to reach his mate?"[77] Theorizing in the humanities or social sciences requires more than scientific objectivity; it also demands "the language of experience"[78]— "grasping the *point* or *meaning* of what is being done or said."[79]

---

cifically to him, and that he also is included in the general promise" (*loc. cit.*).

[77] Peter Winch, *The Idea of a Social Science and Its Relation to Philosophy* (London: Routledge & Kegan Paul, 1958), p. 77.

[78] John Ciardi, "How Does a Poem Mean?", in *An Introduction to Literature,* ed. Gordon N. Ray (Boston: Houghton Mifflin, 1959), p. 666.

[79] Winch, *op. cit.*, p. 115. Winch illustrates with Wittgenstein's hypothetical society where the people sold their wood by piling the timber "in heaps of arbitrary, varying height and then sold it at a price proportionate to the area covered by the piles. And what if they even justified this with the words: 'Of course, if you buy more timber, you must pay more'?" (*Remarks on the Foundations of Mathematics* [Oxford: Blackwell, 1956], pp. 142 ff.). To *understand* such behavior, notes Winch, requires much more than the formulation of statistical laws concerning it. ("Understanding" is here used, let it be noted, not in an abstract, purely cerebral way, but in Max Weber's sense of *Verstehen*— "empathic comprehension"; see Talcott Parsons, "Unity and Diversity in the Modern Intellectual Disciplines: The Role of the Social Sciences," *Daedalus: Journal of the American Academy of Arts and Sciences,* XCIV [Winter, 1965], pp. 59ff.)

Is this also true of theology? We have justified the scientific character of theological theorizing by pointing to the empirical, objective nature of God's historical revelation in Holy Scripture; now we must make the equally important point that, by virtue of its historical character, the biblical revelation lies also in the realm of the social sciences and humanities. Because God revealed Himself in history, and the Bible—the source of all true theological Gestalts—is a historical document, theological theories must partake of the dual science-art character of historical methodology. The historian cannot stop with an external, objective examination of facts and records; as Benedetto Croce and R. G. Collingwood have so well shown, he must relive the past in imagination—reenact it by entering into its very heart.[80] As Jakob Burckhardt's *Civilization of the Renaissance in Italy* and Johan Huizinga's *Waning of the Middle Ages* magnificently delineate their respective historical epochs by cutting to the essence of them, so theological constructions must meet Ernst Cassirer's standard for every "science of culture": they must teach us "to interpret symbols in order to decipher their latent meaning, to make visible again the life from which they originally came into being."[81]

We cannot enter here into the problem of the logical status of subjective artistic assertions;[82] suffice it to say, as has been effectively shown by Ian Ramsey and others, that such judgments follow from the independent, irreducible nature of the "I," which is in fact presupposed in all statements about the world—including scientific statements.[83] What we do wish to emphasize is the necessity of incorporating the artistic element into all theological theories, in order to avoid a depersonalization of theology and the concomitant freezing of biblical doctrine. Concretely, all valid theological theories must be set within

---

[80] On the historical philosophies of Croce and Collingwood, see my *Shape of the Past (op. cit.* in n. 26), pp. 90 ff. Crime detection, like history, is both a science and an art; thus Commissioner Tarquin also recommends in the investigation of a woman's murder: "Put yourself inside this woman's skin, get to know her better than she knew herself, become her twin. Get to understand her from the inside out, if you see what I mean" (Japrisot, *op. cit.*, chap. iii).

[81] Ernst Cassirer, *The Logic of the Humanities*, trans. C. S. Howe (New Haven, Conn.: Yale University Press, 1961), p. 158.

[82] A good beginning can be made with Virgil C. Aldrich's *Philosophy of Art* (Engelwood Cliffs, N.J. Prentice-Hall, 1963).

[83] "In every situation, when 'I' and 'me' have been distinguished, 'I' cannot be given an exhaustive 'objective' analysis without denying ourselves in fact, or without supposing that the subject-object relation in the construction of language is merely subject-predicate, which seems a quite unnecessary, indeed a quite disastrous, assumption. It is what Whitehead calls 'extreme objectivism' which even objectifies the subject" (Ian T. Ramsey, *Miracles; an Exercise in Logical Mapwork. An Inaugural Lecture delivered before the University of Oxford on 7 December 1951* [Oxford: Clarendon Press, 1952], p. 15). Cf. Karl Heim, *Christian Faith and Natural Science*, trans N. Horton Smith (New York: Harper Torchbooks, 1957), *passim*.

the "invisible quotation marks" of belief,[84] must represent the personal, inner involvement of the theologian with Holy Scripture, and must convey a genuine reliving and re-enactment of historical revelation. The presence or absence of such artistic criteria as these is to be determined not by formulae, but by individual sensitivity on the part of theologian and Christian believer. Yet the artistic factor is no less real because of that. Just as a sensitive social scientist can recognize the greatness of William James' *Varieties of Religious Experience* as compared with pedestrian monographs on the same subject, and just as the sensitive literary critic has no doubt as to Milton's stature among epic poets, so the Christian who is in tune with Scripture can readily distinguish between theological theorizing that cuts to the heart of biblical revelation and theological theories that (scientifically correct as they may be) operate on a superficial level. Luther's insistence in presenting the doctrine of the Fall of man that "you should read the story of the Fall as if it happened yesterday, and to you" has this requisite inner quality,[85] as does such a creedal statement as the following, extracted from Johann Valentin Andreae's *Christianopolis* of 1619:

Credimus toto corde in Iesum Christum,[86] Dei & Mariae filium, coaequalem patri, consimilem nobis, Redemptorem, duabus naturis personaliter unitum & utrisque communicantem, Prophetam, Regem, & Sacerdotem nostrum, cujus lex gratia, cujus sceptrum pacis, cujus Crucis est sacr[i]ficium.	We believe with our whole heart in Jesus Christ, the Son of God and Mary, coequal with the Father yet like us, our Redeemer, united as to personality in two natures and communicating in both, our Prophet, King, and Priest, whose law is grace, whose scepter is that of peace, whose sacrifice, that of the cross.[87]

---

[84] Ramsey, *Models and Mystery*, p. 27: "There can — and it is a logical 'can' — be no objects without a subject which cannot itself be reducible to objects. The ideal of logical completion is never a third person assertion; it is first-person assertion. *He does X* necessarily carries with it a pair of invisible quotation marks, so that it is to be set in some such frame as 'I am saying ...', and without this wider frame the third-person assertion is logically incomplete."

[85] Cf. my article, "The Cause and Cure of Sin," *Resource*, III (February, 1962), 2-4.

[86] "*Credimus in*" followed by the accusative is the Latin equivalent of the Greek πιστεύομεν εἰς ..., signifying the highest level of faith *(Fiducia,* confidence). Andreae's Creed thus reaches beyond assent to trust, as must all genuine Christian doctrinal affirmations.

[87] For the full text of this Creed, with accompanying English translation and detailed analysis, see my dissertation for the degree of Docteur de l'Université, mention Théologie Protestante: "Cross and Crucible: Johann Valentin Andreae's *Chymical Wedding*" (3 vols.; University of Strasbourg, France, 1964); published in 2 vols. in the International Archives of the History of Ideas, 55 (The

The Theologian and the Holy. In common with science, theology formulates its theories with a view to the objective fitting of facts (in this case, the facts of Scripture); in common with the arts, theology seeks by its theoretical formulations to enter personally into the heart of reality (God's revelation in the Bible). But theology is more than science or art, for it possesses a dimension unique to itself: the realm of the Holy. By this expression we do not refer merely to the "numinous" quality of religion as analyzed by Rudolf Otto in his epochal work, *The Idea of the Holy*; we refer specifically to the unfathomable nature of the God of Scripture, whose ways are not our ways and whose thoughts are not our thoughts (Isa. 55:8), and who demands of the theologian as of Moses, "Draw not nigh hither: put off thy shoes from off thy feet, for the place whereon thou standest is holy ground" (Ex. 3:5; cf. Acts 7:33). Lack of recognition of the distance between sinful man and sinless God or blindness to the absolute necessity of relying upon His Holy Spirit in theologizing will vitiate efforts in this realm, even though the scientific and artist requirements are fully met. Without *Fiducia, Notitia* and *Assensus* are like sounding brass and tinkling cymbal. O. K. Bouwsma makes this point well in his unpublished allegory, "Adventure in Verification," where his hero encounters difficulties in determining how Zeus makes Olympus quake:

> At a meeting of the P.L.B., the Pan-Hellenic Learning Bust, an annual affair at which the feasters eat each other's work, he confided to fellow-ravishers that at the time he was considering his confrontation with the Makers of Fact or the News, on Mt. Olympus, the difficulty that bothered him most was not the matter of protocol but that of language. It wasn't that, as he anticipated, they, the interviewed divinities, would not understand him — they are adept in understanding four-hundred and twenty-six languages — but that he would not understand them. ...
>
> He went down the mountain disappointed. ... When he got home he wrote an account of his adventure, in order that the future of verification might not lose the benefit of his effort. His own adventure he described as one of weak verification due to sand, quicksand, too quick for the hour-glass. It never occurred to him that, not quicksand, but vanity was the condition which led to his having his eyes fixed on his own good name in the bark of

---

Hague, Netherlands: Martinus Nijhoff, 1973), now available from Springer; I, 272 ff. As a contemporary example of a theological system manifesting biblically sound artistic-subjective quality throughout, I particularly recommend the late Erlangen professor Werner Elert's *An Outline of Christian Doctrine*, trans. C. M. Jacobs (Philadelphia: United Lutheran Publication House, 1927).

the tree when they should have been fixed on Zeus who made Great Olympus shake, not by waving his ambrosial locks, nor by stamping his foot, nor by a crow-bar, nor by a cough but in his own sweet way.[88]

How many theological theorizers have failed in their herculean labors as a result of vanity—as a result of fixing their eyes on themselves "when they should have been fixed on Zeus who made Great Olympus shake"!

In what way is the dimension of the "Sacred" conveyed in theological theory construction? Essentially, by the admission that (in Bouwsma's phrase) we do not fully understand Zeus' language. That is to say, the theological theorist must always indicate in the statement of his doctrines the limited character of them—the fact that ultimately God works "in his own sweet way" (in the double sense of the phrase!). Michael Foster, by his stress on the irreducible mystery in all sound theological judgments,[89] and Willem Zuurdeeg, with his emphasis on the "convictional" nature of theological assertions,[90] endeavor (albeit by overemphasizing a good thing) to drive this point home. The best analysis of the problem, however, comes from Ian Ramsey, who observes the linguistically "odd" character of genuine theological affirmations. These consist of models taken from experience, so qualified to indicate their sacral (logically "odd") character. Such "qualified models" can be found throughout the range of Christian doctrine, e.g., in the phrases "first cause," "infinite wisdom," "eternal purpose" (where the qualifying adjective in each case points the empirically grounded noun in the direction of the sacral, so as to reduce anthropomorphism and increase awareness of God's "otherness"). Another example is "creation *ex nihilo*" where "*ex nihilo*" is the sacral qualifier:

> In all the "creation" stories we have told, there has always been *something* from which the "creation" was effected; there have always been causal predecessors. So that "creation" *ex nihilo* is on the face of it a scandal: and the point of the scandal is to insist that when the phrase has been given its appropriate empirical anchorage, any label, suited to that situation, must have a logical behaviour which, from the standpoint of down-to-earth "creation" language, is odd. When creation *ex nihilo* as a qualified model evokes a characteristically religious situation—a sense of creaturely dependence—it further claims for the word "God," which is then posited in relation to such a situation, that it caps all causal stories and presides over and "completes" all the language of all created things. It places "God" as a "key" word for the universe of "creatures."[91]

---

[88] Bouwsma, (*op. cit.* in n. 8), pp. 8,10.
[89] Michael B. Foster, *Mystery and Philosophy* (London: SCM Press, 1957).
[90] Willem F. Zuurdeeg, *An Analytical Philosophy of Religion* (New York: Abingdon, 1958).
[91] Ian T. Ramsey, *Religious Language: An Empirical Placing of Theological Phrases* (London: SCM Press. 1957), p. 73.

Ramsey's assertion here that the "odd" qualifier, conveying the sacral dimension, can be "any label, suited to that situation," reminds us again of the single source for all sound theological theorizing: Holy Scripture. Only the Bible can serve as an adequate guide for determining what sacral qualifiers are "suitable" to given doctrinal formulations.[92] On this note the present section of the essay can properly be concluded: Sacred Scripture offers the sole criterion for testing the scientific, the artistic, and the sacral health of theological theories. Does a given theory represent objective truth? Does it incorporate the proper kind of subjective involvement? Does it adequately preserve the sacred dimension? To all three of these questions *sola Scriptura* holds the answers.

The Structure of Theological Theories

Theory formation and testing in theology have now been analyzed from the points-of-view of science, art, and the holy. One final question remains—and it is, if possible, the most consequential of all: How do the three methodological aspects of theology relate to each other? Analysis has now been completed; what about synthesis? So important is the synthetic problem that to neglect it or to embrace a false solution to it is to insure failure in theological theorizing, no matter how honorable one's motives and impeccable one's procedures in other respects.

Let us clear the air by making explicit a fundamental principle to which we have already arrived by implication. We have seen, from clear scriptural evidence, that each of the three methodological aspects of theology is absolutely essential. Neither the scientific, nor the artistic, nor the sacral element can be removed from theological theorizing without destroying the possibility of results in harmony with God's Word. Thus we can legitimately expect to find deleterious theological climates wherever, in church history or in the present, reductionism is permitted with reference to one or more of the three methodological elements. The following table will indicate the unfortunate end products of the six possible methodological reductionisms:

---

[92] Unhappily, as we have seen (the text at nn. 35 and 52), Ramsey makes "religious experience" rather than Holy Writ his touchstone for confirming or disconfirming theological models and their qualifiers.

[93] Luther used the expression *Theologia gloriae* to characterize the presumptive, god-like attempts of late medieval scholastic theologians to embrace all reality in their systems; his own approach he designated simply as a *Theologia crucis* ("Theology of the Cross"); see Philip S. Watson, *Let God Be God! An Interpretation of the Theology of Martin Luther* (London: Epworth Press, 1947), p. 78. The scholastics erred through neglecting the *Tentatio* element requisite to the theologian's activity; their impossible endeavor to theologize from, as it were, the perspective of God's throne would not have come about if they had retained awareness of their own subjective involvement in

REDUCTION OF	INTO	PRODUCES
1. Artistic & Sacral	Scientific	Dead Orthodoxy
2. Scientific & Sacral	Artistic	Pietism
3. Scientific & Artistic	Sacral	Mysticism
4. Sacral	Scientific & Artistic	Anthropocentrism
5. Artistic	Scientific & Sacral	"Theology of Glory" [93]
6. Scientific	Artistic & Sacral	Existentialism

In terms of this scheme, many of the unfortunate examples of contemporary theological theorizing already referred to in this paper (G. F. Woods' subjectivism, Hordern's Olympic Game thinking, Bultmannian and "post-Bultmannian" obliteration of the subject-object distinction, etc.) become more understandable: our age is particularly prone to reductionism 6., which eliminates the scientific element from theology, and produces wooly-minded, unverifiable existentialisms that readily pass into the realm of analytic meaninglessness. But let us not lose perspective; this methodological sin, heinous as it is, is only one of several committed through Christian history, and we must link together the scientific, the artistic, and the sacral elements in theology so that *none* of the six methodological blunders will be permitted.

How shall the elements be related? Certainly not in dialectical fashion,[94] for (as we pointed out earlier) a polar dialectic is an open invitation to reductionism, since, as pressure is brought to bear on theology from the sinful cultural situation, the theologian can readily and almost imperceptibly slide from one pole to another, avoiding the serious demands of each. (It is this dialectic approach, so hospitable to Neo-Orthodox and existentialist viewpoints, that has permitted contemporary theology, under pressure from "scientific" critics of the Bible, to avoid the basic issue of the historical and scientific authority of Holy Writ.) And not by an attempt to find a pivot in man's faculties (e.g., Lonergan's striking "insight" motif[95]) by which the several methodological levels can be

---

the theological task.

[94] E.g., "in the tension between analysis and existentialism" (Walter Kaufmann's philosophical maxim, characteristically endorsed by Willem F. Zuurdeeg in his article, "The Implications of Analytical Philosophy for Theology," *Journal of Bible and Religion*, XXIX [July, 1961], 210). In point of fact, only a solid analytical *base* can keep existential affirmations from dribbling off into unverifiable nonsensicality; thus not a "tension" but a *structure* is required for the proper relating of objective analysis and subjective-sacral existentialism. No better illustration of this exists than Wittgenstein's arrival at "das Mystische" at the end of his *Tractatus Logico-Philosophicus*, and the manner in which this work of logical analysis prepared the ground for his later *Philosophical Investigations*.

[95] Bernard J. F. Lonergan, S. J., *Insight: A Study of Human Understanding* (London: Longmans, 1958), *passim*. The Autumn, 1964, number of the Saint Xavier College quarterly *Continuum* is a Festschrift entirely devoted to the exceedingly important work of this Wittgenstein-like profes-

tied together, for such a pivot will inevitably shift the focus of theology from the God of Scripture to sinful man. Rather, we must structure the scientific, the artistic, and the sacral factors in theology so that they have a theocentric, Cross-centered focus, and so that the objective provides an epistemological check on the artistic, and the artistic serves as an entrée to the sacral. Consider, then, this structural model of theological explanation:

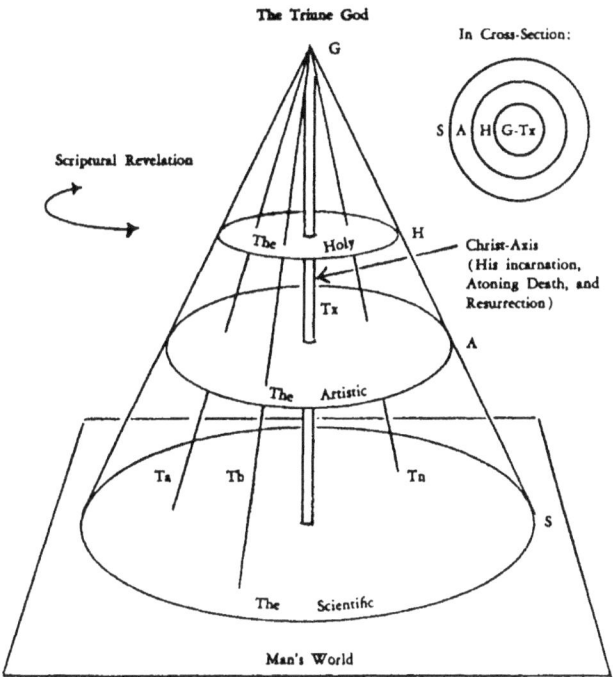

sor at Rome's Gregorian University. In matters of theological methodology, Lonergan is far more worth reading than most contemporary Protestant writers on the subject, since he is well aware of the debilitating effect of current existentialism on theological method, and is thoroughly versed in post-Einsteinian scientific theory. Cf. Lonergan's review of Johannes Beumer's *Theologie als Glaubensverständnis*, in *Gregorianum*, XXXV (1954), 630-48; and see also the accounts of Lonergan's institute on theological methodology held in July, 1962, at Regis College, Toronto (*Sciences Ecclésiastiques*, XV, 291-93 [*op. cit.* in n. 37]). and F. E. Crowe, "On the Method of Theology," *Theological Studies*, XXIII (1962), 637-42.

The cone represents God's revelation to man as expressed in Holy Scripture. This revelation, as we have seen, consists of irreducible, objective facts (the scientific level), to which subjective commitment must be made (the artistic level), and over which the divine majesty hovers in grace and judgment (the sacral level). The truths of which God's revelation is composed are legion (T_a, T_b, … T_n), but they all center upon the great truth which serves as the axis and focal point of the revelation as a whole: the Word become flesh, who died for the sins of the world and rose again for its justification T_x). The task of systematic theology is to take the truths of revelation as discovered by the exegete, work out their proper relation to the focal center and to each other (in the model, these relations are represented by the distances between T_a, T_b, and T_x), and construct doctrinal formulations that "fit" the revelational truths in their mutual relations. In terms of the model, theological theories can be conceived of as cellophane tubes constructed to fit with maximum transparency the truths of revelation; the theologian will endeavor continually to "tighten" them so that they will most accurately capture the essence of biblical truth.

The theological theorist builds his cellophane tubes from bottom to top: he starts in the realm of objective facticity, employing the full range of scientific skill to set forth revelational truth; and he makes every effort not to vitiate his results by reading his own subjective interests into them.[96]

But as he climbs, he inevitably (because of the personal center of biblical truth) reaches a point where he must involve himself subjectively in his material in order to get at the heart of it; here he passes into what we have called the artistic level, where the semi-transcendent, subjective "I" cannot be ignored.

---

[96] The mingling of the subjective with the objective is deadly to any scientific theorizing. Theologians who would disregard this fact in their eagerness to existentialize Christian theology might ponder the following quotation from Rupert T. Gould's *Enigmas* (New Hyde Park, N.Y.: University Books, 1965), p. 321: "A novel and interesting theory respecting the origin—wholly, or in part—of Schiaparelli's (Martian) 'canals' was communicated to me in November, 1944, by Dr. G. S. Brock, F.R.S.E. He draws attention to the possibility that some or all of the appearances which the Italian astronomer believed that he had discovered on the Martian disc were actually situated *in the lens of his own eye*, and were symptomatic of incipient cataract. It is undoubtedly true that in certain conditions of lighting an image of the lens of the eye (together with any defects which this may have) can be projected on to the object which its owner is observing. Dr. Brock informs me that this fact was first announced by an Austrian scientist c.1842, but was afterwards lost sight of in consequence of Helmholtz' invention of the ophthalmoscope some ten years later. He considers it quite possible that some, at least, of Schiaparelli's 'canals' were caused by light from Mars, reflected from his retina, causing defects in the lens of his eye to be apparently projected on to the planet's disc—and, not improbably, blended with markings actually existing there" (italics Gould's). Whether or not this explanation of the famed "canals" of Mars is sound, it should give pause to contemporary theologians; for not a few of the theological theories of our day reflect the inner life of their proponents far more than the objective revealed truth of Holy Writ.

Still he climbs, and eventually—if he is a theologian worthy of the name—he finds that his theory construction has brought him into the realm of the Sacred, where both the impersonal "it" of science and the subjective "I" of the humanities stand on holy ground, in the presence of the living God.

A concrete illustration may be of value here. The doctrine of the Trinity is a theological theory, since the term is not given as a revelational fact. In formulating this theory, the theologian commences by objectively analyzing the biblical data concerning the relations among God the Father, Jesus Christ, and the Holy Spirit—but especially in reference to the character of Jesus Christ, the focal center of theology.[97] He finds that Jesus fully identifies Himself with the Father through His words (e.g., forgiving sin), acts (e.g., miracles), and specific claims ("I and the Father are one"; "he who has seen Me has seen the Father"; etc.), and that He attests His claim to Deity through His resurrection.[98] The theologian discovers, moreover, that this same Jesus asserts that the Holy Spirit is "another of the same kind" (ἄλλον παράκλητον) as Himself,[99] and that in His final charge to His disciples He places Father, Son, and Holy Spirit on precisely the same level.[100] At the same time, the personal identies of Father, Son and Holy Spirit are manifestly evident in Holy Writ, though God is "One" to all the biblical writers. Conclusion: the God of the Bible is (in the words of the Athanasian Creed) "one God in Trinity and Trinity in Unity." The paradoxical character of this theological theory should not disturb us, for it is a conceptual Gestalt demanded by the data; the more "rational" (better: rationalistic) theories of unitarianism and modalism pervert the biblical facts in the interests of a superimposed logical consistency. The orthodox theologian properly and humbly subordinates his theory to the data, as the physical scientist does in formulating the paradoxical "wave-particle" theory to account for the ostensibly contradictory properties of subatomic phenomena:

> Quantum physicists agree that subatomic entities are a mixture of wave properties (W), particle properties (P), and quantum properties (h). High-speed electrons, when shot through a nickel crystal or a metallic film (as fast cathode-rays or even B-rays), diffract like X-rays. In principle, the B-ray is just like the sunlight used in a double-slit or bi-prism experiment. Diffraction is a criterion of wave-like behaviour in substances; all classical wave

---

[97] Historically, as is well known, the Church arrived at its Trinitarian doctrine primarily through just such reflection on the christological problem of Jesus' relation to the Father.
[98] See John 2:18-22, and cf. my *Shape of the Past* (*op. cit.* in n. 26), pp. 138-45. What in our structural model we have called the "Christ-axis" thus becomes the epistemological support for the entire theological endeavor.
[99] John 14:16; ἄλλος is sharply distinguished in the Greek from ἕτερος ("another of a different kind")—cf. Gal. 1:6.
[100] Mt. 28:19.

theory rests on this. Besides this behaviour, however, electrons have long been thought of as electrically charged particles. A transverse magnetic field will deflect an electron beam and its diffraction pattern. Only particles behave in this manner; all classical electromagnetic theory depends upon this. To explain all the evidence electrons must be both particulate and undulatory. An electron is a PWh.[101]

To be sure, the conception of the Trinity in Scripture is not fully or even principally comprehended by an abstract formula. Though on the scientific level "Trinity" is methodologically analogous to "PWh," the comparison ceases when we rise higher. "PWh" is impersonal, but the Trinity is intensely personal and touches the life of the theologian at its very center. Thus in explaining the Trinitarian articles of the Apostles' Creed, Luther reiterates the subjective, "for me" character of the doctrine: "I believe that God has made me. ... I believe that Jesus Christ, true God, begotten of the Father from eternity, and also true man, born of the Virgin Mary, is my Lord. ... I believe that ... the Holy Ghost has called me by the Gospel, enlightened me with His gifts, sanctified and kept me in the true faith."[102] Moreover, as the theologian contemplates the Trinitarian character of Holy Scripture, he is caught up in wonder and amazement, finding himself transported to the very gates of glory; with the Athanasian Creed, therefore, he must express by sacral qualifiers the "otherness" of superlative truth: "The Father uncreate, the Son uncreate, and the Holy Ghost uncreate. The Father incomprehensible, the Son incomprehensible, and the Holy Ghost incomprehensible. The Father eternal, the Son eternal, and the Holy Ghost eternal."[103]

Lost in wonder, then, does theological theorizing find its fulfilment. Commencing in the hard-headed realm of science, moving upward into the dynamic sphere of artistic involvement, it issues forth into a land where words can do little more than guard the burning bush from profanation. Here one can perhaps glimpse theology as its Divine Subject sees it: not as man's feeble attempts to grasp eternal verities, but as a cone of illumination coming down from the Father of lights (Jas. 1:17) — a cone whose sacral level brightens the artistic, and

---

[101] Hanson (*op. cit.* in n. 27), p. 144. Cf. Jean E. Charon, *La Connaissance de l'univers* (Paris: Editions du Seuil, 1963), *passim*. Lutheran theology has always cautioned against violating revelational paradox, while Roman Catholic and Calvinist theologies have emphasized the need of achieving maximum rational consistency in doctrinal construction; the above parallel between the Trinity and PWh illustrates the complementary truth in the two views: the theologian must always strive for rationality in his theorizing, but he must sacrifice this ideal to the accurate "fitting of the facts" when the latter do not permit logically consistent formulation. Reason properly has a ministerial, not a magisterial, role in theology.
[102] Luther, *The Small Catechism*, Arts. 1, 2, and 3 of the Creed.
[103] Cf. Ramsey, *Religious Language*, pp. 174-79.

whose artistic level brightens the scientific level below it. The truly great theologian, like Aquinas, will conclude his labors with the cry: "I can do no more; such things have been revealed to me that everything I have written seems to me rubbish."[104] In the final analysis, the theologian must say of his theologizing what the great Wittgenstein said of his philosophizing:

> My propositions serve as elucidations in the following way: anyone who understands me eventually recognizes them as senseless, when he has used them—as steps—to climb up beyond them. (He must, so to speak, throw away the ladder after he has climbed up it.) He must transcend these propositions, and then he will see the world aright.[105]

---

[104] Cf. Jacques Maritain, *St. Thomas Aquinas* (London: Sheed, 1931), pp. 44-46, 51. The eminent Jesuit philosopher Frederick Copleston writes: "The Christian recognizes in the human nature of Christ the perfect expression in human terms of the incomprehensible Godhead, and he learns from Christ how to think about God. But at the same time it is certainly no part of the Christian religion to say that God in Himself can be adequately comprehended by the human mind. And that He cannot be so comprehended seems to me to be at once a truth vital to religion, in the sense that it prevents us from degrading the idea of God and turning Him into an idol, and a truth which follows necessarily from the fact that our natural knowledge begins with sense-experience. For my own part, I find the thought that the reality, the 'objective meaning,' far exceeds in richness the reach of our analogical concepts the very reverse of depressing. St. Paul tells us that we see through a glass darkly, and the effect of a little linguistic analysis is to illuminate the truth of this statement" (*Contemporary Philosophy: Studies of Logical ... Positivism and Existentialism* [London: Burns & Oates, 1956], pp. 101-102).

[105] *Tractatus Logico-Philosophicus*, 6.54. On the famous concluding assertion (7.0) that immediately follows, Foster (*op. cit.* in n. 89, p. 28), perceptively comments: "When Zechariah says 'Be silent all flesh before the Lord,' this is not wholly different from Wittgenstein's 'Whereof one cannot speak, thereof one must be silent'." And see also Montgomery, *Tractatus Logico-Theologicus* (4th ed.; Bonn: Verlag für Kultur und Wissenschaft, 2009), *passim*.

2. Computer Origins and the Defense of the Faith

Synopsis

In virtually all discussions of the prehistory of computing, the following names are mentioned: Ramon Lull (13th century), Wilhelm Schickard (1592-1635), Blaise Pascal (1623-1662), and Charles Babbage (1791-1871). Their religious orientations, however, are rarely, if ever, discussed. This essay, based on primary as well as authoritative secondary sources, demonstrates that all four were serious, orthodox Christian believers with strong apologetic concerns. The argument is presented that scientific genius—particularly in the computing realm—correlates positively with a sound theology and a concern to discover and present evidence for the faith. Andrew Dickson White's "warfare of science with theology" turns out to be the least satisfying category for understanding computer prehistory.

The first president of my Alma Mater, Cornell University, set an ideological trend which has been generally followed in modern times. Andrew Dickson White's *A History of the Warfare of Science with Theology in Christendom* (1896) endeavored to show that theology was the implacable foe of true science and that, in that fight to the death, science always wins in the end. In the computer sciences, a late twentieth-century monograph follows in White's wake: Geoff Simons attempts to de-theologize computing in his *Is God a Programmer? Religion in the Computer Age*.[1]

It therefore will come as a surprise to many that at least four of the major figures in the prehistory of modern computing were not only serious Christian believers but also directly concerned with the defense of Christian truth. The purpose of this paper is briefly to introduce readers to these individuals and to attempt to determine why computing and apologetics have been—and continue to be—natural bedfellows.

Ramon Lull

L(l)ull—or Lullius (the Latin form of his name)—was a thirteenth-century contemporary of Thomas Aquinas. Like Aquinas, he was a theologian in what

---

[1] Geoff Simons, *Is God a Programmer? Religion in the Computer Age* (Brighton, Sussex, England: Harvester Press, 1988).

one of the Roman Church's eulogists has termed the "greatest of centuries," since it was then that the Church's enduring systematic theological formulations were developed.[2]

Lull, however, was very different from Aquinas. The latter devoted his life to the systematizing of the Church's teaching, based on the philosophical principles of the Aristotelian revival in his time.[3] He wrote for those within the framework of western Christendom. One interpreter has observed, not unjustly, that when Thomas wrote his *Summa contra gentiles* ("Summation Against the Pagans"), he had probably never met a pagan!

Lull, on the other hand, was a polymath[4] who believed that theology could only be properly pursued in the context of missionary endeavor—and that new methods had to be developed to achieve results in contexts where western approaches would not carry the weight they did at home. Lull was ultimately to die a martyr for his beliefs whilst preaching the gospel to that most difficult audience, the followers of Islam. The great nineteenth-century missionary statesman Samuel M. Zwemer characterized Lull as, quite simply, the "first missionary to the Moslems."[5] And, like C. S. Lewis in the twentieth century, Lull's apologetic was not just a tough-minded one; he produced (in his own Catalan tongue) a remarkable missionary novel, *Blanquerna*, which has been compared to Bunyan's *Pilgrim's Progress*.[6]

Lull's theological "Art" or method was scholastic but not Aristotelian—and its unique character has given it a place in the history of logic.[7] Lull is frequently

---

[2] James J. Walsh, *Thirteenth Greatest of Centuries* (New York: Fordham University Press, 1943). Catholic Summer School Press issued this work as early as 1913, and it was reprinted by AMS Press in 1981.
[3] Cf. especially the general studies of Aquinas by Etienne Gilson, A. D. Sertillanges, M. C. D'Arcy, and M. D. Chenu.
[4] Lull's productivity—in the widest range of fields, including medicine—was simply enormous, even after excluding the alchemical works falsely attributed to him. According to the latest catalogue, he produced 265 titles, of which 237 have survived. The *Book of Contemplation* alone contains almost a million words. A large number of Lull's writings remain unedited and in manuscript even today.
[5] Samuel M. Zwemer, *Raymund Lull: First Missionary to the Moslems* (New York and London: Funk & Wagnalls, 1902). Cf. Mark D. Johnston, *The Evangelical Rhetoric of Ramon Llull: Lay Learning and Piety in the Christian West around 1300* (New York: Oxford University Press, 1996).
[6] Ramon Lull, *Blanquerna: A Thirteenth Century Romance*, trans. E. Allison Peers (London: Jarrolds, n.d. [1925/1926]).
[7] For example, in the (rather dismissive) treatment given to Lull in W. and M. Kneale's *The Development of Logic* (Oxford: Clarendon Press, 1964), 241-2, where, however, Lull's influence on Leibniz is at least mentioned. Carl von Prantl's older and far more comprehensive *Geschichte der Logik im Abendlande*, 4 vols. (Leipzig, 1855-1870), III:145-77, is much more informative on the details of the Lullian system.

mentioned by students of the prehistory of computing. Martin Gardner, in his well-received work on *Logic Machines and Diagrams*, begins with Lull and devotes an entire chapter to him.[8] He offers the following illustration of the Lullian method for resolving theological problems by exhaustively interrelating combinations of divine qualities:

> For example, we realize that predestination and free will must be combined in some mysterious way beyond our ken; for God is both infinitely wise and infinitely just; therefore He must know every detail of the future, yet at the same time be incapable of withholding from any sinner the privilege of choosing the way of salvation. Lull considered this a demonstration *"per aequiparantium,"* or by means of equivalent relations. Instead of connecting ideas in a cause-and-effect chain, we trace them back to a common origin. Free will and predestination sprout from equally necessary attributes of God, like two twigs growing on branches attached to the trunk of a single tree.[9]

Lull's approach literally became "a method for 'finding' all the possible propositions and syllogisms on any given subject and for verifying their truth or falsehood."[10]

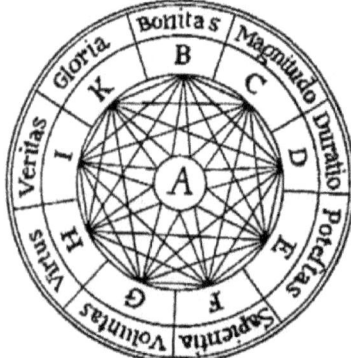

Fig. 1. The Lullian "Dignities".

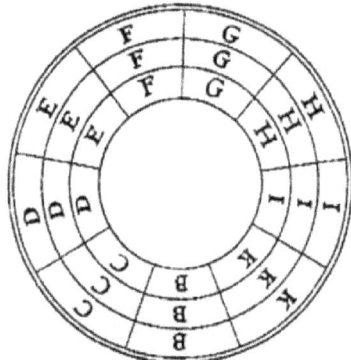

Fig. 2. Lull's Combinatory Art. The fourth figure of the later Art: the inner wheels rotate independently, allowing all possible ternary combinations of the letter BCDEFGHJK to be read off.

---

[8] Martin Gardner, *Logic Machines and Diagrams* (New York: McGraw-Hill, 1958), 1-27.
[9] Ibid., 12.
[10] Anthony Bonner, ed. and trans., *Doctor Illuminatus: A Ramon Llull Reader* (Princeton, NJ: Princeton University Press, 1993), 294. This anthology is a shorter version of Bonner's *Selected Works of Ramon Llull (1232-1316)*, 2 vols. (Princeton, NJ: Princeton University Press, 1985).

Lull saw that everything could be systematically related back to God by examining how Creation was structured by the active manifestation of the divine attributes—which he called Dignities and used as the absolute principles of his Art. Examining their manifestations involved using a set of relative principles; and both sets could be visualized in combinatory diagrams. ...

The most distinctive characteristic of Lull's Art is clearly its combinatory nature, which led to both the use of complex semimechanical techniques that sometimes required figures with separately revolving concentric wheels—"volvelles," in bibliographical parlance ... —and to the symbolic notation of its alphabet. These features justify its classification among the forerunners of both modern symbolic logic and computer science.

Yet the Art can be understood correctly only when viewed in the light of Lull's primary aim: to place Christian apologetics on a rational basis for use in disputations with Muslims, for whom arguments *de auctoritate* grounded on the Old Testament—widely used by Dominicans in disputations with the Jews—carried no weight. ... Lull advanced what he called necessary reasons for accepting dogmas like the Trinity and the Incarnation.[11]

A single example can illustrate Lull's apologetic reasoning, his overarching concern to justify Trinitarian doctrine over against the Muslim refusal to accept it.[12] Lull poses the key question "whether there is plurality in God." To answer this he appeals to a subspecies of one of what he has earlier set forth as the "ten general questions, to which all other possible questions can be reduced," namely Question C (*Quid?*—"What Is It?"). That subspecies deals with the question:

> What does the intellect have coessentially [essentially, naturally] in itself? To which one must reply that it has its correlatives, that is to say, intellectivity, intelligibility, and understanding, without which it could not exist, and would, moreover, be idle and lack nature, purpose, and repose.

Now Lull draws the inevitable logical conclusion on the original issue of plurality within the Godhead:

> One should answer yes, with respect to His correlatives as exemplified in the Second Species of rule C, without which He could not have in Himself

---

[11] R. D. F. Pring-Mill, "Lull, Ramon," *Dictionary of Scientific Biography*, ed. C. C. Gillispie, 16 vols. (New York: Scribner's, 1970-1980), VIII:548-9. The accompanying diagrams have been reproduced from this article.

[12] For the central place of Lull's apologetic for the Trinity in his thought, see his *De Quadratura*, originally written in Catalan and accessible in the excellent French edition titled, *Principes et questions de théologie*, ed. and trans. R. Prévost and A. Llinarès (Paris: Editions du Cerf, 1989), especially pp. 36-57, 95-9, 116-56, 246-54. Lull thoroughly integrates Trinitarian doctrine with Christology (his apologetic also covers the Incarnation, the Resurrection, and the Last Judgment).

an infinite and eternal operation bonifying, magnifying, eternalizing, etc., as a result of which His dignities would be constrained and idle, which is impossible.[13]

What Lull is arguing here is that if God did not consist of more than one Person He could not have manifested from eternity the characteristics such as "understanding" which are essential to an intelligent being. This argument is the logical underpinning of such modern justifications of Trinitarian theology as that which we have presented in our *Tractatus Logico-Theologicus*, 3.747:

> The philosophical importance of Trinitarian doctrine (three Persons in one Godhead) is often overlooked: if God is indeed love, and has always been so (even before he created other persons), he would have to be more than monopersonal.[14]

Wilhelm Schickard

For Protestantism, the seventeenth century corresponded to Roman Catholicism's thirteenth: it was the great period of the Protestant dogmaticians and savants who systematized the results of the Reformation and applied those consequences to cultural life in general. The center of much of that Lutheran activity was the province of Württemberg and its university city of Tübingen. In that region, the learned theologian and littérateur Johann Valentin Andreae (1586-1654) created a *"Societas Christiana"*—a fellowship of likeminded believers in the sciences and the arts for the purpose of transforming society on the basis of sound, confessional Lutheran theology. Though the Thirty Years' War prevented the practical realization of Andreae's utopian dream of a "Christianopolis," that little band accomplished remarkable feats of learning and social amelioration under exceedingly difficult conditions.[15]

---

[13] Lull, *Ars brevis*, in *Opera* (Strasbourg [Argentorati]: Zetzner, 1651), 11, 41. On this influential "final" edition of Lull's works, of which I personally possess a copy, see Bonner, *Doctor Illuminatus*, 67-8. I have modified Bonner's translation at several points on the basis of the original Latin text. The bracketed words appear in the parallel passage in Lull's *Ars generalis ultima*.

[14] John Warwick Montgomery, *Tractatus Logico-Theologicus* (4th ed.; Bonn, Germany: Verlag für Kultur und Wissenschaft, 2009). Available from the Canadian Institute for Law, Theology and Public Policy: http://www.ciltpp.com.

[15] See John Warwick Montgomery, *Cross and Crucible*, 2 vols. (The Hague, Netherlands: Nijhoff [now Kluwer], 1973), 1:55. The Introductory Essay to this work has appeared as a journal article in the *Transactions of the Royal Society of Canada*, 4th ser., I (June 1963): 251-70, as well as in *Ambix: The Journal of the Society for the Study of Alchemy and Early Chemistry*, XI (June 1963): 65-86; and it was published in French in the *Revue d'Histoire et de Philosophie Religieuses* (1966): 323-45. See also the author's reinforcement of his argument in F. A. Janssen, ed., *Das Erbe des Christian Rosenkreuz* (Amsterdam, Netherlands: In de Pelikaan, 1988), 152-69.

Fig. 3. Wilhelm Schickard (1592-1635)

Among the leading members of the *Societas Christiana* was Wilhelm Schickard or Schickhardt (1592-1635).[16] Like Lull, Schickard was a polymath. He was an ordained Lutheran pastor with a scientific background and a knowledge of several oriental languages. He was a long-term friend of Johannes Kepler (also a member of the Andreae's *Societas*) and an early supporter of his astronomical theories. At Tübingen he held professorships in the oriental languages, astronomy, mathematics, and geodesy.

> Schickard ... was a skilled mechanic, cartographer, and engraver in wood and copperplate; and he wrote treatises on Semitic studies, mathematics, astronomy, optics, meteorology, and cartography. He invented and built a working model of the first modern mechanical calculator and proposed to

---

[16] Montgomery, *Cross and Crucible*, I:48, 69, 144, 176-7; II:545. For biographical articles on Schickard, see the *Allgemeine deutsche Biographie;* Hoefer's *Nouvelle Biographie Générale*; and Michaud's *Biographie Universelle*.

Kepler the development of a mechanical means of calculating ephemerides. Schickard's works on astronomy include a lunar ephemeris, observations of the comets of 1618, and descriptions of unusual solar phenomena (meteors and the transit of Mercury in 1631). He also constructed and described a teaching device consisting of a hollow sphere in three segments with the heavens represented on the inside.[17]

What I have written elsewhere of Schickard's friend Kepler could likewise be applied to him:

> Ludwig Guenther has shown in his *Kepler und die Theologie* that this Lutheran father of modern astronomy was consistently and vitally concerned about theological issues; his desire to ground his astronomical work in the biblical revelation is evident.[18]

Schickard's *Purim* (1634)[19] was an attempt of an eschatological and apologetical nature to unlock the numerical prophecies of the Book of Daniel and to develop a philosophy of history on the basis of them; the effort may remind one of Sir Robert Anderson's *The Coming Prince*.[20]

Though it has been maintained by some that Schickard is only "the principal precursor of mechanical calculation but not the inventor of the calculating machine,"[21] the general judgment is that his device was indeed the first working arithmetical calculator, and, as such, a giant step in the future development of the computer. Michael R. Williams, in his *History of Computing Technology*, takes that view.[22] He argues as follows: (1) Two letters from Schickard in Kepler's papers (letters of 20 September 1623 and 25 February 1624) describe the machine in very clear terms: it consisted of eleven "complete" and six "incomplete" or "mutilated" sprocket wheels and "carries by itself from one column of tens to the next or borrows from them during subtraction. [This machine]

---

[17] Wilbur Applebaum, "Schickhard, Wilhelm," *Dictionary of Scientific Biography*, XII:163.
[18] Montgomery, *Cross and Crucible*, I:11.
[19] Wilhelm Schickhard, *"Purim," sive Bacchanalia Judaeorum* (Tubingae: Werlin, 1634).
[20] On Anderson's prophetic apologetic, see John Warwick Montgomery, *The Transcendent Holmes* (Ashcroft, BC, Canada: Calabash, 2000), 129-30, 135-9; and Montgomery, "Prophecy, Eschatology and Apologetics," in his *Christ Our Advocate* (Bonn, Germany: Verlag für Kultur und Wissenschaft, 2002), 255-65, and also in David W. Baker, ed., *Looking Into the Future: Evangelical Studies in Eschatology* (Grand Rapids, MI: Baker, 2001), 362-70.
[21] René Taton, "Sur l'invention de la machine arithmétique," *Revue d'histoire des sciences et de leurs applications*, XVI (1963): 139-60, at 144.
[22] Michael R. Williams, *A History of Computing Technology*, 2ᵈ ed. (Los Alamitos, CA: IEEE Computer Society Press, 1997), 119-24. One of the illustrations to follow (that of Schickard's machine's carry mechanism) has been reproduced from this work; the others have been obtained from Walter Gerblich et al., *Herrenberg und seine Lateinschule. Zur Geschichte von Stadt und Gäu* (Herrenberg, Germany: Theodor Körner, n.d. [1962]), 176-80 (section contributed by Baron von Freytag Löringhoff).

which immediately and automatically calculates with given numbers ... adds, subtracts, multiplies and divides." (2) Though the actual machines constructed by Schickard apparently have not survived, his original sketches turned up as a bookmark in a copy of Kepler's *Rudolphine Tables* in the library of the Pulkovo Observatory near Leningrad/Saint Petersburg. (3) On the basis of the infor-

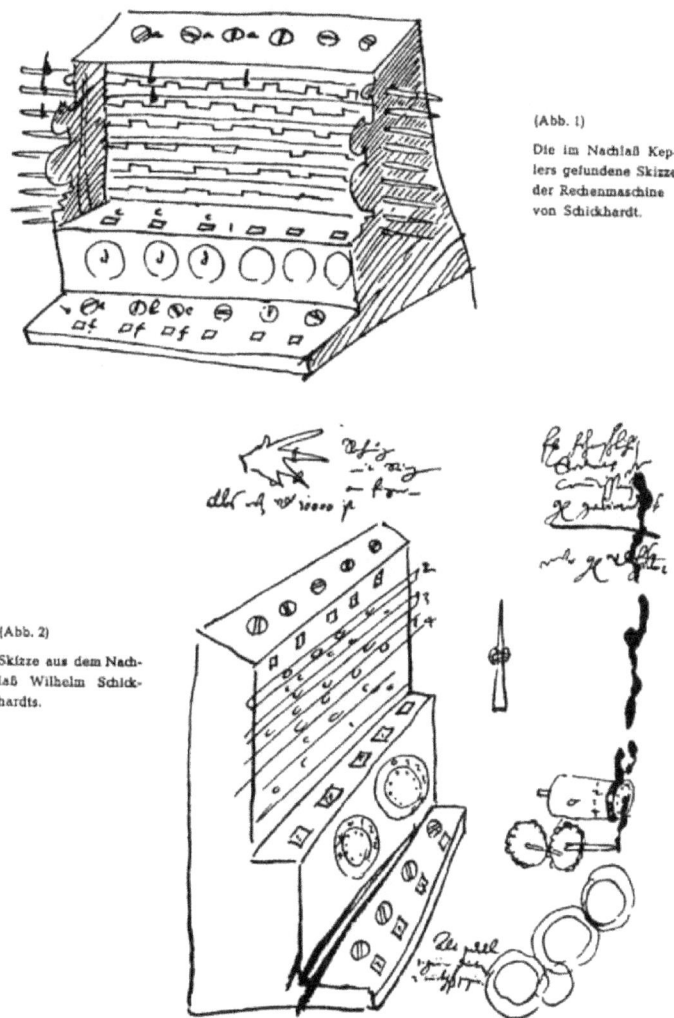

(Abb. 1)
Die im Nachlaß Keplers gefundene Skizze der Rechenmaschine von Schickhardt.

(Abb. 2)
Skizze aus dem Nachlaß Wilhelm Schickhardts.

Fig. 4. The Schickardian Sketches.

mation provided by the letters and the sketches, Professor Baron von Freytag Löringhoff of the University of Tübingen (whose specialities included a knowledge of the techniques of seventeenth-century clockmakers) was able to build a successful working model of the original device.[23]

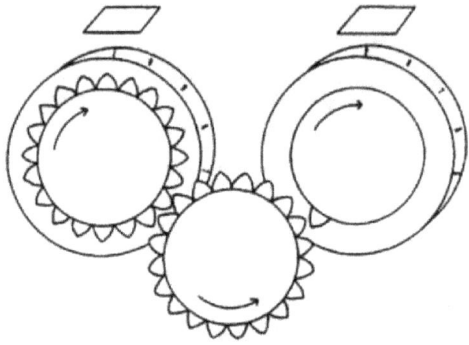

Fig. 5. Schickard's Carry Mechanism.

Fig. 6. The Tübingen Reconstruction of Schickard's Calculating Machine.

---

[23] In 1971, West Germany issued a stamp picturing that reconstruction in honor of the 350th anniversary of Schickard's invention.

The mechanism used to effect a carry from one digit to the next was very simple and reliable in operation. ... Every time an accumulator wheel rotated through a complete turn, a single tooth would catch in an intermediate wheel and cause the next highest digit in the accumulator to be increased by one. ...

The major drawback of this type of carry mechanism is the fact that the force used to effect the carry must come from the single tooth meshing with the teeth of the intermediate wheel. If the user ever wished to do the addition 999,999 + 1, it would result in a carry being propagated right through each digit of the accumulator. This would require enough force that it might well do damage to the gears on the units digit. It appears that Schickard was aware of this particular weakness because he constructed machines with only six-digit accumulators even though he knew that Kepler undoubtedly needed more figures in his astronomical work. If the numbers became larger than six digits, he provided a set of brass rings which could be slipped over the fingers of the operator's hand in order to remember how many times a carry had been propagated off the end of the accumulator. A small bell rung each time such an *overflow* occurred to remind the operator to slip another ring on his finger.[24]

But with all of its limitations, Schickard's calculating machine was a remarkable accomplishment, and one essential for the eventual development of the modern computer. At very minimum, his machine incorporated "both a set of Napier's bones and a mechanism to add up the partial products they produced in order to completely automate the multiplication process."[25]

Blaise Pascal

Schickard's invention had no direct influence, since he made no effort to promote or manufacture it. A generation later, the great French mathematician, scientist, and Christian apologist Pascal (1623-1662), apparently without any knowledge of Schickard's work, developed a similar but more sophisticated calculating machine which had an immediate impact.

Before examining it, we should remind ourselves of Pascal's ideological orientation. He was a Roman Catholic of the school of Port-Royal (the so-called Jansenists). He therefore was deeply committed to an Augustinian theology, to the point of being regarded by many as virtually Protestant in his emphasis on divine grace.[26]

---

[24] Williams, *A History of Computing Technology*, 122-3.
[25] *Ibid.*, 120.
[26] See in particular the excellent treatments of Pascal's thought by Emile Cailliet: *The Clue to Pascal* (London: S. C. M. Press, 1944), *Great Shorter Works of Pascal* (Philadelphia: Westminster

Fig. 7. One of the Surviving Examples of Pascal's Calculating Machine.

Pascal's apologetic activity expressed itself especially in numerous fragments collected after his death. These *Pensées* or thoughts have been ordered in a number of different ways by different editors, ancient and modern, and the arrangements can give quite diverse impressions of Pascal's apologetic method.[27] The most effective ordering is certainly that by the English scholar H. F. Stewart, who used the *entretien, discours,* or lecture on apologetics given by Pascal to friends in 1658 (or the year before or the year after) as a natural structure for arranging the "thoughts."[28] The result shows decisively that Pascal was anything but a modern subjectivist or existentialist.

Press, 1948), etc. It should be noted that, in spite of his Augustinianism, Pascal clearly distinguishes his theology from that of Calvinism, which he regards as a heresy (*ibid.*, 136-42).

[27] Fortunately, there is a standard numbering of the fragments so that one can (usually, but not always!) locate a given *Pensée* regardless of which edition is being consulted.

[28] H. F. Stewart, *Pascal's Apology for Religion Extracted from the Pensées* (Cambridge, England: Cambridge University Press, 1942), especially pp. vii-xxiv ("Preface"). As an Appendix (pp. 203-31), Stewart gives the French texts from which the content of the *entretien* is known: "The *Discours sur les Pensées de M. Pascal* by Filleau de la Chaise compared with the Preface to the Port Royal edition by Etienne Périer." Stewart's posthumous bilingual edition of the *Pensées* (London: Routledge & Kegan Paul, 1950) is to be preferred to all others.

Thus, the Stewart edition of the *Pensées* shows that Pascal never intended his celebrated Wager to be a device to avoid objective evidence of religious truth. That Wager (arguing that even if the evidence for and against Christianity were exactly balanced, one ought still to accept Christ, since if Christianity were false, one would still benefit from the highest moral principles and example, but if true and one rejects it, one goes to hell) was to be used at an intermediate point in witnessing to a non-Christian, not as a final proof of any kind. Its purpose was to counter indifference—to give the unbeliever the maximum motivation to engage in a serious quest for religious truth. Pascal follows the Wager with arguments showing the failure of non-Christian solutions to the human dilemma and the soundness of the case for the unique, revelatory character of Jewish history in the Old Testament and for the prophetically anticipated, miraculous, saving activity of Jesus Christ in the New Testament—as attested by solid eyewitness testimony.[29]

Pascal's father Etienne was an investor, tax collector, and no mean mathematician in his own right. The tedium of assisting his father in the taxation area

Fig. 8. Pascal's Calculating Machine, 1642. Length: 36 cm.

---

[29] Theologians such as Clément Besse (*Le Pari. Avec un Discours critique* [Paris: Gabriel Beauchesne, 1922]) could have avoided much agony over the apparent illogic of the Wager had they paid more attention to the structure of Pascal's 1658 discourse. For a recent and important rehabilitation and defense of Pascal's argument, see Jeff Jordan, *Pascal's Wager: Pragmatic Arguments and Belief in God* (Oxford: Clarendon Press, 2006).

led Blaise, at the age of only nineteen, to design his first calculating machine called the "La Pascaline."[30] Eventually he would produce—and in a number of instances market—some fifty different machines, but they all were refinements of the fundamental design of the original machine.[31]

> Pascal seems to have realized right from the start that the single-tooth gear like that used by Schickard, would not do for a general carry mechanism. The single-tooth gear works fine if the carry is only going to be propagated a few places but, if the carry has to be propagated several places along the accumulator, the force needed to operate the machine would be of such a magnitude that it would do damage to the delicate gear works. Pascal managed to devise a completely new mechanism that was based upon falling weights rather than a long chain of gears. ...
>
> This carry mechanism, which would have been the pride of many mechanical engineers 100 years after Pascal, eliminated any strain on the gears. However, it did have the drawback that the wheels turned in only one direction, and this meant that it was only possible to add and not to subtract with the machine. ... The subtraction problem was solved by simply adding the nines complement of the required number, a process which limited the use of the machine to those with a better than average education.[32]

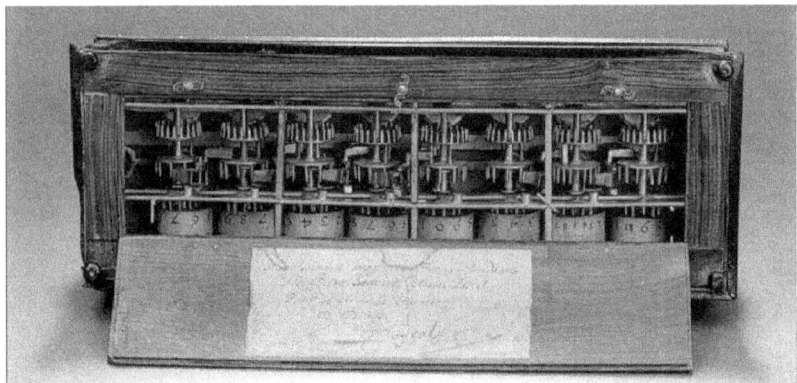

Fig. 9. Pascal's Calculating Machine, detail of the mechanism.

---

[30] He says this specifically in a letter written in the year 1645; the text of this letter is given in Cailliet, *Great Shorter Works of Pascal*, 40-1. For a recent and important rehabilitation and defense of Pascal's argument, see Jeff Jordan, Pascal's Wager: *Pragmatic Arguments and Belief in God* (Oxford: Clarendon Press, 2006).
[31] See Taton "Sur l'invention de la machine arithmétique"; and Jacques Payen, "Les exemples conservés de la machine de Pascal," *Revue d'histoire des sciences et de leurs applictions* XVI (1963): 161-78 (with numerous photographs).
[32] Williams, *A History of Computing Technology*, 128.

Of the Pascaline, his sister Gilberte wrote:

> My brother has invented this arithmetical machine by which you can not only do calculations without the aid of counters of any kind, but even without knowing anything about the rules of arithmetic.[33]

Comments Georges Ifrah in his *The Universal History of Computing*:

> Pascal's sister's letter perceptively foresaw the nature of the era which her brother had just inaugurated ... an era soon to be marked by the rapid development of a great variety of machines which not only eased the heavy burden of tedious and repetitive operations, but, in carrying out automatically an increasingly wide field of intellectual tasks with complete reliability, would come to replace the human being who would be able to use them without having even the slightest knowledge of the physical and mathematical laws which govern their working.[34]

That Pascal anticipated the philosophical issues attendant upon that "new era" is evident from the *Pensées*. He wrote:

> The arithmetical machine produces effects which come closer to thought than anything which animals can do; but it can do nothing which might lead us to say that it possesses free will, as the animals have.[35]

To which Ifrah comments: "[This] is as true today as it was then regarding any calculator or computer."[36]

Charles Babbage

The final figure to be treated here is universally regarded as the most important name prior to the twentieth century in the history of modern computer technology. Babbage's famous Engines were the true ancestor of our modern computers.[37]

---

[33] Mme Périer, "La vie de Monsieur Pascal," in Pascal, *Oeuvres complètes*, ed. Louis Lafuma (Paris: Editions du Seuil, 1963), 19.

[34] Georges Ifrah, *The Universal History of Computing*, trans. and ed. E. F. Harding (New York: John Wiley, 2001), 123-4. It was therefore not without reason that Swiss computer expert Niklaus Wirth named his immensely influential programming language "Pascal."

[35] "La machine d'arithmétique fait des effets qui approchent plus de la pensée que tout ce que font les animaux; mais elle ne fait rien qui puisse faire dire qu'elle a de la volonté, comme les animaux" —Pascal, *Pensées*, 4th ed., 2 vols., ed. Ernest Havet (Paris: Ch. Delagrave, 1887), II:118.

[36] Ifrah, *The Universal History of Computing*, 122. The example of the Pascaline shown here may be seen in the Musée des Arts et Métiers in Paris, where there is also a working reproduction which can be tried by visitors to the museum. Cf. *De la machine à calculer de Pascal à l'ordinateur [exposition du 26 avril au 23 septembre 1990]* (Paris: Musée National des Techniques, CNAM, 1990).

[37] Ifrah, *The Universal History of Computing*, 245.

Charles Babbage, perhaps more than any other person, can be considered to be the grandfather of the computer age. ... His ideas were so far in advance of his time that they would have fit easily into the early computer work being done by people like Konrad Zuse and Howard Aiken in the 1940s.[38]

The reason for this was the unique character of Babbage's "Analytical Engine": though never actually constructed, it was far more than a Schickardian or Pascalian calculator capable of storing and then manipulating data by selecting built-in operations; the Analytical Engine actually *could store the sequence of operations to be performed on the data*, thus displaying the character of a modern computer program. In Babbage's work, we see the first automatic computer conceived by humans.

Charles Babbage (1791-1871) was, like Lull, Schickard, and Pascal, "a vigorous polymath."[39] The son of a well-to-do banker, he took a mathematics degree at the University of Cambridge (Trinity College) and his first scholarly contributions lay in mathematical papers and the construction of computational tables. This led to his years of work designing his "Difference" and "Analytical" Engines to automate the preparation of such tables. Constructing these engines was a task so far in advance of the mechanical skills of his day that he himself had to study the nature of manufacturing machinery and improve upon it. This in turn led to his becoming a lay specialist in economic and industrial theory and the eventual publication of his influential book, *On the Economy of Machinery and Manufactures* (1832).[40]

Fig. 10. Charles Babbage (1791-1871) Daguerreotype by Antoine Claudet, 1847-51.

Babbage became one of the founders of the London Statistical Society, the Astronomical Society, and the British Association. He was elected to the Royal Society as early as 1816. From 1828 to 1839 he held his only paid position during his lifetime—that of Lucasian Professor of Mathematics at Cambridge. He obtained less than sufficient support from the government for the development of his Dif-

---

[38] Williams, *A History of Computing Technology*, 154.
[39] "General Introduction," *The Works of Charles Babbage*, 11 vols., ed. Martin Campbell-Kelly (London: William Pickering, 1989), I:14.
[40] This book constitutes Vol. VIII of Babbage's *Works*, ed. Campbell-Kelly.

ference Engine No. 1 (Figure 11) and none at all for his Analytical Engine or for the Difference Engine No. 2 (Figure 12); by 1842 the government ceased entirely to support his work.[41] Financial considerations were certainly the root cause of his never completing more than a portion of the Difference Engine and the fact that the Analytical Engine remained only a design. After Babbage's death, his labors were virtually forgotten until twentieth-century computer historians recognized his unparalleled genius. This was due in part to Babbage's son's having sent a small demonstration model of the calculating mechanism of Difference Engine No. 1 to Harvard University, where Howard Aiken, the computer pioneer, saw it (as far as we know) in the late 1930s.[42]

A "Difference Engine" is a device which accomplishes multiplication and division by the simpler process of addition, based on the fact that in a series of numbers raised to a given power the differences can be represented by single constants. Thus, for example, the products of a series of numbers squared differ by a constant factor of 2, making the results calculable by machine addition:

2^2 = 4 ["4" and
3^2 = 9 ["9"differ by"**5**"; "9" and
4^2 = 16 ["16" differ by "**7**"; "16" and
5^2 = 25; etc. ["25" differ by "**9**"; etc.]

(Note that the bold-face numbers—5, 7, 9, etc.—are *always* just two apart.)

Babbage's Difference Engine No. 1, if completed, would have required 25,000 parts, weighed several tons, and measured 8 ft. by 7 ft. by 3 ft. Trouble with his toolmaker and the high costs of construction meant that only a single portion of it was ever completed (one-seventh of the whole). That working "finished portion of the unfinished engine" may still be seen at the Science Museum, London, England. Babbage used it at his celebrated Saturday evening soirées to illustrate his argument in behalf of the genuineness of New Testament miracles such as the Resurrection of Christ (more on this below).

The Difference Engine gave Babbage an even more ambitious idea—that of the "Analytical Engine," which, however, never came to realization owing

---

[41] In fairness to Disraeli, the Chancellor of the Exchequer, it should be pointed out that the government's subsidy to Babbage before payments to him ceased was over twenty times what the Crown paid for Robert Stephenson's steam locomotive, the *John Bull*. In his autobiographical *Passages from the Life of a Philosopher* (*Works*, XI:97-111), Babbage shows that he could never excuse the government's cessation of interest in his projects. His machine, after all, could readily "calculate the millions the ex-Chancellor of the Exchequer squandered"!
[42] Doron Swade, *Charles Babbage and His Calculating Engines* (London: Science Museum, 1991), 36 (with excellent bibliography of primary and secondary materials on Babbage's work).

to cost projections and the refusal of the government to finance it. Like the Difference Engine, the Analytical Engine was a sophisticated decimal digital machine.

> The value of a number is represented by the positions of toothed wheels with decimal numerals marked in them. Each digit position in the number has its own wheel and only discrete positions of wheels are valid representations of the numbers.[43]

For the Analytical Engine, Babbage prepared the most extensive set of mechanical drawings ever seen up to his time (they covered 1,000 square feet of paper)[44] and — going far beyond the Difference Engine, which was essentially a high-powered calculator — represented characteristics which we today would associate with full-scale computer sophistication:

1. an *input/output* unit;
2. a unit for setting the machine in motion (for which Babbage did not coin a term), which transferred the numbers from one section to another in order to place them in the correct sequence: it was the machine's *control unit*;
3. a store, which was a numerical memory capable of storing the intermediate or final results of the calculations that had been carried out: it was the machine's *memory*, able to receive the numbers used in the calculations and store the results;
4. a *mill* which was designed to carry out the operations on the numbers that had been introduced into the Analytical Engine: this was the machine's *arithmetic unit*, in which numbers were combined according to the required rules — in other words it was the *processing unit* whose job it was to carry out the calculations by employing the data that had been introduced into the machine and transforming it in order to produce the desired results;
5. finally, a *printing device* to provide the results.[45]

The machine was designed to use punched cards to input data and instructions; it was capable of conditional ("if ... then") branching and looping; and it could handle seventh order polynomials, and would thus have been highly useful in finding trigonometric functions. It benefitted from fail-safe devices: pins and springs forced the wheels back into place if they got out of line and created

---

[43] *Ibid.*, 32. The illustrations in the text are reproduced from this publication (credit: Science Museum/Science & Society Picture Library).
[44] Thirteen plates or sectional plans for the Engine may be seen in the Campbell-Kelly edition of Babbage's *Works*, III:239-53.
[45] Ifrah, *The Universal History of Computing*, 191.

an automatic shutdown of the machine if the problem was very severe. If one were using the machine to compute tables which did not have a constant difference (e.g., a table of logarithms), one could set it so that a bell would ring after a given number of calculations to tell the operator to reset the difference wheels for a new polynomial. The machine was even capable of computing the rational roots of certain functions—and when a function had imaginary roots the first difference bell would ring to indicate that one should stop computing and find the pair of imaginary roots by inspecting the other axles. Printing involved

Fig. 11. Charles Babbage's Difference Engine No. 1 - Portion, 1832. This portion of the engine, assembled by Joseph Clement in 1832, is the first known automatic calculator. It represents about one-seventh of the calculating mechanism of the full size engine which was not completed. The portion shown has nearly 2,000 individual parts, and is one of the finest examples of precision engineering of the time. Size: 72 x 59 x 61 cm. 1862-1889.

wheel cams acting against levers whose ends moved arms containing ten steel punches corresponding to the digits 0 to 9; these punches made impressions on a lead or copper plate, from which a stereotyped printing plate could be cast.[46]

Finally, in 1847-1849, Babbage planned a simpler but more elegant version of his Difference Engine No. 1 which would benefit from some of the characteristics of the Analytical Engine. This also was never constructed by Babbage but the Difference Engine No. 2 was successfully reproduced from his plans in the 1990s and the impressive results can be viewed at the Science Museum, London.

In sum:

> Since Babbage's machine required no human intervention in the carrying-out of its sequences of operations, it thus … synthesized the concept of an automatic sequential digital calculator with a non-cyclical automaton governed by a flexible programming system and equipped with a modifiable control unit, independent of the material structure of the corresponding internal mechanisms.
>
> Even more importantly, Babbage defined, for the first time in history, a true precursor of today's universal computers: general-purpose analytical machines that are not specialized for solving only certain categories of problems, but are conceived to deal with a vast range of computable problems.[47]

Charles Babbage had a fascinating personality. He was a convinced, orthodox Christian believer with a finely tuned sense of humor. He begins his semi-autobiographical reflections with a chapter on his "Ancestry" in which he suggests that his lineage derives from Tubal-Cain, since the latter was "a great worker in iron." He says that the force of evidence is pushing him to believe that the age of humankind on the earth is far greater than Ussher's traditional chronology would put it and that "in this single instance the writings of Moses may have been misapprehended."[48] This, however, does not bring him to "the philosophic, but unromantic, views of our origin taken by Darwin."

As a boy, Babbage's enquiring mind led him to want to test the truths of the faith. He tells us that he once tried to get the devil to appear so as to verify what the Bible said about him—fortunately without success. Then, he writes:

> I resolved that at a certain hour of a certain day I would go to a certain room in the house, and if I found the door open, I would believe in the Bible; but

---

[46] The London Museum of Science version of the Engine, though 10 ft. long and 6 ft. high and containing 4,000 parts, does not include the printing unit, which was omitted for cost considerations.
[47] Ifrah, *The Universal History of Computing*, 191-2.
[48] In his *Ninth Bridgewater Treatise*, chaps. 4-5, Babbage speaks to this point *in extenso*.

that if it were closed, I should conclude that it was not true. I remember well that the observation was made, but I have no recollection as to the state of the door. I presume it was found open from the circumstances that, for many years after, I was no longer troubled by doubts.

At Cambridge, Babbage tells us, "I came into frequent contact with the Rev. Charles Simeon, and with many of his enthusiastic disciples." Indeed, Babbage abstracted the sermons of that great evangelical divine—though sometimes altering their content in an original, scientific direction. (The "Alexander the coppersmith" of 2 Tim. 4:14 led Babbage to the isomorphous character of copper and to a teacher's reaction which Babbage describes as an "awful explosion which I decline to paint."[49])

As an adult, Babbage's great apologetic contribution was his *Ninth Bridgewater Treatise: A Fragment*,[50] the circumstances of whose production need to be mentioned. The eighth Earl of Bridgewater (d. 1829) had bequeathed a princely sum to the Royal Society to encourage the creation of works "on the Power, Wisdom and Goodness of God, as manifested in the Creation," i.e., for the defense of natural theology at a time when it was being threatened by more modern geologic theories. The most impactive of the books written under this grant was William Whewell's *Astronomy and General Physics*. Though a serious believer, Whewell expressed the opinion that "deductive" mathematicians lacked "any authority with regard to their views of the administration of the universe; we have no reason whatever to expect from their speculations any help, when we ascend to the first cause and supreme ruler of the universe."

Whewell had unwittingly thrown down the gauntlet, and Babbage did not hesitate to pick it up. Babbage's *Ninth Bridgewater Treatise*, though indeed fragmentary (with intentional—and sometimes irritating—gaps in the text) is a decisive refutation of this viewpoint. It was a labor of love (or of love and spleen) and was never remunerated as were the eight official Bridgewater productions.[51] Most important, it shows how Babbage's speciality—machine assisted computation—can have significant apologetic relevance.

"If it is meant," says Babbage of Whewell's position, "that there is a 'higher region' of *evidence* than that of 'mathematical proof and physical consequence,' then it is in my opinion utterly and completely erroneous." A most valuable illustration of this point in the *Ninth Bridgewater Treatise* is Babbage's refutation

---

[49] Babbage, "Passages from the Life of a Philosopher," chaps. 2-3, *Works*, XI:7-24.
[50] The 2^d ed. comprising Vol. IX of Babbage's *Works*, ed. by Campbell-Kelly. The *Ninth Bridgewater Treatise* was widely read both in England and in America. I have in my personal library a copy of the Philadelphia printing by Lea & Blanchard (1841), which follows the 2^d London edition.
[51] For the list, see the editor's preface to Babbage's *Works*, IX:6-7.

Fig. 12. Difference Engine No. 2 at the London Science Museum (reproduced by permission of the Museum).

of Hume's classic argument against the miraculous: chapters 10 and 11 and the extended mathematical note "E" to chapter 10 are specifically devoted to this end.

The essence of Babbage's destruction of Hume lies in the latter's inadequate understanding of probability and Babbage's masterly grasp of that mathematical concept. So important is Babbage's argument that it is reprinted in its entirety at the close of Earman's recent, comprehensive critique, *Hume's Abject Failure: The Argument Against Miracles*.[52]

Hume, it will be remembered, declared that it would always be more miraculous if those reporting a miracle such as the Resurrection of Christ were neither deceived nor deceiving (were actually telling the truth) than it would be if the miracle had actually occurred—for "a miracle is a violation of the laws

---

[52] John Earman, *Hume's Abject Failure: The Argument Against Miracles* (New York: Oxford University Press, 2000), 203-12; Earman's mathematical analysis of Babbage's case is given on pp. 54-6. See also Montgomery, *Tractatus Logico-Theologicus*, 3.67 and subpropositions.

of nature; and as a firm and unalterable experience has established these laws, the proof against a miracle from the very nature of the fact, is as entire as any argument from experience can possibly be imagined."[53] After quoting this passage, Babbage writes:

> The word *miraculous* employed in this passage is evidently equivalent to *improbable,* although the improbability is of a very high degree.
>
> The condition, therefore, which, it is asserted by the argument of Hume, must be fulfilled with regard to the testimony, is that the *improbability* of its falsehood must be GREATER than the *improbability* of the occurrence of the fact. ...
>
> The only sound way of trying the validity of this assertion is to *measure* the numerical value of the two improbabilities, one of which it is admitted must be greater than the other; and to ascertain whether, by making any hypothesis respecting the veracity of each witness, it is possible to fulfil that condition by any finite number of such witnesses.
>
> Hume appears to have been but very slightly acquainted with the doctrine of probabilities.

Babbage then subjects the question to a rigorous probabilistic analysis and concludes:

> Pursuing the same reasoning, the probability of the falsehood of a fact which six such independent witnesses attest is, previously to the testimony, $1/100^6$ or it is, in round numbers, 1,000,000,000,000 to 1 against the falsehood of the testimony.
>
> The improbability of the miracle of a dead man being restored, is, on the principles stated by Hume, $1/(20 \times 100^5)$; or it is 200,000,000,000 to 1 against its occurrence.
>
> It follows, then, that the chances of accidental or other independent concurrence of only *six* such independent witnesses, is already *five times* as great as the improbability against the miracle of a dead man's being restored to life, deduced from Hume's method of estimating its probability solely from experience. ...
>
> From this it results that, provided we assume that independent witnesses can be found of whose testimony it can be stated that it is more probable that it is true than that it is false, *we can always assign a number of witnesses which will, according to Hume's argument, prove the truth of a miracle.*[54]

---

[53] David Hume, *Enquiry concerning Human Understanding,* sec. X.
[54] *Ninth Bridgewater Treatise,* in *Works,* IX:122-7 (Babbage's italics). In his more comprehensive mathematical demonstration in Note E to chap. 10 (pp. 201-3), Babbage states the italicized conclusion in a slightly different way: "If independent witnesses can be found, who speak truth more

The *Ninth Bridgewater Treatise* does not limit itself to decimating Hume's argument against the miraculous. It also employs the principles of Babbage's Difference Engine to make a powerful apologetic point over against the general deistic position—that viewpoint which sees God as little more than a "Divine Clockmaker"—that miracles are impossible because they would contradict God's original and perfect arrangement of the universe.

> The object of the present chapter is to show that it is more consistent with the attributes of the Deity to look upon miracles not as deviations from the laws assigned by the Almighty for the government of matter and of mind; but as the exact fulfilment of much more extensive laws than those we suppose to exist ...
>
> Let the reader suppose himself placed before the calculating engine, and let him again observe and ascertain, by lengthened induction, the nature of the law it is computing. Let him imagine that he has seen the changes wrought on its face during the lapse of thousands of years, and that, without one solitary exception, he has found the engine register the series of square numbers. Suppose, now, the maker of that machine to say to the observer, "I will, by moving a certain mechanism, which is invisible to you, cause the engine to make one cube number instead of a square, and then to revert to its former course of square numbers"; the observer would be inclined to attribute to him a degree of power but little superior to that which was necessary to form the original engine.
>
> But, let the same observer, after the same lapse of time—the same amount of uninterrupted experience of the uniformity of the law of square numbers, hear the maker of the engine say to him—"The next number which shall appear on those wheels, and which you expect to find a square number, shall not be so. When the machine was originally ordered to make these calculations, I impressed on it a law, which should coincide with that of square numbers in every case, *except* the one which is now about to appear; after which no future exception can ever occur, but the unvarying law of the squares shall be pursued until the machine itself perishes from decay.
>
> Undoubtedly the observer would ascribe a greater degree of power to the artist who had thus willed that event which he foretells at that distance of ages before its arrival.[55]

Atheist Geoff Simons dismisses this argument as presenting God in the guise of "celestial programmer"; it is, for him, little more than a "redraft of the

---

frequently than falsehood, it is ALWAYS *possible to assign a number of independent witnesses, the improbability of the falsehood of whose concurring testimony shall be greater than that of the improbability of the miracle itself.*"

[55] *Ibid.*, 92-7.

ancient Teleological (design) Argument." "Babbage, like many of his contemporaries, was wedded to the 'other' world, chained to concepts and connotations fashioned in prescientific epochs."[56]

In point of fact, (1) there is nothing logically wrong with the Teleological Argument (particularly when formulated in terms of its foundation, the Argument from Contingency), and (2) more scientific evidence is available today than in Babbage's own time to show the soundness of Intelligent Design in the universe.[57] Sadly, it is those of Simons' persuasion who are living the "prescientific" dream of Naturalism, whilst Babbage stands not only as the grandfather of our computer age but also as a sound apologist for biblical truth which, like its Lord, remains the same yesterday, today, and forever.[58]

Conclusion: Why the Strong Connection between Computing and Apologetics?

In 1973, a Federal District Court rightly ruled that the Sperry Rand Corporation, in spite of having created ENIAC in 1946, could not claim a patent for the electronic computer, thereby obtaining royalties on all electronic data processing from Honeywell and other competitors, since the company had not invented computers as such![59] It is certainly correct that "in this history there cannot be a single invention, still less an inventor."[60]

We are not claiming that Lull, Schickard, Pascal, or even Babbage was *the* inventor of the computer. However, their vital contributions cannot be gainsaid. This being so, the inevitable question arises: Did they have a common motivation in engaging in their scientific work? All four of them were convinced Christian believers who, moreover, were vitally concerned with defending the truth of the "faith once delivered to the saints."

---

[56] Simons, *Is God a Programmer?* 3, 78.
[57] Montgomery, *Tractatus Logico-Theologicus*, 3.8.
[58] Significantly, Babbage concludes his *Ninth Bridgewater Treatise* with a quotation from Anglican Archbishop Whately, the great nineteenth orthodox Christian apologist who wrote a devastating satire against Hume, *Historic Doubts Relative to Napoleon Buonaparte*, and an equally trenchant decimation of Deistic and skeptical historical criticism of the Old Testament, *Historic Certainties Respecting the Early History of America*. Cf. Craig Parton, ed., *Richard Whately: A Man for All Seasons* (Calgary, AB, Canada: Canadian Institute for Law, Theology and Public Policy, 1997).
[59] Bizarrely, however, the judge attributed the invention to a pair of researchers at Iowa State University—whose work was on a very basic device lacking even the structure of an analytical calculator. See Alice Rowe Burks, *Who Invented the Computer? The Legal Battle That Changed Computing History* (Amherst: Prometheus Books, 2003).
[60] Ifrah, *The Universal History of Computing*, 283.

Are we saying that these intellectual pioneers did their scientific work solely because they were committed Christians? It is plain that native intellectual curiosity—what Aristotle at the beginning of the *Metaphysics* called humankind's inherent "desire to know"—played a part. Babbage, for example, noted in his autobiography that as a child his "invariable question on receiving any new toy, was 'Mamma, what is inside of it?'" The intellectual attainments of great mathematicians outside the faith such as Bertrand Russell or modern secularists in the computer field such as Alan Turing attest to the power of such curiosity, wholly apart from religious faith.[61]

At the same time, it should be evident from the foregoing treatments of the lives of Lull, Schickard, Pascal, and Babbage that their faith was intimately connected with their intellectual endeavors. Common to all four was a serious commitment to the fundamental Christian verities: they believed that the Bible was an objectively truthful revelation from God and that Jesus Christ was no less than the God in the flesh, a miraculous Savior.

This brings us to an important *caveat*: the likelihood of engaging in serious or successful work in this field is seriously diminished if one falls into the ideological camp of the "existentialistically motivated churchmen, neo-orthodox theologians, and all those influenced by the current denigration of propositional truth, formal logic, and the subject-object distinction. ... The entire computer concept is founded on the law of non-contradiction: in binary computer language you must choose 'yes' or 'no'—a 'dialectic answer' is no answer at all. There are no neo-orthodox computers."[62]

Moreover, the solidity of Christian conviction on the part of all four of the savants we have treated led them to a cosmic perspective in which it was natural to seek maximum generality: one was not limited to a world of "blooming, buzzing confusion" (to use William James' felicitous expression) or to a universe in which the vast number of particulars (the Many) could never be integrated by way of abstract, general ideas (the One). Babbage, for example, summed up his work in the following terms: "It seems that all of the conditions that

---

[61] However, unfaith cries out for explanation, since Scripture tells us that it is the "fool" who says that there is no God and that there are "many infallible proofs" of the truth of Christ's claims. Serious scholarly work needs to be done on what R. C. Sproul has termed in a book title (but hardly touched on academically), *The Psychology of Atheism* (Minneapolis: Bethany, 1974). The need for such research is particularly evident when one reads in the first volume of Bertrand Russell's autobiography the details of the bizarre anti-religious upbringing he received as a young child.

[62] Montgomery, *Computers, Cultural Change and the Christ* [trilingual: English, French, German] (Wayne, NJ: Christian Research Institute, 1969; now available from the Canadian Institute for Law, Theology and Public Policy, Calgary, AB, Canada: http://www.ciltpp.com), 15. Cf. Montgomery, "Automating Apologetics in Austria," *Christianity Today* (November 8, 1968)—abridged in the *International Christian Broadcasters Bulletin* (January 1969).

allow a finite machine to carry out an unlimited number of calculations have been fulfilled by the Analytical Engine." In other words, Babbage consciously moved from finitude to the realm of unlimited operations, and his unwavering faith in the unlimited God of the Scriptures surely predisposed him to such an endeavor.

Georges Ifrah argues that the combination of *abstraction* and *generalization* were essential to development of the modern computer.

> As abstraction and generalization are closely linked, Babbage accordingly produced a sort of "algebrization" of the fundamental concepts of mechanical calculation. This led him, thanks to his obsession with the difficulties of human calculation and his realization that existing calculators were very inadequate, little by little to a desire to leave behind the great variety of specific data, and so arrive at a much larger construct that approached a universal view.[63]

"Constructs that approach a universal view" are far easier to appreciate when one has met the Christ of the Scriptures, since proper theology is just such a universal construct.[64] And defending that theology intellectually becomes part and parcel of the conviction that God has spoken in both in nature and in history and that his Word is the final truth and must be demonstrated to be such.

Despite the temporal distances separating them, therefore, it is entirely sensible to find much in common as we observe Ramon Lull using his Trinitarian "wheels within wheels" to convert the lost, Wilhelm Schickard calculating the years of Daniel's prophecies, Blaise Pascal figuring not just tax receipts but also the most logical reasons to believe the gospel, and Charles Babbage working out a solid base in mathematical probability for the great miracle of Christ's Resurrection.

---

[63] Ifrah, *The Universal History of Computing*, 246-7.
[64] Montgomery, "The Theologian's Craft: A Discussion of Theory Formation and Theory Testing in Theology," in his *The Suicide of Christian Theology* (Minneapolis: Bethany, 1970), 267-313; also published in the *Concordia Theological Monthly* (February 1966), and in the *Journal of the American Scientific Affiliation* (September 1966); and reprinted in this volume (above, Part Two, chapter 1).

3. God at University College Dublin

On 8 October 2008, the Literary & Historical Society of University College Dublin sponsored a debate on the motion "That this house finds it irrational to believe in God." In the 19th century, philosopher and lay theologian Søren Kierkegaard warned against such occasions; in his *Concluding Scientific Postscript* he asked whether raising such a question was not like standing in the presence of a mighty king and demanding evidence that he exists.

Nonetheless, I accepted the Society's invitation to head the "God side" in this debate. Why? For one thing because of the prestige of the Literary & Historical Society. It was founded in 1855—before University College itself—and by no less a personage than the great Christian apologist John Henry Newman. The Society remains the largest and most distinguished university society in Ireland—comparable to the Oxford Union and Cambridge Union debating societies in England. Among notables who have been invited to speak at the Literary & Historical Society: W. B. Yeats, James Joyce, every President and *Taoiseach* (Prime Minister) of Ireland since the founding of the Republic, Noam Chomsky, John Mortimer (of Rumpole fame), J. K. Rowling (Harry Potter), Oxford philosopher Richard Swinburne, and Harvard philosopher Hilary Putnam. It seemed to me that in that context God deserved a proper hearing—particularly in light of the secular reactions to a legalistic Roman Catholicism which have driven many Irish (for example, James Joyce and Samuel Beckett) to radical unbelief.

There were to be three invitees on each side of the debate. Supporting the proposition: Dr Sean M. Carroll, a theoretical cosmologist, currently senior research associate in the physics department at the California Institute of Technology; Fred Edwords, executive secretary of the American Humanist Association; and Dr Lewis Wolpert, English developmental biologist and Fellow of the Royal Society (who, the day of the debate, notified the Literary & Historical Society that, for reasons of health, he had to cancel; he was replaced by a substitute from University College).

I chose in support of the opposition Dr Angus Menuge, professor of philosophy at Concordia University Wisconsin and fellow and diplomate of the International Academy of Apologetics, Strasbourg, France; and Dr Alistair Noble, chemist and intelligent design expert from Scotland.

The debate took place in a University College auditorium seating 400; roughly 350 students and faculty members attended. Each speaker was given 7 minutes to present his case, and this was followed by questions to the speakers from the audience, and, finally, the audience vote. The order was: Edwords followed by Menuge; Carroll followed by Noble; and the Wolpert substitute followed by Montgomery.

Edwords' argument was simply that humanity is the highest value and that the notion of God is hopelessly confused (theism? pantheism? polytheism?) and thus irrational. Carroll, in line with his published article, "Why (Almost All) Cosmologists Are Atheists," declared that there was no reason why the universe needed to have a beginning; indeed, when he had taught an undergraduate course on the history of atheism at the University of Chicago he had found that reason had little or nothing to do with whether students were believers in God or atheists. As a typical Californian, Carroll dressed informally and quipped that a good reason to disbelieve in God was the presence of Sarah Palin as Republican vice-presidential candidate in the 2008 election! The Wolpert stand-in presented the argument of Wolpert's latest book, *Six Impossible Things Before Breakfast: The Evolutionary Origins of Belief*: "Religious beliefs ... all had their origin in the evolution of causal beliefs, which in turn had its origins in tool use."

How did our "God team" counter these arguments?

Edwords' claim that human values are enough left aside the critical need for an absolute ethic and inalienable rights. Water doesn't rise above its own level—and standards deriving only from the human condition are inevitably limited and tainted by the human beings and societies formulating them. The humanist has no rational way of condemning, for example, the atrocities of the Hitler or Stalinist régimes, since the disvalues at the root of them were also human products. As Ludwig Wittgenstein declared in his *Tractatus*, "Ethics is transcendental"—meaning that values, to be absolute, would have to arise from outside the human situation. Moreover, as is well documented, atheistic régimes in modern times have committed vastly more atrocities and violations of human rights than can be attributed to believers in prior centuries—and the reason is clear: if there is no God, people have no inherent worth and can be manipulated (indeed, eliminated) with impunity to serve any political or ideological end. "Without God," Dostoyevsky, observed, "all things are permissible."

Carroll's claim that the universe can rationally be regarded as infinite—as all there is—runs into gigantic difficulties, and we pointed them out. First, on the basis of the Second Law of Thermodynamics, Olbers' paradox, etc., most cosmologists consider the universe to be finite. The Big Bang, supported by the Hubble/Doppler red-shift, is seen as the beginning of matter, energy, space and time, and thus requires an explanation (which God does not, since he is self-existent, having no beginning). Einstein himself moved from a belief in an eternal universe to an acceptance of Big Bang cosmology—viewing his own effort to correct his General Theory of Relativity to support an eternal, non-expanding universe as his "biggest blunder." Indeed, an actual infinite constitutes an irrational notion (as mathematician Georg Cantor and logician David Hilbert have shown); it follows that the universe cannot have this property, whereas God, as a spirit, is not subject to such a restriction. Further, cosmologist Alan Guth, in an important article, has shown that "inflationary spacetimes are not past-complete," i.e., that "inflationary models require physics other than inflation to describe the past boundary of the inflating region of spacetimes." So, even if the universe is perpetually "inflating," it still had a beginning—which can only be accounted for by the existence of a transcendent God not bound by space-time considerations.[1]

Moreover, as Martin J. Rees and others have so effectively shown, the universe is finely-tuned, requiring an intelligent creator. The so-called Anthropic-principle argument that this may seem to be the case only in our universe as compared with the infinite possibility of "multiverses" is little more than (as convert from atheism Antony Flew has well put it) an example of "escape routes ... to preserve the nontheist status quo." Why? Because the existence of universes other than our own has zero empirical evidence supporting their facticity; and even if they existed we would have no grounds for asserting that they would not be finely-tuned; and, finally, were there to be a multiplicity of universes, we would need a "multiverse generator" to explain them—which would simply push the need to assert God's existence a step backward, in no sense eliminating it.[2]

Fascinatingly, in private discussion, Carroll said that he was now trying to find a way to show that the Second Law of Thermodynamics was not necessarily applicable universally—thus allowing for an eternal universe. This, to be sure, revealed Carroll's underlying metaphysical bias—his commitment to reductionistic naturalism—and the great gulf lying between his atheism and scientific objectivity. Naturally, we are waiting with bated breath for his repeal of the Second Law of Thermodynamics!

My presentation came at the very end. My object was briefly to deal with Wolpert's thesis and, more importantly, to pull together the arguments of the God-side.

---

[1] Bernhard Riemann, the 19th-century German mathematician whose work on non-Euclidean geometry was essential to Einstein's formulation that gravity curves space-time, declared: "If we assume independence of bodies from position and therefore ascribe to space constant curvature, it must necessarily be finite" (Archibald Henderson, "Is the Universe Finite?," 32 *American Mathematical Monthly*, 214 (May, 1925); cf. Jason Socrates Bardi, *The Fifth Postulate* (Hoboken, NJ: John Wiley & Sons, 2009), pp. 196, 208-209.
[2] Cf. note 14 to Part One above.

The notion that tool-making led to an understanding of causation and that in turn led to belief in God suffers from two appalling logical fallacies: *post hoc, ergo propter hoc* (the fact that two things—here, causation and religious belief—happen together does not in any way show that the one produces the other), and the *genetic fallacy* (the idea that the origin of something determines its ultimate truth value). In the latter case, we should remember such examples as the discovery of ammonia by the alchemist Brandt whilst he was boiling toads in urine: the value of ammonia is not (fortunately) dependent on the circumstances of its origin. And suppose we found that mathematical ability had a strictly genetic basis: would that mean that mathematics was invalid? It follows that even if religious beliefs had their source in tool-making *cum* realisation of causation, this would say nothing as to whether those religious beliefs might in fact be true. One must determine whether the object of religious belief (God) is a reality—and that is an entirely separate question from the determination as to how beliefs come about psychologically or developmentally.

As for Wolpert's reductionist-materialist account of the human mind and its beliefs, two further points were worth making. First, such scholars as psychologist Paul Vitz (*Faith of the Fatherless*) have argued that God-denial is a psychological aberration, explicable by the unfortunate experiences of the atheists holding that viewpoint. Secondly, there is powerful evidence that the mind and personality cannot be accounted for by the genetic uniqueness of the brain. Nobel Prize winner in physiology Sir John Eccles, in dialogue with Karl Popper, declared: "I am constrained to believe that there is what we might call a supernatural origin of my unique self-conscious mind or my unique selfhood or soul." The same point has been made by Mario Beauregard in his recent book, *The Spiritual Brain: A Neuroscientist's Case for the Existence of the Soul*.

I then endeavoured to point up the common element in all the atheist arguments presented by the other side. They all were in fact variants on the celebrated comment of Laplace when Napoleon, having read Laplace's groundbreaking *L'Exposition du système du monde* (1796), commented: "Your work is excellent but there is no trace of God in it." Laplace: *"Sire, je n'ai pas eu besoin de cette hypothèse"* [I had no need of that hypothesis]. The issue of God's existence is, at root, whether his existence is or is not needed to account for our world, our history, and our needs.

Fascinatingly (and this came up in the audience question time), the same point was made in the famous Flew-Wisdom parable: "Once upon a time two explorers came upon a clearing in the jungle. In the clearing were growing many flowers and many weeds. One explorer says, 'Some gardener must tend this plot.' The other disagrees: 'There is no gardener.' So they pitch their tents and set a watch. No gardener is ever seen. 'But perhaps he is an invisible gardener.' So they set up a barbed-wire fence. They electrify it. They patrol with bloodhounds. (For they remember how H. G. Wells' Invisible Man could be both smelt and touched though he could not be seen.) But no shrieks ever suggest that some intruder has received a shock. No movements of the wire ever betray an invisible climber. The bloodhounds never give cry. Yet still the Believer is not convinced. 'But there is a gardener, invisible, intangible, insensible to electric shocks, a gardener who has no scent and makes no sound, a gardener who comes secretly to look after the garden which he loves.' At last the Sceptic despairs, 'But what remains of your original assertion? Just how does what you call an invisible, intangible, eternally elusive gardener differ from an imaginary gardener or even from no gardener at all?'"

The striking thing about this parable is that one of its authors, Antony Flew—probably the most influential philosophical atheist of the 20th century—became a believer in God in 2004. Flew's sea change was due to the force of the evidence for intelligent design, especially for the fine-tuning of the universe. The "eternally elusive gardener" was not at all as elusive as the parable suggested!

I concluded with what I see as the most fundamental and most relevant reason for the God hypothesis: the impossibility otherwise of successfully accounting for Jesus Christ. I observed that Harvard astronomer Owen Gingerich (another scientist giving the lie to Carroll's claim that "cosmologist" is virtually synonymous with "atheist") noted in the conclusion to his book, *God's Universe*: "Jesus is the supreme example of personal communication from God. When the apostle Philip requested, 'Show us the Father,' Jesus responded, 'Anyone who has seen me has seen the Father.'"

Jesus' words and acts were reported by reliable, primary-source eyewitnesses in the New Testament records—documents "far better attested than that of any other work of ancient literature," according to Sir Frederick Kenyon and other preeminent textual critics. In these solid historical sources, Jesus rises from the dead, attesting his claim to be God incarnate, come to earth to die for the sins of the world. Humean arguments against the miraculous fall by the wayside in the face of an Einsteinian universe open to the possibility of all events, including miraculous ones—Hume's case having been decimated even by secular philosophers such as John Earman (*Hume's Abject Failure: The Argument Against Miracles*). Indeed, Archbishop Richard Whately—of Dublin fame—produced his wonderful satire, *Historic Doubts Concerning Napoleon Buonaparte*, having the theme that if the Humean arguments against the reliability of the Gospel accounts of Jesus were applied to Napoleon, one would have to deny his existence.

One is reminded of John Stuart Mill's sage observation in his *Three Essays on Religion*: "It is of no use to say that Christ, as exhibited in the Gospels, is not historical, and that we know not how much of what is admirable has been super-added by the tradition of his followers. Who among his disciples or among their proselytes was capable of inventing the sayings of Jesus or of imagining the life and character revealed in the Gospels? Certainly not the fishermen of Galilee; as certainly not St. Paul, whose character and idiosyncrasies were of a totally different sort; still less the early Christian writers, in whom nothing is more evident than that the good which was in them was all derived, as they always professed that it was derived, from the higher source."

I emphasized that proof depends largely on what is to be proved and that there are conditions connected with a given object of proof. If someone in the audience were to deny the fact of electricity, I could of course provide abstract and theoretical arguments in behalf of its reality; but it would be more effective if I stuck his or her finger into a light socket! By the same token, the biblical accounts of Jesus' claim that these texts are the very word of God—constituting the "power/dynamic (Greek, *dynamis*) of God unto salvation." New Testament scholar J. B. Phillips said that translating those documents was like "wiring a house without turning the mains off." And J. R. R. Tolkien, author of *The Lord of the Rings*, said of the Gospel story: "There is no tale ever told that men would rather find was true, and none which so many sceptical men have accepted as true on its own merits."

Are you the audience willing to go to those documents? I asked. No more than a "suspension of disbelief" is required. If you do, you will not be able to account for Jesus apart from God—apart from his in fact being God. Some years ago André Frossard, a French journalist, published his autobiography with the title, *Dieu existe, je l'ai rencontré* [God exists: I've met him]. That can be your story as well.

Ponder two unsettling quotations. Pascal: "There is enough light for those who really want to see—and enough darkness for those with a contrary disposition." And (inevitably) John Henry Newman: "We can believe what we choose. We are answerable for what we choose to believe."

The audience voted to defeat the proposition. For them it was not the case that "this house finds it irrational to believe in God."

4. Dawkins' Irrationality

We are now in France, but in order not to lose our English connections we have managed to obtain by satellite the five main channels of U. K. television—and this without my wife's having to stand on the roof of our house with the TV antenna in her upraised hand.

Is this additional programming necessarily an advantage? We are not sure after seeing evolutionary biologist and atheist Richard Dawkins' two programmes (early January, 2007, Channel 4), titled, "The Root of All Evil?" That root, needless to say, is for Dawkins not the love of money, but religion in general, and more particularly orthodox Christianity.

To be sure, Dawkins has received lengthy critiques of his dogmatic unbelief, e.g., Alister McGrath's *Dawkins' God* (2004). But such criticism really takes Dawkins too seriously. What we wish to do here is to provide, in a few paragraphs, reasons to regard Dawkins' dismissal of historic Christianity as on the same embarrassing plane as Bertrand Russell's simpleminded essay, "Why I Am Not a Christian."

Dawkins' central point is that religion involves faith, and faith by nature is opposed to evidence. In a letter he wrote to his ten-year-old daughter ("Good and Bad Reasons for Believing"), Dawkins writes: "Belief that there is a god or gods, belief in Heaven, ... belief that Jesus never had a human father, ...—not one of these beliefs is backed up by any good evidence. ... Next time somebody tells you something that sounds important, think to yourself: 'Is this the kind of thing that people probably know because of evidence? Or is it the kind of thing that people only believe because of tradition, authority, or revelation?'"

Clearly, Dawkins has never encountered the classic theological formulation that *fides* ("public profession of faith") and *fiducia* ("personal, saving commitment") must always be grounded in *notitia* ("factual knowledge/evidence"). Has he never heard of, much less read, the classical apologists (e.g., Pascal, Grotius, J. H. Newman) or contemporary defenders of the faith (C. S. Lewis, *et al.*)?

The first point, then, in evaluating Dawkins' abysmal failure to criticise biblical Christianity rationally is his out-of-hand *dismissal of the evidence* for the factuality of the historical claims presented in the Christian Scriptures. One cannot rationally dismiss a given revelation-claim as non-evidential when one has *a priori* and by *fiat* refused to investigate the evidence offered for it! Here we are presented with invincible ignorance—nothing more, nothing less.

Secondly, we meet Dawkins' claim, as expressed in the title of his article in the London *Times* (21 May 2005), "Creationism: God's Gift to the Ignorant"—subtitled, "Richard Dawkins speaks up for scientific logic." This of course reflects Dawkins' repeated asseverations that only classical Darwinianism offers a rational explanation of biological origins and that such a viewpoint eliminates the need to believe in a Creator.

Dawkins' most famous book, *The Blind Watchmaker* (subtitle: "Why the evidence of evolution reveals a universe without design"), sets forth this allegedly scientific, rational position. According to Dawkins, biological variations from one generation to the next result from genetic mutations; given enough time, these will produce—indeed, have produced—the remarkable complexity of present-day biological life—and all this without the need for any cosmic intelligence.

To illustrate and demonstrate this thesis, Dawkins developed a "Biomorph" computer program. Nine "genes" are employed (numbers 1 through 9); mutation consists of adding or subtracting 1 from a single gene. The procedure is run a number of times, producing "litters" of mutant offspring. After just a few dozen generations, an amazing variety of shapes emerge—looking like objects in the real world which one might incorrectly attribute to intelligent design or engineering (flowers, insects, birds, animals, lamps, aircraft, etc.). If each of the nine "genes" is allowed to "mutate" from -9 to +9 (19 possible values), each Biomorph has 19^9 possible developments—over 300 billion.

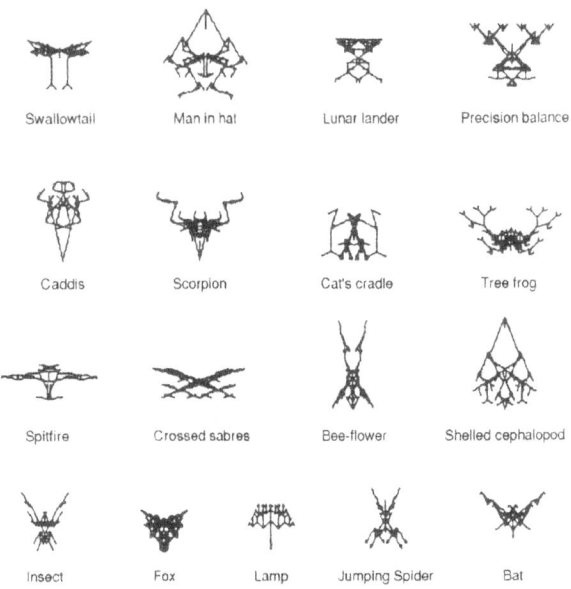

Dawkins' Biomorph program is discussed in detail in Ellen Thro's *Artificial Life Explorer's Kit* (Sams Publishing, 1993). Does the program prove Dawkins' point that intelligent design is irrelevant to biological development? *Quite the opposite—for a high degree of intelligence is required to create and employ the program itself!* Here are a series of quotations from Thro's description of the process (note our italics):

"The system is designed to *require outside intervention* (originally his) in the two main characteristics of natural systems—evolution and self-reproduction."

"Selection here isn't 'natural' but occurs *when a person chooses* an attractive, interesting, or surprising shape—a process that Dawkins likens to the way *people select* roses of a specific, pleasing color or dogs with specific characteristics to reproduce."

"The user *selects* the single Biomorph that will survive and reproduce."

"It takes *several tries* to get the shape right. In fact, Dawkins thinks that this is how evolution has always worked."

Dawkins "decided to take his computer out into the back yard and let insects 'select' screen images by bumping into them. Dawkins *then carried out the insects' selections himself.*"

It is painfully obvious that, apart from Dawkins' own rational, creative activity, the program in question would never have come about—much less have illustrated anything about biological development.

Moreover, the assumption by Dawkins and other doctrinaire evolutionists that, given enough time, natural selection will produce existing biological complexity is entirely gratuitous. Given infinite time, *anything* can theoretically occur—including proof of the falsity of the Blind Watchmaker scenario! "Huxley's notion that monkeys typing at random long enough will eventually produce literature ('the works of Shakespeare') has been tested at Plymouth University, England: over time, the monkeys (1) attacked the computer, (2) urinated on it, and (3) failed to produce a single word (AP dispatch, 9 May 2003)," Montgomery, *Tractatus Logico-Theologicus,* 4th ed., para. 3.86111.

In sum, we must regretfully conclude that it is not Creationism which—but Richard Dawkins himself who—constitutes "God's Gift to the Ignorant."

Part Three
Apologetics Per Se

1. A Short History of Apologetics

The history of the defence of Christian faith is coterminous with the history of Christianity itself.[1] This is the case because Christianity, unlike religions of the East, such as Buddhism and Hinduism, is non-syncretic: Christianity asserts that religious truth can ultimately be found only in Jesus Christ and Christian revelation (John 14:6, Acts 4:12). From this it follows that religious claims contradicting Christian faith cannot be true and must be opposed, and negative criticisms of the truth of the Christian position must be answered.

Covenant theology bifurcates the history of salvation, treating it in terms of Old Testament or Covenant, and New Testament. Dispensationalists prefer to divide salvation history into numerous epochs, often seven in number. We shall try to satisfy both! The major divide in the history of apologetics occurs at the time of the 18th-century so-called "Enlightenment," when secular thinkers such as Thomas Paine endeavoured to replace the "Book of Scripture" with the "Book of Nature"; subsequently, apologetics followed a very different path from that of the preceding centuries. Prior to that massive ideological divide, Christianity had occupied stage centre in Western intellectual history; afterwards, it found itself relegated to the wings.

But the expanse of apologetic history from biblical times to the 21st century can also be discussed in terms of seven epochs or styles of defence, and we shall briefly comment on each of them in turn: (1) Apologetics in the Bible itself; (2) Patristic defence of the faith; (3) Medieval apologetics; (4) Renaissance and Reformation; (5) Apologetics at the zenith of the "classical Christian era"; (6) Response to the Enlightenment in the 18th and 19th centuries; (7) Apologetics today. In our final section, we shall have opportunity to reflect on the weaknesses of the apologetic situation in today's church.

Apologetics in the Bible

Charles Finney was supposed to have downgraded apologetic argument by remarking: "Defend the Bible? How would you defend a lion? Let it out of its

---

[1] Readers interested in the history of apologetics may wish to consult: Bernard Ramm, *Varieties of Christian Apologetics* (rev. ed.; Grand Rapids, MI: Baker, 1961 [evangelical]; Joseph H. Crehan, "Apologetics," *A Catholic Dictionary of Theology*, Vol. I (London: Thomas Nelson, 1962); Avery Dulles, *A History of Apologetics* (New York: Corpus; Philadelphia: Westminster Press, 1971) [Roman Catholic bias—as with Crehan]; L. Russ Bush (ed.), *Classical Readings in Christian Apologetics A.D. 100-1800* (Grand Rapids, MI: Zondervan, 1983) [evangelical]; William Edgar and K. Scott Oliphint (eds.), *Christian Apologetics Past and Present: A Primary Source Reader* (2 vols.; Wheaton, IL: Crossway, 2009-2010) [presuppositionist bias]. It should be noted that these works treat inadequately, or not at all, the 21st century scene.

cage and it'll defend itself!" But, in point of fact, the Bible, unlike the Qur'an and the "holy books" of other religions, does not expect its readers to accept its revelational character simply because the text claims to be true. In the Old Testament, Elijah competes with the false prophets of Baal, and the superior miraculous demonstration by the power of the God of Israel wins the day (I Kings 18). In the Gospels, Jesus makes the truth of his entire ministry depend on a single sign—that of his resurrection from the dead (Matthew 12:39-40). In the Epistles, not only is Christ's physical resurrection asserted, but the Apostle is concerned as well to provide a list of eyewitnesses to the risen Christ (I Cor. 15:4-8).

The biblical apologetic focuses in four areas, and these are subsequently employed throughout Christian history: *miracle, fulfilled prophecy, natural revelation,* and *personal experience* (what the philosophers term "subjective immediacy"). Three caveats: (1) natural revelation (proofs of God from nature), though present in the Bible (e.g., Ps. 19:1), is the least emphasised apologetic; (2) personal experience never "floats free": the subjective is always grounded in one or more of the objective areas of proof—generally miracle and prophecy; (3) occasionally, a "double-barreled" argument is made through *miracle* being the object of *prophecy,* as in the case of the Virgin Birth of our Lord (Isa. 7:14; Mt. 1; Lk. 1-2).

Since the biblical plan of salvation centres on God's revealing himself in real history, through prophets, priests, and finally by the incarnation of his eternal Son, Jesus Christ, the biblical apologetic is essentially one of asserting and demonstrating the *factual* nature of the events recounted. The Apostle is willing to make the entire truth of the faith turn on the reality of Jesus' resurrection (I Cor. 15:17-20). The case for biblical truth, then, connects with the nature of Christianity as "historical religion": it is in principle falsifiable—and, in this case, verifiable—thereby removing Christianity from the analytical philosophers' category of a meaningless metaphysical claim and placing it in the realm of the empirical and the synthetic, along with historical events in general.

Patristic Apologetics

The church fathers closest to the New Testament understandably followed its apologetic lead: prophecy and miracle were their preferred arguments. The earliest of them (Irenaeus, for example) favoured the prophecies of the Old Testament fulfilled in Christ, since in his time the gospel was being proclaimed and defended "to the Jew first." Moreover, the Gnostic heretics employed pseudo-miracles (sherbet in Eucharistic wine!), but had no fulfilled prophecies to support their views. As Christian evangelism reached a predominately Gentile audience, miracle evidence came to the fore. Eusebius of Caesarea, in his *Ecclesiastical History,* employs a testimonial argument in support of Christ's miraculous resurrection from the dead, sarcastically asking whether it would be reasonable to suppose that the Apostles, had they known that Jesus did not rise from the dead, would have lost all they had and ultimately been martyred whilst maintaining that he *had* in fact conquered death. Tertullian's oft-quoted phrase, *"Credo quia absurdum,"* rather than being an invitation to irrationality, expressed the belief that the Christian gospel was almost too good to be true—as the children in C. S. Lewis' Narnian chronicles would later discover.

The bridge between the Patristic and medieval worlds was Augustine of Hippo. He was converted from neo-Platonism to Christianity and offered an apologetic of a Platonic nature to the intellectuals of his time, convinced as they were that Plato was the summation of classical philosophy. For Plato, one must rationally (and for neo-Platonists, rationally *and* spiritually) rise from the world of phenomena to the world of ideas/ideals—of which the highest expression is the Good, the True, and the Beautiful. Augustine identified that realm with the God of the Bible. He also, in his *Confessions,* made a compelling argument from personal experience: "Thou hast made us for thyself, O God, and our hearts are restless until they rest in thee." In the 20th century, Edward John Carnell would expand on this in his axiological apologetic, *A Philosophy of the Christian Religion.*

Medieval Defense of the Faith

Theodore Abu Qurra, an Eastern theologian (9th century) set forth an apologetic parable demonstrating comprehension of the apologetic task well in advance of his time; it raises the critical question as to how one can test multiple revelation claims (in his case, Islam vs. Christianity). For Abu Qurra, one asks each religion what it says of God, what it says of sin, and what sort of remedy it offers for the human condition—thereby demonstrating the superiority of Christianity.[2]

Although a primitive form of the ontological argument for God's existence can be found in St. Augustine, St. Anselm of Canterbury provided its classic formulation in the 11th century. The argument purports to prove God's existence from the concept of God itself: God is "than which no greater can be conceived"; he must therefore have all properties; and since *existence* is a property, God exists! The argument rests on the idealistic assumption that ideas have reality untouched by the phenomenal world (so rational idealists have been somewhat comfortable with it), but the overwhelming fallacy in the argument is sim-

---

[2] See Montgomery, *Faith Founded on Fact* (Nashville, TN: Thomas Nelson, 1978), pp. 119-21.

ply that "existence" is not a property alongside other properties; *existence* is the name we give to something that in fact has properties. To determine whether a something (God?) exists, we need to investigate the empirical evidences of its/his reality. Thus the far better Christian argument is that "God was in Christ, reconciling the world unto himself" (II Cor. 5:19). This critique having been offered, it is worth noting that neo-Orthodox theologian Karl Barth *(Anselm: Fides Quaerens Intellectum)* was quite wrong that Anselm was not trying to do apologetics but was simply preaching to the converted.[3]

The most influential medieval apologist of western Christendom was its most influential theologian: Thomas Aquinas. Though probably having never met a pagan, he wrote his *Summa contra gentiles* ("Summation against the pagans"). By his time—the 13th century—Aristotle had replaced Plato as the most favoured classical philosopher, so Aquinas developed his apologetic along Aristotelian lines. He took over Aristotle's traditional proofs for God's existence, and argued that they can establish a foundation of Reason upon which Faith can operate. This stress on the Aristotelian proofs would have a tremendous influence on all subsequent Christian apologetics.

Contemporaneous with Aquinas was Ramon Lull (or Lullius), a Catalonian who is considered to be the first European missionary to the Moslems. Lull was a philosopher, but not a scholastic in the Aristotelian tradition. He developed an original "method" for the conversion of the infidel through the combining of theological and philosophical concepts and the illustrative use of rotating, interlocking disks. He now figures in the prehistory of the modern computer.[4] Lull also practiced literary apologetics by way of his apologetic novel, *Blanquerna*.

Renaissance and Reformation

By the time of the Italian Renaissance (15th-16th centuries), the world was opening up to exploration and Plato had returned to philosophical prominence. Thus the apologists of that era directed their efforts to adventurous thinkers committed to a Platonic view of the world. Thomas More, in his *Utopia*, well illustrates this. The Utopians pray each night that "if there is a better and truer faith, may God bring it to us." More's explorers reach Utopia and present the Christian religion as that better faith. The Utopians, in seeking the Good, the True, and the Beautiful, accept the God of Christian revelation.

---

[3] Cf. Montgomery, *Where Is History Going?* (Minneapolis: Bethany, 1969), pp. 109-110.
[4] See Montgomery, "Computer Origins and the Defence of the Faith," 56/3 *Perspectives on Science and Christian Faith* (September, 2004), 189-203; and reprinted above (Part Two, chap. 2).

The Protestant Reformers were not concerned with apologetics as such; they had more than enough to do cleaning up the theology of the medieval church. But their work had much indirect value for apologetics. Thus, Luther's insistence on *sola Scriptura* and thoroughgoing christocentricity were healthy counteractives to medieval Aristotelian/Thomistic emphases.[5] And when the Roman Catholic opponents of the Reformation argued that the Bible is an obscure book, requiring the Roman Church to interpret it, Protestants such as Andreas Althamer produced books defending the clarity ("perspicuity") and non-contradictory nature of the teachings of Holy Scripture. Such writings are the forerunners of modern treatises that deal with and refute claims to alleged errors and contradictions in the Bible.

17th-Century Apologetics

This was the last century of "old Western man"—the last century when Christian thought dominated the intellectual landscape of the West. It was the era of "system"—Protestant systematic theology, the musical summation of the Western musical tradition in the labours of Lutheran J. S. Bach, the literary summation in Milton's Paradise Lost, the architectural summation in Wren's magnificent churches constructed after London's Great Fire of 1666.

As for apologetics, Hugo Grotius, the father of international law, published in 1622 his *De Veritate religionis Christianae* ("On the truth of the Christian Religion"). This seminal work was widely translated and in print until the 19th century. It sets forth a modern, historical apologetic for the soundness of Jesus' claims in the New Testament.

Even more famous and influential was the apologetic work of Blaise Pascal, a Roman Catholic but a follower of the Port Royal, Jansenist movement, which was regarded by its conservative Catholic enemies as tantamount to Protestantism—owing to its great appreciation for St. Augustine and central stress on salvation by grace through faith. Pascal's posthumously collected Pensées ("Thoughts") offer a powerful apologetic for the truth of biblical revelation and the saving work of Christ. His "wager" (even if Christianity were false, in accepting it you would be better off, for you would obtain the best ethic and the best human example—Jesus) was not intended as the totality of his apologetic (as his philosophical critics generally maintain, in order to make it appear silly),

---

[5] In an otherwise very useful handbook, Boa and Bowman's classification of Luther as an apologetic "fideist"—and the placing of him in the same bed with Kierkegaard, Karl Barth, and Donald Bloesch— would be ludicrous if it were not so factually wide of the mark: Kenneth D. Boa and Robert M. Bowman, Jr., *Faith Has Its Reasons* (2d ed.; Milton Keynes, UK: Paternoster, 2005).

but only as a device for getting the unbeliever's attention. Having been struck by the force of the wager, the unbeliever would then have powerful reason to examine the full gamut of evidence for the faith and thereby come to see that the probabilities are overwhelmingly in favour of Christian commitment.[6]

The Great Divide and Its Apologetic Aftermath

The 18th century was characterised politically by the French and American Revolutions and ideologically by Deism: the belief that one could and should dispense with the "revealed" religion of historic Christianity, contaminated by superstition (blood sacrifice, miracles, etc.) and substitute a "religion of Nature," focusing on a God of immutable natural law and morality.[7] "Enlightenment" philosophers included Immanuel Kant, who claimed that the traditional proofs of God's existence were inadequate and that only an absolute ethic could be established (the "categorical imperative"); Gotthold Ephraim Lessing, who dug his "Ditch" between absolute, philosophical truth on the one hand, and what he considered the inadequacies of history (including biblical history) on the other; and David Hume, who claimed that, owing to "uniform experience," miracles could always be rejected out of hand, since it would always be more miraculous if the witness were telling the truth than that the miracle actually happened.

These attacks were devastating and historic Christianity lost much intellectual ground as a result of them. The identification of the churches with the privileges of monarchy and the Old Régime only made matters worse. But apologists for the faith heroically entered the fray.

In the 18th century itself, William Paley (*Natural Theology; Evidences*) argued for the soundness of the biblical witness—both as to God's hand in nature and as to the soundness of the New Testament portrait of Jesus[8]; and Thomas Sherlock pointed out, in his legally-orientated work, *The Tryal of the Witnesses of the Resurrection of Jesus,* that people of the 1st century were as capable as those

---

[6] Boa and Bowman also incorrectly classify Pascal as a "fideist"! For a proper understanding of Pascal, see the writings of Emile Cailliet; also, Montgomery, "Computer Origins ..." (*loc. cit.*).
[7] Cf. Montgomery, *The Shaping of America* (Minneapolis: Bethany, 1976).
[8] Paley's continuing relevance is evidenced by the fact that atheist Richard Dawkins makes him his foil in arguing for biological evolutionism (*The Blind Watchmaker*). Paley, incidentally, was a barrister and wrote as a lawyer with Christ as his client; he was roundly (and unfairly) criticised for doing apologetics "in the spirit of the advocate rather than of the judge" by the great classicist Benjamin Jowett: *The Interpretation of Scripture and Other Essays* (London: George Routledge and Sons, n.d.), p. 129.

of his own "enlightened" time to distinguish between a dead body and a live one—and that the case for Jesus' resurrection could not therefore be dismissed philosophically.[9]

The most famous defence of faith in the 18th century was Bishop Butler's *Analogy of Religion,* which attempted to convince the Deist using his own reasoning: the Scriptural teaching, said Butler, was directly *analogous* to the work of God in nature—and since the Deist accepted the latter, he had no ground for rejecting the former. Examples: nature displays seeds falling into the ground and dying, followed by life again every spring, and Scripture presents the crucifixion followed by the resurrection; human society survives only because each person acts for others by doing work the other cannot do, and Scripture makes divine substitution the key to salvation.

The 19th century dealt a further, perhaps even more crushing, blow to the faith. With the publication of Darwin's *Origin of Species* in 1859, even the Deist's God of Nature could be discarded: natural selection could allegedly account for all development. Defenders of the faith offered two very different apologetic approaches to this incipient atheism that culminated, at the end of century, in Nietzsche's famous declaration that "God is dead."

The great Roman Catholic (former Anglican) apologist John Henry Newman doggedly fought the revelational battle on epistemological and historical grounds (*Essays on Miracles; Grammar of Assent*): he refined the notion of historical probability with his concept of the *illative sense*: when "congeries" (concatenations) of facts inexorably point to the same conclusion—as in the testimonies to the resurrection of Christ—they raise the level of the argument to a practical certainty and cannot rationally be dismissed.

Lay philosopher and theologian Søren Kierkegaard, the father of existentialism, took an inner route: for him, "truth is subjectivity." As finite creatures, we cannot, à la Hegel and German idealistic philosophy, discover the "essence" of things; we can only experience our own "existence"—which, owing to the fall, is *Angst* and estrangement without Christ. But his successor existentialists in the 20th century (Heidegger, Sartre), left with only their own subjectivity, did not find Christ, but a valueless, atheistic world, both microcosmically and macrocosmically. By discounting the value of probability and historical reasoning to vindicate Christian revelation, Kierkegaard ended up substituting an unstable, subjective experientialism for the objectivist *hubris* of the unbelieving philosophers he opposed. Modern evangelicalism has frequently made the same mistake.

---

[9] Sherlock's *Tryal* is photolithographically reprinted in Montgomery (ed.), *Jurisprudence: A Book of Readings* (rev. ed.; Strasbourg, France: International Scholarly Publishers, 1980); available from http://www.ciltpp.com.

Apologetics Today

In the early decades of the 20th century, what appeared to be a powerful case against all metaphysical and religious thinking appeared on the scene. This stemmed from Ludwig Wittgenstein's *Tractatus Logico-Philosophicus* and from the so-called Vienna Circle of analytical philosophers and logical positivists. They argued that truth claims, including metaphysical and religious views, were meaningless unless they could be verified. Many theologians and most metaphysicians tried to counter this position by discounting the need for verification (a Pyrrhic victory if there ever was one!). In point of fact, as this essayist has maintained in his major work (*Tractatus Logico-Theologicus*[10]), whereas secular metaphysical systems and virtually all non-Christian religions do in fact entirely lack testability, Christian faith alone offers the solid, empirical, historical evidence of its truth by way of the case for Jesus Christ.

The 20th century and the onset of the 21st have been marked by a number of influential Christian apologists and by several apologetic schools of thought.

Needless to say, the liberal churches did not carry on apologetic activity, since inherent to theological liberalism has always been an accommodating of the faith to secular ideology rather than a defending of it over against secularism (cf. liberal theologian Willard L. Sperry's *"Yes, But"—The Bankruptcy of Apologetics*). The Scopes evolution trial drove many American evangelicals into a radical separation from mainline intellectual life and therefore from apologetic activity: the only choice they saw was to pluck "brands from the burning" through revival campaigns and personal testimony. But even the twelve popular, paperbound volumes that introduced the term "fundamentalist" into the language (*The Fundamentals*, 1910) contained fine apologetic defences of historic Christianity by such notables as James Orr and B. B. Warfield.

Warfield, as a Princeton Theological Seminary professor, commanded great respect. His defence of scriptural inerrancy (*The Inspiration and Authority of the Bible*) had immense impact, especially in Reformed theological circles. Later, this would be blunted by the Westminster Theological Seminary theologian Cornelius Van Til, who criticised Warfield's evidential argumentation as not being sufficiently Calvinistic—since it did not insist on starting from the presupposition of the truth of the faith and God's sovereignty, above and beyond evidential considerations.

In the 1940's, Moody Bible Institute instructor and Bible commentator Wilbur M. Smith wrote his book, *Therefore Stand: A Plea for a Vigorous Apologetic*. Essentially a work of historical apologetics, this book had wide influence:

---

[10] Montgomery, *Tractatus Logico-Theologicus* (4th ed.; Bonn, Germany: Verlag für Kultur und Wissenschaft, 2009), *passim*. Available from http://www.ciltpp.com.

its author could be trusted as not being a closet intellectual or one critical of the evangelical lifestyle. *Therefore Stand* remains a classic, demonstrating on every page the wide learning of the preeminent theological bibliographer of 20th century evangelicalism.

Smith would later accept a chair at the newly founded Fuller Theological Seminary. There (before Fuller gave up its inerrancy position) apologist Edward John Carnell produced exceedingly important works: *An Introduction to Christian Apologetics* and *A Philosophy of the Christian Religion*. The *Introduction* endeavours, without success, to combine a Van Tilian presuppositionalism with E. S. Brightman's truth test of "systematic consistency" (a true assertion must be logically consistent and must also fit the facts of the external world) — but the second part of the book contains masterful responses to a host of common objections to biblical religion: the problem of evil, evolutionary theory, antimiraculous views, etc.

The mid-20th century was also marked by the writings of the most influential of all English-language apologists of the time: C. S. Lewis. To apply the terminology of William James, Lewis successfully practised both "toughminded" and "tenderminded" apologetics. His broadcast talks (later combined under the title *Mere Christianity*) brought many to the faith in England: my Cornell professor, the late literary critic David Daiches, remarked that more had been converted through Lewis than in the British revival campaigns of Billy Graham! *Miracles* dealt with Hume's attempt to short-circuit historical investigation through philosophical speculation[11]; *The Problem of Pain* was a superb popular justification of the God of the Bible against the standard argument that an all-powerful and loving God could not exist in the face of the evils of the world. On the tenderminded front, Lewis' science-fiction trilogy (*Out of the Silent Planet, Perelandra, That Hideous Strength*) and his Narnian chronicles brought many who were indifferent to traditional apologetics to see the truth of the faith on the level of "deep myth."[12]

A number of "schools" of apologetics came into existence in the latter years of the 20th century and continue to influence the intellectual climate. We have mentioned above the *presuppositionalist* approach. Its major representatives have been philosopher Gordon Clark and theologian Cornelius Van Til; its epicentre is the Westminster Theological Seminary (Philadelphia) and its advocates include John Frame and the late Greg Bahnsen. Though there are important

---

[11] Cf. more recent — and systematic — decimations of Hume: philosopher (and non-Christian) John Earman, *Hume's Abject Failure: The Argument Against Miracles* (New York: Oxford University Press, 2000); and David Johnson, *Hume, Holism and Miracles* (Ithaca, NY: Cornell University Press, 1999).

[12] Cf. Montgomery (ed.), *Myth, Allegory and Gospel* (Minneapolis: Bethany, 1974).

differences among these thinkers, they are all convinced that, owing to the fall of man, facts cannot be used to convince unbelievers of Christian truth: as Van Til put it: "All is yellow to the jaundiced eye." Generally (but not in every case) this presuppositionalism is combined with an ultra-Calvinist understanding of predestination.

Philosopher Alvin Plantinga's "Reformed epistemology" can be regarded as a variant of the presuppositionalist position. For Plantinga, historical argumentation is necessarily inadequate and no demonstration that Christianity is true will succeed with the unbeliever: the apologetic task cannot go beyond showing that Christian theism is a legitimate option, plausible and "warranted" — unable to be discounted epistemologically. This position has been severely critiqued for its weakness by non-presuppositionalists[13] — and by presuppositionalists of the stricter variety as well.[14] But Plantinga's *God and Other Minds* is one of the best treatments of the problem of evil, and, almost single-handedly, he has been responsible for making Christian thinking respectable in secular philosophical circles in America.[15]

Over against presuppositionalism are the *evidentialists* and the self-styled *classical apologists*. Evidentialists hold that the fall, though certainly keeping sinful man from re-entering Eden by human effort or will, did not destroy his capacity to distinguish fact from non-fact, even in the religious realm (when God calls to Adam in the garden after he has eaten the forbidden fruit, Adam can still recognise God's voice). The apologetic task consists, then, of marshalling the full panoply of factual evidence to show that Christianity is true and its rivals false. Among prominent evidentialists are the author of this article; Gary Habermas; and the many advocates of the "Intelligent Design" movement (the most important being William Dembski).

"Classical" apologists, such as Norman Geisler, R. C. Sproul, and William Lane Craig, insist that, prior to making a factual, historical case for Jesus Christ, one must establish God's existence — generally using the classical, Aristotelian proofs, or sophisticated variants on those proofs (such as Craig's favourite, the medieval, Arabic *kalam* cosmological argument). Evidentialists almost invariably take the christocentric route, focusing their apologetic on the case for Jesus

---

[13] E.g., Jason Colwell, "The Historical Argument for the Christian Faith: A Response to Alvin Plantinga," 53/3 *International Journal for Philosophy of Religion* (2003), 147-61.

[14] E.g., K. Scott Oliphint, "Plantinga on Warrant," 57/2 *Westminster Theological Journal* (1995), 415-35, and "Epistemology and Christian Belief," 63/1 *Westminster Theological Journal* (2001), 151-82.

[15] In England, respect for the philosophical defence of Christian faith has not needed rehabilitation; see, for example, the valuable apologetic work of Richard Swinburne.

Christ and especially his resurrection—and approaching issues of God's existence by way of the incarnate Christ (Jesus to Philip: "he who has seen me has seen the Father"—John 14:8-9).

As Edward John Carnell once remarked, "There are as many apologetics as there are facts in the world." One should therefore expect specialised apologetic approaches in particular factual areas. Intelligent Design is such an approach—focusing on scientific fact. Other examples include *literary apologetics*, as exemplified by G. K. Chesterton, the Inklings (C. S. Lewis, J. R. R. Tolkien, Charles Williams), and contemporary literary scholars such as Gene Edward Veith[16]; and *juridical* (or *legal*) *apologetics*, where the sophisticated evidential techniques of the law are applied to the collection and interpretation of evidence in behalf of the faith. Historical representatives of legal apologetics would certainly include Thomas Sherlock (*The Tryal of the Witnesses of the Resurrection of Jesus*) and Simon Greenleaf (*The Testimony of the Evangelists*[17]); contemporary work in the field has been carried out by the author of this article, and by others such as Craig Parton and Ross Clifford. A recent survey of the area is William P. Broughton's *The Historical Development of Legal Apologetics, with an Emphasis on the Resurrection*.[18]

And there are what might be termed non-apologetic apologists, such as Regent College's John G. Stackhouse (*Humble Apologetics: Defending the Faith Today*). Stackhouse is highly critical of the kind of decisiveness represented by the title of Josh McDowell's influential book of popular apologetics, *Evidence That Demands a Verdict*, as well as aggressive attempts to defend the faith through public debates with unbelievers (he particularly dislikes William Lane Craig). Stackhouse seems to favour a postmodernist style of non-confrontation: the building of relationships with unbelievers rather than argumentation.[19]

How effective is the contemporary Christian apologetic? In spite of fine examples, there is much room for improvement. Here are three serious difficulties, as the present essayist sees them:

1. A continuing, virtually endemic disinterest on the part of many evangelical denominations, pastors, and laymen for the kind of rigorous academic study apologetics demands—and a corresponding preference for non-intellectual, subjective religiosity ("the devotional life"), group activities

---

[16] See Montgomery, "Neglected Apologetic Styles: The Juridical and the Literary," *Evangelical Apologetics*, ed. Michael Bauman, David Hall, and Robert Newman (Camp Hill, PA: Christian Publications, 1996), pp. 119-133.
[17] Reprinted in Montgomery, *The Law Above the Law* (Minneapolis: Bethany, 1975).
[18] Xulon Press, 2009.
[19] For an interesting critique of this approach, by Canadian judge Dallas Miller, see 4/3 *Global Journal of Classical Theology*, October, 2004: http://phc.edu/gj_1_toc_v4n3.php.

within the church ("fellowship"), and church-growth activism ("megachurchism"). This may appear on the surface as spirituality, but it is just the opposite—since it leaves the seeking unbeliever without an adequate witness.
2. The self-defeating nature of presuppositional and "humble" apologetic approaches. In the Apostolic witness of the New Testament (Paul on the Areopagus, for example), the Christian starts from a common ground with the unbeliever, moving him or her to the cross of Christ. One does not argue that the non-Christian's worldview is utterly inadequate and that only by starting from the Christian presupposition can any proper knowledge be arrived at. And the Apostles certainly did not fear confrontation or insist first on establishing personal "relationships" before the case for Christianity could be made. Our modern secular world is much like the pagan world of the Apostles, and it would behove us to consider seriously their defence of the faith as the proper model for ours.
3. Overemphasis on issues of God's existence rather than on the case for incarnation. We have seen how, owing to Aquinas' baptism of the traditional Aristotelian proofs for God's existence, these proofs became central to Roman Catholic apologetics and to much of Protestant defences of the faith during and even after the 18th-century "Enlightenment." We are not questioning the underlying logic of these proofs, but we are questioning the emphasis placed upon them. Salvation does not depend on believing in God: Scripture tells us that "the devils also believe, and tremble" (James 2:19). Salvation requires coming to terms with Jesus Christ—as the only Saviour from sin, death, and the devil. Thus the Christian apologetic needs to be, root and branch, an apologetic for Jesus Christ—not a disguised exercise in the philosophy of religion.[20]

The history of apologetics is really a special case of the history of evangelism. And the more secular the modern world becomes, the more important it is. If we neglect to answer the legitimate intellectual concerns of the unbelievers of our time, we are admitting that we do not really care about their eternal destiny. Apologetics does not save; only Jesus Christ is able to do that. But apologetics can—and should—serve as a John the Baptist, making the paths straight, facilitating routes to the cross of Christ.

---

[20] Cf. Montgomery, "Apologetics for the 21st Century," *Reasons for Faith*, ed. Norman L. Geisler and Chad V. Meister (Wheaton, IL: Crossway, 2007), pp. 41-52—and included as the next essay (3.2) in the present volume.

2. Apologetics for the 21st Century

Where We Are and Why This Is Important[1]

Christian believers concerned with defending the Faith once delivered to the saints need to recognize the unique cultural situation in which we find ourselves shortly after the turn of the new millennium. This uniqueness stems from a combination of factors, by no means limited to increased secularism and secular self-satisfaction. The major factors are: (1) An enlargement of what Canadian sociologist Marshall McLuhan termed "the Global Village"—the exponential increase in world communications, resulting in continual, unavoidable contact between believers and unbelievers. (2) Pluralism, to an extent unknown in past ages, even during the Hellenistic period; its consequence being a multiplying of sects, religious and philosophical viewpoints, and the interpenetration of worldviews (e.g., Eastern religions transmogrified into Western "New Age" orientations). (3) Increased sophistication on the part of religionists. Examples, among many, include Scientology's use of legal intimidation to stifle criticism of the movement, paralleling the employment of legal teams by multinational corporations to protect their public image[2]; also, al-Qaeda's use of highly sophisticated computer technology to further their interests and terrorist agendas.[3] (4) A growing realization, stemming in large part from the events of 11 September 2001, that all religions are *not* in fact "saying the same thing" in spite of what we were told by generations of liberal clergy and comparative religion teachers.

---

[1] This is a modified version of an essay which was offered as an invitational lecture at the Hope for Europe conference of the Evangelical Alliance, held in Budapest, Hungary, 27 April-1 May 2002. A version of the essay was also published in German as "Die Verteidigung der Hoffnung in uns—Apologetik fuer das 21. Jahrhundert," in Thomas Mayer and Thomas Schirrmacher (eds.), *Europa Hoffnung geben* (Hamburg, Germany: VTR, 2004), pp. 48-61.

[2] As an English barrister, I was consulted on the *Bonny Woods* v. *Church of Scientology* matter a few years ago. Woods and her husband were converted from Scientology to Evangelical Christianity and began a counter-cult ministry to assist others to leave Scientology. Thereupon they were sued for defamation by the Church of Scientology. With its vast financial resources, the Church could easily have bankrupted the Woods, even though the latter were in the right legally. Our strategy was to apply to the Court for discovery of all the foundational records of the Church—on the ground that the only way to know if the Church had in fact been defamed was to find out what it really believed and practiced vis-à-vis its members and how it proselytized. As we expected, the Church dropped the action rather than revealing what it was up to.

[3] Cf. Reuel Marc Gerecht, "The Gospel According to Osama bin Laden," *Atlantic Monthly*, January 2002, pp. 46-48.

Why are these considerations so important? Recognition of the current situation is vital because *only by knowing it will we direct our Apologetic to the real needs of the unbeliever.* The bedrock principle here is: **1. Apologetics is not Dogmatics.**

By this we mean that, whereas Dogmatics begins with God's special revelation of himself in Holy Scripture and expounds its content, Apologetics begins where the unbeliever is: "becoming all things to all people, that we might save some ... a Jew to the Jew and a Greek to the Greeks."[4] This does not mean, to be sure, that in Apologetics we alter the eternal message to fit the unbeliever's situation or needs. That message is the same, yesterday, today, and forever. Our methods of communicating the everlasting gospel will be developed, however, according to the personal, social, and cultural context, which never remains constant. If this fundamental distinction is not understood, *either* Dogmatics will be absorbed into Apologetics (to the loss of the gospel) *or* Apologetics will be swallowed up in Dogmatics (so that the defence of the gospel will make sense only to those who already believe it). The first of these errors is that of the religious liberal; the second is endemic among religious conservatives.[5]

Avoiding 20th Century Mistakes

We have just observed that there are mistakes characteristic of the two chief theological polar-opposites. Let us now observe a few of the other particularly unfortunate errors of doctrinaire religious liberals and conservatives as background to a discussion of how to move forward on a much more solid apologetic basis.

The Conservatives. The "Bible Christian" often sees no distinction between preaching and revivalism, on the one hand, and evangelism and apologetics on the other. He or she will use tracts which do little more than quote Bible passages; one thinks of R. A. Torrey's little booklet consisting of non-Christian

---

[4] Classically, to be sure, Dogmatics and Apologetics were treated as two of the three branches of Systematic Theology (the third being Ethics). Today, in theological faculties, Apologetic instruction has virtually disappeared. At best, it sometimes appears in bastardized form in courses in Philosophy of Religion.

[5] See my book, *Faith Founded on Fact* (available, together with most of my Apologetics writings, from the Canadian Institute for Law, Theology, and Public Policy, Calgary, Alberta, Canada); website: http://www.ciltpp.com. Sadly, the great Calvinist dogmatician Cornelius Van Til believed that his great apologetic accomplishment, over against B. B. Warfield, was to make the God who reveals Himself in Scripture the starting-point for Apologetics as well as for Dogmatics. Warfield, however, knew what he was doing: an Apologetic which insists that the non-Christian start where the Christian starts is really no Apologetic at all. At best it is preaching; at worst it is simply counterproductive.

questions, accompanied with Bible texts supplying the answers. The difficulty (should it not be obvious?) is that today one can hardly assume that the non-Christian is really a lapsed Christian who knows that the Bible is true but has fallen into a life inconsistent with it. With a plethora of alternative "holy books" (Qur'an, Bhagavad-Gita, Book of Mormon, etc., etc.), we presume at our peril that the unbeliever will simply accept whatever we quote from the Bible. The very term "Revival" used so frequently in evangelical circles as equivalent to "Evangelism" shows how unrealistically we view the condition of the average non-Christian today. In point of fact, we must *demonstrate the revelational character of the Holy Scriptures* over against competing claims to inscripturated truth. And our personal "holiness" is hardly a proof of biblical revelation any more than our failings remove from its veracity. As Luther nicely put it: the entire gospel is *extra nos* (outside of us).

Some learned conservatives make the deadly mistake of *confusing Apologetics with Philosophy*. How do they do this? They spend their energies discussing questions which have little or no bearing on the truth of the faith or relevant to the acceptance of it. Example: the relationship of Time to Creation: could God have logically functioned before the creation of temporality? (At a meeting of the Evangelical Philosophical Society in the U.S.A. several years ago, I made myself unpopular by paraphrasing St Augustine, who, when confronted with the question, "What was God doing before He created the world?," replied: "Preparing Hell for people who ask questions like that.") We are thus brought to our next axiomatic truth: **2. Apologetics is not *Philosophy*.**

This is true not merely because, as apologist Edward John Carnell was wont to say, there are as many Apologetics as there are facts in the world; that is to say, Apologetics employs every true fact and every true discipline in its behalf: history, science, jurisprudence, literature, art. The particular reason why Apologetics must not be reduced to Philosophy is that the abstract questions of traditional philosophy are either purely *formal,* dealing with issues of logic and not with issues of fact, or are so arcane that they do not touch the central elements of the gospel (acceptance of the death of our Lord for our sins and His resurrection for our justification).

The gospel is a matter of *fact,* and its acceptance will necessarily depend on whether the documentary records of Jesus' ministry are sound, whether the testimonies to His life and work are accurate, and whether one can accept His claims and His resurrection from the dead. Important philosophical issues do indeed bear on this case (issues such as the legitimacy of miracle evidence), but the case is, in the last analysis, a *factual* one. Metaphysical problems can be discussed from now until just after the Last Judgment and the crucial question of the facticity of the gospel still remain untouched. And it is the gospel's factual truth which constitutes, and has always constituted, the heart of the Christian proclamation and the heart of the Christian apologetic.

Related to the error just discussed is the conservative tendency to think that the best apologetic strategy consists of showing that Christian affirmations are indeed philosophically "meaningful," i.e., not irrational or technically nonsensical. One of the most influential and important Christian philosophers of our time has succeeded in showing, for example, that the existence of evil is not logically incompatible with the existence of an omnipotent, omniscient Deity. Fine! But logical possibility is hardly the same as de facto existence! There is nothing *logically* absurd in a claim that the Big Bang was the product of a Divine Burp, but that hardly means that such occurred.

There is no substitute for evidence in our defense of the faith. Life is bigger than logic; and, again and again, things apparently irrational have turned out to be true on the basis of the factual evidence in their behalf. Thus, the physical characteristics of light (particulate and undulatory) are mutually inconsistent, since waves are not particles and particles are not waves. But the evidence is incontrovertible, and so the Photon. The parallel issue of the Trinity will be assisted only peripherally by philosophical discussions of the meaningfulness of the concept. Our apologetic thrust must be the historical evidence that Jesus, in rising from the dead, validated His claim to Deity, and thus His affirmations that He and the Father are One,[6] that the Holy Spirit is "another" (Gk., *allos*, "of the same kind qualitatively") as Himself,[7] and that the church is to baptize in the name (*one* name) of the Father, and of the Son, and of the Holy Spirit. If these facts are genuine, we have put paid to the question. We do not understand the mechanism any more than we do in the case of the nature of light, but that does not alter the factual character of things in the least.

The Liberals. We have already noted that the religious liberal's overwhelming tendency is that of accommodation to the secular climate, thus losing the message which he is endeavoring to communicate. Here is a sad example: In 1950, the Reverend Leslie Badham published a solid volume of Christian Apologetics, titled *Verdict on Jesus: A New Statement of Evidence*. Badham was a distinguished conservative churchman and a fine communicator. For some thirteen years he was Vicar of Windsor and Chaplain to Her Majesty the Queen (who has never been happy with broad-church liberalism). During his ministry he was equally at home in the pulpit and on the airwaves as a radio broadcaster. *Verdict on Jesus* was expanded in a second edition in 1971. After Badham's death, his son, presently Dean of Theology in the University of

---

[6] John 14:8-11.
[7] John 14:16.

Wales at Lampeter, took over the book. There followed third (1983) and fourth (1995) editions, the text of which remained substantially that of the original author. However, Badham's son supplied new introductions to these editions, purportedly to update the book. The point of the original volume was to argue for the de facto reliability of the biblical accounts of the life of Christ and the consequent veracity of His claims. Badham's son, however, having accepted the so-called "historical criticism" of the biblical narratives, supports John Hick's position in his work, *The Myth of God Incarnate,* that incarnation is but metaphorical in character. "Hence," the reader is told, "it is possible to make a total faith commitment to Jesus as God Incarnate while believing that the language is true in a metaphorical rather than an ontological sense."[8] This, of course, not only constitutes heresy by the standards of the Ecumenical Creeds of the Universal Church, but also entirely evacuates of meaning his father's powerful original argument for Christian faith. As I have maintained elsewhere in my critique of Hick's position: once one accommodates to the poor scholarship of higher criticism, the loss of fundamental Christian teaching is logically inevitable and an effective Apologetic rendered impossible.[9]

A second gross error of the religious liberal is to capitulate to Postmodern thinking in its refusal to take seriously the objective character of external reality. It is the position of contemporary thinkers such as Jacques Derrida that to try to find a core of objective meaning in the world or in literary materials such as the Bible is a chimerical quest. There are necessarily as many valid interpretations as there are interpreters, we are told, and interpreters always approach objects of study from their own personal, cultural, and presuppositional viewpoints. Moreover, in the case of literary works, meanings are always multilayered and can never be fully understood by efforts to get at an author's original intention or purpose.[10]

Such a perspective is, of course, very hospitable to the religious liberal, who has never had a serious view of the unity of the Scriptures; has always regarded the Bible as a product of diverse human cultural experiences; and has had a powerful tendency to substitute for the doctrine that God created us in His image a humanistic theology of *our* creating God (and theology) in *our* image.

---

[8] Paul Badham, Introduction to Leslie Badham, *Verdict on Jesus* (4th ed.; Wantage, U.K.: Ikon Productions, 1995), p. xv.

[9] John Warwick Montgomery, "Why Has God Incarnate Suddenly Become Mythical?," in *Perspectives on Evangelical Theology,* ed. Kenneth S. Kantzer and Stanley N. Gundry (Grand Rapids, Michigan: Baker Book House, 1979), pp. 57-65; reprinted in C. E. B. Cranfield, David Kilgour, and J. W. Montgomery, *Christians in the Public Square* (Calgary, Alberta, Canada: Canadian Institute for Law, Theology and Public Policy, 1996), pp. 307-316.

[10] See, *inter alia,* Stuart Sim (ed.), *The Icon Critical Dictionary of Postmodern Thought* (Cambridge, England: Icon Books, 1998).

Religious liberals have never seemed to see the fundamental illogic in the view that reality outside of us—including biblical narrative—has no objective meaning, and that each person can never go beyond the limits of his or her own "personal story" in understanding the world, the Bible, or religious truth. In fact, this approach falls into an infinite regress of solipsism if carried to its logical conclusion.[11] If the Bible (or anything else) has no objective meaning, neither do the writings and assertions of the Postmodernists! To communicate at all, we must assume that at least our own oral and written statements can be understood in the sense in which we have intended them. But if so, we can hardly claim that this is not the case for the communications of others, including those of our Lord, who said, "He who has ears to hear, let him hear," and condemned those who perverted the clear word spoken by his Father through Moses and the prophets.[12] A sound Christian Apologetic requires a serious view of objective reality and of a Bible which does not speak with forked tongue.

Additionally, religious liberals (especially in England) readily succumb to a "Via Media" style of thinking. By this we mean the ability not to come down too hard on any side of any disputed question for fear of offending someone, particularly the popular or lionized secularist. Here, again, the byword is accommodation: the utterly false assumption that Christianity can gain friends and converts by modifying its teachings to make them more palatable to the secular mindset.

Unhappily, this tendency is by no means limited to the religious liberal. In evangelical circles, especially in the United Kingdom and the European continent, it is becoming harder and harder to find those who will unqualifiedly affirm biblical inerrancy. "After all," we are told, "the word isn't mentioned in the Bible; and the gospel and Christian experience cannot be hurt by minor historical errors or contradictions in the Scriptures." To which we reply: neither does the word "Trinity" appear in the Bible, but we dismiss it at our theological peril. And: if the biblical writers cannot accurately describe the Temple in Jerusalem, for example, what makes anyone think that they are correct when they talk about the Heavenly Jerusalem? One would think that the former would be far less demanding than the latter! Did not our Lord say, "If I have told you earthly things and you believe not, how shall you believe if I tell you of heavenly things?"[13]

---

[11] Two excellent counteractives to such thinking are: Noretta Koertge (ed.), *A House Built on Sand: Exposing Postmodernist Myths About Science* (New York: Oxford University Press, 1998); and Kevin J. Vanhoozer, *Is There a Meaning in This Text? The Bible, the Reader and the Morality of Literary Knowledge* (Leicester: Apollos/Inter-Varsity Press, 1998).
[12] Cf. Luke 16:29-31.
[13] John 3:12.

We also have the sad, mediating concessions recently made by some evangelical thinkers to the so-called "Openness of God" theology, whereby, in the supposed interest of preserving human freedom, God's omniscience is jettisoned. Certain charismatics, in particular, have thought that this provides a more human face for God and a more attractive Deity in the eyes of potential converts. Hardly! One ends up with a God who cannot promise anything on which poor sinners can depend since He, no less than His creatures, is limited to statistical prediction of the future. One of the greatest genuine apologetic appeals continues to be that which, according to the Venerable Bede, converted the Northumbrians in the 7th century: the argument that our life, like that of a sparrow flying briefly into a lighted hall and quickly disappearing again into darkness, is one of utter uncertainty and that "if this new teaching has brought any greater certainty, it seems fitting that it should be followed."[14]

The Way Forward

To avoid the errors—both liberal and conservative—just delineated, what must we do? How can we achieve a vigorous, sound Apologetic for the 21st century? Consider five minimal requisites.

First, there must be *a vigorous attack on the utterly fallacious notion that one does not need Jesus Christ for a fulfilled life*. It has often been observed that those who cannot be convinced that they are sick will not go to a doctor. We need to employ the writings of the existentialists (Sartre, and especially Camus[15]) and of the depth psychologists and psychoanalysts to point out the misery of the human condition apart from a relationship with Christ. This should not be in the least difficult, since these thinkers have rung the changes on the meaninglessness of life and the void at the centre of the human heart. Carl Gustav Jung, to take one example, has analogized the human condition to that of the nursery character Humpty Dumpty: broken and unable to put himself back together again.[16] And, what is even worse, as Jacques Lacan points out, "The analysand's basic position is one of a refusal of knowledge, a will not to know

---

[14] Bede, *Ecclesiastical History*, ii. 13. Cf. John Warwick Montgomery, *The Suicide of Christian Theology* (Minneapolis: Bethany, 1970; reprinted 1998), especially pp. 42-43. The great contemporary English Christian jurist Lord Hailsham of St Marylebone titled his second autobiography, *The Sparrow's Flight*; at his Memorial Service a poem of his composition was read at his request in which he referred to himself as just such a sparrow.

[15] Though Camus is universally regarded as a secular existentialist, at the time he was killed in a car accident he was seriously considering Christian baptism from one of my students, then guest preacher at the American Church in Paris: see Howard Mumma, *Albert Camus and the Minister* (Brewster, Massachusetts: Paraclete Press, 2000).

[16] Cf. John Warwick Montgomery, *Myth, Allegory and Gospel* (Minneapolis: Bethany, 1974).

(a *ne rien vouloir savoir*)." The analysand (that is, the one who is undergoing psychoanalysis) wants to know nothing about his or her neurotic mechanisms, nothing about the why and wherefore of his or her symptoms. Lacan even goes so far as to classify ignorance as a passion greater than love or hate: "a passion not to know."[17] "How," the jocular question is put, "does a psychiatrist differ from a coal miner?" Answer: "The psychiatrist goes down deeper, stays down longer, and comes up dirtier." One of the very few positive results of the 11 September 2001 horror was that it drove many Americans back to church (at least for a time!). Why? Because they were reminded of the fragility of life, the inevitability of death, and their inability to control their own destinies. The 21st century apologist needs to drive these truths home, based upon universal human experience.

In the second place, the effective apologist *must be willing to engage in an uncompromising, frontal attack on prevailing non-Christians worldviews.* Liberal accommodationism has to be rejected out of hand. Any gains from compromise are trivial when compared to the losses—losses in integrity and in the power of the gospel message.

How do we attack secular viewpoints? Not on peripheral issues (their failure to live up to their own principles, for example), but *at the presuppositional heart of their beliefs*. The efficient way to destroy a condemned building is not to start on the roof, removing the tiles one by one; it is to blow up the foundations, after which the entire building will fall. Take the case of Marxism: its fundamental error is to assume that modifications in the means of production in society will produce "new men," a proletariat capable of creating a perfect, classless society.[18] But, through human history, modifications of the environment external to man have *never* changed man's selfish nature. The precise same fallacy lies at the heart of liberal Western, utopian social planning. Tear down slums; replace them with clean, new buildings; put the same people into the new buildings and the buildings soon become slums again. As Jesus summed it up (and human experience entirely confirms this): "That which comes out of the man, that defiles the man. For from within, out of the heart of men, proceed evil thoughts, adulteries, fornications, murders, thefts, covetousness, wickedness, deceit, lasciviousness. ... All these evil things come from within, and defile the

---

[17] Bruce Fink, *A Clinical Introduction to Lacanian Psychoanalysis: Theory and Technique* (Cambridge, Massachusetts: Harvard University Press, 1997), p. 7.
[18] See John Warwick Montgomery, "The Marxist Approach to Human Rights: Analysis and Critique," 3 *Simon Greenleaf Law Review* (1983-84), *passim*.

man."[19] Only a personal, living relationship with Jesus the Savior can transform the heart: "If any man be in Christ he is a new creature: old things are passed away; behold, all things are become new."[20]

Moreover, we must not be afraid to *attack the fallacious logic of non-Christian positions.* Even though, as pointed out earlier, the refutation of unsound viewpoints does not establish the truth of one's own, it is vital to remove the false hopes which often keep non-Christians from even considering the case for Christianity. Take, as an obvious example, the Quranic picture of Jesus, contradicting the very essence of the New Testament description of Him as the unique Son of God, come to earth to die for the sins of the world. Since the New Testament testimony comes from eyewitnesses or close associates of eyewitnesses, whereas Mohammed's material appears on the scene six hundred years later, no-one with any historical sense would prefer the latter to the former.[21]

Another classic piece of non-Christian illogic is the oft-heard argument that belief in a creator God solves nothing, since one is still left with the question, "Who created God?" However, since an infinite regress solves nothing, one must stop the reasoning process either with the universe or with a Creator of the universe; and since the universe is patently contingent (nothing in it can explain itself), it is far more sensible to appeal beyond it to a non-contingent, absolute, creator God than to deify the universe by pretending, mythologically, that it really *isn't* contingent at all! Those who do the latter show that it is the unbeliever who is the myth-maker, not the theist (demonstrating, not so incidentally, that Freud had it exactly reversed when he asserted that believers in God mythologically create an illusion of divine existence). In point of fact, it is the theist who is the realist, not the atheist who creates the illusion that the world is self-sufficient, self-explanatory, and therefore absolute.[22]

In the third place, besides being willing and prepared to press home the hopelessness and illogic of non-Christian worldviews, the 21st century apologist *must offer positive, compelling evidence in support of the Christian claim.* Note carefully the Apostle's language: "Be ready always to give an answer [Gk., *apologia*] to every person who asks you a reason for the hope that is in you."[23] Merely

---

[19] Mark 7:20-23.
[20] 2 Corinthians 5:17.
[21] See John Warwick Montgomery, "How Muslims Do Apologetics," 51 *Muslim World* (April and July 1961), reprinted in his *Faith Founded on Fact* (Nashville and New York: Thomas Nelson, 1978); and his London debate with Imam Shabir Ally, available on audiotape from the Canadian Institute for Law, Theology and Public Policy (http://www.ciltpp.com).
[22] John Warwick Montgomery, *Christianity for the Toughminded* (Minneapolis: Bethany, 1973), pp. 21-34.
[23] 1 Peter 3:15.

preaching the good news or announcing the hope is *never* enough! One must *always* give a *reason* for the hope. This can be stated axiomatically: *3. Apologetics is* **not** *Preaching.*

What kind of positive evidence is to be presented? The focus must be a demonstration of the soundness of our Lord's claim to be "the Way, the Truth, and the Life," so that the seeker can appreciate why He declared that "no man comes to the Father but by Me." We are not in the business of persuading people to become deists, theists, or members of particular religious organizations. We are in the business of persuading people to accept Jesus as personal Saviour—as the only One who can "save them from their sins." To make this case, there is no way to avoid arguing for the soundness of the New Testament documents, the reliability of the testimony to Jesus contained therein, and the facticity of His resurrection from the dead as the final proof of His claims.[24]

Such argumentation can benefit greatly from, for example, Theodor Zahn's great commentary on the Gospel of John, establishing the Apostolic authorship of the book; and Adolf Harnack's reasoning to support the dating of the Synoptic Gospels within the generation of Jesus' crucifixion (the Acts of the Apostles must have been written before A.D. 64-65, since it does not record the death of Paul, its central personage; Luke's Gospel, by the same author, had to have been written before Acts; and Luke employed Mark as one of his sources, driving the date of composition of Mark back even farther). In general, the pretensions and the subjective, bad scholarship of the form- and redaction-critics must be fought on every front. Higher criticism is the single most deadly foe which the 21st century apologist must defeat.[25] To retreat into pietism or an Averroës-like doctrine of "two-fold truth" ("yes, the Gospels are historically unreliable, but no, our faith experience of Jesus remains firm") is to destroy all the credibility of the Christian message and eliminate any meaningful Apologetic for its truth.

A fourth essential requisite for an effective contemporary Apologetic is the *willingness to address the most difficult issues troubling the unbeliever.* So often, Christians offer pat answers to minor difficulties (reconciliations of the king lists in the books of Kings and Chronicles; explanations for the apparent tension between "faith" in Paul and "good works" in James; etc.) whilst ignoring or bypassing that which really keeps the non-Christian from becoming a

---

[24] See John Warwick Montgomery, *History, Law and Christianity* (Calgery, Alberta: Canadian Institute for Law, Theology and Public Policy, 2002); *Where Is History Going? Essays in Support of the Historical Truth of the Christian Revelation* (Minneapolis: Bethany, 1969). *Where Is History Going?* has been published in German under the title, *Weltgeschichte wohin?* (Stuttgart-Neuhausen: Haenssler Verlag, 1977).

[25] The German works of Gerhard Maier are particularly to be commended in this regard; in English, see his *The End of the Historical-Critical Method*, trans. E. W. Leverenz and R. F. Norden (Eugene, Oregon: Wipf and Stock, 2001).

Christian. We must be prepared to face such issues as the perceived irrationality and lack of justice in the world (the Holocaust; 11 September 2001). The unbeliever will balance these against our case for Jesus' claims, and may think that the horrors entirely outweigh any argument for "God in Christ, reconciling the world to Himself." Here we will need to break new ground. For example, we can point out that the critical consideration is not the number of horrific events in history weighed against the single event of Jesus Christ (a matter of quantity), but the *qualitative* issue of whether, even if only one instance of evil and irrationality existed in human history, would that be consistent with the existence of a loving God coming to earth to die for a fallen race? Since love entails freewill, and since the God of the Bible reveals Himself as perfectly good, irrationality and evil (on whatever scale) will be the creature's fault, not the Creator's; and God's willingness to suffer undeservingly for us should fill us with gratitude, rather than eliciting criticism of his morality. Such argumentation may not exhaust the question, but it at least does not sidestep the non-Christian's genuine concerns.

Finally, the 21st century Apologist needs to take Apologetics far more seriously. He needs to *incorporate Apologetics into* every *aspect of his or her ministry: every* sermon, *every* class, *every* evangelistic activity. We have woefully neglected our responsibility to train our young people in the solid case for Christianity, and then we wonder why they depart from the faith under the influence of secular university instruction. We give our parishioners and our missionaries no foundation in the defence of the faith, and then wonder why our evangelistic efforts show so little fruit in a world where people have long moved beyond accepting something just because someone else believes it.

In a word, we need to return to our biblical and theological foundations to find the place which Apologetics should have in Christian ministry. That place is absolutely clear. We are to do as the Apostle did: "While Paul waited for them at Athens, his spirit was stirred in him when he saw the city wholly given to idolatry. Therefore disputed he in the synagogue with the Jews ... [and] in the market daily with them that met with him, [and with] certain philosophers of the Epicureans and of the Stoics. ..."[26] We are to become "all things to all people, that some might be saved, a Jew to the Jew and a Greek to the Greeks," which necessarily entails giving reasons for the faith, since that is what so many of our contemporaries, Jews and Gentiles, require before they will commit themselves to a faith-position. We must not reduce the faith once delivered to the saints to a cultic matter of inner experience and personal testimony. There are enough irrational religions and sects in our 21st century world

---

[26] Acts 17:16 ff.

without giving the unbeliever the impression that Christianity is just another one of them. And so, a final (and, this time, positive) axiom: *4. **Apologetics** is **Always Giving a Reason for the Hope**.*

Appendix: The Axiom Set

*1. **Apologetics** is* not *Dogmatics*
*2. **Apologetics** is* not *Philosophy*
*3. **Apologetics** is* not *Preaching*
*4. **Apologetics** is Always Giving a Reason for the Hope*

3. The Holy Spirit and the Defence of the Faith

Many evangelicals express the view that evidences for the truth of Scripture or for the saving events recorded in it are never adequate in themselves; only through the work of the Holy Spirit in the heart of the unbeliever will such evidences carry conviction.

Particularly in traditional Calvinist circles (though by no means limited to those in the Reformed camp), this theological judgment is embraced in the concept of the *testimonium internum Spiritus Sancti* ("the inner testimony of the Holy Spirit"). Calvin expounded this teaching in a chapter of his *Institutes* titled, "Scripture Must Be Confirmed by the Witness of the Spirit."

> *4. The witness of the Holy Spirit: this is stronger than all proof*
> ... If we desire to provide in the best way for our consciences—that they may not be perpetually beset by the instability of doubt or vacillation, and that they may not also boggle at the smallest quibbles—we ought to seek our conviction in a higher place than human reasons, judgments, or conjectures, that is, in the secret testimony of the Spirit. ... The testimony of the Spirit is more excellent than all reason. For as God alone is a fit witness of himself in his Word, so also the Word will not find acceptance in men's hearts before it is sealed by the inward testimony of the Spirit. The same Spirit, therefore, who has spoken through the mouths of the prophets must penetrate into our hearts to persuade us that they faithfully proclaimed what had been divinely commanded.
>
> *5. Scripture bears its own authentication*
> Let this point therefore stand: that those whom the Holy Spirit has inwardly taught truly rest upon Scripture, and that Scripture indeed is self-authenticated; hence, it is not right to subject it to proof and reasoning. And the certainty it deserves with us, it attains by the testimony of the Spirit. For even if it wins reverence for itself by its own majesty, it seriously affects us only when it is sealed upon our hearts through the Spirit.[1]

The great Rostock theologian Friedrich Adolph Philippi expressed this position in the following terms in his posthumously published *Symbolik*:

---

[1] John Calvin, *Institutes of the Christian Religion*, trans. Ford Lewis Battles, ed. John T. McNeill (Philadelphia: Westminster, 1960), 1.7.4-5. For the French text of this key passage, with the variants in the several editions of the *Institutes* during Calvin's lifetime, see E. Doumergue, *Jean Calvin* (Lausanne: Bridel, 1910), 4:59.

That the Word is self-evidencing is equivalent to saying that the Spirit of God, of Whom the Word is the bearer, shows the truth of the Word to man's spirit. No one, therefore, is a competent judge of the divine origin, truth, clearness and sufficiency of the Word, unless he have experienced its enlightening and quickening power.[2]

An even stronger statement of the same viewpoint was given by the Dorpat theologian Alexander von Oettingen.

Every theoretical proof which may be attempted, every logical demonstration of truth, yea even the practical appeal to experience is vain, without the presupposition of a receptive organ, of a developed sensorium for the particular sphere of life that is concerned. Who can explain to the blind or even to the aesthetically unreceptive the true beauty of a painting, or bring to scientific understanding the aesthetical principles which here prevail? Who can disclose to the deaf or even to those without musical talent the deep mysteries of the great musical masterpieces? Who is in a condition to convince materialistic stupidity which regards only that which is comprehensible and sensually perceptible as true, of the overwhelming power of the architecture of the world? The worlds of Nature and of Spirit, their reciprocally conditioning and connecting laws remain dead and unintelligible, where our sense is dead.[3]

Problems with the "Testimonium" Teaching

It is clear, particularly in Calvin's treatment of the subject, that a prime motivation for stressing the *testimonium* has been the desire to oppose all forms of semi-Pelagian synergism, especially as manifested in Roman Catholic theology. Calvin was not about to concede that Scripture's veracity depends on the church or on clever ecclesiastical arguments; the Bible's sole authentication must come directly from God Himself, and thus the acceptance of its truth will ultimately derive from the work of God the Holy Spirit in the heart of the believer, and from no other source.

Unfortunately, however, this particular medicine for fighting synergism has serious negative side effects. The *testimonium* teaching, applied strictly, would eliminate all serious efforts to convince unbelievers of biblical truth by the presentation of factual evidence in its behalf. Why? Because it would follow that any and all such evidence could never succeed; conviction would depend not on it but on the Holy Spirit's direct action on an unbeliever. True, even Calvin

---

[2] Friedrich Adolph Philippi, *Symbolik, akademische Vorlesungen*, ed. Ferdinand Philippi (Gütersloh: Bertelsmann. 1883).
[3] Alexander von Oettingen, *Lutherische Dogmatik* (Munich: Beck, 1897), 1:8.

spent a chapter setting forth objective evidences for the divine character of the Bible (1. viii), but there and elsewhere he was at pains to emphasize the inadequacy of all such reasoning.

> This bare and external proof of the Word of God should have been amply sufficient to engender faith, did not our blindness and perversity prevent it. But our mind has such an inclination to vanity that it can never cleave fast to the truth of God; and it has such a dullness that it is always blind to the light of God's truth. Accordingly, without the illumination of the Holy Spirit, the Word can do nothing.[4]

Reconciling *testimonium* theology with Scripture's own teaching encounters overwhelming obstacles. If evidence can never convince an unbeliever, what is the point of the Petrine injunction to be "ready to make a defense [ἀπολογία] to everyone who asks you to give an account for the hope that is in you" (1 Pet. 3:15)? Why did Jesus, at the beginning of His earthly ministry, heal a paralytic so as to demonstrate objectively that He has divine miraculous power, thereby convincing His hearers that He can also forgive sin (Mark 2)? What is the significance of the detailed, physical descriptions of the resurrected Christ, if not to convince doubters ("a spirit does not have flesh and bones as you see that I have," Luke 24:39; cf. the doubting Thomas incident, John 20)? Why would Luke bother to stress that there were "many infallible proofs" of Christ's resurrection (Acts 1:3, KJV)? And what reason would there be for Paul's emphasis on the risen Christ having been seen by over five hundred witnesses (1 Cor. 15:6)? Indeed, the Apostle's entire apologetic strategy on the Areopagus at Athens (Acts 17:16-33) would have been meaningless if evidence presented to unbelievers had no power to convince.[5]

Efforts have been made to explain *testimonium* thinking to reduce the tension with passages like those cited in the paragraph above. Doumergue, following de Witt,[6] argues dualistically:

> It would be plainly absurd to say that the Spirit conveys even the smallest bit of information or that His work furnishes a testimony—except indirectly—as to any literary issues raised by the biblical text on the matter of its veracity. The Spirit's witness concerns the saving truth of the entire text and does not embrace the document which incorporates that truth. The Holy

---

[4] Calvin, *Institutes of the Christian Religion*, 3.2.33.
[5] Even Westminster Seminary New Testament scholar Ned B. Stonehouse recognized that Paul's address to the philosophers at Athens was by no means a failure or misconceived, versus the often-heard claim that Paul later repented of it in 1 Corinthians 1 (*Paul before the Areopagus* [London: Tyndale, 1957]).
[6] John de Witt, "The Testimony of the Holy Spirit to the Bible," *Presbyterian and Reformed Review* 6 (1895): 80-82.

Spirit testifies with power to the truth of the Bible and its authority, not to its inspiration or its canonicity. It is history which attests the canon; it is the Bible which attests its own inspiration. The Holy Spirit attests the Bible's divine character and the absolute authority of the saving truth contained in the Bible.[7]

For Doumergue, Calvin's teaching on the *testimonium* is simply a special case of the Reformer's general principle that the Holy Spirit is the sole Teacher in matters of faith.[8]

This, however, will not do. One cannot dualistically split the "truth" and "authority" of the Bible from its "inspiration" and "canonicity," claiming that the witness of the Spirit applies to the former and not to the latter. This is because truth, authority, inspiration, and canonicity are integrally connected (a problem with any one of them will be a problem for all); if the Holy Spirit is the sine qua non for establishing one, He will likewise be essential for validating the rest. The fundamental issue remains: Can evidence per se put the non-Christian in a position where he ought reasonably to accept the saving facts of the gospel and the truth, authority, inspiration, and canonicity of Scripture—or does he need the Spirit's illumination as a prerequisite for doing so?

Moreover, the question is not whether the Holy Spirit is the sole Master in spiritual things. Of course He is. What has to be determined is whether He works mediately—through the Scriptures (whose veracity can be independently established)—to change people's hearts, or whether His work in the human heart is a precondition for the recognition of the Bible's veracity. It is doubtful that Calvin was correct in declaring that "without the illumination of the Holy Spirit, the Word can do nothing."

Distinctions

One of the strengths of medieval scholastic learning was the methodology of so-called "distinction." Seemingly intractable dilemmas could be solved by "distinguishing" the different senses in which words or concepts were used or should be used. The conflict between an evidential apologetic and the work of the Holy Spirit in conversion, as heightened by the *testimonium* doctrine, can be resolved biblically if four distinctions are made.

First, in salvation it is surely true that God's Holy Spirit is the sole efficient cause. Salvation is by grace alone, and even saving faith is an unmerited gift of

---

[7] Doumergue. *Jean Calvin*, 4:67.
[8] *Ibid.*, 68.

the same Spirit (John 1:12-13; Eph. 2:8-9). Because of original sin, human beings are in no position to "cooperate" with God in salvation. Synergistic, semi-Pelagian understandings of the salvatory process are unbiblical.

Second, the Scriptures are authoritative and veracious. The Holy Spirit does not make the Bible more true, more factual, or more objectively persuasive. The Spirit normally works through the Word, not independently as do supposed "spiritual influences" in other religions.

Third, Jesus said the Holy Spirit testifies of Him (John 15:26). The Spirit does not create the Word or the gospel—or the evidence for them—but witnesses to the person and work of the second person of the Trinity and to the Scriptures, which also testify of Him (5:39). The Spirit's activity is essentially derivative where revelation is concerned (16:13-15)[9] and must not be elevated to a primary role, as is done in some charismatic circles.

Fourth, if the Spirit does not create evidence for faith—if the evidence is already present—what does He do in relation to the potential convert? He convicts "the world concerning sin, and righteousness, and judgment" (John 16:8), that is, He lays on the individual the conviction of sin and its consequences. Also He guides "into all the truth" (v. 13), that is, He motivates the potential convert to consider the claims of Christ and the evidence for them—and He implants saving faith in the heart. In a word, the Holy Spirit makes the gospel personally meaningful. This is the true sense of the *testimonium internum Spiritus Sancti*—that "the Spirit Himself bears witness with our spirit that we are children of God" (Rom. 8:16). Putting it otherwise, the *testimonium* has to do with soteriology (how one is saved), not with bibliology (how Scripture is validated). Calvin was right when he declared that "Scripture will ultimately suffice for a saving knowledge of God only when its certainty is founded upon the inward persuasion of the Holy Spirit";[10] he was not correct, however, when he suggested that the objective evidence for scriptural truth is inadequate in itself apart from the Spirit's working. One must be scrupulous in distinguishing

---

[9] On the procession of the Spirit from both Father and Son (as declared in the Western form of the Nicene Creed), see John Warwick Montgomery, "Evangelical Unity and Contemporary Ecumenicity," in *Ecumenicity, Evangelicals and Rome* (Grand Rapids: Zondervan, 1969), 13-44. For a complete picture of the Holy Spirit's relationship to revelation, one also needs to recognize the truth emphasized by the major Reformers that the Spirit is in fact the ultimate Author of the Scriptures (see John Warwick Montgomery, "The Fourth Gospel Yesterday and Today," in *The Suicide of Christian Theology* [Minneapolis: Bethany, 1970], 428-65, esp. 454). On the person and work of the Holy Spirit in general, see Montgomery, "Choice Books on the Holy Spirit," in *ibid.*, 480-87.

[10] Calvin, *Institutes of the Christian Religion*, 1.8.13.

the Spirit's subjective work of applying existing evidence to the heart from the question of the value, persuasiveness, and demonstrability of that evidence as such.

On the basis of the distinctions just formulated, it follows that the Holy Spirit's work in conversion ought not inhibit the apologist's activity of offering persuasive evidence for the truth of the gospel and the Scriptures. Why should the unbeliever respond to the evidence? Theologically, of course, because it is true. But—even from his own, unbelieving standpoint—because in ordinary affairs, in order to survive in the real world, he has to accept the same kinds of evidence. For example courts of law must rely on good testimony to the events recounted; scientists cannot ignore the results of sound observation; people who eat fish—as Jesus did after His resurrection—have to be considered alive, not dead.

Ultimately a non-Christian must make a moral choice as to what he will do with the objectively sound case for Christianity. If he exercises his will to accept the Christ of the Scriptures, that act must be attributed to the Spirit alone as a pure gift of grace. But the monergistic event of conversion no more denigrates or renders superfluous the work of the apologist than it does the work of the preacher or evangelist who presented the saving message to the individual in the first place. The Holy Spirit does not create the gospel or the evidence for it; He applies what is preached and defended to produce salvation.

What, then, are the dangers of *testimonium* theology? Two risks, in particular, are evident, and they both stem from the "inner," subjective character of the viewpoint. First, if the evidence for scriptural truth is regarded as somehow deficient without the additional work of the Spirit in the individual, this will inevitably give the impression that the Scriptures and their message are "true" only for those who already believe them.[11] This is the very morass into which Barthian neoorthodoxy has fallen in its claim that Christ's resurrection occurred not in ordinary history (*Historie*), susceptible to historical investigation, but in "supra-history" or "faith-history" (*Geschichte*), available only to those who believe.[12]

Ramm, certainly an evangelical and not a Barthian, nonetheless clearly illustrates this danger. Having thoroughly committed himself to *testimonium* thinking in his book *The Witness of the Spirit*,[13] he wrote a year later, "Only if

---

[11] Doumergue simply concedes that this was Calvin's position (*Jean Calvin*, 4:66).
[12] See John Warwick Montgomery, *Where Is History Going?* (Minneapolis: Bethany, 1969), 100-117. That Barthian neoorthodoxy has its ideological roots firmly planted in Reformation Calvinism has been thoroughly demonstrated by Herman Sasse, *Here We Stand*, trans. T. G. Tappert (Minneapolis: Augsburg, 1938).
[13] Bernard Ramm, *The Witness of the Spirit: An Essay on the Contemporary Relevance of the Internal*

there were no presence of the Holy Spirit or of God or of the community of the covenant could we think of historical revelation in terms of documented court evidence."[14] In effect, Ramm is here arguing a "circularity" principle which has more than a little in common with Karl Barth and Rudolf Bultmann, for he is saying that the Scriptures do not have demonstrable reality as historical revelation apart from the covenantal community and the *testimonium* of the Spirit. In actuality, however, the reality of historical revelation in Scripture is fully objective—and the Spirit and the community bear witness to this fact; they do not in any sense bring about the Bible's veracity. For Calvinist Gordon Clark, though an implacable foe of Barth, the only assured proof of Christian revelation is supplied by "the inward work of the Holy Spirit."[15] Obviously such approaches are the death of any meaningful apologetic to those who are not already Christians—yet the non-Christians are the ones who principally need it.

Secondly, in the pluralistic, secular environment at the beginning of the 21st century, any unnecessary theological emphasis on the subjective is a distinct liability. The Eastern religions, the cults, and liberal Christianity have little to offer but "experience," which is continually touted as self-validating. The *testimonium* approach falls unwittingly into this same abyss of unverifiability, dragging the gospel down to the level of its nonrevelatory competitors for people's hearts and minds. Kuyper attempted to blunt the charge of subjectivism by noting that the *testimonium* is not really an "internal argument" (since the Spirit does not arise from within individuals) but an *argumentum externum* (because the Spirit comes from above, from God).[16] This, however, is of little consequence when presenting and defending the gospel in a secular world, for there is no objective way of testing the Spirit's inner presence. The "inward witness" remains as subjectively unverifiable as the Mormon claim to a "burning in the bosom." Granted, the *testimonium* advocate maintains the ontological objectivity of Christian revelation; but what good is this in witnessing to outsiders if there is no corresponding epistemological objectivity by which ontological reality can be distinguished from pure religious wish-fullfilment?

Witness of the Holy Spirit (Grand Rapids: Eerdmans, 1959).
[14] Bernard Ramm, *Special Revelation and the Word of God* (Grand Rapids: Eerdmans, 1961), 99.
[15] Gordon Clark, "Holy Scripture," *Bulletin of the Evangelical Theological Society* 6 (Winter 1963): 4. Cf. Montgomery, *Where Is History Going?* 141-81, esp. 178.
[16] Abraham Kuyper, *Encyclopaedie der heilige Godgeleerdheit* (Amsterdam: Wormser, 1894), 2:505.

An Analogy: The House of Salvation

The preceding analysis may be illustrated by a model called "the house of salvation." Viewed from outside the house, a path leads to it and the entire fallen race travels that road. Sadly, many people stop their spiritual journey without ever arriving at true salvation. Not a few are put off by the condition of the road (potholes and obstructions), representing the real (and specious) objections to the faith they encounter. The apologist's prime task is to clear away the intellectual blockage and also give the best reasons for continuing to move forward toward the house of salvation.[17] He functions as a kind of road mender, like a John the Baptist, making paths straight and rough places plain (Isa. 40:3-4; Luke 3:3-5).

If an unbeliever arrives at the house of salvation, he sees a sign on the door with two references, John 3:16 and Acts 16:30-31, informing him or her in no uncertain terms that one must believe in the Lord Christ to enter. An act of the will is demanded, and if it occurs, a person finds himself inside the house; he is saved.

Once inside the house of salvation, the new believer learns from the Scriptures (if he or she is not already aware of it experientially) that what has occurred is not due to personal effort in any sense. Posted inside the house is John 1:12-13 (salvation is "not by the will of man, but of God") as well as Ephesians 2:8-9 (even the faith the believer now exercises is solely the product of divine grace).

Clearly this is a mystery. On the one hand one must "do something" to be saved (Acts 16:30-31); on the other hand the act of faith turns out to be exclusively the work of God the Holy Spirit. This "mystery of faith" (to use the felicitous expression of Lutheran theologian Gustaf Aulén) must not be blunted in an effort to resolve the humanly unresolvable. Hyper-Calvinists, by way of the doctrine of double predestination, have tried to resolve it by putting, as it were, John 1:12-13 and Ephesians 2:8-9 on the *outside* of the house of salvation; people are thus led to believe that nothing they do can influence their eternal destiny. Hyper-Arminians have done the opposite, placing John 3:16 and Acts 16:30-31 *inside*, so as to justify a semi-Pelagian view of salvation. But the signs must not be reversed. Otherwise either the unbeliever will not be confronted with the proper biblical "hour of decision," or the believer will be led to false reliance on his own act of will, faith-exercise, or spiritual condition.

---

[17] To be sure, there are many more kinds of obstruction than intellectual objections to the faith; some are psychological and sociological reasons for unbelief. Apologists, however, specialize in dealing with the intellectual (and pseudo-intellectual) roadblocks that keep non-Christians from accepting the truth of the gospel and the Scriptures.

Why retain this mystery? Simply because the Scriptures require it. To subordinate "outside" passages to "inside" passages or to do the opposite is to eliminate crucial biblical teaching. If this is disturbing (since people legitimately try to reduce paradox and mystery as much as possible), a consolation is to recognize that the nature of this mystery focuses on the interrelationship of God's will and man's will—and humans do not even understand the depths of human volition, much less God's (Rom. 11:33-34).

The application of the house of salvation analysis to the preceding *testimonium* discussion should be obvious. The "internal witness of the Spirit" has been used by many as a device for the laudable end of eliminating synergism from the evangelistic-apologetic task, but this has been done at the price of emasculating the case for biblical reliability. Not only is this price far too much to pay in a secular world desperately needing a solid, objective apologetic for scriptural truth, but the device is unnecessary, since it fundamentally misconstrues the problem.

Synergism does not come about when unbelievers are expected to accept persuasive, objective evidence for the truth of the Bible or its gospel message, any more than it is synergistic for evangelists to call for decisions for Christ. Apologists (and evangelists) operate outside the house of salvation; they are not pastors or systematic theologians interpreting the conversion experience after it has come about. "Synergism exists only when, following conversion, the justified man is led to believe that in any way whatever (rational, moral, volitional) he contributed to his own salvation."[18]

Believers therefore need to be especially careful not to water down the effectiveness of their apologetic in a misguided effort at conquering semi-Pelagianism. *Sola gratia* and powerful apologetic evangelism are entirely compatible. Christians should place before unbelievers the "many infallible proofs" of God's revelation of Himself in Christ and in the Scriptures, and the Holy Spirit, working through the objective gospel and the inherently persuasive evidence for it, will assuredly apply it; for God's Word never returns void.

---

[18] John Warwick Montgomery, "The Apologetic Thrust of Lutheran Theology," in *Lutheranism and the Defense of Christian Faith*, a special number of the *Lutheran Synod Quarterly* XI/1 (Fall 1970): 34. (That essay, under the title "Lutheran Theology and the Defense of Biblical Faith," also appears in Montgomery, *Faith Founded on Fact* [New York and Nashville: Thomas Nelson, 1978], 129-53.)

4. Christian Apologetics in the Light of the Lutheran Confessions

"What indeed has Athens to do with Jerusalem?" queried the church father Tertullian,[1] expecting a negative as the only possible answer. In the same vein one might ask, "What indeed has apologetics to do with the Lutheran Confessions?" A confession is, after all, a public declaration of belief, not an argument. The very title given in 1580 to the official collection of Lutheran confessional writings was *Concordia: Book of Concord*—suggesting the peace and unity of common belief, not the disputatious refutation of other viewpoints.

And even if the controversial nature of material in the *Concordia* is recognized, must one not also admit that the controversies leading up to it occurred strictly within Christendom—between the Lutherans, on the one hand, and the Roman Catholics, the Sacramentarians, etc., on the other—not between Christians and unbelievers?[2] Aside from a few passing references to the "Turks," the Lutheran Confessions seem largely unaware of the existence, beyond the confines of internal Christian doctrinal discussion, of a world of unbelief to which apologetic argument ought to be addressed. Could one not apply to the Confessions with even greater force the tongue-in-cheek remark made concerning Thomas Aquinas, that when he wrote his *Summa contra gentiles* (his apologetic against the pagans) he had never met a pagan? In short, is not the *Book of Concord* simply a compendium of Christian belief-statements, written for an audience of believers, and is not its range of controversy limited to the correction of false doctrine within the narrow sphere of Christian profession? If so, the apologetic significance of the *Concordia* would seem, *ipso facto*, to be minimal at best.

There is another side to the matter, however. It is widely agreed that even the Ecumenical Creeds of the Patristic age, which are incorporated into the *Book of Concord* and form its first section, arose in a context of disputation and set forth orthodox doctrine in specific contradistinction to such heresies as Arianism and non-Christian belief-systems as Gnosticism.[3] Could not one go so far as to say that a true confession is always at the same time an apologia?

---

[1] Tertullian, *De praescriptione haereticorum*, VII.
[2] Cf. Johann Georg Walch, *Introductio in Libros Ecclesiae Lutheranae Symbolicos, observationibus historicis et theologicis illustrata* (Ienae [Jena]: sumtu viduae Meyer, 1732).
[3] See, *inter alia*, the writings of J. N. D. Kelly (*Early Christian Creeds; Early Christian Doctrines: The Athanasian Creed*).

The very title of one of the chief Lutheran confessional writings, the *Apology of the Augsburg Confession*, displays a concern that goes well beyond the mere proclamation of a theological position. Professor Allbeck does not exaggerate when he declares:

> Looking back from our time to the sixteenth century, we see the Apology as an outstanding example of the theological writing of the Reformation age. Those who would sample the literary style and the patterns of thinking of that day would do well to read the Apology. ... The purpose of the Apology to defend the Confession, and with it the gospel doctrine, against a specific opponent was accompanied by a vigorous mood. For the Apology is a piece of polemical writing.[4]

Indeed, the tone of the Reformation Lutheran Confessions in general, with their constant stress on refuting "antitheses" as well as setting forth "theses," reveals a veritable preoccupation with the defense of sound teaching over against falsehood. Leonhard Hutter's great work, *Concordia concors: de origine et progressu Formulae Concordiae*, appropriately begins with a book-length "Praefatio Apologetica," refuting views such as those of the Calvinist Hospinian.[5]

And if such considerations are regarded merely as further proof that the Lutherans, even when engaged in controversy, never went beyond intra-Christian disputation, it must not be forgotten that in those days doctrinal dispute was taken so seriously that particularly offensive views, even though maintained by professing Christians, were refuted as non-Christian. At Marburg Luther did not shrink from declaring that the sacramentarian views of Zwingli manifested another Christ from his own, and the Confessions retain this same perspective.[6] The *Book of Concord*, holding that justification by grace through faith is the "article by which the church stands or falls," classes Roman Catholic doctrinal works-righteousness as nothing short of Antichristic. When the Lutheran Confessions engage in apologetic controversy, they speak not primarily to minor internal differences within Christendom but more especially to fundamental issues dividing the true church from varieties of pseudo-Christian religiosity. The Lutheran Confessions do not tilt against windmills; they endeavor to storm the bastions of serious religious aberration.

And is this not what one would expect, after all? In my essay, "Lutheran Theology and the Defense of Biblical Faith," I have shown that both Luther himself and the Lutheran theologians of the Age of Orthodoxy maintained

---

[4] W. D. Allbeck, *Studies in the Lutheran Confessions* (Philadelphia: Muhlenberg Press, 1952), pp. 142-43.
[5] Leonhard Hutter, *Concordia concors: de origine et progressu Formulae Concordiae* (Witebergae [Wittenberg]: Clement Berger, 1614).
[6] See Hermann Sasse, *This Is My Body* (Minneapolis: Augsburg, 1959), pp. 148-55.

vigorous apologetic principles.[7] It would be strange indeed if the Lutheran Confessions—which historically link Luther and the Orthodox theologians together and whose authors include students of Luther and Melanchthon (such as David Chytraeus) and Orthodox fathers in their own right (e.g., Martin Chemnitz)—were not to display the apologetic perspective and concerns of those who preceded and followed them in the same theological tradition.[8]

But deduction from "historical necessity" is a notoriously unreliable way to answer factual questions. We must turn from general speculation to the Lutheran Confessions themselves to see what degree of apologetic insight they manifest.

How Apologetic Are the Lutheran Confessions?

The task of the Christian apologist may be said to embrace three major activities: (1) clarification (he defends the faith by disabusing the unbeliever of misconceptions concerning its nature), (2) refutation (he defends the faith by showing the fallacies and unworthiness of opposing positions), and (3) positive argumentation (he defends the faith by offering positive reasons to accept the Christian world-view in preference to other philosophical or religious options).[9] To what extent, if any, does the *Book of Concord* engage in apologetic activity along these lines?

Undeniably present throughout the Lutheran Confessions are arguments of a clarifying and refutory nature in defense of biblical religion. Among innumerable examples of attempts to defend the orthodox position by clarifying its true nature is the following:

> We herewith condemn without any qualification the Capernaitic eating of the body of Christ as though one rent Christ's flesh with one's teeth and digested it like other food. The Sacramentarians deliberately insist on crediting us with this doctrine, against the witness of their own consciences over

---

[7] Published in Swedish in *Ditt Ord ar Sanning: En Handbok om Bibeln, tillagnad David Hedegaard*, ed. Seth Erlandsson ("Biblicums Skriftserie," 2; Uppsala: Stiftelsen Biblicum, 1971), pp. 234-58. Available in English in the *Lutheran Synod Quarterly*, XI, 1 (Special Issue; Fall, 1970), and in John Warwick Montgomery, *Faith Founded on Fact* (New York and Nashville: Thomas Nelson, 1978).

[8] Cf. Montgomery, *Chytraeus on Sacrifice* (St. Louis, Mo.: Concordia, 1962); Montgomery, *Cross and Crucible* ("Archives Internationales d'Histoire des Idees," 55; The Hague: Martinus Nijhoff [now New York: Springer], 1973), 2 vols.; and Montgomery, "Chemnitz on the Council of Trent," in *Soli Deo Gloria: Essays in Reformed Theology; Festschrift for John H. Gerstner*, ed. R. C. Sproul (Nutley, N.J.: Presbyterian and Reformed Publishing Co., 1976), pp. 73-94. (The latter essay is reprinted in this volume, Part Six, chap. 4 below.)

[9] See Montgomery, *Christianity for the Toughminded* (Minneapolis: Bethany, 1973) and *Myth, Allegory and Gospel* (Minneapolis: Bethany, 1974).

our many protests, in order to make our teaching obnoxious to their hearers. On the contrary, in accord with the simple words of Christ's testament, we hold and believe in a true, though supernatural, eating of Christ's body and drinking of his blood, which we cannot comprehend with our human sense or reason.[10]

Negative, refutory arguments are even more frequent. We have already noted the standard inclusion of "antitheses" throughout the *Concordia*. In the Preface written both for the *Formula of Concord* and for the whole *Book of Concord*, Jakob Andreae and Martin Chemnitz spend considerable time expressly justifying such material. "Condemnations," they declare, "cannot by any means be avoided," for (as Andreae noted in a marginal revision to the printed draft) "the responsibility devolves upon the theologians and ministers duly to remind even those who err ingenuously and ignorantly of the danger to their souls and to warn them against it, lest one blind person let himself be misled by another." Typical of the refutory argumentation of the Confessions is the *Formula of Concord*'s direct citation of Luther (WA, XXVI, pp. 321-22):

> If Zwingli's *alloeosis* stands, then Christ will have to be two persons, one a divine and the other a human person, since Zwingli applies all the texts concerning the passion only to the human nature and completely excludes them from the divine nature. But if the works are divided and separated, the person will also have to be separated, since all the doing and suffering are not ascribed to the natures but to the person. It is the person who does and suffers everything, the one thing according to this nature and the other thing according to the other nature, all of which scholars know right well. Therefore we regard our Lord Christ as God and man in one person, neither confounding the natures nor dividing the person.[11]

To be sure, those who question the apologetic character of the Lutheran Confessions will not be especially disturbed by the presence of clarifying or refutory arguments in these documents—even when such arguments appear there with great frequency (as they do). The real issue will be said to lie with the third type of apologetic reasoning as set forth above, viz., the presence or absence of *positive proofs*, consciously designed to convince an unbelieving opponent through the marshalling of facts and evidence in behalf of orthodox religious truth. Proofs of this kind are held by many to be not only absent but in fact utterly foreign to the teaching of the Confessions. "Proving the faith," we

---

[10] F. C. Ep. VII, 42 (486.42). Throughout this essay, citations to the *Concordia* follow the standard system employed by Schlink in his *Theologie der lutherischen Bekenntnisschriften*. For convenience we have also added in parentheses page and paragraph references to the Tappert edition of the *Book of Concord* (Philadelphia: Muhlenberg Press, 1959), and, unless otherwise indicated, English translations of Confessional sources have been quoted from that edition.

[11] F.C. S.D. VIII, 43 (599.43).

are told, contradicts confessional Lutheranism in the following respects: (1) it gives reason a place in man's salvation and therefore constitutes a return of the dog to the vomit of works-righteousness; (2) it elevates "historical knowledge" (*fides historica*) to the level of saving faith and ignores the monergistic work of the Holy Spirit in salvation; (3) it disregards the total depravity produced by the fall and the noetic effects of original sin; and (4) it is oblivious of the fact that Scripture does not make sense to the unbeliever through argumentation but solely through illumination of the Spirit and the influence of justification by grace through faith.

If this is indeed the viewpoint of the Confessions, a positive Lutheran apologetic would admittedly be excluded on principle: at best the confessional Lutheran could only defend his position by attempting to remove misconceptions concerning it or by endeavoring to point out fallacies in his opponents' reasoning. (Indeed, as I have maintained elsewhere,[12] the problem for the witnessing Christian would be far more acute, for the just-stated understanding of total depravity as precluding meaningful positive argument to the sinner would *also* make any clarifications or refutations correspondingly ineffective when presented to him!) But we shall quickly see that the Confessions do not at all require us to avoid positive apologetic argument. Let us analyze confessionally each of the four points raised.

(1) *The problem of reason*. Every Lutheran is familiar with Luther's explanation of the Third Article of the Apostles' Creed in his *Small Catechism:* "I believe that by my own reason or strength I cannot believe in Jesus Christ, my Lord, or come to him."[13] Does this mean that a rational defense of the faith—any positive apologetic for Christian truth—turns out to be superfluous at best and highly dangerous at worst? Edmund Schlink comments:

> The opinion that man can arrive at a true knowledge of divine matters on the basis of human thought and emotion is again and again traced in the most diverse doctrines of the opponents, refuted, and finally made ridiculous. All this is only *"multa fingere,"* to "invent many things in one's own brain," which leads only to such opinions as are "totally unfounded in Scrip-

---

[12] See my essays, "Clark's Philosophy of History," in *The Philosophy of Gordon H. Clark: A Festschrift*, ed. Ronald H. Nash (Nutley, N.J.: Presbyterian and Reformed Publishing Co., 1968), pp. 353-90, 505-11; and "Once Upon an A Priori," in *Jerusalem and Athens: Critical Discussions on the Theology and Apologetics of Cornelius Van Til*, ed. E. R. Geehan (Nutley, N.J.: Presbyterian and Reformed Publishing Co., 1971), pp. 380-92, 482-83. (These essays have been reprinted, respectively, in Montgomery, *Where Is History Going?* and *Faith Founded on Fact*.)
[13] S.C. II, 6 (345.6).

ture and touch neither above nor below" (Ap. XII, 178). Reason cannot even come to a knowledge of original sin, but this "must be believed because of the revelation in the Scriptures" (S.A. III, i, 3).[14]

Indeed, the Confessions seem to exclude reason from even a preparatory role in the evangelistic task: "There is no power or ability, no cleverness or reason, with which we can prepare ourselves for righteousness and life or seek after it."[15]

But a closer look at the Confessional passages just cited will show that they do not condemn reason (in the sense of the rational process) as such: they condemn a particular *misuse* of man's rational faculty. What this misuse is will become plainer from other references in the *Concordia*.

The *Apology* roundly criticizes those "scholastics, Pharisees, philosophers, and Mohammedans" who "reason" that justification can be attained through the law. Such "reasoning" is just another name for "human wisdom," and is the exact opposite of "the foolishness of the Gospel": "We know how repulsive this teaching is to the judgment of reason and law and that the teaching of the law about love is more plausible; for this is human wisdom."[16] What is being condemned here is a non-Christian value system which passes itself off as "rational" but which in reality is one hundred and eighty degrees removed from true wisdom. As would later occur in the eighteenth century "Age of Reason, (the misnamed "Enlightenment"), the idea of rationality was being elevated to the status of a philosophy of life, and an anti-Scriptural philosophy at that. The Lutheran Confessions are simply declaring that they will tolerate no such competition with God's saving message.

What did the scholastics' pseudo-rational value system entail? In a word, works-righteousness. When the Confessions set the Gospel over against "reason," they are employing the word "reason" as a synonym for works-righteousness. "Blind reason," says Luther in the *Smalcald Articles*, "seeks consolation in its own works."[17] Throughout the long article on Justification in the *Apology* the same emphasis is to be found: "The scholastics have followed the philosophers. Thus they teach only the righteousness of reason—that is, civil works—and maintain that without the Holy Spirit reason can love God above all things."[18] "It is false that by its own strength reason can love God. ... Reason cannot free

---

[14] Edmund Schlink, *Theology of the Lutheran Confessions*, trans. P. F. Koehneke and H. J. A. Bouman (Philadelphia: Muhlenberg Press, 1961), pp. 3-4.
[15] F.C. S.D. II, 43 (529.43).
[16] Ap. IV, 229-30 (139.229-30).
[17] S.A. III, iii, 18 (306.18).
[18] Ap. IV, 9 (108.9).

us from our sins or merit for us the forgiveness of sins."[19] "Being blind to the uncleanness of the heart, reason thinks that it pleases God if it does good."[20] Here, reason is not being rejected *per se*; it is being rejected only when it evinces the irrational pretention to self-salvation.

Since man is incapable of saving himself, his only hope lies in a revelation from God. God's thoughts are higher than man's thoughts (Isa. 55:9), so God's Word will necessarily contain truths that go beyond man's comprehension. The *Book of Concord*, while never suggesting that Christian revelation contradicts good reasoning, emphasizes that when Scripture does transcend man's rational categories it must be accepted anyway. Thus human reason needs to bow to God's transcendent truth in such areas as the depth and extent of original sin,[21] predestination,[22] our Lord's descent into hell,[23] and his real presence in the Holy Eucharist.[24]

In technical theological parlance, the *Concordia* rejects not the *ministerial*, but the *magisterial* use of reason. "We take our intellect captive in obedience to Christ," declare the authors of the *Formula*.[25] As long as reason is brought into genuine captivity to Christ, and is not allowed to usurp a self-justifying role in the salvatory operation, the Confessions in no way exclude its apologetic use. Indeed, major confessional authors such as David Chytraeus were so emphatic in marshalling proofs for biblical revelation that they have made orthodox Lutherans of our own day a bit uncomfortable.[26]

(2) *The problem of "historical knowledge."* Nonetheless, it is argued that the depreciation of *fides historica* by the Lutheran Confessions renders apologetic argument of little or no consequence. If the Holy Spirit and not factual knowledge does the saving, what possible good can apologetics serve?

One must note first of all that the *Concordia* does not reject historical knowledge as such, any more than it rejects reason as such. In virtually every instance where the *Book of Concord* speaks negatively of the *fides historica*, it carefully qualifies the condemnation (generally by the words "merely" or "only"), as in the following typical examples from the *Apology*: "Our opponents imagine that faith is *only* historical knowledge"; "The faith of which the apostles speak is not

---

[19] Ap. IV, 27-31 (111.27-31).
[20] Ap. IV, 288 (151.288).
[21] F.C. Ep. I, 9 (467.9); F.C. S.D. I, 8 (510.8); F.C. S.D. II, 60 (519.60).
[22] F.C. Ep. XI, 9, 16 (495.9; 497.16); F.C. S.D. XI, 26, 91 (620.26; 631.91).
[23] F.C. Ep. IX, 4 (492.4); F.C. S.D. IX, 3 (610.3).
[24] F.C. S.D. VII, 102-106 (587.102-588.106).
[25] F.C. Ep. VII, 42 (486.42); F.C. S.D. VIII, 96 (609.96).
[26] Robert D. Preus, *The Theology of Post-Reformation Lutheranism* (2 vols.; St. Louis, Mo.: Concordia, 1970-1972), I, pp. 100-103; II, p. 35.

idle knowledge, but a thing that receives the Holy Spirit and justifies us"; "As we have often said, faith is not *merely* knowledge but rather a desire to accept and grasp what is offered in the promise of Christ"; "We are not talking about *idle* knowledge, such as even the demons have"; "Faith is not *merely* knowledge in the intellect but also trust in the will"; "The scholastics ... interpret faith as *merely* a knowledge of history or of dogmas, not as the power that grasps the promise of grace and righteousness, quickening the heart amid the terrors of sin and death."[27]

What is here being taught becomes particularly plain in the Latin text of the *Augsburg Confession*, where we read: "The term 'faith' does not signify *merely* knowledge of the history (such as is in the ungodly and the devil), but it signifies faith which believes not only the history but also the effect of the history."[28] The Roman Catholic opposition had restricted the meaning of "faith" to factual, historical knowledge of saving truth so as to be able to argue that works were also essential to salvation; therefore the Confessional writers had to point out that the proper biblical understanding of faith, as set forth by Saint Paul, embraced "not only the history but also the effect of the history."[29] This did not mean, however, that the Confessions were denigrating historical knowledge! The Lutheran fathers were anything but *Schwaermer* or modern existential mystics. They believed thoroughly that the assent (*assensus*) and trust (*fiducia*) elements of faith had to be grounded in objective knowledge (*notitia*).[30]

Such kndwledge could go only so far: it could not justify or save; only the Holy Spirit imparting faith to the heart could do that. But since the Spirit works through the Word, and since the Word sets forth accurate historical knowledge of Christ's life and saving work, the Confessions hardly preclude the apologetic use of such evidence. Historical knowledge, like reason, can be misused by sinful man; but it—again like reason—can be brought into obedience to Christ and employed ministerially to persuade men to accept the historical Christ as Lord of their personal history.

(3) *The problem of original sin.* But what value can apologetic arguments have—even if based upon sound logic and historical fact—when the sinner

---

[27] Ap. IV, 48, 99, 227, 249, 304, 383 (113.48; 121.99; 139.227; 142.249; 154.304; 165.383).

[28] A.C. XX, 23 (44.23).

[29] See Carpzov's discussion of this point: Johann Benedict Carpzov, *Isagoge in Libros Ecclesiarum Lutheranarum Symbolicos*, ed. Johann Olearius and Johann Benedict Carpzov, Jr. (3^d ed.; Lipsiae [Leipzig]: David Fleischer, 1699), pp. 206-207, 224, 286.

[30] Cf. John Warwick Montgomery, *The Suicide of Christian Theology* (Minneapolis: Bethany, 1970), pp. 289 ff.

is incapable of appreciating them and is actively engaged in twisting them to justify himself? Schlink understands the Confessions to paint such a picture; his discussion is worth quoting *in extenso*:

> God is hidden from the empirical observation of human reality. He is completely hidden behind the *simul* of creatureliness and corruption. Neither God the Creator nor God the exacting Lawgiver, neither God's love nor God's wrath can be recognized in this fallen world. ...
>
> At first glance this seems to be contradicted when it is occasionally said of "man's reason or natural intellect" in a subordinate clause, "... although man's reason or natural intellect still has a dim spark of the knowledge that there is a God, as well as of the teaching of the law (Rom. 1:19 ff.)" (S.D. II, 9; cf. V, 22). A similar thought is hidden in the expressions concerning the loss of the *"notitia Dei certior"* of paradise (Ap. II, 17), where already the German text, however, passes over the problem of the comparative. How do the Confessions arrive at equating this "spark" of the knowledge of God with ignorance of God?
>
> This question occupied the Confessions surprisingly little. They give no direct answer. The problem involved in the natural knowledge of God is treated in the Confessions as so unimportant and insignificant that apparently no need of harmonizing the opposing formulations was felt. Only indirectly can we seek to attain clarity in the matter. ...
>
> By analogy, then, we may say of the natural knowledge of God in general:
>
> a) Man has a "dim spark of the *knowledge that there is a God*" (S.D. 11,9).
>
> b) This knowledge, however, is only "a dim spark," an indefinite and general knowing.
>
> c) As soon as man tries to take this vague knowing seriously and to put it into practice concretely by calling God by name and devising a ritual for him, he only falls more deeply into sin with his natural obedience to the law and does not come to God but to idols. ...
>
> Thus natural man knows that there is a God but not who God is, and so he does not know God the Creator. He knows in part what is demanded but not who demands it, and therefore he does not recognize God's wrath. He knows neither God nor his own reality; the innate internal uncleanness of human nature is not seen by him, and "this cannot be adjudged except from the Word of God" (Ap. II, 13; cf. 34). "This hereditary sin is so deep a corruption of nature that reason cannot understand it. It must be believed because of the revelation in the Scriptures" (S.A. III, i, 3; cf. also Ep. I, 9; S.D. I, 8). Original sin is "ultimately the worst damage ..., that we shall not

only endure God's eternal wrath and death but that we do not even realize what we are suffering" (S.D. I, 62). Thereby our creatureliness too is hidden from the natural knowledge.[31]

Schlink's catena of passages from the *Book of Concord* showing the effect of man's fall upon his natural knowledge of God is a fair and accurate one, but the general interpretation he places upon these passages is too extreme. The Confessions deal with this issue to make clear beyond all doubt that no natural knowledge on the part of fallen man is capable of bringing him to salvation. Natural knowledge has precisely the same limitations as reason or historical knowledge: not one of them or all of them in combination can form a ladder reaching to heaven. The *Smalcald Articles* declare it to be "nothing but error and stupidity" to hold "that after the fall of Adam the natural powers of man have remained whole and uncorrupted, and that man by nature possesses a right understanding and a good will, as the philosophers teach."[32] Salvation is a gift, and is brought home to the heart only by the sovereign work of God the Holy Spirit.

But it by no means follows that in the *Concordia* "God is hidden from the empirical observation of human reality." As Schlink admits (grudgingly), the authors of the Confessions allow the natural man knowledge that there is a God; and their overwhelming emphasis on the reality of the incarnation—the personal union of the divine and human natures—makes them the strongest possible supporters of the biblical affirmation that God submitted to the "empirical observation of human reality" by becoming true Man in Jesus Christ.

Thus there is nothing in the Confessions which would in principle militate against the use of apologetic arguments for God's existence from nature, or for the deity of our Lord and Savior Jesus Christ from empirical observation of His resurrection appearances, or for the inspiration of Scripture from fulfilled prophecy and other external proofs—as long as such arguments do not purport to substitute for the Spirit's converting work in the heart. As already noted, the orthodox Lutheran theologians of the post-Reformation time—including the authors of the confessional documents—feel comfortable with apologetic arguments of this kind; indeed they seem driven to use them because of their great concern to employ every legitimate means to bring men to the Savior and to His revealed truth (cf. I Cor. 9:22; I Pet. 3:15).

(4) *The problem of spiritual illumination.* Yet does not the *Book of Concord* teach that the very scriptural revelation God gives to a fallen race remains a

---

[31] Schlink, *op. cit.* (in note 14 above), pp. 48-52.
[32] S.A. III, i, 3-4 (302.3-4).

closed book until the sinner's eyes have been opened—not by argument, but by God's Spirit who teaches him to read it from the vantage point of justification by grace through faith? Again let us hear Schlink:

> Without the knowledge of the Gospel the Bible remains unintelligible and useless. Only from the Gospel do all individual statements of Scripture receive their proper place and meaning. Erasmus, Zwingli, the peasants, and the Enthusiasts had also waged their battle with Bible quotations, as did also the Roman adversaries. By means of Scripture texts employed "in either a philosophical or a Jewish manner" it is possible to abolish the certainty of faith and to exclude Christ as mediator (Ap. IV, 376). Only in the light of the Gospel can we determine which words of Scripture are commands and promises, which words serve to terrify or to comfort, which words are valid for us as God's commandments, and which commandments of the Old Testament have been abolished by Christ. Only by faith in the Gospel can Scripture be interpreted correctly, that is, by receiving the benefits secured for us by the crucified Christ.[33]

What we have said repeatedly earlier in this paper applies here with equal force: the Confessions will not allow a man to save himself by any work, rational, cognitive—or even biblical! The sinner cannot pull himself up to heaven by the bootstraps of his own ability to interpret the Scriptures. God alone can give fallen man the illumination necessary to comprehend the Bible in a salvatory way.

However, the *Book of Concord* never suggests—as Schlink does—the modern Neo-Orthodox teaching that the Bible possesses no inherent clarity, but somehow waits for the Spirit's work on the heart to acquire the meaning God intended for it. After discussing a number of biblical passages and their relationship to justification by grace through faith, the *Apology* bluntly says: "No sane man can judge otherwise."[34] Then Melanchthon goes on to quote Romans 10:10 and states: "Here we think that our opponents will grant that the mere act of confessing does not save, but that it saves only because of faith in the heart."[35] Later the same confessional writing utters the following imprecation: "May God destroy these wicked sophists who so sinfully twist the Word of God to suit their vain dreams!"[36]

Such passages from the *Concordia* show beyond question that the confessional authors believed that Scripture is inherently perspicuous—that it speaks clearly and ought to say exactly the same thing to their opponents as it did

---

[33] Schlink, *op. cit*, p. 7.
[34] Ap. IV, 375 (164.375).
[35] Ap. IV, 383-84 (166.383-84).
[36] Ap. XII, 123 (200.123).

to them. If it did not, the reason was simply that the opposition twisted it by sinful sophistry. Indeed, it should be obvious that had the confessional writers not been convinced that the Bible could speak clearly and persuasively to their opponents, they would not have gone to the trouble of continually presenting and arguing from Scriptural texts!

And since their opponents were particularly of the Roman Catholic camp and therefore did not believe in justification by grace through faith, the confessional authors could not have cited Scripture against them and at the same time have held the Bible to be a closed book to those who had not already accepted the Scriptural teaching on justification. They believed that the Bible itself was capable of convincing their opponents as to the proper view of justification, and they quoted it to that end.

Likewise with the Sacramentarians. In arguing for Christ's real presence in the Holy Eucharist, the *Formula of Concord* stresses that the words of Scripture are clear and plain and that the only reasonable course for any Bible reader to take is to accept Jesus' own understanding and interpretation of Scripture:

> There is, of course, no more faithful or trustworthy interpreter of the words of Jesus Christ than the Lord Christ himself, who best understands his words and heart and intention and is best qualified from the standpoint of wisdom and intelligence to explain them. In the institution of his last will and testament and of his abiding covenant and union, he uses no flowery language but the most appropriate, simple, indubitable, and clear words, just as he does in all the articles of faith and in the institution of other covenant-signs and signs of grace or sacraments, such as circumcision, the many kinds of sacrifice in the Old Testament, and holy Baptism. And so that no misunderstanding could creep in, he explained things more clearly by adding the words, "given for you, shed for you."[37]

In sum, though only the Holy Spirit can apply Biblical texts in a salvatory way to human hearts, believers can and should employ Scripture to convince unbelievers of the nature and truth of God's message. Good interpretation can be distinguished from bad interpretation in such a way as to lead opponents to discover the meaning of the Biblical texts. Both an apologetic for Scripture and an apologetic through Scripture must be seen as compatible with the *Book of Concord*.

---

[37] F.C. S.D. VII, 50 (578.50). See also Gottfried Olearius, *Isagoge Anticalvinistica secundum Formulae Concordiae* (Lipsiae [Leipzig]: Johann Wittigau, 1662), pp. 91-114; and Sebastian Schmidt, *Articulorum Formulae Concordiae repetitio* (Argentorati [Strasbourg]: Josias Staedel, 1696), pp. 348-74.

Fundamental Apologetic Axioms in the Lutheran Confessions and Their Contemporary Application

Admittedly, we have done no more than to show that the *Concordia* opens the door to apologetic operations. Can we go beyond this point (which, *nota bene*, should not be minimized, considering the number of anti-apologetic Lutherans who have tried to eliminate all apologetics on the basis of supposed confessional teaching!), and find positive apologetic substance in the *Book of Concord*? To be sure, we should not expect to discover any general programmatic against unbelief in confessional documents composed before the rise of modern secularism in the eighteenth century.[38] But we can derive from the *Concordia* a fundamental apologetic axiom-set which will serve as a kind of template outlining the characteristics which a truly confessional apologetic would need to display. Wittgenstein observed that though the propositions of logic do not describe the world they do serve as a "scaffolding" to show the shape of the world;[39] the Lutheran Confessions, *mutatis mutandis*, do not provide an apologetic for an age of unbelief, but they can display the shape such an apologetic ought to have to be Scripturally meaningful and doctrinally sound. We shall list the fundamental apologetic axioms derivable from the *Book of Concord*, and then, on the basis of them, say a few words as to the apologetic challenge facing confessional Lutheranism today.

(i) *Fallen man retains the ability to reason deductively — to employ logic.* Note how, throughout the Confessions, when bad reasoning is condemned, proper logic is offered as a substitute and opponents are expected to respond to its force:

> If the old witch, Dame Reason, the grandmother of the *alloeosis*, would say that the deity surely cannot suffer and die, then you must answer and say: That is true, but since the divinity and humanity are one person in Christ, the Scriptures ascribe to the deity, because of this personal union, all that happens to the humanity, and vice versa. And this is likewise within the bounds of truth, for you must say that the person (pointing to Christ) suffers, dies. But this person is truly God, and therefore it is correct to say: the Son of God suffers. Although, so to speak, the one part (namely, the deity) does not suffer, nevertheless the person who is true God suffers in the other

---

[38] Cf. Montgomery, *The Shaping of America* (Minneapolis: Bethany, 1976).
[39] "Die logischen Sätze beschreiben das Gerüst der Welt, oder vielmehr, sie stellen es dar. Sie 'handeln' von nichts" (Ludwig Wittgenstein, *Tractatus Logico-Philosophicus*, 6.124; cf. 3.42 and 4.023).

part (namely, in the humanity). For the Son of God truly is crucified for us—that is, this person who is God, for that is what he is—this person, I say, is crucified according to the humanity.[40]

(ii) *Fallen man also retains the ability to reason inductively—to draw correct factual inferences from empirical data.* The Augsburg Confession quotes approvingly from the pseudo-Augustinian *Hypognosticon*: "We concede that all men have a free will which enables them to make judgments according to reason,"[41] and the *Apology* comments: "Human nature still has reason and judgment about the things that the senses can grasp."[42] The Confessions evidently regard the inferential functioning of man's mind, in regard both to logic and to facts, as an aspect of the human essence. Man did not lose this essence when he fell, for had he done so he would have ceased to be human. The *Concordia* guards itself carefully from the Flacian error—the gross doctrinal mistake of Matthew Flacius, who in attempting definitively to answer the semi-Pelagians and synergists, toppled into the opposite error of holding that Adam's fall resulted in a different essence in man.[43]

(iii) *A common ground of logic and fact unites believer and unbeliever, so that the believer can persuasively employ the unbeliever's own reasoning against him.* Note how the *Apology* engages in just such an argumentative process in the following passage:

> Where is the "divinely instituted order that we should take refuge in the help of the saints"? ... Perhaps they derive this "order" from the usage at royal courts, where friends must be used as intercessors. But if a king has appointed a certain intercessor, he does not want appeals to be addressed to him through others. Since Christ has been appointed as our intercessor and high priest, why seek others?[44]

(iv) *The common ground of logic and fact uniting believer and unbeliever permits the effective use of analogy-reasoning to convince the unbeliever.* In the same section of the *Apology* from which the preceding illustration is taken, Melanchthon offers this persuasive analogy-argument for the biblical doctrine of propitiation, as against the invocation of saints:

---

[40] F.C. S.D. VIII, 41-42 (599.41-42). The *Formula of Concord* is here quoting Luther (*WA*, XXVI, 321-22).
[41] A.C. XVIII, 4 (39.4); we follow the Latin text here.
[42] Ap. XVIII, 4 (225.4).
[43] Cf. Henry W. Reimann, "Matthias Flacius Illyricus," *Concordia Theological Monthly*, XXXV (February, 1964), pp. 69-93.
[44] Ap. XXI, 24 (232.24).

If one pays a debt for one's friend, the debtor is freed by the merit of another as though it were his own. Thus the merits of Christ are bestowed on us so that when we believe in him we are accounted righteous by our trust in Christ's merits as though we had merits of our own.[45]

(v) As demonstrated in detail in the previous section of this paper, the Confessions hold that *fallen man is capable of acquiring natural knowledge of God's existence, historical knowledge ("fides historica") of Biblical events, and understanding as to the meaning of the perspicuous Scriptural text.*

(vi) However, the Confessions are even more concerned to emphasize, as we have seen, that *none of the above capacities of the unregenerate man* (or any other abilities he may possess, for that matter) *are such as to permit him to mend his broken God-relationship: the Holy Spirit and the Holy Spirit alone, converts men to Christ.* "To be born anew, to receive inwardly a new heart, mind, and spirit, is solely the work of the Holy Spirit."[46]

Now what kind of apologetic approach ought today's confessional Lutheran to build on this axiomatic foundation? Let us be very clear, first of all, as to what approach he must *not* take. He must not fall into the trap of *presuppositionalism* or *apriorism* so attractive to orthodox Calvinists of the Dutch school (Van Til, Dooyeweerd, *et al.*). Even the ostensibly milder, revisionist presuppositionalism advocated in Reymond's provocative little work, *The Justification of Knowledge*, cannot be accepted by a confessional Lutheran. Reymond correctly sees that Van Til's epistemology destroys the divinely created common ground between believer and unbeliever: "The solution to all of Van Til's difficulties is to affirm, as Scripture teaches, that both God and man share the same concept of truth and the same theory of language."[47] But Reymond still rejects any positive apologetic to the unbeliever on the theory that the universe of facts and possible interpretations is so vast that the unbeliever can consistently interpret all evidence in line with his sinful presuppositions.

The *Book of Concord* much more wisely perceived that the unbeliever, living in the same universe with the Christian and using the same inferential faculties of mind, should respond to reasoning that proceeds by analogy from ordinary decision-making in secular affairs to the meaning and significance of biblical

---

[45] Ap. XXI, 19 (231.19).
[46] F.C. S.D. II, 26 (526.26).
[47] Robert L. Reymond, *The Justification of Knowledge: An Introductory Study in Christian Apologetic Methodology* (Nutley, N.J.: Presbyterian and Reformed Publishing Co., 1976), p. 105. Dr. Robert H. Countess provides an excellent review of this work in *Christianity Today*, November 18, 1977, pp. 34-35.

evidence. If the unbeliever refuses to do so, he acts irrationally by analogy with his ordinary experience and displays his *real* reason for rejecting the truth—not intellectual dissatisfaction but willful egocentricity.

Here, on the basis of the apologetic axioms of the *Concordia*, the contemporary Lutheran apologist begins to discover his battle plan. What will be its characteristics?

The Lutheran apologist will not be afraid to "become all things to all men that by all means some may be saved": convinced of the common ground of logic and fact between believer and unbeliever, he will argue by analogy that bad reasoning leads to religious heresy just as it produces catastrophe in the secular realm, and that the same good reasoning as is essential to survival in ordinary life, if applied to religious issues, will vindicate the Holy Scriptures and their Christ.

The contemporary confessional apologist will not be afraid of developing effective modern arguments for God's existence (such as is afforded by the application of the classical contingency proof to the Second Law of Thermodynamics, or such as Peter Berger creates on a sociological base in his *Rumor of Angels*); but—in line with the fundamental stress of Lutheran theology on the incarnation, the Gospel, and the Cross—he will especially endeavor to provide a case for the deity of our Lord and Savior Jesus Christ beginning from, but not limited to, the *fides historica*.[48]

Rather than giving today's religious seeker the impression that the Missouri Synod's uncompromising stand on the inerrancy of the Bible is an aprioristic asylum of invincible ignorance, the Lutheran apologist will offer the best evidence in support of our Lord's own assertion that Scripture cannot be broken.

Finally, the confessional apologist will see himself not as a Holy-Spirit-substitute but as a John the Baptist in the wilderness of a secular age, preparing the way of the Lord, making the paths intellectually straight which lead to the Lamb of God—to the only One who can take away the sins of the world.

Admittedly, such an apologetic is not provided, full-blown, in the *Book of Concord*. Apologetics speaks to the fallen man, and the *Zeitgeist* constantly changes. There is no absolute apologetic; the apologetic task faces each generation of Christians anew. But we of the Lutheran Church-Missouri Synod have taken a giant step forward to meet that challenge. A Lutheran Council in the U.S.A. news release of December 1, 1977, quotes the report of a five-year official LCUSA theological study observing that "the LCA and ALC have not felt it

---

[48] See Montgomery, *Sensible Christianity* cassette series (3 vols.; Santa Ana, Ca.: Vision House/ One Way Library, 1976); now available from the Canadian Institute for Law, Theology and Public Policy (http://www.ciltpp.com).

necessary to adopt doctrinal statements in addition to the confessional articles. The LCMS, on the other hand, has reserved for itself the right to restate its positions on doctrinal matters throughout its history."

The Missouri Synod has rightly seen that modern secularism requires new confessional responses; she has not been intimidated into accepting modern heresies such as result from the application of historical-critical hermeneutics just because the 16th century Confessions antedated them. Surely, then, in the realm of apologetics—a domain far less static than dogmatics—we can no longer employ our theology as the fundamentalists do their sociological blue laws, to wall the church off from the real challenges of the age. Only the Word of God remains forever; nothing else is changeless. Now that our battle for the Bible has been won, let us with apologetic vigor show modern secular man that the Holy Scriptures still have the last Word.

5. Pain in Theological Perspective

The Issue

Though our subject is far from humorous, we begin with a quotation from Matthijs van Boxsel's *The Encyclopaedia of Stupidity*—a passage in which he commences his discussion of "No Pleasure Without Pain" with Menander and relies, at the end, on Slavoj Zizek's *Le plus sublime des hystériques* (Paris, 1988):

> I learned my greatest lessons
> from the distress of others.
> *Menander, Sententiae ...*

> All of us dwell in the confused realm of beneficial blunders, of actions that succeed because of their failure. We operate in the area that lies between wise intention and mere fluke. And that lends an unintentionally comic aspect to all our actions. Every action that crosses the threshold of possibility and is realised in the full sense of that word, contains at bottom an element of idiocy.[1]

Van Boxsel, whether he understands it or not, is here accurately describing one of the numerous manifestations of life in a fallen world. But our concern in this paper is not with pain as a positive phenomenon, or even with pain per se, but with *seemingly irrational pain*. Neither theologically nor in other respects does the kind of pain which warns of danger or which is a necessary concomitant of healing create difficulty.

> "Senseless" suffering, such as we see when innocent children are destroyed or mutilated in war, sickness, plague or famine, makes our anger and impatience rise. ... When senseless pain is apparently not merely adventitious, but designed, the average honest-thinking person tends to lose restraint in considering it.

> A good example of this arises in considering, as did C. S. Lewis, the deafness of a musical genius such as Beethoven. An absolute master of the art and science of sound struck down with stone deafness! Could a greater refinement of apparent sadism be conceived? Hence the impatience of many when they merely begin to consider the problem of suffering.[2]

---

[1] Matthijs van Boxsel, *The Encylopaedia of Stupidity*, rev. ed. trans. from the Dutch by Arnold and Erica Pomerans (London: Reaktion Books, 2003), p. 35.
[2] A. E. Wilder-Smith, *The Paradox of Pain* (Wheaton, Illinois: Harold Shaw, 1972), pp. 91-92. The reference to C. S. Lewis is to his *A Grief Observed* (New York: Seabury, 1961), p. 31.

In the face of such apparently irrational or designed miseries, four major approaches have been taken: (1) Evil is not ontologically real—it only seems to be such. (2) There is no God. (3) There is a God, but he is indifferent to such pain and/or lacks the moral quality to eliminate it. (4) There is a God, but he lacks omnipotence and is thus unable to prevent pain of this nature. (5) There is a God who is both infinitely powerful and infinitely good, and such miseries are in fact logically compatible with his existence.

The view that evil is not real but only appears to be such is doubtless the least attractive of these options, since it flies in the face of universal human experience. One thinks of the Christian Scientist who declared, after being stuck with pin: "The illusion of pain was as bad as the pain would have been." If one must predicate of an illusion all the qualities of reality, there is little point in treating it as illusory.

In spite of the fact that unbelievers such as John Mortimer invariably fall back on the "problem of evil" as their major justification for denying God's existence,[3] the atheistic answer faces overwhelming difficulties. Philosophically, a contingent universe by definition requires an explanation outside of it—that is to say, a transcendent explanation. Scientific illustrations abound: Olbers' paradox; the Second Law of Thermodynamics; the impossibility of accounting for mind by the characteristics of the human brain. The case for "intelligent design" is so powerful that even lifelong atheist Antony Flew has moved to a Deistic worldview.[4]

One of the most serious practical problems with the secularist approach to pain is that since nothing (including pain) has inherent moral value in an atheistic universe, suicide and assisted suicide are legitimate responses to excessive suffering. The loss of respect for human life is a natural consequence of such a worldview. Thus it was not in the least strange for Deistic skeptic David Hume, the 18th-century critic of biblical miracles, to assert in his essay *Of Suicide* that "the life of a man is of no greater importance to the universe than that of an oyster."[5]

As between (3) and (4)—an immoral God or a finite God—it is hard to decide which is less satisfactory. An Aristotelian Deity, indifferent to the plight

---

[3] See John Mortimer's interviews with clerics such as Archbishop Runcie (*In Character* [Harmondsworth, Middlesex: Penguin Books, 1984], pp. 27 ff.).

[4] On all of the above, see Montgomery, *Tractatus Logico-Theologicus* (4th ed.; Bonn: Verlag für Kultur und Wissenschaft, 2009), proposition 3.8.

[5] *Of Suicide* is included in Hume's *Essays Moral, Political and Literary* (London: Oxford University Press, 1963), pp. 585-96. See Montgomery, "Whose Life Anyway? A Re-Examination of Suicide and Assisted Suicide," in his *Christ Our Advocate* (Bonn: Verlag für Kultur und Wissenschaft, 2002), pp. 169-195.

of his creatures, is hardly an attractive option. Even less attractive is the God of personalist philosopher Edgar Sheffield Brightman or process philosopher Charles Hartshorne—a God who is doing the best he can in the face of cosmic misery and would appreciate all the help we can give him.[6] In point of fact, any rational choice between these two highly questionable alternatives would be impossible unless God revealed his true nature to finite beings obviously incapable of arriving at independent, transcendent knowledge of him.

This brings us to the classic Christian position, namely, that the existence of apparently irrational and certainly genuine evil in the world is logically reconcilable with the existence of the God of the Bible, who is there presented as both omnipotent and perfectly good.

The Christian Response

Two major approaches to resolving the problem of evil have been employed in the history of Christian theology. The first is that of the sovereignty of God; the second locates the cause of evil in the freedom of the creature to act against divine standards. These two approaches are not incompatible and, as we shall see, both have a part to play in aiding our understanding of this acute issue of theodicy.[7]

Because arguments based on God's sovereignty can seem to exclude the moral dimension, modern apologists for the faith have generally relied more on the creature's misuse of freewill to explain how the evil in the world could come about and persist even when that world is in the hands of a loving, all-powerful God. C. S. Lewis' little book, *The Problem of Pain*, is perhaps the best known and most attractive contemporary example.[8] More recent endeavours along the

---

[6] Cf. Charles Hartshorne, *Omnipotence and Other Theological Mistakes* (Albany: State University of New York Press, 1984).
[7] For a wide-ranging treatment of the subject, see John S. Feinberg, T*he Many Faces of Evil: Theological Systems and the Problems of Evil* (rev. ed.; Wheaton, Illinois: Crossway Books, 2004).
[8] C. S. Lewis, *The Problem of Pain* (London: Geoffrey Bles, 1940), and frequently reprinted. It is worthwhile emphasising (contra the theatrical and cinematographic pictures of Lewis presented in recent years) that Lewis' later book, *A Grief Observed*, though written from the standpoint of the personal tragedy he experienced on the death of his wife, does not alter his fundamental argument: it simply refines and personalises it.

same line include Richard Swinburne's claim that evil plays an essential role in creating a context for moral and spiritual development,[9] and the revival of the "greater good"/ "fortunate fall" argument.[10]

Because of the critical importance of this issue not only for the case for the existence of the Christian God but also for the validity of the biblical *Heilsgeschichte*, we are taking the liberty of reproducing here the detailed argument contained in our *Tractatus Logico-Theologicus*.[11] At very least, this should stimulate the reader to examine the problem in depth and to appreciate how effectively Christian revelation deals with it.

4.8   *Over against the biblical worldview—indeed, contra the very existence of the God of the Bible—looms the Problem of Evil: how can there be a God who is both perfectly good (and therefore opposed to evil) and all-powerful (and therefore capable of eradicating evil), when the world displays the presence of evil on so many levels?*

4.801   As we shall soon see, and as Wittgenstein himself emphasised, absolute moral judgments can only be justified transcendentally; it follows that the atheist, having by definition no such absolute source of morality, is in a particularly disadvantageous position logically to offer ethical criticism of the actions of Deity.

4.802   We have already noted the inadequacy of trying to handle this issue by maintaining that God lacks omnipotence (Brightman): such a finite god is not the God of Scripture or the Father of our Lord Jesus Christ; and he does not in any event constitute an attractive object of worship.

4.81   The earliest chapters of the Bible inform us that evil in the human sphere originated because the first humans chose to violate God's express will, and that in consequence, they and their descendants suffered pain and death, and the natural world itself lost its perfection (Genesis 3:15-19).

4.811   The tempter in that scenario is identified elsewhere in Scripture as the devil, a former angel who himself fell as a result of a similar insistence on following his own way rather than acknowledging the sovereign will of God (Isaiah 14:12-15; Revelation 12:9, 20:2).

---

[9] Richard Swinburne, *The Existence of God* (rev. ed.; Aberdeen: Aberdeen University Press, 2004). Cf. Alvin C. Plantinga, *God, Freedom, and Evil* (Grand Rapids, Michigan: Eerdmans, 1974), Part I.

[10] See especially Melville Y. Stewart, *The Greater-Good Defence: An Essay on the Rationality of Faith* (New York: St. Martin's Press, 1993).

[11] *Op. cit.*, proposition 4.8.

4.82   It follows that evil was not created by God but came about as the result of God's creatures' misuse of their freewill.

4.821 Evil is neither a mere "absence of good" (Augustine) nor a substance: it refers to a *broken relationship* between the creature and the Creator; from that broken relationship follow concrete evil*s* (plural)—sickness, death, crime, environmental catastrophe, etc.

4.822 Evil is not something God created; it is a perversion of the right relationship with him, for which the creature is responsible.

4.83   Natural evils can follow from perverse human decisions, just as physical illnesses are often produced psychosomatically by wrong psychological attitudes.

4.831 Many so-called "natural catastrophes" today (such as African famines) are in fact the product of human neglect of the environment or bad use of natural resources.

4.84   When the Bible asserts that the sin of Adam passed to his descendants, so that the entire human race is corrupted and needs salvation (Romans 5:12), it speaks both biologically and sociologically: every human generation is born into the sinful context created by past generations, is impacted by them, and adds to the burden for the future.

4.841 The Hebrew word *Adam*, like the Greek *anthropos* and the Latin *homo*, means "mankind"; in that sense, the first man was a representative of the entire race—a kind of perfect statistical sampling of mankind in general.

4.8411 Thus the truth of the old school-book doggerel: "In Adam's fall, we fell all": had you or I been in the Garden, we would have done the same as Adam and Eve did, so we are in no position to blame someone else for our condition.

4.8412 Moreover, if we are honest with ourselves, we know that we have, by our own personal, conscious decisions, gone against the best dictates of our own conscience—to say nothing of divine standards (cf. J. S. Feinberg, *The Many Faces of Evil*).

4.85   The key to understanding why the continuing presence of evil in the world is not a bar to the existence of the God of the Bible is, then, *the reality of freewill*.

4.8501 Even if one operates with a Calvinist understanding of God as the predestinarian Sovereign, the Problem of Evil is not insoluble, since God (not man) sets the standards of cosmic morality (Plantinga).

4.85011 "C'est le Père Noël qui fait la classe aux lutins. Quelquefois, il perd patience et les menace d'appeler le directeur, mais les lutins savent bien que c'est pour rire; c'est lui, le directeur" (G. Solotareff, *Dictionnaire du Père Noël*).

4.8502 Scripture, as a matter of fact, presents the interrelationship of predestination and freewill as a mystery: man's freewill is genuine and one must believe in order to be saved (John 3:16; Acts 16:30-31), yet salvation is God's work alone — even faith being the gift of God (John 1:12-13; Ephesians 2:8-9).

4.85021 As Luther put it, fallen humanity has all the freewill needed to choose a preferred path to hell — but not the capacity to climb to heaven — since salvation is a matter of God's grace alone.

4.85022 "Double" predestination (God's choosing not only the saved but also the damned) is an obnoxious and unbiblical doctrine; and so is the Arminian teaching that we have the capacity to assist in our salvation by contributing our faith (or our "predisposition toward faith") to the salvatory process.

4.85023 The revelatory facts take precedence over the logical difficulty; as already noted, when fact and logic conflict, facts win.

4.851 God is love (1 John 4:8, etc.), and love entails freewill (John 7:17): the biblical God is not a puppet master, pulling strings so as to force his creation to do what he wishes (C. S. Lewis).

4.852 Enforced love would not be love at all; it is rape — metaphysically even if not physically.

4.8521 Every lover (and parent) knows this, or should know it: you want your intended or your child to love you in return, and to do what is best, but to force this upon the object of your love is to destroy the possibility of a genuine, reciprocal love-relationship.

4.853 Freewill means the possibility of rejecting love as well as of accepting it — with all the negative consequences which flow from such rejection.

4.8531 If the rejection is everlasting, the negative consequences will likewise be eternal and everlasting; such a choice cuts one off from all goodness and love, and leaves one with only one object of worship: the egocentric self which has been the source of the problem from the outset.

4.854 But does not determinism — biological or otherwise — prevent our recourse to freewill as an explanation for the Problem of Evil? Certainly not; for:

4.8541 Determinism contradicts human experience (even the determinist functions as if he were making free decisions); and

4.8542 Determinism is self-defeating (were it universally true, then the determinist philosophy *itself* would have been predetermined and could not claim to be objectively true); and

4.8543 So-called "chaotic dynamics" shows that we are operating in an open universe: though God has set out a pattern of general cosmic laws, he has indeed "left himself and us room to maneuver" (Polkinghorne).

4.86 Did not God foresee the negative effects of sin, and, if so, why—among the infinite possible worlds he could have created—did he not create one where Adam would *not* have fallen?

4.861 To eliminate all possible fallen worlds in favour of one that would not fall must be seen as the functional equivalent of eliminating freewill from the creation in the first place.

4.8611 Even the non-religious find couples morally unpalatable who obtain "perfect" offspring by systematically destroying nested embryos when ultrasound shows that, if born, they would display characteristics the parents dislike.

4.87 If freewill is essential to love, would this not mean that in eternity there would always have to be the possibility of new falls into sin—contrary to the assurances of a perfect "new heaven and new earth," given, for example, in the Book of Revelation?

4.871 As Augustine argued, the redemption of the world in Christ moves the relationship between creature and Creator to a new level—that of *non posse peccari*.

4.872 "We love because he first loved us" (1 John 4:19), so the likelihood of a repeat of the fall drops to zero as a limit in the face of an undeserved redemption of infinite consequence.

4.88 Even granting the essential tie between love and freewill, could—and, therefore, *should*—God not have limited the *effects* of man's sin?

4.881 But if the consequences of moral acts are removed, their moral character disappears: the language game changes from ethics to play or to strategy: in our own interests, we will try more and more clever ways to circumvent the law, knowing that a term in gaol is no longer in the offing.

4.882 Why do not the consequences of sin fall only on the wicked? Why does not God preserve the innocent from sin's miseries? Why does the godfather die comfortably at an advanced age while the good citizen is struck down by the early onset of cancer?

4.8821 Unfortunately, since "all have sinned and come short of the glory of God" (Rom. 3:23; cf. Psalm 53:3; Isaiah 53:6; 1 John 1:8), there are *no* innocents.

4.88211 As John Donne put it, the human race is inseparably interconnected: "Never send to know for whom the bell tolls: it tolls for thee."

4.8822 Sin, by its very nature, is irrational, and its consequences likewise.

4.88221 Sinful consequences in a broken world are like the effects of a terrorist's bomb, striking anyone within range, not necessarily specific political opponents (cf. 11 September 2001).

4.8823 Even genuine Christian believers are not exempted from the effects of a fallen world — the promise to them is, not that they will never suffer but that "all things work together for good to them that love God" (Romans 8:28).

4.883 But God could certainly have *diminished* the consequences of sin without removing them entirely? Scripture teaches that:

4.8831 He has already done so, since if he had removed his hand from the world after the fall, all would have returned to its original state of chaos (Colossians 1:16-17); and

4.8832 In spite of our killing his prophets and even his own Son, he has provided the only way of salvation out of the misery we have created for ourselves (Matthew 21; Mark 12; Luke 20; Romans 5:8); and

4.8833 He promises an ultimate restoration of all things (Revelation 21-22); and

4.8834 Those who have created the mess are in a particularly poor position to criticise the only One who is doing anything cosmically about it — simply because he is not working on their schedule; and

4.8835 Oddly enough, God, not ourselves, remains the sovereign in these matters (Job 38-42).

4.89 Granted, the evils of this world are evident on every hand; but the issue is: does their existence negate the clear evidence of God's love for us in coming to earth in Jesus Christ to deal with this very problem?

4.891 One must not regard this matter as a question of weighing quantities (deaths in the Holocaust, for example, against the single death of Christ): *if* the case for Incarnation is a good one (and we have seen just how excellent it is), that case stands regardless of the existence of human misery, whatever its degree.

4.892 Indeed, the greater the misery, the greater should be our gratitude to the One who loves us and gave himself for us.

4.893 "Scarcely for a righteous man will one die: yet perhaps for a good man some would even dare to die" — one thinks of Sidney Carton in Dickens' *Tale of Two Cities* — "but God commends his love toward us, in that, while we were yet sinners, Christ died for us" (Romans 5).

Conclusion

To be sure, the argument as just presented is a biblical argument, and, as such, requires justification for the revelatory character of Holy Scripture. That case is made elsewhere in the *Tractatus Logico-Theologicus*,[12] and space forbids our presenting it here. In broad sweep, we maintain that the soundness of the historical records and eyewitness testimony concerning Jesus Christ leads to the conclusion that he was in fact what he claimed to be: God incarnate, come to earth to die for the sins of the world and to offer eternal life to a fallen race. Since Jesus' view of Scripture (the existing Old Testament, together with the forthcoming New Testament as the product of the Holy-Spirit-led Apostolic company) was that it represented the very word of God, and since Jesus was himself God incarnate, the revelatory value of the Bible and its teachings follows inexorably.

Among those central biblical teachings is that of God's goodness towards a creation whose miseries came about—and continue to plague a fallen race—through selfishness and the disregard of the will of its loving Creator. But the final chapter to the story is still to be written. As Sonia declares in the last act of "Uncle Vania"—it serves as the conclusion of Samuel Benchetrit's *Moins 2*, starring Jean-Louis Trintignant:

> Nous nous reposerons! Nous entendrons les anges, nous verrons tout le mal terrestre, toutes nos souffrances noyées dans la miséricorde qui va emplir l'univers tout entier, et la vie deviendra douce, tendre, bonne, comme une caresse. J'y crois, j'y crois … Tu n'as pas connu de joies dans ta vie, oncle Vania, mais patiente un peu, patiente … Nous nous reposerons … Nous nous reposerons … Nous nous reposerons … [13]

---

[12] *Ibid.*, propositions 3 and 4.
[13] *L'Avant-Scène Théâtre*, No. 1188 (1 septembre 2005), p. 66. The play was first performed at the Hébertot theatre, Paris, on 26 August 2005.

Part Four
Legal Evidence, Resurrection and Human Rights

1. Legal Evidence for the Truth of the Faith

The Apostle exhorts Christians to "be ready always to give an answer to everyone who asks you a reason for the hope that is in you" (1 Peter 3:15). The word translated "answer" here is the Greek *apologia*, "defense," and from it comes the name of the theological discipline concerned with defending Christian truth-claims: Apologetics.

Through church history apologists for the faith have often relied on philosophical styles of reasoning to bolster their efforts; thus Augustine depended heavily on Plato, and Aquinas borrowed extensively from Aristotle. With the decline of these classical philosophies and particularly since the rise of modern rationalism in the eighteenth century (Kant, Lessing, Hume), non-Christians have generally presumed that no meaningful defense of Christian faith is possible — that religion is, in the final analysis, only a question of personal feeling — and Christians themselves (the so-called presuppositionalists, existentialists, and pietists) have often unwittingly aided and abetted such a presumption by declaring that Christianity starts from its own presuppositional faith-experience and cannot be either proved or disproved by factual evidence.[1]

Worth emphasizing is the legal flavor of the Greek word *apologia*: the Apostle consciously employed a technical term of ancient Greek law, having reference to the answer given by a defendant before a tribunal. One should not therefore be surprised to discover that the Law of Evidence offers innumerable valuable insights for the defense of historic Christian faith. Our expectations in this regard are particularly heightened when we consider that the evidential machinery of the law has been developed, as the 1975 *Federal Rules of Evidence* state, "to the end that the truth may be ascertained."[2] All societies, whether civilized or primitive, require legal techniques for getting at the truth when disputes arise, and these techniques are refined through experience until they reach a level of sophistication satisfying to litigants who otherwise would breach the peace to settle their conflicts. Small wonder that philosopher Stephen Toulmin argues that philosophical inquiry itself could be considerably improved if it would look to legal reasoning as a model.[3]

---

[1] J. W. Montgomery, *Christianity for the Toughminded* (1973); J. W. Montgomery, *Faith Founded on Fact* (1978).
[2] *Fed. R. Evid.* 102; on the *Rules* in general, see *ALI-ABA Federal Rules of Evidence Resource Materials, with October 1975 Supplement* (1975).
[3] S. E. Toulmin, *The Uses of Argument* (1958); cf. J. W. Montgomery, *The Law above the Law* 84-90 (1975).

Early Christianity based its case for divine truth on the deity of Jesus Christ, and its claim to His deity on His resurrection from the dead (1 Corinthians 15). The Law of Evidence well sustains this argumentation as will be seen from the application of several specific evidential rules.

1. Decisions on questions of fact must be made by the trier of fact on the basis of the weight of relevant evidence, defined by the *Federal Rules* as "evidence having any tendency to make the existence of any fact that is of consequence to the determination of the action more probable or less probable than it would be without the evidence."[4] Christians are therefore precisely on the right track when they defend their position in terms of the weight of factual evidence for Christ's deity. A disputed question of religious truth must not be prejudged in a presuppositional manner: no one can expect that judicial notice will be taken for or against Christian truth, since "a judicially noticed fact must be one not subject to reasonable dispute."[5] The outcome of the case will depend, rather, on evidential probability.[6] And probability has to do with the weight of evidence for the particular claim at issue, without reference to general or collateral considerations. Thus just as "evidence of a person's character or a trait of his character is not admissible for the purpose of proving that he acted in conformity therewith on a particular occasion,"[7] so the non-Christian will be prevented from arguing against Christ's resurrection on the ground that regular events in general make a particular miracle too "improbable" to consider. The law refuses to obscure concrete evidence of the particular by the introduction of collateral generalities, for it recognizes that "there are too many differences to insure that what holds true in one case will apply in the other."[8]

2. "The common law system of proof," writes McCormick in his standard treatise on Evidence, "is exacting in its insistence upon the most reliable sources of information. This policy is apparent in the Opinion rule, the Hearsay rule, and the Documentary Originals rule. One of the earliest and most pervasive manifestations of this attitude is the rule requiring

---

[4] *Fed. R. Evid.* 401. This definition of relevant evidence derives from Professor Thayer's classic *Preliminary Treatise on Evidence* (1898).
[5] *Fed. R. Evid.* 201. Indeed, statutes undertaking to establish conclusive presumptions with respect to material facts are held unconstitutional—on the ground that they deprive the accused of due process of law (Caroline Products Co. v. McLaughlin, 365 Ill. 62).
[6] Cf. V. C. Ball, "The Moment of Truth: Probability Theory and Standards of Proof," in *Essays on Procedure and Evidence* 84-107 (T. G. Roady and R. N. Covington ed. 1961).
[7] *Fed. R. Evid.* 404.
[8] H. P. Chandler and S. D. Hirschl, "Evidence," 11 *American Law and Procedure* 21 (1910, rev. ed. 1955).

that a witness who testifies to a fact which can be perceived by the senses must have had an opportunity to observe, and must have actually observed the fact." In strict conformity to these requirements, the Christian properly focuses attention on the New Testament documents relating to the life of Christ as the best evidence concerning Him, since these can be shown to be primary sources — either written by those, such as Matthew and John who had immediate, firsthand, eyewitness contact with Jesus, or by others (Mark, Luke, Paul) who were intimately acquainted with the original apostolic circle. Moreover, as Simon Greenleaf of Harvard, author of the nineteenth century classic on Evidence stressed, any common-law court would favor the New Testament writings with a presumption of authenticity as ancient documents regular on their face and preserved through the centuries in a place of natural custody. The burden of proof thus rests upon the unbeliever to disprove the testimonial value of these apostolic books, not upon the Christian to build up support for documents already having prima facie legal authenticity.[9]

3. Where direct evidence is not available, the law allows circumstantial evidence, and also proof by *res ipsa loquitur*. The latter is often resorted to in negligence cases where no one directly observed the act in question but where, by process of elimination, only the defendant was in a position to have done it.[10] Likewise, no one was present at the moment of Christ's resurrection, but the events surrounding it were testified to by careful eyewitnesses (Jesus was in fact put to death by crucifixion; Jesus afterwards made numerous, physical post-resurrection appearances over a forty-day period).

Res ipsa loquitur in a typical negligence case

1. Accident does not normally occur in the absence of negligence.
2. Instrumentality causing injury was under the defendant's exclusive control.
3. Plaintiff did not himself contribute to the injury.

Therefore, defendant negligent: "The event speaks for itself."

---

[9] Professor Greenleaf makes this important point in his *Testimony of the Evangelists*, now reprinted in J. W. Montgomery, *The Law above the Law* 91-140, 149-63 (1975). On the historical soundness of the New Testament writings, see F. F. Bruce, *The New Testament Documents: Are They Reliable?* (5th ed. 1960), and cf. J. A. T. Robinson, *Redating the New Testament* (1977).
[10] M. Shain, *Res Ipsa Loquitur, Presumptions and Burden of Proof* (1945).

Res ipsa loquitur as applied to Christ's resurrection

1. Dead bodies do not leave tombs in the absence of some agency effecting the removal.
2. The tomb was under God's exclusive control, for it had been sealed, and Jesus, the sole occupant of it, was dead.
3. The Romans and the Jewish religious leaders did not contribute to the removal of the body (they had been responsible for sealing and guarding the tomb to prevent anyone from stealing the body), and the disciples would not have stolen it, then prevaricated, and finally died for what they knew to be untrue.

Therefore, only God was in a position to empty the tomb, which He did, as Jesus Himself had predicted, by raising Him from the dead: "The event speaks for itself."

This reasoning process has close affinities with the method of *reductio ad absurdum*, which Professor Daube has shown to have been common in Greek and Roman law: supporting a case "by shewing the alternative to be in striking contrast to the declared specific objective of the enterprise."[11] If the object of examining the primary-source documentary evidence for Christian claims is to determine what in fact happened, one cannot arrive at an "explanation" of the resurrection which contradicts what these documents have to say about the historical circumstances and about the personalities and motivations of the people involved in them.[12]

And here, in contact with Greco-Roman jurisprudence, we see that the Law of Evidence is not a self-serving technique developed by common-law jurists in subtle support of Christian theology! The fundamental canons of evidence which we have employed in defense of biblical faith are found with remarkable consistency in all legal systems—from primitive to civilized, from ancient to modern. Max Gluckman writes of the Lozi people of Northern Rhodesia: "The Lozi distinguish between different kinds of evidence as hearsay, circumstantial, and direct, and attach different degrees of cogency to these and different degrees of credibility to various witnesses."[13] The ancient Persian *Digest of a Thousand Points of Law* begins with a detailed chapter on the Law of Evidence, insisting, as does the common law, on "independent and convincing proof" to

---

[11] D. Daube, *Roman Law: Linguistic, Social and Philosophical Aspects* 180 (1969).
[12] J. W. Montgomery, *History, Law and Christianity* (2002).
[13] M. Gluckman, *The Judicial Process among the Barotse of Northern Rhodesia* 82 (1955).

support allegations, and setting forth detailed criteria for distinguishing reliable from unreliable testimony (declarations against interest as opposed to self-serving declarations, etc.).[14] In Roman law,

> When the witnesses for the parties gave conflicting testimony on any point, it was the duty of the judge, not to count the number on each side, but to consider which of them were entitled to the greatest credit, according to the well-known rule, *"Testimonia ponderanda sunt, non numeranda."* It rarely happens that the evidence is so nicely balanced as not to preponderate on one side or the other. But questions of fact may be supported and opposed by every degree of evidence, and sometimes by that degree of evidence of which the proper effect is to leave the mind in a state of doubt, or in an equipoise between two conclusions. Where such a case occurred, the Roman law provided that the benefit of the doubt should be given to the defendant rather than to the plantiff.[15]

Jewish evidential standards were, if anything, even more rigorous than those of Roman law at the time of Christ. For Jewish tribunals of the first century, "all evidence must be direct, and not circumstantial or presumptive. Be the chain of evidence every so strong, if not all links are forged by direct eye-testimony, and that of at least two competent witnesses, the accused cannot be adjudged guilty".[16]

Where unsatisfactory or bizarre evidential standards have been developed in a society, these have generally been due to religious influences of an unfortunate kind. Thus among the Muslims one finds not only severe deficiencies in substantive law (e.g., the inferior legal position of women) but also sad procedural standards:

> One of the most serious limitations upon the practical efficiency of the Shari'a courts lay in the rigid system of procedure and evidence, applicable both in civil and criminal cases, by which they were bound. The burden of proof was strict, and the party who bore it, usually the plaintiff, was obliged to produce two male, adult, Muslim witnesses, whose moral integrity and religious probity were unimpeachable, to testify orally to their direct knowledge of the truth of his claim. If the plaintiff or prosecution failed to discharge this burden of proof the defendant or accused was offered the oath of denial. Properly sworn on the Qur'an, such an oath secured judg-

---

[14] 1 *The Laws of the Ancient Persians* pt. 1, 12, 26-27 (S. J. Bulsara ed. 1937).
[15] Lord Mackenzie, *Studies in Roman Law, with Comparative Views of the Laws of France, England and Scotland* 382 (7th ed. J. Kirkpatrick 1911). Cf. H. F. Jolowicz, *Roman Foundations of Modern Law* 102 (1957).
[16] S. Mendelsohn, *The Criminal Jurisprudence of the Ancient Hebrews, Compiled from the Talmud and Other Rabbinical Writings, and Compared with Roman and English Penal Jurisprudence*, para. 82 (1891).

ment in his favour; if he failed to take it, judgment would be given for the plaintiff or prosecution, provided, in some circumstances, this side in turn took the oath. Such a system of procedure and evidence may have reflected the religious idealism of the scholars: but it was largely because of the often impractical burden of proof that was imposed upon a plaintiff, and the corresponding ease with which unscrupulous defendants might avoid a civil or criminal liability which reason declared to exist, that the Shari'a courts proved an unsatisfactory organ for the administration of certain spheres of the law.[17]

What, then, are the evidential standards pertinent to the question of the reliability of the testimonies to Jesus Christ as found in the primary documents of the New Testament?

In courts of law, admissible testimony is considered truthful unless impeached or otherwise rendered doubtful. This is in accord with ordinary life, where only the paranoic goes about with the bias that everyone is lying. The burden, then, is on those who would show that the New Testament testimony to Jesus is not worthy of belief.

In their standard work on the subject, McCloskey and Schoenberg offer a fourfold test for exposing perjury, involving the determination of *internal* and *external* defects in the *witness himself or herself* on the one hand and in the *testimony itself* on the other.[18] Can the New Testament witness to Jesus be impeached by way of these standard criteria?

(1) Internal defects in the witness refer to any personal characteristics or past history tending to show that the witness is inherently untrustworthy, unreliable or undependable. There is no reason whatsoever to conclude that the apostolic witnesses to Jesus were tainted with criminal records or suffered from pathological lying. If anything, their simple literalness and directness is almost painful. Nor do they have any of the characteristics of mythomanes (2 Pet. 1:16-18).

(2) Did the apostolic witnesses suffer from external defects, that is, motives to falsify? Surely no sensible person would argue that they would have lied about Jesus for monetary gain or as a result of societal pressure. After all, they lost the possibility both of worldly wealth and of social acceptability among their Jewish peers because of their commitment to Jesus. But might that very af-

---

[17] N. J. Coulson, "Islamic Law," in *An Introduction to Legal Systems* 67-68 (J. D. M. Derrett ed. 1968). For an expanded treatment of the same subject, see N. J. Coulson, *A History of Islamic Law* 124-27 (1964).
[18] McCloskey and Schoenberg, 5 *Criminal Law Advocacy*, para. 12.01-12.03 (1984).

fection for and attachment to Jesus serve as a motive to falsify? Not when we remember that their Master expressly taught them that lying was of the devil (John 8:44).

(3) Turning to the testimony itself, we ask if the New Testament writings are internally consistent or self-contradictory. Certainly, the four Gospels do not give identical, verbatim accounts of the words or acts of Jesus. But if they did, that fact alone would make them highly suspect, for it would point to collusion. The several accounts are complementary, not contradictory. To use New Testament translator J. B. Phillips' expression, the internal content of the New Testament records has "the ring of truth."

(4) Finally, what about external defects in the testimony itself, i.e., inconsistencies between the New Testament accounts and what we know from archaeology or extra-biblical historical records? Unlike typical sacred literature, myth and fairytale ("once upon a time ..."), the gospel story begins and ends in history (Luke 3:1-3). Modern archaeological research has confirmed again and again the reliability of New Testament geography, chronology and general history.

Thus, no one of the four elements of the McCloskey-Schoenberg construct for attacking perjury allows us to impugn the veracity of the New Testament witnesses to Jesus.

Furthermore, a point well understood by trial lawyers but seldom by laymen needs to be stressed, namely, the extreme difficulty of successful lying in the presence of a cross-examiner. As the late F. F. Bruce declared:

> It was not only friendly eyewitnesses that the early preachers had to reckon with; there were others less well disposed who were also conversant with the main facts of the ministry and death of Jesus. The disciples could not afford to risk inaccuracies (not to speak of wilful manipulation of the facts), which would at once be exposed by those who would be only too glad to do so. On the contrary, one of the strong points in the original apostolic preaching is the confident appeal to the knowledge of the hearers: ... Acts 2:22. Had there been any tendency to depart from the facts in any material respect, the possible presence of hostile witnesses in the audience would have served as a further corrective.[19]

In short, even if the New Testament witnesses to Jesus were the kind of people to engage in deception (which they surely were not), *had* they attempted it, they could not have gotten away with it. Admittedly, they were never put on a literal witness stand, but they concentrated their preaching on synagogue audiences, thus putting their testimony at the mercy of the hostile Jewish religious

---

[19] F. F. Bruce, *The New Testament Documents: Are They Reliable?* 45-46 (5th ed. 1960).

leadership. That audience had the *means, motive* and *opportunity* to expose the apostolic witness as inaccurate and deceptive if it had been such, and the fact that they did not can only be effectively explained on the ground that they *could not.*

Legal standards of evidence, such as have here been applied to the New Testament witnesses to Jesus Christ, must not be ignored by believers or unbelievers: since courts of law exist to decide the most intractable conflicts in society, to jettison legal methodology is to melt the very glue that holds society together.

Simon Greenleaf, the greatest of the 19th century common-law experts in legal evidence, summarises in the following terms:

> Let the [Gospel] witnesses be compared with themselves, with each other, and with surrounding facts and circumstances; and let their testimony be sifted, as if it were given in a court of justice, on the side of the adverse party. … The result, it is confidently believed, will be an undoubting conviction of their integrity, ability, and truth.

It is almost universally agreed that to solve disputes over truth questions in society, factual evidence — not mere sincerity — must carry the day. In the words of the pre-Christian Roman dramatist Plautus,

> *Pluris est oculatus testis unus, quam auriti decem: Qui audiunt, audita dicunt, qui vident, plane sciunt.*
> One eyewitness is worth more than ten purveyors of hearsay;
> Those who only hear about things say what they've heard, but those who see, know the score![20]

Christian faith, alone among the religious claims of history, is able to stand in the dock and be vindicated evidentially.[21] For only Christianity rests its case on the divine life, sacrificial death, and miraculous resurrection of the Incarnate God — events witnessed to by those who had direct contact with them and who in consequence "knew the score" (Acts 1:1-3; 2 Peter 1:16-18). May serious Christian belivers — those concerned to bring the secularists of our day to the Cross of Christ — therefore employ the solid canons of evidence by which this truth can be effectively shown. May we never lose an opportunity to serve as advocate for the One who has Himself promised to plead our cause before His heavenly Father.

---

[20] Plautus, *Truculentus* Act ii, sc. 6, 11.8-9 (our translation).
[21] Cf. C. S. Lewis, *God in the Dock* (W. Hooper ed. 1970).

2. A New Approach to the Apologetic for Christ's Resurrection by way of Wigmore's Juridical Analysis of Evidence

Synopsis

Philosophical and theological arguments for Christ's deity based on his miracles have not always had the convincing force expected of them. As epistemological efforts in general move more and more in a juridical direction, we apply for the first time the most sophisticated of these — Wigmorean analysis — to the central apologetic for the resurrection of Jesus from the dead.

In my books, *Human Rights and Human Dignity* and *Tractatus Logico-Theologicus*,[1] I emphasised the shift on the part of distinguished philosophers such as Mortimer Adler and Stephen Toulmin toward a juridical approach to the solving of epistemological problems. At a recent conference at the Institute of Advanced Legal Studies at the University of London, Professor David Schum of George Mason University, who instructs at the U.S. Joint Military Intelligence College, pointed to the same phenomenon in the field of military strategy: juridical argument, particularly Wigmorean argument construction, is now being employed in the analysis of potential insurgency operations and analogous tactical themes.[2]

The prime reason for the move toward juridical thinking in these fields is the sophistication with which lawyers must deal with evidence questions. Decisions of law can only be made once facts have been established, so lawyers and legal scholars must employ the most effective techniques possible in arriving at factual conclusions on which life or death may depend — and these must be sufficiently persuasive to convince the "triars of fact" (juries and judges) to arrive at just verdicts.

Moreover, the factual decisions to be reached in the courts are seldom of a single-issue character; they generally involve a great number of factual particu-

---

[1] John Warwick Montgomery, *Human Rights and Human Dignity* (2ᵈ ed.; Calgary, Alberta, Canada: Canadian Institute for Law, Theology and Public Policy, 1995), pp. 134-36; *Tractatus Logico-Theologicus* (3ᵈ. ed; Bonn, Germany: Verlag für Kultur und Wissenschaft, 2004), para. 3.126.
[2] "Teaching Evidence and Fact Analysis," 9 June 2006.

lars and the interlacing of numerous sub-arguments. Even Toulmin, who argued so eloquently in his classic, *The Uses of Argument,* for replacing the epistemological models of "psychology, sociology, technology and mathematics" with "the discipline of jurisprudence,"[3] when he produced his highly useful text, *An Introduction to Reasoning,* never went beyond two levels of analysis.[4]

In diametric contrast, John Henry Wigmore (1863-1943), the greatest common-law specialist on the law of evidence after Harvard's Simon Greenleaf,[5] endeavoured to treat what he termed "the ultimate and most difficult aspect of the principles of Proof; namely, the method of solving a complex mass of evidence in contentious litigation."

> Nobody yet seems to have ventured to offer a method. ... The logicians have furnished us in plenty with canons of reasoning for specific single inferences; but for a total mass of contentious evidence, they have offered no system. ...
>
> The problem of collating a mass of evidence, so as to determine the net effect which it should have on one's belief, is an everyday problem in courts of justice. Nevertheless, no one hitherto seems to have published any logical scheme on a scale large enough to aid this purpose.[6]

Wigmore produced what is still the most comprehensive work in the field of legal evidence, his *Evidence in Trials at Common Law*; the 4th edition (1985) runs to eleven volumes,[7] plus a massive 1999 supplementary volume.[8] Even Wigmore's sharpest critic, one Edmund Morgan, called it "the best work ever produced on any comparable division of American Law."[9]

We therefore have every good reason to examine Wigmore's method of proof, and, having done so, to discover its relevance to the question of the facticity of the resurrection of Jesus Christ.

---

[3] Stephen E. Toulmin, *The Uses of Argument* (Cambridge: Cambridge University Press, 1958), p. 7.
[4] Stephen E. Toulmin, Richard Rieke, and Allan Janik, *An Introduction to Reasoning* (New York: Macmillan, 1978). An apparently unchanged "second edition" was issued in 1984 by the same publisher.
[5] See Greenleaf's "Testimony of the Evangelists," reprinted in Montgomery, *The Law Above the Law* (Minneapolis: Bethany, 1975), pp. 91 ff.
[6] John Henry Wigmore, *The Principles of Judicial Proof: As Given by Logic, Psychology, and General Experience, And Illustrated in Judicial Trials* (Boston: Little, Brown, 1913), pp. 3-4, 747.
[7] Published by Little, Brown, with various editors following Wigmore's death.
[8] Published by Aspen Law & Business; edited by Professor Arthur Best.
[9] Quoted by William L. Twining, "Wigmore, John Henry," in A. W. B. Simpson (ed.), *Biographical Dictionary of the Common Law* (London: Butterworths, 1984), p. 533.

Wigmorean Chart Analysis

In his biographical sketch of Wigmore, Professor William Twining comments that Wigmore's *Principles of Judicial Proof* "remains largely forgotten, perhaps because it placed too much emphasis on an ingenious system of analysing masses of evidence through elaborate charts that involved resort to unfamiliar symbols."[10] Yet Twining himself, in his own publications in field of reasoning and legal evidence, has seen the tremendous value of this complex analytical technique and has endeavoured to explain it to the *non cognoscenti*.[11] In the explanations to follow, we rely heavily on Twining's materials, developed largely to present the Wigmorean method to law students unacquainted with it.

One begins with an overall analysis of the problem. Here is Twining's seven-step summary of the methodology:

1. Clarification of standpoint, purpose, and role;
2. Formulation of potential ultimate *probandum* [that which is to be proven] or *probanda* [those things which are to be proven];
3. Formulation of potential penultimate *probanda*;[12]
4. Formulation of theory and themes of the case: choice of strategic ultimate, penultimate, and intermediate *probanda*;[13]
5. Compilation of a key-list;
6. Preparation of the chart(s); and
7. Completion of the analysis.

Twining illustrates by way of a simple criminal case. The *ultimate probandum* is that "X murdered Y," or, stated more formally, that "(A) Y is dead; (B) Y died as a result of an unlawful act; (C) it was X who committed the unlawful act

---

[10] Twining, *op. cit.*, p. 534.
[11] Twining, *Theories of Evidence: Bentham and Wigmore* (London: Weidenfeld & Nicolson, 1985), pp. 125 ff.; *Rethinking Evidence* (2ᵈ ed.; Cambridge: Cambridge University Press, 2006), pp. 426-28 *et passim*; Terence Andreson, David Schum, and William Twining, *Analysis of Evidence* (2ᵈ ed.; Cambridge: Cambridge University Press, 2005), pp. 123-44 *et passim*.
[12] The "penultimate *probanda*" remind one of mathematical philosopher Imre Lakatos' use of the term *proof* for "a thought-experiment—or 'quasi-experiment'—which suggests a decomposition of the original conjecture into subconjectures or lemmas" (Imre Lakatos, *Proofs and Refutations: The Logic of Mathematical Discovery*, ed. John Worrall and Elia Zahar [Cambridge: Cambridge University Press, 1977], pp. 9, 13-14). On Lakatos, see John Worrall's article in the *Concise Routledge Encyclopedia of Philosophy* (London: Routledge, 2000), pp. 449-50.
[13] Step 4 is clearly unique to advocacy and persuasion: choosing the strategy most likely to convince the trier of fact and win the case; it would presumably not figure into a straight investigation of a factual issue.

that caused Y's death; and (D) X intended (i) to commit the act and (ii) thereby to cause Y's death." The coroner's report and observations at the scene satisfy all concerned that "Y died at approximately 4:45 p.m. on 1 January in his house as the result of an unlawful act committed by another." We thus develop a key-list and corresponding chart involving some five testimonial assertions and related inferences that appear relevant to the *penultimate probandum* (C) that "It was X who committed the unlawful act that caused Y's death."

The Key-List

1. X was in Y's house at 4:45 P.M. on January 1.
2. X entered Y's house at 4:30 P.M. on January 1.
3. W_1 saw X enter Y's house at 4:30 P.M. on January 1.
4. W_1: I saw X enter Y's house at 4:30 P.M. on January 1 as I was walking on the sidewalk across the street.
5. X left Y's house at 5:00 P.M. on January 1.
6. W_3 saw X leave Y's house at 5:00 P.M. on January 1.
7. W_3: I saw X leave Y's house at 5:00 P.M. on January 1.
8. X was *not* at Y's house on January 1.
9. X did not enter or leave Y's house on January 1.
10. X: I never went to Y's house on January 1.
11. X was at her office at 4:45 P.M. on January 1.
12. X was working at her office from 9:00 A.M. to 5:00 P.M. on January 1.
13. X: I was working at my office from 9:00 A.M. to 5:00 P.M. on January 1.
14. A claimed eyewitness identification by a pedestrian walking on the other side of the street is doubtful.
15. It may be someone other than X whom W_1 saw enter Y's house.
16. The sun had set before 5:00 P.M. on January 1.
17. A claimed eyewitness identification made after the sun has set is doubtful.
18. It may have been someone other than X whom W_3 saw leave Y's house.
19. W_1 saw X enter Y's house at 4:30 P.M. on January 1.
20. W_2: I saw X enter Y's house at 4:30 P.M. on January 1.
21. X's testimony should not be accepted.
22. X is lying about her actions and whereabouts on January 1.
23. A person accused of a crime has a strong motive to fabricate testimony that might exonerate her.
24. X is the accused in this case.
25. X was probably not in her office on January 1.
26. January 1 is New Year's Day and a legal holiday in this jurisdiction.
27. Few people go to their office and work all day on New Year's Day in this area.

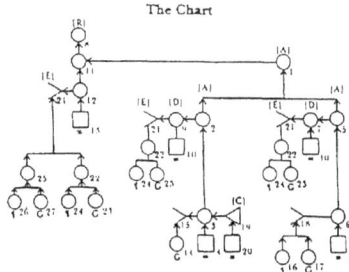

The Chart

A = assertion; E = explanation; R = rival; and D = denial. Note that a defendant becomes a "proponent" of rival and denial assertions, and thus the prosecutor may use the process of "opponent's" explanation to undermine these assertions.

We do not need to go into the details of this illustration. Just a few basic points require clarification.

The chart symbols vary somewhat from one Wigmorean analysis to another. In general, a *circle* represents evidence; more explicitly (and not used in this chart), a *filled-in circle* is used to depict factual, empirical data—what Sherlock Holmes called the "trifles" which are capable ultimately of deciding issues[14]—as contrasted with *unfilled-in circles*, representing circumstantial evidence or mere inferences; a *square* depicts testimonial assertions (it does not have to be used when the entire case is a matter of testimony or conflicting testimony); a *triangle* identifies an argument that corroborates a fact or inference to which it is related; an *open angle* represents an alternative explanation for an argument given by the other side; *arrows* show the direction of an inferential relationship between one fact or fact to be proven and another; and the letter *G* is used for generalisations which are taken (correctly or incorrectly) as not requiring proof because they are accepted as such and would supposedly be received by a tribunal as worthy of judicial notice.

It will be observed that in the illustration one single chart has been used to show both the "prosecution" and the "defense" arguments (thus, for example, items 1 and 8 are mutually contradictory and cannot both be true). A clearer picture and a more effective analysis is usually possible by separating the pro- and the con- streams of argument by the use of separate, parallel charts. Either way, it is vital to chart the strongest arguments both *for* and *against* the ultimate *probandum*.

Here, in an unpublished chart which avoids the use of symbols, Twining separates pro- and con- lines of argumentation, designating the opposition case with the term "infirmative":

---

[14] "You know my method. It is founded upon the observation of trifles" (*The Boscombe Valley Mystery*). "It is, of course, a trifle, but there is nothing so important as trifles" (*The Man with the Twisted Lip*). Cf. John Warwick Montgomery, *The Transcendent Holmes* (Ashcroft, British Columbia, Canada: Calabash Press, 2000), especially pp. 97-139.

A New Approach to the Apologetic ...

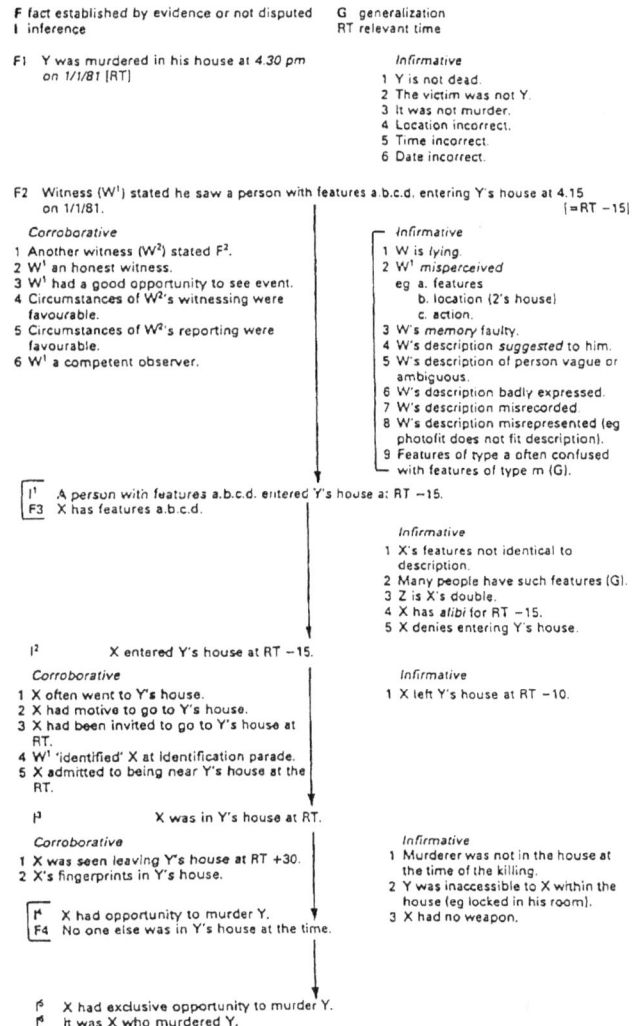

Inference upon inference (source: Twining, unpublished)

F fact established by evidence or not disputed
I inference
G generalization
RT relevant time

F1 Y was murdered in his house at *4.30 pm on 1/1/81* [RT]

Infirmative
1. Y is not dead.
2. The victim was not Y.
3. It was not murder.
4. Location incorrect.
5. Time incorrect.
6. Date incorrect.

F2 Witness (W¹) stated he saw a person with features a.b.c.d. entering Y's house at 4.15 on 1/1/81.   [=RT −15]

Corroborative
1. Another witness (W²) stated F².
2. W¹ an honest witness.
3. W¹ had a good opportunity to see event.
4. Circumstances of W²'s witnessing were favourable.
5. Circumstances of W²'s reporting were favourable.
6. W¹ a competent observer.

Infirmative
1. W is *lying*.
2. W¹ *misperceived*
   eg a. features
      b. location (Z's house)
      c. action.
3. W's *memory* faulty.
4. W's description *suggested* to him.
5. W's description of person vague or ambiguous.
6. W's description badly expressed.
7. W's description misrecorded.
8. W's description misrepresented (eg photofit does not fit description).
9. Features of type a often confused with features of type m (G).

I¹ A person with features a.b.c.d. entered Y's house at RT −15.
F3 X has features a.b.c.d.

Infirmative
1. X's features not identical to description.
2. Many people have such features (G).
3. Z is X's double.
4. X has *alibi* for RT −15.
5. X denies entering Y's house.

I² X entered Y's house at RT −15.

Corroborative
1. X often went to Y's house.
2. X had motive to go to Y's house.
3. X had been invited to go to Y's house at RT.
4. W¹ 'identified' X at identification parade.
5. X admitted to being near Y's house at the RT.

Infirmative
1. X left Y's house at RT −10.

I³ X was in Y's house at RT.

Corroborative
1. X was seen leaving Y's house at RT +30.
2. X's fingerprints in Y's house.

Infirmative
1. Murderer was not in the house at the time of the killing.
2. Y was inaccessible to X within the house (eg locked in his room).
3. X had no weapon.

I⁴ X had opportunity to murder Y.
F4 No one else was in Y's house at the time.

I⁵ X had exclusive opportunity to murder Y.
I⁶ It was X who murdered Y.

Note that the "RT" (relevant time) category would be employed only when the issue in question turned on a matter of chronology.

Application to the Claim That Jesus Christ Was Resurrected

We are now in a position to use the foregoing style of analysis to evaluate the evidence for Christ's resurrection.

Before we do, however, it may be well to observe the desirability of employing this approach rather than the Bayesian probability calculus. Bayes' theorem, in essence, asserts that the probability of an event can be calculated by multiplying posterior odds by prior odds to obtain a likelihood ratio. But as Earman (the secular author of a devastating critique of Hume's argument against the miraculous[15]) observes:

> Attempts to objectify priors run into notorious difficulties. ... The anomalous advance of the perihelion of Mercury was known to astronomers long before Einstein formulated his general theory of relativity. A naïve application of Bayes's theorem would seem to imply that no incremental confirmation takes place, despite the fact that physicists uniformly claim that general relativity receives strong confirmation from the explanation of the perihelion advance.[16]

True, the Bayesian approach has been usefully employed by Richard Swinburne in his book, *The Resurrection of God Incarnate*.[17] But a particular problem with using it in arguing for the resurrection of Christ (or any miracle, for that matter) is the number of prior events which do not have a miraculous character. Wigmore's approach, based solidly in historical and testimonial evidence for events themselves rather than in philosophical speculation or probabilistic calculation involving prior events, bypasses this problem.

In arguing for the resurrection of Christ, our terms are as follow:

Ultimate probandum [UP]: "God raised Jesus from the dead as Saviour of the world."
Penultimate probandum [PP]: "Jesus rose from the dead."

Stated more formally:

---

[15] John Earman, *Hume's Abject Failure: The Argument Against Miracles* (New York: Oxford University Press, 2000).
[16] John Earman, "Bayesianism," *The Encyclopedia of Philosophy Supplement*, ed. Donald M. Borchert (New York: Macmillan Reference, 1996), p. 52. Cf. Earman's book-length treatment of the problem: *Bayes or Bust? A Critical Examination of Bayesian Confirmation Theory* (Cambridge, Mass.: MIT Press, 1992).
[17] Richard Swinburne, *The Resurrection of God Incarnate* (Oxford: Clarendon Press, 2003), especially pp. 206 ff. I have cited Swinburne's conclusions positively in my *Tractatus Logico-Theologicus* (*op.cit.*), para. 3.8732.

[PP(A)]: "Jesus died on the Cross."

[PP(B)]: "On and after the first Easter morning, Jesus was physically alive."

[PP(C)]: "Jesus' transition from death to life occurred miraculously—without third-party human agency."

The Positive Key-list:

1. All events related to Christ's death and resurrection were reported by eyewitnesses or associates of eyewitnesses.
2. Jesus is said by these witnesses to have been born miraculously and performed numerous impressive miracles, including the raising of Lazarus, during his public ministry.
3. On several occasions, Jesus predicted his resurrection.
4. Jesus was tried publicly by Jewish and by Roman leaders, given a death sentence, and executed by crucifixion.
5. On the cross, a sword was driven into his side to assure the soldiers in charge that he was indeed dead.
6. Jesus' crucifixion occurred publicly in Jerusalem at the high season of the Jewish religious year.
7. Jesus' body was then placed in a well-known tomb belonging to a prominent Jewish religious personality.
8. Efforts were made by the Jewish religious leaders to prevent a stealing of Jesus' body and to surpress any rumours of resurrection.
9. On the first Easter morning, Jesus' disciples encountered a Jesus who was alive.
10. Jesus appearsed subsequently to his followers over a 40-day period, followed by his public ascension into heaven.
11. Jesus' disciples did not believe that he would rise prior to the event having occurred—as evidenced, for example, by "doubting Thomas."
12. Jesus' resurrection appearances were physical in nature (Jesus eating fish, Thomas able to touch wounds in Jesus' hands and side).
13. Paul testified to having seen and spoken to the risen Christ on the Damascus road.
14. Paul provided a list of named witnesses to the risen Christ and claimed that over 500 were still alive to testify to it in A.D. 56 (1 Cor. 15)—as well as claiming when on trial before the Roman governor that Christ's death and resurrection were "not done in a corner" (Acts 26:26).
15. Absence of motive to steal Jesus' body on the part of the Romans or the Jewish religious leaders, and every reason on their part not to do so.

16. Irrationalism of any argument that Jesus' disciples or followers would have stolen his body and then claimed he rose from the dead—thus inviting persecution and death.
17. Irrationality of any unnamed third parties stealing the body or inventing such a story.
18. No contemporary refutations or attempted refutations of the fact of the resurrection by those with means, motive, and opportunity to do so.
19. Explanations of the event other than that by Jesus and the firsthand witnesses have no cogency and should be rejected.
20. Jesus claimed to be God incarnate, raised up by his Father, and the unique Saviour through his death and resurrection.

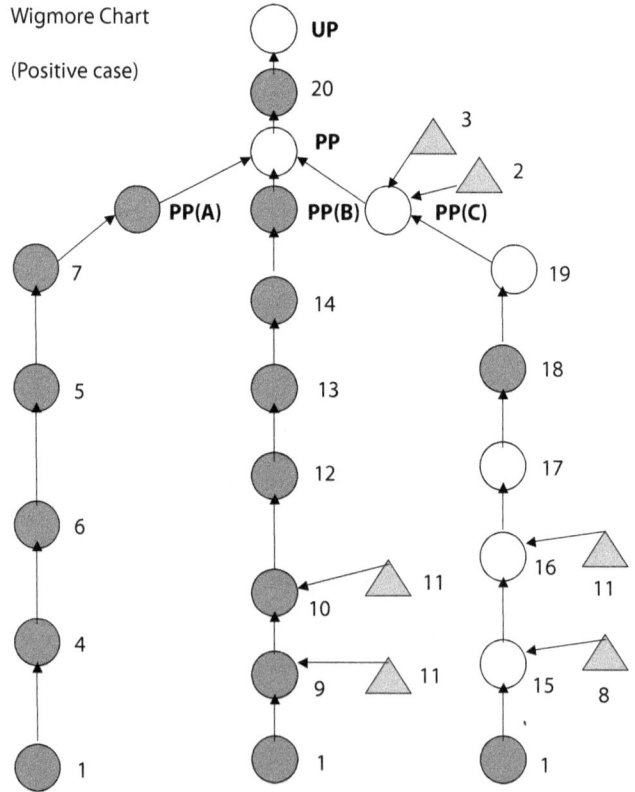

Note: In the positive Chart (above), red filled-in circles (facts) and white unfilled-in circles (circumstantial evidence or inferences) need to be distinguished, and it is important also to observe the difference between the circles and the pink triangles (=corroborations).

The Negative Key-list (based on Twining analysis):

F Fact established by evidence
I Inference

                                  Infirmative

F-1 [PP(A)]   1. He did not die on the cross (**2**)
Jesus died   2. Victim was someone else (**3**)
on the cross   3. He died later under other circumstances (**4**)
                        4. One cannot trust the documents/witnesses (**1**)

F-2 [PP(B)]   1. Disciples mistook someone else for Jesus (**5**)
On and after the first   2. Disciples had a mystical vision (**6**)
Easter morning, Jesus   3. Disciples suffered from a collective
was physically alive   hallucination (**7**)
                               4. Disciples stole the body (**8**)
                        5. Unnamed persons stole the body (**9**)
                               6. Jesus rose "spiritually" but not physically (**10**)
                               7. One cannot trust the documents/witnesses (**1**)

I-1 [PP(C)]   1. Miracles simply do not happen: people who
Jesus' transition from   die stay dead (**11**)
death to life occurred   2. To prove an extraordinary event, you would
miraculously – without   need extraordinary evidence – which we
third-party human   don't have (**12**)
agency   3. Any natural explanation is preferable to a
↑   supernatural, miraculous explanation (**13**)
                               4. One cannot trust the documents/witnesses (**1**)

I-2 [UP]   1. Jesus was lying or lacking in
God raised Jesus from   self-knowledge/knowledge of the true
the dead as Saviour of   explanation of his resurrection (**14**)[18]
the world   2. One cannot logically move from a miracle –
                               even a resurrection – to divine truth; cf. Lessing's
                               ditch & the naturalistic fallacy (**15**)
                               3. One cannot trust the documents/witnesses (**1**)

192   Part Four – Legal Evidence, Resurrection and Human Rights

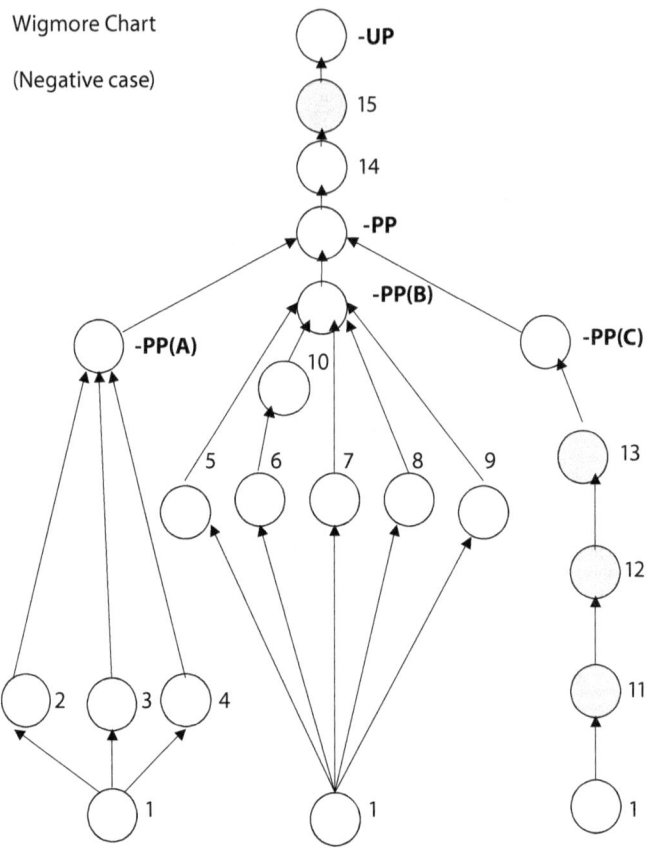

Note: In the Chart of the negative case (above), numbers correspond to the *italicised* figures in parentheses which appear at the end of each **Infirmative** in the corresponding Key-list. Yellow filled-in circles represent generalisations (*G*) — items which the proponent assumes to be universally accepted without requiring proof.

Conclusion: What This Evidential Approach Reveals

It would be inappropriate here to present the data underlying each of the items in the Key-lists. Such data can readily be obtained elsewhere, and I myself have devoted a fair number of my writings to this very purpose.[19] What we wish to do instead is note how the Wigmorean method assists in revealing the core issues at stake in reaching a proper decision on a vital factual issue—here, the central epistemological question of Jesus' resurrection and divine claims.

First, as we compare the negative with the positive Key-lists by way of the Charts, we observe that the objector to the facticity of the resurrection relies entirely, not on factual data, but on conjecture, inference, and supposed universal generalisations. This in itself places the negative case in the worst possible light.

Secondly, it is plain that in the final analysis the issue of the truth of the resurrection and of Christ's claims depends squarely on the reliability of the New Testament records—not on philosophical, presuppositional, or sociological argument. It follows that the apologetic task is best carried on in an evidential context, and that any and all dehistoricising and higher critical dismembering of the New Testament documents must be shown as erroneous methodologically—as bad scholarship—rather than being somehow baptised as theologically legitimate.

Finally, the Wigmorean approach keeps the resurrection question focused on those considerations which are truly determinative: a genuine death, a subsequent living, physical presence, the absence of human third-party agency, and the Subject's (Christ's own) explanation as to the Divine source of this miraculous event—an event on which depended nothing less than the salvation of the human race.

---

[18] It is worth stressing that (1) he who rises from the dead is in a far better position to explain how this happened than are those who have not (cf. Montgomery, *Tractatus Logico-Teologicus* [*op. cit.*], para. 3.72-3.7321), and (2) Jesus' factual claim can be accepted without prior proof of God's existence—*pace* Norman Geisler, R. C. Sproul, William Lane Craig and the so-called "classical" apologists (see Gary R. Habermas, *The Risen Jesus & Future Hope* (Lanham, Maryland: Rowman & Littlefield, 2003), especially chaps 2-3; also Habermas's contribution to *Five Views on Apologetics*, ed. Steven B. Cowan (Grand Rapids, Michigan: Zondervan, 2000), pp. 91 ff.).

[19] Montgomery, *Tractatus Logico-Theologicus* (*op. cit.*); *Human Rights and Human Dignity* (*op. cit.*); *The Law Above the Law* (*op. cit.*); *History, Law and Christianity* (Calgary, Alberta, Canada: Canadian Institute for Law, Theology and Public Policy, 2002); *Faith Founded on Fact* (Nashville: Thomas Nelson, 1978); etc., etc.

3. The Need for Epistemological Sophistication in Human Rights Teaching[1]

I. Setting the Stage

A proliferation of textbooks and practitioners' manuals have appeared since the Human Rights Act entered into force. These focus almost exclusively on substantive law, procedure, and technique. Almost never is there a discussion of the justification of human rights principles in general or of the contents of the Act in particular. Remarkably, even when the director of Liberty, the prominent British activist organisation, did such a book, it contained not a word on the foundations of the human rights discussed.[2] Older teaching materials in the field quite generally treat foundational principles,[3] but the trend seems clearly away from such an approach.

This shift away from the "theoretical" to the "practical" may be observed throughout the legal education sphere; it is by no means limited to the teaching of human rights. The Association of Law Teachers is overwhelmingly concerned with "skills"—as if law were essentially a trade rather than a learned profession. We can understand, in light of university funding problems (which seem to increase in seriousness every year), that recruiters want to demonstrate to potential applicants that a university education is worth the time and the money; but such a perspective is highly dangerous in the long run. For it suggests that the point of a legal education (or university education in general) is to earn money, whereas that should be a by-product of professional service by a truly educated, cultured graduate.

And professional service requires a sharp distinction between *education* and *training*. The latter (like television repair) requires only cookbook knowledge of techniques; the former (like engineering) requires a far broader knowledge base and the ability to think critically in new situations.

To a certain extent, what we face here is an attitudinal problem. At a law faculty where I once taught, the head of the department, who taught contract law, once said to me that not only did he know nothing about the history of contract, he didn't care in the least about it: his function was to teach students how to handle current contract litigation. At the same institution, the teacher

---

[1] An invitational presentation at the conference on Global Challenges for Legal Education and Human Rights Teaching, University of Warwick, 8 March 2003.
[2] John Wadham and Helen Mountfield, *The Human Rights Act 1998* (London: Blackstone, 1999).
[3] E.g., Julian R. Friedman and Laurie S. Wiseberg, *Teaching Human Rights* (Washington, D.C.: Human Rights Internet, 1981).

of human rights declared that he found all philosophical discussion of rights questions incomprehensible: the issue was simply how to learn to apply existing human rights protections.

At this point, it might be well to ponder Socrates' axiom, "The unexamined life is not worth living." Or to reflect on an exchange between C. S. Lewis and a critic at a library conference:

> Mr. L. M. Bickerton (Worthing) considered that Dr. Lewis's paper had raised points that we as librarians must consider—our policy had been to provide more and more of the practical type of book written by authors like Ransome and De Sellincourt that taught children how to handle boats, etc., but he wondered what practical use fantasy, such as Dr. Lewis advocated, could have for the child. Dr. Lewis agreed that practical things were first class, but that although fantasy might not help a boy to build a boat, it would help him immensely should he ever find himself on a sinking boat.[4]

It is the contention of this paper that law teaching in general, and instruction in the international and comparative law of human rights in particular, must deal not just with the *what* and the *how,* but also and especially with the *why.* A proper university education never stops with the *descriptive*; it always confronts the *normative* as well. We need to deal with fundamentals and to teach the student how to engage in critical thinking about those fundamentals.

In this essay, we shall illustrate this pedagogical philosophy by taking up the most common theoretical justifications of human rights and suggest the kinds of critical questions to which the student (and the practitioner) should be directed in reference to those theories.

II. Major Human Rights Theories and the Questions To Raise About Them

There are at least six major approaches to the justification of human rights on the scene today, and any responsible instruction in the field will introduce the student to them. They are: legal positivism or realism; natural law theory ("jusnaturalism"); Marxism; neo-Kantian ethical theory; postmodernism and constructivism; and transcendental/religious human rights theories.[5]

---

[4] C. S. Lewis, "On Three Ways of Writing for Children," *Library Association. Proceedings, Papers and Summaries of Discussions at the Bournemouth Conference 29 April to 2nd May 1952* (London: Library Association, 1952), p. 28 ("Discussion"). Cf. Montgomery, *Myth, Allegory and Gospel* (Minneapolis: Bethany, 1974), pp. 115-16.
[5] This is obviously not an exclusive list; we could also have included, for example, feminist human rights theory. But our central point as to the necessity of raising hard questions should be sufficiently illustrated by way of the theories we have chosen to treat.

A. Legal Positivism/Realism.

Even at the present day, the most commonly accepted theory of human rights on the English scene is one form or another of 19th legal positivism (or "realism" as is it usually denominated on the European continent). The classic statement of this approach, as formulated by John Austin, with considerable help from utilitarian philosopher Jeremy Bentham, is that law is but a species of command: the only true rights are the rights given by the positive law of the state or by treaties among nations. Law and rights stem from the sovereign's commands and from that source alone; they are self-justifying and must not be evaluated from the standpoint of any external value-system. Understandably, such a viewpoint encourages legal instruction which focuses almost solely on substantive law and procedure and excludes serious discussion of foundational issues.[6]

In the 20th century, the most renowned advocate of classical positivism was the Austrian jurisprudent Hans Kelsen. He maintained that each legal system is unique and logically uncriticisable from the outside or from the standpoint of any other legal system. A legal system (*Stufenbau*) will necessarily have a fundamental root principle grounding it (the *Grundnorm*) and one cannot subject that basic norm to any higher standard. In Kelsen's own words: "The search for the reason of a norm's validity cannot go on indefinitely like the search for the cause of an effect. It must end with a norm which, as the last and highest, is presupposed."[7] Law thus constitutes a "coercive order" and is—literally—a law unto itself. The "first cause" is not a transcendent God but rather a necessitarian ultimate norm of the human legal system.

When this classic theory is presented, students need to face such critical questions as these: Since there are numerous sovereign powers and "coercive orders" (not just ours), with laws and formulations of rights which contradict each other, how can we determine if any are deserving of acceptance? Surely, the fact that—say—a cannibal legal system formulates "the right to eat one's neighbour" does not justify including that right in a proper catalogue of human rights? But, if not, is positivism logically capable of offering any kind of solid basis for human rights?

Influential refinements of positivist legal and human rights theory have been attempted by H. L. A. Hart and by his successor at Oxford, Ronald Dworkin. Hart saw that the Austinian notion of all law being direct commands

---

[6] For primary and secondary source references on the human rights theories discussed in this paper, see Montgomery, *Human Rights and Human Dignity* (3d printing; Calgary, Alberta, Canada: Canadian Institute [http://www.ciltpp.com], 1995), pp. 82 ff.

[7] Hans Kelsen, *The Pure Theory of Law*, trans. Max Knight (Berkeley: University of California Press, 1970), p. 194. Cf. Montgomery, *The Law Above the Law* (Minneapolis: Bethany, 1975), pp. 32 ff.

was much too simplistic. Many genuine laws (as in the constitutional, "bill of rights" realm) do not function that way at all. He therefore maintained that not only is there a direct application of law by way of what he calls "primary rules," but also there are "secondary rules" which determine ultimately what goes into the system and whether and how the system can be changed. Hart identified three kinds of "secondary rules": the rule of change; the rule of adjudication; and—most important—the rule of recognition, by which decisions are made as to what is and what is not a true part of the legal system. But these secondary rules, like the primary rules, cannot be criticised from without. One can critique the lesser rules in the system for their lack of conformity with the rule of recognition, but since each legal system exists *sui generis*, there is no way to question the system's rule of recognition itself. To use Hart's own analogy, it is like the standard metre bar in Paris by which all metre sticks are measured: there is no sense in asking if *it itself* is of the right length.

> We only need the word 'validity', and commonly only use it, to answer questions which arise within a system of rules where the status of a rule as a member of the system depends on its satisfying certain criteria provided by the rule of recognition. No such question can arise as to the validity of the very rule of recognition which provides the criteria; it can neither be valid nor invalid but is simply accepted as appropriate for use in this way. To express this simple fact by saying darkly that its validity is "assumed but cannot be demonstrated," is like saying that we assume, but can never demonstrate, that the standard metre bar in Paris which is the ultimate test of the correctness of all measurements in metres, is itself correct[8]

Students need to reflect as to whether Hart's refinement of classical legal positivism really achieves anything in the realm of human rights theory. Cannot exactly the questions posed above to the Austinian be asked of advocates of Hart's position? Human rights law is closely analogous to constitutional law, and if the validity of the "secondary rules" is as arbitrary as the length of the metre bar, how can they be accepted as an inalienable standard of human conduct and deserve universal protection?

Dworkin takes Hart's positivism a step further. He says: to understand a legal system, you cannot even stop with *rules*; you must go on from rules, primary and secondary, to *principles*. Rules, he notes, are all-or-nothing, whereas the principles behind the rules "incline" toward particular legal results. Illus-

---

[8] H. L. A. Hart, *The Concept of Law* (Oxford: Clarendon Press, 1961), pp. 105-106. A 2^d ed. was published in 1997; this second edition is particularly valuable as it combines Hart's original text with a postscript, in which he responds to criticisms of his theory levelled by such notable scholars as Dworkin, Fuller, and Finnis. Written by him but only discovered after his death, it has been edited by Joseph Raz and Penelope Bulloch of Balliol College, Oxford.

tration: the legal principle that no-one must profit from his or her own wrong. That is *not* all-or-nothing. Why? Because of the rule of adverse possession (often wryly called "legal theft")—the rule that says that if you can occupy in an open, uninterrupted, and hostile manner for a sufficient length of time a particular piece of land under the conditions the common law sets forth, you may obtain the legal title or interest to it. In such an instance, you will profit from your own wrong. So, behind the rule there lie general principles, inclining to but not forcing particular legal consequences. And where do these fundamental principles come from? Here, Dworkin introduces the ideal judge—a kind of Platonic philosopher-king in judicial garb. Judge Hercules develops the needed principles in the course of his judicial activity.

> You will now see why I call our judge Hercules. He must construct a scheme of abstract and concrete principles that provides a coherent justification for all common law precedents and, so far as these are to be justified on principle, constitutional and statutory provisions as well.[9]

How does the godlike Hercules find these essential principles?

> We could not devise any formula for testing how much and what kind of institutional support is necessary to make a principle a legal principle, still less to fix its weight at a particular order of magnitude. We argue for a particular principle by grappling with a whole set of shifting, developing and interacting standards (themselves principles rather than rules) about institutional responsibility, statutory interpretation, the persuasive force of various sorts of precedent, the relation of all these to contemporary moral practices, and hosts of other such standards.[10]

Here, the student of human rights must ask herself: How can such vague "principles" possibly be justified? How could they be distinguished from mere sociological products of the culture in which the legal system operates—the *vox populi* (which, last we heard, is not synonymous with the *vox Dei*)? And, in general, where multiple sources of principles are in the picture, what is to be done when one source conflicts with others ("precedent" *versus* "contemporary moral practices," etc., etc.)? Examples such as that of the Nazi legal system need to be introduced, and the student asked to determine whether, in fact, one could argue that the "principles" of that system were entirely justified by the general sociological milieu in which they arose; and—if so—what does that say as to positivistic legal and human rights theory even in its most refined form? The student should also be expected to reflect on whether any kind of positivist jurisprudence is capable of sustaining such international human

---

[9] Ronald Dworkin, *Taking Rights Seriously* (London: Duckworth, 1977), pp. 116-17.
[10] *Ibid.*, pp. 40-41.

rights tribunals as that at Nuremberg—where the defendants argued that they had done no more than implement the rules and principles which followed from the *Grundnorm* of National Socialist legality.

B. Jusnaturalism

Until the appearance of positivism in the 19th century, the prevailing philosophy of law and rights in the Western world was so-called "natural-law" theory. Originating with the Greeks in classical times (Aristotle; the Stoics), it profoundly influenced the Roman world (Cicero; Seneca) and was baptised by the great theologians of medieval Christendom (Augustine; Thomas Aquinas). The essence of the Greco-Roman position was that the human race benefits from natural, built-in standards of justice and human laws need to conform to them. Cicero put it thus:

> I find that it has been the opinion of the wisest men that Law is not a product of human thought, nor is it any enactment of peoples, but something eternal which rules the whole universe by its wisdom in command and prohibition.[11]

Aquinas defined true law as "an ordinance of reason for the common good"[12]—meaning that even if a law were jurisdictionally justified (passed by the appropriate law-making body or the result of proper judicial decision-making) it would not constitute genuine law if it violated our built-in understanding of reasonableness or was contrary to the good of the community.

The 18th century theoreticians of the French and American revolutions were deeply influenced by such natural-law thinking. It directly impacted the French Declaration of the Rights of Man and the American founding documents such as the Declaration of Independence, which sees the source of civil liberties in "Nature and Nature's God," as well as the American Bill of Rights (the first ten Amendments to the Federal Constitution). By the end of the 19th century, under the influence of growing secularism, natural-law theory became entirely anthropocentric: mankind was supposed to manifest, on an entirely naturalistic basis, the ethical principles—or the ability to arrive at such—which could serve as an adequate criterion for judging positive law and existing legal systems and ground a solid understanding of human ("natural") rights.

At the present time, the most distinguished advocate of jusnaturalism is doubtless John Finnis of Oxford. Following Aquinas, he attempts to show that "practical reasonableness" in ordering human affairs requires an approach to the state, law, and human rights that will preserve and extend universal hu-

---

[11] Marcus Tullius Cicero, *De legibus*, Bk. 2, chap. 4.
[12] Thomas Aquinas, *Summa Theologica*, Bks. I-II, QQ 90-97.

man goods (defined as life, knowledge, play, aesthetic experience, friendship or sociability, religion, etc.). "There are human goods," he declares, "that can be secured only through the institutions of human law, and requirements of practical reasonableness that only those institutions can satisfy."[13]

> What Finnis is trying to show is how any common enterprise of human beings aims at achieving a common good, and hence demands something which can only be called political or governmental authority. Nor is the function of such authority to be understood exclusively, or even primarily, in terms of any mere exercise of coercive force. No, it is rather for the necessary and indispensable coordination of the efforts of the different agents of the community that the authority is instituted in the first place; and it is only through the exercise of such a directing and coordinating authority that the common good of the community can even be concretely determined, much less achieved. And as for law—human law or positive law—it is nothing if not the indispensable instrument of such a public or governmental authority, aimed at the attainment of the good of the community. Moreover, since the good of the community is not literally collective good, or even an additive good but simply the well-being of each and all of the members of the community individually, the law needs to be so constituted as to respect the rights of the individual members of the community. And here again, in his discussion of the rights, i.e. the natural rights, of citizens, Finnis is very careful to construe such rights—e.g. common law rights, such as the right to property, to a fair trial, to protection against self-incrimination, to safeguards against viol—not as absolute rights, in the way in which this term is so often understood now-days, but rather as rights that are justified in terms of the natural needs and requirements of the individual, if he is ever to be able to live the life of a truly moral and autonomous human person.[14]

The student needs to analyse most carefully the inherent difficulties with natural law thinking. She must not rush to accept this approach simply because positivism fails as an adequate justification of human rights. Here are several of the key questions requiring answers if one is to accept jusnaturalism as the solution to the human rights dilemma: (1) Modern anthropology has shown the tremendous diversity of standards, ethical norms, and moral practices in the world's cultures; how, then, is it possible to sustain the idea of common human "conscience" adequate to judge positive legislation and provide an agreed picture of "practical reasonableness" for defining human rights? (2) Moreover, even supposing that such a common standard could be demonstrated, would that make it right? In 1903, English philosopher G. E. Moore identified as the

---

[13] John Finnis, *Natural Law and Natural Rights* (Oxford: Clarendon Press, 1980), p. 3.
[14] Henry B. Veatch, Review of *Natural Law and Natural Rights* by John Finnis, 26 *American Journal of Jurisprudence* 253 (1981).

"naturalistic fallacy" the assumption that an "is" (here, common ethical beliefs) can be regarded *ipso facto* as the equivalent of an "ought" (here, proper natural laws and human rights principles). (3) Must one not agree that Finnis "is better at showing how law needs to be grounded in ethics than he is at showing how the principles of ethics are discoverable right in the very facts of nature and reality"[15]? (4) What assistance can natural law theory offer to the day-to-day work of the legislator, judge, or human rights advocate when it defines true law in such vague, formal and general terms as "the art of what is good and equitable" (Celsus) or "the abstract expression of the general will existing in and for itself" (Hegel) or "the organic whole of the external conditions of the intellectual life" (Krause)?[16] (5) Indeed, cannot the very formality and vagueness of natural law principles serve the very opposite purpose—that of condoning human rights violations? Is it not disquieting that one of the key elements in the Justinian Code's classic definition of the natural law ("Give to each his own/ what he deserves") was inscribed in German translation (*"Jedem das Seine"*) on the metal doors leading into the Buchenwald death camp?[17]

C. Marxist Human Rights Theory

Though with the fall of the Iron Curtain and the disappearance of the U.S.S.R. Marxism's official influence has been reduced considerably (leaving only China, Cuba, and a few small third-world countries as nations committed to it), the Marxist political philosophy has had remarkable impact in the modern world, and its human rights theory has been one of the dominant viewpoints in the preceding half century.

The Marxist view of human rights entails commitment to the following basic doctrines:[18] (1) human rights depend on social and economic factors, (2) private property is per se detrimental to human rights, (3) the state creates whatever human rights in fact exist, (4) international organisations, governments, and individual interest groups have no business interfering in the domestic affairs of a state on the pretense of correcting alleged human rights violations (the "noninterference principle"), (5) the individual is not a proper subject of international law or international human rights protection.

---

[15] *Ibid.*, p. 250.
[16] Cf. John Chipman Gray, *The Nature and the Sources of the Law*, ed. Roland Gray (2⁴ ed.; Boston: Beacon Press, 1963), pp. 88-89, 96-99.
[17] Personal observation of the author. The tripartite definition of the natural law appears in the *Digest*: *"Honeste vivere, neminem laedere, suum cuique tribuere."*
[18] For my detailed treatment of the Marxist conception of human rights, see Montgomery, "The Marxist Approach to Human Rights: Analysis & Critique," 3 *Simon Greenleaf Law Review* (1983-1984), whole number.

These principles, to be sure, do not arise out of nothing. They derive from the monolithic, architectonic Marxist worldview, characterised by a materialistic metaphysic, the materialistic-economic reinterpretation of Hegel's dialectic, an ethic of the end justifying the means, and an apocalyptic view of history in which class struggle will inevitably pass through the phase of a temporary dictatorship of the proletariat to a classless society in which both the state and law will have withered away, being no longer necessary.

Students must think critically both about the Marxist human rights principles themselves and concerning the presuppositions which underlie those principles. Indeed, this is an ideal opportunity to teach the student that it is never enough simply to raise questions about the derivative practices of a worldview; one must always penetrate to the (often unstated) assumptions of the system to determine its validity or invalidity. In this instance, the student should ask herself: How would one demonstrate that material (and especially economic) factors are *always* determinative—that law and human rights are a mere "superstructural" build upon the "base" of economic materialism? If the real source of all violations of human dignity must be sought externally in bad economic conditions and not in man himself, how did these conditions arise in the first place? Is a classless society in fact possible? Can the manipulation of socio-economic conditions actually change human nature? What are the consequences for a legal system if the end is allowed to justify the means? If law and human rights are mere instruments for the achieving of ultimate societal goals, can any human rights be inviolate? What are the consequences of exempting governments from criticism for human rights violations on the basis of "national sovereignty" and the "noninterference principle"? What happens if individuals, not being the subjects of international law, have no standing to bring governments to task before international human rights tribunals?

The posing of such issues is a far cry from the typical law school exercise in construing existing case and statute law; but such a pedagogical approach is absolutely vital if we expect our students to analyse human rights issues in a mature way.

D. Neo-Kantian Approaches

Faced by the problems in positivism, traditional natural law thinking, and revolutionary Marxism, influential Western thinkers are endeavouring to justify human rights by going back to the rationalistic ethic of the 18th century German Enlightenment philosopher Immanuel Kant. In political philosophy, this is the approach of the late John Rawls; in legal philosophy Alan Gewirth represents this orientation.

For Rawls, employing the model of the 17th-18th century contract theorists (Hobbes, Locke, Rousseau), human beings, if placed under a "veil of ignorance" as to their special advantages, will, by rationalistic necessity, arrive at his two fundamental Principles of Justice (embracing civil and social rights) and thus establish a rationally-sound political and legal order.[19] In Gewirth's case, this same result is supposedly achieved by a modern argument paralleling Kant's assertion of his Categorical Imperative ("act only on that maxim which you can will to be a universal law"): human beings, as purposive agents, require freedom and well-being to function, so they must rationally concede such freedom and well-being (i.e., fundamental civil and social rights) to others as well. Result: a just legal and political order and a rationally sound justification of human rights.[20]

Gewirth's position offers the opportunity for students to engage in serious logical analysis, for he formulates his human rights argument syllogistically:

(1) Human beings always act purposively.

(2) To act purposively, human beings must have freedom (embracing civil and political rights) and well-being (entailing social and economic rights).

(3) They must therefore object to the removal of or the interference with their freedom and well-being by others.

(4) The ground of one's freedom and well-being is the mere fact that one is a "prospective personal agent"; that ground does not lie in any special strengths or characteristics one may possess.

(5) *Ergo, all* prospective personal agents have rights to freedom and well-being; and

(6) One ought to act in accord with the generic rights of one's recipients as well as of oneself—thereby establishing the general moral principle:

(7) Act in accord with the generic rights of your recipients as well as of yourself.

In dealing with such an argument, the student needs to ask, for example in respect to point (4), whether human rights abuses do not *generally* result from

---

[19] John Rawls, *A Theory of Justice* (Oxford: Oxford University Press, 1972); *Political Liberalism* (New York: Columbia University Press, 1993); "The Law of Peoples," in *On Human Rights: The Oxford Amnesty Lectures 1993*, ed. Stephen Schute and Susan Hurley (New York: HarperCollins BasicBooks, 1993), pp. 41-82, 220-30; "Reply to Habermas," 92/3 *Journal of Philosophy* 132-80 (March 1995).

[20] Alan Gewirth, *The Community of Rights* (Chicago: University of Chicago Press, 1996), especially pp. 16-20; *Gewirth's Ethical Rationalism*, ed. Edward Regis Jr. (Chicago: University of Chicago Press, 1984); Deryck Beyleveld, *The Dialectical Necessity of Morality* (Chicago: University of Chicago Press, 1991).

the fact that the violator maintains that her special position, not any notion of common humanity, justifies the action performed. From here, one moves inevitably to such foundational issues as whether, à la Rawls's contract theory, it is realistic to expect human beings to disregard the knowledge of their own special characteristics and so commence treating others with equal respect; and whether, à la Kant, one can realistically expect people in general to accept ethical universalisation when it works to their personal or national disadvantage.

It is often helpful to present a trenchant critical comment on the human rights theory under discussion, asking the students to react to it with specific reasons for agreement or disagreement. Thus, in regard to Rawls's approach, one might quote critic Robert Paul Wolff: "Even if Rawls's theorem can be established, the self-interested moral skeptic may still decline to make a once-and-for-all commitment, even to a principle chosen from self-interest. Fidelity to principle is not, after all, deducible from bare formal rationality."[21]

The use of hypothetical situations (cf. the employment of hypothetical questions in advocacy) can also be an exceedingly useful tool in the analysis of attempts to justify human rights. For example, in regard to the entire range of neo-Kantian positions, one can ask the student to consider the case of "Ghengis Khan": Would Ghengis (as representative of history's tyrants and human rights violators) be persuaded by the Categorical Imperative to stop raping and pillaging when presented with the rational argument that he and others are equal members of a common humanity and thus deserve equal concern and respect?

E. Postmodern and Constructivist Justifications

The most recent effort at providing a theoretical basis for human rights arises out of contemporary postmodernist thinking and has close affinities with the Critical Legal Studies movement (Roberto Unger, Duncan Kennedy). Here is a typical statement of it from the pen of philosopher Morton E. Winston:

> The attempt to ground the doctrine of human rights on a universal conception of human nature or or to provide an objective basis, purportedly outside of the stream of history, is a sham and an illusion, and reflects the attempt to endow the doctrine with an authority and universality which it does not and cannot possess. Since it is impossible to escape one's own historical vantage point, one's own ethnicity, gender, and class, any attempt to reaffirm the universality of rights by claiming them to be universal moral truths is only a tired repetition of the same old European cultural arrogance that brought the world colonialism, imperialism, and the ongoing domination by the

---

[21] Robert Paul Wolff, *Understanding Rawls* (Princeton, N.J.: Princeton University Press, 1977), p. 20.

North of the South. The basic standpoint of the postmodern conception of rights, that human rights are socially-created, historically-evolved, cultural entities is the view that will be defended here. ... The doctrine of human rights is not just a set of arbitrary, culturally-relative conventions; rather it is a normative *theory* of the organization of social relations in human societies. The ideas of human dignity, equality, and freedom, and the notions of rights and correlative responsibilities which the theory proposes are theoretical constructs, and the standards and norms embodied in human rights declarations, treaties and covenants are particular hypotheses concerning preferred ways in which to construct humane and decent governments and vibrant and creative civil societies.[22]

To which the student should pose such questions as: Why *this* "theory" or "construct" rather than another (such as those previously discussed)? How can any postmodern theory *not* be "arbitrary" if it necessarily reflects the particular social and cultural stance of the formulator of the theory? Why *this* postmodern "story" of human rights rather than, say, the Nazi or Marxist "stories"? Could universal tribunals of human rights ever function adequately on such a basis?

Closely related to the postmodern approach is the so-called "constructivist" theory of human rights. Here is Jack Donnelly's formulation of it:

> I shall argue that the source of human rights is man's *moral* nature, which is only loosely linked to the 'human nature' of basic human needs. ... Human rights are not 'given' to man by God, nature, or the physical facts of life; to think of them in such terms is to remain tied to a vision of human rights as things. Like other social practices, human rights arise from human action. Human rights represent the choice of a particular moral vision of human potentiality and the institutions for realising that vision.[23]

But why, the student must ask, should we "construct" human rights in this fashion rather than in other ways? Why this "moral vision" rather than another? Is not "human potentiality" quite diverse—with potential for savagery as well as potential for civilised development? Why is the latter preferable to the former? Do not both postmodernism and constructivism essentially beg the question, namely, *which* rights should be properly classified as genuine human rights?

The student needs to react to such criticisms of postmodernism and constructivism as offered by law professor Michael J. Perry:

---

[22] Morton E. Winston, "Philosophical Conceptions of Human Rights," *Summary of Lectures, July 5-9, 1993* (Strasbourg, France: International Institute of Human Rights, 1993), pp. 22-23.
[23] Jack Donnelly, *The Concept of Human Rights* (London: Croom Helm, 1985), p. 31.

1. "No culture is better than any other. (Therefore, no culture is worse than any other.) Every culture is as good as every other." From *what* or *whose* evaluative standpoint—on the basis of what or whose norms or criteria—is every culture supposed to be as good as every other? Yours? Mine? Theirs? God's? From any particular evaluative standpoint, every culture is obviously not as good as every other. ...
2. "No evaluative standpoint is better than any other. In particular, the evaluative standpoint of no culture is better than that of any other. Every evaluative standpoint is as good as every other." Same problem: From *what* or *whose* evaluative standpoint is every evaluative standpoint supposed to be as good as every other? From any particular evaluative standpoint, every evaluative standpoint is not as good as every other.[24]

F. Religious Justifications

The importance of religious argument in behalf of human rights lies especially in the principle enunciated by Ludwig Wittgenstein in his *Tractatus Logico-Philosophicus* that "ethics is transcendental."[25] Metaphorically expanding on this theme in his posthumously published "Lecture on Ethics," Wittgenstein says: "[W]e cannot write a scientific book, the subject matter of which could be intrinsically sublime and above all other subject matters. I can only describe my feeling by the metaphor, that, if a man could write a book on Ethics which really was a book on Ethics, this book would, with an explosion, destroy all the other books in the world."[26] In other words, to arrive at inalienable rights one would have to move beyond the limited, finite perspective of human opinion and go "outside the world" to a "transcendental" realm of values. Only there could "intrinsically sublime" standards be found. Wittgenstein's insight seems entirely in accord with common sense. Water does not rise above its own level; why should we think that absolute legal norms could arise from relativistic human situations? Archimedes said that if he were given a lever long enough and a fulcrum outside the world he could move it—but the *sine qua non* is that the fulcrum be located outside the limited world of human experience.

On this basis, religious traditions have asserted that their revelations (Bible, Qur'an) constitute that transcendent source of absolute ethical principles and human rights. Islam, for example, offers to the human rights community "the sublime morality and legal precepts of the Qur'an"—to use the language of the Kuwait seminar on human rights in Islam, held in December, 1980, under the

---

[24] Michael J. Perry, *The Idea of Human Rights* (New York: Oxford University Press, 1998), p. 80.
[25] Wittgenstein, *Tractatus Logico-Philosophicus*, §§ 6.41-6.421.
[26] Wittgenstein, "Lecture on Ethics," 74 *Philosophical Review* 3,7 (1965).

co-sponsorship of the International Commission of Jurists, the University of Kuwait, and the Union of Arab Lawyers.[27] Christians affirm not only that the Old and New Testaments constitute the transcendent basis of an absolute ethic (the Ten Commandments, the Sermon on the Mount) but also that a personal relationship with Jesus Christ is the only way to transform human nature so that the human being will indeed consider the rights of others as deserving of equal recognition with her own rights.[28]

But religious declarations certainly cannot be accepted on the basis of the claims themselves. After all, the religions of the world present views of the world which are mutually incompatible, so they cannot all be true.[29] Thus the student must pose the key epistemological question: Is there any way to test these incompatible revelational claims to see if any one of them might be veracious? Were the latter to be the case, a solution to the problem of justifying human rights would indeed be possible. But only serious work on the student's part in checking the evidence for revelational claims could legitimate such a conclusion.[30]

III. Pedagogical Advice in Conclusion

If this paper has persuaded the reader that serious epistemological questions need to be an integral part of human rights instruction, a few words of practical advice are called for at its close.

First, in order to bring students of human rights to the desired level of epistemological sophistication, there is no substitute for the Socratic method of posing difficult questions—of the kind we have introduced throughout this article. Granted, the use of this technique in American law schools, stemming from the pedagogical revolution under Dean Christopher Columbus Langdell at Harvard, has gone much too far there, and when employed throughout the law school curriculum produces a fragmented picture of the law.[31] But the British commitment to black-letter, lecture-style instruction is definitely not sufficient when dealing with the foundations of human rights law—or with

---

[27] The quoted words are those of A. K. Brohi in his keynote address, "The Nature of Islamic Law and the Concept of Human Rights," in *Human Rights in Islam* (Geneva: International Commission of Jurists, 1982), p. 51.
[28] Montgomery, *Human Rights and Human Dignity* (*op. cit.*), especially chap. 6, pp. 131 ff.
[29] Montgomery, *Tractatus Logico-Theologicus* (Bonn, Germany: Verlag für Kultur und Wissenschaft, 2002).
[30] Montgomery, *Christ Our Advocate* (Bonn, Germany: Verlag für Kultur und Wissenschaft, 2002), especially chap. 1, pp. 13 ff.
[31] Cf. Montgomery, "The American Law Teaching Experience," *Law & Justice*, No. 126/127 (Trinity/Michaelmas 1995), pp. 120-37.

jurisprudential issues in general. Here, it is imperative that the student herself reflect critically upon a diversity of mutually incompatible viewpoints, working through these to arrive (hopefully) at a sound personal philosophy. That result, needless to say, will not be achieved by a supposed direct transfer of information from the mind of the lecturer to the mind of the lectureee.

Secondly, in the planning of a human rights course the instructor needs specifically to introduce units dealing with the foundations and justification of human rights. This will doubtless entail assigning more than one textbook, since, as we noted at the outset, most of the standard law school texts on human rights law do not even include the epistemological dimension. Ideally, students will be expected to read more widely than just in their assigned texts; they should be brought into contact both with the primary-sources (the writings of the prominent human rights theorists themselves) and with quality secondary sources (critical examinations of those views by responsible scholars).

Thirdly, the epistemological dimension, though well deserving its own unit in the human rights course, must not be restricted to a discrete portion of the course. Since fundamental questions of justifying human rights relate to the entire field, they should be raised throughout the course in conjunction with the discussion of the substantive and procedural law. Thus—to take but one example—when the Nuremberg trials are discussed, the students should be asked why it was that Justice Robert H. Jackson, in his summing up for the prosecution, felt compelled to argue:

> ... At this stage of the proceedings I shall rest upon the law of these crimes as laid down in the Charter [of the International Military Tribunal]. ... In interpreting the Charter, however, we should not overlook the unique and emergent character of this body as an International Military Tribunal. It is no part of the constitutional mechanism of internal justice of any of the Signatory nations. ... As an International Military Tribunal, it rises above the provincial and transient and seeks guidance not only from International Law but also from the basic principles of jurisprudence which are assumptions of civilization.[32]

In general, we must remember that the positive law is constantly changing, and that therefore there is no way we can stuff into the heads of our students a complete picture of it. What lasts—and what makes a true professional in any field of endeavour—is the ability to engage in critical thinking and analysis whatever the changes that occur in the chosen field. In the case of the interna-

---

[32] Robert H. Jackson, Closing Address in the Nuremberg Trial, in 19 *Proceedings in the Trial of the Major War Criminals Before the International Military Tribunal* 397 (1948). Cf. Montgomery, *The Law Above the Law* (*op. cit.*), pp. 22-26.

tional and comparative law of human rights, that critical skill will be directly proportional to the epistemological sophistication which the lecturer has imparted to future practitioners.

4. The Rights of Unborn Children[1]

"The most dangerous place in the world is in the womb," asserted Cardinal Sin of the Philippines in a widely quoted statement. How accurate is this judgment? What, in fact, are the rights of the unborn?

It is common to deal with this question philosophically. The most recent comprehensive effort along philosophical lines has yielded disquieting conclusions. Michael Tooley, professor of philosophy at the University of Western Australia, argues that "neither abortion, nor infanticide, at least during the first few weeks after birth, is morally wrong."[2] He arrives at this conclusion by such reasoning as the following: "Basic moral principles should involve neither terms referring to particular biological species, nor the general concept of membership in a biological species. It follows that the fact that abortion and infanticide result in the destruction of innocent human beings cannot, in itself, be a reason for viewing such actions as wrong." Also: "An entity cannot be a person unless it possesses, or has previously possessed, the capacity for thought. And the psychological and neurophysiological evidence makes it most unlikely that humans, in the first few weeks after birth, possess this capacity."[3]

As thought-provoking as such philosophical studies may be—and the present writer confesses that he has been responsible for more than one himself[4]—it would appear that considerable light could be shed on the subject of the rights of the unborn by approaching the subject from the juridical side. In contrast with ethical or moral analysis, as Farrar and Dugdale have well noted, "law has clearly recognized authoritative sources and can fall back on institutionalized coercion and force."[5] This is not to accept a naive jurisprudence of positivism or "realism": it is simply to appreciate the value for any discussion

---

[1] Sudarshan Kapila Memorial Prize essay, Council of Legal Education's Inns of Court School of Law, England, 1984. Presented as the 1985 Dwight Lecture in Christian Thought at the University of Pennsylvania. Also presented as an invitational lecture at the American Scientific Affiliation-Research Scientists' Christian Fellowship International Conference, St. Catherine's College, Oxford, England, July, 1985; and at the Faculty of Law, University of Essex, England, October, 1985.
[2] Michael Tooley, *Abortion and Infanticide* (Oxford: Clarendon Press, 1983), p. 419.
[3] *Ibid*, p. 421.
[4] I was one of four chosen to contribute to the "American Medical Association Symposium: When Does Life Begin?" 214 *Journal of the American Medical Association* (JAMA) 1893-95 (1970). See also John Warwick Montgomery, *Slaughter of the Innocents: Abortion, Birth Control and Divorce in Light of Science, Law and Theology* (Westchester, Illinois: Crossway Books, 1981).
[5] John H. Farrar and Anthony M. Dugdale, *Introduction to Legal Method* (2^d ed.; London: Sweet & Maxwell, 1984), p. 10.

of the rights of the unborn of seeing how those rights are understood in clearly recognized and authoritative legal sources, backed up by the institutional sanctions of society.

This we shall endeavour to do, with particular reference to the English (including Commonwealth and American) common law, but also touching at appropriate points the European civil law tradition and the international and comparative law of human rights. And having provided an overview of the juridical rights (and non-rights) of unborn persons, we shall be in a position, at the close of this essay, to return briefly to the ethical issues raised by Professor Tooley. For whatever one may think about Ronald Dworkin's critical philosophy of law, he is surely correct in maintaining that at the end of the day law and morals cannot be relegated to hermetically sealed compartments.[6]

Unborn Children in the English Legal Tradition

The question of the rights of the unborn is today almost exclusively treated from the standpoint of the abortion question, i.e., in terms of the criminal law. This is a sound starting-point, and we shall begin there for the sake of convenience. However, of equal or greater significance for a comprehensive understanding of the subject is the legal recognition of the rights of the unborn in the areas of tort, land law, and inheritance. Our discussion of foetal rights will therefore also focus on these topics.

Abortion in English Law

The common law background. Procuring an abortion was not made a statutory felony until as late as 1803. Does this suggest that the older English common law took a fairly relaxed attitude toward foetal rights? That such an inference cannot properly be drawn is evident from the classic commentators. Fleta, in his epitome of Bracton (ca. 1290) writes:

> He, too, in strictness is a homicide who has pressed upon a pregnant woman or has given her poison or has struck her in order to procure an abortion or to prevent conception, if the foetus was already formed and quickened, and similarly he who has given or accepted poison with the intention of preventing procreation or conception. A woman also commits homicide if, by a potion or the like, she destroys a quickened child in her womb.[7]

---

[6] Ronald M. Dworkin, *Taking Rights Seriously* (rev. ed.; Oxford: Clarendon Press, 1978), *passim*. Cf. J. W. Harris, *Legal Philosophies* (London: Butterworths, 1980), pp. 177 ff.
[7] *Fleta, seu Commentarius iuris Anglicani*, Bk. I, chap. 23-12 ("De homicidio"); Selden Society trans. (Vol. 72).

Blackstone, by characterising abortion as a common-law misdemeanor, has sometimes been taken as evidence that prior to the 19th century the crime was not regarded with much seriousness. But his remarks need to be read more carefully.

> Life ... begins in contemplation of law as soon as an infant is able to stir in the mother's womb. For if a woman is quick with child, and by a potion or otherwise, killeth it in her womb; or if any one beat her, whereby the child dieth in her body, and she is delivered of a dead child; this, though not murder, was by the antient law homicide or manslaughter (Bracton). But Sir Edward Coke doth not look upon this offence in quite so atrocious a light, but merely as a heinous misdemeanor.[8]

In point of fact, Coke does not use the word "misdemeanor": he describes abortion as "a great misprision"[9]—and Blackstone himself notes in his *Commentaries* that "misprisions ... are, in the acceptation of our law, generally understood to be all such high offences as are under the degree of capital, *but nearly bordering thereon*."[10] So Coke regarded abortion as bordering on a capital crime. And it should not be forgotten that Blackstone himself does not make the sharp modern distinction between misdemeanors and felonies; says he, "crimes and misdemeanors ... properly speaking, are mere synonymous terms."[11]

Little case authority exists on the crime of abortion prior to its statutory criminalisation, but this is due to the fact that the offence was ecclesiastically cognisable, not to its supposedly trivial nature. Writes Bernard Dickens: "There are scanty records of this crime, because it was mainly regarded as a matter for the ecclesiastical courts."[12] So one cannot draw the conclusion that in pre-19th century England the unborn child had virtually no right to life; far from it. "The protection the Common Law afforded to human life certainly extended to the unborn child."[13]

The Offences against the Person Act. In modern English law, the crime of abortion is a statutory offence, involving the interpretation of three major statutory instruments: the Offences against the Person Act 1861, the Infant Life (Preservation) Act 1929, and the Abortion Act 1967.

s. 58 of the Offences against the Person Act 1861 declares:

> Every woman, being with child, who, with intent to procure her own miscarriage, shall unlawfully administer to herself any poison or other noxious

---

[8] Bl. Comm. I, 129 (1765).
[9] Coke, *Institutes*, III, 50.
[10] Bl. Comm. IV, 119 (italics ours).
[11] *Ibid.*, IV, 5.
[12] Bernard M. Dickens, *Abortion and the Law* (London: MacGibbon & Kee, 1966), p. 23.
[13] *Ibid.*, p. 20.

thing, or shall unlawfully use any instrument or other means whatsoever with the like intent, and whosoever, with intent to procure the miscarriage of any woman, whether she be or be not with child, shall unlawfully administer to her or cause to be taken by her any poison or other noxious thing, or shall unlawfully use any instrument or other means whatsoever with the like intent, shall be guilty of felony, and being convicted thereof shall be liable ... to be kept in penal servitude for life ...

It will be noted that the Act makes a distinction between the pregnant woman and any other defendant—a distinction not heretofore part of English law: when the woman herself is charged, she must actually be with child; this need not be shown in the case where another person is charged with the offence. (Nonetheless, the woman may, even if not pregnant, be charged either with conspiracy to commit the offence[14] or with aiding and abetting its commission.[15]) This distinction is not maintained in s. 59 of the Act, which asserts:

Whosoever shall unlawfully supply or procure any poison or other noxious thing, or any instrument or thing whatsoever, knowing that the same is intended to be unlawfully used or employed with intent to procure the miscarriage of any woman, whether she be or be not with child, shall be guilty of a misdemeanor, and being convicted thereof shall be liable ... to be kept in penal servitude ...

Does the "noxious thing" referred to in both sections of the Act have to be noxious *per se*? It has been settled law since *R v Cramp* (1880)[16] that this need not be so. In that case, it was said: "Some things administered in small quantities are useful, which when administered in large quantities are noxious. In the present case the oil of juniper as administered was noxious."

The 1861 Act offers powerful protection to the unborn: it does not specifically contain any qualifications (such as the age of the foetus or even the health of the mother) to its general proposition that procuring abortion is a felonious act and supplying the means to accomplish it is a misdemeanor. However, it is noteworthy that the Act repeatedly employs the adverb "unlawfully," suggesting the possibility of "lawful" abortion—though not in any fashion defining what that might consist of.

Such definition came about by judicial decision in the leading case of *R v Bourne* (1938)[17], in which an eminent surgeon aborted a fourteen year old multiple rape victim, and reported that he had done so in order to clarify the law on the subject. The *Bourne* case makes sense only if it is seen as the narrowest

---

[14] *R v Whitchurch*, 24 Q.B.D. 420 (1890).
[15] *R v Sockett*, 72 J.P. 428 (1908).
[16] 5 Q.B.D. 307.
[17] 3 A.E.R. 615.

opening of the door in the direction of therapeutic abortion. Macnaghten J allowed for this exception solely "if the doctor is of the opinion, on reasonable grounds and with adequate knowledge, that the probable consequence of the continuance of the pregnancy will be to make the woman a physical or mental wreck" (this was Bourne's claim, backed up by expert testimony, concerning the pregnant girl). Bernard Dickens, in his careful analysis of this case, observes that the exception is "limited to pathological indications": "social indications" would be "too remote, even if generally prejudicial to health"; moreover, "the defence of necessity can scarcely be used, as necessity only justifies acts to preserve life when endangered, not to end the possibility of life which jeopardises no other."[18] Macnaghten J's efforts to restrict the scope of the exception are plain from his statutory argument that the legality of abortion "for the purpose only of preserving the life of the mother" can be derived from the later Infant Life (Preservation) Act 1929, and that the wording of the proviso in that Act equally applies to the 1861 Act.

The Infant Life (Preservation) Act 1929. This Act deals, not with abortion in the very widest sense, but with the crime of "child destruction"—with the killing of "a child capable of being born alive." s. 1 provides:

> (1) Subject as hereinafter in this subsection provided, any person who, with intent to destroy the life of a child capable of being born alive, by any wilful act causes a child to die before it has an existence independent of its mother, shall be guilty of felony, to wit, of child destruction, and shall be liable on conviction thereof on indictment to penal servitude for life:
>
> Provided that no person shall be found guilty of an offense under this section unless it is proved that the act which caused the death of the child was not done in good faith for the purpose only of preserving the life of the mother.

In spite of the anomalous description of this Act in s. 5(1) of the Abortion Act 1967 as "protecting the life of the viable foetus," no such limitation of viability appears in the 1929 Act itself.[19] The only limitation is that the child must

---

[18] Dickens, *op. cit.* [in note 12], pp. 46, 49.
[19] See the careful discussion of the viability question by Gerard Wright, "Capable of Being Born Alive?," *New Law Journal*, Feb. 19,1981. He writes: "Save in the curious parenthesis to s 5(1) of the Abortion Act 1967, the phrase "viable foetus" is not to be found in any English statute nor indeed in any reported decision of the courts. It is, however, a phrase which can be found in American jurisprudence. Indeed, in the famous case in which the Federal Supreme Court defined a woman's constitutional right to have an abortion, *Roe v Wade* 410 US 113, Justice Blackmun defined the point at which the State has an interest in preserving the foetus as 'viability', which he said was when the foetus is 'potentially able to live outside the mother's womb albeit with artificial aid' (410 US, at 160). There is no reason, however, why this concept of American jurisprudence should be imported into English law and no justification for using it as a means of interpreting an English

be "capable of living for however short a time — maybe only a few hours or even minutes — after the process of birth is completed."[20] To aid the prosecution in discharging its burden of proof, the section continues:

> (2) For the purposes of this Act, evidence that a woman had at any material time been pregnant for a period of twenty-eight weeks or more shall be prima facie proof that she was at that time pregnant of a child capable of being born alive.

Bowles and Bell observe that "this length of time appears to have been selected in the light of the medical knowledge of 50 years ago, and it is thought that it would have little relevance in a modern case except to shift the burden of proof."[21]

As already noted, the 1929 Act explicitly decriminalises child destruction performed "in good faith for the purpose only of preserving the life of the mother," and, on the authority of the *Bourne* case, this proviso has been taken to apply to ss. 58-59 of the Offences against the Person Act 1861 as well. Except in this one narrowly defined instance, the 1929 Act endeavours to accomplish precisely what its title states: the preservation of unborn infant life.

The Abortion Act 1967. The 1967 Act must be read in conjunction with foregoing statutes: it serves to qualify the 1861 Act, and states expressly in s. 5(1) that "nothing in this [1967] Act shall affect the provisions of the Infant Life (Preservation) Act 1929."

The 1967 Abortion Act sets forth certain delimited situations in which "a person shall not be guilty of the offence under the law relating to abortion" (s. 1[1]).

Where these conditions do not apply, termination of pregnancy is still illegal under ss. 58-59 Offences against the Person Act 1861, if not under the provisions of the Infant Life (Preservation) Act 1929. We shall not give the complete text of the Abortion Act here, but merely summarise the qualifying procedures stipulated in the Act.[22]

---

statute."

[20] T. G. A. Bowles and M. N. M. Bell, "Abortion—A Clarification," *New Law Journal*, Sept. 27, 1979.

[21] *Ibid*. Indeed, the Royal College of Obstetricians and Gynaecologists has just recommended to the government that the 28 week figure, as set forth in the Infant Life (Preservation) Act 1929, should be reduced to 24 weeks, since "advances in care for the very premature baby ... have been such that foetuses under 28 weeks now regularly survive. The implication, therefore, is that very late abortions are being carried out on some foetuses which, given appropriate care, have a good chance of surviving. Such abortions are thus ethically dubious and probably illegal" (Nicholas Timmins, "Late Abortions: A New Dilemma for Doctors," *The Times, July* 26, 1985, p. 13).

[22] For the annotated text of the Abortion Act 1967, see 8 *Halsbury's Statutes of England* 682-86 (3^d ed. 1969).

Most significantly, the Act gives protection against criminal prosecution for abortion only when the "pregnancy is terminated by a registered medical practitioner" (s. 1[1]) in an approved hospital or facility (s. 1[3]). The physician need not obtain a second concurring opinion (and the hospital requirement is dispensed with) in the single instance where "he is of the opinion, formed in good faith, that the termination is immediately necessary to save the life or to prevent grave permanent injury to the physical or mental health of the pregnant woman" (s. 1[4]). Since most commentators on the *Bourne* case are of the opinion that Macnaghten J thought only in terms of physicians' benefiting from the case-law exception he created to the 1861 Act, it would appear that s. 1(4) of the Abortion Act 1967 does little more than codify what had already become common law by way of *Bourne*.

However, the Abortion Act goes well beyond the situation where the mother's life is in immediate jeopardy — though in the instances it enumerates the physician performing the abortion, to benefit from the Act's protection, must have obtained a second concurring medical opinion, also "formed in good faith" (s. 1[1]). The conditions requiring the agreement in good faith of two registered medical practitioners to the abortion are of greater or lesser stringency. The two physicians must be of the good faith opinion that absent an abortion "there is a substantial risk that if the child were born it would suffer from such physical or mental abnormalities as to be seriously handicapped" (s. 1[1][b]). The words "substantial" and "seriously" here show plainly that in the case of potentially handicapped children Parliament was allowing for abortion only in those instances where the resulting handicap would be of an extreme nature. On the other hand, the other qualifications do not have to involve "substantial" or "serious" risk, but only a straightforward balance of risk: an abortion is decriminalised if two physicians hold the good faith opinion that "the continuance of the pregnancy would involve risk[23] to the life of the pregnant woman, or of injury to the physical or mental health of the pregnant woman or any existing children of her family, greater than if the pregnancy were terminated" (s. 1[1][a]).

Now, to be sure, even the least stringent of these conditions is anything but an open sesame to irresponsible abortion. The "good faith" requirement must certainly be understood according to settled common law principle: unreasonableness of an opinion allegedly formed in good faith could count evidentially against its good faith character.[24] And the "statistical argument" Professor

---

[23] But not "immediate" risk: if termination of pregnancy is "immediately necessary", as we have seen, a single physician may perform the abortion without a second concurring opinion and outside an approved hospital (s 1[4]).

[24] *R v Morgan*, A.C. 182(1976).

Glanville Williams included in strong form in the first edition (and in chastened form in the most recent edition) of his *Textbook of Criminal Law*[25] has been thoroughly exploded: to argue from (fairly old) East European statistics that since first semester abortions are (allegedly) safer than to allow pregnancy to continue, a doctor may under certain circumstances lawfully terminate a pregnancy even if he finds no specific grounds to do so, is to substitute statistical generality for the factual particularity the statutory law requires.[26] "The Act does not say pregnancies may be terminated if in general childbirth represents a greater risk to the mother than abortion. It could have said that, but it did not. To obtain the protection of the Act, the doctor has to consider the health of the pregnant woman before him, and form an opinion in good faith about the risk to the health of the particular woman."[27] The same authors reinforce this argument elsewhere:

> Statistics may be of help to doctors in situations where they show that death is almost certain to result if an operation is not provided, but in a situation such as abortion, where in more than 90% of cases the operation is medically wholly unnecessary, it is absurd to suggest that doctors should use them as a guide. If it is the statistics that make the abortion legal, then a doctor would have to know first how many deaths were caused by abortion in the year in question, and secondly how many deaths by childbirth, and then compare the two figures, before he could form a view as to whether the act he was proposing to perform was legal or illegal. This might make a good plot for a Gilbert and Sullivan Opera, but as a guide to either law or medicine it can only be described as ridiculous.[28]

Thus the Abortion Act 1967 certainly cannot be said to establish "abortion on demand" in England. Yet it has unarguably diminished the common-law and earlier statutory protections afforded to the child not yet "capable of being born alive" (in the terms of the 1929 Act). Such an unborn child suffering from "substantial" or "serious" risk of being born handicapped today has virtually lost his or her right to life—and in light of eugenic attempts under other political systems to eliminate the "unfit", this should give sensitive Englishmen

---

[25] Glanville Williams, *Textbook of Criminal Law* (London: Stevens, 1978), p. 258; 2ᵈ ed. (London: Stevens, 1983), p. 299.

[26] The common law has rightly looked with grave suspicion on statistical-style evidence. Thus, in a very recent tort case, efforts to introduce actuarial reasoning to quantify future loss led to a judicial comparison of actuaries with astrologers: *Auty v National Coal Board* (*The Times*, April 3, 1984). One is also reminded of the sad but apocryphal case of the statistician who drowned wading across a river with an average depth of three feet.

[27] T. G. A. Bowles and M. N. M. Bell, "Abortion on Demand or on Request: Is It Legal?", 77 *Law Society's Gazette* 938 (1980).

[28] M. N. M. Bell and T. G. A. Bowles, "The Statistical Argument," *News and Comment* (Association of Lawyers for the Defence of the Unborn), No. 21 (Spring, 1984), 3-4.

more than a little disquiet. Moreover, the right to life of the unborn has made a decided shift in the direction of the relativistic calculus of risk, where the balance is no longer limited to the extreme case in which the mother's life may need to be chosen over against the life of the child (as in the 1929 Act): now the child incapable of being born alive may be sacrificed on the ground, inter alia, of mere "injury to the physical or mental health of ... existing children" in the family. The right of unborn children to life itself is seen less and less as an absolute value in English law, but rather as a value legitimately capable of sociological subordination to the general well-being or happiness of those whose lives his existence or presence would influence. In the same vein it is highly significant that, whatever other rights the unborn person possesses, "he has no legal right to have his interests represented at the time when a decision whether or not to abort him or her is being taken."[29]

Abortion Law in the Commonwealth and in America

The Commonwealth. Although there is predictable diversity in the criminal laws of Commonwealth and post-Commonwealth countries in regard to abortion, the most impressive fact is the degree of basic uniformity of approach stemming from the influence of the English Offences against the Person Act 1861. In the most comprehensive recent study of Commonwealth abortion laws, the authors write:

> Too much should not be made of the diverse and geographically eclectic origins of abortion laws in the Commonwealth. Basic laws differ upon whether a woman commits the offence by operating upon herself when she is not pregnant, the 1861 Act considering her not to be liable, the historically influential Code of Cyprus imposing liability "whether she is or is not with child." The Penal Code of Sri Lanka, however, renders both the woman herself and any other person operating upon her liable only when she is "with child." Other minor variants concern punishment, a few laws providing for greater punishment when the woman is "quick with child." In general, however, the atmosphere of the 1861 Act is pervasive, even where its words are differently ordered or, for instance, the two halves of section 58, concerning a woman acting upon herself and another acting upon her, are presented in separate sections, as they not uncommonly are.[30]

At the same time, a number of Commonwealth and post-Commonwealth countries have passed what Dickens and Cook term "advanced laws," allowing

---

[29] M. N. M. Bell, *Abortion Law Simply Explained* (2ᵈ ed.; Bournemouth, n.d.), p. 3.
[30] Bernard M. Dickens and Rebecca J. Cook, "Development of Commonwealth Abortion Laws," 28 *International and Comparative Law Quarterly* 424-57 (1979), at 427-28.

(as does the British Abortion Act 1967) for abortion on grounds other than the preservation of the life of the mother. The "advanced" indications sometimes reflect indigenous social concerns, such as a contraceptive failure vis-à-vis overpopulation. S. 3(2) (i) of India's Medical Termination of Pregnancy Act 1971 states that "where any pregnancy occurs as a result of failure of any device or method used by any married woman or her husband for the purpose of limiting the number of children, the anguish caused by such unwanted pregnancy may be presumed to constitute a grave injury to the mental health of the pregnant woman."

The conservative character of such "advanced laws," however, should be carefully observed. Thus the Indian statutory subsection just cited is restricted in its application to married women, and creates no more than an evidentiary presumption (doubtless a rebuttable presumption at that). Indeed, the only Commonwealth jurisdiction where the law allows abortion on demand—i.e., without any indication other than the woman's request or consent—is Singapore (s. 3[1] Abortion Act 1974), and even "this provision is hedged around by many conditions,"[31] such as consent in writing; citizenship or residency; and pregnancy under 24 weeks (otherwise, a strict necessity indication must be satisfied). All in all, one is impressed by the degree to which respect for the life of the unborn in English criminal law has been effectively transplanted or found congenial soil in which to grow in so many diverse cultures around the globe.

The United States of America. We are informed by Mohr, in his standard work, *Abortion in America*, that "in the period from 1880 to 1900 the United States completed its transition from a nation without abortion laws of any sort to a nation where abortion was legally and officially proscribed."[32] This is, however, a dangerous half-truth,[33] for prior to the enactment in 1828 of the New York anti-abortion statute which became a model for those of many other states, the common law existed—and that common law was essentially the English common law as set forth by such classic commentators as Blackstone. Thus the state anti-abortion statutes, which became more and more severe by the end of the 19th century, gradually eliminating the earlier statutory distinction between the foetus before or after quickening, were a genuine reflection of the respect for unborn life in the English common law. By the end of the 1950's, most U.S. jurisdictions banned abortion completely except to preserve the life of the mother.

---

[31] *Ibid.*, p. 449.
[32] James C. Mohr, *Abortion in America: The Origins and Evolution of National Policy, 1800-1900* (New York: Oxford University Press, 1978), p. 226.
[33] See the critique of Mohr's study contained in John T. Noonan's *A Private Choice: Abortion in America in the Seventies* (New York: Macmillan-Free Press, 1979), *passim*.

In 1973, this pattern was radically changed, not by statute but by U.S. Supreme Court decision in the well-known case of *Roe v Wade*.[34] A Texas anti-abortion statute (typical of most existing state statutes criminalising abortion) was struck down as unconstitutional, specifically in that it violated the "right to privacy" of the plaintiff, a single pregnant woman. Henceforth, American women would have an absolute right to physician-performed abortions during the first trimester of pregnancy, and state legislatures attempting to regulate abortion during the second and third trimesters would be radically limited in the extent to which they could do so. In actual effect, *Roe v Wade* judicially created abortion on demand in the United States.

Blackmun J wrote for the majority in this leading case, and his opinion remains a jurisprudential mystery to many on both sides of the Atlantic. The "right to privacy" on which the decision chiefly relies is nowhere mentioned in the U.S. Constitution; it was first argued for as a constitutional right in a *Harvard Law Review* article in 1890 by Warren and Brandeis.[35] But Blackmun's use of the doctrine in *Roe v Wade* bears virtually no relation to the original meaning of that legal principle. (The Court would hardly argue that whenever one's privacy is potentially disturbed — e.g., by prying neighbors or obnoxious newsmen — one may kill the source of the disturbance and the result will be justifiable homicide!) Understanding *Roe v Wade* requires, not jurisprudential acumen but sociological perception: as is so often the case with contemporary U.S. Supreme Court decisions, social and policy considerations played the primary role. The majority in *Roe v Wade* say as much: "This holding is consistent with the relative weights of the respective interests involved ... and with the demands of the profound problems of the present day."[36]

The case-law picture in the United States since *Roe v Wade* can best be seen by a short catalogue of the most important U.S. Supreme Court decisions on the subject from 1973 to the present.

> **Doe v Bolton,** 410 U.S. 179 (1973) (companion case to *Roe*) — requirements that a hospital committee or a second doctor approve an abortion are unconstitutional; state residence cannot be required to obtain an abortion.

---

[34] 93 S. Ct. 705 (1973); also 410 U.S. 113 (1973).
[35] Cf. M. L. Ernst and A. U. Schwartz, *Privacy* (New York: Macmillan, 1962); H. Gross, *Privacy — Its Legal Protection* (Dobbs Ferry, N.Y.: Oceana, 1964); G. D. Glenn, "Abortion and Inalienable Rights in Classical Liberalism," 20 *American Journal of Jurisprudence* 62-80 (1975).
[36] *Roe v Wade*, 93 S. Ct. 705 (1973), at 733. Cf. Janet LaRue, "Abortion: Justice Harry A. Blackmun and the *Roe v Wade* Decision," 2 *Simon Greenleaf Law Review* 122-45 (1982-1983).

Planned Parenthood of Central Missouri v Danforth, 428 U.S. 52 (1976)—spousal consent and blanket parental consent requirements unconstitutional; requirement woman certify "that her consent is informed and freely given and is not the result of coercion" is constitutional.

Maher v Roe, 432 U.S. 464 (1977)—federal Constitution does not require that tax dollars be used to pay for nontherapeutic abortions for the poor.

Poelker v Doe, 432 U.S. 519 (1977) (companion case to *Maher*)—public hospitals need not provide nontherapeutic abortions in their facilities.

Bellotti v Baird (II), 443 U.S. 622 (1979)—for a parental consent statute to be constitutional, a minor must be given the alternative of going before a judge or administrator to show either 1) that she is mature enough to decide about abortion without parental involvement or 2) that even if immature, an abortion without parental involvement would be in her best interest.

Harris v McRae, 448 U.S. 297 (1980), and **Williams v Zbaraz,** 448 U.S. 358 (1980)—neither Medicaid statute nor U.S. Constitution requires tax dollars to be spent for "medically necessary" abortions for the poor.

City of Akron v Akron Center for Reproductive Health, 103 S.Ct. 2481 (1983)—*Roe v Wade* reaffirmed. Informed consent ordinance unconstitutional: physician must have discretion to decide what information to give or withhold from a woman considering an abortion. Parental involvement statute constitutionality standards reaffirmed. Legislative regulations concerning maternal health constitutional only when they comply with standards established by professional medical organizations. 24 hour waiting period unconstitutional. Requirement for "humane and sanitary" disposal of aborted unborn child unconstitutionally vague.

Planned Parenthood Association of Kansas City, Mo. v Ashcroft, 103 S.Ct. 2517 (1983) (companion case to *Akron*)—requirement that a second doctor be present in a post-viability abortion to aid a live-born child, requirement that a pathology report be completed after each abortion, and parental consent statute with proper judicial consent alternative constitutional; second trimester hospitalisation requirement constitutional.

Simopoulos v Virginia, 103 S.Ct. 2532 (1983) (companion case to *Akron* and *Ashcroft*)—requirement that second trimester abortions be performed in licensed clinic constitutional.

The viewpoint is frequently expounded that the U.S. Supreme Court has been moving in a more conservative direction on abortion since *Roe v Wade*. The cases belie that conclusion. True, the court has ruled against a constitutional right to publicly funded abortions (*Maher, Poelker, Harris*); and it has allowed for a limited range of parental consent statutes, as well as a requirement that second trimester abortions be performed in hospitals or licensed clinics

(*Bellotti, Ashcroft, Simopoulos*). But spousal consent, and legislative efforts to set forth the substantive content of the woman's own "informed consent" have been roundly rejected (*Danforth, City of Akron*). Most significantly, *Roe v Wade* was reaffirmed in the *City of Akron* case (1983) — but with a powerful dissent by Justice O'Connor, who clearly would like to see the decision reversed.[37] Unless and until the composition of the Court changes, however, the American legal landscape offers virtually no right to life to the unborn child.

Pre-Natal Torts in Contemporary English Law

Discussion of the rights of the unborn must not be limited only to the criminal law, though such limitation seems the rule rather than the exception. Much can be learned of the common law's underlying valuation of the unborn through an examination of tort, land law, and inheritance.

In the modern law of tort, rights of the unborn have been declared by statute in the Congenital Disabilities (Civil Liability) Act 1976.[38] By the terms of this Act, a minor can sue for torts committed against him before his birth — as long as he was born alive after June 22, 1976, the date when the Act came into force on receiving the Royal Assent.

Under s. 1 damages can be recovered against any third party (including the father but excluding the mother) under the following two conditions: there must have been an occurrence preventing either party from having a normal healthy child (e.g. irradiation) or which affected the mother during the course of the birth; and the defendant tortfeasor must have breached some legal duty to the parent. It is expressly stated that if the parent shared the responsibility for the child being born disabled, recoverable damages are to be reduced correspondingly (a contributory negligence defence).

s. 2 deals with the case of a disability to the child arising proximately from the mother knowingly driving a motor vehicle when pregnant, and covers also the situation where she causes such injury when she ought reasonably to have known that she was pregnant. She "is to be regarded as being under the same

---

[37] On March 31, 1984, an important national conference was held in Chicago on the subject, "Reversing *Roe v Wade* through the Courts," sponsored by the Legal Defence Fund of Americans United for Life. Speakers included, *inter alia*, John M. Finnis, professor of jurisprudence at Oxford, and John T. Noonan, professor of law at the University of California, Berkeley. The present writer was privileged to attend.
[38] Arising out of and giving effect to the recommendations of the Law Commission's Report on Injuries to Unborn Children (Law Com. No. 60, August, 1974; Cmnd. 5709).

duty to take care for the safety of her unborn child as the law imposes on her with respect to the safety of other people"; if the mother breaches this duty, she is liable in tort to her child for consequential disabilities.

The unborn child is brought within the scope of the Nuclear Installations Act 1965 by s. 3 of the 1976 Act. Where the child's birth defects were proximately caused by violations of the Nuclear Installations Act, these injuries are to be regarded, in terms of compensation, as "caused on the same occasion, and by the same breach of duty, as was the injury to the parent."

Two common misunderstandings of the Act need to be laid to rest. First, s. 1(6) appears to take away from the unborn child with one hand what was given with the other: "Liability to the child ... may be treated as having been excluded or limited by contract made with the parent affected, to the same extent and subject to the same restrictions as liability in the parent's own case." But this defence by exclusion clause must now be seen in light of s. 2(1) of the Unfair Contract Terms Act 1977, which rejects such exclusion clauses within the scope of that Act: business liability for a person's death or personal injury resulting from negligence cannot be so excluded or restricted.[39] Wherever this applies to injuries to the parent, it will apply, by the terms of the Congenital Disabilities Act, to the unborn child's resulting injuries as well.

Secondly, one goes much too far in arguing that the rights of the unborn under the Act are merely "derivative"—in that liability to the child depends only "on a pre-existing liability to one or other of the parents in respect of the matters giving rise to the disabled birth." It is simply not the case that thus "there is no nexus of legal duty, whether at common law or under statutes, as between the defendant and the child '*in utero*'."[40] The liability of the defendant to the unborn child is indeed linked to his liability to the parent, but clearly the unborn child himself or herself is the focus of the Act, and s. 2 creates a specific instance (liability of a woman driving when pregnant) in which the mother may herself become liable in tort to her child. It is of more than passing significance that s. 2 imposes on the woman precisely the same standard of care for the safety of her unborn child as it "imposes on her with respect to the safety of *other people*" (italics ours). Ergo, the unborn child who is subsequently born alive is here regarded as having precisely the same rights as any adult person not to be subjected to another's negligence and to be appropriately compensated for breaches of that duty. Moreover, even in reference to s. 1, "the child's right of action is not prejudiced by the inability of the mother to sue, as for example

---

[39] To be sure, the provisions of the Unfair Contract Terms Act do not cover international trade contracts, or contracts only subject to English law by choice of the parties.
[40] "The Congenital Disabilities (Civil Liability) Act 1976," *Miscellaneous Acts: Annotated Legislation Service*, Vol. 244 (London: Butterworths, 1977), p. 20.

where she immediately pre-deceased the child, or can claim no actionable damage (because the occurrence in question was not one which caused any injury to her)."[41]

Very much the same jurisprudential sensitivity to the needs of the child born alive who has suffered tortious injury pre-natally can be found in the recent case law of Commonwealth countries.[42] In the United States, there is a steady movement toward giving children wider legal opportunities to bring a cause of action to recover for pre-natal injuries; indeed, viability—which has played such a strong role in American abortion law in contrast with the English pattern—is less and less regarded as a meaningful criterion of recovery where prenatal torts are at issue.[43] Surveying not only the common law world but also the French civil law tradition, Somerville, in a study prepared for the Law Reform Commission of Canada, concludes: "Today there is no doubt whatever that, in all the countries with which we are concerned, the foetus who is born alive enjoys legal protection and has at his or her disposal legal recourse for prenatal injuries."[44]

To complete our discussion of the rights of the unborn in English tort law, a word needs to be said about the so-called tort of "wrongful life." Does the unborn child have a right to die, so that in cases such as a failed contraceptive preventing termination of pregnancy and resulting in the birth of a deformed child, the latter can maintain a right of action? The answer is no. The Congenital Disabilities (Civil Liability) Act 1976 "gives the child no right of action for 'wrongful life',"[45] and contemporary English case authority is uniformly and eloquently against the whole idea. In *McKay v Essex Area Health Authority*,[46] defendant Health Authority was sued in tort for negligence for the faulty testing of the mother's blood samples, which, properly tested, would have revealed German measles; as a result, no abortion took place and the child—six years of age at the time of the trial—was born mentally and physically handicapped, blind, and deaf. The Appeal Court allowed that the defendant owed a duty

---

[41] *Ibid.*, p. 21.
[42] E.g., *Watt v Rama*, V.R. 353 (Australia, 1972); *Duval v Seguin*, 26 D.L.R. 3^d 418 (Ontario, 1972).
[43] Cf. M. L. Closen and J. D. Wittenberg, "Recovery for Preconception Negligence," *Case & Comment*, Sept.-Oct., 1979, pp. 34-38.
[44] Margaret A. Somerville, *Le consentement à l'acte médical: Série Protection de la vie* (Ottawa: Law Reform Commission of Canada, 1980), p. 100 (translation ours).
[45] *Butterworths Annotated Legislation Service*, Vol. 244 (*op. cit.* [in note 40]), p. 21.
[46] 2 WLR 890 (1981). Cf. John Finch, "No Wrongful Life," *New Law Journal*, Mar. 11, 1982, pp. 235-36.

to the child, but on the ground, not that she was born, but that she was born with deformities; plaintiff, however, insisted that her claim should be based on "wrongful life."

Lord Justice Lawton's analysis is well worth pondering not only on the narrow issue of a "right to die" but also on the larger question of the effect of the Abortion Act of 1967 on the right to life of the unborn:

> The Abortion Act 1967 gave mothers a right to terminate the lives of their unborn children and made it lawful for doctors to help to abort them. By that Act, the legislature made a notable inroad on the sanctity of human life by recognising that it would be better for a child, born to suffer from such abnormalities as to be seriously handicapped not to have been born at all. ... But because a doctor can lawfully do to a foetus what he cannot lawfully do to a person who has been born, it does not follow that he is under a legal obligation to a foetus to terminate its life, or that the foetus has a legal right to die. ...
>
> To impose such a duty towards the child would make a further inroad on the sanctity of human life which would be contrary to public policy. It would mean regarding the life of a handicapped child as not only less valuable than the life of a normal child but so much less valuable that it was not worth preserving.

A more recent case, *Udale v Bloomsbury Health Authority*[47] makes an even more preposterous claim. Here, the child was born in perfect health, but the birth took place because of allegedly negligent sterilisation by defendant Health Authority. Plaintiff mother claimed damages for (i) the pain and distress caused by the pregnancy (here she succeeded), (ii) the expenses of bringing up an unwanted child, and (iii) the anxiety of having another child, with the loss of the free time this would involve. The latter two claims were roundly rejected by Jupp J on grounds of public policy. American cases have likewise condemned the notion of a right to die and the idea that a court should try to weigh the relative merits of life vs. nonexistence. And "in American cases that bear some similarity to the *McKay* case, the tendency is to reject the child's claim to 'wrongful life' but to focus on the family as the true object of the claim."[48]

---

[47] 1 WLR 1098 (1983).
[48] Michael Slade, "The Death of Wrongful Life: A Case for Resuscitation?", *New Law Journal*, Sept. 16, 1982, pp. 874-76, citing recent American case authority.

Property and Inheritance Rights of the Unborn

No areas of English law have maintained such a consistent regard for foetal rights—from the very moment of conception—as have land law and the law of wills and trusts. "In contrast to abortion and homicide, property law has long been one where the foetus at its earliest stages has been given recognition."[49]

The Rule against Perpetuities is a prime illustration of the central place the *en ventre sa mère* doctrine holds in English property law. The child *en ventre sa mère* has always been treated as a life in being at the death of the testator, so as to extend the classic perpetuity period to 21 years plus the 9 month period of gestation. Thus the leading case of *Thellusson v Woodford* (1805)[50] enumerated foetal rights as including recovery, execution, devise, and injunction. Kindersley V-C declared in *Knapping v Tomlinson* (1864): "In the case before me, all the children were *in esse*, because I consider the child *en ventre sa mère* at the death of the testator, was, for the purpose of the rule as to perpetuities, a child *in esse*."[51] And in *Villar v Gilbey* (1907), Lord Atkinson succinctly stated the general principle: "The cases ... establish this, that in construing the rule [against perpetuities] a child *en ventre* may be deemed to be a "life in being," and the period of gestation may be added at both ends of the period of twenty-one years mentioned in the rule."[52]

In the English law of wills and trusts the *en ventre sa mère* doctrine is as firmly established: upon the testator's death a child may inherit before he or she is born, and on the settlor's death a child may become an income recipient of the trust while still in the womb. In the leading case of *Doe d Clarke v Clarke* (1795), lands were devised to B for life and after his decease to all and every such child or children of B as should be living at the time of his decease; it was held that a posthumous child of B should share equally with those who were born in his lifetime, and the principle was explicitly set forth that an infant *en ventre* is considered born for all purposes which are for his benefit.[53] *Re Wilmer's Trusts, Moore v Wingfield*[54] made clear that the principle was not to be restricted to cases where it was to the advantage of, or immaterial to, the infant to apply it: in other words, the English rule of foetal property rights that an infant *en ventre sa mère* is a life in being was so fundamental that it transcended even the best interests of the child in question.

---

[49] Section III ("Property Law") of the essay, "The Commencement of Life: An Historical Review," forthcoming in the *Pepperdine University Law Review*.
[50] 11 Ves. 112 (1805).
[51] 34 LJ Ch. 3 (1864).
[52] AC 139 (1907).
[53] 2 Hy Bl 399; subsequent proceedings sub nom *Clarke v Blake*, 2 Ves. 673 (1795).
[54] 2 Ch. 411 (1903).

Two additional cases will illustrate the general working of the principle:

> Testator directed his executors to pay "the sum of £500 apiece to each child that may be born to either of the children of either of my brothers lawfully begotten": *Held* the child of a niece born within eight months after testator's death was entitled to the legacy, and the gift was not as to such niece void for remoteness. *Storrs v Benbow* (1853).[55]

> A testator by his will dated October 17, 1904, gave a number of pecuniary legacies and £500 to each of his great-nephews and great-nieces "born previously to the date of this my will, to whom no other pecuniary bequest is given by this my will or any codicil thereto." He made two codicils, dated respectively October 18, 1904, and February 17, 1905, and died on April 19, 1905. One of his great-nieces was not born until March 14, 1905, and she was therefore *en ventre sa mère* at the date of the will and codicils: *Held* the rule of construction, that a child *en ventre sa mère* at a particular time, who is subsequently born alive, is to be considered as "born" at that time, where such construction is for the benefit of the child, applied; no contrary intention was indicated in the will; there was no ground for the suggestion that the rule only applied to a class of children to be ascertained at some future date as distinguished from a class of children born at the date of the will, and the infant was entitled to a legacy of £500. *Re Salaman, De Pass v Sonnenthal* (1908).[56]

On the other side of the Atlantic, American courts likewise made the *en ventre sa mère* principle a cornerstone of the common law of property, inheritance, and trusts. The leading case is *Hall v Hancock* (1834)[57], where it was held that a grandson born almost nine months after the testator's death was a beneficiary under a bequest to such grandchildren "as may be living at my death."

In contemporary English law, the historic concern for the property rights of the unborn child is reflected statutorily. A good example is s. 1 Variation of Trusts Act 1958, which gives wide powers to the court to permit changes in the terms of a trust where beneficiaries are of full age and agreeable to those alterations. The court is empowered to act on behalf of other beneficiaries who for a variety of reasons cannot consent personally. However—and this is the significant point for our purposes—the Act must not be used to prejudice the rights of such beneficiaries as the unborn who are incapable of giving their personal consent to the variation. A good example of the operation of the Act in practice is the case of *Re Cohen* (1965)[58]:

---

[55] 22 LJ Ch. 823 (1853).
[56] 1 Ch. 4 (1908).
[57] 32 Mass. (Pick.) 2-5, 26 AD 598 (1834).
[58] 1 WLR 1229 (1965).

Income was payable to a son and the issue of four deceased sons. When the surviving son died, the capital was to devolve on all grandchildren and their issue alive on that date. In order to save estate duty it was suggested that 30 June 1973 be substituted for the date of the son's death. In fact the son was unlikely to live until the stipulated date. *Held* approval would not be given on behalf of unborn persons. The son might live beyond the stipulated date, and if so the proposed variation would not benefit persons born thereafter and before his actual death who would have taken a benefit except for the variation.

The Rights of the Unborn in Wider Perspective

Our survey of the rights of unborn children in the English legal tradition has shown that whether one looks back to ancient authorities and early case law or focuses attention on modern statutes, one finds that the sanctity of unborn life has generally been held very high. To be sure, differences exist, the most striking being the contrast between recognition of lives in being from the very moment of conception (in property law, trusts, and inheritance), as compared with vastly attenuated rights for the child not yet capable of being born alive (as in the criminal law by way of the Abortion Act 1967) or the non-recognition of rights if the child has not actually been born alive (the usual locus standi requirement for bringing pre-natal tort actions).

In endeavouring now to place the rights of the unborn in wider perspective, we shall first attempt to provide assistance in making an informed choice between the contrasting positions of criminal law and property law as to when the unborn child should first receive legal protection. Then we shall offer some insights from the standpoint of the international and comparative law of human rights. Finally, we shall speak briefly to the philosophical and ethical issues raised by Professor Tooley in his remarks quoted at the outset of this paper, thereby arriving at the place where we can offer a concrete suggestion or two for strengthening the rights of the unborn.

The Significance of the "En Ventre Sa Mère" Doctrine in Anglo-American Property and Inheritance Law

Even those favouring the relaxed abortion standards of the modern law must concede, as we have been at pains to demonstrate, that in the areas of property and inheritance law Anglo-American jurisprudence has maintained a scrupulous concern for the rights of the unborn, recognizing that human lives in being begin at conception. "However," the argument goes, "this means little or nothing, since where the right to life per se is at issue (the criminal law) full protection for the unborn is unavailable in England today at least until the foetus is capable of being born alive, and in America the rights of the unborn have often been made a function of 'viability.' After all, we are dealing with a question of personhood, so property issues will perforce have little bearing."

This depreciation of the significance of property law for abortion discussion overlooks the place of property law in common law jurisprudence. In point of fact—as apologists for the socialist philosophy of law[59] and as American radical lawyers[60] have not ceased to declare (with disgust)—traditional Anglo-American law elevates the concept of property to a sacred level. Holdsworth speaks of "the most unique branch of the common law—the law of Real Property."[61] One of the ways in which that uniqueness manifested itself was in the high value placed upon property and the corresponding reticence of the courts or legislatures to tamper with existing property law. Writes Simpson in the concluding chapter of his standard *Introduction to the History of the Land Low*:

> Those who did understand the system encouraged the view that it was dangerous to meddle with so elaborate a structure, upon which the sacred property rights of people were based. ...
>
> ... The old concepts of the law are not roughly handled; the definitions of Littleton and Coke still find their place in the modern textbook; lawyers can still gravely dispute the modern effects of *Quia Emptores*. For all the legislative interference which it has suffered, the law of property continues to display an extraordinary measure of historical continuity.[62]

Why do property rights carry a sacral quality in the common law? Let us hear from the two most influential writers of general legal textbooks in the history of the common law: Blackstone and Kent.

Blackstone, after discussing "The Rights of Persons" in Book I of his *Commentaries*, proceeds in Book II to treat "The Rights of Things." Book II, Chapter 1 deals with "Property in General," and there we read:

> There is nothing which so generally strikes the imagination and engages the affections of mankind, as the right of property; or that sole and despotic dominion which one man claims and exercises over the external things of the world, in total exclusion of the right of any other individual in the universe. ...

---

[59] E.g., V. M. Chkhikvadze, ed., *The Soviet State and Law* (Moscow: Institute of State and Law, 1969).
[60] Cf. Jonathan Black, ed., *Radical Lawyers* (New York: Avon, 1971).
[61] W. Holdsworth, *A History of English Law*, II (3ᵈ ed.; London: Methuen, 1923), 78.
[62] A. W. B. Simpson, *An Introduction to the History of the Land Law* (London: Oxford University Press, 1967), pp. 253, 261.

> In the beginning of the world, we were informed by holy writ, the all-bountiful Creator gave to man "dominion over all the earth; and over the fish of the sea, and over the fowl of the air, and over every living thing that moveth upon the earth." This is the only true and solid foundation of man's dominion over external things, whatever airy metaphysical notions may have been started by fanciful writers upon this subject. ...
>
> ... In the case of habitations in particular, it was natural to observe that even the brute creation, to whom everything else was in common, maintained a kind of permanent property in their dwellings, especially for the protection of their young; that the birds of the air had nests, and the beasts of the fields had caverns, the invasion of which they esteemed a very flagrant injustice, and would sacrifice their lives to preserve them. Hence a property was soon established in every man's house and homestall. ... [63]

It will be noted that Blackstone unequivocally establishes property rights on a revelatory foundation, citing Genesis 1:28 and alluding to Jesus' words in Matthew 8:20 (parallel passage, Luke 9:58) as a source of his argument. For Blackstone, property law had divine sanction. Applying modern philosopher of religion Rudolf Otto's terminology, property in Blackstone's view was embraced in "the idea of the holy": it was sacral, an aspect of the *numen tremendens et fascinosum*.

Chancellor Kent, whose influence on American law in many ways corresponds to Blackstone's on English jurisprudence,[64] likewise sets forth a numinous conception of property rights.

> The sense of property is inherent in the human breast, and the gradual enlargement and cultivation of that sense, from its feeble force in the savage stage, to its full vigor and maturity among polished nations, forms a very instructive portion of the history of civil society. Man was fitted and intended by the Author of his being for society and government, and for the acquisition and enjoyment of property. It is, to speak correctly, the law of his nature; and by obedience to this law, he brings all his faculties into exercise, and is enabled to display the various and exalted powers of the human mind.
>
> ... The right of property, founded on occupancy, is suggested to the human mind by feeling and reason prior to the influence of positive institutions.[65]

---

[63] Bl. Comm. II, 4.
[64] To be sure, one must never forget that Blackstone had the most profound effect on the education of American lawyers in the 18th and 19th centuries; see, e.g., J. S. Waterman, "Thomas Jefferson and Blackstone's *Commentaries*," in D. H. Flaherty, ed., *Essays in the History of Early American Law* (Chapel Hill, N.C.: University of North Carolina Press, 1969), pp. 451-88.
[65] J. Kent, *Commentaries*, 318-19.

Particularly illuminating is Kent's citation of authorities for his position. He quotes Selden's definition of natural law and refers to Aristotle, Plato, Cicero, and to Hooker's *Ecclesiastical Polity* in the same connection. On the principle of occupancy as establishing property rights, he quotes the fundamental aphorism from Justinian's Digest, "*Quod enim nullius est id ratione naturali occupanti conceditur*";[66] the significance of this reference lies in the fact that Roman law distinguished between "civil" and "natural" acquisition of property, and classed acquisition by occupancy as "natural" (i.e., "recognized by the *jus gentium*"[67]). Since the *jus gentium* is "that law which natural reason has established among all men, is equally observed among all nations, and is called the 'law of nations,' as being the law which all nations use,"[68] Kent is saying that the root concepts of property ownership are part of the natural law deriving from no less a source than "the Author of [man's] being." Thus the Chancellor held no less than Blackstone to a sacral view of property and of its concomitant legal relations.

Whatever may be the case in other legal systems, therefore, one cannot dichotomize person and property, to the detriment of the latter, in the context of common law. Property, no less than personhood, is regarded as sacred—for both are part of the "natural law" and originate from the divine will.

Indeed, there is a sense in which property rights are superior to personal rights! Blackstone has already expressed his awe at "the right of property ... that sole and despotic dominion which one man claims and exercises over the external things of the world, in total exclusion of the right of any other individual in the universe." Here he alludes to the distinction between rights *in rem* as contrasted with rights *in personam*: whereas personal rights (rights in contract, etc.) are available only against some particular or determinate person or persons, rights *in rem* are available against the whole world. Digby observes that "the law dealing with rights *in rem* may be called—using the term 'property' in a large sense—the law of property, or the law dealing with property rights."

> The rights and their corresponding duties which form the matter of English private law are first to be divided into two great classes, differing from each other in respect of the persons on whom the duties, which correlate the rights, are incumbent. A person may have a right the essence of which consists in the fact that *all* other persons whatsoever are under a duty corresponding to the right; or he may have a right the essence of which consists in the fact that the corresponding duty is incumbent on some one or more *determinate* person or persons. An example of the first class of rights is the

---

[66] Justinian, *Digest*, 41.1.3.
[67] R. D. Melville, *A Manual of the Principles of Roman Law Relating to Persons, Property, and Obligations* (Edinburgh: W. Green, n.d.), pp. 213, 217.
[68] *Black's Law Dictionary* (4th ed. 1957), p. 997.

right of property which a person has in or over a piece of land or a herd of cattle. *All* other persons whatsoever are bound to abstain from acts injurious to his power of dealing as he pleases with his own. In other words, he may enjoy, use, and, if he pleases, if the thing is perishable, use up, the thing which is the subject of the right, subject only to certain general limitations, and also to certain special limitations prevailing in particular cases, where his rights are limited by conflicting rights possessed by other persons over the same subject. Rights of this class have received the name of rights *in rem*, an expression which means, not rights over things, but rights *available against all the world*, i.e., where a duty is incumbent on all persons whatsoever to abstain from acts injurious to the right.[69]

He continues, "If the word 'property' were not so ambiguous, one might venture to suggest that the 'law of property,' or 'of property rights,' should be substituted for the obscure expression 'rights *in rem*.'"

In other words, common-law jurisprudence imparts an absolute quality to property rights ("against all the world") which it hesitates to find in the realm of personal rights as such. We may of course disagree with such a jurisprudential philosophy, but we can hardly deny that this is what the common law is saying.

Nor can we deny the implications of this high view of property for the issue at hand; namely, the extent to which the common law regards the foetus as a person. In that realm of common law—property rights—where the protections afforded are the most unqualified and absolute (*in rem*), the foetus has most consistently been given recognition from the moment of conception. Putting it otherwise, when the common law has had its most unqualified rights at stake—inheritance, etc.—it has been the least willing to place the beginning of human life later than conception itself.

Should not this give us good reason to seek to bring modern abortion law into line with the history and spirit of the common law as reflected in that fundamental principle of *in rem* property rights which declares that human beings are to be recognized as such from the very moment of conception?

The International Human Rights Perspective

Property and inheritance rights take one back to the beginnings of the common law; the international and comparative law of human rights represents, if any legal field may be said to do so, the cutting edge of contemporaneity. But in

---

[69] K. E. Digby, *An Introduction to the History of the Law of Real Property with Original Authorities* (4th ed.; Oxford: Clarendon Press, 1892), pp. 298-300.

the latter, as in the former, the message concerning the rights of the unborn is the same: maximal protection should be afforded to unborn children.

On February 25, 1975, the Federal Constitutional Court (*Bundesverfassungsgericht*) of the Federal Republic of Germany (BRD) struck down the relaxed abortion provision of the Federal Diet's Fifth Law for the Reform of the Penal Code. In doing so, the German Court reached a conclusion diametrically opposed to that of the U.S. Supreme Court in *Roe v Wade*[70], and inconsistent with limited protections given to the child not yet "capable of being born alive" in the English Abortion Act 1967. The Federal Constitutional Court held that unborn human life represents an independent legal value enjoying protection under Article 2 of the German Basic Law (the German federal constitution), that the state is under a duty to protect unborn human life from attacks not only from the state but also from individuals, including the mother, and that this duty exists throughout pregnancy and even takes precedence over the mother's rights to self-determination.[71]

> In construing Article 2, Paragraph 2, Sentence 1, of the Basic Law, one should begin with its language: "Everyone has a right to life." ... The process of development ... is a continuing process which exhibits no sharp demarcation and does not allow a precise division of the various steps of development of the human life. The process does not end even with birth; the phenomena of consciousness which are specific to the human personality, for example, appear for the first time a rather long time after birth. Therefore, the protection of Article 2, Paragraph 2, Sentence 1, of the Basic Law cannot be limited either to the "completed" human being after birth or to the child about to be born which is independently capable of living. The right to life is guaranteed to everyone who "lives"; no distinction can be made here between various stages of the life developing itself before birth, or between unborn and born life. "Everyone" in the sense of Article 2, Paragraph 2, Sentence 1, of the Basic Law is "everyone living"; expressed in another way: every life possessing human individuality, "everyone" also includes the yet unborn human being.[72]

---

[70] See Harold O. J. Brown, "Abortion: Rights or Technicalities? A Comparison of *Roe v Wade* with the Abortion Decision of the German Federal Constitutional Court," *Human Life Review*, Summer, 1975, pp. 60-85; and D. P. Kommers, "Abortion and Constitution: United States and West Germany," 25 *American Journal of Comparative Law* 255-85 (1977).

[71] See the full translated text of the decision in Robert E. Jonas and John D. Gorby, "West German Abortion Decision: A Contrast to *Roe v Wade*—with Commentaries," 9 *John Marshall Journal of Practice & Procedure* 551-695 (1976).

[72] *Ibid.*, p. 638 (the key phrase in the Basic Law is: "*Jeder hat das Recht auf Leben*"). Even the dissenting justices agreed with the majority on this point; they assert: "The life of each individual human being is self-evidently a central value of the legal order. It is uncontested that the constitutional duty to protect this life also includes its preliminary stages before birth" (*ibid.*, p. 663).

Defendants in the case, not satisfied with this decision, took the matter to the European Commission on Human Rights in Strasbourg, arguing that the judgment of the Federal Constitutional Court was incompatible with the provisions of the European Convention on Human Rights. Defendants' application was declared admissible,[73] but they were unsuccessful on the merits: no incompatibility between the Convention and the judgment of Germany's highest Court could be found.[74]

This result should not appear in the least strange. The European system for the protection of human rights originated in large measure in reaction to the devaluation of human life and the atrocities which Europe experienced during the Second World War.[75] The Basic Law of the German Federal Republic—the source of the Federal Constitutional Court's authority—had precisely the same historical antecedents. In its decision of February 25, 1975, the Constitutional Court declared:

> Underlying the Basic Law are principles for the structuring of the state that may be understood only in light of the historical experience and the spiritual-moral confrontation with the previous system of National Socialism. In opposition to the omnipotence of the totalitarian state which claimed for itself limitless dominion over all areas of social life and which, in the prosecution of its goals of state, consideration for the life of the individual fundamentally meant nothing, the Basic Law of the Federal Republic of Germany has erected an order bound together by values which places the individual human being and his dignity at the focal point of all of its ordinances. At its basis lies the concept, as the Federal Constitutional Court previously pronounced (Decisions of the Federal Constitutional Court, 2, 1. 12), that human beings possess an inherent worth as individuals in order of creation which uncompromisingly demands unconditional respect for the life of every individual human being, even for the apparently socially "worthless," and which therefore excludes the destruction of such life without legally justifiable grounds. This fundamental constitutional decision determines the structure and the interpretation of the entire legal order. Even the legislature is bound by it; considerations of socio-political expediency, even necessities of state, cannot overcome this constitutional limitation (Decisions of the

---

[73] *X. and Y. against the Federal Republic of Germany*, Application No. 6959/74, decision of May 19, 1967 (19 Yearbook 382-416).

[74] Cf. T. R. Sealy, III, "Abortion Law Reform in Europe: The European Commission on Human Rights Upholds German Restrictions on Abortion," 15 *Texas International Law Journal* 162-86 (1980).

[75] See, in particular, A. H. Robertson, *Human Rights in Europe* (2ᵈ rev. ed.; Manchester: Manchester University Press, 1977), pp. 3-4.

Federal Constitutional Court, 1, 14. 36). Even a general change of the viewpoints dominant in the populace on this subject—if such a change could be established at all—would change nothing.[76]

The overall picture of foetal rights in the international and comparative law of human rights has become clear through a landmark analysis by two French legal scholars, Alexandre Kiss and Jean-Bernard Marie.[77] They point out, *inter alia*, that even though it is true that the foetus does not automatically benefit from all the protections and freedoms afforded by international conventions, nevertheless, since the foetus is part of the mother's body, it "benefits by way of the mother from the protections accorded to her—specifically including the right to life" (example: Article 6 of the United Nations Covenant on Civil and Political Rights, prohibiting the execution of the death penalty pronounced against a pregnant woman; the same principle would apply *a fortiori* to torture and to cruel or inhuman treatment).

Moreover, the most recent international human rights agreements show increasing sensitivity to and concern for the protection of the human person from the very moment of conception. Thus the (nonobligatory) Declaration of the Rights of the Child states in its Preamble that the child "requires appropriate juridical protection before as well as after birth."[78] The American Convention of Human Rights, which entered into force in 1978, declares (Article 4) that

---

[76] 9 *John Marshall Journal of Practice & Procedure*, op. cit. [in note 71], p. 662. It should be pointed out that since this 1975 decision, abortion law has in fact been relaxed in West Germany by means of legislation that has survived the constitutional test; but the significance of the Court's reasoning in the 1975 decision is not lessened thereby. Indeed, the Spanish Constitutional Court used much the same *ratio* in its decision of April 11, 1985 (Sentencia No. 53/1985: text in BOE 119 Suplemento, para. 9096 [May 18, 1985]), declaring unconstitutional a proposed new law depenalizing abortions under certain circumstances; see the well documented articles in *ABC* [Madrid], April 12 and 18, 1985, analyzing in detail the legal, social, moral, and political consequences of the decision. In brief, the Spanish Constitutional Court's ruling rejected the law passed in October, 1983, by the (Socialist) Parliament, but not put into effect pending the outcome of an appeal against it: the Court ruled that the law violated Art. 15 of the 1978 Spanish Constitution (introduced after the death of Franco and the termination of his dictatorship) which declares: "Everyone has a right to life and physical and moral integrity" (*"Todos tienen derecho a la vida y a la integridad física y moral"*). As in West Germany, so in Spain, the Constitutional Court decision was followed by the passage of a more nuanced abortion law; but its implementation is being vigorously opposed by the Spanish medical profession and prominent jurists.

[77] Alexandre Kiss and Jean-Bernard Marie, "Le droit à la vie: rapport juridique," 7 *Human Rights* 338-53 (1974).

[78] Cf. Guy Raymond, *Droit de l'enfance, de la conception à la majorité* (Paris: LITEC/Libraire de la Cour de Cassation, 1983), pp. 141 ff.

> Every person has the right to have his life respected. This right shall be protected by law and, in general, from the moment of conception. No one shall be arbitrarily deprived of his life.

The United States has not ratified the American Convention, and the strong wording of this right-to-life article has worried more than a few congressmen: might not the United States, after ratification, find itself a defendant before the Inter-American Court of Human Rights because of *Roe v Wade*? But whether such a worry is realistic or not (and the U.S.—if it does ratify the Convention—may well take the coward's way out by qualifying its ratification of Article 4 by a "reservation" or "statement of understanding"), the American Convention sharply illustrates the tension between, on the one hand, all statutory and case-law attempts to limit the right to life of the unborn, and, on the other, the powerful trend toward maximizing human rights on the international scene. In international human rights law, the rights of the unborn are gaining ground continually.

The Beginning of Human Life and Its Ethical Consequences for the Law

Perhaps the most quoted line in *Roe v Wade* is that in which the Court said, "We need not resolve the difficult question of when life begins."[79] But, with respect, that is the very question which cannot go unresolved if the rights of the unborn are properly to be protected and the interests of society adequately served at the same time. If the unborn are indeed human persons, any society aiming to realize the non-discriminatory ideals of natural justice will aim to give them the same legal rights and protections afforded to other human beings. If the unborn are not human beings, or do not become human until a particular point in their development (commencement of brain function, capability of being born alive, viability, birth itself, etc.), then the law must take this into account in order not to give the non-human rights which will perforce limit the rights of those (such as the pregnant woman or other family members) who are truly human.

The problem of locating a developmental point where the foetus can be regarded as having passed from pre-human to human is truly insolvable. The German Federal Constitutional Court saw the issue clearly when it wrote (as we already observed): "The process of development ... is a continuing process which exhibits no sharp demarcation and does not allow a precise division of the various steps of development of the human life. The process does not end even with birth; the phenomena of consciousness which are specific to the hu-

---

[79] 93 S. Ct. 705 (1973) at 730.

man personality, for example, appear for the first time a rather long time after birth." On the basis of exactly such reasoning does Professor Tooley, whom we quoted at the beginning of this essay, argue that "neither abortion, nor infanticide, at least during the first few weeks after birth, is morally wrong," since "an entity cannot be a person unless it possesses, or has previously possessed, the capacity for thought."

In point of fact, a satisfactory legal understanding as to the beginning point of human life will necessitate reliance upon empirical, scientific evidence of human personhood. One must not create a legal definition of personhood which flies in the face of medical evidence as to what a person in fact is. In National Socialist law, the Jew—regardless of genetic evidence of his humanity—was deprived of his legal personhood and destroyed like worthless offal.[80] Prior to the American Civil War and the antislavery Amendments to the U.S. Constitution, such judicial decisions as *Dred Scott* relegated slaves to the status of legal nonpersons in spite of clear biological evidence of their humanity.[81] Wherever legal personhood has been defined without reference to objective genetic criteria, the door has been opened to the most frightful consequences.

And what is the testimony of contemporary genetics? The current biological evidence is unequivocal; here is a summary of it by Jules Carles, director of research at France's National Center for Scientific Research (CNRS):

> This first cell [formed by sperm-and-egg union] is already the embryo of an autonomous living being with individual hereditary patrimony, such that if we knew the nature of the spermatozoid and the chromosomes involved, we could already at that point predict the characteristics of the child, the future colour of his hair, and the illnesses to which he would be subject. In his mother's womb, where he will grow, he will not accept everything she brings to him, but only that which is necessary to his existence; thereby he will realize his hereditary patrimony. In that first cell the profound dynamism and the precise direction of life appears. ... In spite of its fragility and its immense needs, an autonomous and genuinely living being has come into existence. ... It is rather surprising to see certain physicians speak here of "potential life" as if the fertilized egg began its real life when it nests in the uterus. Modern biology does not deny the importance of nidation, but it sees it only as condition—indispensable, to be sure—for the development of the embryo and the continuation of a life already in existence.[82]

---

[80] Cf. J. W. Jones, *The Nazi Conception of Law* (New York: Oxford University Press, 1939).
[81] *Dred Scott v Sandford*, 19 Howard 393 (1857).
[82] Jules Carles, *La fécondation* (Paris: Presses Universitaires de France, 1967), pp. 81-82 (translation ours). Strange to say, in spite of the general soundness of its judgment, the German Federal Constitutional Court emphasises, not conception but nidation in its discussion of the origin point of human life: 9 *John Marshall Journal of Practice & Procedure, op. cit.* [in note 71], p. 638.

The law must therefore aim at protecting the rights of the unborn from the moment of conception, not merely from some subsequent point of human development. The law must set its face against functional definitions of personhood. People function as humans *because* they are human; they do not become human by performing human functions. Professor Finnis[83] has rightly shown the fallacy of functional argumentation in criticizing Peter Singer's view that, since we commonly locate the death of a person at the point of brain death, we should locate the beginning of human life at the point when the brain first begins to function; says Finnis: if you feed a conceptus, you get a brain and possibly a philosopher, whilst if you feed someone whose brainstem has been severed, you get nothing. The BRD's Federal Constitutional Court rightly observed that "the security of human existence against encroachments by the state would be incomplete if it did not also embrace the prior step of 'completed life', unborn life."[84]

The practical implications of such a jurisprudential approach, firmly grounded in the empirical evidence of modern genetics, will embrace such considerations as the following: (1) Even when the life of the unborn needs to be sacrificed for the sake of the life of the mother, this will not be justified by the view that the unborn child is somehow "sub-human." As the leading case of *R v Dudley and Stephens*[85] (the cannibalism case) established, the killing of an innocent human being even to save the life of another person does not trigger the defence of "necessity." As in that case, abortions to save the life of the mother should be treated by the law as lesser-of-evils (lesser, because of the greater nexus of responsibility of the mother), not as neutral acts.[86] (2) Therapeutic abortions should be viewed with the greatest jurisprudential suspicion. Even Dickens and Cook, who favour a relaxed policy toward them, admit that "the degree of

---

[83] In his unpublished lecture on "Natural Law and the Rights of the Unborn," delivered at the Chicago conference on "Reversing *Roe v Wade* through the Courts," March 31, 1984 (see above, note 37).

[84] 9 *John Marshall Journal of Practice & Procedure, op. cit.* [in note 71], p. 638.

[85] 14 Q.B.D. 273 (1884). For a recent, comprehensive treatment of this case, see A. W. B. Simpson, *Cannibalism and the Common Law* (Chicago: University of Chicago Press, 1984).

[86] Indeed, "there are some killings fairly within the net-saving-of-lives, lesser-evil doctrine that it is very doubtful courts would sanction—for example, killing a person to obtain his organs to save the lives of several other people or even removing them for that purpose against his will without killing him. The unreadiness of the law to justify such aggression against non-threatening bystanders reflects a moral uneasiness with reliance on a utilitarian calculus for assessing the justification of intended killings, even when a net saving of lives is achieved": Sanford H. Kadish, "Respect for Life and Regard for Rights in the Criminal Law," in O. Temkin, W. K. Frankena, and S. H. Kadish, *Respect for Life in Medicine, Philosophy, and the Law* (Baltimore and London: Johns Hopkins University Press, 1977), p. 83; Professor Kadish's valuable article was also published in 64 *California Law Review* 871-901 (1976).

congenital disadvantage that may justify abortion is unavoidably contentious, since it touches upon evaluating the worth of a human life."[87] (3) The law will indeed have to "take on the test-tube," as Ian Kennedy, professor of medical law & ethics at King's College, London, has recently written[88]: it will need to deal with issues of genetic experimentation, embryo banks, etc. The only satisfactory map through this difficult, unexplored thicket is the genetic-chromosomal map of the human person, showing that the unborn child is a genuine human being from the moment of conception. Once this is recognized, it follows that

> it should be unlawful to induce super-ovulation and to fertilise multiple ova where there is no possibility of the fertilised ova being implanted immediately in the womb of the woman from whom they came. It should also be unlawful to take any steps:
>
> (a) To alter genetically the fertilised ovum
>
> (b) To test the sex of a fertilised ovum with the intention of rejecting a zygote of the unwanted sex
>
> (c) To test a fertilised ovum with the intention of destroying the zygote if it proves to be defective or susceptible to certain diseases. ...[89]

In expressing deep concern over the Warnock report, Robert Snowden, director of the Institute of Population Studies at the University of Exeter, has well expressed the position which a sound jurisprudence should also affirm:

> To experiment on live embryos, whether they are deliberately created for the purpose, or "spare" embryos left over from another procedure, is to treat them as a sub-human species. A live human embryo, however early its stage of development, has all the potential of a unique human being.[90]

---

[87] Dickens and Cook, *op. cit.* [in note 30], p. 445.
[88] Ian Kennedy, "Let the Law Take on the Test-tube," *The Times*, May 26, 1984, p. 6. Among the bons mots in this penetrating article are: "Intuitively we do not equate a fertilized human egg with a hamster or a piece of mouse tissue"; and "no human life should be used as a means to an end." A longer version of Professor Kennedy's article, with his trenchant criticisms of the Warnock report, appears under the title, "The Moral Status of the Embryo," in 34 *King's Counsel* [Faculty of Laws, King's College, London] 21-29 (1984-1985).
[89] "In Vitro Fertilisation," *News and Comment* (Association of Lawyers for the Defence of the Unborn), No. 21 (Spring, 1984), 5. We do not deal here with questions of sperm banks or surrogate motherhood, since these (admittedly important) legal and ethical issues are out of the scope of this essay: no one claims that the sperm or unfertilized ovum constitutes a human person/unborn child.
[90] *The Times*, Aug. 9, 1984, p. 11.

Constitutional Suggestions by Way of a Conclusion

Unborn children are in no position to assert their own rights—indeed, they are incapable of even thinking about them. Does this mean, as Professor Tooley would certainly maintain,[91] that they are devoid of rights? Professor Neil MacCormick has successfully argued that children's rights are an ideal test-case for the validity of "interest theories" as against "will theories" of right, since the rights of children do not depend upon the conscious choices they make.[92] Professor Melden makes the same point: "To assert that awareness is a necessary condition of the possession of rights is to lay down too strong a condition, either in law or morals. Children, for example, possess legal and moral rights even before they are aware of them."[93] Indeed, one of the chief glories of the English legal tradition is that it has been acutely sensitive to the need to protect the rights of the weak and of those who because of disability have not been able to protect themselves.

How best can Anglo-American law assert and protect the rights of the unborn today? In the United States, there is virtual unanimity among those supporting the right to life of the unborn that Acts of Congress in behalf of the unborn child, though politically more practicable, will not be sufficient at the end of the day: what one Session of Congress enacts, another can as readily repeal. The solution is thus a right-to-life Amendment to the federal Constitution, which would function much as did the post-Civil War 14th Amendment, declaring that the unborn—like former slaves—are indeed "persons" within the meaning of the Constitution and therefore entitled to its protections.[94]

In England, the ultimate answer would also appear to be constitutional, in that the rights of the unborn require a more solid base than the changing will of Parliament. No student of Bennion's *Statute Law*[95] can be sanguine about Parliamentary legislation, and the weaknesses of the Abortion Act 1967 may well precursor a general legislative inability under contemporary societal pressures to keep a clear eye on the unwritten verities of English constitutionalism. Not without reason, an impressive number of luminaries of the English bench have argued eloquently for a written, if not entrenched, Bill of Rights: Lord

---

[91] See above, our text at note 3.
[92] Neil MacCormick, "Children's Rights: A Test-case for Theories of Right," in his *Legal Right and Social Democracy: Essays in Legal and Political Philosophy* (Oxford: Clarendon Press, 1982), pp. 154-66.
[93] A. I. Melden, *Rights and Persons* (Oxford: Basil Blackwell, 1977), p. 200.
[94] See R. A. Destro, "Abortion and the Constitution: The Need for a Life Protective Amendment," 63 *California Law Review* 1250 (1975).
[95] Francis A. R. Bennion, *Statute Law* (2d ed.; London: Oyez Longman, 1983), especially "doubt-factors" 3 ("politic uncertainty") and 5 ("the fallible draftsman"), pp. 157-61, 167 ff.

Scarman in his 1974 Hamlyn lectures; Professor Wade in his Hamlyn lecture of 1980; and Lord Hailsham in his *Elective Dictatorship* (1976), *The Dilemma of Democracy* (1978), and his Hamlyn lecture of 1983.[96]

To be sure, a written and entrenched constitution is no panacea for all legal ills (witness the *Roe v Wade* decision flying in the face of the U.S. Bill of Rights), but one is deeply impressed by what the Federal Constitutional Court of West Germany was able to do in behalf of the rights of unborn children through its interpretation of the German Basic Law. And Strasbourg, by refusing to find incompatibility between that constitutional decision and the European Convention on Human Rights, reaffirmed the belief of many that incorporation of the Convention into English law might well fill the need for an entrenched Bill of Rights in the United Kingdom. However this may be, those who create, interpret, and apply English law today must surely endeavour to do all that they can in the difficult days of social change now upon us to reinforce and extend the historic sensitivity of the common law tradition to the rights of unborn children.

---

[96] See, in general, *Do We Need a Bill of flights?*, ed. Colin M. Campbell (London: Temple Smith, 1980), and Michael Zander, *A Bill of Rights?* (3ᵈ ed.; London: Sweet & Maxwell, 1985). The year 1998 saw the passing of the U.K. Human Rights Act, which effectively incorporated the European Convention of Human Rights into English law. Most of the provisions of the Act came into force on October 2, 2000.

Part Five

A Bit of Systematic Theology

1. Did Christ Die for E.T. as well as for *Homo Sapiens*?

Winning Contribution in the 2003-2004 Essay Competition of The Victoria Institute (The Philosophical Society of Great Britain)

Synopsis

The essay begins with a brief discussion of the dangers of theological speculation. It then presents the major opposing positions on the question of the redemption of other fallen worlds. The issue is then treated in terms of the nature of sin, the significance of the Incarnation, and the character of the Atonement. Atonement theories are seen to offer the best route to a solution to the vexed issue. Finally, the suggestion is made that God's grace may be such that earthly redemption might even impact unfallen worlds.

The issue before us in this paper is the applicability—or non-applicability—of the salvatory work of Christ on earth to rational creatures on other worlds.

Introduction: The Danger of Speculation?

When such a topic is broached, the immediate reaction may well be: "How sad! Another example of the irrelevance of theological speculation! Will Christians never get beyond medieval theorising of the kind which endeavoured to determine the number of angels able to dance on the head of a pin?" Or one may think of the 18th century mystic Emanuel Swedenborg, who provided remarkable detail concerning the spiritual nature of life on other worlds—all without a shred of supporting evidence for his "visions."[1]

Indeed, even the kind of serious biblical discussion to follow might appear to attract the answer recounted by Augustine in his *Confessions* to the query, "What was God doing before he made heaven and earth?": "He was preparing hell for pryers into mysteries."[2]

However, it is well to observe that Augustine himself rejected such a cavalier approach to difficult issues, since they "elude the pressure of the question." And,

---

[1] Swedenborg, *Earths in the Universe* (London: Swedenborg Society, 1970).
[2] *Confessions*, XI. 14.

as to our present discussion, two points are worth noting in its defence: (1) The meaning, significance, and extent of Christ's atonement can hardly be regarded as peripheral. Christocentric matters lie at the very heart of Christian faith. As Luther well put it, "The whole of the Scripture is about Christ alone, everywhere." (2) The interest in space travel and other worlds continually increases as astronomical investigations and modern technology become more and more sophisticated,[3] so such questions as that posed here may be of interest not just to Christian believers but also to secularists seeking a coherent worldview. It follows that we must not aprioristically rule out, as Aquinas did, following Aristotle, the very existence of other inhabited worlds[4] — or the possibility of their needing a Saviour.

A preliminary caveat: in this paper we restrict ourselves to the theological question posed in its title. We do not treat the wider question of the plurality of inhabited worlds, or the history of the controversies concerning the existence of such worlds. For those more general topics, readers should consult the excellent published studies available in the history of ideas.[5]

The Opposing Positions

Throughout the Christian era, theologians have differed on the issue of whether Christ's redemption could apply to the rational inhabitants of other worlds. We shall illustrate with two representatives of the negative and two representatives of the positive viewpoint.

---

[3] Cf. Ronald N. Bracewell, *The Galactic Club: Intelligent Life in Outer Space* (San Francisco: W. H. Freeman; New York: Scribner's, 1975).

[4] *Summa Theologica*, Pt. I, Q. 47, Art. 3. Needless to say, Aquinas was not adverse to undemonstrable theological speculations — for example his assertion, again following Aristotle, that the male receives his "rational soul" forty days after conception whilst the female has to wait eighty to ninety days for hers (cf. John Warwick Montgomery, "The Christian View of the Fetus," in: W. O. Spitzer and C. L. Saylor (eds.), *Birth Control and the Christian* (London: Coverdale House; Wheaton, Illinois: Tyndale House, 1969), p. 69.

[5] In particular: Steven J. Dick, *Plurality of Worlds: The Origins of the Extraterrestrial Life Debate from Democritus to Kant* (Cambridge: Cambridge University Press, 1982); and Michael J. Crowe, *The Extraterrestrial Life Debate 1750-1900* (reprint ed. with addendum; Cambridge: Cambridge University Press, 1988). Professor Crowe's work is especially valuable, and has been of great assistance in the preparation of this paper, since (quite obviously as a believing Christian) he fully appreciates the theological aspects of the question as to the existence of intelligent life on other worlds.

On the negative side, Philip Melanchthon, Luther's closest associate, the author of the *Augsburg Confession* (the first of the Protestant Confessions) and an educator and Renaissance classicist whose impact on subsequent theology and European church life was enormous:[6]

> The Son of God is One; our master Jesus Christ was born, died, and resurrected in this world. Nor does He manifest Himself elsewhere, nor elsewhere has He died or resurrected. Therefore it must not be imagined that Christ died and was resurrected more often, nor must it be thought that in any other world without the knowledge of the Son of God, that men would be restored to eternal life.[7]

Isaac Watts, the great evangelical hymn writer of the 18th century, took essentially the same position—as have many others:

> Thy voice produc'd the seas and spheres,
> Bid the waves roar, and planets shine;
> But nothing like thy Self appears,
> Through all these spacious works of thine.[8]

In contrast, the opposing viewpoint—that holding either the genuine possibility or the virtual certainty that Christ's atoning work on earth would also redeem extraterrestrial rational creatures—has had such representatives as the 17th century Christian philosopher Descartes and the late 19th century Roman Catholic popular theologian J. De Concilio. In a letter of 6 June 1647, Descartes wrote: "I do not see at all that the mystery of the Incarnation, and all the other advantages that God has brought forth for man obstruct him from having brought forth an infinity of other very great advantages for an infinity of other creatures."[9] In the same spirit, but in much more specific terms, De Concilio argued that "when Christ died and paid the ransom of our redemption, He included [extraterrestrials] also in that ransom, the value of which was infinite and capable of redeeming innumerable worlds."[10]

---

[6] See Clyde L. Manschreck, *Melanchthon: The Quiet Reformer* (New York and Nashville: Abingdon, 1958); John Warwick Montgomery, "Luther, Libraries, and Learning," in his *In Defense of Martin Luther* (Milwaukee: Northwestern Publishing House, 1970), pp. 123-25; and Montgomery, *Heraldic Aspects of the German Reformation* (Bonn: Verlag für Kultur und Wissenschaft, 2003).
[7] Trans. and quoted by Dick, *op. cit.*, p. 89.
[8] David P. French (ed.), *Minor English Poets 1660-1780*, Vol. III (New York, 1967), p. 635. See also, on Watts's lines, A. J. Meadows, *The High Firmament: A Survey of Astronomy in English Literature* (Leicester, 1969), p. 131.
[9] *Oeuvres*, ed. C. Adams and P. Tannery, Vol. V (Paris, 1903), p. 54.
[10] J. De Concilio, *Harmony Between Science and Revelation* (1889), p. 232. See also Concilio, "The Plurality of Worlds," 9 *American Catholic Quarterly Rev.* 193-216 (April 1884).

Which of the two diametrically contrasting positions is correct? To answer this, we shall have to engage in some in-depth theological thinking.

Unfallen Worlds?

Why did Christ die? The Scriptures are unequivocal: *for the sins of the world.* Jesus is so named in the Gospels because "he shall save his people from their sins." And it is no exaggeration to say that Paul's Epistle to the Romans and the Book of Hebrews (perhaps the most theologically systematic books of the entire Bible) have Christ's sacrificial death for the sins of a fallen race as their central themes. It follows that Christ's death could not be directly relevant to an *unfallen* world. "Those who are well," Jesus taught, "have no need of a physician." As Renaissance littérateur Tommaso Campanella, author of the utopia, *City of the Sun*, recognised: "If the inhabitants which may be in other stars are men, they did not originate from Adam and are not infected by his sin. Nor do these inhabitants need redemption, unless they have committed some other sin."[11]

To be sure, Christ's teaching and example could have positive influence on unfallen terrestrials. Thus Swedenborg argued that

> It pleased the Lord to be born, and to assume the Human, on our Earth, and not on any other. THE PRINCIPAL REASON *was for the sake of the Word, that it might be written on our Earth; and when written might afterwards be published throughout the whole Earth; and that, once published, it might be preserved for all posterity; and thus it might be made manifest, even to all in the other life, that God did become Man.*[12]

Professor Crowe rightly notes, however, that "a striking feature of this is that Christ's communicative function in his terrestrial incarnation seems to be given primacy over his redemptive role."[13] Not "seems" but "is"! Swedenborg, having rejected atonement as satisfaction for sin and having limited himself to a purely subjective view of redemption, replaces it with the "communicative" role of the Word.[14] Our subject in the present essay is the potential impact of the *death* of Christ on other worlds—not the impact of the Second Person of the Trinity on the universe in any other respect; and his death would have no directly

---

[11] Tommaso Campanella, "The Defense of Galileo," trans. Grant McColley, 22/3-4 *Smith College Studies in History* 66 (1937).
[12] Swedenborg, *op. cit.*, para. 113.
[13] Crowe, *op. cit.*, p. 100.
[14] See Walter R. Martin's treatment of Swedenborgianism in his classic, *The Kingdom of the Cults* (London: Marshall, Morgan and Scott, 1967), chap. 11, pp. 241-51. (This chapter appears as an Appendix in the "revised and expanded" edition of 1985.)

redemptive function for rational creatures on other worlds if they were not, like us, fallen creatures.[15]

So is it likely that extraterrestrials would not in fact need the redeeming work of Christ? Were that the case, then the question posed in this essay would have already found its answer!

C. S. Lewis consciously produced his space trilogy as "a kind of theologised science-fiction."[16] In the first two of these novels (*Out of the Silent Planet* and *Perelandra*—the latter published in America under the title, *Journey to Venus*), he employed the theme of fallen terrestrial invaders discovering unfallen rational beings on other worlds.[17] This possibility of human space travellers corrupting unfallen worlds also preoccupied Lewis in his non-fiction writings and in his letters.[18] For example, in his essay "Religion and Rocketry" (published also under other titles), he wrote: "I have wondered before now whether the vast astronomical distances may not be God's quarantine precautions. They prevent the spiritual infection of a fallen species from spreading."[19]

Lewis's notion of other inhabited worlds being unfallen had prior support from both Protestants and Roman Catholics. Distinguished 18th century American astronomer David Rittenhouse wrote—with illustrations hardly designed to improve American-British relations then or now:

> Happy people [on other worlds]! and perhaps more happy still, that all communication with us is denied. We have neither corrupted you with our vices nor injured you by violence. None of your sons and daughters ... have been doomed to endless slavery by us in America, merely because *their* bodies may be disposed to reflect or absorb the rays of light, in a way different from *ours*. Even you, inhabitants of the moon, ... are effectually secured, alike from the rapacious hand of the haughty Spaniard, and of the unfeeling British nabob. Even British thunder impelled by British thirst of gain, cannot reach you.[20]

---

[15] *Indirect* redemptive benefits, however, might exist for unfallen extraterrestrials; see below, note 59.

[16] C. S. Lewis, *Letters* (New York: Harcourt Brace Jovanovich, 1966), p. 260.

[17] Cf. Martha C. Sammons, *A Guide through C. S. Lewis Space Trilogy* (Westchester, Illinois: Cornerstone Books, 1980); and John Warwick Montgomery (ed.), *Myth, Allegory and Gospel: An Interpretation of J. R. R. Tolkien, C. S. Lewis, G. K. Chesterton, Charles Williams* (Minneapolis: Bethany, 1974).

[18] See the following writings by Lewis: *God in the Dock* (Grand Rapids, Michigan: Eerdmans, 1970), p. 267; *Reflections on the Psalms* (New York: Harcourt Brace Jovanovich, 1958), p. 103; *Letters (op. cit.)*, p. 210; *Problem of Pain* (New York: Macmillan, 1978), pp. 62-64, 85.

[19] C. S. Lewis, *Fern-seed and Elephants and Other Essays on Christianity* (London: Fontana/HarperCollins, 1975), p. 93. This essay also appeared under the title, "Will We Lose God in Outer Space?," 81 *Christian Herald* (April, 1958), and was published under a similar title as a pamphlet by S.P.C.K. in 1959. It also appears in Lewis's *The World's Last Night*.

[20] David Rittenhouse, *An Oration* (Philadelphia, 1775), pp. 19-20; see the facsimile reprint in

Joseph Pohle (d. 1922), a distinguished German dogmatician of the Roman Church and one of the founding faculty of the Catholic University of America, wrote prolifically on the plurality of worlds. In his *Die Sternenwelten und ihre Bewohner*, Pohle declared: "Concerning the dogma of the Redemption of fallen men through the God-man Christ, it is not necessary to assume as probable also the fall of species on other celestial bodies. No reason ... obliges us to think others as evil as ourselves."[21]

Of course, we are not *obliged* to think in such terms; and E.T. is such a charming, apparently unfallen little fellow![22] But E.T. is not the only cinematographic extraterrestrial: there is also, for example, Alf—whose rapier sense of humour only thinly disguises a remarkably single-minded concern with his own interests, at the expense of the household with which he lives.[23] Why should we exclude the possibility—or even the likelihood—that other rational creatures (possessed of freewill as are all creatures of a loving God)[24] might have misused that freedom to violate the will of their Creator?

Thomas Rawson Birks, 19th century professor of moral philosophy at Cambridge and the earliest ally of William Whewell, argued in much stronger terms: since our actual knowledge extends to only two races, men and angels, and they are both fallen, the notion that "ours is the only world where sin has entered" violates "the plainest lessons of moral probability."[25] Twentieth-century Roman Catholic theologian Teilhard de Chardin put the matter even more powerfully: the idea that "alone among all inhabited planets the earth has experienced original sin and needs redemption" is "scientifically *absurd*—since it implies that death (the theological index of the presence of original sin) could not exist in certain locations in the universe—in spite of the fact that those locations (and we know it for a fact) submit to the same physio-chemical laws as the earth does."[26]

Brooke Hindle (ed.), *The Scientific Writings of David Rittenhouse* (New York, 1980).

[21] Joseph Pohle, *Die Sternenwelten und ihre Bewohner* (2^d ed.; Köln: Bachem, 1899), pp. 457-58.

[22] E.T.'s winning character is one of the chief factors in the great appeal of Steven Spielberg's 1982 film.

[23] Alf (from the planet Melmac) was the subject of highly successful American TV series (NBC, 1986-90) and at least one motion picture (shown also in a German version). His magazine was published for several years in the United States. The dubbed French version of his television series is still shown on French TV in the afternoons; and his popularity extended to the Scandinavian countries and to Italy. Recently, he has been revived in American television commercials.

[24] A point powerfully made by C. S. Lewis in his *Problem of Pain:* genuine love logically implicates freedom of choice as to whether to love in return—or not.

[25] Thomas Rawson Birks, *Modern Astronomy* (London, 1850), pp. 53-54.

[26] This passage appears in an essay of Teilhard de Chardin on the plurality of inhabited worlds; it is dated 5 June 1953 and was left unpublished at his death in 1955. Chardin's essay was published for the first time by Henri Duquaire in his book, *Si les astres sont habités ...* (Paris and Geneva: La

Is Sin on Earth Sin Elsewhere?

Leaving aside the statistical question as to how many other worlds are fallen (*pace* Chardin, the universal application of the Second Law of Thermodynamics and entropy hardly means that death must everywhere prevail in the cosmos!), we must surely entertain the hypothesis that we are not the only world which has disappointed its Creator. Would the atoning sacrifice of Christ on earth impact another fallen world? Answering that question requires us to deal with at least three fundamental underlying matters: the nature of *human sin*, the nature of *incarnation*, and the nature of the *atonement*.

Since Christ died "for sin," we must determine whether biblical revelation views Christ's sacrifice as touching only those who are genetically members of the human race. Put otherwise, is the sin for which Christ died the sin of humans—and their sin alone?

In a discussion of "Original Sin and Contemporary Anthropology," a theologian summarises what "Scripture (both in Genesis and in Romans) requires":

1. Man is accountable for what went wrong in the beginning. What does go wrong is inescapably part of his history.
2. What went wrong in the beginning is universal in its consequences.
3. All men are born alienated and breathe the air of alienation all life long.
4. Both original sin and personal sin conspire in the creation of the death we all inherit and ratify. The only way out of both is Christ.[27]

This summary quite clearly points up the "human" dimension of the sin problem. But just how racially inherent is it? Here we need to listen to the major theologians of classical Christianity, both Catholic and Protestant.[28]

Ludwig Ott's standard *Fundamentals of Catholic Dogma,* succinctly states the Roman Catholic view: "The Council of Trent says: *propagatione, non imitatione transfusum omnibus.* ... As original sin is a *peccatum naturae,* it is transmit-

---

Palatine, 1963); the passage we have translated appears on pp. 120-21.
[27] Anthony T. Padovano, *Original Sin and Christian Anthropology* ("Corpus Papers"; Washington, D.C.: Corpus Books, 1969), pp. 6-7.
[28] But not to modern representatives of the craft whose views of biblical reliability are so negative that we cannot be sure that they are endeavouring to determine "the *whole* counsel of God" on the matter in question. Thus we omit from our overview such well-known names as Karl Barth (who held that sin was an "absence" of good—like a "hornet without a sting") and Paul Tillich (whose ontological God—"Being Itself"—leaves us with a strange identification of sin with idolatry, including the "idolatry" of taking the Bible or Jesus as infallible truth). See John Warwick Montgomery, *The Suicide of Christian Theology* (Newburgh, Indiana: Trinity Press, 1998), and *Where Is History Going?* (Minneapolis: Bethany, 1969). For an interesting treatment of the shift from classical to modern views, see H. Shelton Smith, *Changing Conceptions of Original Sin: A Study in American Theology since 1750* (New York: Scribner's, 1955).

ted in the same way as human nature, through the natural act of generation. ... In each act of generation human nature is communicated in a condition deprived of grace."[29] Sin, then, is not the product of imitating one who has already sinned; it is inherent to the race, following the sin of our first parent, and is communicated genetically by the act of generation.

The Lutheran position focuses more on the scriptural grounding of the doctrine, emphasising, for example, Acts 17:26 (God "has made of one blood all nations of men"), but differs little from that just stated. The great 16th century Lutheran theologian Martin Chemnitz—who, incidentally, was one of the chief opponents of the theologising of the Council of Trent[30]—wrote: "The guilt must not be understood as only on account of another's (i.e. Adam's) sin, without any guilt of one's own. Paul affirms that the world is guilty from the one sin of the first man; and because all have sinned, they have all become sinners. ... He describes the way in which original sin is propagated: 'Through one man,' he says. And because posterity is reckoned through men, carnal propagation is understood."[31] Thus, guilt has its source in the original sin of Adam, compounded by the volitional acts of disobedience committed by his progeny, all of whom are identified with him.

The American Lutheran theologian Francis Pieper reinforces this position in his standard work, *Christian Dogmatics*:

> Original sin, which is the sin which is not committed but which is inborn in man since Adam's Fall, embraces two things: a) hereditary guilt (*culpa hereditaria*), the guilt of the one sin of Adam which God imputes to all men; and b) hereditary corruption (*corruptio humanae naturae kereditaria*), which by imputation of Adam's guilt is transmitted to all his descendants through the natural descent from the first fallen pair. ...
>
> With regard to hereditary depravity erroneous views are held ... by all those who deny it altogether when they assert that children do not inherit the corruption from their parents through their birth (*generatione*), but learn it by following the evil example (*exemplo*), which is contrary to John 3:6: "That which is born of the flesh is flesh."[32]

---

[29] Ludwig Ott, *Fundamentals of Catholic Dogma*, trans. P. Lynch, ed. J. Bastible (St. Louis, Missouri: B. Herder, 1958), p. 111.
[30] Cf. John Warwick Montgomery, "Chemnitz on the Council of Trent: An Evaluation of Chemnitz's *Examen Concilii Tridentini*," in R. C. Sproul (ed.), *Soli Deo Gloria: Essays in Reformed Theology; Festschrift for John H Gerstner* (Nutley, N.J.: Presbyterian and Reformed Publishing Company, 1976), pp. 63-94 [and *infra* as Part Six, chap. 4 in the present volume]; also, Montgomery, *Heraldic Aspects of the German Reformation* (*op. cit.*).
[31] Quoted in Herman A. Preus and Edmund Smits (ed.), *The Doctrine of Man in Classical Lutheran Theology* (Minneapolis: Augsburg, 1962), pp. 144-45.
[32] Francis Pieper, *Christian Dogmatics* (4 vols.; St. Louis, Missouri: Concordia, 1950-1957), I, 538-

Calvin's treatment of the matter is not dissimilar (whilst combined with a rather uncomfortable predestinarianism):

> Adam, when he lost the gifts received, lost them not only for himself but for us all. ... There is nothing absurd, then, in supposing that, when Adam was despoiled, human nature was left naked and destitute, or that when he was infected with sin, contagion crept into human nature. Hence rotten branches came forth from a rotten root, which transmitted their rottenness to the other twigs sprouting from them. For thus were the children corrupted in the parent, so that they brought disease upon their children's children. That is, the beginning of corruption in Adam was such that it was conveyed in a perpetual stream from the ancestors into their descendants. For the contagion does not take its origin from the substance of the flesh or soul, but because it had been so ordained by God that the first man should at one and the same time have and lose, both for himself and for his descendants, the gifts that God had bestowed upon him.[33]

One of the very finest of 20th century evangelical dogmaticians was J. Oliver Buswell, Jr, my colleague when at the end of his life he taught at the Trinity Evangelical Divinity School. On the basis of Scripture and classic theology, Buswell condemns what Charles Hodge termed "mediate imputation" —

> the theory that all mankind have become sinners through the influence of Adam's sin, and that the guilt imputed to us is based, not immediately upon the original act of human sin, but mediately upon the sinfulness which has developed in us. This doctrine would imply that we are not guilty sinners because our representative sinned, but we are guilty sinners only because we ourselves are individually corrupt.
>
> It is quite apparent that such an interpretation of the sin of Adam would destroy the analogy of original sin to the atonement of Christ. If we are not guilty sinners because our representative sinned, then we are not justified because our Representative, our Substitute, "bore our sins in His own body on the tree" (I Peter 2:24).[34]

From the systematicians of dogma just surveyed — and they are a fair sampling of those treating the subject through Christian history — one must conclude that the substitutionary sacrifice of Christ requires his identification with a race whose inherent corruption derives from the sin of its first member and the passing on of that corruption by natural generation. Adam's sin is of course re-

---

42. In support, Pieper cites Rom. 5:18-19 and Ps. 51:5.
[33] John Calvin, *Institutes of the Christian Religion*, II. i. 7; trans. F. L. Battles, ed. J. T. McNeill ("Library of Christian Classics"; 2 vols.; Philadelphia: Westminster Press, 1960), I, 249-50.
[34] J. Oliver Buswell, Jr, *A Systematic Theology of the Christian Religion* (2 vols.; Grand Rapids, Michigan: Zondervan, 1962-1963), I, 298.

inforced by the subsequent sinful decisions of his progeny, but it is their genetic connection with him which makes them what they are. (It is highly relevant that the Hebrew word "Adam" is the generic word for "mankind.") This does not of course deny the effects of a sinful environment as contributing to the sins of each subsequent generation; human sin is both hereditary and environmental. But it is the unity of the race in sin through our first parent which lies at the heart of the problem—and this is equally true if we choose to regard Adam as the perfect statistical sampling of the race and conclude that had we been in his shoes we would have done as he did.[35] The children's primer is theologically quite correct: "In Adam's fall, we sinned all." The Second Adam (Christ) came to rectify what the first Adam had done; he accomplished this by taking the sin of Adam on himself, thereby expiating the sins of the human race.

We are now in a position to understand the virtually universal negative response of theologians to the question of whether Christ's atoning sacrifice could have covered the sins of non-humans. Thus, it is maintained, fallen angels were not redeemed at the Cross, and neither were any (if they exist) fallen "intermediate beings" such as the races of dwarfs and fairies.[36]

All of which would seem to afford little consolation to sinning extraterrestrials, since they, like angels and fairies, are not children of Adam. But, as we shall see later, the substitutionary understanding of the atonement is not the only way in which Scripture presents Christ's work on the Cross.

How Many Incarnations?

If Christ as Second Adam, substituting his innocent death for the well-deserved death of human sinners, cannot be applied to benefit fallen non-humans, what about the possibility of "incarnations" specifically for them? Is this perhaps a route by which God's love for the fallen could be vindicated even if his incarnation on this earth could not be helpful to extraterrestrials? The Roman Catholic poets Aubrey de Vere and Alice Meynell certainly thought so:

> Judaea was one country, one alone:
> Not less Who died there died for all. The Cross

---

[35] See John Warwick Montgomery, *Tractatus Logico-Theologicus* (2ᵈ printing with corrections; Bonn: Verlag für Kultur und Wissenschaft, 2003), para. 4.84 ff.
[36] Cf. John Warwick Montgomery, *Principalities and Powers: The World of the Occult* (3ᵈ rev. ed.; Calgary, Alberta, Canada: Canadian Institute for Law, Theology and Public Policy, 2001), especially chap. 5, pp. 132 ff. To be sure, the question of the redemption of J. R. R. Tolkien's hobbits (such as Bilbo and Frodo) remains an open question, since they are clearly semi-human!

> Brought help to vanished nations: Time opposed
> No bar to Love: why then should Space oppose one?[37]

> ... in the eternities,
> Doubtless we shall compare together, hear
> A million alien Gospels, in what guise
> He trod the Pleiades, the Lyre, the Bear.
>
> O, be prepared, my soul!
> To read the inconceivable, to scan
> The million forms of God those stars unroll
> When, in our turn, we show to them a Man.[38]

However, the "million forms of God" have consistently given intractable problems to the theologians, as well as providing grist for pagan mills. In his *Age of Reason,* Deistic sceptic Thomas Paine queried: "Are we to suppose that every world in the boundless creation had an Eve, an apple, a serpent, and a redeemer? In this case, the person who is irreverently called the Son of God, and sometimes God himself, would have nothing else to do than to travel from world to world, in an endless succession of death, with scarcely a momentary interval of life."[39] Alexander Von Humboldt wrote to Gauss that Christian polymath William Whewell agreed: "The redemption (crucifixion) can not be repeated on the many millions of nebulae observed by Rosse."[40]

Paine's statistical argument may be easy to answer, but the theological problems with multiple incarnations cannot so easily be dismissed. Thomas Rawson Birks, the earliest supporter of Whewell, rejects any "series of revelations" on the scriptural ground that Christ "is the Son of God and the Son of man, in two distinct natures and one person, forever."[41] A 19th century contemporary of Whewell and Birks, Presbyterian William Leitch, principal of Queen's College, Kingston, Ontario, was in full agreement: multiple incarnations cannot be reconciled with "Scripture, which declares that He [Christ] will forever bear His

---

[37] Aubrey de Vere, "The Death of Copernicus," 57 *Contemporary Review* 421 f. (September, 1889).

[38] Alice Meynell, *Poems* (New York: Scribner's, 1923), p. 92.

[39] Thomas Paine, *Age of Reason* (New York: Freethought Press Association, n.d.), p. 57.

[40] Kurt R. Biermann (ed.), *Briefwechsel zwischen Alexander von Humboldt und Carl Friedrich Gauss* (Berlin, 1977), p. 116. There is some question as to the accuracy of Von Humboldt's characterisation of the views of Whewell, which underwent a sea change from supporting a plurality of worlds to opposing that position. It was, incidentally, Whewell's opposition to employing the physical sciences and mathematics apologetically which led Charles Babbage, the great precursor of today's computer revolution, to produce his great *Ninth Bridgewater Treatise*; see above, Part Two, chap. 2 of the present work.

[41] Birks, *op. cit.*, p. 55.

human nature."⁴² Roman Catholic theologians of the time were no less decisive on the point: François Xavier Burque stressed the impossibility of sustaining multiple incarnations in the face of Hebrews 9 which teaches that Christ did not "suffer often since the foundation of the world [*cosmos*]" but rather was "once offered to bear the sins of many."⁴³ In the next century C. S. Lewis would agree:

> I do not think it at all likely that there have been many Incarnations to redeem many different kinds of creature. One's sense of *style*—of the divine idiom—rejects it. The suggestion of mass-production and of waiting queues comes from a level of thought which is here hopelessly inadequate. If natural creatures other than Man have sinned we must believe that they are redeemed: but God's Incarnation as Man will be one unique act in the drama of total redemption.⁴⁴

Doubtless, the Divine "style" is not the best way of deciding the issue (how much, really, do we know about the aesthetics of God?), but Lewis surely has a point. In commenting on a heterodox 18th century treatment of the question, which held that the Second Person of the Trinity "united to himself Jesus: and for the same or similar Ends he may have, and probably hath, united to himself other rational Creatures in other Planets,"⁴⁵ Professor Crowe rightly observed: "The idea of turning Christ into a cosmic Krishna was then, and remains, a notion that Christian theologians, as well as such critics of Christianity as Tom Paine, have judged to be irreconcilable with that religion."⁴⁶

We can, then, agree with Frederick William Cronhelm when he dismisses "a Bethlehem in Venus, a Gethsemane in Jupiter, a Calvary in Saturn."⁴⁷ Such notions go well beyond William Blake's query, "And was the holy Lamb of God on England's pleasant pastures seen?"—since England (whatever Frenchmen may say) is indeed part of the human landscape and not an alien world!

But the refusal theologically to countenance multiple incarnations is not equivalent to saying that fallen extraterrestrials are per se without hope. Perhaps the atonement which occurred on our earth has larger dimensions than we ordinarily think.⁴⁸

---

⁴² William Leitch, *God's Glory in the Heavens* (3ᵈ ed.; London: Strahan, 1866), pp. 322 ff.

⁴³ François Xavier Burque, *Pluralité des mondes habités considérée au point de vue négatif* (Montréal, 1898), pp. 246 ff.

⁴⁴ C. S. Lewis, *Miracles* (New York: Macmillan, 1960), pp. 51 ff.

⁴⁵ William Hay, *Religio Philosophi* (London: R. Dodsley, 1753), p. 139.

⁴⁶ Crowe, *op. cit.*, p. 87. Cf. Charles Davis, "The Place of Christ," 45 *Clergy Review* 706-718 (1960).

⁴⁷ Frederick William Cronhelm, *Thoughts on the Controversy As to a Plurality of Worlds* (London, 1858), p. 17.

⁴⁸ There is also, to be sure, the slim possibility of employing the motif of "multiple universes"

Is the Atonement Exportable?

Is the meaning of the redemptive sacrifice of Christ limited to substitution for the sins of humanity? Might the atonement not also operate on a level which would be transferable to races other than our own?

The most helpful modern treatment of atonement theory in the history of doctrine was achieved by the Swedish Lutheran theologian Gustaf Aulén in his book, *Christus Victor*. Because of the importance of the subject, we have provided, in the Appendix to this essay, our detailed review and analysis of this book.[49] Aulén describes three main atonement theories in the history of the church: (1) the "Christus victor" theory, maintained especially by the Patristic church and the Reformers, which stresses that on the Cross God-in-Christ monergistically conquered the evil powers arrayed against the fallen creature (those powers being sin, death, the devil, and the law); (2) the "Anselmian" or "substitutionary" theory, characteristic of the Medieval church, Anglo-Catholics, and evangelicals, which sees the atonement as God the Father punishing God the Son as perfect representative man (the Second Adam) who has taken on himself the sins of mankind; and (3) the "subjective" or "Abelardian" theory, held by the liberal and broad-church streams, to the effect that the atonement provided a basis for the "imitation of Christ" and the moral regeneration which would follow from it.

Now it should be clear from inspection (and much more from the analysis provided in the Appendix material) that all three of these theories can be justified within Holy Writ — though their relative importance varies considerably. The second (substitutionary) theory has the most weight scripturally, being featured in Romans and Hebrews (and Hebrews shows the intimate connection between this theory and the entire history of sacrifice in the Old Testament). The first (Christus victor) theory receives second place, being clearly taught in diverse passages throughout the New Testament (Ephesians 4:8, Colossians

---

(as discussed in contemporary cosmology) to get around the limitation on multiple incarnations created by such biblical teachings as that Christ is "the same yesterday, today and forever" and that his human incarnation is permanent (since "this same Jesus, which is taken up from you into heaven, shall so come in like manner as ye have seen him go into heaven"). The seemingly insurmountable problem with such theological speculation (and it remains pure speculation in secular cosmology as well) is that it would seem to produce "multiple" Deities — as against the overwhelming biblical prohibitions against all forms of polytheism ("Hear, O Israel: the Lord our God is one Lord"). On "a proliferation of universes" see John Gribbin, *Schrödinger's Kittens and the Search for Reality* (London: Orion Phoenix Books, 1996), pp. 160-66.

[49] First published in John Warwick Montgomery, *Chytraeus on Sacrifice: A Reformation Treatise in Biblical Theology* (2^d ed.; Malone, Texas: Repristination Press, 2000), pp. 139-46.

2:14-15, Revelation 12:9-11, etc.). The third (subjective) theory can be justified by way of a few verses (principally 1 Peter 2:21), but quite obviously receives the least emphasis of the three theories in biblical teaching.

As to the applicability of atonement to fallen creatures other than human beings, theory (3) would certainly work, since extraterrestrials could imitate the selfgiving of Christ just as we can. But, of course, they could only do so on receiving knowledge of what he had done on earth for the human race (cosmic evangelism through future space exploration from earth?).[50] Theory (2) could not apply to extraterrestrials, since Christ functions as Second *Adam*: he is a representative of the progeny of Adam and takes on the sin of Adam, not the sins of any other race. Theory (1) could embrace extraterrestrials insofar as the evil powers conquered on the Cross are understood in a broad or cosmic sense: sin, death, the law (as these would operate in other worlds), and the Book of Job and the Book of Revelation clearly teach that the devil's infernal activities are by no means limited to earth, but have cosmic repercussions.

The problem, however, is that biblically *all three of these theories* are correct—all provide valid understandings of the atonement. It might therefore appear that we are left with only two alternatives: *either* to say that since at least one of the theories (the one most emphasised biblically!) could not apply to extraterrestrials, the atonement per se could not do so; *or* to say that the atonement was only *partially* applicable outside the human sphere. But such a conclusion would not be required logically. One could better argue that for the atonement to be valid and applicable it is not necessary that *all* biblically justified theories of it apply in every context; it should be enough that any *one* correct theory genuinely apply. If, for example, the evil powers arrayed against the cosmos were successfully conquered through what Christ did on earth, would it really matter that some of the beneficiaries could not place themselves within the ambit of the race identified with the Second Adam?

An Answer for E.T.

What can be done for a fallen E.T.? Not an incarnation in his world; and the substitutionary aspect of the atonement for humankind on our earth would not help him. But surely a positive solution can be arrived at?

We should expect so, on the basis of the character of God, as revealed in the Holy Scriptures. The God of the Bible is a God of love who weeps over Jerusalem and "will have all to be saved and to come unto a knowledge of the truth"

---

[50] See below, our text at note 60.

(1 Timothy 2:4). It follows that the burden of proof should lie with those who would argue against any salvation for fallen inhabitants of other worlds, not with those suggesting positive solutions.

But what can be said concretely? We begin with a general consideration and then move to a more specific solution.

Even if we were to hold that the Anselmian, substitutionary understanding of the atonement must be essential to any efficacious application of the Cross, and therefore that Christ's work on earth could not be directly relevant to the sinful plight of extraterrestrials, it would not follow that fallen creatures on other worlds could not be saved. To hold otherwise is tantamount to maintaining that God is limited to only one means of redemption. But the God of the Bible declares: "As the heavens are higher than the earth, so are my ways higher than your ways, and my thoughts than your thoughts" (Isaiah 55:9).

This point has been made by a number of students of the matter. Rittenhouse writes: "Neither Religion nor Philosophy forbids us to believe that infinite wisdom and power, prompted by infinite goodness, may throughout the vast extent of creation and duration, have frequently interposed in a manner quite incomprehensible to us, when it became necessary to the happiness of created beings of some other rank or degree."[51] Pohle's opinion is similar: "Even if the evil of sin had gained its pernicious entry into those worlds, so would it not follow from it that also there an Incarnation and Redemption would have to take place. God has at his disposal many other means to remit a sin that weighs either on an individual or on an entire species."[52]

And C. S. Lewis: "To different diseases, or even to different patients sick with the same disease, the great Physician may have applied different remedies; remedies which we should probably not recognise as such even if we ever heard of them."[53] Lewis deals with the matter in more detail elsewhere:

> We might find a race which, like ours, contained both good and bad. And we might find that for them, as for us, something had been done: that at some point in their history some great interference for the better, believed by some of them to be supernatural, had been recorded, and that its effects, though often impeded and perverted, were still alive among them. It need not, as far as I can see, have conformed to the pattern of Incarnation, Passion, Death and Resurrection. God may have other ways—how should I be able to imagine them?—of redeeming a lost world. And Redemption in that alien mode might not be easily recognisable by our missionaries, let alone by our atheists.

---

[51] Rittenhouse, *loc. cit.*
[52] Pohle, *loc. cit.*
[53] Lewis, *Fern-seed and Elephants* (*op. cit.*), p. 90.

We might meet a species which, like us, needed Redemption but had not been given it. But would this fundamentally be more of a difficulty than any Christian's first meeting with a new tribe of savages? It would be our duty to preach the Gospel to them. For if they are rational, capable of both of sin and repentance, they are our brethren, whatever they look like. ...[54]

In short, God is certainly capable of redeeming other fallen worlds by means entirely different from the one he has used on earth to save fallen humanity. A loving God may well provide other means of redemption totally beyond our ken.

But there may be a solution for E.T. which follows directly on what God in Christ has done for us on earth. That is to say, God's redemptive work in Christ on earth may itself have a secondary salvatory impact on other worlds.

We have already suggested that the "Christus victor" dimension of the atonement could have significance beyond our own world. Biblical passages such as Colossians 1:19-20 and Ephesians 1:10 seem to say that the effect of the Cross was not limited to our human situation: "It pleased the Father that in him [Christ] should all fulness dwell; and, having made peace through the blood of his cross, by him to reconcile all things unto himself; by him, I say, whether they be things in earth, or things in heaven." "In the dispensation of the fullness of times he [God the Father] might gather together in one all things in Christ, both which are in heaven, and which are on earth."[55] And the Greek word *cosmos* in the phrase, Christ died "for the sins of the *world*" — though generally taken to mean "the earth" or "humanity, fallen creation, the theatre of salvation history" — may linguistically have a wider referent ("the universe, the sum of all created being").[56]

Even the "subjective," Abelardian understanding of the atonement — though hardly adequate by itself — might extend the application of the atonement to other worlds. Eighteenth-century Scottish moral philosopher and poet James Beattie argued that extraterrestrials

---

[54] Lewis, *Christian Reflections* (Grand Rapids, Michigan: Eerdmans, 1967), p. 175 (cf. the entire discussion, pp. 173-76).
[55] Abbott, in the respected *International Critical Commentary* series, suggests that the "things in the heavens" in Col. 1:21 (the Greek is in the plural) may be inhabitants of other worlds. A. S. Peake, commenting on the same passage in W. Robertson Nicoll's *Expositor's Greek Testament* ([5 vols., reprint ed.; Grand Rapids, Michigan: Eerdmans, 1951], III, 509; cf. pp. 261-62), observes: "The natural sense is that this reconciliation embraces the whole universe, and affects both things in heaven and things on the earth, and that peace is made between them and God (or Christ)."
[56] Gerhard Kittel, *Theological Dictionary of the New Testament*, trans. and ed. G. W. Bromiley (6 vols.; Grand Rapids, Michigan: Eerdmans, 1964-1968), III, 868 ff. (art. *Kosmos*).

will not suffer for our guilt, nor be rewarded for our obedience. But it is not absurd to imagine, that our fall and recovery may be useful to them as an example; and that the divine grace manifested in our redemption may raise their adoration and gratitude into higher raptures and quicken their ardour to inquire ... into the dispensations of infinite wisdom.[57]

The "French Burke," Count Joseph de Maistre (d. 1821), argues eloquently for the wider application of Christ's redemptive work in the course of refuting "certain theologians" who could not stomach the idea of other inhabited worlds:

> If the inhabitants of the other planets are not like us guilty of sin, they have no need of the same remedy, and if, on the contrary, the same remedy is necessary for them, are the theologians of whom I speak then to fear that the power of the sacrifice which has saved us is unable to extend to the moon? The insight of Origen is much more penetrating and comprehensive when he writes: "The altar was at Jerusalem, but the blood of the victim bathed the universe."[58]

C. S. Lewis goes considerably further along the same line:

> It might turn out that the redemption of other species differed from ours by working through ours. There is a hint of something like this in St Paul (Romans 8:19-23) when he says that the whole creation is longing and waiting to be delivered from some kind of slavery, and that the deliverance will occur only when we, we Christians, fully enter upon our sonship to God and exercise our 'glorious liberty'.
>
> On the conscious level I believe that he was thinking only of our own earth: of animal, and probably vegetable, life on earth being "renewed" or glorified at the glorification of man in Christ. But it is perhaps possible—it is not necessary—to give his words a cosmic meaning. It may be that Redemption, starting with us, is to work from us and through us.[59]

---

[57] James Beattie, *Evidences of the Christian Religion* (Annapolis, 1812), p. 184. This work is a refutation of David Hume; it employs in its apologetic the Scottish Common Sense philosophy of Thomas Reid.

[58] Joseph de Maistre, *Soirées de Saint-Petersbourg*, Vol. II (Paris, n.d.), pp. 319-20.

[59] Lewis, *Fern-seed and Elephants* (*op. cit.*), pp. 90-91. In his book *Miracles* Lewis even hypothesises that redemption on earth could positively influence *unfallen* worlds: "It would be all of a piece with what we already know if ninety-and-nine righteous races inhabiting distant planets that circle distant suns, and needing no redemption on their own account, were remade and glorified by the glory which had descended into our race" (*loc. cit.*). This point was earlier made *in extenso* by the 18th century German Christian poet Klopstock: "The triumph of Christ extended to the stars of innocent persons/And of immortals" (*Der Messias*, XX, 578-579).

Would the extraterrestrial need to have knowledge of salvation history on earth to benefit from it? Not in the "Christus victor" understanding of the atonement, for the victory over the evil powers is an objective fact whether one knows of it or not. Pierre Courbet (admittedly from a Roman Catholic, sacramentarian standpoint) maintained that "extraterrestrials would not need to know of these actions to derive their benefits, any more than the infant must understand baptism."[60] Such an approach must not be allowed to descend into *ex opere operato* formalism, but the point is sound that Christ's victory is objective and its effects should not depend on specific knowledge of it. In contrast, the Abelardian, "imitation" interpretation of the atonement would require that the extraterrestrial know what Christ had suffered on earth for humankind, for without such knowledge "following Christ's steps" would be impossible.

And so, in sum, there is indeed hope for a fallen E.T. We have excellent reason to agree with the 19th century Anglican clergyman Robert Knight, who declared that although the Scripture teaches us that the "Incarnation is unique," it gives us every reason to believe that its "influences are universal."[61]

Perhaps the best illustration of this great truth—and a fitting conclusion to this essay—is the Resurrection panel of Grunewald's great Isenheim altarpiece, now in the Unterlinden Museum in Colmar, France. Here, Christ, having conquered the powers of death, rises in triumph from the tomb. The grave clothes fall away from the sheer power of his victory, and the nimbus around his head has been expanded so as to show that the effects of the victory spread out into the starry heavens, even to the limits of the universe.[62]

---

[60] Crowe, *op. cit.*, p. 417. The reference is to Courbet's essay, "De la redemption et de la pluralité des mondes habités," *Cosmos*, 4th ser., 28 (19 May 1894), 208-211; (2 June 1894), 272-76.

[61] Robert Knight, *The Plurality of Worlds: The Positive Argument from Scripture* (2d ed.; London, 1878), p. 16. We should, however, guard against explaining that "universal influence" in the terms of Teilhard de Chardin's mystical "hyperphysics," wherein the Incarnation impacts cosmic history by a built-in evolutionary development (absorbing and counteracting the entropic effect of the Second Law of Thermodynamics!) and the entire universe evolves to an ultimate "Omega-point" in Christ (see Chardin in Duquaire, *op. cit.*, p. 122; also, J. E. Jarque, *Foi en l'homme: l'apologétique de Teilhard de Chardin* (Paris: Desclée, 1969); and John Warwick Montgomery, *The Suicide of Christian Theology* [*op. cit.*], pp. 8, 124, 171).

[62] The reproduction here has been taken from Marcel Brion, *Les peintres de Dieu* (Paris: Philippe

Appendix

Evaluation of the Three Atonement Theories as Characterized by Aulén

In order to offer the clearest possible picture of Aulén's argument in *Christus Victor*, we present the following tabular schema of the three atonement theories with which he deals. It should be emphasized that the data given in the table represent Aulén's descriptions of these atonement theories [1] and that these descriptions are not necessarily accepted as factually accurate or complete by the present author.

"Classic" theory (Fathers, Luther)	*"Latin doctrine"* (Anselm, Lutheran Orthodoxy)	*"Subjective"* view (Abelard, Schleiermacher, Ritschl)
1. Continuity of divine operation	1. Discontinuity of divine operation	1. Human operation (conversion or amendment)
a. Atonement planned by God	a. Atonement planned by God	a. No consistent stand taken on the source of the "atonement" plan
b. Accomplished by God in the person of Christ	b. Accomplished by Christ as sinless Man suffering God's wrath against sins of the world	b. Accomplished by Jesus as exemplary Man
c. God approaches (▼) man	c. Man approaches (▲) God	c. Man approaches (▲) God

[1] The data in the table are derived principally from pp. 145—158 of *Christus Victor: An Historical Study of the Three Main Types of the Idea of the Atonement*, trans. A. G. Hebert (New York: Macmillan, 1956). The reader is referred to this section for detailed explanations of assertions in the table. Helpful collateral reading may be found in Aulén's *Faith of the Christian Church*, trans. E. H. Wahlstrom and G. E. Arden (Philadelphia: Muhlenberg Press, 1948), pp. 223—241, and in Nels F. S. Ferré's *Swedish Contributions to Modern Theology, with Special Reference to Lundensian Thought* (New York: Harper, 1939), pp. 153—165 ("The Religious View of the Atonement"). Bishop Aulén himself, incidentally, read portions of Ferré's manuscript and offered suggestions on it before its publication.

Lebaud, 1996), facing p. 89.

d. Incarnation and atonement closely related	d. Incarnation separated from atonement	d. Neither incarnation nor atonement stressed; Jesus the Pattern Man
e. Atonement, justification, sanctification seen as different aspects of virtually the same thing	e. Atonement, justification seen as successive, separate operations	e. Sanctification stressed, with atonement and justification playing little part
2. Discontinuity of merit and justice; grace and love stressed	2. Continuity of merit and justice; Law stressed	2. Neither justice nor grace receive much emphasis; human love stressed
3. Dualistic emphasis — ransom paid to the devil (yet God all-sovereign)	3. Monistic emphasis — ransom paid to God	3. Monistic emphasis — devil not regarded with much seriousness
a. The sinner freed from the power of sin, death, devil	a. Christ's merits imputed to the sinner	a. Man given a new motive for obedience
b. Sin, death, devil all stressed as powers to be dealt with	b. Sin stressed as the power to be dealt with	b. Little stress on evil power
c. Triumphal, positive emphasis	c. Negative emphasis (man's penalty legally removed)	c. Optimistic emphasis
4. Paradoxical tensions maintained	4. Attempt at rational construction	4. Attempt at rational construction

What light will an examination of Scripture shed on the truth value of these three atonement doctrines? Let us consider in turn each of the four main characteristics of these theories: (1) In a larger sense, *sub specie aeternitatis*, the atonement was surely a continuous work of God, as the "classic" doctrine asserts. Acts 2:22, 23: "Jesus of Nazareth ... being delivered by the determinate counsel and foreknowledge of God, ye have taken and by wicked hands have crucified." John 6:38: "I [Christ] came down from heaven, not to do Mine own will but the will of Him that sent Me." Luke 22:42: "Father, if Thou be willing, remove this cup from Me; nevertheless not My will but Thine be done."

However, in a more narrow (but no less real) sense, Scripture presents a sharp discontinuity which reaches its climax in the agonized words of Christ on the cross: ὁ θεός μου ὁ θεός μου, εἰς τί ἐγκατέλιπές με; Christ did in fact, as man, suffer the full effect of God's wrath directed against the sins of the world. 2 Cor. 5:21: "For our sake He [God] made Him [Christ] to be sin who knew no sin, so that in Him we might become the righteousness of God." 1 Peter 3:18: "Christ also hath once suffered for sins, the Just for the unjust, that He might bring us to God." Gal. 3:13: "Christ hath redeemed us from the curse of the Law, being made a curse for us." There is perhaps no clearer doctrine expressed in Scripture than Paul's delineation of Christ as the "Second Adam" — as the Representative Man who reconciled the race to God. 1 Cor. 15:45: "The first man, Adam, was made a living soul; the last Adam was made a quickening spirit." Rom. 5:15: "If through the offense of one many be dead, much more the grace of God, and the gift by grace, which is by one Man, Jesus Christ, hath abounded unto many." In this (admittedly secondary) sense, man did approach God in the atonement. Moreover, though incarnation, atonement, justification, and sanctification are generally presented in Scripture as mere aspects of a single great plan, the very fact that separate words such as δικαίωσις and ἁγιασμός are employed indicates that these concepts are sometimes thought of as separate, discrete operations (cf. Rom. 8:30).

And when we consider the "subjective" doctrine, we find not merely the inadequacies which Aulén sees in it but definite Scriptural merits as well. Charles M. Sheldon *(In His Steps)* has shown beyond a doubt the power in that Scriptural text which reads: "Christ also suffered for us, leaving us an example, that ye should follow His steps" (1 Peter 2:21). The "subjective" view rightly sees that Jesus' work on the cross is of no value to an individual or a society without repentance and faith. Luke 13:3: "I tell you . . . Except ye repent, ye shall all likewise perish." Acts 16:31: πίστευσον ἐπὶ τὸν κύριον Ἰησοῦν, καὶ σωθήσῃ σύ.[2] Finally, the "subjective" theory places an emphasis on sanctification which is very Scriptural and very healthy. 1 Thess. 4:3: "This is the will of God, even your sanctification." James 2:26: "Faith without works is dead."

It thus becomes evident that with regard to point (1) each of the atonement theories as presented by Aulén has definite values not possessed by the others. Conversely, each lacks emphases which are Scriptural and vital — for the "classic" view does not sufficiently stress Christ as Representative Man offering Himself to God for the sins of the world; the "Latin doctrine" myopically fails to see the all-over continuity of the divine redemptive plan; and the "subjective" view, as the word "subjective" indicates, superficially misses the objective and profoundly efficacious character of the atonement as it is presented in Holy Writ.

(2) As in the preceding case, the atonement doctrine which Aulén terms "classic" presents the more ultimate Scriptural truth: Grace and love did in fact triumph over law and justice on the cross. The words of Hugh of St. Victor cross the centuries with undiminished power: "Non quia reconciliavit amavit, sed quia amavit reconciliavit."[3] But this is hardly the whole story. Law and

---

[2] Note the aorist imperative and future passive indicative. Both the aorist and future tenses have punctiliar *Aktionsart,* and the indicative in the apodosis of this implied condition carries with it a feeling of great certainty and definiteness.

[3] Quoted on the title page of George Cadwalader Foley, *Anselm's Theory of the Atonement* (New York: Longmans, 1909).

justice had profound roles to play in the drama whose last act (or rather, next-to-last act!) was played out on Golgotha. Christ did act as a substitute for sinful mankind, as we have already pointed out (2 Cor. 5:21; 1 Peter 3:18; Gal. 3:13). He fulfilled the demands of the Law and then died so that those who had broken the Law might not have to die. Unless substitutionary, "legalistic" (if you will) sacrifice is retained as an element in the atonement, the New Testament book of Hebrews becomes meaningless, and the vital connection between the Old Testament sacrificial system and the perfect sacrifice of Christ in the New Testament is lost. One who doubts the deep significance of the "Latin doctrine" in this regard need only read James Denney's *Death of Christ*.[4] The "subjective" doctrine again stresses the necessity of human response to the act of God in Christ, but needless to say, it runs the risk of perverting the total atonement picture, because Law and grace are not emphasized as well.

(3) When we come to matters of dualism-monism, we find Scripturally that the "Latin doctrine," rather than the "classic" theory, provides the more ultimate interpretation. The existence of a personal devil and a host of evil forces is clearly asserted in Scripture (temptation of Christ passages; Eph. 6:12), but these powers of darkness are never viewed as eternal opposites to God, as was Ahriman in Zoroastrianism. The evil forces in the universe exist only because God permits it; here the opening chapters of the Old Testament book of Job can be consulted profitably and compared with New Testament passages such as Col. 1:16. Thus, even though some of the fathers do say that Christ paid His ransom to the devil, yet in a more fundamental sense the ransom was paid to God (Heb. 9:14), who, in His *opus alienum*, allowed the evil powers to gain a certain legitimate sway over sinful mankind.

The "classic" view rightly stresses the unholy triad of evil influences — sin, death, and the devil; and not to do so is to restrict the scope of the Biblical plan of salvation (Heb. 2:14-17). On the other hand the "Latin doctrine" is very correct in centering attention on the sin factor, for unless this is done, one's conception of the atonement becomes grossly "physical" (where death is emphasized), or the vital issue of personal human responsibility for sin becomes neglected (where satanic activity is stressed). The triumphal, positive mood of the "classic" theory is of course thoroughly Biblical and is illustrated in such magnificent New Testament passages as Rom. 8:37-39; 1 Cor. 15; and Rev. 20 and 21.

(4) The "classic" theory sees deeply into Scriptural doctrine when it makes no attempt rationally to resolve the paradoxical character of the

---

[4] E. g., as edited by Prof. R. V. G. Tasker of the University of London (Chicago: Inter-Varsity Christian Fellowship, 1952). Cf. Eugene R. Fairweather, "Incarnation and Atonement: An Anselmian Response to Aulén's *Christus Victor*," *Canadian Journal of Theology*, VII (July 1961), 167—175.

atonement. Isaiah, shortly after giving us his great "substitution" chapter (Is. 53), utters one of the profoundest sentences in all of Scripture: לֹא מַחְשְׁבוֹתַי מַחְשְׁבוֹתֵיכֶם וְלֹא דַרְכֵיכֶם דְּרָכָי נְאֻם יְהוָה: (Is. 55:8). And yet (existentialism notwithstanding) paradoxes are not to be made more severe than Scripture makes them. There is no utility in a contradiction *qua* contradiction. The "credo quia absurdum" type of theology is repugnant not only to the serious believer but also to the inquiring unbeliever. Both the "substitutionary" and the "new motive" rationales for the atonement are clearly present in Holy Writ, as we have attempted to show, though they are not intended to remove the ultimate "offense of the cross" (1 Cor. 1:22-25). In explaining the atonement to the Galatians by means of legal analogy, Paul clearly states the limitations of his explanation, but the fact that limitations necessarily exist does not prevent him (as it does many moderns) from giving any explanation at all. Paul writes: "Brethren, I speak after the manner of men: though it be but a man's covenant, yet if it be confirmed, no man disannulleth or addeth thereto" (Gal. 3:15; note the context of this verse). The "Latin doctrine" and the "subjective" view do not become unbiblical simply because they attempt to understand the atonement; they do, however, lose their right to speak authoritatively when they assert or imply that their rational explanations constitute the total picture. Any "explanation" of kerygmatic doctrine must always, by the nature of the case, "speak after the manner of men."

Aulén's Cross-Division
The Crucial Difficulty in Lundensian Theology

The preceding discussion has made rather clear that Aulén's partiality for what he calls the "classic" atonement doctrine is not fully justified on Scriptural grounds. On issues (1), (2), and (4) the "classic" doctrine states the more ultimate truth — *sub specie aeternitatis;* but this does not mean that the emphases of the other two theories on these very issues do not have Scriptural sanction. On the monism-dualism problem we have in the "Latin doctrine" (and to a lesser extent in the "subjective" view) a more fundamental Biblical viewpoint presented than that given by the "classic" theory; yet on this issue as well, the "classic" view offers healthy insights. The point we wish to make is that no one of the three theories delineated by Aulén contains the whole Biblical picture of the atoning work of Christ.

Now since our author is more interested in the truth value of atonement theories than in the bare historical presentation of them, we have in *Christus Victor* a patent case of what the logicians, taxonomists, and library classifiers term "cross-division" or "cross-classification." Let us hear L. S. Stebbing on the theory of classification:[5]

The basis of division (i. e., the differentiating characteristics) is

---

[5] L. Susan Stebbing, *A Modern Introduction to Logic* (London: Methuen, 1930), p. 435.

often called by the Latin name *"fundamentum divisionis."* The principles regulating a logical division are usually summed up in the following rules:

1. There must be only one *fundamentum divisionis* at each step.
2. The division must be exhaustive.
3. The successive steps of the division (if there be more than one) must proceed by gradual stages.

From Rule 1 there follows the corollary that the classes must be mutually exclusive. Violation of this rule results in the fallacy of *cross-division,* or overlapping classes. For example, if *vehicles* were divided into *public vehicles, private vehicles, motor-cars* and *lorries,* there would be more than one basis of division, with the result that the classes would overlap.

Bishop Aulén has inadvertently allowed himself two *fundamenta divisionis* at his first step of classification — the *fundamentum* of theological truth and the *fundamentum* of historical coherence. In attempting two things at once, he has really succeeded in neither. As we have said, we are concerned more chiefly with the truth-value issue, but it is well to note in passing that purely from a historical standpoint the three atonement views given by our author cannot be considered as distinct as he would have us believe. Luther did not present solely "classic" ideas of the atonement,[6] nor was Anselm entirely free from "classic" influences in *Cur Deus Homo;*[7] and the same could be said for practically all other writers on the atonement through Christian history. The reason for this is obvious: the ultimate source of atonement doctrine is Holy Writ, and Holy Writ is not exclusively "classic," "Latin," or "subjective" in its view of Christ's work on the cross.

Since he is primarily interested in the truth value of atonement theories, our author should certainly have used "Scriptural soundness" and "Scriptural unsoundness" as his two main genera of classification, and then (if he wished) various "historical types" of atonement theory as species under each of these

---

[6] Read, for example, Luther's exposition of Ps. 51:7 (in *Luther's Works,* ed. Jaroslav Pelikan, XII [St. Louis: Concordia, 1955], 359—367). In this exposition both "Latin" and "subjective" elements are clearly present.

[7] Note, e. g., Bk. I, chaps. 5 and 6, whose titles are respectively: "How the redemption of man could not be effected by any other being but God"; "How infidels find fault with us for saying that God has redeemed us by his death, and thus has shown his love toward us, and that he came to overcome the devil for us" (St. Anselm, *Cur Deus Homo?,* trans. Sidney Norton Deane [Chicago: Open Court, 1903], pp. 184 to 186). Walter Marshall Horton is of course correct when he says *(Our Eternal Contemporary)* that Aulén considers the "classic" atonement view to be more inclusive than the others, rather than completely distinct from them; yet in the last analysis *Christus Victor* is Aulén's attempt to separate the "classic" theory from the two theories which have held the field in the past and to place the "classic" view on a par with them — treating it as the "genuine, authentic Christian faith" (p. 159).

two genera. Yet he did not do this; in fact, no thorough Biblical analysis of atonement theories appears in *Christus Victor*. There is no chapter at all devoted to the "Old Testament," and the "New Testament" chapter appears — and this is very significant when we consider Aulén's attitude toward patristics — *after* a chapter on "Irenaeus" and one on "the Fathers in East and West." At this point we begin to grasp a basic problem both in Aulén's theological approach and in that of the Lundensian theology of which he has been a prime spokesman.[8]

Aulén's blunder of "cross-division" is due to the lack of a clear-cut Biblical standard of theological evaluation — and this same difficulty plagues all of modern Lundensian thought. The Lundensians refuse to employ the historical criterion of conformity to the Christian Scriptures as interpreted by the *analogia fidei*. Anders Nygren writes:[9]

> The reason that historical truths are insufficient as a foundation for faith is their relative degree of certainty. Even the facts most definitely ascertained possess but relative certainty, while the very nature of faith requires absolute certainty for its foundation. . . . Only the a priori has apodictic certainty.

And what is the principal a priori involved in Lundensian thought? It is the concept of *sola gratia* and its motivating force, agape love (as Nygren's *Agape and Eros* clearly states). When one realizes this, it becomes easy to see why Aulén stresses the atonement characteristics he describes as "classic": all four of the "classic" characteristics, as we have listed them above, emphasize God's unmerited grace and love toward His fallen creatures. We should note that the inadequacy of our author's position becomes evident at this very point where its greatest strength lies; for even if we admit (as we in fact do) that agape-motivated grace is the most fundamental and ultimate theological principle, this principle is *not* the whole theological story, and therefore, if it is taken completely by itself, it will inevitably pervert one's conception of the divine plan of salvation.[10]

It was not for nothing that the Reformers employed three great theological principles — not only *sola gratia* but also *sola fide* and *sola Scriptura*. The only effective counteractant to Lundensian one-sidedness is to return to the historical Scriptures (and to the *historical* Christ on whom they center) as the formal

---

[8] "Gustaf Aulén, whose imprint on Lundensian ideology is in certain aspects the heaviest. . . ." (Ferré, op. cit., p. 26)

[9] In *Religiöst apriori*, pp. 15, 16 (quoted by Ferré, op. cit., p. 55).

[10] We are of course acquainted with the fact that the Lundensian school arose "as a reaction to the indefiniteness of a confused liberalism" which manifested "bewildered relativism" (Ferré, op. cit., p. 23). Thus the Lundensian position was itself a healthy counteractant to a far more theologically questionable extreme; yet two wrongs do not make a right, even when considered from the standpoint of Hegel's thesis-antithesis-synthesis dialectic!

principle — the source and norm — of all theological doctrine;[11] and to return to the *sola fide* principle as the means of appropriating the grace of God in individual lives. Had Aulén stressed Scriptural authority more, he would not have passed such a negative verdict on the substitutionary "Latin doctrine" of the atonement; had he stressed the *sola fide* principle more, he would have seen more clearly the profound truth resident in the "subjective" theory, namely, that "without faith it is impossible to please Him."

In conclusion, then, we give credit to our author where credit is due — we praise his insight into the fundamental and vital "classic" aspects of the atonement; but at the same time we plead for a return to the complete Reformation motto of *sola gratia, sola fide, sola Scriptura.* Only when such a return is made will we avoid the theological blunder of pitting good things against each other, and only then will we be willing to accept all the facets of evangelical Christian doctrine.

[11] We should fully realize that, unless the Scriptures are taken as the theological *principium cognoscendi,* Aulén's a priori of *sola gratia* cannot be defended against any other theological a priori (for example, the exact opposite of *sola gratia,* Pelagio-Arminian synergism!).

2. The Freewill Issue in Theological Perspective[*]

Synopsis

The freewill/determinism issue has not been a concern solely of secular metaphysicians and philosophers of law. Theologians also have wrestled with this intractable problem. The present paper considers the three major approaches to the issue as presented in Western theology: that of Roman Catholicism/Protestant Arminianism, Lutheranism, and Calvinism. A sound theological approach is seen to have distinct advantages over against secular treatments, both in general terms and in the sphere of legal philosophy.

Part One of the *The Oxford Handbook of Freewill* is devoted to "Theology and Fatalism."[1] The *Handbook* quite properly recognises the place of freewill discussions in the history of Christian theology and their potential value to the analysis of that crucial issue in other domains such as legal theory. The purpose of this essay is to outline the positions classically taken on the freewill issue in Christian dogmatics and to see whether they can shed light on the freewill/determinism controversy in general.

Before presenting the theological alternatives, however, it may be worthwhile to observe the state of the question in secular thought. On the one hand, it seems logical to assume that the genetic makeup of the individual covers all aspects of his or her actions; were we to have a complete map of that genetic situation in the case of any given person, we could presumably predict all of that individual's life decisions.

However, such a deterministic conclusion flies in the face of our need to establish responsibility for human action—particularly in the case of antisocial behaviour, where one can hardly be allowed to push responsibility back upon one's progenitors and thereby avoid the consequences of one's acts. To take but one legal example, the French *Cour de cassation* in the important *Laboube* case declared:

---

[*] This paper was presented at the 23rd World Congress of Philosophy of Law and Social Philosophy (IVR World Congress), Cracow, Poland, 4 August 2007.
[1] Robert Kane (ed.), *The Oxford Handbook of Freewill* (New York: Oxford University Press, 2002).

Encore faut-il, conformément aux principes généraux du droit, que le mineur dont la participation à l'acte matériel à lui reproché est établi, *ait compris et voulu cet acte*; toute infraction, même non intentionnelle, suppose en effet que son auteur *ait agi avec intelligence et volonté*.[2]

In short, in spite of herculean efforts to arrive at rational compatibility between genetic determinism and freely chosen human actions,[3] the paradox remains: in theory, our acts are predetermined, yet in practice we must take personal responsibility for them in order to maintain a functioning civilised society. Einstein put it succinctly: "I am a determinist, compelled to act as if free will existed, because if I wish to live in a civilized society, I must act responsibly. I know philosophically a murderer is not responsible for his crimes, but I prefer not to take tea with him."[4]

The Three Classic Theological Approaches

The history of Christian thought has provided three major understandings of the relationship between divine providence and human freedom: the Roman Catholic/Arminian view; the Calvinist view; and the Lutheran view.[5] Notably, since the *point de départ* of Christian theology is divine revelation rather than human speculation, these approaches are not general attempts to resolve the destiny/freewill issue, but focus (as does Holy Scripture) on the matter of personal salvation. The question for the theologians has been "What, in the final

---

[2] Crim. 13 déc. 1956, *Recueil Dalloz*, 1957.349, note Patin (italics ours). "It is still necessary, in conformity with the general principles of law, that the minor whose participation in the *actus reus* has been established, should have understood and willed this act; every offence, even nonintentional ones, suppose in effect that its author has acted with intelligence and will."

[3] One of the most striking is the argument for psychological dualism/interactionism by Nobel prize winning neurophysiologist Sir John C. Eccles: "If my uniqueness of self is tied to the genetic uniqueness that built my brain, then the odds against myself existing in my experienced uniqueness are $10^{10,000}$ against" (Karl R. Popper and John C. Eccles, *The Self and Its Brain* (New York: Springer International, 1985), p. 559.

[4] Albert Einstein, quoted in Denis Brian, *Einstein: A Life* (New York: John Wiley, 1996), p. 185. Quantum theory, to be sure, does not support such determinism. "As in Newton's world, the actors in Einstein's world parrot their lines from a script that was written beforehand. But in a quantum play, the actors suddenly throw away the script and act on their own. The puppets cut their strings. Free will has been established" (Michio Kaku, *Parallel Worlds* (New York: Random House Anchor Books, 2006), p. 149. Einstein would of course reply that without consistent physical laws, one could not establish the soundness of quantum theory in the first place.

[5] A valuable historical survey of western Christian approaches to the freewill issue (though lacking in sympathy for Protestant viewpoints and appreciation for the logical irreconcilability of the Lutheran approach with the classic Roman Catholic position) is Bernard Quilliet, *L'Acharnement théologique: Histoire de la grâce en Occident IIIe-XXIe siècle* (Paris: Fayard, 2007).

analysis, accounts for the saved person being saved, and what accounts for the unbeliever remaining in his or her unbelief?" The following diagram sets forth the three classic positions:

Election/Predestination and Freewill in Human Salvation

	RC/Arminian	Lutheran	Calvinist
The Saved	~~Election~~	**Election**	**Election**
	Freewill	~~Freewill~~	~~Freewill~~
The Unsaved	~~Election~~	~~Election~~	**Election**
	Freewill	**Freewill**	~~Freewill~~

Several clarifications are immediately necessary to make this conceptualisation understandable. These are best presented by way of the three confessional positions represented in the chart.

The Roman Catholic view has always emphasised the controlling place of the human will in salvation. God's grace alone provided the means of human salvation through the gift of His Son Jesus Christ, but to benefit from this gift one must exercise his or her freewill—by personally accepting the Church's sacramental provisions whereby the "treasury of Christ's merits" becomes available to those who repent and agreeing to the penitential ministries of the Church as the extension of Christ's body in history. An interesting recent illustration of this viewpoint is seen in a comment by Monseignor Ravasi, prefect of the Ambrosian Library, Milan, and member of the Pontifical Biblical Commission, when asked why Judas' betrayal of Jesus has been included in the recent revision of the Stations of the Cross; said he: "The episode shows that we all have been given free will and a conscience."[6]

The freewill explanation of both salvation and damnation has also been maintained by the followers of Dutch Protestant theologian Jacob Arminius (1560-1609), who developed his position over against that of the strict Calvinism of his time. It is also represented by the so-called "Freewill Methodists," "Freewill Baptists," and Arminian Evangelicals who assert a direct causal relationship between making a "decision for Christ" and salvation.

Polar opposite to the Roman Catholic/Arminian view is that of classic Calvinism, which holds that the efficient cause of both salvation and of damnation is the "election" (i.e., decision) of God in eternity. Predestinarian Calvinism

---

[6] "Way of Sorrows To Call at New Stations," *The Times* [London], 6 April 2007.

comes in two varieties: "supralapsarian" (God's decision preceded even the Fall of man) and "infralapsarian" (that decision was not made until after our first parents sinned).

Not all Calvinists by any means take these positions today. A number of Presbyterian church bodies have removed the predestination article from the text of the Westminster Confession of Faith (a prime Calvinist doctrinal statement). Historically, the French Calvinist theologian Moïse Amyraut or Amyraldus (1596-1664) formulated a theology of freewill virtually indistinguishable from the Lutheran view.

The Lutheran position, which is also that of mainline Anglican theology,[7] endeavours to take into account the full range of biblical teaching on the election/freewill issue. On the one hand, Scripture is definitive in its teaching that no one can save himself or herself by any good work, including any act of human will (John 1:12-13, Ephesians 2:8-9). The believer must not therefore attribute his or her salvation to any other source than God Himself, working through His Holy Spirit. On the other hand, unbelief is never presented as the result of God's decision to damn; damnation is the product of the misuse of the creature's freewill (Matthew 23:37).

Efforts have been made to assimilate the Lutheran view to that of Calvinism. Thus James Packer, in his edition of Luther's *De servo arbitrio*, presents Luther as holding that "the cause of salvation and damnation alike is the sovereign will of God."[8] However, this interpretation of Luther simply does not wash. True, Luther fought tooth and nail against the Roman Catholic and Renaissance humanist position of Erasmus that freewill is the effective cause of salvation; and, so important to Luther was the doctrine of salvation by grace alone through faith, that he sometimes expressed that teaching in extreme terms. But if we compare Luther with Calvin, Robert Will is surely correct in seeing "une différence de tempérament très nette (...) entre la liberté [de Luther] (...) et la détermination avec laquelle Calvin, dans l'intransigeance de sa raison française, mit en pratique ses principes de liberté."[9] As Robert Kolb has emphasised, for Luther, "God is not responsible for evil. No explanation of the existence of evil and its continuation in the lives of believers is possible." We are to recognise

---

[7] I.e., the Anglican mainstream which is neither "low church" (essentially Calvinistic) nor "high church" (essentially Roman Catholic in its theology—without, to be sure, accepting the authority of the Pope).

[8] J. I. Packer and O. R. Johnston (eds. and trans.), *The Bondage of the Will* by Martin Luther (London: James Clarke, 1957), p. 55.

[9] Robert Will, *La liberté chrétienne. Etude sur le principe de la piété chez Luther* (Strasbourg: Istra, 1922), pp. x-xi; cf. Gerhard O. Forde, *The Captivation of the Will: Luther vs. Erasmus on Freedom and Bondage* ("Lutheran Quarterly Books"; Grand Rapids, Michigan: Eerdmans, 2005), especially pp. 32 ff.

how "unsearchable are God's ways" (Romans 11) and be driven "to reliance on the goodness of God and to trust in Jesus Christ."[10] If further evidence of Luther's true position were needed, one could simply go to his Theses for the Heidelberg Disputation of April 1518, where he states in Thesis 14 that "'Freewill' after the fall has the potentiality toward good as an unrealisable capacity only [*subiectiva potentia*]; towards evil, however, always a realisable one [*activa potentia*]."[11]

The Lutheran position—often referred to as "single predestination," since divine election applies only to the saved—lacks the consistency of the Roman Catholic/Arminian viewpoint (freewill across the board) and that of the Calvinist "double predestination" (divine election across the board, affecting both the saved and the lost). But it has the great merit of taking into account all the biblical data. An interesting illustration in this regard is the passage in the Acts of the Apostles (16:30-31) recounting the Apostle Paul's encounter with his Philippian jailer. The jailer asks, "What must I *do* to be saved?" Paul (who wrote Ephesians, declaring that one is saved solely by God's grace and not by what one does or wills and that faith itself is God's gift) replied: "Believe in the Lord Jesus Christ and you shall be saved." An act of will is required; but once that act has taken place, it must be attributed to God the Holy Spirit and not to the individual—"lest anyone should boast."[12]

Further Analysis and a Conclusion

Several questions are worth raising at this point.

(1) Could one not eliminate the paradox in the Lutheran viewpoint (and vindicate the Roman Catholic/Arminian approach) by observing that in Scripture predestination is made conditional upon divine foreknowledge (Romans 8:29)? The problem here is that the biblical understanding of "foreknowledge" entails the notion of divinely created knowledge—and is thus simply another way of expressing divine sovereignty. God's foreknowledge "is an election or foreordination of His people (R. 8:29; 11:2) or Christ (1 Pt. 1:20)."[13] The idea is not that God looks forward in time to see who will believe and who will not and then ratifies what the hu-

---

[10] Robert Kolb, *Bound Choice, Election, and Wittenberg Theological Method* ("Lutheran Quarterly Books"; Grand Rapids, Michigan: Eerdmans, 2005).
[11] *WA* [the standard, authoritative Weimarer Ausgabe of Luther's Works], I, 353-54.
[12] See John Warwick Montgomery, "The Holy Spirit and the Defense of the Faith," 154 *Bibliotheca Sacra* (October-December 1997), 387-95; reprinted above: Part Three, chap. 3.
[13] Gerhard Kittel (ed.), *Theological Dictionary of the New Testament*, trans. Geoffrey W. Bromiley (10 vols.; Grand Rapids, Michigan: Eerdmans, 1964-1976), I, 715.

man creature decides, but rather that divine election/predestination takes place as a result of the action of the divine mind. In short, one cannot solve the paradox by pitting foreknowledge against election.

(2) Can one not get around the problem by Ockhamist thinking or by Molinist "middle knowledge"? (After all, Luther himself had Ockhamist instructors early in his theological and philosophical education!) Zagzebski points up the great difficulties with both of these approaches. "In my opinion a serious problem with Ockhamist solutions is that even if they can produce an account of temporal asymmetry that has the consequence that God's past beliefs do not have the necessity of the past, it is unlikely that this can be done in a way that is independently plausible."[14] On Molinism, Zagzebski cites Walls who "argues that since Molina maintained that God chooses to put people in situations in which he knows they will choose damnation, Molinism is as morally abhorrent as the Calvinist doctrine of predestination."[15]

(3) Should not the Lutheran approach be rejected simply on the ground that it embraces a formal contradiction? If one subtracts the saved elect from the totality of the human population, must not the lost be regarded as in that category because they are the non-elect? Or if one subtracts the lost—who misused their freewill—from the sum total of humanity, must not the saved be seen as having arrived there through a different but equally real act of will (they did *not* reject the grace of God)? Luther's answer is simply that since "God's thoughts are higher than our thoughts" (Isaiah 55:9), one must stick with the Word of God in Holy Scripture no matter what, and must never draw inferences from one passage of Scripture which would contradict the clear teaching of other biblical passages. Putting it another way, Luther places fact (here biblical fact) above formal questions of contradiction. Life, for him, is bigger than logic. This may seem initially irrational, but at the frontiers of science, the same approach operates. Thus, though the properties of particles are not those of waves (and the two are in various respects logically incompatible), where two sets of equally good experiments lead to the conclusion that light is both particulate and undulatory, one works with the "photon" (a "wave-particle") regardless of the logical difficulties present in such a solution. The alternative is clearly unacceptable, for it would involve refusing to recognise one set of sound experiments or the

---

[14] Linda T. Zagzebski, "Recent Work on Divine Foreknowledge and Free Will," in Kane, *op. cit.*, pp. 54-55.
[15] *Ibid.*, p. 57. Jerry Walls, "Is Molinism as Bad as Calvinism?," 7 *Faith and Philosophy* (1990), 85-98.

other.¹⁶ Of course, Luther's reasoning is founded on a confidence that the Bible is indeed God's Word and therefore that none of its asseverations can rightly be ignored. Support for that claim would take us well beyond the bounds of this paper.¹⁷

(4) What can a theological approach — and, specifically, the Lutheran — offer to the general and the legal discussion of the freewill issue? We shall make four suggestions in conclusion. First, freewill is established on a transcendent foundation — on the basis of clear revelatory teaching, and each individual is held responsible morally and legally for his or her acts (Galatians 6:7). Secondly, because the most important possible decision in life, that of entering into a saving relationship with God, does not have its ultimate explanation in man's freewill but rather in God's sovereign love, humans are given every reason not to exercise *hubris* in thinking that they can build towers of Babel so as to climb up to God by their own self-centred efforts. Thirdly, the promise of a Last Judgment means that where judicial error has occurred or for any other reason human beings have escaped the consequences of the misuse of their freewill on earth, they will not escape those consequences in eternity. Finally, though the theological answer does not resolve the paradox of determinism/freewill as it exists in secular thought, it places it in the context of a loving God who sent His only Son to die for an undeserving race and "who will have all people to be saved and to come to the knowledge of the truth" (1 Timothy 2:4).¹⁸

How much more satisfactory is the biblical gospel than the conclusions to which secular theorising leads in an attempt to resolve the destiny/freewill issue. Consider again Einstein: "Human beings, vegetables, or cosmic dust, we all dance to a mysterious tune, intoned in the distance by an invisible player."¹⁹ Or playwright Glen Berger (*Underneath the Lintel*): "A magician tells you to choose

---

[16] Cf. Kip S. Thorne, *Black Holes and Time Warps*, Foreword by Stephen Hawking (New York: W. W. Norton, 1994), especially p. 147.

[17] For a full-scale argument to this effect, see John Warwick Montgomery, *Tractatus Logico-Theologicus* (4th ed.; Bonn, Germany: Verlag für Kultur und Wissenschaft, 2009); also, his *History, Law and Christianity* (Calgary, Alberta: Canadian Institute for Law, Theology and Public Policy, 2002).

[18] This essay is not the place to enter into casuistical areas such as that represented by a recent Roman Catholic work: Simon Francis Gaine, O.P., '*Will There Be Free Will in Heaven?' Freedom, Impeccability and Beatitude* (London: T & T Clark, 2003). The answer to that question, by the way, is Yes: owing to a radical character-change in the saved individual (2 Corinthians 5:17), he/she in eternity will no longer seek to use freewill negatively so as to reach sinful decisions. Augustine properly described this as the state of *non posse peccari*.

[19] Einstein, *loc. cit.*

any card in the deck, (*Increasingly bitter*) and so with free will you do choose ... but you don't realize the magician has already subtly forced you to pick the exact card he wanted you to pick. Magicians call that a 'Hobson's Choice.' And in life we think we make choices ... but they're Hobson's Choices. So who is this Hobson? Who is this magician gulling us? That's the question. Simply something named Chance? Or Fate? (*Looking up*) Or Something Else?"[20]

"Something Else," indeed. Rather, Some*one* Else. And Someone who says that not a sparrow falls from a tree without the knowledge of our Heavenly Father and that we are of more value than many sparrows. The sovereign decisions of this "magician" are saving acts, and if we insist on employing our genuine freewill to thwart His love and grace, we have only ourselves to blame for the results, both in time and in eternity.

---

[20] Glen Berger, *Underneath the Lintel* (New York: Broadway Play Publishing, 2003), pp. 28-29. Currently (April 2007) Richard Schiff is starring in the play at the Duchess Theatre in London's West End.

3. Some Remarks on Punishment and Freewill in Legal Theory & Classical Christian Theology*

Can—and should—societal punishment operate in the absence of freewill on the criminal's part? Should punishment exist only if rehabilitation can be achieved? In this paper, we contend (1) that Christian theology answers these questions in the negative, and (2) that a proper jurisprudence does likewise.

The Criminological Scene

Utilitarian theories of punishment, so popular in the latter half of the 20th century, do not rely for their justification on the freewill of the criminal. Just as social philosophies such as Marxism and Environmentalism believe that altering the physical or natural climate will change human behaviour, rehabilitative theories of punishment maintain that an enlightened punitive system can per se lead to positive change in the criminal.

Retributive theories, however, are based squarely on the reality of freewill. Classically, Immanuel Kant argued:

> Juridical punishment (*poena forensis*) … can never be administered merely as a means for promoting another Good either with regard to the Criminal himself or to Civil Society, but must in all cases be imposed only because the individual has committed a Crime. … The Penal Law is a Categorical Imperative; and woe to him who creeps through the serpent-windings of Utilitarianism to discover some advantage that may discharge him from the Justice of Punishment, or even from the due measure of it, according to the Pharisaic maxim: 'It is better than one man should die than that the whole people should perish.'[1]

Fleischacker comments:

> Retributive punishment serves a moral function for Kant by making the criminal live under the law he implicitly sets up in his criminal act. The criminal acts on a maxim that he would not will as a universal law; we apply

---

*An invitational essay presented at the 24th World Congress of Philosophy of Law and Social Philosophy (IVR Congress), Beijing, China, 15-20 September 2009.

[1] Immanuel Kant, *The Philosophy of Law: An Exposition of the Fundamental Principles of Jurisprudence As the Science of Right* [The Metaphysics of Morals, Pt. II, 6:331], trans. William Hastie (Edinburgh: T. & T. Clark, 1887).

the law of that maxim to him, as thought he had willed it universally. ... We are merely following out the rational interpretation of his irrational act, and he should have no reason to complain.[2]

Even though there are serious problems with the logic of Kant's categorical imperative,[3] a steady movement away from utilitarian to retributive approaches to punishment can be observed in contemporary criminology. Easton and Piper describe this shift in the following terms:

> In the UK and the USA criticism [of the utilitarian approach] focused on the 'inequities' and ineffectiveness of rehabilitation, and on wide judicial discretion. ... The leading voice for modern retributivist theory ... was von Hirsch who argued that fairness and justice should be the key elements of a coherent penal theory. In *Doing Justice* (1976), he maintained that the aim of the penal system should, then, be to 'do justice' rather than to maximise utility. In other words he construed justice—in line with classical retributivism—as giving offenders punishments in proportion to their crimes *and, in doing so, recognising them as moral agents possessing autonomy.*[4]

Necessarily, a retributivist view of punishment requires as its justification the belief that the criminal is an autonomous entity, possessing a freewill that he or she has employed in a socially deleterious manner. Retributivism thus presupposes that the criminal has knowingly or recklessly committed a serious fault and thus deserves an appropriate and proportional punishment.

In point of fact, when one analyzes the modern penal law of any civilised nation, the retributive basis of the legislation is clearly seen.[5] Take, as a single but typical example, the French criminal law of intentional harm to others ("wilful attacks on the integrity of the person"), as set out in Articles 222-1 through 222-5 of the new (1994) *Code pénal*:

Art. 222-1 Subjecting a person to torture or barbarous acts is punishable by fifteen years of imprisonment.

Art. 222-2 The offense in Article 222-1 is punishable by imprisonment for life when it precedes, accompanies, or follows a felony other than murder or rape. [Murder and rape carry their own severe penalties, set out elsewhere in the *Code pénal*.]

---

[2] Samuel Fleischacker, "Kant's Theory of Punishment," 79/4 *Kant-Studien* (1988), 442.
[3] Montgomery, *Tractatus Logico-Theologicus* (4th ed.; Bonn, Germany: Verlag für Kultur und Wissenschaft, 2009), sec. 5.5-5.6.
[4] Susan Easton and Christine Piper, *Sentencing and Punishment: The Quest for Justice* (2d ed.; Oxford: Oxford University Press, 2008), p. 63; italics ours.
[5] It should not be necessary to point out that a retributivist philosophy does not necessarily entail acceptance of capital punishment. "Just deserts" must be determined in a proportionate manner, taking into account all factors relative to the given case and the perpetrator. Cf. Montgomery, "Capital Punishment," Part Ten, chap. 5, below.

Art. 222-3 The offense in Article 222-1 is punishable by twenty years imprisonment when it is committed:

1. On a minor less than fifteen years old;
2. On a person whose special vulnerability, due to age, sickness, infirmity, physical or mental deficiency, or pregnancy, is apparent or known to the perpetrator;
3. On an ascendant, either legitimate or natural, or on a father or mother by adoption;
4. When the status of the victim is apparent or known to the perpetrator, on a magistrate, juror, lawyer, public or ministerial officer, officer of the gendarmerie, agent of the national police force, customs official, prison administration official, or any other person exercising governmental authority or entrusted with a mission of public service, in the performance or on the occasion of performing his or her duties or mission;
5. On a witness, victim, or civil party [in a legal action];
5b. On a victim who is thought to belong, or not to belong, to a given race, nationality, ethnic group, or religion—whether he or she does in fact so belong;
6. By the spouse or concubine of the victim;
7. By a person exercising governmental authority or entrusted with a mission in the public service, in the performance or on the occasion of performing his or her duties or mission;
8. By several persons acting as perpetrators or accessories;
9. With premeditation;
10. By using or threatening to use a weapon.

Art. 222-4 The offense in Article 222-1 is punishable by thirty years imprisonment when it is committed habitually on a minor less than fifteen years old or on a person of special vulnerability.

Art. 222-5 The offense in Article 222-1 is punishable by thirty years imprisonment when it results in a mutilation or permanent infirmity.

It will be observed that an effort is made here to relate penalties directly to the actual harm caused, i.e., to give the perpetrator a sentence proportionately reflecting the seriousness of his or her volitional act. Granted, the judge may as a general rule reduce a given sentence in light of mitigating circumstances, but even that discretion is being continually circumscribed—as in the 10 August 2007 *"Peines-plancher"* law, incorporated into the *Code pénal* as Articles 132-18-1 and 132-19-1, which largely eliminates sentence reductions and mandates jail time for repeat offenders.

Apart from the assumption of freewill exercisable and exercised by the criminal, such penalties would be meaningless at best and immoral at worst. Indeed, the *Code pénal* expressly declares as a principle underlying all of its provisions: "A person is criminally responsible only for his or her own conduct" (Article 121-1).

A Theological Perspective

What is the biblical view of punishment and freewill and the connections between them?

Holy Scripture—the formal basis of all Christian theology—presents God's human creation as morally responsible and subject to punishment for violations of the Creator's revealed will. From the fall of mankind's first parents in the Garden of Eden to the casting of Satan into the Lake of Fire at the end of time, God holds his creatures responsible for their acts. Jesus weeps over Jerusalem: "O Jerusalem, Jerusalem, thou that killest the prophets, and stonest them which are sent unto thee, how often would I have gathered thy children together, even as a hen gathereth her chickens under her wings, *and ye would not!* Behold, your house is left unto you desolate" (Matthew 23:37-38; italics ours).

The Apostle Paul begins his Epistle to the Romans with a sad description of the fallen human race: Gentile peoples volitionally chose to violate the moral law written on their hearts, committing idolatry and engaging in unnatural practices such as homosexuality, and the Jews volitionally broke the revealed law given to them by God in the Old Testament (Romans 1-2); in sum, "All have sinned, and come short of the glory of God" (Romans 3:23). The consequence follows inexorably: "Be not deceived; God is not mocked: for whatsoever a man soweth, that shall he also reap" (Galatians 6:7).

Throughout the Bible, human freewill and moral choice are asserted, and the violation of God's will leads inevitably to proportionate punishment—if not in this life then at the Last Assize when all evils will be judged and all wrongs righted.[6]

To be sure, this theology has met with strong objection ever since the rise of modern secularism during the 18th century Enlightenment. "An eye for an

---

[6] Indeed, the source of the legal concept of *mens rea* is a sermon by St Augustine. "Coke, Third Inst. 6, gives '*Et actus non facit reum nisi mens sit rea.*' Coke knew the Red Book of the Exchequer which contains the Leges Henrici where the maxim stands '*Reum non facit nisi mens rea.*' The original source is S. Augustinus, Sermones, No. 180, c. 2 (Migne, Patrol. vol. 38, col. 974): '*Ream linguam non facit nisi mens rea.*' This passes into the Decretum, c. 3, C. 22, qu. 2. The author of the Leges took it from some intermediate book": Sir Frederick Pollock and Frederic William Maitland, *The History of English Law Before the Time of Edward I* (2 vols., 2ᵈ ed.; Washington, D.C.: Lawyers' Literary Club, 1959), II, 476.

eye and a tooth for a tooth" has been condemned as barbaric, and 20th century liberal theological ethicists such as Joseph Fletcher have attempted to replace the alleged "prescriptive legalism" of biblical revelation with forms of "situation ethics" which rely not on principle but on existential decision-making and ill-defined notions of "love."[7] But such efforts have devolved into relativism and subjectivism, leaving Christian believers with no ethical moorings in the face of more and more agonising moral dilemmas (stem cell research on embryos, gun control, capital punishment, etc.).

And serious philosophical and jurisprudential defences of "eye for an eye" retributive punishment have come on the scene. Thus University of Michigan law professor William Ian Miller argues:

> The deuteronomic talion adds the notion of "teaching a lesson" to the notion of "getting even" that characterizes the formulations in Exodus and Leviticus, just as in our own speech we will often find both idioms — getting even and teaching a lesson — to be equally appropriate to explain the ministering of justice.[8]

But are there not serious theological objections to the position here described? Let us briefly consider three such problem areas.

Firstly, does not the transmission of original sin from Adam to his descendants rule out the principle of personal responsibility and therefore the legitimacy of individualised punishment? True, according to clear biblical teaching, the sin of Adam passed to all his descendents (Romans 5), but this simply means, as Augustine put it in his phrase, *non posse non peccari*, that human beings in this fallen world never reach perfection (1 John 1:8); it does not mean that one is forced by one's humanity to commit any particular sin. If one does choose to commit a sin or do an illegal act, one's personal responsibility for it remains.

Secondly, did not Jesus replace the Old Testament lex talionis by a new, loving, constructive, forgiving approach to punishment? Did he not say to the judgmental crowd ready to stone an adulteress, "He who is without sin, cast the first stone" and to the adulteress, "Go and sin no more" (John 8)? But the fact that Jesus condemns mob justice and offers a new way of life to a fallen woman does not in any way suggest that he is discarding the Old Testament law or its standards of justice. He plainly stated in the Sermon on the Mount: "Think not that I am come to destroy the law, or the prophets: I am not come to destroy, but to fulfil. For verily I say unto you, Till heaven and earth pass, one jot or one tittle shall in no wise pass from the law, till all be fulfilled. Whosoever therefore shall

---

[7] Cf. Joseph Fletcher and John Warwick Montgomery, *Situation Ethics: Is It Sometimes Right to Do Wrong? A Debate* (2d ed.; Calgary, Alberta: Canadian Institute for Law, Theology and Public Policy, 1999).

[8] William Ian Miller, *Eye for an Eye* (Cambridge: Cambridge University Press, 2006), p. 68.

break one of these least commandments, and shall teach men so, he shall be called the least in the kingdom of heaven: but whosoever shall do and teach them, the same shall be called great in the kingdom of heaven. For I say unto you, That except your righteousness shall exceed the righteousness of the scribes and Pharisees, ye shall in no case enter into the kingdom of heaven" (Matthew 5:17-20).

The point is well made by the late American theologian Carl F. H. Henry:

> The specific references make it apparent that Jesus is not changing the Law, but rather unveiling its inner requirements. The prohibition against murder ([5:]21ff.) and adultery ([5:]27ff.) apply to the life of thought as well as of deed; the moral obligation they impose is spiritual, and not merely external. Jesus does not set forth a higher law of his own to discredit the Old Testament law, but declares that the requirement of Old Testament law was more exacting than the current tradition taught.[9]

Thirdly, does not the atoning death of Christ for the sins of the world unjustly shift the subject of punishment from the deserving sinner to a sinless victim—thus countermanding the principle of proper retribution? In biblical perspective, one here encounters Grace as the fulfilment of the Law: the Creator God, in his infinite mercy, comes down from heaven and takes the sins of the fallen world on himself, expiating them and saving all those who do not reject his gift. Anselm, in *Cur Deus Homo?*, persuasively argued that this was in fact not an abrogation but a cosmic illustration of proper retribution, Christ being both God and man: as a human being, he could represent the entire race (as Adam had done), whilst, as God, he had the capacity to cancel out the penalty of sin for all mankind through his sacrificial death—thereby fulfilling the legal condition that "without shedding of blood is no remission" (Hebrews 9:22).[10] Personal responsibility and freewill remain, for the effectiveness of redemption for the individual depends on his or her not rejecting God's grace: "Without faith it is impossible to please him [God]: for he that cometh to God must believe that he is, and that he is a rewarder of them that diligently seek him" (Hebrews 11:6).

These difficulties bring us quite naturally to a more profound comment relating to the theology of punishment—specifically, a word about the relationship between Law and Gospel. The *lex talionis* functions as an aspect of the *Schöpfungsordnungen*, or "Orders of Creation" imbedded in our world by God to permit human survival in our fallen state of radical self-centredness.[11] The

---

[9] Carl F. H. Henry, *Christian Personal Ethics* (Grand Rapids, Mich.: Eerdmans, 1957), p. 307.
[10] Cf. Montgomery, *Chytraeus on Sacrifice* (2ᵈ ed.; Malone, Texas: Repristination Press, 2000), especially pp. 139-46; also, Milton S. Terry, *The Mediation of Jesus Christ* (New York: Eaton & Mains, 1903), *passim*.
[11] See especially, Werner Elert, *The Christian Ethos*, trans. Carl J. Schindler (Philadelphia: Muhlen-

politico-legal order requires proportionate, retributive justice; otherwise, pragmatism and naked power prevail. But on the model of God's redemptive order, there is place for mercy and forgiveness. This is the foundation for Equity in the Anglo-American common law tradition, and the basis in the criminal law in all civilised nations for the employment of mitigation in sentencing, judicial discretion, amnesty, and the fitting of the punishment to the condition of the offender (individualisation of penalty).[12]

Central to all this, however, is *the relationship of the utilitarian/rehabilitative factor to the retributive*. It is the biblical view—and, in our judgment, the necessary jurisprudential approach—to make retribution the foundation and rehabilitation the second-, *not* the first-, storey of the punitive structure:

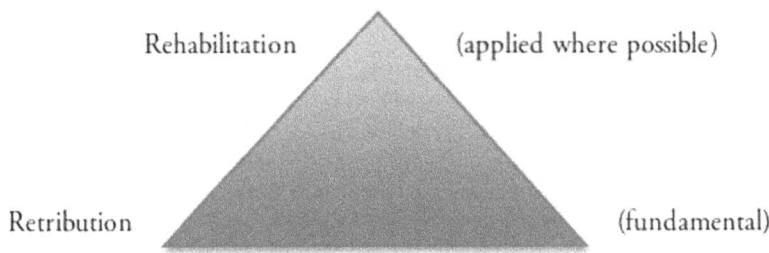

Rehabilitation (applied where possible)

Retribution (fundamental)

The chief reasons why one must not make utilitarian/rehabilitative considerations primary in a justice system are:

(1) Without clear evidence that justice is done through "making the punishment fit the crime," the society loses its moral foundation and there will inevitably be more and more creative attempts to circumvent the law through utilitarian techniques.[13]

---

berg Press, 1957), pp. 101 ff.

[12] In marked contrast, we have the recent example of the application of Shari'a law in Saudi Arabia: A 75-year-old widow has been condemned to forty lashes and four months in prison followed by expulsion from the country for having allowed two young men not of her immediate family to visit her in her home (they were doing shopping for her). A local lawyer offered as justification of the penalty that the Shari'a is the Shari'a and even though a women of 75 years of age is "not normally regarded as seductive, nevertheless age is not a sufficient condition for acquittal" (*Figaro*, 18 March 2009).

[13] It will be noted that our position agrees in its essentials with that of C. S. Lewis, as presented in his essay, "The Humanitarian Theory of Punishment" and "On Punishment: A Reply to Criticism," included in Lewis's *God in the Dock*, ed. Walter Hooper (Grand Rapids, Michigan: Eerdmans, 1970), pp. 287-300. Concludes Lewis: "All I plead for is the *prior* condition of ill desert; loss

(2) Rehabilitative theories invariably reduce the level of personal responsibility for wrongdoing by deemphasising the importance of freewill in the performance of criminal acts.

(3) Rehabilitation simply does not work in the majority of cases, the root cause being that the self-centredness of the criminal can only be changed by a radical, spiritual conversion. Only the gospel of the grace of God in Jesus Christ—not any human system of punishment—has proven capable of achieving this.

---

of liberty justified on retributive grounds *before* we begin considering the other factors."

4. Legal Hermeneutics and the Interpretation of Scripture

The Hermeneutical Impasse

What divides Christian theology and turns the theological landscape into a battlefield today is not so much confessional differences as hermeneutical perspectives. On the one side, regardless of denominational commitment, are those who insist on interpreting the biblical text in its natural (not necessarily literal) sense; on the other, those who flatly deny that any such objective interpretation is possible and who therefore see the text as a reflection of its original environment and in dialectic interaction with the contemporary interpreter. The conflict may almost be reduced to: Billy Graham ("The Bible says ...") vs. Robert Funk's Jesus Seminar.

One might even go so far as to claim that biblical hermeneutics constitutes the great gulf dividing the church at the end of the twentieth century. As illustrated by Robert Campbell, O.P.'s companion volumes, *Spectrum of Protestant Beliefs* and *Spectrum of Catholic Attitudes*,[1] far more basic than Protestant-Catholic doctrinal differences today is the cleavage between those who take revelational sources as objectively true and those who relativize and subjectivize them. The conservative-liberal split on how to read the Bible cuts across all denominational lines, and directly or indirectly colors the theology and church life of every church person. Clearly, if the Bible does not mean what it appears to mean and does not teach what it seems to teach, the door opens wide for an infinite number of new interpretations, teachings, and styles of church life.

The essential difference between historical-grammatical interpretation and the new hermeneutic is not difficult to describe. The former, set out in such classic treatises as Milton S. Terry's *Biblical Hermeneutics*, maintains that the scriptural text can be objectively known, that it has a clear, perspicuous meaning, and that that meaning can be discovered if the text is allowed to interpret itself, without the adulteration of the interpreter's personal prejudices. Professor Eugene F. A. Klug summarizes this approach, which dominated the field of scriptural interpretation at least from the Reformation to the rise of modern biblical criticism, as follows:

> It is a fundamental principle to assume that there is one intended, literal, proper sense to any given passage in Scripture ("sensus literalis unus est"); also that the Scripture is its own best interpreter ("Scriptura Scripturam in-

---

[1] Published by Bruce in Milwaukee in 1968 and 1969 respectively. The present writer was one of the five contributors to *Spectrum of Protestant Beliefs*.

terpretat' or 'Scriptura sui ipsius interpres"). ... The literal sense thus always stands first and each interpreter must guard against cluttering that which is being communicated with his own ideas, lest the meaning be lost.[2]

In diametric contrast to this classic hermeneutic is the so-called "hermeneutical circle" of Rudolf Bultmann and the contemporary followers of *formgeschichtliche Methode* and related higher-critical philosophies. Here, the text and the interpreter are locked together in such a way that a purely objective, "presuppositionless" understanding of the text is out of the question. The interpreter always brings his own understanding to the text, and interpretation is the product *both* of the text working on the interpreter *and* the interpreter working on the text.[3] And this will be true not only of the current interpreter vis-à-vis the text but also of the original writer or editor of it: neither the events described in the text nor the resulting description of them can ever represent objective truth in any absolute sense. A text is ultimately inseparable from its *Sitz im Leben* in the widest sense of that term.

Philosopher Roy J. Howard thus sets forth "three important aspects of contemporary hermeneutics": (1) "There is no such thing as presuppositionless knowing." (2) "Just as there is no uniform stance from which to begin thinking, so there is no uniform term in which to end it. Hermeneutics is willing to rethink the dialectical logic of Hegel but not to accept his conclusion of an absolute mind." (3) "Hermeneutics' recognition that intentionality is present and operative and effective on both sides ... and in a dialectical way. This effectiveness might be resident in the social condition of the researcher (cf. Habermas and Winch) or in the very logic of his research activity (cf. von Wright), or in the choice and manner of the questions he addresses to experience (cf. Gadamer)."[4]

The impasse between classical and contemporary hermeneutic approaches is well illustrated by the current controversy engendered by Adrian Desmond's and James Moore's biography, *Darwin* (1991). The authors set Darwin in his 19th century context, relating the development of his theory of organic evolution to the social influences that played upon him. Evangelical reaction has been mixed: on the one hand, there is joy that evolutionary theory is now less

---

[2] Eugene F. A. Klug, "'Sensus Literalis'—das Wort in den Wörtern, eine hermeneutische Meditation vom Verstehen der Bibel," 12/5 *Evangelium* (December, 1985), 165-75.
[3] Cf. Bultmann's seminal essay, "Is Exegesis Without Presuppositions Possible?," conveniently available in English translation in Kurt Mueller-Vollmer, ed., *The Hermeneutics Reader: Texts of the German Tradition from the Enlightenment to the Present* (Oxford: Basil Blackwell, 1986), 241-48.
[4] Roy J. Howard, *Three Faces of Hermeneutics: An Introduction to Current Theories of Understanding* (Berkeley: University of California Press, 1982), 165-66. On the varieties of contemporary higher criticism, see Steven L. McKenzie and Stephen R. Haynes, eds., *To Each Its Own Meaning: An Introduction to Biblical Criticisms and Their Application* (London: Geoffrey Chapman, 1993).

able to be regarded as scientific fact than as "the contingent product of complex inferences between the Victorian natural and social orders"; on the other, there is much disquiet that such sociological reductionism is the very thing that has characterized the treatment of the Bible by the modern critics! Moore, in responding to the evangelicals on the latter point, puts it bluntly: "Can texts interpret themselves? If the Bible's don't, why *a fortiori* should Darwin's?"[5]

To determine whether or not texts such as Scripture can or cannot interpret themselves, we may perhaps benefit from a perspective other than that afforded by theology or even the liberal arts. Theological discussions of the hermeneutical impasse tend to become mired in dogmatic considerations; and philosophical, historical, and literary treatments of the question are often highly abstruse and far removed from the practicalities.

In the present essay we shall offer assistance by way of legal hermeneutics—and that for two reasons. First: Lawyers—perceived through the centuries as motivated by filthy lucre and woefully deficient in moral character and spirituality—can hardly be thought to be offering surreptitious theological solutions to the hermeneutic dilemma! Secondly, and far more important: As I have pointed out elsewhere,[6] law is necessitarian, coloring all aspects of societal life; so its solutions to fundamental problems carry powerful weight. On the interpretation of contracts, wills, statutes, and constitutions hang the lives and property of all of us. A legal hermeneutic will not represent mere academic theory: it will have developed a necessary response to resolving peaceably the otherwise intractable conflicts within society. A legal hermeneutic, in short, constitutes the interpretive cement by which society is kept from fragmenting.[7] The plain consequence is that the theologian has every reason to observe law's hermeneutic methodology with care.

---

[5] James Moore, "Cutting Both Ways—*Darwin* Among the Devout: A Response to David Livingstone, Sara Miles, and Mark Noll," 46/3 *Perspectives on Science and Christian Faith: Journal of the American Scientific Affiliation* (September, 1994), 169-72.

[6] John Warwick Montgomery, *Human Rights and Human Dignity*, 2nd ed. (Calgary, Alberta: Canadian Institute for Law, Theology and Public Policy, 1995), 134-36.

[7] In legal literature there are occasional references to possible connections between legal hermeneutics and theological interpretation—for example, Per Olof Ekelof, "Teleological Construction of Statutes," 2 *Scandinavian Studies in Law* (1958), 88-89—but the subject remains undeveloped. Moises Silva, in his brief work, *Has the Church Misread the Bible? The History of Interpretation in the Light of Current Issues* (Grand Rapids: Zondervan Academic Books, 1987), includes as fields creating "Today's Hermeneutical Challenge" (chap. 1): Philosophy, Literary Criticism, Linguistics, History, Science, and Theology. Law is conspicuous by its absence!

How Lawyers Construe Documents

It is a truism that written instruments have played and continue to play a central role in legal activity. Legal historian Frederic William Maitland argued that the "forms of action"—the documentary writs—were the most important single factor in the development of the Anglo-American common law tradition.[8] As early as the 17th century, written evidence of contractual relations, as compared with purely oral contracts, was deemed so important that in certain key areas only contracts in writing or evidenced by written memoranda could any longer be enforced.[9] Written instruments such as contracts, deeds, wills and trusts, legislative statutes, and constitutions represent the very essence of the law, and their proper interpretation is a *sine qua non* for the effective operation of the machinery of justice.

Not surprisingly, therefore, canons for the proper construction of legal documents were developed early in the history of the law and remain with us to this day. The Oxford *Concise Dictionary of Law* lists the six "principal rules of statutory interpretation" as follows.

(1) An Act must be construed as a whole, so that internal inconsistencies are avoided.

(2) Words that are reasonably capable of only one meaning must be given that meaning whatever the result. This is called the *literal rule*.

(3) Ordinary words must be given their ordinary meanings and technical words their technical meanings, unless absurdity would result. This is the *golden rule*.

(4) When an Act aims at curing a defect in the law any ambiguity is to be resolved in such a way as to favor that aim (the *mischief rule*).

(5) The *ujusdem generis rule* (of the same kind): when a list of specific items belonging to the same class is followed by general words (as in "cats, dogs, and other animals"), the general words are to be treated as confined to other items of the same class (in this example, to other *domestic animals*).

(6) The rule *expressio unius est exclusio alterius* (the inclusion of the one is the exclusion of the other): when a list of specific items is not followed by general words it is to be taken as exhaustive. For example, "weekends and public holidays" excludes ordinary weekdays.[10]

---

[8] Frederic William Maitland, *The Forms of Action at Common Law* (Cambridge: Cambridge University Press, 1936).

[9] The so-called Statute of Frauds, 29 Car. II, c.3, s.17 (1676). Though modified in various particulars, sections of this historic Statute remain in force today in all common law jurisdictions.

[10] Elizabeth A. Martin, ed., *A Concise Dictionary of Law* (Oxford: Oxford University Press, 1987), 189. For a fuller discussion of these canons, see, *inter alia*: Herbert Broom, *Legal Maxims*, ed. W.

In the law of contracts, the *parol evidence rule* sets forth the same hermeneutic philosophy: Integrated writings cannot be added to, subtracted from, or varied by the admission of extrinsic evidence of prior or contemporaneous oral or written agreements; extrinsic evidence is admissible to *clarify* or *explain* the integrated writing, but never when it would *contradict* the writing.[11] The construction of deeds follows the same approach: the parties "are presumed to have intended to say that which they have in fact said, so their words as they stand must be construed."[12] And at the loftiest point of American constitutional interpretation the identical philosophy prevails; thus Chief Justice John Marshall in *Gibbons* v. *Ogden*:

> As men whose intentions require no concealment, generally employ the words which most directly and aptly express the ideas they intend to convey, the enlightened patriots who framed our Constitution, and the people who adopted it, must be understood to have employed words in their natural sense, and to have intended what they have said. If, from the imperfection of human language, there should be serious doubts respecting the extent of any given power, it is a well-settled rule that the objects for which it was given, especially when those objects are expressed in the instrument itself, should have great influence in the construction. ... We know of no rule for construing the extent of such powers, other than is given by the language of the instrument which confers them, taken in connection with the purposes for which they were conferred.[13]

Concerning the interpretation of legal documents in general, Lord Bacon summed up aphoristically.[14]

> Non est interpretatio, sed divinatio, quae recedit a litera. (Interpretation that departs from the letter of the text is not interpretation but divination.) Cum reciditur a litera, judex transit in legislatorum. (When the judge departs from the letter, he turns into a legislator.)

More recently, Sir Roland Burrows drives the same point home with admirable clarity:

J. Byrne, 9th ed. (London: Sweet & Maxwell, 1924), chap. 8 ("The Interpretation of Deeds and Written Instruments"), 342-444; P.B. Maxwell, *The Interpretation of Statutes*, ed. G. Granville Sharp and Brian Galpin, 10th ed. (London: Sweet & Maxwell, 1953); Rupert Cross, *Statutory Interpretation*, ed. John Bell and George Engle, 2nd ed. (London: Butterworths, 1987).
[11] Cf. *Uniform Commercial Code*, sec. 2-202.
[12] Charles E. Odgers, *The Construction of Deeds and Statutes*, 4th ed. (London: Sweet & Maxwell, 1956), 21. The cited statement offers a direct challenge to and refutation of the so-called "intentional fallacy" as commonly practiced in contemporary biblical interpretation; see John Warwick Montgomery, ed., *God's Inerrant Word* (Minneapolis: Bethany, 1974), 30-31, 41.
[13] "*Gibbons* v. *Ogden*, 9 Wheaton, 187-89 (1824).
[14] Francis Bacon, *The Advancement of Learning*, II. 20. viii.

> The Court has to take care that evidence is not used to complete a document which the party has left incomplete or to contradict what he has said, or to substitute some other wording for that actually used, or to raise doubts, which otherwise would not exist, as to the intention. When evidence is admitted in connection with interpretation, it is always restricted to such as will assist the Court to arrive at the meaning of the words used, and thus to give effect to the intention so expressed.[15]

Now it is certainly true that among contemporary thinkers in the fields of political theory and jurisprudence (philosophy of law) the classical hermeneutic approach just described has not received uniform approbation. The most radical of today's legal philosophies, the Critical Legal Studies (CLS) movement, which reached its high water mark in the 1970s in the work of Roberto Unger and Duncan Kennedy, argues in deconstructionist fashion against the face-value of virtually all legal instruments. Carrying American Legal Realism's doubts about the objectivity of legal operations virtually to the point of existential solipsism, CLS regards the legal interpreter as all-important and the text as infinitely malleable grist for the mill of political activism.[16] But CLS has been decisively shown to be incapable of practical application in the legal field, since its position undercuts the very Rule of Law.[17] The impact of CLS on day-to-day judicial activity has been virtually nil.

Professor Ronald Dworkin, H. L. A. Hart's successor in the chair of jurisprudence at Oxford, maintains that interpretation, in law and other fields, is essentially concerned with *purpose*: "but the purposes in play are not fundamentally those of some author but of the interpreter. Roughly, constructive interpretation is a matter of imposing purpose on an object or practice."[18] On the surface, this suggests that Dworkin is prepared to sacrifice the text to the interpreter, but he insists that "constructive interpretation" does not mean that "an interpreter can make of a practice or work of art anything he would have wanted it to be."[19] The text or object of interpretation is a residual given which limits what the interpreter can do to it.

Moreover, Dworkin is so unhappy with American Legal Realism and so horrified by Critical Legal Studies—and quite rightly, in our view—that he has

---

[15] Roland Burrows, *Interpretation of Documents*, 2nd ed. (London: Butterworth, 1946), 13.
[16] Roberto Unger, *The Critical Legal Studies Movement* (Cambridge: Harvard University Press, 1986); Mark Kelman, *A Guide to Critical Legal Studies* (Cambridge: Harvard University Press, 1987); Peter Fitzpatrick and Alan Hunt, eds., *Critical Legal Studies* (Oxford: Basil Blackwell, 1987).
[17] See especially J. W. Harris, "Legal Doctrine and Interests in Land," in *Oxford Essays in Jurisprudence, Third Series*, ed. John Eekelaar and John Bell (Oxford: Clarendon Press, 1987), 167-97.
[18] Ronald Dworkin, *Law's Empire* (Cambridge: Harvard University Press, 1986), 52.
[19] *Ibid.*

set forth his "one right answer" thesis: the view that, in deciding cases, judges can indeed arrive at a single correct answer, based objectively on the existing legal tradition.[20] Such a view, inconsistent though it may be with Dworkin's concept of "constructive interpretation," nonetheless shows that he is at heart an objectivist who refuses to sacrifice the integrity of the legal documentary tradition to the subjective whims of the interpreter.

The most powerful contemporary theoreticians of legal hermeneutics are certainly those in the "original intent" camp—thinkers who argue (as did Chief Justice John Marshall) that texts must be understood in their original sense, not twisted to fit the interpreter's agenda. Robert Bork, for example, admits to the difficulty of psychoanalyzing the Founding Fathers to discover what they really "intended" in framing the American Constitution (the dilemma thrown up by liberal constitutionalists such as Laurence Tribe), and so prefers the expression "original understanding": "What we're really talking about [is] not what the authors of the Bill of Rights had in the backs of their minds, but what people who voted for this thing understood themselves to be voting for."[21]

If, however, trying to determine the "original intent" of the author over and above his text poses extreme problems (Sibelius, for example, was hopeless at explaining the true intent and significance of his *Finlandia!*), the same dilemma attaches to the original audience of the text: they, too, may have misunderstood it—for any number of personal, societal or cultural reasons.

Thus the most sophisticated academic analysis of legal interpretation would appear to focus on the Wittgenstein-Popper approach: the analogy of the shoe and the foot. Interpretation is like a shoe and the text like the foot. One endeavours to find the interpretation that best fits the text (allowing the text itself to determine this). Here, "intent" or "understanding" is decided by the text itself.[22]

Such an approach fully supports the principle that the text must be allowed to interpret itself—in the sense that when different or contradictory interpretations of it are offered, each will be brought to the bar of the text to see which

---

[20] Ronald Dworkin, in *Law, Morality and Society: Essays in Honour of H. L. A. Hart*, ed. Hacker and Raz (Oxford: Oxford University Press, 1977), 58-83.

[21] Robert Bork, interview in "Bork v. Tribe on Natural Law, the Ninth Amendment, the Role of the Court," *Life* (Fall Special, 1991): 96-99. For his position in detail, see Bork, "Neutral Principles and Some First Amendment Problems," 47/1 *Indiana Law Journal* (Fall, 1971); Bork, *The Tempting of America* (New York: The Free Press, 1990); and cf. Ethan Bronner, *Battle for Justice: How the Bork Nomination Shook America* (New York: W.W. Norton, 1989).

[22] For examples of the contribution of Wittgensteinian analysis to legal hermeneutics, though centering more on the *Philosophical Investigations* than on the *Tractatus Logico-Philosophicus*, see Jim Evans, *Statutory Interpretation: Problems of Communication*, corrected ed. (Auckland, New Zealand: Oxford University Press, 1989), 16-19, 25-26, 29-30, 188.

fits best. Interpretations therefore function like scientific theories which are arbitrated by the facts they endeavour to explain: the facts ultimately decide the value of our attempts to understand them.[23]

In the Wittgenstein-Popper model, the interpreter of course brings his prejudices (*aprioris*, presuppositions, biases) to the text, but it is the text that judges them also. And the meaning of the text is not to be established by extrinsic considerations, for that would yield an infinite regress. (If the given fact or text has no inherent meaning and one must appeal beyond it for its true signification, then that must *also* be true of the extrinsic facts to which one appeals. "Bigger bugs have littler bugs upon their backs to bite them/And littler bugs have littler bugs/And so—*ad infinitum*.") Of course, extrinsic considerations can be used to clarify ambiguity, but never to contradict the clear meaning of a text.[24]

Free Legal Advice for Theologians

What has our discussion of legal hermeneutics to do with the interpretation of Scripture? Could it not be argued that Christian faith is a matter of grace and not law and that therefore the preceding analysis, interesting as it may be for the history of ideas, is irrelevant to the Bible interpreter?

Hardly, for (1) the Bible—as a matter of fact—presents *both* gospel *and* law, and, as Luther stressed, the theologian's task is not to eliminate either one for the sake of the other, but properly to distinguish them;[25] and (2) a confusion

---

[23] See John Warwick Montgomery, "The Theologian's Craft," in his *The Suicide of Christian Theology* (Minneapolis: Bethany, 1970), 267-313, and above, Part Two, chap. 1, in the present volume.
[24] The corresponding principle of classical biblical hermeneutics is that extra-biblical materials may be used *ministerially*, but never *magisterially*, in the interpretation of the sacred text. On the English legal scene, the opinion prevails in some quarters that the recent House of Lords decision in *Pepper (Inspector of Taxes) v. Hart and Others* (*Times* Law Report, 30 November 1992) erodes the fundamental hermeneutic principle that statutes must interpret themselves, since it allows the record of Parliamentary debate ("Hansard") to assist in interpreting them. However, *Pepper* emphatically does not displace the classic rule, for the decision expressly makes "a limited modification to the existing rule, subject to strict safeguards." These are: (1) use of Hansard is allowed only "as an aid to construing legislation which [is] ambiguous or obscure or the literal meaning of which led to absurdity" and only "where such material clearly discloses the mischief aimed at" by the legislation; and (2) even in such instances, it is highly unlikely that any use can legitimately be made of a Parliamentary statement "other than that of the minister or other promoter of a Bill." Thus *Pepper* is little more than a gloss on the *golden rule* and the *mischief rule* of the classic canons of legal hermeneutics (see rules 3. and 4. in the list corresponding to note 10, *supra*).
[25] See C. F. W. Walther, *The Proper Distinction Between Law and Gospel*, ed. W. H. T. Dau (St. Louis, Mo.: Concordia, 1928); John Warwick Montgomery, "Luther's Hermeneutic vs. the New Hermeneutic," in his *Crisis in Lutheran Theology*, I, 2nd ed. (Minneapolis: Bethany, 1973), 45-77—also in his *In Defense of Martin Luther* (Milwaukee: Northwestern Publishing House, 1970),

of categories occurs when we do not recognize that Scripture, which indeed centers on grace and salvation, is first of all a collection of *writings*. If we do not employ a proper hermeneutic to discover what the Bible says, we cannot be sure of its message at all, whether it deals with grace or law.

Legal hermeneutics offers the most powerful reinforcement for traditional, grammatical-historical interpretation of Holy Writ. And why is such reinforcement important? Because of the tragic departure from such standards of literal, textual interpretation of the Bible in the church today. Modern theology has done perhaps its greatest harm to classical Christian faith through the new hermeneutic. In general, modern interpreters refuse to be held to the fundamental rule of classical biblical hermeneutics that "Scripture must interpret itself." Because the contemporary theologian does not regard the Bible as a qualitatively unique divine revelation, he constantly employs extra-biblical materials (ancient non-biblical Near Eastern documents, modern scientific and social theories, etc.) to structure and recast the scriptural data.

Thus the Creation account in Genesis is construed—on the basis of extrinsic evolutionary considerations—not to intend to teach *how* the world came about (but only *that* God created it), in spite of its clear and repeated stress on the creation of each species "after its kind"; alleged scientific "impossibilities" transmute the account of Noah and the Flood—which could hardly teach more plainly a universal deluge—into a minor Near Eastern drizzle; ancient extra-biblical literary parallels are allowed (by fallacious *post hoc, ergo propter hoc* reasoning) to contradict the veracity of Jesus' own affirmations of the Mosaic and Davidic authorship of Old Testament books; and modern rationalistic antipathies to the supernatural provide hermeneutic justification for construing our Lord's miraculous ministry as little more than a morality play. These are but illustrations of the fact that practitioners of the new hermeneutic operate on the general assumption that no biblical text is capable of objective interpretation but must be construed in a "dynamic life-relation" with extra-biblical materials of the past and present and with the presuppositions of the contemporary interpreter.[26]

Here indeed we have the "divination"—as opposed to interpretation—Lord Bacon warned against. Such an approach is the death of all meaningful under-

---

pp. 40-85; and John Warwick Montgomery, *Law & Gospel: A Study for Integrating Faith and Practice*, 2nd ed. (Calgary, Alberta: Canadian Institute for Law, Theology and Public Policy, 1994), especially 5-10, 23-26.

[26] On the scholarly problems with form- and redaction-criticism, see the references in John Warwick Montgomery, Letter to the Editor, 3/12 *Ecclesiastical Law Journal* 45-46 (January, 1993); and John Warwick Montgomery, "Why Has God Incarnate Suddenly Become Mythical?," in *Perspectives on Evangelical Theology: Papers from the 30th Annual Meeting of the Evangelical Theological Society*, ed. K. S. Kantzer and S. N. Gundry (Grand Rapids: Baker Book House, 1979), 57-65.

standing of Scripture—as it would be in reference to legal documents too, were jurists to enter on the same suicidal hermeneutic course. They do not, of course, since if they did they would be disbarred or removed from the bench; our courts would crumble. And the society which depends on the Rule of Law would collapse with them—or be transformed into something closer to barbarism and anarchy than to civilization.

In theology, however, defrocking is virtually impossible today (witness the late Bishop James Pike and the just-retired Bishop of Durham); and the effects of textual destruction are far less visible. Apathy and invisibility, however, have never prevented fatal diseases from spreading or reduced the numbers of their victims. We conclude, therefore, with two words of advice for the theologian interpreting Scripture today: *Gardez bien!*[27]

---

[27] The Montgomery clan motto.

Part Six
Reformation Heritage

1. The Celebration of the Lord's Supper according to Calvin: A Study of His Genevan Rite of 1542 (etc.)

Introduction

As the title of this paper indicates, we shall be concerned here with John Calvin's views on the administration and reception of the Eucharist, as these views are reflected in his *Forme des Prières* published at Geneva in 1542 (etc.). Let us specifically define our subject—first by setting forth its limits, and then by outlining the manner in which we intend to pursue it.

At the outset it should be carefully noted that we are not (necessarily) dealing here with the eucharistic views either of Reformed theology or of Calvinism. One does not automatically treat *Calvinism* by treating Calvin, as Professor McNeill indicates when he concludes his presentation of "Calvin and the Reformed Churches" with these words: "Much of 'Calvinism' has deviated from Calvin, for better or for worse" ("Christianity in the Reformation Era," p. 117).[1] *Reformed theology*, moreover, influenced as it has been by Zwingli *et. al.* as well as by Calvin, cannot even be equated with Calvinism—to say nothing of identifying it with Calvin's own views. Modern Calvinist theologians such as Berkouwer demonstrate this clearly as they attempt to distinguish carefully between Zwingli and Calvin—on such matters as the nature of Christ and His presence in the eucharistic meal.[2] In the study which comprises this paper, we shall concern ourselves only with Calvin himself—not with later blends or modifications of his views.

A second point which should be kept in mind while reading this paper is that we are dealing here primarily with the *liturgical* rather than the *theological* aspects of Calvin's eucharistic position. Obviously, however, since liturgies cannot be divorced from theology, the latter will have some part to play in our discussion—especially in the final section of the paper.

A final delimiting consideration must also be mentioned. This paper will concentrate on the Genevan Rite which Calvin published in 1542 and which

---

[1] Throughout this paper, citations to pertinent literature will be given in very brief form. The reader is referred to the Bibliography (at the close of the paper) for complete bibliographic details on any item mentioned.

[2] "There is every reason to assume that Luther, in his resistance to the spiritualistic tendencies of Zwingli, drew Calvin too much into Zwingli's Nestorianizing atmosphere. To Luther *this* Christology and the doctrine of the Lord's Supper were inseparably linked together. He believed that Calvin also paid tribute to spiritualism and that, in fact, he repudiated the 'real presence.' But in reply one may say precisely that Calvin remained loyal to Chalcedon and that in his line he was able to overcome spiritualism in the doctrine of the Lord's Supper" (Berkouwer, pp. 280-81).

he revised slightly in succeeding years. This Rite is, strictly speaking, the only form of service we possess from Calvin's pen: and, as Brilioth says, it is "the type and model of the Calvinistic liturgy" (p. 174).[3] Since space limitations prevent us from even attempting to present a comprehensive picture of all Calvin had to say on the celebration of the Lord's Supper,[4] we are forced by the nature of the case to narrow our sphere of concentration to some extent. It has seemed most logical and fruitful, therefore, to center our attention on Calvin's own eucharistic Rite. This does not mean that we shall disregard other pertinent, available material which Calvin has written (see Bibliography), but we shall view such material in the light of the form of service which he actually prepared and used.

This paper will be divided into two main sections, which will attempt to answer the following two basic questions concerned with Calvin's Genevan Rite: (1) Is this Rite, generally speaking, a poor representation of Calvin's eucharistic views? (2) Does this Rite have significant liturgical and doctrinal value? These questions have of course been posed by others; but in giving *a negative answer to both* we shall differ markedly from the majority of scholars who have studied Calvin's liturgical efforts.

Calvin's Genevan Rite—a Poor Reflection of His Eucharistic Views?

A prevalent opinion seems to exist among liturgical scholars and students of Calvin that the latter's Genevan Rite is not a fair standard by which to judge his philosophy of eucharistic celebration. Brilioth writes: "We come now to our question: Can the communion service which thus took shape at Geneva be called an adequate expression of the idea of the sacrament which we find in Calvin's dogmatic writings? The answer must be a decided negative" (p. 177). A veritable battery of reasons has been adduced in support of this contention. Let us first list them (quoting as far as possible from the writers who present them), and then proceed to examine their validity.

(1) Doumergue writes (p. 502): "Il (Calvin) s'était accommodé au culte de Genève, à tel point que ce culte mérite le titre de genevois beaucoup plus que de calviniste." (a) "Calvin s'était accommodé pour la sainte Cène" (by complying with the Genevan magistrates' wish to have Communion quarterly rather than

---
[3] "It became the standard of Reformed worship" (Maxwell, *The Book of Common Prayer and the Worship of the Non-Anglican Churches*, p. 3).
[4] For a convenient list of Calvin's numerous writings, see pp. 465-97 (following Prof. Tholuck's article) in Calvin's *Commentaries on the Book of Joshua*.

weekly), (b) "Calvin s'était accommodé pour l'absolution" (by not employing an Absolution after the Confession of Sins), (c) "Calvin s'était accommodé pour la communion aux malades" (by not demanding that a reserved sacrament be taken to them).[5]

Brilioth lists two other reasons (besides the influence of Geneva) to support the view that the Genevan Rite is far more "low-church" than one would expect of Calvin: (2) Calvin's "biting scorn" toward the Roman mass (p. 171), and (3) "The influence of Strassburg. ... There is no doubt at all that the forms of service used in the French congregation at Strassburg, of which he took charge in 1538, had a marked influence on his liturgical work" (p. 173). Maxwell, on the other hand, argues that the Rite which Calvin supposedly prepared at Strassburg in 1539 or 1540 provides a more faithful picture of his liturgical philosophy than does the Genevan Rite: "We may take the Strasbourg rites as being a better indication of Calvin's own mind" (*An Outline of Christian Worship*, p. 115).

On pp. 177-78 Brilioth lists the specific ways in which the Genevan Rite fails to attain the liturgical heights scaled elsewhere by Calvin:

(4) "The chief special feature of the Calvinistic service is the psalm-singing; but even this finds only scanty room in the eucharistic rite." (5) "The long exhortation which takes so large a part of the rite not only introduces into the central act of Christian devotion the unedifying list of open sins, and goes off into a controversial digression; but it is in itself a liturgical monstrosity, or rather a piece of preaching, and it fails to give a worthy expression of the strong positive elements of the Reformed view: eucharistic praise, communion-fellowship, commemoration, and the offering of personal devotion. ... Commemoration is all but absent, and the ancient traditional forms of the liturgy, rich in links with the past, are more completely abolished than even by Zwingli. ... Most of the space is taken up with giving a correct definition of the mystery of the sacrament. But even here the emphasis on God's transcendence above the whole material creation robs the element of Mystery itself of its deepest meaning."

Having now presented at length this formidable list of arguments, let us attempt to determine in fact whether the Genevan Rite should be considered as an inadequate expression of Calvin's eucharistic views. We shall deal in turn with each of the five main arguments just given.

(1) We must agree with Doumergue's three specific assertions (a, b, and c), but we do not feel that these provide sufficient support for his generalization that the Genevan Rite "mérite le titre de genevois beaucoup plus que de calviniste." It should be noted at the outset that point (1c) has nothing to do with the text of the eucharistic Rite, and therefore may be disregarded for our purposes.

---

[5] See also Maxwell, *John Knox's Genevan Service Book*, pp. 13 (note 17), 70.

Points (1a) and (1b) do in fact indicate a limited compromise of Calvin's liturgical ideals,[6] but one certainly cannot conclude from this that his Genevan Rite is simply a version of Farel's *Manière et fasson* which was "in existence, if not in regular use at Geneva, at Calvin's first visit; and on his return in 1541 it was in possession of the field" (Brilioth, p. 172).[7] Even the most cursory comparison of the Genevan Rite[8] with the outline of *La Manière* given by Brilioth (*ibid*.) shows the great dissimilarity of the two rites. It is significant in this connection that whereas "Farel's service had allowed no singing, at least in the Lord's Supper" (*ibid*., p. 174), Calvin's Genevan Rite carried the title "La forme des prières et chantz ecclésiastiques!" Maxwell states flatly that Farel's *La Manière* was "an utterly barren rite, a result of Zwinglism influence" and "had no influence whatever upon any succeeding rites except that Calvin borrowed from it considerably for his Marriage Service" (*An Outline of Christian Worship*, p. 112).[9] To argue, therefore, that Calvin's Genevan Rite of 1542 merely reflects earlier, un-Calvinian liturgical practice in the city, or that it largely reflects the demands of the Genevan magistracy, is to go well beyond historical fact.

(2) We can summarily dismiss the argument that Calvin's "biting scorn" toward the Mass influenced him to produce a low-church service at Geneva which did not come up to his ideals. Either Calvin honestly held such scorn for the Mass or he did not. If he did honestly feel such scorn, then any liturgical effort of his which reflects this scorn will be *consistent* with his principles, not contrary to them. If he did not feel such scorn, then the argument naturally loses all its force. (In point of fact, of course, he did despise the Roman Mass, and his Genevan Rite consistently reflects this scorn.)

(3) Calvin himself admits that he was greatly influenced by the form of service already in use at Strassburg when he arrived there in 1538. He writes: "As for the Sunday prayers, I took the form of Strasbourg, and borrowed the greater part of it" (quoted in Maxwell, *An Outline of Christian Worship*, p. 113). The question we must ask, however, is: whether this borrowing was carried on

---

[6] Calvin himself admits this. See Doumergue, p. 502; Maxwell, *An Outline of Christian Worship*, pp. 117-18; Maxwell, *John Knox's Genevan Service Book*, pp. 97-98.
[7] The text was edited by J. G. Baum and published at Strassburg and Paris in 1859. For bibliographic information, see Maxwell, *John Knox's Genevan Service Book*, pp. 68-69.
[8] The French text of the Genevan Rite of 1542, together with the changes made by Calvin in the later editions, is given in Vol. 6 of Calvin's *Opera quae supersunt omnia* (*Corpus Reformatorum*, v. 34). The portions of the *Forme des prières* with which we are concerned in this paper may be found on columns 172-84 and 195-202 of that volume. A somewhat unsatisfactory English translation of these sections of the Rite is given in Calvin's *Tracts*, v. 2, pp. 100-12, 119-22. For outlines of the contents of Calvin's Genevan Rite, see Maxwell, *John Knox's Genevan Service Book*, p. 18; and Maxwell, *An Outline of Christian Worship*, pp. 114-15.
[9] Note that Reed falls into error on this point (p. 81).

in a manner consistent with Calvin's total liturgical philosophy. Brilioth (pp. 173-74) says that it was not, and asserts that Bucer's German rite of 1539[10] (which was in use in Strassburg when Calvin arrived, and which he translated or paraphrased into French) was a low-church rite unworthy of Calvin. But Maxwell (who constantly tries to defend Calvin as a Reformed "high-churchman" — in contrast, say, to Zwingli) makes out a far better case for Bucer's rite being of a (relatively) high-church character. Even Brilioth has to admit that Bucer was the one responsible for introducing psalm-singing into the Reformed church — a development which (from Zwingli's standpoint) would hardly have been considered low-church.

As for Maxwell's comparison of Calvin's "Strassburg Rite" with the Genevan Rite (to the detriment of the latter), we hasten to point out that the alleged "Strassburg Rite" may be merely a hypothetical construction having no real existence — and even if it did exist, no copy of it has apparently been preserved. Maxwell uses the 1542 service book[11] of Pierre Brully (who succeeded Calvin at Strassburg in 1541), together with an assertion made in 1542 (allegedly by Brully) stating that this 1542 book was a second edition, to show "what Calvin's rite while in Strasburg must have been" (*John Knox's Genevan Service Book*, p. 69). Maxwell even goes so far as to assert (*ibid.*, p. 21): "That it (Brully's book) was in point of fact a reprint of Calvin's lost edition (1539 or 1540) is made clear beyond all doubt by Brully's statement concerning it, as follows: 'Ich habe die französischen gesang psalmen, gemeine gebet vnd formular der Sacrament handlungen diser kirchen alhie, weil keine büchlin mehr vorhanden, widerumb inn Druck verfertiget.'"

But one should note carefully that this statement of Brully's (if it is his statement[12]) informs us only that his 1542 *La Manyere* was a second edition; the statement does not mention Calvin, nor even imply that the latter was responsible for the first edition. If anything, the statement suggests that Brully himself prepared the first edition ("Ich [Brully] habe ... widerumb inn Druck verfer-

---

[10] For bibliographic data on Bucer's rite (entitled "Psalter mit aller Kirchenuebig die man bey der Christlichen Gemein zu Straszburg vnd anders wa pflaegt zu siingen"), see Maxwell, *John Knox's Genevan Service Book*, p. 69.

[11] Entitled, "La manyere de faire prières aux églises francoyses." The colophon can hardly be regarded as a model of dispassioniate honesty ("Imprimé à Rome par le commandement du pape, par Theodore Brüsz allemant, son imprimeur ordinaire. Le 15 de feburier.")! For bibliographic information on this book, see Maxwell, *John Knox's Genevan Service Book*, pp. 69-70.

[12] Maxwell quotes the statement from A. Erichson's *Die calvinische und die altstrassburgische Gottesdienstordnung* (Strassburg, 1894), p. 10. Baum, Cunitz, and Reuss (Calvin's *Opera*, v. 6, p. xv) maintain that the statement comprises part of an "epistolam quandam Petri Alexandri, ecclesiae gallicanae argentoratensis pastoris, ad magistratum reipublicae nostrae datam d. 25. Maii 1542 et in archivis civitatis asservatam." (See also Doumergue, p. 489, note 1.) Thus there is at least a real possibility that Brully never made the statement in question.

tiget"). One may perhaps argue that Brully had not been in charge in Strassburg long enough to have brought out both the first and second editions of *La Manyere*—since (a) he arrived at the end of July, 1541 (Doumergue, pp. 358-59) and (b) Calvin did not leave for Geneva until early in September of that year, and (c) the second edition of *La Manyere* was published on February 15, 1542. However, we may answer that it is by no means impossible for a congregation to find itself in need of more hymnals within a six months period. Moreover, during the time between Calvin's return to Strassburg from the Colloquy at Ratisbon (June 25, 1541; *ibid.*, p. 638) and his departure from Strassburg for Geneva (i.e., during the time Brully was also in Geneva), Calvin was deeply troubled as to whether he should, after all, return to Geneva. It is reasonable to suppose that even though he was still in official charge in Strassburg during July and August of 1541, he would not have been psychologically capable of producing the first edition of *La Manyere* during this period.[13]

The foregoing discussion should make quite clear that Maxwell (*Outline*, p. 113) has no real basis for treating as "a third edition of the Strasbourg rite" the 1545 service which Calvin prepared in Geneva for his old congregation at Strassburg. If the very existence of the "first edition" of the "Strassburg Rite" depends chiefly on Brully's (?) statement quoted above, and if the "second edition" is actually Brully's 1542 *La Manyere,* then one is on much firmer ground if he considers Calvin's 1545 rite to be merely a later variant of the Genevan Rite of 1542, rather than part of a more-or-less independent group of Calvinian liturgies. After all, Calvin produced the 1545 rite at Geneva, just as he did the 1542 rite, the 1547 rite, etc., etc. Baum, Cunitz, and Reuss (in the *Corpus Reformatorum*, v. 34) logically present the 1545 and all later Calvinian rites in the form of variant readings to the basic 1542 Genevan Rite.

We thus conclude that it is illogical to split Calvin's liturgical efforts into a "Strassburg" and a "Genevan" rite, and by such a split to attempt to prove that the latter is an unfaithful representation of Calvin's true liturgical philosophy.

(4) On the matter of psalm-singing in Calvin's Genevan Rite, Brilioth apparently overlooks the rubric which reads: "Les Ministres distribuent le pain et le Calice au peuple, ayant adverty qu'on y vienne avec révérence et par bon ordre. Cependant on chante quelques Psalmes ou on lit quelque chose de l'Escripture,

---

[13] Doumergue describes Calvin's last two months in Strassburg thus (p. 708): "Il avait hâté son retour de Ratisbonne à Strasbourg, et là, l'indécision lui était tout de suite devenue insupportable. Le sort de Genève, impliquée dans de si graves difficultés avec Berne, le troublait. Son 'anxiété' croît. Que vont décider les surarbitres bâlois? Est-ce que nous ne faisons pas défaut aux 'nôtres?' La crainte des Bernois le retient encore; cependant il announce, le 13 août, à Viret, qu'il a suspendu ses leçons, et averti les étudiants qu'il ne les reprendra pas avant nouvel ordre. Le 29, le Conseil de Genève s'occupe de son logis, car il 'doybt arryver l'un de ses jours.'"

convenable à ce qui est signifié par le Sacrement" (Calvin's *Opera quae supersunt omnia*, v. 6, column 200). Moreover, no less than thirty-five psalms are appended to the liturgy (Maxwell, *John Knox's Genevan Service Book*, p. 70). It is interesting in this connection that "Calvin's First Psalter (1539)"[14]—printed at Strassburg—contained only nineteen psalms!

(5) We are very willing to admit that Calvin's Genevan Rite is largely taken up with exhortation (including a list of open sins), controversial material, and theological definition of the sacrament. We wish only to say that such emphases are *typically* Calvinian, and are completely *consistent* with the Reformer's other writings concerning the sacrament.

When in his Genevan Rite Calvin says "I excommunicate all [here follows a list of nineteen distinct varieties of open sinners]; declaring to them that they must abstain from this holy table, for fear of polluting and contaminating the sacred viands which our Lord Jesus Christ gives only to his household and believers" (Calvin's *Tracts*, v. 2, p. 120)—when he says this, Calvin is consistently reflecting the strong connection between the eucharist and excommunication which exists in his other writings. To take a single example; Calvin's "Articles concerning the Organization of the Church and of Worship at Geneva" (1537) have at their very outset the following two sentences:

> Right Honourable Gentlemen: it is certain that a Church cannot be said to be well ordered and regulated unless in it the Holy Supper of our Lord is always being celebrated and frequented, and this under such good supervision that no one dare presume to present himself unless devoutly, and with genuine reverence for it. For this reason, in order to maintain the Church in its integrity, the discipline of excommunication is necessary, by which it is possible to correct those that do not wish to submit courteously and with all obedience to the Word of God.[15]

With the great amount of doctrinal exhortation and definition in Calvin's Genevan Rite, compare the following statements from his "Short Treatise on the Holy Supper":

> To come to an end, we comprehend under one article what could be considered separately.
>
> The article is that the devil introduced the manner of celebrating the Supper without any doctrine, and in place of the doctrine substituted ceremonies, partly unfitting and useless, and partly even dangerous, from which much ill has followed—to such an extent, that the mass, which takes the place of

---

[14] Edited in facsimile by Sir Richard R. Terry.
[15] Calvin's *Theological Treatises* (Library of Christian Classics, v. 22), p. 48. See also pp. 50-53, 67, 70, 71, 79. (For the French text of the passage quoted above, see Calvin's *Opera Selecta*, v. 1, p. 369.)

the Supper in the popish Church, when strictly defined, is nothing but pure apishness and buffoonery. ... This being so, the chief thing which our Lord recommends to us, is to celebrate this mystery with true intelligence. It follows then that the substance of it all consists in the doctrine.[16]

Brilioth himself destroys much of the force of his own argument, as a matter of fact, by pointing out the particular ways in which "eucharistic praise, communion-fellowship, commemoration, and the offering of personal devotion" do appear on a limited scale in Calvin's Genevan Rite. Moreover, Brilioth has to admit that the emphasis given in the Rite to God's transcendence is "genuinely Calvinistic" (p. 178).

In concluding this first portion of our paper, therefore, we may confidently assert that Calvin's Genevan Rite provides a good, concrete example of his eucharistic philosophy in action. Because of Calvin's great logical abilities—his eminence in the field of systematic theology—the burden of proof has lain with those who claim that his Genevan Rite is inconsistent with his eucharistic views as he expressed them elsewhere. We have attempted to show that, except for the two matters of absolution and frequency of communion, such claims are unfounded; now, therefore, we may assert the truly Calvinian character of the Genevan Rite, and move on to a liturgical and doctrinal evaluation of it.

Calvin's Genevan Rite—a Valuable Contribution Liturgically and Doctrinally?

Liturgical Evaluation of the Genevan Rite. Having determined that Calvin's Genevan Rite is a fair standard by which to judge his liturgical philosophy, let us briefly attempt to make a value judgment with regard to the liturgical significance of this Rite.

Doumergue thinks highly of the Rite, to say the least. He writes (p. 504):

> Dira-t-on ... que le vrai culte calviniste était, par nature, pauvre et froid? Ceux qui y ont assisté nous ont raconté qu'ils ne pouvaient souvent retenir leurs larmes d'émotion et de joie. Chants et prières, adoration et édification, ... actes rituels et actes spontanés, tous les éléments essentiels existaient; et, fait peut-être non moins important, ils étaient réunis dans un organisme très simple, mais souple et fort.

We find, moreover, that Maxwell approves of Doumergue's evaluation (*An Outline of Christian Worship*, p. 119).

---

[16] *Ibid.*, p. 161. (For the French text of this passage, see Calvin's *Opera Selecta*, v. 1, p. 524.)

However, it should be noted that both of these men have strong Calvinist sympathies. Outside the Calvinist fold, opinions as to the liturgical worth of Calvin's Rite are far less complimentary. We have already quoted Brilioth, who describes the Rite as "a liturgical monstrosity, or rather a piece of preaching." An honest and unprejudiced reading of the Rite can hardly bring one to disagree with Brilioth's remark. We noted above the disgusting list of open sins which forms an integral part of the eucharistic service. Another very unpleasant inclusion should be mentioned. In the morning service (at which communion may or may not be given), the minister delivers a long and tiresome prayer following his sermon. The text of this prayer covers four full pages in volume two of Calvin's *Tracts* (pp. 101-05), and one of these four pages is completely devoted to a *paraphrase* of the Lord's Prayer!

Little further evidence is needed to justify Brilioth's condemnatory opinion of Calvin's Rite. Calvin demonstrates well the grave difficulties attendant upon liturgical innovation (even if it is disguised as returning to "la coustume de l'église ancienne"[17]); a rite produced by such innovation will almost certainly bear the image of the individual producing it — rather than of the historic body of believers.[18]

Doctrinal Evaluation of the Genevan Rite. From the doctrinal standpoint Calvin's eucharistic service is also deserving of severe criticism, for his Rite centers on a scripturally-imsupportable interpretation of the Sacrament. We quote from the exhortation which immediately precedes the distribution:[19]

> Let us raise our hearts and minds on high, where Jesus Christ is, in the glory of his Father, and from whence we look for him at our redemption. And let us not amuse ourselves with these earthly and corruptible elements which we see with the eye, and touch with the hand, in order to seek him there, as if he were enclosed in the bread or wine. Then only will our souls be disposed to be nourished and vivified with his substance, when they are thus

---

[17] This phrase occurs in the title of Calvin's Genevan Rite. He obviously did not mean the phrase to be taken literally — unless we are to assume that the early church used tiresome paraphrases of the Lord's Prayer in its services!

[18] Maxwell (*John Knox's Genevan Service Book*) argues very unconvincingly that Knox's and Calvin's rites are merely modifications of the historic Mass. It is true that he traces "step by step the history of the Sunday Morning Service of (Knox's) *Forms of Prayers*, 1556 ... till we have been led back through the Sunday Morning Services of Calvin and Bucer to the first German Mass of Diebold Schwarz at Strasburg, and thence to the Mass itself" (p. 32). But it should be obvious to all that a great deal can happen to a rite during such a process as this. Maxwell (pp. 66-70) designates Schwarz's Mass by the letter "A", and by the time he reaches Calvin's 1542 *Forme des Prières*, he has come to the letter "M" — with each of the intervening letters referring to a distinct step in the process!

[19] Calvin's *Tracts*, v. 2, pp. 121-22. (For the French text, see Calvin's *Opera quae supersunt omnia*, v. 6, column 200).

raised above all terrestrial objects, and carried as high as heaven, to enter the kingdom of God where he dwells. Let us be contented, then, to have the bread and wine as signs and evidences, spiritually seeking the reality where the word of God promises that we shall find it.

Calvin's doctrine of "sursum corda," as described in this quotation from the Genevan Rite, lies at the very heart of his whole eucharistic teaching.[20] Wallace well describes Calvin's view of the eucharistic communion when he says (p. 206): "Communion with the body of Christ is effected through the descent of the Holy Spirit, by whom our souls are lifted up to heaven, there to partake of the life transfused into us from the flesh of Christ." In his *Commentary on I Corinthians* Calvin himself says: "For as to him communicating himself to us, that is effected through the secret virtue of his Holy Spirit, which cannot merely bring together, but join in one, things that are separated by distance of place, and far remote" (p. 380). And Wendel argues (p. 271): "L' intervention du Saint-Esprit comme agent d'union entre le croyant et le Christ aboutit en effet à établir une symétrie entre la doctrine du baptême et celle de la Cène."

It should be obvious even to the most casual reader of the Lord's Supper accounts as given in the Synoptic Gospels and in I Corinthians, that no mention whatever is made of the "secret virtue" of the Holy Spirit, or of a "lifting up" of the believer's soul to heaven upon partaking of the Holy Meal. How, then, did Calvin arrive at this strange interpretation? The answer is not, as one might possibly gather from Sasse's otherwise excellent treatment of Calvin's eucharistic position, simply a conscious attempt to arrive at a *media via* between Luther on the one hand and Zwingli and Oecolampadius on the other.[21] To say that is to imply that Calvin's aim was primarily mediative. In actuality, Calvin's purpose in formulating his doctrine of the Lord's Supper was (as in the case of all of his theological work) the commendable one of setting forth the true scriptural view on the subject.[22] But since the Lord's Supper accounts in the New Testament nowhere mention a "sursum corda" or a special work of the Holy Spirit in lifting up believers to heaven, why did Calvin believe that these emphases were more truly biblical than other interpretive options?

Calvin rejected Zwingli's "spiritualistic" view because a purely spiritual presence of Christ in the Supper would deny the incarnation and because the eu-

---

[20] See especially Calvin's *Institutes*, Bk. 4, Chs. 14 and 17.

[21] "He (Calvin) wanted to do justice to Zwingli and Oecolampadius, whose figurative understanding of the words of institution he had accepted. On. the other hand, he felt himself to be closer to Luther, with whom he shared the conviction that the body of Christ is received 'substantially'" (Sasse, *This Is My Body*, pp. 325-26).

[22] Calvin, *Opera quae supersunt omnia*, v. 16, column 450. "Calvin said that he clung to his particular form of sacramental doctrine not from obstinacy but because he believed himself to be bound by the authority of Scripture" (Niesel, *The Theology of Calvin*, p. 228).

charistic texts patently show that "those who exclude the substance of vivifying flesh and blood from the communion defraud themselves of the use of the Supper."[23] He rejected Luther's "materialistic" view because:

(1) The rule of faith—proper hermeneutics—requires us to interpret the obscure passages of Scripture by the clear passages, and not the reverse, and "when our Lord instituted the Supper, He spoke briefly, as is usually done in federal acts, whereas in the sixth chapter of John, He discourses copiously and professedly on that mystery of sacred conjunction of which He afterwards held forth a mirror in the Sacraments."[24] John 6 makes clear that we are to interpret the *verba*, not literally, but sacramentally (*sacramentali modo*).

(2) In Scripture, sacraments invariably involve a sign and a gift, but to held that the sign itself *is* the gift negates the sign *per se*; rightly understood, the sacramental sign points us to the gift, which is Christ in heaven.[25]

(3) The Lutheran doctrine endangers "the truth of the human nature in which our salvation is grounded,"[26] for "the true humanity of Christ is threatened if we suppose that Christ, invisibly omnipresent, corporeally indwells the bread and wine."[27] This latter point was especially important to Calvin, for he wished at all cost to preserve God's absolute sovereignty over His creation, and he felt that the Lutheran doctrine of the real presence meant in fact a blending of the divine and human natures of Christ, so that the human nature became in a sense divine; otherwise, he argued, how could Christ's flesh be present simultaneously at many Communion tables? A classic modern treatment of Luther's theology carries the title, *Let God Be God*; in his eucharistic doctrine Calvin intended precisely this—and he was convinced that Luther was reviving the age-old error of the Doeetists by making of Christ's glorified human nature a mere semblance. Calvin's conclusion was that scriptural teaching could be preserved only if the Holy Spirit bridged the gulf between Christ in heaven[28]

---

[23] Calvin, *Opera quae supersunt omnia*, v. 9, column 76.
[24] *Ibid.*, column 200.
[25] See the excellent discussion of Calvin's general concept of sacrament in Dankbaar's dissertation, *De Sacramentsleer van Calvijn*, passim.
[26] Calvin, *Opera quae supersunt omnia*, v. 9, column 208; cf. v. 16, column 678.
[27] Niesel, *The Theology of Calvin*, p. 224.
[28] It is true.that Calvin believed in a spatial heaven, but (contra Sasse, *This Is My Body*, p. 323, n. 50) I believe that modern Calvinist theologians such as Niesel are quite within their rights to translate this spatial heaven into a metaphysical heaven, for such translation accords perfectly with Calvin's central concern for the sovereignty of God and His absolute "otherness."

and the believer participating in the Eucharist here on earth, and he was sure that by this rational construct he could remove the difficulties attendant upon the alternative approaches.

Credit certainly must be given to Calvin—who was probably the greatest Protestant systematic theologian in church history—for this attempt to deal with an exceedingly important and controversial doctrinal issue, and for his forthright inclusion of his sacramental interpretation in his eucharistie Rite. But, unhappily, his view suffers from serious difficulties, and these difficulties are grave enough to vitiate his Rite on theological grounds. Let us take each of his arguments in order. (1) Calvin's hermeneutical principle is eminently sound, but he goes wrong in the application of it. One cannot argue that John 6 is clearer than the *verba*, for (a) there is by no means unanimity among biblical scholars that John 6 has reference to the Eucharist;[29] (b) even if John 6 does refer to the Eucharist, the passage has nothing to do with a lifting of the believer to heaven, but—to the contrary—reiterates no less than seven times that Christ is the "bread which *came down from heaven*" (ὁ ἄρτος ὁ ἐξ οὐρανοῦ καταβάς)—see vv. 33, 38, 41, 42, 50, 51, 58; (c) if, as Calvin claims, "brevity is obscure" in the *verba*, we have Paul's detailed and inspired commentary on the *verba* in I Cor. 11, including the decisive assertion: "He that eateth and drinketh unworthily, eateth and drinketh damnation [κρίμα, judgment] to himself, not discerning the Lord's body. For this cause many are weak and sickly among you, and many sleep" (vv. 29-30).

(2) In arguing from the nature of sacraments in general to the meaning of the sacrament of the Lord's Supper, Calvin errs logically and hermeneutically. Logically, one can in this case establish the nature of the *genus* only by inductive examination of the *species*, for Scripture nowhere defines a sacrament in abstract terms. But if this is true, one must inductively discover the nature of the eucharistic sacrament from the passages describing it, not interpret those passages by a presumed invariable definition of what constitutes a sacrament. A definition of sacrament-in-general, in other words, can be arrived at only *after* discovering the nature of particular scriptural sacraments. Hermeneutically Calvin errs by using the Old Testament to interpret the New Testament, rather than the reverse; as Wallace readily admits (pp. 223-24): "Calvin's view of the New Testament sacraments is largely determined by the use made of signs in Old Testament revelation." Yet there is real question as to whether any "sacramental" teaching exists in the Old Testament; and if in fact such teaching is present

---

[29] For example, C. K. Barrett, in his commentary on John (1955), denies the validity of such eucharistic interpretation.

there, it must be interpreted by the New Testament. Symbolic "sacraments" of the Old Covenant (if such existed) must not be allowed to determine in an *a priori* manner the character of clearly-expressed New Testament sacraments.

(3) Christology is indeed vitally connected with sound eucharistic doctrine, and the sovereignty and "otherness" of God must be retained in any Christian theology worthy of the name. But proper Christology and a proper understanding of divine sovereignty must themselves derive from scriptural teaching. To know what it means that ὁ λόγος σὰρξ ἐγένετο (Jn. 1:14) requires us inductively to examine New Testament accounts of the ministry of the Christ, not excluding His post-Resurrection ministry. Even before His Resurrection, Christ's body possessed remarkable characteristics, for though His enemies were all about Him and intended to kill Him, He "passed through the midst of them [διελθὼν διὰ μέσου αὐτῶν] and went His way" (Lk. 4:28-30). After the Resurrection, as is well known, He passed through doors without opening them. Calvin is clearly rationalizing when he has to resort to such explanations as the following: "To enter while the doors remained shut, does not imply His penetrating through the solid matter, but His opening an entrance for Himself by His divine power, so that, in a miraculous manner, He instantaneously stood in the midst of His disciples, though the doors were shut."[30] But if Christ had the power to transform doors, why did He not have the power to transform Himself? One's doctrine of the relation of the two natures in the incarnated Christ must be determined by Scripture, not by *a priori*—even if Chalcedonian *a priori* is marshalled. Here again Calvin errs by reasoning from the general to the particular, when he should have formulated his abstract and general principles on the basis of particular scriptural teaching.

Just as Luther has been falsely accused of irrationalism, so Calvin has been falsely accused of rationalism. In actuality, Luther carefully distinguished the right uses of reason (reason as logical method; reason as the normative principle in social life) from the wrong use of it (reason as the norm in the realm of salvation).[31] Likewise, Calvin distinguished the right and wrong uses of reason; he saw the difference between the reason which "is manifested when mortal man, instead of receiving divine things with reverence, would subject them to his own judgment" and the "reason which both the Spirit of God and the Scripture sanction" (i.e., the reason which requires the conformity of each statement of doctrine with the rest of the Christian faith).[32] True, Luther on occasion made unguarded criticisms of reason, and Calvin tended to overrate the

---

[30] Calvin, *Institutes*, Bk. 4, Ch. 17, par. 29.
[31] Cf. Robert H. Fischer, "A Reasonable Luther," in Littell (ed.), *Reformation Studies*, pp. 32-33.
[32] Calvin, *Opera quae supersunt omnia*, v. 9, column 474.

efficacy of the rational faculties,[33] but, in all fairness, both Reformers honestly attempted to subject themselves to biblical teaching in the determination of doctrine.

It is the conviction of the writer of this paper that Calvin's failure to achieve a satisfactory eucharistic Rite and a sound doctrine of the Eucharist was due, not to intentional rationalism, but to a *misuse* of reason—to the systematician's natural tendency to reason from the general to the specific and particular, rather than the reverse. Whereas Luther in his *Formula missae* (and even in his *Deutsche Messe*) began with the actual, particular historic usage of the church, and tried to purify it by conformity with Holy Writ, Calvin began with general reforming principles and created a Rite which was an extension of his own personality and interests more than a reflection of the corporate worship experience of the church. And whereas Luther, in his doctrine of the Lord's Supper, always began with the specific words of institution—"the plain words just as they stand"[34]—and conformed general doctrines (e.g., the mutual relation of Christ's natures; God's sovereignty over His creation) to them, Calvin forced the *verba* into line with generalized, *a priori* doctrines which really should have been influenced by the *verba*. Luther was not by vocation a "systematic theologian"; as Kooiman correctly notes, he would today probably be regarded as a professor of Bible—indeed, of the Old Testament.[35] Significantly, however, it was Luther's very biblical orientation which gave him his theological strength, for he invariably began with the text and generalized from it, instead of beginning with a generality and examining Scripture in relation to it. Calvin always reminds the church of the towering magnificence of theological construction; but, as this paper has been at pains to point out, he should likewise warn us of the importance of examining our theological starting-points with great care.

---

[33] Cf. Calvin's unfortunate use of the simple syllogism: "A doctrine carrying many absurdities with it is not true. The doctrine of the corporeal presence of Christ is involved in many absurdities; therefore it follows that it is not true" (*ibid.*, column 233). Quirinus Breen notes that Calvin had bees "almost entirely committed to the humanistic ideal until his twenty-fourth year" and that it left him with a valuable "mental set" (*John Calvin: A Study in French Humanism*, p. 146); it may be debated just how valuable this mental set actually was.

[34] Luther, "Confession concerning Christ's Supper" (1528), in *Luther's Works*, v. 57 (ed. Robert H. Fischer), p. 165. On the relation between Luther's and Calvin's doctrines of the Lord's Supper, with special reference to Calvin, see Grass, *Die Abendmahlslehre bei Luther und Calvin, passim*.

[35] Kooiman, *Luther and the Bible*, p. 197 (citing Heinrich Bornkamm's *Luther und das Alte Testament*).

Bibliography

Berkouwer, G. C. *The Person of Christ*. Trans. by John Vriend. Grand Rapids, Eerdmans, 1955 (Studies in Dogmatics.)

Breen, Quirinus. *John Galvin: A Study in French Humanism*. A dissertation submitted to the Graduate Faculty (of the University of Chicago) in candidacy for the degree of Doctor of Philosophy, Department of Church History. Grand Rapids, Eerdmans, 1931.

Brilioth, Yngve. *Eucharistic Faith and Practice, Evangelical and Catholic*. Trans. by A. G. Hebert. London, Society for Promoting Christian Knowledge; New York, Macmillan; 1939.

Bruce, A. B. "The Synoptic Gospels." *In*: Nicoll, W. Robertson, ed. *The Expositor's Greek Testament*. Vol. I. Grand Rapids, Eerdmans, 1951.

Calvin, John. *Commentary on a Harmony of the Evangelists, Matthew, Mark, and Luke*. Trans. by William Pringle. Vol. 3. Edinburgh, Calvin Translation Society, 1846.

Commentary on the Epistles of Paul the Apostle to the Corinthians. Trans. by John Pringle. Vol. 1. Edinburgh, Calvin Translation Society, 1848.

Institutes of the Christian Religion. Trans. by John Allen. 8th American ed., rev. and corrected, with an account of the literary history of the *Institutes* by Benjamin B. Warfield, and an introduction by John Murray. Grand Rapids, Eerdmans, 1949. 2 vols. (Bound at the back of Vol. 2 is Nixon, Leroy. *Complete Indexes to the Institutes of the Christian Religion by John Calvin*. Grand Rapids, Eerdmans, c1950.)

Opera quae supersunt omnia. Ed. by Guilielmus (Wilhelm) Baum, Eduard(us) Cunitz, and Eduard(us) Reuss. Brunsvigae (Brunswick), C. A. Schwetschke, 1867 (Vol. 6), 1876 (Vol. 15). (*Corpus Reformatorum*, vols. 34, 43.)

Opera selecta. Ed. by Petrus (Peter) Barth. Vol. I: Scripta Calvini ab anno 1533 usque ad annum 1541 continens. Monachii (Munich), Chr. Kaiser, 1926.

Theological Treatises. Trans. by J. K. S. Reid. Philadelphia, Westminster Press, 1954 (Library of Christian Classics, Vol. 22.)

Tracts. Trans. by Henry Beveridge. Edinburgh, Calvin Translation Society, 1844-51. 3 vols.

Dankbaar, Willem Prederik. *De Sacramentsleer van Calvijn*. Proefschrift ter Verkrijging van den Graad van Doctor in de Godgeleerdheid [Th.D.] aan de Rijksuniversiteit te Leiden. Amsterdam, H. J. Paris, 1941.

Doumergue, E. *Jean Calvin*: les hommes et les choses de son temps. T. 2: Les premiers essais. Lausanne, Georges Bridel, 1902.

Fischer, Robert H. "A Reasonable Luther." *In*: *Reformation Studies*: Essays in Honor of Roland H. Bainton. Edited by Franklin H. Littell. Richmond, Va., John Knox Press, 1962. Pp. 30-45, 255-56.

Grass, Hans. *Die Abendmahlslehre bei Luther und Calvin*. Beiträge zur Förderung christlicher Theologie, 2. Reihe, 47. Bd. Gütersloh, C. Bertelsmann, 1954.

Luther, Martin. *Works*. Vol. 37: Word and Sacrament, III. Edited by Robert H. Fischer. Philadelphia, Muhlenberg Press, 1961. (American Edition of Luther's Works.)

McNeill, John T. "Christianity in the Reformation Era," *In*: *A Short History of Christianity*. Edited by Archibald G. Baker. Chicago, University of Chicago Press, 1940. Pp. 99-134.

Maxwell, William D. *The Book of Common Prayer and the Worship of the Non-Anglican Churches*. London, Oxford University Press, 1950. (Friends of Dr. Williams's Library, 3rd Lecture.)

John Knox's Genevan Service Book, 1556. The liturgical portions of the Genevan Service Book used by John Knox while a minister of the English congregation of Marian exiles at Geneva, 1556-1559. Edinburgh and London, Oliver and Boyd, 1931.

An Outline of Christian Worship; its developments and forms. London and New York, Oxford University Press, 1952.

Niesel, Wilhelm. *The Theology of Calvin*. Trans. by Harold Knight. Philadelphia, Westminster Press, 1956.

Reed, Luther D. *The Lutheran Liturgy*. Philadelphia, Muhlenberg Press, 1947.

Sasse, Hermann. *This Is My Body*; Luther's contention for the Real Presence in the Sacrament of the Altar. Minneapolis, Augsburg, 1959.

Terry, Richard R., ed. *Calvin's First Psalter (1539)*. London, E. Benn, 1932.

Tholuck, F. A. G. "Calvin As an Interpreter of the Holy Scripture." Trans. by Prof. Woods of Andover. *In*: Calvin, John. *Commentaries on the Book of Joshua*. Edinburgh, Calvin Translation Society, 1854. Pp. 337-375.

Wallace, Ronald S. *Calvin's Doctrine of the Word and Sacrament*. Edinburgh and London, Oliver and Boyd, 1953.

Wendel, François. *Calvin: sources et évolution de sa pensée religieuse*. Paris, Presses Universitaires de France, 1950. (Etudes d'histoire et de philosophie religieuse publiées par la Faculté de Théologie Protestante de l'Université de Strasbourg, No. 4l.)

2. The Life of Paul Luther, Physician*

The importance of Martin Luther's son Paul to the history of medicine and to the history of theology does not lie in the uniqueness of his views or in extraordinary personal accomplishments, for in neither of these respects was he outstanding. His value to historical enquiry stems rather from the fact that he is an excellent representative of the sixteenth-century German court physician and of the educated Protestant layman of the Reformation period. Because people of the time were fascinated by the progeny of the great, they frequently took care to record biographical details concerning them. It is of great advantage to us that they did so, for by way of such progeny we often gain historical insight which would otherwise not come easily. In the case of Paul Luther, we have a previously untranslated literary time-machine that can carry a contemporary reader back into that period of history when empirical medicine was emerging, and when the clarion call of *"sola gratia, sola fide, sola scriptura"* fired believers' hearts.

The present translation has been made from Melchior Adam's *Vitae Germanorum medicorum* (Heidelberg: Impensis heredum Jonae Rosae, 1620) in the possession of Columbia University's College of Physicians and Surgeons. This quarto volume consists of over one hundred twenty-five brief "Lives," of which Paul Luther's occupies pages 338-341. Melchior Adam (d. 1622) was a German biographer whose chief characteristics were great literary industry and a strongly Protestant (Calvinistic) frame of reference.

> Baillet said that the Lutherans criticized our author [Adam] for having several times insulted the memory of those who had rendered the greatest services to the new faith; but the Calvinists whose teachings he followed did not reproach him on these grounds. For the rest, one must acknowledge that these biographies of great men (all Protestants, with the exception of about twenty Germans and Flemings) are a work that involved a great deal of labor (Michaud I: 145; cf. Hoefer I: 226).

At the end of this text Melchior Adam states that he derived his biographical information from the funeral oration of Matthew Dresser. This oration is printed in Dresser's biography of Martin Luther, *Historia Lutheri* (Leipzig, 1598) (see Ukert I: 18). Dresser (1536-1607), being a contemporary of Paul Luther and one who frequented his circles, was undoubtedly in a position to describe accurately his subject's activities. Michaud says of Dresser:

---

*This research essay was originally submitted to the College of Physicians and Surgeons, Columbia University, for course credit, and led to the author's receiving the Grade I Certificate of Medical Librarianship from the (U.S.) Medical Library Association (14 March 1955).

This Lutheran scholar ... was first educated at Eisleben, and then returned to Wittenberg to study under Melanchthon and Luther. ... He was called to Jena to fill the chair of history, which had been vacant since the death of Justus Lipsius, and he delivered his inaugural address in 1574. However, he preferred the position of dean of the college at Meissen to the position at Jena, and he left Meissen in 1581 to assume the chair of humanities at the University of Leipzig. ... He became one of the most ardent advocates of forbidding the teaching of the new doctrine [i.e., Calvinism] (Michaud XI: 302).

It should be noted that Dresser, unlike Adam, was Lutheran rather than Calvinistic in his doctrinal position. The very fact that Paul Luther appears in Melchior Adam's work indicates the regard in which he was held by scholarly authors in early modern times, whatever their theological position.

Melchior Adam's Latin must certainly be regarded as classical rather than medieval. It contains none of the grammatical "errors" which crept into the language during the Middle Ages. Ciceronian influence is present to a marked degree. One of the many examples of this classicism is found in the line reading: "He considered that he now had an open field in which his own ability could show itself and be recognized." This sentence parallels very closely the wording of a line in Cicero's *Speech on Behalf of Lucius Murena* (8.18), which reads "a field, in which his excellence could show itself." One of the clearest expressions of the classical revival in Melchior Adam's Latin is the use of Grecisms. The reader will note a quotation from Euripides' *Rhesus*, the English translation of which we have taken from Arthur S. Way's *Euripides* in the Loeb Classical Library. But the Greek influence extends even to direct transliteration of Greek words into Latin. An example is the word for "[physician's] fee": the "Latin" word used here is *sostra*—which is in fact a Greek term used by Pollux, Archaeologus (c. AD 180). There are, of course, a few medieval words and loose constructions in the biography of Paul Luther, but these are the exceptions. *Archiepiscopatus* ("Archbishopric") is an obvious example.

In order not to disturb the flow of the narrative, I have avoided footnotes to the translation and instead have provided appendices. These appendices give additional data regarding various persons mentioned in the biography; the chemicals and herbs used by Paul Luther in his practice; and Paul Luther's chief personal characteristic, designated in Greek by Melchior Adam as *parresia*.

Lexical Resources

Dictionaries employed in making the translation were: for classical Latin, Harpers' Latin Dictionary (*ed. Lewis and Short*) *and* Cassell's Latin Dictionary; *for classical Greek*, Liddell and Scott's Greek-English Lexicon (*ed. Henry Stuart Jones*);

for medieval Latin, Baxter and Johnson's Medieval Latin Word-List, *Du Cange's* Glossarium mediae et infimae Latinitatis, *and Maigne d'Arnis'* Lexicon manuale ad scriptores mediae et infimae Latinitatis. *In order to find the German equivalents of Latin place names mentioned in the biography, J. G. Th. Graesse's* Orbis Latinus oder Verzeichnis der wichtigstens lateinischen Orts- und Ländernamen *(Berlin, 1909) was employed.*

Luther's son Paul by Johann Georg Menzel.

Life of Paul Luther

Paul Luther was born at Wittenberg in the year of Christ 1533, on the twenty-eighth day of January. His parents were Martin Luther, that heroic theologian, and Catherine von Bora, an excellent woman. He spent his boyhood years in the discipline of the home and in the school of the fatherland; and he conducted himself in such a manner that even then he brought to his parents great hope of his having outstanding erudition and virtue. From that school he transferred to the university, where he drew forth Latin and Greek literature, not out of pools, but from living springs; that is, from the writings of the philosophers, the orators, the poets, and the historians, as interpreted by Melanchthon, Vitus Winshemius, and others.

A certain natural ability particularly showed forth with regard to the virtue which is called "magnanimity," as well as an ability for that study which explains the meaning and nature of things, and provides remedies for preventing diseases. Indeed, he gave many evidences of a keen and noble character—and by these indications his father was able to see that he was being driven on to commendation for his seriousness and perseverance. Therefore Martin loved him even more deeply as he perceived his greater strength of character and spirit. But Paul was driven by an even greater force (or, as Plato said of Isocrates, by a more divine impulse of the soul) to the study of nature, and of the power of remedies which apply to the body. For this reason his parent certainly approved, if he did not advocate and urge, the commencement and pursuit of that study to which his nature led him. His father took such wonderful delight in these graces of character that he kept his son before his eyes; he did not allow him to depart from his side. For his part, Paul observed and welcomed all the words and deeds of his parent so well that he considered it his task to imitate them. Therefore, that which is most highly desirable for all good children happened to him: he was even present at his father's death.

For Paul went with his father when the latter was summoned to Eisleben by the counts of Mansfeld, and with such care and devotion did he attend him in his illness that in the arms of this son Martin Luther expired with the utmost serenity, and his son heard his last breath. This took place when Paul had just entered upon his thirteenth year.

In this regard, moreover, we should note that examples of paternal piety and magnanimity which have been infused into children cannot but take root and bear fruit throughout the whole of life. Thus patterns of seriousness and steadfastness on the father's part result in the child's being found serious and steadfast in religious conviction even to death. For although Paul did not teach and propagate religion as his father had done, nevertheless he always professed one and the same faith; and indeed he did not cease to defend it if anywhere the occasion demanded.

After these events, Paul deepened his studies of philosophy and of Latin and Greek literature on the advice of Melanchthon, thereby contributing to his progress in the art of medicine. His scholarship was publicly recognized by the University of Wittenberg; and in the year 1557, with Jacob Milichius serving as Dean, he was declared a Doctor of Medicine.

This learning had already produced in him a certain stability and reasoning power which complemented his extraordinary natural ability. For this reason he appeared thereafter as remarkable and unique. To begin with, he undertook to teach medicine at the University of Jena. From this position he was summoned to the bodily care of the most important dukes and electors of the Holy Roman Empire. First he was called by the Dukes of Upper Saxony at the court at Weimar, where he showed his wisdom in preventing illness and exceptional industry in curing it. He remained at this court until the surrender of the city of

Gotha in Thuringia on April 13, 1567. So unreservedly had he given his pledge to Duke John Frederick that he did not break it even in peril of siege and in imminent danger. Indeed, he suffered with a resolute spirit all annoyances, terrors, assaults, and the most violent siege tactics which the strength of Mars and the rage of arms are wont to produce.

But when the duchy's stronghold had been forced to surrender, Luther went over to the court of Elector Joachim II at Brandenburg. He had been commissioned as Joachim's "protophysicus," or primary physician and medical doctor. To this end he engaged in the performance of his duty with extraordinary concentration, vigilance, and scrupulousness of mind; more and more he demonstrated every day both integrity of judgment and candor of speech. At that time the Elector, in his sixty-fourth year, unexpectedly contracted a very severe disease and longed for a remedy both powerful and ingenious. Therefore Luther brought forth everything he had learned from the precepts and practice of medical men. The outcome did not disappoint him. For by the work of God and the skill of physicians the Duke was restored to good health — not without praise and honor to Luther. The Duke not only gave testimony of his activity, but also paid him a very handsome fee. For he bestowed on him two gold decorations of great value, with the name of the donor and the reason for bestowal inscribed upon them; above and beyond this he commanded that Luther should be given a sum of money worthy of the munificence of a prince such as himself.

But at length when Joachim II was called to leave this life on January 3, 1571, at the age of sixty-six, Luther left the province of Brandenburg, and served Augustus, Duke Elector of the Saxons. He moved to Augustus' court in 1571. Here at last he employed all his powers of mind and talent, considering that he now had an open field in which his own ability could show itself and be recognized. He conformed himself fully to the virtue and to the character of Augustus, his prince being a man of the most ardent virtue. The Elector loved uprightness of character: Luther was eager to prove himself upright in word and deed. The Duke hated pretense: therefore Luther himself fled all hypocrisy — to the point of actually preferring to hate in the open rather than conceal his true feelings behind appearances. Augustus was a lover of art to the greatest degree: therefore Luther so exerted himself in the art he himself professed that he investigated all aspects of it and did not consider anything to be so remote or so profound that he could not comprehend it with ingenuity and work it out with diligence.

At this time, that which they call the "spagiric" or chemical art was daily emerging. Already it had penetrated into the very courts of princes; and indeed several had been convinced that the drugs prepared by that art possessed great abilities to cure certain human misfortunes. Luther earnestly devoted himself to this study so that he might test it in theory as well as in practice. Indeed, he considered that neither effort nor expense should be spared. He thought that he ought not to rest until he had penetrated the inmost aspects of that subject and—if I may put it this way—acquaint himself with its very juice and marrow. And he did not misplace this zeal and labor. For to theoretical medicine he also joined that branch of the subject which embraces certain chemical substances discovered and developed in an ingenious and clever manner. He did this in order that nothing might remain in any quarter that was not understood by the mind and tested in practice.

Therefore Luther accepted quite a number of medicines into his laboratory, as ointment from niter, mother of pearl, mother of coral, drinkable gold, remedies against the stone; and also many extracts from herbs—blessed thistle, scabiosa, angelica, pimpinella, and others of the same kind. Added to this was a personal acquaintance and contact with all the most learned physicians, but also with the wisest princes; and the practical judgment of these men was brought to greater exercise in his art. Not surprisingly, therefore, he was compared to the masters in this discipline and became very highly esteemed by princes themselves—especially by Augustus, Elector of the Saxons. Since Augustus loved every art to an amazing degree, so also he magnified and honored artists. Hence it happened that along with other favors Luther was even presented with a spacious estate and with a gold ornament that bore Augustus' name and likeness. Besides this love of art, Augustus possessed not only love and concern but also considerable ardor for the true faith. Stirred and driven by this feeling, therefore, he also loved those servants of his in whom he found a free and sincere profession of the Christian religion. In this respect Luther stood out most conspicuously, since no religion was acceptable to him except the one that his own father, under divine influence, had drawn forth from the founts of Israel and, with courageous perseverance, summoned again from darkness into light. Indeed, as he had drunk of this faith in the home schooling his father had given him, so he held firmly to it through all his life.

Hence Paul Luther devoted as much labor and planning as he was able to the improvement of the churches of the Saxon Electorate under Administrator Frederick William. And nothing was more his wish than that any suspicion of defection from Luther's doctrine be removed. He was truly a *parresiastes*—one who loves the freedom to speak as he wishes—a stranger to the charge of adulation and flattery—an exact representation of Euripides' Rhesus, who says of himself in the tragedy of the same name:

Toioutos eimi kautos, eutheian logon
Temnon keleuthon, kou diplous pephuk'aner.

Even such am I: no devious track of words
I follow: no man I of double tongue.

Indeed, this Luther had many other great virtues; but I do not know whether any ought more to be commended in him than this very *parresia* in which he appeared to the greatest degree like his father.

After the death of Augustus on February 11, 1586, at the age of sixty, Luther devoted more than three years of his service to Christian I, Duke and Elector of Saxony. Thereupon he bid a long farewell to the court on account of religious suspicion and moved to Leipzig. He lived piously and uprightly among the citizens there from the year 1587. In 1592, however, he was called back with a generous and creditable stipend by Frederick William, the Administrator of the Saxon Electorate, as much for the care of the Administrator himself as for the care of the ducal wards.

Luther spent many years as a widower with the sweetest of children. He had sired six children by Anna (of the ancient and noble Warbeck family in Swabia), whom he had married in the year 1553. He left three sons, of whom the eldest, Ernest, was admitted into the evangelical college of canons in the diocese of Siza. Moreover, he brought about most creditable marriages for his two daughters: Margaret to Simon Gottsteig, a high official of the Magdeburg Archbishopric, and Anna to the noble Nicolas Marschalck in Oberschar.

Finally, after he had piously and uprightly lived for a sufficiently long time, had helped people in their difficulties, and had practiced medicine against as many sufferings as he was able, he contracted an illness from which it was not possible to recover. For although he took diligent care of himself, and made use of the advice and efforts of other physicians, nevertheless he was from day to day in poorer and poorer health. And so, not without reason, he prepared himself completely for the blessed journey and for life's metamorphosis. He wished for nothing more than to be freed the more swiftly from the troublesome burden of the body. To this end he desired more quickly to come into the bosom and embrace of the Son of God, our Savior and sweetest brother. At length this wish was granted; and on the eighth of March in the year 1593 (at the age of sixty), a little after the eighth hour, he was called forth out of this impure and chaotic world and received into the celestial fatherland by this very sweetest of brothers Jesus Christ.

Luther made frequent remarks full of the spirit and faith of Jesus Christ as long as he lay on his deathbed. Nor was he reluctant to repeat quite often and to declare eloquently in what faith he wished to die and come to Christ—to repeat and declare specifically those things which have been fixed and established in the sole merit of Christ alone. In fact, with regard to the doctrine of the Holy Supper, he asserted with all earnestness that he was not satisfied with any other view than that which had hitherto been declared and defended out of the holy Word of God by Martin Luther his father. Let people believe otherwise; he himself continually and earnestly declared that in his heart and in his public profession he shrank from the views of such people. He was buried with a great number present—not only of townspeople but also of the University of Leipzig, which bestowed upon the dead man the last service and honor.

Matthew Dresser, in his funeral oration, stated these facts about Luther the physician.

Paul's father Martin Luther and mother Catherine von Bora by Lucas Cranach (1526).

Appendices

Paul Luther's Teachers

Vitus-Ortelius Winsheimius or Windsheim (1501-1570). "Having finished his studies at the University of Wittenberg, he received the degree of Doctor of Medicine. But he was offered the chair of Greek shortly afterward, and he gave up practicing [the art of] medicine to devote himself completely to teaching literature" (Michaud XLIV: 702; for a list of the numerous editions, translations, and orations by Winsheimius, see Michaud and also Melanchthon's *Declamations*, vol. V).

Jacob Milichius or Milich (1501-1559) came to Wittenberg in 1524. "Here he was first a philosopher [i.e., a member of the faculty of philosophy], then later a professor in the faculty of medicine" (*Allgemeine Deutsche Biographie* XXI: 745). When Melanchthon was preparing his systematic account of Aristotle's physical theories and the current state of knowledge in that area, he sought out and benefited from Milichius' scientific expertise (Scheible, *Encyclopedia* III: 43).

Political Figures Whom Paul Luther Served
Duke John Frederick (and the Fall of Gotha). "John Frederick (1529-1595), called *der Mittlare*, duke of Saxony, was the eldest son of John Frederick, who had been deprived of the Saxon electorate by the emperor Charles V in 1547. ... The duke was a strong, even a fanatical, Lutheran, but his religious views were gradually subordinated to the one idea of regaining the electoral dignity then held by Augustus I. ... In 1566 his obstinacy caused him to be placed under the imperial ban. Its execution was entrusted to Augustus who, aided by the duke's brother, John William, marched against Gotha with a strong force. In consequence of a mutiny the town surrendered in April 1567, and John Frederick was delivered to the emperor Maximillian II. He was imprisoned in Vienna, his lands were given to his brother, and he remained in captivity until his death at Steyer on the 6th of May 1595" (*Encyclopedia Britannica* [11th ed.] XV: 458f.).

Joachim II (1506-1571) introduced the Reformation into his lands in 1539. "While stressing the centrality of the evangelical doctrine of justification by faith alone, the elector, a ceremonial traditionalist, sought to maintain continuity with the old church by preserving both its liturgical heritage and the episcopal form of church government" (Nischan, *Encyclopedia* I: 208). Franz Lau considered Joachim's approach in Brandenburg a "unique type of Reformation" (*Wissenschaftliche Zeitschrift* III: 139-152), but one should remember that this was very much consistent with Martin Luther's conservative reforming style—over against left-wing, radical *Schwärmerei* as represented by Karlstadt and Müntzer (cf. Krauth).

Augustus I (1526-1586). "The elector imposed a strict form of Lutheranism in his dominion, and tortured and imprisoned the ‚Crypto-Calvinists' who followed the teaching of Melanchthon" (*Encyclopedia Britannica* [14th ed.] II: 689f.). "Political factors played a role in August's act: even greater Lutheran aversion to Calvinism and the desire to protect its legality in the wake of the Saint Bartholomew's Day Massacre in France (1572)" (Peterson, *Encyclopedia* III: 260). At the same time, Augustus I "was one of the best domestic rulers that Saxony ever had. ... He devoted his long reign to the development of its resources" (*Encyclopedia Britannica* [11th ed.] XXIV: 270).

Christian I (1560-1591), son of and successor to Augustus I, did not share his father's strict Lutheranism (see *Allgemeine Deutsche Biographie* IV: 172). During his reign, Nikolas Crell or Krell, the Chancellor, was really in control. "Crell's religious views were Calvinistic or Crypto-Calvinistic, and both before and after his appointment as chancellor in 1589 he sought to substitute his own form of faith for Lutheranism which was the accepted religion of electoral Saxony. ... When the elector died in October 1591 he was deprived of his offices and thrown into prison by order of Frederick William, duke of Saxe-Altenburg, the regent for the young elector Christian II" (*Encylopedia Britannica* [11th ed.] VII: 402). Crell was subsequently "executed for his part in the adventure after a long trial and imprisonment" (Peterson, *Encyclopedia* III: 261).

Frederick William (1562-1602) — just mentioned — is the "Administrator" referred to in Adam's life of Paul Luther (see *Allgemeine Deutsche Biographie* VII: 791f.). One of the "ducal wards" in Frederick William's care was the future Elector Christian II. As a result of this guardianship, orthodox Lutheranism was brought back to electoral Saxony (Junghans, *Encyclopedia* IV: 285).

Concerning the electoral system in the Holy Roman Empire, the body of Electors who chose the Holy Roman Emperor consisted of seven men (thus the term *Septemvirs*). The number was fixed around 1260 and remained unchanged until 1623. These men were originally described as "princes entitled to vote in this election, who were seven in number" (*principes vocem in huiusmode electione habentes, qui sunt septem numero*) in an official letter to the Pope (c. 1260).

Paul Luther's Wife and Children
Paul and Anna Luther had four sons and two daughters. The reason that only three of the sons are mentioned by Melchior Adam is that the first boy, Paul, died on February 23, 1558 at the age of four or five. Ernest was the oldest son to reach maturity. For detailed histories of Paul Luther's wife and children, see David Richter's *Genealogia Lutherorum* (Berlin & Leipzig, 1733), which contains portraits of Paul Luther and his wife.

Paul Luther's Chemical Interests
Webster defines "spagiric" (a word that is obsolete except in historical usage) as equivalent to "alchemy" or "iatrochemistry." "Iatrochemistry" in turn is described as "chemistry united with medicine; applied to the chemistry of the period (about 1525-1660) which was dominated by the teachings of Paracelsus: that the activities of the human body are chemical, that health depends on the proper chemical composition of the organs and fluids, and that the object of chemistry is to prepare medicines" (see also my article on Paracelsus in *Cross and Crucible*). In connection with the mention of Paracelsus here, we should note the inclusion of a biography of him in Adam's volume (pp. 28-38).

Paul Luther was not only well grounded in theoretical, classical medicine, but also had an interest in the new experimental, empirical, chemical medicine that appeared during the Renaissance-Reformation period. We shall therefore take a closer look at the chemicals and herbs used by Paul Luther in his practice. What were they considered good for, and are any of them used in modern medicine and pharmacy?

Ointment from niter (unguentum de nitro). "Nitro" of course refers to saltpeter. "In the 16th century the ancient nitrum becomes altered to natron, a term still used for native sodium carbonate, while nitrum, and its adaptation nitre, were retained for potassium nitrate or saltpetre" (*Encyclopedia Britannica* [14th ed.] XVI: 466). The closest to an ointment of niter that I was able to discover in early works on *materia medica* is described as follows: "There is also a Sort of Butter prepar'd of Nitre, by the Means of Tartar; the Process whereof may be seen in Monsieur *Charas's* Chymistry, p. 853 (Pomet 379). In contemporary medical practice, saltpeter is considered very "irritating to the stomach and is not now used internally, but is used for inhalation in the treatment of asthma" (*Black's Medical Dictionary*).

Magistery of pearl and magistery of coral (magisterium perlarum, corallorum). At the back of the 1658 Geneva edition of Paracelsus' *Opera Omnia* there is a glossary of medical and chemical terms prepared by Rochi le Baillif. In this glossary we find *magisterium* defined as "what remains after it has been extracted from other ingredients, without the elements used in preparation and separation, so that its [properties] are preserved if the other materials from which it was extracted are added to it [again]" (*Magisterium, est quod ex rebus extractum stet, sine elementali preparatione et separatione, ut fit additione aliarum rerum, in quibus quod extrahitur, conservatur*). This definition corresponds with the one given in the *Oxford English Dictionary*—"the residuum obtained by precipitation from an acid solution, e.g., magistery of bismuth, pearls, etc.; a precipitate." Pomet specifically mentions both magistery of pearl and magistery of coral, but does not consider them of much medical value (pp. 97, 302).

Drinkable gold (aurum potable). Pomet writes: "The Aurum Potabile of the Chymists is nothing but a Chimaera; they pretend that they can resolve Gold into its first Principles, and separate the Salt and Sulphur of it. ... They call these pretended Salts and Sulphurs of Gold, Potable Gold, because they can be dissolved in all Sorts of Liquors, and be taken as a Potion: They attribute to it the Virtue of being a Preservative against all sorts of Illness, that it cures all Diseases, prolongs Life, and in a Word, is the Universal Medicine" (pp. 311f.). *Aurum potabile* was prepared somewhat differently by different alchemists (for various recipes see Wecker 407-28; also Hill 51).

Before we dismiss as bizarre the "drinkable gold" of Paul Luther and his contemporaries, we should give some thought to the "chrysotherapy" of our own day. The modern use of gold therapy began with Robert Koch's discovery in 1890 of the bacteriostatic properties of Au(CN). In the 1920s and 1930s gold thiolates were used to treat tuberculosis, and in the late 1920s Forstier noted that patients with arthritis showed improvement on receiving chrysotherapy. Today, five complexes are used, each containing gold(I) coordinated to sulphur, the sulphur often bridging two gold atoms; most of the compounds are injected. According to Dr. Stephen Ralph of the Faculty of Science of the University of Wollongong (N. S. W., Australia), in his 2002 Medical-Chemical Lectures, the mechanisms of chrysotherapeutic action include, among others, anti-inflammation, inhibition of lysosomal enzymes, and immunomodulatory activity. "We conclude that glucocorticoids given as intermittent, intramuscular depot injections have a significant short term benefit which can be maintained by concomitant administration of intramuscular gold" (Corkill 274-279). Besides their value in treating rheumatoid arthritis, gold drugs have been shown to inhibit growth of HIV in cultured cells, to fight P399 leukemia in vivo, and to be active against two strains of Plasmodium responsible for malaria.

The extracts from herbs. All four of those mentioned are found in modern *materia medica.* The following information is derived from *Stedman's Medical Dictionary. Carduus benedictus* (blessed thistle), the plant *Cnicus benedictus:* a bitter tonic in doses of 2.0-4.0. (A "bitter tonic" is a tonic of bitter taste, such as quinine, which acts chiefly by stimulating the appetite and improving digestion.) *Scabiosa* or Scabious or Erigeron, the dried leaves and flowering tops of *Leptilon canadense* (*Erigeron canadense*): a diaphoretic and expectorant in doses of 15.0-30.0 of a decoction (half-ounce to the pint), or 2 to 4 drops of the eclectic specific medicine in water every hour. *Angelica,* a genus of umbelliferous plants, found mainly in northern temperate regions; *Angelicae fructus* (angelica fruit or seed) is given in doses of gr. 15 or 1.0; *Angelicae radix* (angelica root) in doses of gr. 30 or 2.0. The roots of *Angelica sylvestris* (wild angelica) are also used. The drug is a tonic and stimulant in the doses given here. *Pimpinella* (pimpernel), the rhizome and root of *Pimpinella saxifraga* (burnet saxifrage) is a carminative, diuretic, and emmenagogue in doses of gr. 15 (1.0).

Paul Luther's Chief Personal Characteristic: *Parresia*

Liddell and Scott define a *parresiastes* as one manifesting *parresia,* or "outspokenness, frankness, freedom of speech, claimed by the Athenians as their privilege." We should be careful to note that *parresia* has reference not to its possessor's attitude toward others but to his own character, that is, it does not refer to "freedom of speech" or "tolerance" for everyone, but instead describes the person whose character manifests frankness and absence of hypocrisy. Certainly the Athenians felt no compulsion to give their slaves free speech just because they enjoyed it themselves. Paul Luther was frank and outspoken in his beliefs; he was not a man of "double tongue," but this did not mean that he was a crusader for universal toleration of diverse views or for "freedom of speech" in eighteenth-century Enlightenment terms.

Paul Luther was intensely devoted to his father's doctrinal position—strict Lutheranism—and would not accept even the mild Lutheranism of Melanchthon, to say nothing of outright Calvinism. This explains why he found Augustus I and Administrator Frederick William so congenial, but he did not get along well with Christian I. His departure from the court of Christian I ("on account of religious suspicion") is explained more fully in the *Biographie médicale* (*Dictionnaire des sciences médicales*):

> Paul, who had accepted his father's teachings, upheld his preeminence, and wanted to take down Melanchthon to the lesser position of one of his father's many disciples, as he thought people had overestimated Melanchthon. His usual character emerged in this debate; he demonstrated the hot temper and tendency to exaggeration that characterized Martin's lectures and writings. The passage of time had already lowered the intensity of people's feelings, however, and the same people found blameworthy in the son what they had admired or put up with in the father. Meanwhile history had already given place to the more moderate author of the *Augsburg Confession* (VI: 134f.).

On this incident, see also the articles on Paul Luther in Richter. It should now be evident why Melchior Adam felt that Paul Luther's *parresia* made him appear "to the greatest degree like his father." Paul Luther was certainly faithful in conviction and character to the man who caused the medieval world to crumble by his words, "Here I stand. God help me. Amen."

Sources Cited

Allgemeine Deutsche Biographie. Leipzig, 1885.

Biographie médicale (*Dictionnaire des sciences médicales*). Paris, 1824.

Black's Medical Dictionary. Ed. John D. Comrie and William A. R. Thomson (21st ed.). London, 1953.

Corkill, M. M., et al. "Intramuscular Depot Methylprednisolone Induction of Chrysotherapy in Rheumatoid Arthritis: A 24-week Randomized Controlled Trial" in *British Journal of Rheumatology* XXIX/4 (1990).

Encyclopedia Britannica (11th & 14th ed.).

Hill, John. *A History of the Materia Medica.* London, 1751.

Hoefer. *Nouvelle biographie générale.* Paris, 1853-1866.

Junghans, Helmar. "University of Wittenberg" in *Oxford Encyclopedia of the Reformation*, Vol. IV. Oxford, 1996.

Krauth. Charles Porterfield. *The Conservative Reformation and Its Theology.* Philadelphia, 1871.

Lau, Franz. "Georg III. von Anhalt" in *Wissenschaftliche Zeitschrift der Karl-Marx-Universität Leipzig*, Vol. Ill (1953-1954).

Liddell-Scott. *Greek-English Lexicon.* Ed. Henry Stuart Jones. Oxford, 1948.

Michaud. *Biographie universelle* (2nd ed.). Paris, 1843-1865.

Montgomery, John Warwick. *Crisis in Lutheran Theology* (rev. ed.). Minneapolis, 1973.

Montgomery, John Warwick. *Cross and Crucible.* "International Archives of the History of Ideas," 55. The Hague, 1973. (Now available from Springer International.)

Montgomery, John Warwick. *In Defense of Martin Luther.* Milwaukee, 1970.

Nischan, Bodo. "Brandenburg" in *Oxford Encyclopedia of the Reformation*, Vol. I. Oxford, 1996.

Peterson, Luther D. "Philippists" in *Oxford Encyclopedia of the Reformation*, Vol. III. Oxford, 1996.

Pomet. *A Compleat History of Druggs … to which is added what is further observable on the same Subject, from Messrs. Lemery, and Tournefort.* London, 1712.

Richter. *Genealogia Lutherorum.* Berlin & Leipzig, 1733.

Scheible, Heinz. "Philipp Melanchthon" in *Oxford Encyclopedia of the Reformation*, Vol III. Oxford, 1996.

Stedman's Medical Dictionary. Ed. Norman Burke Taylor (18th rev. ed.). Baltimore: Williams and Wilkins. 1953.

Ukert, G. H. U. *Dr. Martin Luthers Leben mit einer kurzen Reformationsgeschichte Deutschlands und der Litteratur.* Gotha, 1817.

Wecker, John Jacob. *De Secretis Libri XVII. Ex variis Auctoribus Collecti.* Basel, 1701.

3. John Gerhard: Theology and Devotion

Synopsis

A comparison of the theological and the devotional activity of John Gerhard, discussed with special reference to his Sacred Meditations and to passages here rendered into English for the first time from his Loci Theologici *and* Homiliae XXXVI

It is generally agreed that John Gerhard's magnum opus is his multivolume systematic theology entitled *Loci Theologici*. Charles S. Albert, in his introduction to the Heisler translation of Gerhard's *Meditationes Sacrae*, says: "His great work, the *Loci Theologici*, begun in 1610 and completed in 1621, in which the theology of the Lutheran Church is set forth, is his theological masterpiece, and is marked by fulness of learning, logical force, clearness, thorough elaboration of every question, and by a practical and spiritual use of dogma."[1] However, Gerhard's fame and influence do not rest so much upon the *Loci Theologici* as upon his *Sacred Meditations*, a little book of devotional selections which has been compared with a Kempis' *Imitatio Christi*, and which has been honoured with translations into many languages.[2] Recognizing the possibility that fame and quality do not always go together, we shall make an attempt in this brief paper to compare these two chief aspects of Gerhard's work — the theological and the devotional, in an effort to determine where Gerhard's true strength lay. In making our comparison, we shall refer to three works of Gerhard's — the two already mentioned, and also his *Homiliae XXXVI seu meditationes breves diebus dominicis atque festis accomodatae*, a work not published until 1898,[3] very little-known even at the present time, and not to my knowledge ever translated from its original Latin.

---

[1] Gerhard's *Sacred Meditations* (Introduction), p. 9. Cf. also *Concordia Cyclopedia*, art. "Gerhard, Johann," p. 410.
[2] Gerhard's *Sacred Meditations* (Introduction), p. 7.
[3] "In perlustrandis codicibus Gerhardinis a ducali bibliotheca Gothana asservatis in unum autographum incidisse videor, cujus argumentum si non plane incognitum tamen quoad ego scio in notitiam ecclesiae nostrae evangelicae nondum pervenerit." — George Berbig, in his "Prologus" to the *Homiliae XXXVI*, published in *Studien zur Geschichte der Theologie und der Kirche*. III (5), p. vii.

We shall come to two conclusions in this paper, both of which we hope to validate sufficiently by reference to the primary source literary material involved: (i) On the basis of the *Loci Theologici* and *Meditationes Sacrae* alone, Gerhard's theological work was of greater value than was his devotional activity. The *Sacred Meditations* have perhaps received more attention than they have deserved, at least in comparison with the *Loci*. (ii) However, on the basis of the little-known *Homiliae XXXVI*, Gerhard has proven himself to be a devotional writer of great stature—a writer well-deserving of the reputation gained him by the *Meditationes Sacrae*, the quality of which, ironically, is inferior to that of the *Homiliae XXXVI*.[4]

The "Sacred Meditations"

Let us first consider Gerhard's *Meditationes Sacrae*. his famous devotional work composed in 1603 when he was only 21 years old.[5] Since the *Sacred Meditations* precedes the *Loci Theologici* and the *Homiliae XXXVI* in point of time, it is perhaps wise to consider it first in our discussion.

In order to evaluate the quality of the work, we must have criteria against which to judge it. Many criteria might well be proposed, but certainly two vital ones for a Christian devotional work are (1) consistency with the spirit and letter of God's written Word, the Holy Scriptures;[6] and (2) deep spiritual insight into the Christian life. If either of these two characteristics is lacking from a supposed work of Christian devotion, the work either is not fully Christian (criterion 1), or is not devotional in the ordinary sense of the term (criterion 2).

Our contention is that although Gerhard's *Meditationes Sacrae* often manifest real devotional content, there are tendencies present in the work to go dangerously beyond Scripture, to employ allegory excessively, and to use as motivations for action, and present as desirable patterns of conduct, suggestions which are more in keeping with a Roman Catholic than an evangelical frame of reference.

---

[4] It should perhaps be stated at the outset that this paper will stay quite strictly on the delimited subject just described. I have not attempted here a general discussion of Gerhard's "Life and Work," for there is little reason to rehash biographical information on Gerhard which is easily available elsewhere. (See the Bibliography at the end of the essay.)
[5] Berbig, *op. cit.*, pp. vii, viii.
[6] Cf. Revelation 22:18-19.

First let us present by direct quotation some of the positive attributes of the *Sacred Meditations*—attributes which have rightly endeared the work to countless Christian hearts. The *Meditationes Sacrae* give us sound warnings and exhortations:

> Why therefore do we delay repentance? Why put it off until tomorrow? Neither tomorrow nor true repentance is in our own power. For we must render an account at the final judgement not only for tomorrow, but for today as well. That tomorrow shall come is not certain, but that everlasting destruction shall overtake the impenitent is certain. God has promised grace to the penitent soul, but He does not promise a tomorrow.
>
> Those thoughts which have become bad by our familiar use of them will not go unexamined by the judgment. What advantage is there then in concealing thy sins of lust for awhile from the eyes of men, when after awhile at the judgment they must be brought to light before the assembled universe.[7]

Less known (or perhaps forgotten) spiritual truths are uncovered for us from the Scriptures:

> Truly, my whole life is, on the one hand, sinful and worthy of Thy condemnation, and on the other unfruitful and wretched. But why do I distinguish between unfruitful and worthy of condemnation? For certainly if it is unfruitful it is to be condemned; for every tree that bringeth not forth good fruit shall be cast into the fire (Matt. iii, 10).[8]

Great truths of the Bible are reiterated forcibly:

> But faith is not mere opinion or empty profession; it is a living and efficacious apprehension of Christ as He is set forth in the gospel. It is a most hearty conviction of God's grace to us, a confident tranquillity of heart, and an undisturbed peace of conscience relying upon the merit of Christ.[9]

Finally, Gerhard gives us many practical helps for our everyday Christian lives. For example, in Meditation XLI ("The Principles of Christian Patience"), one is told that to achieve Christian patience, (i) "Meditate upon the awful passion of Christ, thy spiritual spouse"; (ii) "Think of the inconceivable reward held out to thee"; (iii) "Consider ... the tribulation which the saints of the past have endured"; (iv) "Consider the blessed advantages of the cross [which you have to bear]."[10]

---

[7] Gerhard's *Sacred Meditations* (Meditation III.), p. 22; (Meditation XXXVII), p. 213.
[8] *Ibid.* (Meditation VI.), pp. 37-38.
[9] *Ibid.* (Meditation XII.), p. 68.
[10] *Ibid.*, pp. 235-241.

Unfortunately, however, we find not only deep spiritual insights such as the above in the *Sacred Meditations*; we also find less satisfactory passages—which reduce the over-all quality of the devotional work.

We note a use of allegory that may seem "charming" on the surface, but that has a real connection with an insidious type of Scriptural interpretation prevalent in the Middle Ages which made the Bible an obscure book:

> Christ desired to be present at the marriage in Cana of Galilee (John ii. 2), so as to show us that He had come to the earth to celebrate His spiritual nuptials with believing souls.
>
> He [Christ] is born in Bethlehem, the house of bread, who brought with Himself from Heaven the bread of life for our souls.
>
> Our Saviour chose to ascend to Heaven from the Mount of Olives (Acts i. 12); the olive branch is the emblem of peace and joy; it was fitting, therefore, that He who through His bitter passion brings peace to terrified and troubled consciences, and is received into the skies with most jubilant joy by the heavenly hosts, should ascend from the mount called the Mount of Olives.
>
> Bethany signifies the village of humility and affliction through which the way to the heavenly kingdom lies open to us, just as Christ through the severest sufferings entered into His glory (Luke xxiv, 56).[11]

More reprehensible by far than the use of questionable allegory is Gerhard's willingness in the *Sacred Meditations* to go beyond the Biblical revelation in some of his assertions. Meditation XXVI ("The Guardianship of Angels") is a particularly clear instance of this. In this devotion Gerhard makes numerous statements which cannot be supported by the few statements concerning angels in Scripture. For example:

> Consider, O devout soul, that these angels are holy; strive then after holiness so thou wouldest enjoy their blessed fellowship. Similarity of character is especially favourable to friendship; accustom thyself to holy deeds if thou wouldst have their guardianship. Everywhere show due reverence to thine angel, and never do anything in his presence thou wouldst blush to do in the sight of men. These angelic spirits are chaste and pure, and therefore are driven away by impurity in thought and deed. As foul smoke drives away bees, so these angelic guardians of our lives are put to flight by foul and grievious sin; and having once lost their protecting power, how wilt thou be safe from the snares of the devil, or the various perils that may beset thee?[12]

---

[11] *Ibid*. (Meditation XIII.), p. 71; (Meditation XIV.), p. 77; (Meditation XXL), pp. 114, 115.
[12] *Ibid.*, p. 147.

Perhaps in some cases we can say that Gerhard has been carried away by over developing a perfectly sound Scriptural point; but the fact remains that one of the *sine quibus non* of any Christian devotional work is the absolute faithfulness of the work to the source of all Christian doctrine and devotion, the Bible.

The above over-statements concerning angels suggest and logically lead into our final negative criticism of the *Meditationes Sacrae*: the presence of some Romanist and Pelagian-Arminian[13] sentiments in it—sentiments hardly consistent with a peculiarly evangelical faith. Such, for example, is the impression given by Meditation XXV, entitled "The Saving Efficacy of Prayer." Here we seem to see man striving upward to reach God through the power of man's own prayer, rather than God reaching down by grace to man. In this Meditation we specifically read statements like "It [prayer] is a ladder by which we ascend to heaven."[14] Along the same line we note the great emphasis in the *Meditationes Sacrae* on man's confession and man's repentance, and what these acts accomplish.[15] We are also confronted by rubrics such as "An Acknowledgement of a Fault Heals It,"[16] a dubious assertion indeed in the light of the evangelical doctrine of the forgiveness of sins. Besides this sort of over-emphasis upon the part man plays in his own spiritual life, the *Sacred Meditations* tend to encourage a withdrawal from the world which reminds one more of the Romanist *Weltanschauung* than of the biblical one. We read such bland assertions as this: "The more thou art separated from the world, the more pleasing thou wilt be to God."[17] It seems that Gerhard would have done better to place more emphasis in the *Sacred Meditations* on the type of life which is definitely in the world but not of it.

Having considered in some detail the deficiences as well as the merits of Gerhard's *Sacred Mediations*, we might ask ourselves why, in spite of its great worth, the book has the faults it does. I submit three reasons.

(1) Gerhard's age at the time he wrote the *Meditationes Sacrae*. He was only 21, and, as we shall see below, had not matured spiritually to the level he was to reach through further experiences in life.

(2) As a youth he was undoubtedly quite impressionable, and we know that the writer of *True Christianity*, John Arndt, had a profound effect on him early in life. Twice Arndt powerfully influenced Gerhard's career: first, at the age of fifteen, when Gerhard suffered a severe illness, Arndt helped him to reach a

---

[13] Coincidentally, it was in 1603 that Jacob Arminius charged the Calvinist predestination view with making God the source of sin. (See *Documents of the Christian Church*, pp. 375-376.)
[14] Gerhard's *Sacred Meditations*, p. 138. The whole Meditation covers pp. 137-143.
[15] *Ibid.* (Meditations I-III), pp. 11-26.
[16] *Ibid.* (Meditation I), p. 11.
[17] *Ibid.* (Meditation XXVIII), p. 160. See also pp. 128, 159.

decision to enter the ministry[18]; second, Arndt's counsel came back to him early in 1603, aiding him to return to theological study after he had left his original goal and spent two years studying medicine.[19] We should note that it was in December of this same year 1603, again as the result of a very grave illness, that Gerhard wrote the *Meditationes Sacrae*.[20] One is struck by the parallels between the *Sacred Meditations* and Arndt's *True Christianity*[21], and the two more serious defects in Gerhard's work are especially evident in Arndt's devotional treatise. Arndt is not loathe to go beyond the divine revelation of Scripture in his assertions; witness for example his three hierarchial levels of prayer — oral, internal, and supernatural — and his description of the highest level of the three:

> A soul once arrived at this happy state, gives little or no employment to the tongue: it is silent to the Lord: it pants after, and thirsts for God: it longs, yea, even faints for him: it loves him only, rests in him alone, disregarding and not minding the world, nor any worldly affairs. Whence it is still more and more filled and possessed with an experimental savoury knowledge of God, with love and joy to such a degree, as no tongue is able to express. For whatever the soul then perceives, is beyond all possibility of being explained by words. In so much that if one should ask a soul wrapped up in these sublime contemplations, what she thinks on, or what she perceives? She would certainly answer: a good that is above all good. What seest thou? A perfection of beauty transcending all created forms. What feelest thou? A joy surpassing all joys. What dost thou taste? The inexpressible delights of love. Nay, such a one would tell you, that all the words that could possibly be framed, were but a shadow, and came infinitely short of the comprehensive-

---

[18] *Ibid.* (Introduction), p. 8. See also J. F. Cotta's "De vita, fatis et scriptis Io. Gerhardi", in *Loci Theologici*. I, pp. xii, xiv.

[19] Cotta, *ibid.* Berbig, *op. cit.*, p. viii.

[20] Berbig, *ibid.*, pp. vii-viii.

[21] Compare for example the titles and contents of the sections cited side by side below:

Sacred Meditations	True Christianity
I, II, III	Bk I, Chs. 4, 8, 20, 39; Bk II, Chs. 8, 9, 10;
V, VI, VII	Bk II, Chs. 2, 18, 19;
X	Bk I, Ch. 3;
XII	Bk I, Ch. 5;
XV	Bk I, Ch. 3; Bk II, Chs. 1, 2, 3;
XXV	Bk II, Ch. 20;
XXVIII	Bk I, Ch. 40;
XXX	Bk I, Chs. 11, 37; Bk. II, Chs. 13, 17;
XXXIV	Bk I, Chs. 19, 31, 42; Bk I, Chs. 22, 24, 25, 26, 27, 28, 30, 31, 32; Bk II, Ch. 18;
XXXIX	Bk I, Chs. 13, 14, 17, 18, 23; Bk II. Chs. 14, 15.

ness of what was inwardly felt and sweetly suffered; nothing but the actual sense and perception itself, being capable to give us a sound impression of it.[22]

This sort of mysticism (to say nothing of the hierarchy of prayer that precedes it) goes far beyond the statements in Holy Writ concerning prayer, and would be more appropriate in a work by Plotinus than in one by a Christian pastor. (Note also the attitude toward "worldly affairs" in the above selection.)[23] Arndt's over-emphasis on the work of man in the Christian life (which is perhaps the great fault of the Pietistic movement which Arndt influenced through P. J. Spener)[24] is also very evident in *True Christianity*. He seems obsessed with what he terms "true repentance," and other similar concepts.[25] In his chapter on "What the True Cross of Christ Is," he presents this astounding definition of the Cross of Christ:

> You have it now declared to you what it is to deny yourself; even to acknowledge yourself unworthy of every good thing, and worthy of all evils that may or can befall you. And this is the cross of Christ which he has commanded and encouraged us to carry, saying to us, "he that will be my disciple, let him deny himself, and take up my cross.[26]

As with the *Sacred Meditations*, we are not here attempting to conceal the good qualities so evident in Arndt's *True Christianity*, but we are trying to point out similar defects in the two works which may account in part for some of Gerhard's false emphases.

Finally (3), as we have pointed out above, Gerhard in 1603 had just returned to his theological studies after a two-year sojourn in the medical field. He was in no sense a fully trained theologian at this time, having received less that half of his university-level theological training (two years at Wittenberg—1599-1600). Therefore we may not go wrong in supposing that tendencies in his thinking had not had the benefit of the rigorous pruning that the University of Jena was sure to provide in the years 1603-1605.

---

[22] John Arndt, *True Christianity* (trans. A. W. Boehm; Boston, 1809), Bk II, Ch. 20, pp. 482-483.
[23] The *Concordia Cyclopedia* says of *True Christianity* that it "in some parts, however, is drawn from medieval writers like Tauler and not always sound" (p. 59). Arndt himself in his Preface to *True Christianity*, admits his obligation to medieval Romanist writers and anticipates some of our criticisms of his work, but this does not of course *per se* negate the force of these criticisms (Arndt, *op. cit.*, p. xxxi).
[24] K. S. Latourette, *A History of Christianity*, pp. 894-895.
[25] Arndt, *op. cit.*, Bk. I, Chs. 4, 8, 20, 39; Bk. II, Chs. 8, 9, 100.
[26] *Ibid.*, Bk. I, Ch. 15, p. 135.

Gerhard's "Loci Theologici"

Let us now turn to John Gerhard's great work in the field of systematic theology, and see how it compares qualitatively with his *Meditationes Sacrae*. By way of background, we should note that Gerhard began the *Loci Theologici* in 1610, at the age of 27, while at Heldburg.[27] After completing his theological training at Jena, Gerhard had given lectures there for a short time (1605)[28], and had then (1606) accepted the Duke of Coburg's invitation to become a professor at the Coburg Gymnasium as well as Superintendent of Heldburg. In 1615 he was made General Superintendent of Coburg.[29] In 1616 Gerhard became a professor at Jena, in which position he remained until the end of his life.[30] In 1621 or 22 he completed the *Loci Theologici*. In comparing it with Gerhard's other works, Cotta simply says: "Primum inter illa locum merito damus eiusdem *locis theologicis*."[31]

What are the criteria by which we shall judge the merit of the *Loci Theologici*? Certainly the following must be taken into account in determining the value of a systematic theology: faithfulness to the spirit and letter of Scripture; comprehensiveness; consistency and soundness in reasoning; clarity of outline and style. It is our opinion that the *Loci Theologici* is one of the greatest Christian systematic theologies of all time—in short, that it fulfills those criteria superbly. In proving our point, we shall let Gerhard's work speak for itself. As an Appendix to this paper we have translated into English a considerable part of the detailed "Conspectus" or Table of Contents of the first volume of the *Loci*. We ask the reader to study it carefully, especially the contents of Topics I ("Concerning Sacred Scripture") and III ("On the Nature of God"). This should provide adequate enough illustration of the comprehensiveness, logic of outline, and all-over clarity of presentation which the entire work possesses.[32] In order also to make it possible for the reader himself to determine whether Gerhard's work is faithful to the biblical revelation and maintains a high standard of logic and clarity in its discussions of specific issues, I have translated a rather lengthy

---

[27] Cotta, *op. cit.*, p. xxxvi.
[28] Gerhard's *Sacred Meditations* (Introduction), p. 8. Gerhard also studied theology at Marburg, probably for a brief time in 1605.
[29] "En 1606 il devint surintendant (évêque protestant) à Heldbourg. Il professa aussi la théologie à Cobourg. En 1615 Gerhard eut la surintendance générale (archévêché) de cette ville." (*Nouvelle biographie générale*. Ed. Hoefer. 1858. V. 20, col. 213)."
[30] *Concordia Cyclopedia*, p. 409.
[31] Cotta, op. cit., p. xxxvi. One should note that Gerhard's *Loci* was in part an answer to the Jesuit theologian Bellarmine's chief work, entitled *Disputationes de controversiis Christianae Fidei*. See the *Concordia Cyclopedia*, art. Bellarmine, p. 102.
[32] Note also in the "Conspectus" the strong spiritual content of such chapters as Topic III, Ch. XXV. Would that more works of systematic theology had this kind of emphasis included!

section from one of the chapters in the *Loci Theologici*. This translation appears as Appendix I. One can hardly avoid the impact of Gerhard's relentless destruction of a false position, and his own humility before God's written Word.

It is not expected that everyone will agree with our judgment of Gerhard's *Loci*. Since Kant in philosophy, and Kierkegaard and the Neo-Orthodox school in Protestant theology, traces of "Aristotelianism" in a theologian's work have often been sufficient to condemn him. And certainly we will admit to the presence of Aristotelian-scholastic influences in Gerhard's *Loci*. The very plan of the work, and the numerous catalogs of patristic and even medieval authorities interspersed through it attest to such scholastic influence. But we caution the reader not to let "Aristotelian" or "scholastic" become terms of derision which can be applied with little or no thought as to their content. Regardless of the inadequacies of some of the later "orthodox" Lutheran theologians, we hasten to point out that Gerhard's *Loci Theologici* does not possess the negative characteristics of Aristotelian scholasticism which rightly deserve the criticisms leveled against it by evangelical Christians. First, the *Loci* starts with Scripture as its foundation (*principium*)[33]; Gerhard does not attempt to construct a rational edifice for theology. Secondly, as the translated section I have included shows, the *Loci* does not concern itself with the minutiae of scholastic theology—the "angels on the head of a pin" type of subject. Gerhard deals rather with those issues having scriptural importance. Thirdly, although he sometimes quotes non-biblical authorities in support of a point, Gerhard does so only as a supplement to a sound scriptural proof. In conclusion, we may note that even Jaroslav Pelikan, whose theological tendencies are clearly anti-Aristotle, anti-17th century Lutheran "orthodoxy," and pro-Kierkegaard, speaks of Gerhard as one "in whom the evangelical intentions of the Reformation find articulation more clearly than in most of the other dogmaticians."[34]

Our conclusion at this point in the discussion of Gerhard's devotional and theological work is that the *Loci Theologici*. much more successfully than the *Meditationes Sacrae*, fulfils the standards by which we have attempted to judge its quality. Regardless of the popularity of Gerhard's *Sacred Meditations*, we should have to say, if this were the only devotional work of Gerhard's available, that Gerhard was a far greater theologian than a devotional writer.

---

[33] See "Conspectus" (the introductory remarks to Topic I), in Appendix III to this paper. For Gerhard's view of Holy Scripture, see Hagglund, *Die Heilige Schrift und ihre Deutung in der Theologie Johann Gerhards*.

[34] Jaroslav Pelikan, *From Luther to Kierkegaard*, p. 147. See also p. 62.

Gerhard's Homiliae XXXVI

Fortunately, however, Gerhard's reputation as a great devotional writer can be completely vindicated through his little-known *Homiliae XXXVI seu meditationes breves diebus dominicis atque festis accomodatae*. These wonderful sermons or meditations cover the Sundays and feast days from the 1st Sunday of Trinity through the last Sunday after Epiphany. Each is based on the Gospel text for the particular Sunday or feast day. Concerning the style of these homilies, their editor writes: "Stylo in nostris quoque homiliis Gerhardus brevi, sed fluido ac piano atque artificis instar utitur."[35]

I have translated into English two homilies typical of the thirty-six. These appear as Appendix II. The meditation for the 1st Sunday of Trinity is based on Luke 16:19-31 (the story of Lazarus and the rich man); that for the 23rd Sunday after Trinity deals with the "Render unto Caesar" episode (Matt. 22:15-22). It will be advantageous to review in one's Bible these Gospel sections before reading the homilies themselves.

One of my purposes in presenting translations of these representative homilies is to give the reader a crystal-clear picture of their wonderful quality, and to make it easy for him or her to compare them with the *Meditationes Sacrae*. Since the *Homilies* and the *Sacred Meditations* are similarly devotional in character (note the subtitle of the *Homilies*), the same criteria of evaluation can apply to both. Thus, in dealing with the *Homilies*, we should ask, on the positive side, whether they (1) exhibit consistency with the spirit and letter of God's written Word, and (2) give deep spiritual insight into the Christian life.[36] Since we are here dealing with homilies, or sermons, delivered on a specific text of Scripture, the first criterion will be especially important. It is our contention that a serious and careful reading of the two translated homilies will indicate beyond the shadow of a doubt how admirably they fulfil both of these requirements. They (and all of the other homilies) succeed in the difficult task of catching the spirit—not merely agreeing with the letter—of the Scripture texts on which they are based. From the standpoint of the second criterion, we find in both of

---

[35] Berbig, *op. cit.*, p. viii. On this same page Berbig describes the MS copy of the *Homiliae XXXVI* as follows: "Sed intueamur codicem nostrum **), cujus inscriptio auctoris manu propria a fronte legitur: Meditationes Theologicae ad Doctrinam et Veram consolationem. Folio altero sequuntur meditationes sacrae contra mortis terrorem profuturae, numero XIX, quas omnes in illo libro citato [*The Sacred Meditations*] paulo modo auctiores et quibusdam verbis mutatas videre licet. Jam vero in codice nostra, a folio XLII usque ad folium LXXXVIII homiliarum exercitium seu meditationes breves legimus dignas adeo quae vulgentur. **) Codex sub Lt. Chart. B. No. 894 a bibl. Ducali Gothana continetur." We consider the value judgement in this last sentence as a great understatement!

[36] For these criteria, see above, p. 2.

the translated homilies sound exhortations and practical helps for the Christian life, together with great scriptural truths reiterated and less known ones uncovered. Beyond even these things, we find a profound application of scriptural truths to the political phase of life (23rd Sunday), and one of the most beautiful statements I have ever read of faith in God's omniscient and paternal benevolence in relation to man's needs (1st Sunday).[37]

From the negative side, although we do still find cases of objectionable allegory in the *Homilies*,[38] the more serious criticisms we leveled against the *Sacred Meditations* definitely do not apply here. In the *Homilies* we do not find Gerhard presenting expositions which go beyond Scripture. For example, in his homily for the 2nd Sunday of Advent, he mentions various individuals who had attempted to calculate the date of Christ's Second Coming and the end of the world (e.g. Pico of Mirandola, who placed the date at 2004 A.D.). What better opportunity for Gerhard himself to do some figuring! But he simply quotes the statements of our Lord to the effect that it is not for us to know the times and the seasons, and no one except the Father knows the hour of Christ's coming. Gerhard's advice is that instead of attempting such calculation we should await our Lord's Coming with (i) vigilance of heart, (ii) perseverance in prayer, and (iii) temperance.[39] We are also hard put to find any instances of Romanist or Arminian attitudes in the *Homilies*. For the 11th Sunday after Trinity Gerhard presents a sermon on the Pharisee-and-the-publican text (Luke 18:9-14). In it prayer is not dealt with in any sense as a way of propitiating God.[40] Furthermore, we are not confronted by a contempt of the world when we read the homilies for the 25th Sunday after Trinity and for the 2nd Sunday of Advent (texts dealing with the last days, the end of the age, etc.), nor even in the sermon for the 15th Sunday after Trinity, on the text, "Seek ye first the Kingdom of God."[41] Thus we conclude that in the *Homiliae XXXVI* we have a devotional work of great stature, possessing more than all of the good qualities of the *Meditationes Sacrae*, and very few of its deficiencies.

---

[37] In connection with the last line of this Homily for the 1st Sunday of Trinity, it is interesting to note that of Gerhard the *Allgemeine Deutsche Biographie* says: "'komm Herr, komm!' waren seine letzten Worte" (VIII, pp. 767-71).

[38] E.g., in the Homily for the 1st Sunday of Advent (text: Matt. 21:1-9) the ass represents "caro nostra et homo exterior, qui legum vinculis et poenarum verberibus ad Christum cogendus" (*Homiliae XXXVI*, p. 31); and in the Sermon for the 2nd Sunday after Epiphany (on John 2:1-11) the marriage at Cana still represents Christ's spiritual marriage with the faithful soul (*ibid.*, pp. 39-40).

[39] *Ibid.*, pp. 32-33.

[40] *Ibid.*, pp. 11-12.

[41] *Ibid.*, pp. 29-30, 32-33, 16.

Since the *Sacred Meditations* and the *Homilies* were written by the same person, it would be interesting to compare the dates of composition of the two. We of course know when Gerhard wrote the *Sacred Meditations* (December 1603); the problem is to determine the date of the *Homilies*. Berbig conjectures "initium anni MDCIII,"[42] apparently basing this on the fact that the MS is found in a codex which also contains nineteen meditations which appear in augmented and altered form in the *Meditationes Sacrae*.[43] But this is manifestly weak, for the title of the whole codex obviously refers more—if not entirely—to the nineteen meditations that immediately follow (*folio altero*) the title page than to the *Homiliae XXXVI* which come later in the codex. The homilies could easily have been written later in the same codex.

But how can we determine the date of the *Homilies*? If they were in fact written before the *Sacred Meditations*, Gerhard's Christian life showed a very early high (devotionally), then a trough, followed by another high (theologically). This does not on the surface seem very probable. It seems even less probable that Gerhard would have written a series of thirty-six sermons as early as 1603 when (a) we remember that he was at that time less than halfway through his theological training, and when (b) we read that when he was appointed Superintendent at Heldburg (1606) he was also "made Doctor of Divinity, having preached only four times."[44]

Since the *Homiliae* are not only "meditationes breves" but also *sermons*, it does not seem improbable that they were written to be preached. On this assumption, I have tried to discover years in Gerhard's life to which his particular group of thirty-six homilies (covering the Sundays from Trinity of one church year through Epiphany of the next) might have corresponded. The number of Sundays in Trinity and in Epiphany and the presence or absence of Sundays after Christmas and after New Year's day (before Epiphany begins), can determine the dates of Easter in two contiguous years,[45] and since the Pascal Cycle is 532 years in length, the chances are not great of two given Easter dates occurring contiguously with much frequency.

---

[42] *Ibid.*, p. viii.
[43] See above, note 33.
[44] *Concordia Cyclopedia*, p. 409.
[45] Using, for example, the Table on preliminary page 158 of *The Lutheran Hymnal* (Concordia Publishing House, c1941), together with the Easter-day Tables in Bond's *Handy-book of Rules and Tables for Verifying Dates with the Christian Era*, pp. 138, 405-16. One must remember, of course, that "The Gregorian calender, or 'New Style', was almost immediately adopted by Roman Catholic nations. In Germany the Emperor Rudolf II. and the Roman Catholic States accepted it in 1583, but the Elector of Saxony and the Protestant States adhered to the Old Style, objecting to the New, not merely as coming from Rome, but because of certain defects which Scaliger and other authorities pointed out in its astronomical accuracy. This difference of calendar was

I shall not go into detail in this matter of dating the Homilies, but shall merely indicate the results of my calculations. (1) No two years in Gerhard's life (except when he was five years old!) correspond exactly to the sequence of 25 Sundays in Trinity, no Sundays after Christmas and New Year's day (before Epiphany begins), and 5 Sundays in Epiphany. However, (2), there is no homily given for the 1st Sunday after Epiphany, so we may assume that some other omissions might have been made due to illness, etc. Such omissions would have to consist either (a) of Sunday(s) after the last (25th) Sunday after Trinity for which there is a homily given, or (b) of Sunday(s) between Christmas and Epiphany; if any other omissions had been made, they would be clearly indicated by gaps (like that of the 1st Sunday after Epiphany) in the thirty-six Homilies as we have them.[46] (3) The chances of more than one further omission are very small, obviously, so I have tried each of the two possible types of omission (a and b) separately. The single resulting years (Old Style calendar) were 1608-1609 (assuming 26 rather than 25 Sundays in Trinity, and with all other Sundays and feasts exactly as given in the Homilies). On the basis of the New Style calendar (much less probable, because of Gerhard's Protestant sphere of activity), 1608-1609 again comes out (this time assuming the omission of meditations for Sundays between Christmas and Epiphany rather than at the end of Trinity season), and 1622-1623 or 1633-1634 (again assuming only that the sermon for a 26th Sunday after Trinity was omitted). If we take the 1608-1609 years,[47] then the two homilies we have translated were given on May 29 and October 30, 1608 (Old Style), or possibly June 8 and November 9, 1608 (New Style).

Regardless of which sets of years we pick of those just listed, we see that the probability is extremely small that the *Homiliae* were written before the *Sacred Meditations* had been published (early in 1606).[48] In 1608-1609 Gerhard's for-

---

productive of much discussion and inconvenience, especially in places where populations were mixed." (Hastings, *Encyclopedia of Religion and Ethics* (1919), III, p. 90.) The Protestant States did not make the change to the New Style calendar until 1700, and then did so only "at the instance of Leibnitz" (*ibid.*).

[46] A 6th Sunday after Epiphany would not have been omitted from the Homilies because the Gospel lesson for Transfiguration is used on the last Sunday of Epiphany, and Gerhard gives a Transfiguration meditation for his 5th Sunday after Epiphany. See Reed, *The Lutheran Liturgy*, p. 449.

[47] It will be remembered that in Germany the years 1608-09 saw the formation of the Protestant Union (under Elector Frederick IV of the Palatinate) and the Catholic League (under Duke Maximillian of Bavaria), in preparation for the holocaust of the Thirty Years' War which was soon to break out. This was a "Munich" period; the Donauworth incident had occurred in 1607, infuriating Protestant Germany (note in this connection the statements about Tyranny in the Homily for the 23rd Sunday after Trinity, translated above in the text); Simplicissimus would soon have his day.

[48] Berbig, *op. cit.*, p. vii.

mal theological study was behind him and he was engaged in professorial and administrative duties for the Duke of Coburg. In 1610 he would begin the *Loci Theologici*. If we should assume a date later than 1608-1609 (which would necessitate a justification of that use of the New Style dating), the *Homiliae* would be placed after the completion (1621-1622) of the *Loci*.

We therefore not only feel able to assert with confidence the two theses stated at the outset of this paper, but at the same time see a linear progress in John Gerhard's devotional and theological stature—from the *Sacred Meditations* to the *Homiliae* and the *Loci Theologici*. Gerhard gradually threw off the harmful aspects of Arndt's influence, and came into his own as one of the greatest Lutheran thinkers and saints of all time.

Appendix I

A Translation of Part of Chapter XI (on the Use of Reason in the Analogy of Faith) of Topic II ("On the Interpretation of Holy Scripture") from Gerhard's Loci Theologici *(ed. J. F. Cotta, 1767), Vol. I, pp. 79-80*

Grynaeus * (disp. Heid. De coena thes. 25 and 26) and Bucanus (*ibid*. 48, p. 711) distinguish between corrupted reason and reason which after regeneration has been made spiritual. To the former they refer the things which are said in the Scriptures about the need for making thought captive under the obedience of Christ [II Cor. 10:5]; about the need for guarding against the spoiling prey of philosophy [Col. 2:8]; etc. They say, however, that reborn reason should not detract from faith, since after regeneration it has been made spiritual. What ought we to conclude with regard to this matter?

We answer: Human reason rightly can, and should, be considered in two senses. One way is in terms of its resources (which it possesses because of its very own nature, and has made use of in deriving its own principles)—resources such as ordinary ideas, perception, experience, induction, acquisitiveness; another way of considering reason is in terms of those things which it eagerly takes to its bosom from another source—from divine revelation, to be sure. Or, on the one hand, you can look at reason as it is left to itself and unfettered; on the other hand, as it is enclosed and restrained within the orb of the divine word. Or, reason can be considered from one standpoint as it runs to and fro without a bridle, when it is borne away by its own dialectics, "whithersoever its feet carry it" [Horace]; from another standpoint, as it runs about beneath the bridle, curbed through the word of GOD and restrained under the obedience of Christ. Or, one can first view reason such as is in both the man and the philosopher, insofar as he is man or philosopher; and one can also view reason such as is in the Christian man and/or philosopher, not insofar as he is simply man or philosopher, but as he is Christian man and Christian philosopher. (See Dn. Schroder (de princ. Fid.; cap. I, sect. 2, 3), who most skillfully sets forth and explains these very matters.)

Now, therefore, the question is: When a man already reborn attacks from the principles of reason the literal sense in articles of faith, whether he ought to be said to do this according to reborn reason? We answer: Certainly not, for even if the reason of such a man is reborn, nevertheless to the extent that from its own principles it wishes to argue against articles of faith, to that extent it is no longer reborn, for reborn reason argues from the principles of the word. Because he argues from the principles of reason against the mysteries of faith, he does this, not insofar as he is a Christian, but insofar as he is a man misapplying philosophy. As, therefore, we read in I John 3:9, "He who has been born of God, does not commit sin." (Of course this is true to the degree that one is really born of God, and to the degree that he retains the grace of regeneration.) But if he wishes to follow the desires of the flesh, he sins and becomes liable to death (Rom. 8:13). So reborn reason does not oppose articles of faith, certainly insofar as it is such, and follows the leading of the word; but if it wishes from its own principles to attack the word of God, it errs and is no longer reborn.

Let us clarify the matter by an example, which we have also brought forward previously. It is asked, "May the body of Christ truly, really and substantially be present in the Lord's Supper?" Our churches answer affirmatively, because Christ says, "Take, eat, this is my body." Our opponents take the opposite position on the basis of this principle, that a true and natural body cannot at a single time be simultaneously in several places. They add that reborn reason cannot state otherwise concerning a body, and that therefore its testimony ought to be heard. But, I say, reborn reason (insofar as it is such) makes statements concerning articles of faith on the basis of the word of GOD, and does not exceed its limits. Now assurdly this is the word of God: "Take, eat, this is my body." If reason argues against this word of Christ from its own principles, it is no longer reborn, but follows its own leading, and so ought not to be heard, any more than should the philosopher who argues against the resurrection of bodies from the principle: "no entity that has once perished, can as the same entity return to its position"; or any more than the Antitrinitarian who argues against the mystery of the Trinity on the basis of this principle: "One cannot be triple"; or the Arian who argues against the eternal generation of the Son from this principle: "The one born comes after the one who bears him."

But, you say, reason which argues against the presence of the body of Christ in the Supper does not support itself simply by its own principles, but by the declaration of Scripture concerning the reality of Christ's body. We answer:

One ought to listen to Scripture not only when it speaks on one matter, that certainly Christ has a real body, but also when it speaks on another, that certainly the real body of Christ is present in the Supper. The analogy of faith must be accepted as a whole. It is not the question here whether the body of Christ is a real body; rather, the question is: whether, the reality of the body holding true, one may thereupon rightly conclude that God cannot cause that real body to be present in the Supper. They say: the nature of the body does not admit of this, for it is finite. I ask: How may they know that this is opposed to Christ's body being simultaneously present in several places? Surely from the principles of reason, for Scripture says the opposite. Therefore the final resolution of their argument goes back to a proposition deduced from a principle of reason, and one that is viciously opposed to the words of Christ. Hence the sophist-like refuge may be removed which they wish to contrive for themselves in that distinction between unregenerate reason, and reborn (or, as they say, spiritual) reason.

* Simon Grynaeus (1493-1541), Calvinist theologian, Prof. of Greek and Latin at Heidelberg, one of the authors of the First Helvetic Confession. (See *Concordia Cyclopedia*, pp. 437, 892-93.)

Appendix II

*Homily or Short Meditation for the 1ˢᵗ Sunday of Trinity**

Lord Jesus we are all paupers in thy sight: paupers in works, paupers in paying the debt of sins. How could our basest poverty merit those supreme riches of eternal glory? How could our extreme need pay that exceedingly great debt of sins which has been conveyed to us by hereditary right—and which we have over and above this enlarged by our own personal sins? Thou Lord Jesus, by the countless favors of thy grace, hast relieved our need, and although rich, wast made poor in our behalf, that through thy poverty we might be restored as sharers in eternal riches. Paupers we are Lord; grant that we may imitate the life of the devout poor, and that pride may be far distant from our every work and thought. Indeed, what is ours, by reason of which we can boast? Nothing is ours by reason of our sins, and these are from the devil and ourselves: for the good things and all gifts are from God alone, not from us. Lord Jesus guard my soul in this age full of wickedness, lest it come into the place of torments; guard me God, and give bountifully to me whatsoever thou knowest will be beneficial to eternal salvation: I shall gladly endure that instructress in patience, a holy poverty. Alas, Lord Jesus, what do I say—"I shall endure"? Do thou grant that I may be able to endure if thou dost judge this poverty more salutary and advantageous in seeking to reach eternal life. Behold, thy slave am I; let it be to me in all things according to thy will, and may I be not only a slave, but more a son and friend, for of this most honorable and dearest name thou dost deem us worthy — us who are degenerate and exceedingly wicked. Ah Lord, thou art Father, thou dost bear a father's heart; how then couldst thou not give the things thou knowest will be of benefit — knowledge, ignorance, wealth, poverty, health, sickness, life, death, joy and sadness — all things are in thy hand — thou dost distribute to each one severally; distribute both to me a slave and to me thy son the things thou knowest will be profitable for me. This only I ask and in it I know most certainly that I shall be clearly heard — do thou support me by thy Holy Spirit in the hour of death, and, I beg, send the holy Angels to convey my soul into Abraham's bosom. Come Lord Jesus, come quickly, that our sins and whatever in us displeases thee may die in us. Amen.

* Translated from John Gerhard, "Homiliae XXXVI," *Studien zur Geschichte der Theologie und der Kirche* (Leipzig, 1898), III (5), pp. 1-2.

*Homily or Short Meditation for the 23rd Sunday after Trinity**

The things that are Caesar's, give to Caesar; the things that are God's, give to God. Let us divide the duties and also the functions of our work, beginning with the truth that we are wholly from God. To God therefore we owe the whole of ourselves; for Him let us expend the whole of ourselves: let us bring before Him spiritual sacrifices. The soul, from its inmost being, brings prayer to God as a spiritual gift. A content heart, a humble heart, a faithful heart, are sacrifices most acceptable to God. And assuredly also in others there is something of God, and these we should not defraud of the honor that is due them. Instead we shall honor them with our words, our deeds, our works. For our religion does not destroy reverence for Magistrates and superiors, but elevates it. The laws of Christ do not subvert states; on the contrary, obedience which is offered to the mighty is presented to God. Consequently, obedience there should be, but obedience bounded and encompassed by definite limits. If something is commanded against God, against a true doctrine of the faith, against good morals, it is not obligatory. For just as what is wrongly vowed is more wrongly completed, so what is wrongly commanded is more wrongly carried out.

Nor does the Christian fear to lay aside the love of parents, spouses, children in the cause of Christ, since he loves all of them through Christ. He does not fear by a confession of the truth to offend the Lords in earthly regions, since they certify to a higher Someone in the heavens. Indeed, as for them, their authority concerns the outer man; him they may govern, for him they may prescribe laws, his passions they may restrain. The inner man, however, serves

God alone, the inner man is understood only by God, and there is no more intolerable Tyranny than that which wishes to have dominion over consciences. Therefore, the things that are Caesar's give to Caesar; the things that are God's are to be preserved inviolate and undefiled for God.

* Translated from John Gerhard, "Homiliae XXXVI," *Studien zur Geschichte der Theologie und der Kirche* (Leipzig, 1898), III (5), pp. 27-28.

Appendix III

A Conspectus of the Topics, Chapters, and Assertions Occurring in Volume One of John Gerhard's Loci Theologici *(ed. John Federick Cotta, 9 vols., 1767)*

PRELIMINARY NOTE: This Appendix comprises a partial translation of the "Conspectus" found at the end of Vol. 1 of the *Loci Theologici*. Topic I. is translated in its entirety. For Topic III. only the rubrics for the contents of the paragraphs are omitted. Topics II., IV., and V. are listed solely by title.

Topic I. Concerning Sacred Scripture (pp. 1-41)

The guidance for theological investigations is obtained from the foundation of theology, which is the word of God, or *sacred scripture*. # 1, 2 (p. 1)

Reasons are adduced why this scripture may be called *sacred*. # 3 (p. 1) Although no Christian denies that this scripture is a foundation for theology, some deny that the same is the *sole* foundation for theology, # 4 (p. 1)

Chapter I. On the Canonical and Apocryphal Books (pp. 1-7)

The *canonical* books of the Old Testament are enumerated, together with the various classes of them established by the ancient Hebrews. # 5 (pp. 1, 2)

We show which books may be called *apocrypha* and two classes of them are drawn up. # 6-9 (p. 3)

The arrangement of the Bible books and the authority of the canonical books is shown by various arguments. # 10-13 (pp. 3-5)

Objections of the popes are dissolved, and the distinction between the canon of the Jews and the canon of the Christians is also examined. # 14-16 (pp. 5, 6)

We investigate whether a distinction of this kind between *canonical* and *apocryphal* books ought also to be established among the books of the New Testament. # 17 (pp. 6, 7)

Chapter II. On the Authority of Sacred Scripture (pp. 7-13)
So that the authority of the canonical scripture may be rightly understood, several distinctions are observed, as well as various classes of *witnesses* testifying as to the authority of scripture. # 18 (pp. 7, 8)

The authority of all scripture is derived from God alone. # 19 (pp 8, 9)

We inquire how the authority of scripture may *become evident* [to us]. # 20, 21 (p. 9)

We show how one ought to *convince* of the authority of the scripture those who deny it. # 22-24 (pp. 9-10)

The church has not established the *canonical* authority of scripture, but merely witnesses to it. # 25, 26 (pp. 10-11)

Whether and in what way the dogma of the *canon* is found in scripture. # 27-29 (p. 11)

We set forth whether the question of which books are *canonical* may be settled from the testimony of the church alone. # 30 (p. 11)

Persuasive arguments, that we may believe the writings of the apostles. # 31, 32 (pp. 11, 12)

Scripture is worthy of belief *per se* # 33 (p. 12)

To what end do the popes derive the authority of scripture from the testimony of the church alone? # 34, 35 (pp. 12, 13)

Chapter III. On the Perfection of Sacred Scripture (pp. 13-22)
The *perfection* of scripture—what is meant by it, # 36 (pp. 13-14)

It is demonstrated by a general syllogism # 37, 38 (p. 14)

In particular, scripture

1. *is called* perfect. # 39 (pp. 14, 15)

2. By reason of its *subject-matter*. #40-50 (pp. 15-17)

3. And by reason of its *purpose*, it is perfect. # 51, 52 (pp. 17, 18)

Testimonies are summoned from the fathers, from the scholastics, and from the popes themselves on behalf of the perfection of scripture. # 53 (pp. 18-22)

Chapter IV. Concerning Traditions (pp. 22-25)
What has been decreed *traditions* by the Council of Trent. # 54 (p. 22)

Arguments are delivered against *traditions*. # 55-67 (pp. 23-25)

Chapter V. On the Clarity of Sacred Scripture (pp. 26-28)
What kind of clarity is meant? # 68-71 (p. 26)

The clarity of Scripture is *twofold*. # 72 (pp. 26-27)

Arguments are adduced for the clarity of Scripture, together with a discussion of *objectives*. # 73-83 (pp. 27-28)

Chapter VI. Concerning the Norm in Controversies (pp. 28-30)
Sacred Scripture is *the norm in theological controversies*. # 84 (pp. 28-29)

Hence it is called *canonical*. # 85 (p. 29)

This property of Scripture is established by various arguments. # 86-90 (pp. 29-30)

Chapter VII. Concerning the Judge in Controversies (pp. 31-33)
Sacred Scripture, because it is the norm, is by this very fact also the judge in *controversies*. # 91 (p. 31)

This is demonstrated. # 92-96 (pp. 31-32)

The popes disagree. # 97 (pp. 32-33)

Chapter VIII. That the Reading of Scripture Extends Also to Laymen (pp. 33-37)
Laymen also ought to read and meditate on Sacred Scripture. # 98 (p. 33)

This is proven by many arguments, and the *objections* of opponents are dissolved. # 99-110 (pp. 33-37)

Chapter IX. On Translations of Scripture (pp. 37-39)
The *translation* of the Scripture into everyday languages ought not to be condemned. # 111 (p. 37)

The *Hebrew* idioms characteristic of the Old Testament, and the *Greek* idioms characteristic of the New. # 112, 113 (pp. 37-39)

Various *translations*. # 112, 113 (pp. 37-39)

Chapter X. Concerning an Authoritative Edition of Sacred Scripture (pp. 39-41)

Only the Hebrew text in the case of the Old Testament, and the Greek text in the case of the New, is *authoritative*. # 114 (pp. 39-40)

Scripture in its *sources* is not corrupt. # 115-117 (p. 40)

The *vulgate* Latin version is not authoritative, and abounds in errors # 118-120 (pp. 40-41)

A definition of *canonical* Scripture is presented. # 121 (p. 41)

Topic II. On the Interpretation of Holy Scripture (pp. 42-91) 15 Chapters

Topic III. On the Nature of God (pp. 91-184)

Chapter I.	Whether and to what extent can God be known? (*cognosci*) (pp. 91-93)
Chapter II.	From what source is knowledge (*cognito*) of God to be sought? (p. 93)
Chapter III.	On natural knowledge (*notitia*) of God. (pp. 93-98)
Chapter IV.	Concerning the Names of God. (pp. 98-102)
Chapter V.	On certain expressions frequently used in reference to the mystery of the Trinity [e.g. hypostasis; person]. (pp. 102-104)
Chapter VI.	On the Unity of God. (pp. 105-108)
Chapter VII.	On the Divine Attributes. (pp. 108-115)
Chapter VIII.	On the Spirituality of God. (pp. 115-117)
Chapter IX.	On the Invisibleness of God. (pp. 118-119)
Chapter X.	On the Simplicity [uncompounded nature] of God. (pp. 119-121)
Chapter XI.	On the Eternal Nature of God. (pp. 121-122)
Chapter XII.	On the Immutability of God. (pp. 122-124)
Chapter XIII.	On the Immortality of God. (pp. 124-125)
Chapter XIV.	On the Infiniteness of God. (pp. 125-126)
Chapter XV.	On the Omnipresence of God. (pp. 126-130)
Chapter XVI.	On the Omnipotence of God. (pp. 130-135)
Chapter XVII.	On the Goodness of God. (pp. 135-140)
Chapter XVIII.	On the Justice of God. (pp. 140-145)
Chapter XIX.	On the Wisdom and Knowledge (*scientia*) of God. (pp. 145-150)
Chapter XX.	On God's Freedom of Action. (pp. 150-152)
Chapter XXI.	On the Truthfulness and Veracity of God. (pp. 152-154)
Chapter XXII.	On the Perfection of God. (pp. 154-156)

Chapter XXIII. On the Majesty of God. (p. 156)
Chapter XXIV. On the Blessedness of God. (p. 157)
Chapter XXV. On the Use of the Doctrine of Divine Attributes. (pp. 158-159)

The *use* of this doctrine is summarized thus: that we unite *practice* with *theory*. [A wonderful section. Shows how completely Gerhard integrated the theological and the devotional aspects of the Christian life. He quotes such Scripture passages as Mal. 1:6, and closes with these words, "Therefore O Fire, O Love, illumine and inflame us; to thee be glory and honor forever, Amen."]

An Appendix, Presenting the History of the Doctrine of God. (pp. 159-184) [A very detailed and valuable section inserted by the editor, consisting of 28 columns in small type, which presents through direct quotation the false views of God held by almost any one of importance (and by many not so important) from Aristotle to Spinoza.]

Topic IV. Concerning the Most Sacred Mystery of the Trinity (pp. 185-223) 14 Chapters

Topic IV. Part II. Concerning God the Father, and His Eternal Son (pp. 223-296) 7 Chapters

Topic IV. Part III. Concerning the Holy Spirit (pp. 296-342) 7 Chapters; Chapter VII: On the Use of this Doctrine (pp. 340-342)

Topic V. Concerning the Person and Office of Christ (pp. 343-378) 8 Chapters

(Appended to this Topic is a doctoral oration of Gerhard's on the subject "Whether all, or some, or in fact no divine attributes were communicated to Christ's human nature"—pp. 372-378.)

Bibliography

Allgemeine Deutsche Biographie: herausgegeben durch die Historische Commission bei der K. Akademie der Wissenschaften. Leipzig, 1875-1912. Article: Gerhard, Johann. Vol. VIII, pp. 767-71. (Article contains excellent brief bibliography of material about Gerhard, but only German and Latin writings are included.)

Allgemeines Gelehrten Lexicon: herausgegeben von Christian Gottlieb Jocher. Leipzig, 1750-51. Article: Gerhard, Johann. Vol. II, columns 948-50. (Article includes a list of Gerhard's writings, but no further bibliographic references.)

Arndt, John. *True Christianity: or, The Whole Economy of God towards Man, and the Whole Duty of Man, towards God*. In Four Books. Trans. by the Rev. Anthony William Boehm. First American edition, rev. and corrected by the Rev. Calvin Chaddock. Books I and II. Boston, 1809.

Barraclough, G. *The Origins of Modern Germany*. Oxford, Blackwell, 1952.

Biographie universelle ancienne et moderne. Nouv ed., publiée sous la direction de M. Michaud. Paris, 1843-65. Article: Gerhard, Jean. (No further bibliographic references given with article.)

Bond, John J. *Handy-Book of Rules and Tables for Verifying Dates with the Christian Era*. 4th ed. London, Bell, 1889. (Cited in C. M. Winchell's *Guide to Reference Books*. 7th ed., as N160, under "Chronology.")

(Concordia) Lutheran Cyclopedia. Editor-in-chief: Erwin L. Lueker. Saint Louis, Concordia Publishing House, c1954.

Documents of the Christian Church. Ed. by Henry Bettenson. New York and London, Oxford University Press, 1947.

Gerhard, John. *Confessio Catholica ... in quatuor tomos distributa*. Frankfurt and Leipzig, 1679.

Gerhard, John. *Gerhard's Sacred Meditations*. Trans. by the Rev. C. W. Heisler. Intro. by Chas. S. Albert. Philadelphia, Lutheran Publication Society, c1896.

Gerhard, John. *Harmonia Evangelistarum*. Begun by Martin Chemnitz, continued by Polycarp Lyser (Leyser), and finished by John Gerhard. [Vol. I] Frankfurt and Hamburg, 1653.

Harmoniae quatuor Evangelistarum. Chemnitio-Lysero-Gerhardinae. Tomus Secundus [et Tertius.], qui D. Johannis Gerhardi continuationis Partes Primam et Secundam [et Tertiam, Quartam, Quintam, Eamque postremam] complectitur. Hamburg, 1704.

Homiliae XXXVI seu meditationes breves diebus dominicis atque festis accomodatae. Ed. with Prologue by Georg Berbig. In: *Studien zur Geschichte der Theologie und der Kirche*, herausgegeben von N. Bonwetsch und R. Seeberg. Leipzig, 1898. Band III, Heft 5, S. viii, 43.

Loci Theologici. Ed. with Preface "De vita, fatis et scriptis Io. Gerhardi" by John Frederick Cotta. 2nd ed. Tübingen, 1767-81. Vols. I-XX. (Cotta's Preface in Vol. I, pp. x-lii, contains an excellent bibliographic essay or classified catalog of Gerhard's writings.)

Hägglund, Bengt. *Die Heilige Schrift und ihre Deutung in der Theologie Johann Gerhards*. Eine Untersuchung über das altlutherische Schriftverständis. Lund, CWK Gleerup, 1951. (Contains a fine bibliography of material by and about Gerhard.)

Hastings, James, ed. *Encycopedia of Religion and Ethics*. New York, Scribner's 1919.

Hayes, Carlton J. H. *A Political and Cultural History of Modern Europe*. Vol I (1500-1830). New York, Macmillan, c1932.

Keil, Richard and Keil, Robert. *Geschichte des Jenaischen Studentenlebens von der Gründung der Universität bis zur Gegenwart (1548-1858)*. Eine Festgabe zum dreihundertjährigen Jubiläum der Universität Jena. Leipzig, Brockhaus, 1858. (Unfortunately has no index.)

Langer, William L., ed. *An Encyclopedia of World History*. Rev. Ed. Boston, Houghton Mifflin, c1948.

Latourette, Kenneth Scott. *A History of Christianity*. New York, Harper, c1953.

The Lutheran Hymnal. Authorized by the Synods Constituting the Evangelical Lutheran Synodical Conference of North America. Saint Louis, Concordia Publishing House, c1941.

Nouvelle Biographie Générale. Ed. by M. le Dr. Hoefer. Paris, Firmin Didot, 1853-66. Article: Gerhard, Jean. (One bibliographic citation given at end of article.)

Pelikan, Jaroslav. *From Luther to Kierkegaard*. Saint Louis, Concordia, c1950.

Reed, Luther D. *The Lutheran Liturgy*. Philadelphia, Muhlenberg Press, c1947.

Troeltsch, Ernst. *Vernunft und Offenbarung bei Johann Gerhard und Melanchthon*. Inaugural-Dissertation. Göttingen, 1891.

4. Chemnitz on the Council of Trent: An Evaluation of Chemnitz's *Examen Concilii Tridentini*

The Purpose, Scope, and Justification of the Present Study

Near the close of his "vita Martini Chemnicii," Eduard Preuss writes: "Erat in ecclesia proverbium: Si Martinus (Chemnicius) non fuisset, Martinus (Lutherus) vix stetisset. Hanc sententiam probabit, quicunque historiam reformationis accurate perpendit."[1] The basis for these assertions lies chiefly in Chemnitz's great *Examination of the Council of Trent*, which was published during the years 1565 to 1573.[2] The *Examen*, "than which no book of the period was more damaging to Roman claims,"[3] deserves far more attention than it has received in recent days; it is therefore my purpose in the present study briefly to evaluate Chemnitz's great work, in an effort to interest others in the theological merits of the "Alter Martinus."

Since this essay is concerned specifically with Chemnitz's *Examen*, the reader should not expect to find here either a general discussion of the Council of Trent (although some background material on the Council will of course appear), or a biographical treatment of Chemnitz himself. For those interested in the details of Chemnitz's life, we merely suggest bibliographic leads: Preuss for those who read Latin;[4] Pressel, or perhaps Frank, for those who read German;[5] the brief articles in the *Biographie universelle* and the *Nouvelle biographie générale* for those who prefer French; and Kunze or Gordon or the *Lutheran Cyclopedia* for those limited to English sources.[6] There is, however, one biographical fact

---

[1] Preuss, *Examen Concilii Tridentini per Martinum Chemnicium*, p. 956. It is a sobering fact that Preuss, the great editor of Chemnitz's *Examen*, became "a Romanist at St. Louis (1871)"—ten years after his edition of the *Examen* was published (Schaff, *Creeds of Christendom*, v. 1, p. 96, n. 1).
[2] For an "historia libri impressi" see the Preuss edition, pp. 959-64.
[3] Johannes Kunze, *The New Schaff-Herzog Encyclopedia of Religious Knowledge*, v. 3, p. 25.
[4] The basic source is P. J. Rehtmeyer's *Antiquitates Ecclesiasticae inclytae urbis Brunsvigae* (*Der beruehmten Stadt Braunschweig Kirchen-Historie*), Braunschweig, Friedrich Zilligers, 1707-10 (vol. 3, pp. 273-536).
[5] Frank's biography of Chemnitz appears at the beginning (pp. v-xx) of his German translation of pt. I, chapters 1 and 2 of the *Examen*. There are short German sketches of Chemnitz's life in the *Allgemeine Deutsche Biographie*, the *Allgemeines Gelehrten Lexicon*, and in Herzog and Hauck's *Realencyklopädie*.
[6] Gordon's article appears in the *Encyclopaedia Britannica*, 11th ed. Reference should also be made here to the recent (1971) and excellent English translation of Chemnitz's *De duabis naturis* (*The Two Natures in Christ*) by Dr. J. A. O. Preus, then president of the Lutheran Church—Missouri Synod.

concerning Chemnitz which is worth mentioning at the outset, for it provides real insight into the manner of life which produced a man of Chemnitz's great accomplishments:

> His theological attainments ... were largely the result of private study. An opportunity for this was afforded him by his appointment as librarian of Duke Albert of Brandenburg. Here he remained until 1552, faithfully studying the Word of God, and the writings of the Fathers and Reformers.[7]

An evaluation of Chemnitz's *Examen* may seem unnecessary in light of the universal acclaim both it and its author have received. Krauth refers to Chemnitz as "the greatest of the dogmatic theologians of the sixteenth century" and speaks concerning "the weight which his name bears" and "the exquisite combination of sound judgment, erudition, profound thought and clear reasoning, with great mildness, and a simple scriptural piety which characterized him."[8] Schmid considers the *Examen* "the ablest defence of Protestantism ever published," and says of Chemnitz: "Wealth of Scriptural learning, profoundness of reasoning, clearness and accuracy of statement, well-balanced judgment, simplicity and freshness of style, a constantly practical tendency, and devout feeling, are the prominent characteristics of his works."[9] And even Jaroslav Pelikan, who smells the musty odor of Aristotelian scholasticism in almost every Lutheran theologian who had the misfortune to come on the scene between Father Luther's time and that of "S. K." — even Pelikan has a good word to say for Chemnitz:

> The early Lutheran critics of Roman Catholicism, like Chemnitz in the *Examen*, were ... rather suspicious of scholastic philosophy. ... Like most of the humanists, these early Lutherans believed that medieval scholasticism had not only perverted the Christian Gospel, but also that it had not done justice to Greek philosophy. ... Poor theology and poor philosophy seemed to go hand in hand, and critiques like those of Chemnitz were equally opposed to both.[10]

Such praise of Chemnitz as we have just cited does not, we believe, render unnecessary further evaluations of his work. The very fact that only a small portion of the *Examen* — Chemnitz's greatest work — has until very recently

---

[7] H. E. Jacobs, "Martin Chemnitz and the Council of Trent," *Evangelical Quarterly Review* (1870), p. 410.
[8] *The Conservative Reformation and Its Theology*, p. 466.
[9] *The Doctrinal Theology of the Evangelical Lutheran Church*, trans. Hay and Jacobs, p. 666.
[10] *From Luther to Kierkegaard*, p. 54. Chemnitz does not entirely escape censure at Pelikan's hand, however, for "the dominance of Aristotelian terminology in the theological classroom which Melanchthon had achieved managed to survive Chemnitz's repudiation of some of Melanchthon's theological vagaries" (p. 46). More about this later.

been available in English translation (and no complete translation has as yet been published in the Romance languages[11]) makes clear that in this country few scholars, and far fewer parish clergy, know Chemnitz firsthand. The present essay is an attempt to evaluate Chemnitz anew, through the medium of primary contact with his *Examen*. The resultant picture will be neither completely positive nor completely negative, but, we hope, honestly objective. In dealing both with the records of the Tridentine Council and with the contents of the *Examen*, we can do no better than to follow the advice given by Ignatius Loyola to the Jesuits who were to attend the Council of Trent:

> Just as it is profitable to be slow to speak, so it is profitable to listen quietly in order to understand the kind of mind the speakers have, their feelings, and their wills.[12]

---

[11] Three editions of the *Examen*, as a whole or in part, have appeared in German: (1) that of Georg Nigrinus (1530-1602)—a folio volume (which I have not seen), published at Frankfurt in 1576 (*vide* Preuss, p. 962, and the *Lutheran Cyclopedia*, art., "Nigrinus, Georg); (2) that of C. A. Frank (1875)—see note 5; (3) that of Bendixen and Luthardt (1844). Oddly enough, Pelikan seems not to have heard of (1) and (3)! (*From Luther to Kierkegaard*, p. 139, n. 22). In French, however, only two chapters from part IV of the *Examen* are apparently available. The *British Museum Catalogue* (1943, v. 36, col. 675) reveals that French translations of part IV, chapter 3 ("De indulgentiis") and part IV, chapter 1 ("De reliquiis sanctorum") were published at Geneva in 1599. The latter chapter appeared together with Calvin's *Traitté des reliques*. The only portions of the *Examen* to have been published in English prior to Hassold's complete translation seem to be the following: A translation of part I, chapter 2 ("De traditionibus"), issued in London in 1582 (*British Museum Catalogue, ibid.*). (Incidentally, the "traditions" section of the *Canons and Decrees of the Council of Trent* seems to incite more than ordinary interest—see the first part of Solana's *Estudios sobre el Concilio de Trento*.) An abbreviated translation by H. E. Jacobs of part I, chapter 1 ("De Scriptura Sacra") of the *Examen*. (Jacobs, H. E., "Chemnicius Redivivus," *Evangelical Quarterly Review*, 1870, pp. 553-98.) An abbreviated translation, also by H. E. Jacobs, of part I, chapter 9, section 3 ("utrum vera fides justificans sit fiducia, an dubitatio") of the *Examen*. (Jacobs, H. E., "The Assurance of Faith," *Evangelical Quarterly Review* (*Lutheran Quarterly*), 1871, pp. 290-99. Translations of brief quotations from the *Examen* appear in such books as Schmid (*op. cit.*), and in such articles as the following by H. E. Jacobs: "The Lutheran Doctrine of the Sabbath, and the Lord's Day" (*Evangelical Quarterly Review*, 1869, pp. 125-52), "The Doctrine of the Ministry as Taught by the Dogmaticians of the Lutheran Church," *Evangelical Quarterly Review* (*Lutheran Quarterly*), 1874, pp. 290-99. A translation of part I (dealing with Scripture, traditions, original sin, freewill, justification, and good works—and embracing roughly one-fourth of the total work—by Fred Kramer (1971). This publication—the most ambitious to date—is based upon a MS translation of the entire *Examen* by Dr. Henry Hassold, a Lutheran pastor of Adelaide, South Australia. This full translation of the Examen is now available from the Concordia Publishing House, St. Louis Missouri, in four volumes.

[12] Loyola, "Instructions for Debate," quoted in Perkins, *At Your Ease in the Catholic Church*, p. 193.

Some Preliminary Remarks on the Council of Trent

Philip Schaff provides a useful orientation for this section of our paper when he writes:

> The Council of Trent (1543-63) is reckoned by the Roman Church as the eighteenth (or twentieth) ecumenical Council. It is also the last, with the exception of the Vatican Council of 1870, which, having proclaimed the Pope infallible, supersedes the necessity and use of any future councils, except for unmeaning formalities. It was called forth by the Protestant Reformation, and convened for the double purpose of settling the doctrinal controversies, which then agitated and divided Western Christendom, and of reforming discipline, which the more serious Catholics themselves, including even an exceptional Pope (Adrian VI.), desired and declared to be a crying necessity.[13]

Needless to say, however, the fact that Rome considers the Tridentine Council "ecumenical" has not carried much weight with a rather imposing number of Christians from the sixteenth century to the present day. Dean Stanley, in discussing the background of the Council of Nicaea, makes the following suggestive statement:

> This leads us to ask what caused the selection of the locality. In General Councils, as in battles, this has always been a very important question. Look at Trent. Its situation immediately under the Alps, yet on the Italian side, exactly expresses the peculiarity of the assembly convened there. It was to be as near the dominions of the Emperor as was possible, without being altogether out of reach of the dominions of the Pope. It was to come as close to the confines of Protestantism as it could without crossing the barriers which parted it from them.[14]

And Bungener's editor (John M'Clintock) is even more specific:

> The doctrine of Rome should be called Tridentine rather than Catholic. It was the Council of Trent which gave them their form and pressure. Dogmas which had for ages floated in the uncertainty were at Trent stereotyped for ever; the theories of the schools were trimmed, revised, composed, and arranged, until at least a semblance of harmony was obtained, and they were then stamped by the Council with infallibility.[15]

---

[13] *Creeds of Christendom*, v. 1, pp. 91-92. To be sure, the Second Vatican Council (1962-1965) has shown how dangerous it is to predict, as Schaff does here, what can or cannot occur in subsequent church history!

[14] *Lectures on the History of the Eastern Church* (1884), p. 83.

[15] *History of the Council of Trent* (1855), p. xvii. Schaff includes this edition of Bungener's work in his brief bibliography of the "History of the Council" (of Trent), *Creeds of Christendom*, v. 1,

As a backdrop for our discussion of Chemnitz's *Examen* (and as a help in evaluating it), we wish to deal briefly with the question of the ecumenicity or catholicity of the Council of Trent. We intend, in other words, to present here some points of factual information on the Council which will help to put it in proper historical perspective. The first and most perplexing problem one encounters in studying the history of the Council of Trent is that of sources. The two great published histories—Sarpi's and Pallavicini's—have the irritating habit of contradicting each other. Some have gone so far as to argue that the work "of Sarpi, written from a professedly Romish standpoint, with the design of attacking the Council, in all fairness, must be rejected as an impartial history," and "neither is the reply of the Jesuit Pallavicini to be accepted as any more trustworthy."[16] Schaff takes a less extreme, and on the whole more satisfactory, view of the two historians:

> The history of the Council was written chiefly by two able and learned Catholics of very different spirit: the liberal, almost semi-Protestant monk Fra Paolo Sarpi, of Venice (first, 1619); and, in the interest of the papacy, by Cardinal Sforza Pallavicini (1656), who had access to all the archives of Rome. Both accounts must be compared.[17]

Unfortunately, no objective historical interpretation of the Tridentine Council has yet appeared which is comparable in scope to the biased treatments by Sarpi and Pallavicini, though Hubert Jedin's *Geschichte des Konzils von Trient* may eventually fill the gap.[18] For the time being it seems best to use Sarpi and Pallavicini with caution,[19] supplementing them with, and checking them against, such material as is found in Joseph Mendham's *Memoirs of the Council of Trent; Principally Derived from Manuscripts and Unpublished Records*.[20] Mod-

---

p. 91.
[16] Jacobs, "Martin Chemnitz and the Council of Trent," p. 408.
[17] *Creeds of Christendom*, v. 1, pp. 95-96. For a detailed criticism of Sarpi and Pallavicini, see Ranke's *History of the Popes*, v. 3, pp. 103-38.
[18] In reviewing the first volume ("Der Kampf um das Konzil") of Jedin's work, John T. McNeill writes: "So far as the Council of Trent is concerned, it is devoted to background material only. ... His balanced judgment in this treatment of Conciliarism gives promise of an exposition of Trent itself that will at last rescue that important council from the cross-fire of a debate begun long ago by Sarpi and Pallavicini" (*Church History*, Dec, 1951, p. 87).
[19] We can hardly discard Sarpi when even in Italy he is looked upon by some as a good Catholic herald of Italian nationalism! In an article entitled "Paolo Sarpi," appearing in *Contributi alla Storia del Concilio di Trento e della Controriforma* (Firenze, 1948), Luigi Salvatorelli writes: "E proprio qui che si chiarisce l'estrema questione: 'Sarpi fu o non fu protestante?' E si chiarisce nel senso che Sarpi, nonostante ogni specifica affinita, non e sulla linea storica del protestantesimo, ma sull'altra, antecedente e anche più tardi distinta, del cattolicesimo riformista italiano, la quale ha il suo punto di partenze alle origini stesse, se puo dire, della nazione italiana moderna, cioe agli inize del periodo comunale, e si prolunga fin entro il secolo XIX" (p. 144).
[20] Mendham's work is included in Schaff's bibliography (*Creeds of Christendom*, v. 1, p. 91), and

ern secondary source works, e.g., James Anthony Froude's *Lectures on the Council of Trent*, can also be of value to the student.[21] Our policy will be to quote *ad libitum* from Froude in this section of our essay, and to employ material from Pallavicini, Mendham, etc., when in the last part of the paper we come to treat in detail certain specific sessions of the Council and Chemnitz's examination of the canons and decrees resulting from these sessions. Professor Froude has made quite clear that the Tridentine Council was in no real sense "catholic" or "ecumenical." Papal policy at the time was unscrupulous but simple: to make it as difficult as possible, if not completely impossible, for Protestants safely to attend the Council until all of the important doctrinal issues had been railroaded through and the Council's decisions had been declared irrevocable.

> The Emperor had to deal with an antagonist as determined as himself, and a great deal more subtle. Paul III. had no intention of being reformed; he knew well enough what would happen to him if the bishops began upon reform and were reinforced by rebellious Protestants. He knew that his own bishops resented his encroachments, and resented the oath extorted from them of obedience to the Papacy. He had packed the council with Italians, but with all his skill he could not prevent spurts of mutiny. The bishops alone he might still hope to control, and, therefore, since a council there had to be, all his efforts from the first had been to make the coming of the Lutherans impossible. His legates directed the proceedings, and scarcely touched reform with the points of their fingers. They played on the appetite of the fathers for doctrinal discussions. Disregarding absolutely the Emperor's orders, they had hurried through decree on decree, definition on definition, on the points on which the Lutherans were most sensitive. These once settled, the legates hoped that the Lutherans might refuse to appear, or that if they did come, it would be only to find that all was over, and that they were committed to the council's decisions.[22]

M'Clintock says, "No writer of recent times has done more to throw light upon the history of the Council, and to furnish materials for its study, than the Rev. Joseph Mendham" (Bungener, *History of the Council of Trent*, p. xxii). Ranke states that "in Mendham's 'Memoirs of the Council of Trent,' there is much that is new and good" (*History of the Popes*, v. 3, p. 138).

[21] The Romanists are not particularly happy with Froude's treatment of the Invincible Armada, and an English Jesuit (J. H. Pollen) claims that in Froude's *History of England and English Seamen of the Sixteenth Century* he relies "upon coloured, and even prejudiced, evidence" (*Catholic Encyclopedia*, art. "Armada, the Spanish," v. 1, p. 729). There is certainly truth in Charles Kendall Adams' criticism of Froude: "The likes and dislikes of the author are too intense to allow him ever to be strictly judicial" (*A Manual of Historical Literature*, p. 482). However, we today are in a better position than nineteenth-century historians to see that the real issue is not bias *per se*, but the evidence marshalled in support or vindication of the bias. All historians write with bias—the question is simply, how sound an evidential argument does the given writer present in behalf of his bias?

[22] Froude, *Lectures on the Council of Trent*, pp. 276-77.

In discussing the matter of safe-conduct for Protestants who wished to attend the Council, Froude writes:

> Meanwhile the Germans were preparing leisurely to keep their engagement. Melanchthon drew up a body of Lutheran doctrine which was to be submitted to the council. Several of the Catholic German bishops, the three Archbishop Electors at their head, made their way to Trent in the course of the summer, and at length Maurice informed the Emperor that the Protestant divines were ready to start. There was still, however, a preliminary question to be settled about their safe-conduct. Trent was occupied by troops under the council's orders. These divines in the eyes of the Church were condemned heretics liable to seizure and execution. The Emperor had given them a safe-conduct, but Sigismund had granted John Huss a safe-conduct at the Council of Constance, and yet Huss was burnt. Luther came to Worms with a safe-conduct, and the Roman cardinals and bishops had urged Charles to disregard it and burn Luther also. Very naturally, therefore, and as will be seen with excellent reason, Maurice required security in the name of the council itself. ...
>
> The Pope ... drew a form on the lines recommended, which was sent to the council and was read in session. By this document the council was to grant, *so far as lay in its power*, security to all Germans, secular or spiritual, of what degree, condition, or quality soever, to appear at the council, assist in its debates, propose, treat, and even, if they wished, dispute with the fathers, provided it was done with decency, as well as to withdraw at any moment if they should think fit.
>
> Such a safe-conduct might have seemed sufficient, and the Germans might have overlooked the phrase which concealed so sinister a meaning. Constance, however, had made them suspicious. They observed the words. They again referred to Augsburg, and the Diet agreed unanimously that the safe-conduct must be further amended.
>
> The fathers, supposing that they had extricated themselves from the difficulty, went on with their ordinary work. They defined the power of the keys as committed exclusively to priests. Priests had it, however wicked; laymen had it not, however holy. Absolution was a judicial act, not a mere declaration, and contrition was of little value without it. This was all easy sailing. ...
>
> Orders came at length to the ambassadors to apply for an alteration of the safe-conduct to the presiding Legate in person. Crescentio was difficult to approach. They had been told to be conciliatory, and the Cardinal of Trent being on better terms with them than the rest, they asked him to procure them an audience. On their arrival, they had themselves refused to wait on the Legate. They were told now that they could not be received till they had stated what they wanted. They said their business was to demand a safe-conduct with no doubtful meanings in it, and to present again the Lu-

theran confession of faith, which their theologians would defend when they arrived. The Cardinal of Trent carried the message to the Legate and the Legate broke into most unapostolic rage. He said he would have no heretic articles of faith presented or defended in a holy ecumenical council. ... If the Protestants would state their difficulties in a spirit of humility, and with a willingness to receive instruction, the council would teach them the truth; but he said he would rather forfeit his life than permit strangers to advance doctrines of their own in a synod of Christ's ministers. As to the safe-conduct, the ambassadors' language was an insult to the council's honour; all had been granted that could be granted, and every Catholic would resent a demand for further security as a personal outrage. The truth was now coming out. The legates had never intended that the Protestants should be heard in the council at all. The Emperor had promised that they should be heard. The council itself had seemed to promise it in the sham safe-conduct which had been offered; but all was illusion.[23]

Finally, too late to do any real good (and then only due to heavy pressure from Emperor Charles), a somewhat tolerable safe-conduct for Protestants was secured, and a group of them was actually given an audience at the Council.

> The ambassadors were to be heard, and heard in full congregation before the assembled fathers. The occasion was felt to be momentous. In all Church history there had been nothing like it. The foreign ministers attended in their robes of state. The fathers of the council sat ranged along the benches, hiding thoughts in their tonsured heads which few of them would have dared to utter. The ambassadors — plain, honest, German laymen — were introduced into the splendid assembly, and did not seem to have been particularly awed by it. One of them, Leonard Badehorn, spoke for the rest.
>
> He began by addressing the fathers as "Reverendissimi Patres ac Domini." He would not call them a council, for Germany had not yet recognised them, and France had disputed their title. ... He said that the States of Germany had intended from the first to send representatives to a General Council, but it was to be a council where Scripture was to be the rule of controversy, where all persons present were to have liberty to speak, and where the head of the Church was to be called to account as well as its members. They had hoped that the time had come when these conditions would be fulfilled. Unfortunately the time had not come. ... He had been told that the definitions already made were not to be revised.[24]

And the end result of the Tridentine Council's work?

---

[23] *Ibid.*, pp. 255, 261-62, 263-64.
[24] *Ibid.*, pp. 268-69.

Luther's propositions were duly condemned. The Vulgate was canonised, tradition and Church authority were declared to rank with Scripture as the rule of faith, and the vulgar were forbidden to think that they would understand Scripture for themselves. ... Three cardinals and forty bishops, mostly persons of no consideration, had laid down the law upon questions which had been agitating the ablest minds in Europe.[25]

Thus Luther's statements at the end of Part Two, Article Four of the Smalcald Articles (written by him in December, 1536) were truly prophetic as to the true character of the forthcoming Council of Trent:

> In these four articles they will have enough to condemn in the Council. For they cannot and will not concede us even the least point in one of these articles. Of this we should be certain, and animate ourselves with the hope that Christ, our Lord, has attacked His adversary, and he will press the attack home both by His Spirit and coming. Amen. For in the Council we will stand not before the Emperor or the political magistrate, as at Augsburg (where the Emperor published a most gracious edict, and caused matters to be heard kindly and dispassionately), but we will appear before the Pope and devil himself, who intends to listen to nothing, but merely when the case has been publicly announced to condemn, to murder and to force us to idolatry. Therefore we ought not here to kiss his feet, or to say: "Thou art my gracious lord," but as the angel in Zechariah 3,2 said to Satan: "The Lord rebuke thee, O Satan."[26]

We conclude this second section of our essay, as we began it, with a quotation from Professor Schaff:[27]

> The Council of Trent, far from being truly ecumenical, as it claimed to be, is simply a Roman Synod, where neither the Protestant nor the Greek Church was represented; the Greeks were never invited, and the Protestants were condemned without a hearing. But in the history of the Latin Church, it is by far the most important clerical assembly, unless the unfinished Vatican Council should dispute with it that honor, as it far exceeded it in numbers. It completed, with the exception of a few controverted articles, the doctrinal system of mediaeval Catholicism, and stamped upon it the character of exclusive Romanism. It settled its relation to Protestantism by thrusting it out of its bosom with the terrible solemnities of an anathema. Papal diplomacy and intrigue outmanaged all the more liberal elements.[28]

---

[25] *Ibid.*, p. 179.
[26] *Concordia, or Book of Concord* (1952), pp. 141-42.
[27] *Creeds of Christendom*, v. 1, p. 95.
[28] One is probably not fully aware of the far-reaching influence of the Council of Trent until he peruses such a work as Dejob's *De l'influence du Concile de Trente sur la littérature et les beaux-arts chez les peuples catholiques.*

Chemnitz's *Examen* Examined

Having acquired some degree of historical perspective on the Council of Trent, and having seen its true character as a Roman rather than an ecumenical assembly, we are now in a position to consider, in a rather detailed manner, Chemnitz's *Examen Concilii Tridentini*. First we shall describe the work, and then we shall attempt to determine its positive and negative qualities on the basis of a firsthand study of passages from it.

The Nature and Origin of Chemnitz's Examen

The *Examen Concilii Tridentini*, as its title suggests, is a detailed examination of the Council of Trent; what the title does not reveal, however, is that the *Examen* deals with only the *doctrinal* matters contained in the canons and decrees of the Tridentine Council. Chemnitz is not concerned with the internal reforms which the Council of Trent effected; his interest is entirely centered upon the truth-value of the Council's doctrinal decisions. In examining these doctrinal pronouncements, moreover, he spares no effort to be comprehensive and meticulous. The Preuss edition of the *Examen* is a formidable tome—containing 920 double-columned super octavo pages, with seven-and-a-half-point type throughout. The *Examen* is really a four-volume work; its four main parts were issued separately over an eight-year period. Part One appeared in 1565, only two years after the Council had ended. It contained "chapters upon Traditions, Original Sin, Concupiscence, the Word Sin, the Conception of the Virgin Mary, the Works of Unbelievers, the Free Will, Justification, Faith, and Good Works. The succeeding year he published the second part, treating of the Sacraments *in genere*, Baptism, Confirmation, the Holy Supper, the Communion under one kind, the Mass, Repentance, Contrition, Confession, Satisfaction, Extreme Unction, Ordination and Marriage. In January, 1573, the third part followed, on Chastity, Celibacy, Purgatory and the Invocation of Saints; and in August of the same year, he finished his work, with chapters on the Relics of the Saints, Images, Indulgences, Fasts, Choice of Food, and Festivals."[29] The *Examen*'s arrangement does not exactly correspond to that of the canons and decrees of the Tridentine Council; Chemnitz first of all aimed for a systematic, orderly presentation of doctrinal material (both Roman and Lutheran), and, within this order, followed the sessions of Trent as closely as he could. His success in systematizing, incidentally, is well attested by the fact that the Frankfurt 1599 edition of the *Examen* came to be used as a Protestant textbook in systematic theology.[30]

---

[29] Jacobs, "Martin Chemnitz and the Council of Trent," p. 414.
[30] *Biographie universelle ancienne et moderne*, ed. Michaud, v. 8, pp. 74-74.

The circumstances which led Chemnitz to produce his *Examen* are of more than routine interest.[31] In 1560 the Jesuit faculty at Cologne brought out a work entitled *Censura de praecipuis doctrinae coelestis capitibus*. Upon reading it, Chemnitz gave (to put it mildly) a rather low "censuram" of his own; said he: "I can truly affirm that nothing in the Romish Church, be it ever so notoriously false, or shamelessly impudent, was ever thought, or dreamed of, which this judgment did not dare openly to approve, and defend with still greater impudence." He proceeded in 1562 to publish an abridged edition of the Jesuit *Censura*, illumined by his own highly satirical and extremely humorous notes. The Romanists, as one might expect, could not let Chemnitz's edition of the *Censura* go by unchallenged. The most formidable attempt at refutation was a work entitled *Decem libri orthodoxarum explicationum* (1564 etc.), written by a Portuguese theologian named Diego Andrada (Andradius de Payva (1528-1575), who had played an important role at the Council of Trent.[32] Jacobs considers the *Decem libri* "more remarkable for its bombast than for anything else," and Chemnitz at first ignored it. Then he decided that there was a real need not merely for a rebuttal to Andrada, but, more important, for a decisive refutation of the doctrinal decisions of the whole Tridentine Council. And so he produced his *Examen Concilii Tridentini*. Andrada came back with his *Defensio Tridentinae fidei Cath.* (published posthumously in 1578 and 1595), but it had little effect. Reinhard Mumm, in concluding his section on Chemnitz as "polemiker," nicely sums up history's verdict on Andrada—in contrast to the judgment of history on Chemnitz:

> Über Andrada, den bittersten Feind unseres Chemnitz, hat die Geschichte ganz anders geurteilt als jener Lobredner, der dem Braunschweiger zurief:
>
> > Bis Martine paras bello certare nefando
> > Bis victus, Payva bis superante cadis.
>
> Andradas Werk ist selbst für einen Leibnitz verschollen gewesen und sein Name ist nur durch den des Chemnitz bekannt geblieben.[33]

The Merits of Chemnitz's Examen

The positive, as well as the negative, qualities of the *Examen Concilii Tridentini* can be seen best from the work itself; we shall therefore provide the reader with a few examples of Chemnitz's technique, and then draw conclusions from

---

[31] Through most of this paragraph we follow Jacobs, "Martin Chemnitz and the Council of Trent," pp. 412-14.
[32] See McCaffray's (rather colored) biographical sketch of Andrada in the *Catholic Encyclopedia* (v. 1, p. 469). Also see the article on Andrada in Hoefer's *Nouvelle biographie générale*, v. 2, p. 533.
[33] Reinhard Mumm, *Die Polemik des Martin Chemnitz gegen das Konzil von Trient*, pp. 54-55.

these representative portions of the *Examen*. As an indication of the merits of Chemnitz's work, we offer material from Part One, chapter seven ("De Libero Arbitrio"), in which he discusses the following canons, approved on January 13, 1547, by the Council of Trent meeting in its Sixth Session:

> Can. 2. If anyone says that divine grace through Christ Jesus is given for this only, that man may be able more easily to live justly and to merit eternal life, as if by free will without grace he is able to do both, though with hardship and difficulty, let him be anathema.
> Can. 3. If anyone says that without the predisposing inspiration of the Holy Ghost and without His help, man can believe, hope, love, or be repentant as he ought, so that the grace of justification may be bestowed upon him, let him be anathema.
> Can. 4. If anyone says that man's free will moved and aroused by God, by assenting to God's call and action, in no way cooperates toward disposing and preparing itself to obtain the grace of justification, that it cannot refuse its assent if it wishes, but that, as something inanimate, it does nothing whatever and is merely passive, let him be anathema.
> Can. 5. If anyone says that after the sin of Adam man's free will was lost and destroyed, or that it is a thing only in name, indeed a name without a reality, a fiction introduced into the Church by Satan, let him be anathema.
> Can. 6. If anyone says that it is not in man's power to make his ways evil, but that the works that are evil as well as those that are good God produces, not permissively only but also *proprie et per se*, so that the treason of Judas is no less His own proper work than the vocation of St. Paul, let him be anathema.[34]

Chemnitz's method of examining these canons concerning freewill is typical of the thoroughgoing scholarship employed everywhere in the *Examen*. First he quotes verbatim the canons (and corresponding decrees) which he intends to discuss. Then come two short paragraphs of introduction, followed by six major sections, whose titles reveal the comprehensiveness and logic with which he treats the canons quoted above: (1) "Various Related Questions concerning Freewill" (i.e., questions not specifically raised in the canons quoted, but implicitly present in them); (2) "The Basic Point of Dispute on the Freewill Issue"; (3) "The View of the Council of Trent with regard to Freewill, according to Andrada's Interpretation"; (4) "The View of Scripture with regard to Freewill";

---

[34] H. J. Schroeder, ed., *Canons and Decrees of the Council of Trent*, pp. 42-43 (English translation, which we have quoted), 321 (Latin text). I have used Schroeder's edition of the Canons and Decrees since it has the Roman *imprimatur*, rather than employing Schaff's *Creeds of Christendom*.

(5) "Augustine's View on Freewill, and How Andrada Perverts It"; (6) "How Insidiously the Tridentine Decrees on Freewill Are Stated."[35] Let us observe the second and sixth sections at close range.

In treating "The Basic Point of Dispute on the Freewill Issue," Chemnitz masterfully clears away great loads of argumentative rubbish which have done nothing more than to obscure the real problem on the freewill issue. For example, he cites Lorenzo Valla (1405-1457), whose humanistic "Dialogue on Freewill" had wide influence duing the Renaissance:[36] "Valla argues whether man's will has the power to determine whether he shall move his foot to the right, or to the left. And in the Dialogues of Jerome, Pelagius asks: 'If I wish to bend my finger, do I always need the special help of God?'"[37] Chemnitz makes it quite plain that this is hardly the problem:

> The point of this dispute ... does not have to do with the nature of the mind, of the will, or of the heart, nor is it that these faculties of the soul can act in a way different both from their natural way of acting and from the way they act when excited and driven by violent, brute passion ... ; nor does the basic question have to do with the training of our rational faculty or with the problem of depraved actions. ... The question really concerns *spiritual* emotions or actions—in the realm of contrition, faith, and new obedience—*as those are presented to us in the Word of God.* ... It is certain that conversion and renovation do not occur without some action or activity of the mind, will, and heart. ... But the question is: *From what source* does man have or acquire the power, strength, or ability to begin to carry through such emotions or actions?[38]

The beauty of this argument lies in the way Chemnitz has cut to the very heart of the freewill issue. From Pelagius to the present-day Roman theology, the problem of grace versus freewill in conversion simply comes down to the question: Who is *finally responsible* for man's salvation? God alone, or man in some degree? And the answer to such a lofty problem must come from special revelation, not from scientific or philosophical speculation.

In the last section of his chapter on freewill, Chemnitz points out eight ways in which the Tridentine canons and decrees on freewill are insidiously stated. One of these is the following:

---

[35] I translate from the Preuss edition of the *Examen*, pp. 129-44. My renderings are entirely independent of Kramer-Hassold (see above, note 11).
[36] Valla's "Dialogue" is now available in English, thanks to Cassirer, Kristeller, and Randall's *The Renaissance Philosophy of Man* (University of of Chicago Press, c. 1948), pp. 145-82.
[37] *Examen*, p. 133.
[38] *Ibid.*, p. 134. Italics mine.

They even satirize what Luther says: that man is merely passive in regeneration, renovation, or conversion. And any one not accustomed to the ways of speaking which are employed by the Scholastic Authors could indeed be offended at this expression—as if the meaning were that the Holy Spirit so manages conversion that not the slightest new affections result in the will which begins to be renovated, and that the will is simply unresponsive and inert, and is beaten down and pushed forward only by brute force. This never entered Luther's mind. But the theologians who were summoned in the Council of Trent, since they were both brought up on and accustomed to that manner of speaking which the Scholastic Writers employ, without doubt understood well what "to be merely passive" meant; but they have not succeeded in hiding the issue by their sophistry. ....[39]

Thus our author catches verbal trickery as astutely as a modern semanticist. Chemnitz recognized clearly what later critics of the Council of Trent also came to see: that in the canons and decrees "the Protestant doctrines ... are almost always stated in an exaggerated form, in which they would hardly be recognized by a discriminating evangelical divine."[40]

Chemnitz's critical method, as illustrated by the above passages from his *Examen*, has two further merits which we should by no means overlook. The first of these is Chemnitz's straightforward examination of the Roman position on its own ground. Chemnitz was willing to take the time and trouble to understand his adversary and deal with him as one worthy of careful scholarly consideration. Too few of us today, unfortunately, are willing to expend the effort required to understand our theological opponents; we prefer to refute the straw men we ourselves have created, rather than go to the trouble of dealing with actual beliefs of those outside our doctrinal communion. And then we wonder why our opponents despise us instead of expressing interest in what we have to say. Chemnitz was feared by the Roman Church, but he was never despised by her.

The other great positive quality exhibited in Chemnitz's *Examen* is closely connected with the preceding one. I refer to Chemnitz's confidence in searching for and defending objective truth. He was not afflicted with the post-Kantian, existentialist, neo-orthodox fear of propositional truth.[41] The welter of diverse

---

[39] *Ibid.*, p. 144.
[40] Schaff, *Creeds of Christendom*, v. 1, p. 94.
[41] For an excellent treatment showing the influence of Kant on modern philosophy, theology, and culture in general, see J. H. Randall, Jr., *The Making of the Modern Mind* (rev. ed.), pp. 304-06, and chapters 16-21. Jaroslav Pelikan's *From Luther to Kierkegaard*, while having numerous scholarly merits, uncritically accepts the viewpoint expressed in Kant's *Critique of Pure Reason*, and looks at the subjective, experience-centered theology of Kierkegaard as the starting point for a "Lutheran philosophy" (see chapter 5, pp. 97-120). Such a statement as the following (p. 113) must

views present even in his day did not reduce him to skepticism or drive him to excessive subjectivity. He had an unshaken belief that in the realm of theology and religion, as much as in any other realm, truth could be distinguished from error, if one were willing to put real effort into the study of conflicting and contradictory views. In my opinion, one of the main reasons why books like the *Examen* are virtually ignored today, and have largely been replaced by the trivial, subjective "positive-thinking" type of religious publication, is that we have lost faith in our ability to arrive at objective religious truth and a solid theological *Weltanschauung*. Oddly enough, the only realm of modern life which has gone on almost as if Kant had never existed is that of physical science and technology;[42] and it is also this field of endeavor which has made greater strides than any other in the last century and a half. One reason for this, I am convinced, is that the scientist is confident that he *can* discover truth and apply it; would that in theology we would cease our myopic introspection, and would again come to view the Holy Scriptures as a valid source of objective truth concerning God and His will for us. Chemnitz's *Examen* is an excellent illustration of the fact that theology could still be queen of the sciences, if we would allow her to be.

The Defects of Chemnitz's Examen

The great merits of the *Examen Concilii Tridentini* should not blind us to its defects. Three negative characteristics in Chemnitz's work appear important enough to discuss here. The first two are sins of "omission" rather than of "commission"; the third will require our presenting evidence from the text of the *Examen* itself.

(1) Chemnitz's polemic technique in the *Examen* never goes beyond a specific refutation of Tridentine canons and decrees. He never questions the philosophical validity of the whole Council as an authoritative body pronouncing on Christian doctrine. We have already seen, in the second major section of this paper, that the Council of Trent was not really an ecumenical assembly in any legitimate sense of the term; had Chemnitz placed emphasis upon this fact, the strength of his refutation would have been greatly increased. As an illustration of the kind of supporting evidence he neglected, I shall quote from a few standard sources which describe the circumstances surrounding

---

be regarded as hopelessly naive: "A reprisination of classical Lutheran Orthodoxy was impossible after Kant; he had destroyed the epistemological presuppositions upon which Orthodoxy had built its system." For an excellent criticism of Kant by one not so naive (who calls the *Critique of Pure Reason* a "confused book"), see Randall, *op. cit.*, pp. 411-15, 599-600.

[42] *Ibid.*, p. 469.

the Sixth Tridentine Session. (This Session, the reader will remember, formulated the canons and decrees on freewill, Chemnitz's refutation of which we discussed above.) Mendham points out the disreputable character of the pope's conduct preceding the Sixth Session, and the lack of truly ecumenical participation in the Session:

> The author of the Diary, immediately after mentioning the fifth session, relates, that the emperor, being informed how much the protestants were dissatisfied with the decrees which had been passed in the council, wrote to his ambassadors and prelates at Trent to urge by all means an attention to reform, and the postponement of doctrines, which, as they had been established, deterred the protestants from attending the council. He then states, that the cardinal of Trent had arrived at Rome, and concluded a league with the pope against the protestants of Germany. ... For this purpose the pope remitted to his ally 200,000 crowns, upon condition, that his majesty should not make peace with the protestants.[43]

Ranke makes clear that the decisions of the Sixth Session on the freewill-justification issue by no means reflected the views of all the delegates present—nor were the decisions reached in a dispassionate, "truth-for-truth's-sake" atmosphere:

> Among the members of this council there were many who held opinions on this point entirely similar to those of the Protestants. The archbishop of Sienna, the bishop della Cava, Giulio Contarini, bishop of Belluno, and with them five theologians, ascribed justification to the merits of Christ and to faith alone and wholly; charity and hope they declared to be the attendants, and works the proof of faith, but nothing more,—the basis of justification must be faith alone. But was it to be expected, at a moment when pope and emperor were attacking the Protestants with force of arms, that their primal doctrine—that on which the whole existence of their creed was founded—should be received as valid by a council assembled under the auspices of these two powers? It was in vain that Pole exhorted them not to reject an opinion simply because it was held by Luther; too much of bitter and personal animosity was connected with this tenet. ...
>
> And thus were the Protestant opinions altogether excluded from Catholicism, all mediation was utterly rejected. This occurred precisely at the moment when the emperor was victorious in Germany, the Lutherans were submitting in almost every direction, and preparations were being made to subdue those who still hoped to hold out. The advocates of moderate views, Cardinal Pole and the archbishop of Sienna, had already quitted the council,

---

[43] *Memoirs of the Council of Trent*, p. 79.

but as might be expected, under different pretexts; instead of guiding and moderating the faith of others, they had cause to fear, lest their own should be assailed and condemned.[44]

So far from manifesting a loving, Christian atmosphere, the Sixth Session was the occasion for the following pleasant little incident (recorded by Pallavicini) which started when the bishop of Chiron made the following remark to the bishop of Cava:

> "Certo Monsignore, voi non potete scusarvi o d'ignoranza, o di protervia." L'altro allora, secondo il costume de'passionati nella collera, precipitò in una vendetta assai più nociva al vendicatore, che l'ingiuria vendicata. Imperocchè scagliate le mani alla barba del Chironese, no strappò molti peli, ed immantenente partissi. Concorse gran gente al romore: Il Chironese non se altro risentimento salvo che ad alta voce rinovò il suo detto, e s'offerì di provarlo. I Legati e i Padri so commossero incredibilmente a quello scandaloso specttacolo.[45]

Chemnitz should really have expanded his critical approach by including facts of this sort — even as Calvin did in his *Antidote of the Council oj Trent*.[46]

(2) The second "sin of omission" committed by Chemnitz in the *Examen* is his neglect of certain important decrees, not strictly of a doctrinal nature, which were passed at the Council of Trent and which offer a real opportunity for pointing up the negative character of the Council. The example we

---

[44] *History of the Popes*, v. 1, pp. 152-53, 155-56. These statements from Ranke show how misleading is Jedin's assertion concerning the Sixth Session: "The actual unanimity of the Council was not disturbed by any political considerations; of the seven dissenting votes cast in the sixth session, not one contained any opposition to the dogmatic substance of the decree on justification" (*Papal Legate at the Council of Trent: Cardinal Seripando*, p. 391).

[45] *Istoria del Concilio di Trento* (1757), v. i, p. 557 (bk. 8, chap. 6). This incident reminds us of another — which Döllinger mentions in discussing the Council of Trent: "When on one occasion, a foreign bishop mentioned an historical fact which would not fit in with the Papal system the storm broke out. Vosmediano, Bishop of Cadiz, had observed that formerly metropolitans used to ordain the bishops of their provinces by virtue of their own authority. Cardinal Simonetta promptly contradicted him, and then the Italian bishops raised a wild cry, and put him down by stamping and scraping with their feet. They cried out that this accursed wretch must not speak; he should at once be brought to trial. That was the Concilar freedom of speech at Trent!" (*The Pope and the Council*, by Janus, p. 368). Döllinger's authority for this incident is Le Plat, which Schaff refers to as "the most complete documentary collection" on the Council of Trent (*Creeds of Christendom*, v. 1, p. 91).

[46] See especially Calvin's "Preface to the Antidote," and his section entitled "On the Prefatory Discourse by the Legates in the First Session, and other Preliminary Matters of the Council" (Calvin's *Tracts*, v. 3, pp. 30-54).

cite is one that Chemnitz, having himself served as a librarian, should certainly have noted: the decrees concerning the Index of Books, and the "Ten Rules concerning Prohibited Books."[47] Probably no decrees passed at Trent have had such an unfortunate effect on culture as these.[48]

(3) The third defect in the *Examen* can best be shown by quoting Chemnitz directly. In Part two, chapter 6, section 3 ("De Canone Missae"), Chemnitz criticizes the following decree of the Tridentine Council:[49]

> And since it is becoming that holy things be administered in a holy manner, and of all things this sacrifice is the most holy, the Catholic Church, to the end that it might be worthily and reverently offered and received, instituted many centuries ago the holy canon, which is so free from error that it contains nothing that does not in the highest degree savor of a certain holiness and piety and raise up to God the minds of those who offer. For it consists partly of the very words of the Lord, partly of the traditions of the Apostles, and also of pious regulations of holy pontiffs.

Chemnitz gleefully lists seventeen separate errors in the Roman Canon of the Mass, of which number fifteen reads as follows:

> Pope Julius declared that intinction of the Eucharist was not according to the institution of Christ, the tradition of the Apostles, or the custom of the Church. ... Moreover, in the Canon the Priest not only puts part of the consecrated host into the chalice, but adds "that this mingling is to those who receive it the salvation of the soul and body to life everlasting." Thus the Canon of the Mass agrees neither with Scripture, nor with the Fathers, nor with the ancient Roman Popes themselves.[50]

This argument illustrates Chemnitz's tendency to "over-refute" the Roman position on occasion. He seems to forget here that Lutheranism does not have to reject a rite, etc., unless it is actually *condemned* in Scripture. Chemnitz,

---

[47] These decrees were passed at the Eighteenth and Twenty-fifth Sessions of the Council (texts in Schroeder, pp. 125-26, 254-55, 399-400, 519-20). The "Ten Rules" are given in Schroeder, pp. 273-78 (English), 545-50 (Latin).

[48] See Dejob, *De l'influence du Concile de Trente sur la littérature et les beaux-arts chez les peuples catholiques*, chapters 3 and 5.

[49] This decree was approved at the Council's Twenty-second Session (Sept. 17, 1562). English translation from Schroeder, pp. 146-47 (Latin text, pp. 419-20).

[50] *Examen*, pp. 414. Chemnitz's definition of the Canon of the Mass is broader than that of modern liturgical scholars. Whereas the latter mean by it all that "comes between the Sanctus and the Lord's Prayer" (Reed, *The Lutheran Liturgy*, p. 643), Chemnitz considers the Canon to include everything from the Sanctus to the end of the Mass. The phrase Chemnitz refers to is found as follows in the modern text of the Roman Mass: "May this mingling and consecration of the Body and Blood of our Lord Jesus Christ be to us who receive it effectual to life everlasting" (Reed, p. 613).

like Father Luther, rejected some beautiful portions of the Roman Canon of the Mass which really did not need to be discarded at all.[51] Intinction, for example, beautifully symbolizes "the reunion of our Lord's body and spirit at the resurrection."[52]

Summary and Conclusion

The three defects in Chemnitz's *Examen Concilii Tridentini* should not be allowed to cast more than a fleeting shadow over the great merits of the work—merits which we have discussed and illustrated above. Jacobs did not exaggerate in the least when he wrote that "as a treasury of the pure gold of God's Word, and the sanctified experience of all preceding ages of the Church, it stands next to our Confessions among the classics of Lutheranism."[53]

And let it be reiterated that in perhaps no generation since the *Examen* was written has its testimony to the objective validity of religious knowledge been more needed than in ours. Why is this so? We shall conclude this paper with Screwtape's description of Satanic strategy:[54]

> The use of Fashions in thought is to distract the attention of men from their real dangers. We direct the fashionable outcry of each generation against those vices of which it is least in danger and fix its approval on the virtue nearest to that vice which we are trying to make endemic. The game is to have them all running about with fire extinguishers whenever there is a flood, and all crowding to that side of the boat which is already nearly gunwale under. Thus we make it fashionable to expose the dangers of enthusiasm at the very moment when they are all really becoming worldly and lukewarm; a century later, when we are really making them all Byronic and drunk with emotion, the fashionable outcry is directed against the dangers of the mere "understanding."

---

[51] *Ibid.*, pp. 72-73, 643.
[52] *Ibid.*, p. 72. Today even Lutherans sometimes employ intinction in hospitals and army camps (*ibid.*, p. 648), but obviously for reasons of expediency rather than out of liturgical principle!
[53] "Martin Chemnitz and the Council of Trent," p. 399. On p. 412 Jacobs makes this added observation concerning Chemnitz's *Examen*: "So thorough is the treatment of every subject which it undertakes, and so little does the personal mingle in the discussion, that the value of the book is not to be measured by its merits as a controversial work. Were the Roman Catholic Church blotted out of existence, the faithful study of this most masterly refutation of her doctrine, would not be of less importance, as an exhibition of the pure faith of God's word."
[54] C. S. Lewis, *The Screwtape Letters*, pp. 128-29.

Bibliography

Bungener, L. F. *History of the Council of Trent, from the French with the Author's last Corrections and Additions communicated to the Translator.* Edinburgh: Constable, 1852.

Calvin, John. *Tracts & Treatises.* Trans. Henry Beveridge. Reprint ed. Eugene, OR: Wipf & Stock, 2002. 3 vols. Vol. 3: *Antidote to the Council of Trent.*

Canons and Decrees of the Council of Trent: Original Text with English Translation. Ed. H. J. Schroeder. St. Louis, MO: Herder, 1941.

Chemnitz, Martin. *Examen Concilii Tridentini.* Ed. Eduard Preuss. Berlin: Schlawitz, 1861.

Chemnitz, Martin. *Examination of the Council of Trent.* Trans. Henry Hassold and Fred Kramer. 4 vols. St. Louis, MO: Concordia, 1971-1986.

Chemnitz, Martin. *Loci Theologici.* Ed. and trans. J. A. O. Preus. St. Louis, MO: Concordia, 1989. (Contains Parts I-III of Chemnitz's *Loci*, with omissions within those Parts of *Loci* 9-12, 20-21, and the concluding Theses to Part III. Concordia later issued a more complete version as Vols. 7-8 in their series "Chemnitz's Works.")

Chemnitz, Martin. *The Two Natures in Christ.* Ed. and trans. J. A. O. Preus. St. Louis, MO: Concordia, 1971.

Dejob, Charles. *De l'influence du Concile de Trente sur la littérature et les beaux-arts chez les peuples catholiques.* Reprint ed. Whitefish, MT: Kessinger, 2009.

Döllinger, Johann Joseph Ignaz von. *The Pope and the Council*, by Janus. Reprint ed. n.p.: BiblioLife, 2009.

Froude, James Anthony. *Lectures on the Council of Trent, delivered at Oxford, 1892-3.* London: Longmans, Green, 1896.

Jedin, Hubert. *Papal Legate at the Council of Trent: Cardinal Seripando.* St. Louis, MO: Herder, 1947.

Krauth, Charles Porterfield. *The Conservative Reformation and Its Theology.* Philadelphia: J. B. Lippincott, 1871.

Lewis, C. S. *The Screwtape Letters.* New York: Macmillan, 1944.

Mendham, Joseph. *Memoirs of the Council of Trent.* London: James Duncan, 1834.

Mumm, Reinhard. *Die Polemik des Martin Chemnitz gegen das Konzil von Trient.* Reprint ed. Whitefish, MT: Kessinger, 2009. Part I (1905).

Pallavicini, Sforza. *Histoire du Concile du Trente*. Montrouge: Migne, 1844-1845. 3 vols. (Translated from the original Italian version.)

Pelikan, Jaroslav. *From Luther to Kierkegaard*. St. Louis, MO: Concordia, 1950.

Perkins, Mary. *At Your Ease in the Catholic Church*. New York: Sheed & Ward, 1938.

Randall, John Henry, Jr. *The Making of the Modern Mind*. Rev. ed. Boston: Houghton Mifflin, 1940.

Reed, Luther D. *The Lutheran Liturgy*. Philadelphia: Muhlenberg Press, 1947.

Sarpi, Paolo. *The History of the Council of Trent*. London: Maycock, 1676.

Schaff, Philip (ed.). *The Creeds of Christendom*. 6th ed. New York: Harper & Row, 1931. 3 vols.

Schmid, Heinrich. *The Doctrinal Theology of the Evangelical Lutheran Church, Verified from the Original Sources*. Ed. and trans. Charles A. Hay and Henry E. Jacobs. 5th ed. rev. Philadelphia: United Lutheran Publication House, 1899.

5. An Historical Study of the *"Dignus Est Agnus"* Canticle

Unlike such familiar canticles as the *Magnificat* and the *Te Deum*, the *Dignus Est Agnus* poses a challenging and perplexing historical problem. Detailed historical information, together with further bibliographical leads, may easily be found by anyone wishing to study the more well-known canticles (see, for example, the *Catholic Encyclopedia*, Grove's *Dictionary of Music and Musicians*, Julian's *Dictionary of Hymnology*). Such sources, however, yield no data whatsoever on the *Dignus Est Agnus*.[1] Further checking reveals that *Dignus* is not used in the liturgies of the Roman Catholic, Greek Orthodox, or Anglican Communions.[2]

From the standpoint of the present-day liturgical situation, therefore, the *Dignus Est Agnus* is a peculiarly Lutheran canticle. But when we turn to Lutheran sources of information, we are again faced with a dearth of concrete data on this canticle. The 1917-1918 *Common Service Book* includes the text of the *Dignus*.[3] The general rubrics inform us that in Matins and Vespers the *Dignus* is "proper during the Easter season and Ascensiontide" and "may also be used during the Trinity-season," and that this or another canticle or hymn of praise may be substituted for the *Gloria in Excelsis* in the service except on "Festival Days or when there is a Communion."[4] "The Explanation of The Common Service," however, does not refer once to this canticle. The *Lutheran Hymnal* of the Synodical Conference gives the text of the *Dignus*, but permits its use only in weekday Matins.[5] The handbook to this hymnal deals only with the historical background of the hymns that are found in the hymnal, so again we are uncertain as to when or why the *Dignus* appeared in Lutheran liturgy.[6]

---

[1] The *Dignus* also fails to appear in Herzog and Hauck's *Realencyklopaedie* (and its English abridgment, the *New Schaff-Herzog*); Meusel's *Kirchliches Handlexikon*; *Die Religion in Geschichte und Gegenwart*; Hastings' *Encyclopedia of Religion and Ethics*; the *Encyclopaedia Britannica*.

[2] Note, for example, the absence of any reference to this canticle in Pierre Batiffol, *History of the Roman Breviary*, translated from the third French edition, ed. Atwell M. Y. Baylay (London: Longmans and New York: Green, 1912), W. K. Lowther Clarke, ed., *Liturgy and Worship: A Companion to the Prayer Books of the Anglican Communion* (New York: Macmillan, 1932), or the *Hymnal of the Protestant Episcopal Church in the United States of America* (New York: Church Pension Fund, 1940, 1943).

[3] The *Dignus* is the final canticle of twelve included there; it may be found on page 215 of the *Common Service Book of the Lutheran Church*, authorized by the United Lutheran Church in America (Philadelphia: Board of Publication of the ULCA, 1917, 1918).

[4] *Common Service Book*, 291-292.

[5] *Lutheran Hymnal*, authorized by the Synods Constituting the Evangelical Lutheran Synodical Conference of North America (St. Louis: Concordia Publishing House, 1941), 122, 34.

[6] *The Handbook to the Lutheran Hymnal*, comp. W. G. Polack (St. Louis: Concordia Publishing

Luther D. Reed, in his classic *The Lutheran Liturgy*, repeats the information given in the *Common Service Book* on the use of this canticle, and provides as further data on the canticle only the fact that neither the Roman Breviary nor the Common Service text of 1888 contains it (the impression is given that the *Dignus* was first added in the *Common Service Book* of 1917).[7] Strodach makes the tantalizing statement, "It is one of the later Canticles," but gives no authority for this assertion, nor any indication of what he means by "later."[8] Neither Horn, in *Outlines of Liturgies*, nor Alt, in *Der Christliche Cultus*, makes any reference to the *Dignus Est Agnus*.[9] The same is true of R. Morris Smith, who claimed "to trace the origin and give a partial history of the various parts of these [the minor] services."[10]

Moreover, the liturgical volume in the Philadelphia edition of *Luther's Works* gives no indication that the Reformer was acquainted with the *Dignus Est Agnus*.[11] An examination of Sehling revealed that the *Dignus* is not employed in the church orders of the Lutheran Church in the sixteenth century.[12] A study of Section V of Horn's article on "The Lutheran Sources of the Common Service" confirmed Sehling's omission of references to the *Dignus*.[13] A check of various works by Wilhelm Löhe for some mention of the *Dignus Est Agnus* turned out to be a blind alley as well.[14]

In the face of such an absence of information, is it possible for us to discover when and how and by whom the *Dignus Est Agnus* entered the liturgy of the Lutheran Church? Moreover, can we justify the continued use of this canticle

---

House, 1942).

[7] Luther D. Reed, *The Lutheran Liturgy: A Study of the Common Service of the Lutheran Church in America* (Philadelphia: Muhlenburg Press, 1947), 381, 413.

[8] Paul Zeller Strodach, *A Manual on Worship*, rev. ed. (Philadelphia: Muhlenberg Press, 1946), 276.

[9] Edward T. Horn, *Outlines of Liturgics* (Philadelphia: Lutheran Publication Society, 1910); Heinrich Alt, *Der Christliche Cultus*, 2 volumes (Berlin: Müller, 1851-1860).

[10] R. Morris Smith, "The Sources of the Minor Services," *Lutheran Liturgical Association: Memoirs*, ed. Luther D. Reed (Pittsburgh: Lutheran Liturgical Association, 1906), 2:35-56, at 38.

[11] I have checked all the references under "Matins" and "Vespers" in the index at the back of this volume. The heading "Dignus Est Agnus," needless to say, does not appear in the index. Under "Canticles" in the index one reads "see Benedictus; Nunc Dimittis; Magnificat; Te Deum."

[12] The only church order to mention canticles other than the four listed in the previous note is that of Pomerania (1535), which gives a total of ten canticles, none of which happens to be the *Dignus*. Emil Sehling, *Die evangelischen Kirchenordnungen des XVI. Jahrhunderts* (Leipzig: O.R. Reisland, 1902-1913).

[13] Edward T. Horn, "The Lutheran Sources of the Common Service," *Lutheran Quarterly* 21 (1891): 239-268.

[14] Those responsible for the Common Service relied heavily on Löhe, who lived 1808-1872. For a recent biography of Löhe, see David Ratke, *Confession and Mission, Word and Sacrament: The Ecclesial Theology of Wilhelm Löhe* (St. Louis: Concordia Publishing House, 2001).

or its variations in Lutheran worship? These two questions are integrally connected, for liturgical form is determined not only by scriptural content, but also by historical usage in the church, which is the body of Christ. The remainder of this paper will be devoted to answering these questions.

The Entrance of the *Dignus Est Agnus* into Lutheran Liturgical Usage

Entrance into American Lutheran Liturgy

As pointed out above, the *Dignus Est Agnus* is present in the *Common Service Book* (1917), but was not included in the Common Service of 1888.[15] The first question we face, therefore, is: Why was it included in the former but not the latter? In a significant article in the *Lutheran Church Review* for July 1901, Luther D. Reed informs us that the General Council *Church Book* of 1900 "furnishes twelve Canticles, which are not given in the Standard edition, except as some of them appear in the various Services."[16] Neither the United Synod of the South (which reprinted the Common Service exactly) nor the General Synod made a similar inclusion. This section of twelve canticles (which of course includes the *Dignus Est Agnus*) did not, however, appear in the General Council *Church Book* for the first time in 1900. The editions of the *Church Book* of 1868, 1875, 1891 and 1892 also contain the twelve canticles section (and therefore the *Dignus*). In these editions, the *Dignus* may be used only in Matins, in the (Morning) Service (as an alternative for the *Gloria in Excelsis*), or in the old "Evening Service" (which was later dropped from the hymnal entirely). The Vesper service permits only the *Magnificat* or *Nunc Dimittis*.

Who in the General Council was responsible for the addition of the *Dignus* to the *Church Book*, and why was the addition of this and other canticles made? Two quotations from an article by Henry E. Jacobs in the *Lutheran Church Review* offer suggestions toward an answer:

> The General Council Committee, in preparing the text of the edition of the Church Book published in 1892, after the death of Dr. Schmucker [Oct. 15, 1888], was persuaded in a few instances by several of its older members not to make changes in the text of 1868 until it was certain that the Common

---

[15] The Common Service was developed by a Joint Committee of the General Council, the General Synod, and the United Synod of the South—the bodies that merged to form the United Lutheran Church in America (ULCA) on November 14, 1918.
[16] Luther D. Reed, "The Standard Manuscript of the Common Service and Variata Editions," *Lutheran Church Review* 20 (1901): 469. See also 460, 472.

Service would actually have wide use in the other Bodies. ... The prediction was even made in the discussion within the committee of the General Council, that there would not be over a half dozen English congregations in the General Council in which the Vesper Service would be introduced.

A great change in the methods of the committee followed the death of Dr. Schmucker. The "copy" ready for the printer, which "fell from his hands" as he died, was never published in the form in which he had left it. ... Dr. Seiss, as chairman of the editorial committee, applied his industrious energy and his acknowledged gifts as a writer, to a revision of parts of the book. ... With his classmate, Dr. Schmucker, as his critic and counselor, the contributions of Dr. Seiss to the Church Book were of decided importance. But associated only with those who were less free to offer their objections, his influence has introduced into the issues of the Church Book since 1892 some elements that are individual rather than such as really were determined by the Church. This has been noticed above in the reference made to the variations of the Church Book of 1892 from the standard text of the Common Service ... as a comparison with the original text, as determined by the committee, in the *Kirchenbuch* will show.[17]

So: why the incorporation of the canticle and who was responsible for it? Again we quote Jacobs: "It seems, therefore, as though the change from the liturgy of 1860 to the form in which it is found in the Church Book [of 1868] was determined principally by the influence of Dr. Krauth, while the chief agent in the preparation of the scheme of details, thus outlined, was always, and to the close of his life, Dr. Schmucker."[18] Dr. Schmucker, moreover, became the leading light on the committee appointed in 1866 to prepare the *Kirchenbuch* (1877).[19] "By his tact, he reconciled conflicting interests, and brought order out of confusion; and by his activity, at the same time, on both the English and German committees, gave assurance that the two books would harmonize."[20] As we have already seen, the General Council *Church Book* published after Dr. Schmucker's death showed variations from the text of the Common Service on whose committee he had been a most influential member. The *Kirchenbuch*, which was completed under Dr. Schmucker's guidance, shows accurately the liturgy he would also have desired in the English *Church Book* (1891 and

---

[17] Henry E. Jacobs, "The Making of the Church Book," *Lutheran Church Review* 31 (October 1912): 615, 618-619.
[18] Jacobs, "Making of the Church Book," 612.
[19] *Kirchenbuch für Evangelisch-Lutherische Gemeinden*. Hrsg. von der Allgemeinen Versammlung der Evangelisch-Lutherischen Kirche in Nord Amerika (Philadelphia: United Lutheran Publication House, 1877).
[20] Jacobs, "Making of the Church Book," 613.

1892).[21] The *Kirchenbuch* does not include the canticle section. Moreover, there is no rubric permitting the use—either in the Service, the Matins, or the Vespers—of an alternative canticle section. Clearly, then, Beale Schmucker was not the source for the inclusion of the *Dignus*.[22]

Who, then, was? It appears that Dr. Joseph Augustus Seiss (1823-1904) was chiefly responsible for the entrance of the *Dignus Est Agnus* into the *Church Book* (and therefore into the *Common Service Book*).[23] Three further items of evidence support this claim. First, the "Additional Prayers" in the "Pulpit Edition" of the *Church Book*:

> To the individual efforts of Dr. Seiss, and not to the work of the Church Book Committee, the so-called "Pulpit Edition" of the Church Book and its "Additional Prayers" must be ascribed. At Erie, in 1897, the preparation of this edition was taken out of the hands of the Church Book Committee and given to the Board of Publication. With this authority an entire pamphlet of forty-four pages, which Dr. Seiss had compiled from various unknown sources and published a few years before, was bodily transferred to the Church Book without submission to the Church Book Committee or revision of any kind whatsoever by it or any of its members.[24]

If this could happen with numerous prayers, why should we doubt an innovation on Dr. Seiss's part with regard to a few canticles?

Second, certain statements by Dr. Theodore E. Schmauk in his obituary notice for Dr. Seiss:

> It is the common impression that the General Council Church Book in its liturgical portions are almost entirely the work of Dr. B. M. Schmucker, and, in its hymnological portion, the work of Dr. Seiss. Almost the reverse is the case as far as Dr. Seiss is concerned. ... It is quite true that ... improvements and alterations were made as a result of their [the Committee's] united consideration. But the moving mind and the formative hand were those of Dr. Seiss. ... It will be remembered that when Dr. Schmucker died, nothing but the Morning Service and what belonged to it was complete. ... Though we have never been able to give complete assent to all the principles of Dr. Seiss

---

[21] "The text found in the *Kirchenbuch* must be used as the standard to determine the ultimate decision of the General Council upon the recommendation of the committee under his [Dr. Schmucker's] guidance." Jacobs, "Making of a Church Book," 617.

[22] See *Kirchenbuch* 5, 22, 27; compare 276.

[23] For biographical information on Seiss, see Lawrence R. Rast Jr., "Joseph A. Seiss and the Lutheran Church in America," Ph.D. diss., Vanderbilt University, 2003; Samuel R. Zeiser, "Joseph Augustus Seiss: Popular Nineteenth-century Lutheran Pastor and Premillennialist," Ph.D. diss., Drew University, 2001. I take this opportunity to thank Dr. Rast for his assistance in researching the present chapter.

[24] Jacobs, "Making of the Church Book," 619.

... and, on important points we take the position of the *Kirchenbuch*, yet it is our firm belief that ... the present English Church Book of the General Council, which was the pioneer work in the field, owes much to Dr. Seiss in substance, and more in form, than to any other writer.[25]

Finally, the *Dignus Est Agnus* is taken entirely from the Revelation of St. John, and Dr. Seiss was almost certainly the greatest Lutheran commentator on this Bible book during the nineteenth century. Thirty-thousand sets of his three volume *Lectures on the Apocalypse* had been published by 1917, and the work is still in print. Although chiliastic in point of view, this book is even today held in high esteem in many quarters. The writing of this book spanned fifteen years (1865-1880) of Dr. Seiss's life, and would obviously have influenced him in areas other than the strictly expository.[26]

The Dignus Est Agnus *and Continental Lutheran Liturgy*

We should also briefly face the problem of a possibly continental liturgical origin for the *Dignus*. It seems doubtful that American Lutherans — or even an individual American Lutheran — would have introduced this canticle into our liturgy without continental tradition favoring such action. Two possible continental origins suggest themselves, and we can only make cursory mention of them here.

The first is the Western Breviary tradition. Clarke writes: "The Monastic Breviary, and the French diocesan Breviaries issued in the seventeenth and eighteenth centuries, are rich in canticles."[27] But note that Batiffol nowhere mentions the *Dignus*.

The second origin is that of individual European Lutheran liturgists and church musicians of the Reformation period, such as Lukas Lossius (d. 1582) or Johann Spangenberg (d. 1550). Archer and Reed mention both of these men in their preface to *The Psalter and Canticles Pointed for Chanting*, which contains a musical setting for the *Dignus*.[28] Wackernagel's bibliographic description of

---

[25] Theodore E. Schmauk, "The Death of Dr. Seiss," *Lutheran Church Review* 23 (July 1904): 619-622.

[26] Where Dr. Seiss himself got the notion of introducing into the Church Book the *Dignus* (and, for that matter, the whole twelve canticle sections) is a question the answer to which we cannot attempt to give here. Rast argues that the incipient form of the *Dignus Est Agnus* appeared already in the hymnal that Seiss developed for St. John congregation in Philadelphia in 1859, the *Evangelical Psalmist*. See Rast, "Joseph Seiss," 154-159.

[27] Clarke, *Liturgy and Worship*, 273. See also Reed, *The Lutheran Liturgy*, 381, 354.

[28] Harry G. Archer and Luther D. Reed, eds., *The Psalter and Canticles Pointed for Chanting* (New York: Christian Literature Company, 1897), ix, x.

Lossius' four volume *Psalmodia* (Nürnberg, 1553 edition) indicates that the entire second book is devoted to "cantica veteris ecclesiae selecta de praecipuis festis sanctorum Jesu Christi."[29] It certainly seems more likely that the Lutherans who first introduced the *Dignus* in this country would have read Lossius than that they should have been influenced by Roman or Gallican Breviaries.

Historical Justification for the Continued Use of the *Dignus Est Agnus* in Lutheran Worship

Regardless of the somewhat individualistic manner in which the *Dignus* canticle entered the Common Service Book tradition, and in spite of the absence of this canticle from the 1888 text of the Common Service, I believe that sufficient historical evidence exists for its retention in succeeding Lutheran service books. I base this contention on four arguments.

First, Rietschel considers that the very verses in the Apocalypse which make up the *Dignus Est Agnus* are in the nature of New Testament Psalms, and he associates these verses with the *Magnificat*, the *Benedictus*, and the *Nunc Dimittis* passages.[30] Weizsäcker goes even further, and states concerning these and a few other similar verses in the Apocalypse: "The separate short songs ... fit into one another like strophes of a complete ode."[31] He says that they may be "traditional songs," and quotes the famous line from Pliny's letter to Trajan, "Carmenque Christo quasi Deo dicere secum invicem."[32] Thus from a liturgical standpoint the *Dignus Est Agnus* seems to have a precedent in very early church usage.

Second, even if the *Dignus* were not used in the Lutheran Church during the early years of the Reformation, "the rubrical permission to use another Canticle or Hymn" for the *Gloria in Excelsis* in the Service "except on occasions when a full Service is desirable, accords with Lutheran usage" during the Reformation period.[33] This being true, there has been a place in Lutheran liturgy ever since the Reformation for alternative canticles having the quality of the *Dignus*.

---

[29] Philipp Wackernagel, *Bibliographie zur Geschichte des deutschen Kirchenliedes im XVI. Jahrhundert* (Frankfurt: Heyder und Zimmer, 1855), 253-254.
[30] Georg Rietschel, *Lehrbuch der Liturgik*, 2. neubearb. Aufl. von Paul Graff, 2 vols. (Göttingen: Vandenhoeck und Ruprecht, 1951 [Bd. I], 1952 [Bd. II]), 201.
[31] Carl von Weizsäcker, *The Apostolic Age of the Christian Church*, vol. 2, trans. from the 2nd, rev. ed. by James Millar (New York: G. P. Putnam's Sons, 1895), 260.
[32] Weizsäcker, *The Apostolic Age*, 262.
[33] Horn, "The Lutheran Sources of the Common Service," 251.

Third, even from the standpoint of the Common Service tradition the use of the *Dignus* can be defended. Reed may have written in 1901 concerning the Common Service of 1888, "every variation from the standard form is alike unpardonable," but even before this (in 1897) he had set the *Dignus* and other canticles to music in his Psalter and Canticles.[34] He refers to this work frequently, moreover, in his later publications.[35] The *Dignus Est Agnus*, regardless of the rather arbitrary way it entered the Church Book liturgy, was here to stay. In 1917 the same Lutheran bodies that had approved the Common Service of 1888 (without the *Dignus*) placed their stamp of approval on the Common Service Book (which includes this canticle).[36] Here we have an excellent example of the ongoing force of a Spirit-motivated tradition in its continual process of refining and perfecting.

Finally, we note the tremendous value of having a canticle of Johannine authorship in Lutheran liturgy. Our Church has always had at the center of its theology the Lamb of God who shed his blood upon the Cross to save a fallen race; it is therefore only fitting that this sentiment should be expressed in canticle form for use in our services of worship.

---

[34] Reed, The Common Service and Variata Editions," 472.
[35] See Archer and Reed, eds., *The Choral Service Book* (Philadelphia: General Council Publication Board, 1901); Harry G. Archer and Luther D. Reed, eds., *The Music of the Responses* (Philadelphia: General Council Publication Board, 1903); and Harry G. Archer and Luther D. Reed, eds., *Season Vespers* (Philadelphia: General Council Publication Board, 1905).
[36] See Strodach, *A Manual on Worship*, 188.

Appendix

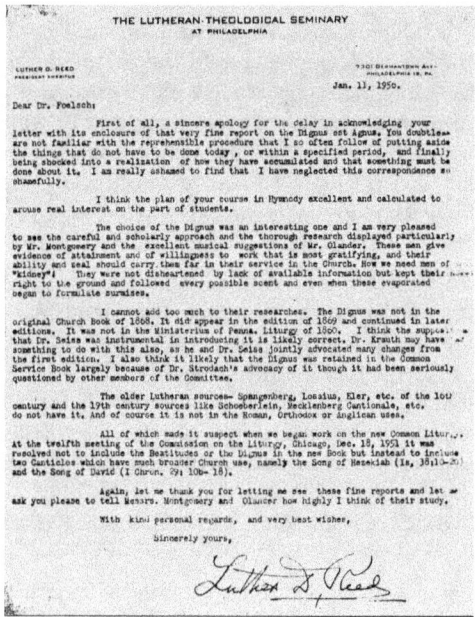

The Lutheran Theological Seminary at Philadelphia

Luther D. Reed
President Emeritus

7301 Germantown Ave.
Philadelphia 18, PA
Jan. 11, 1956.

Dear Dr. Foelsch:

First of all, a sincere apology for the delay in acknowledging your letter with its enclosure of that very fine report on the Dignus est Agnus. You doubtless are not familiar with the reprehensible procedure that I so often follow of putting aside the things that do not have to be done today, or within a specified period, and finally being shocked into a realization of how they have accumulated and that something must be done about it. I am really ashamed to find that I have neglected this correspondence so shamefully.

I think the plan of your course in Hymnody excellent and calculated to arouse real interest on the part of students.

The choice of the Dignus was an interesting one and I am very pleased to see the careful and scholarly approach and the thorough research displayed particularly by Mr. Montgomery and the excellent musical suggestions of Mr. Olander. These men give evidence of attainment and of willingness to work that is most gratifying, and their ability and zeal should carry them far in their service in the Church. How we need men of their "kidney"! They were not disheartened by lack of available information but kept their noses right to the ground and followed every possible scent and even when these evaporated began to formulate surmises.

I cannot add too much to their researches. The Dignus was not in the original Church Book of 1868. It did appear in the edition of 1869 and continued in later editions. It was not in the Ministerium of Penna. Liturgy of 1860. I think the supposition that Dr. Seiss was instrumental in introducing it is likely correct. Dr. Krauth may have had something to do with this also, as he and Dr. Seiss jointly advocated many changes from the first edition. I also think it likely that the Dignus was retained in the Common Service Book largely because of Dr. Strodach's advocacy of it though it had been seriously questioned by other members of the Committee.

The older Lutheran sources- Spangenberg, Lossius, Eler, etc. of the 16th century and the 19th century sources like Schoeberlein, Mecklenberg Cantionale, etc. do not have it. And of course it is not in the Roman, Orthodox or Anglican uses.

All of which made it suspect when we began work on the new Common Liturgy. At the twelfth meeting of the Commission on the Liturgy, Chicago, Dec. 18, 1951 it was resolved not to include the Beatitudes or the Dignus in the new Book but instead to include two Canticles which have much broader Church use, namely the Song of Hezekiah (Is. 38:10-20) and the Song of David (I Chron. 29:10b-18).

Again, let me thank you for letting me see these fine reports and let me ask you please to tell Messrs. Montgomery and Olander how highly I think of their study.

With kind personal regards, and very best wishes,
Sincerely yours,

Luther D. Reed

6. Robert Preus (1924-1995)

I very much enjoy good science fiction. One perennial science-fiction theme is that of cloning: just suppose that we were able to clone an individual, thereby reduplicating him or her in a future generation ... To be sure, problems would arise, such as the mammoth interest the said individual's bank account would have accrued over the years! In any case, if cloning were possible scientifically, the theologian first on my list to clone would be Robert Preus.

The remarks to follow should not be construed as a mini-biography; others are in a far better position than I to provide such. What I want to do here is, rather, to give just a few of the many reasons why Robert Preus is the ideal candidate for cloning — or, putting it otherwise, why he stands as an archetypal theologian and churchman for our time. What follows will necessarily be personal, and anything but politically correct, but, in our post-modern era, how can one argue against "my telling my story" where Robert is concerned?

A serious theologian. Robert never wavered in his commitment to the faith once delivered to the saints. When he was alive (and this applies equally to the present moment), there was staggering pressure to liberalise, and that pressure did not by any means come only from ecumenical and broad-church theologians. Just as evangelicalism saw Fuller Theological Seminary remove biblical inerrancy from its doctrinal statement, and the Eerdmans Publishing Company shift its emphasis to Barthian and mediating books, so even the Concordia Theological Seminary, St. Louis, found itself with a president — John Tietjen — and a majority of faculty members who were prepared to embrace so-called "higher criticism" of the Bible and a relativistic approach to the Lutheran Confessions.

Robert recognised that to move in these directions was to destroy classic Lutheranism and, indeed, to remove the foundations of Christian faith itself. The four essays he contributed to the second volume of my *Crisis in Lutheran Theology,* considered by many to have had a decisive impact on the Seminex controversy, bear eloquent witness to his stand in this regard. Here is a sample: "Let us build on the foundation of the apostles and prophets, on the authoritative and inerrant Word of God, and let us resolve to dig deeper and deeper into this word of eternal life which, as Luther said, is like the swaddling clothes of Jesus; and we will not fail to find the Savior lying there. This is the only answer to our present dilemma and to every problem facing us."

A serious intellectual. For Robert, the anti-intellectualism so typical of many conservative evangelicals was simply incomprehensible. Never did he set the heart against the head or tolerate the sloppiness of those who unthinkingly and lazily reproduce sermons from the *Concordia Pulpit.* Robert benefited from a solid classical education: the biblical languages, German, and a fluent reading knowledge of Latin. The latter gave him access to the neglected world of the 17th century Lutheran systematicians, which he made his special province. The result was the production of two works of permanent importance: *The Inspiration of Scripture: A Study of the Theology of the Seventeenth Century Lutheran Dogmaticians* and *The Theology of Post-Reformation Lutheranism*. In these studies, he operated in depth, refusing to drive an unscholarly wedge (as Jaroslav Pelikan did in *From Luther to Kierkegaard*) between an allegedly "existential" Luther and "fundamentalist" 17th century orthodox theologians. He rightly saw that the authors of the *Formula of Concord* and their successors were simply expressing in a more systematic way the theology they derived from Luther himself—just as the creedal theologians of Nicaea had done no more than to systematise the Trinitarian doctrine they found in the teachings of Jesus himself.

And, in diametric contrast to televangelists and the producers of trivial devotional literature so rampant in conservative religious circles, Robert put his stamp of approval on formal academic study and quality university degree programmes. He was not content with one doctorate—even from as distinguished a university as Edinburgh. I had little trouble persuading him to devote a sabbatical year to taking a second doctorate in Strasbourg—no little accomplishment, since it involved tackling yet another language (French) and stuffing his wife and large brood of children into our favourite building in the university quarter!

A serious appreciation of Protestant evangelicalism. In general, the stronger one's own denominational connection, the less one is willing to make contact with the life of other churches, even those similarly strong theologically. Thus, in my experience, Southern Baptists tend to limit their theological contacts and reading to Southern Baptist circles. The same is certainly true within the Lutheran Church-Missouri Synod. Even professors at Missouri Synod colleges and seminaries are, in general, woefully ignorant of what is going on in evangelical but non-Lutheran settings, where, however, biblical inerrancy is generally of utmost importance and the scholarly productions are of considerable importance.

Robert, however, did not suffer from this kind of myopia. He was active in the International Council for Biblical Inerrancy; he spoke frequently at evangelical occasions and published outside the narrow confines of his own denomination. In doing this, he never compromised Lutheran teaching; what he did do was to demonstrate in his own person that Lutheranism does not have to be a narrow, ethnic phenomenon. For many evangelicals, Robert was a kind of revelation: they had thought that the only orthodox Protestant theologies were Calvinism and Arminianism. Robert offered them a third way—one far more in accord with the thrust of biblical revelation. A single illustration: my late, dear friend Walter Martin, author of *The Kingdom of the Cults,* became a kind of baptistic Lutheran through contacts with Robert and myself.

A serious appreciation of high culture. The last time I had contact with Robert was in London when his wife and he were visiting there. My wife and I took them to my club, The Athenaeum. This club, founded in the 19th century, has been the haunt of the cultured and boasts a slew of Nobel prize winners amongst its membership. A century ago, Thackeray and Dickens finally resolved their longstanding feud at the foot of the monumental staircase leading to one of the finest private libraries in England. Robert was in seventh heaven. I thought back to a time in Strasbourg, years before, when Robert and I invited a visiting Missouri Synod seminary professor to dine with us at a fine restaurant in Strasbourg, and the professor arrived in the dress of a lumberjack and displayed all the characteristics of the typical "ugly American." Robert was the diametric opposite: a gentleman in the best sense of the term—and thus a model for his students and acquaintances. For him, the gospel had nothing to fear from culture; quite the opposite. One did not need to be a bumpkin to be follower of our Lord.

Not politically correct, but faithful to his church. During his later years, Robert put up with a most distressing treatment from seminary colleagues, board members, and the administration of his denomination. Through all of this he never wavered in his commitment to his students or to the grass roots of the church at large. Personally, if I had had a modicum of the difficulties he faced while at the helm of the Concordia Seminary, Ft. Wayne, I would have contacted *mafiosi* friends in Sicily and had a number of people relegated permanently to the foundations of public buildings. Robert's admirable level of sanctification was illustrated by his dogged determination to do the right thing, and in this he was ultimately vindicated. He had every reason to dump the church that treated him so shabbily, but this he did not do. He preferred to suffer indignity rather than to contribute in any way to schism.

Along similar lines (and this takes us back to what we said at the outset), Robert stood for the truth and did not really care if by doing so he brought criticism down upon his own head. He saw, for example, that Herman Otten's *Lutheran* (now *Christian*) *News* was the key element in conveying an understanding of Seminex errors to the attention of the laity of the Lutheran Church-Missouri Synod. True, Otten was just to the right of Ghenghis Khan politically and socially, and was thoroughly hated by the Synod's bureaucrats (since he had the effrontery to call a spade a spade and even to criticise the St. Louis Lutheran "papacy"), but the importance of the periodical meant that Robert wrote frequently for it and refused to shove Otten into outer darkness as did many who were embarrassed by him. This took real courage on Robert's part—but, where courage was concerned, he never faltered.

Can we find theologians like Robert today? Very rarely. When one does find them, their professional lives are not generally within denominational structures, for institutions do not readily tolerate high purpose, high scholarship, high culture, and—perhaps most troubling—non-politically correct gadflys on the collective, institutional rump. Maybe this is why our church institutions are so often pallid, lifeless, and seem to reflect the lowest common denominator. Surely our seminary students deserve the kind of role model Robert provided. How badly we all need Robert Preus and his ilk!

Ah, for successful cloning …

Part Seven
Literature and the Aesthetic in Christ's Service

1. Chesterton the Apologist

> The sages have a hundred maps to give
> That trace their crawling cosmos like a tree,
> They rattle reason out through many a sieve
> That stores the sand and lets the gold go free:
> And all these things are less than dust to me
> Because my name is Lazarus and I live.
> — *G. K. Chesterton (1922)*

When we think of Chesterton today, we think of Father Brown, the quintessential priest-detective. But, like Conan Doyle, who believed his more serious writings were more important than his Sherlock Holmes stories, Chesterton's central thrust (even in the persona of Father Brown) was elsewhere. At heart, Chesterton was a controversialist, or, better, an apologist. What he really wanted to achieve was to bring his contemporaries (and us!) back to sanity by showing the truth of classic Christian orthodoxy.

True, he seems to discount his apologetic role. In one of his most important books, *Orthodoxy*, he claims that he is doing spiritual autobiography, not apologetics. He goes so far as to declare: "I never read a line of Christian apologetics." But in effect this put him in the same category of originality as Wittgenstein, who refused to read traditional philosophy and thereby created something truly original himself.

Chesterton's apologetic impact

The proof of the pudding in Chesterton's case is the influence he has had on contemporary and subsequent defenders of the faith. Étienne Gilson, the great medievalist, said that *Orthodoxy* was the best apologetic the 20th century had yet produced. When Chesterton died, Charles Williams of the Oxford *Inklings* lamented, "The last of my Lords is dead." In his obituary for Chesterton, T. S. Eliot stated flatly that Chesterton "did more than any man of his time" to "maintain the existence of the [Christian] minority in the modern world."

Chesterton's impact on C. S. Lewis and J. R. R. Tolkien was immense. When Lewis asserts concerning the gospel story that "here and here only in all time the myth must become fact; the Word, flesh; God, Man," and Tolkien declares, "this story is supreme; and it is true. Art has been verified. Legend and history have met and fused," they are echoing Chesterton:

> "In answer to the historical query of why it was accepted, and is accepted, I answer for millions of others in my reply: because it fits the lock; because it is like life. It is one among many stories; only it happens to be a true story. It is one among many philosophies; only it happens to be the truth."

And when C. S. Lewis, in the final volume of the *Narnian Chronicles,* has the children find in Narnia companions they thought they would never see again and learn that in God's kingdom "no good thing is ever lost," he picks up from where Chesterton left off:

> "Paradise is somewhere and not anywhere, is something and not anything. And I would not be so very much surprised if the house in heaven had a real green lamp-post after all."

Chesterton's attack on enemy territory

Chesterton's influence apologetically was—and is—due to his special approach to the defence of the faith. Several elements come together to produce a unique apologetic style.

First, though the word "apologetics" means literally "defence," Chesterton was never defensive. As one commentator put it, he "wrestled the initiative from the skeptics and presented the historic faith upon a note of triumphant challenge."

Thus, Chesterton goes after the fallacious and irrational presuppositions of unbelief, showing, often by way of epigrammatic gems, that the self-styled rationalist is as naked as Hans Christian Andersen's emperor in the tale of "The Emperor's Clothes." An example or two will show Chesterton's withering logic.

He observes that "the man who denies original sin believes in the Immaculate Conception of *everybody.*"

Over against the argument that we must remain agnostic and never claim that God has in fact revealed himself in this world: "We don't know enough about the unknown to know that it is unknowable."

To those who think Evolution eliminates God's creative activity: "It is absurd for the Evolutionist to complain that it is unthinkable for an admittedly unthinkable God to make everything out of nothing, and then pretend that it is more thinkable that nothing should turn itself into everything."

Chesterton never tires in pointing out the unjustified and unrecognised dogmatism of the unbeliever—in contrast with the open and attractive worldview of the orthodox Christian: "The Christian is quite free to believe that there is a considerable amount of settled order and inevitable development in the universe. But the materialist is not allowed to admit into his spotless machine the slightest speck of spiritualism or miracle."

Chesterton's concern with facts

In today's apologetic climate, there are two major schools of thought: the *Presuppositionalists* (who hold that because of sin, the unbeliever always starts from his or her presuppositions of unbelief, and that only by starting from the true presupposition of Christian truth can one achieve anything) and the *Evidentialists* (who argue that we can and must convince the unbeliever of revelational truth by presenting the factual evidence for Christian verities).

Chesterton would certainly have joined the Evidentialist camp.

True, he was concerned with the unbeliever's presuppositions—but only to demonstrate the fallacious nature of them. He did not think that believers and unbelievers operate, as it were, in hermetically sealed philosophical compartments. His apologetic echoes St Paul's concern to become "a Jew to the Jew and a Greek to the Greeks"—"all things to all persons, that by all means some might be saved."

Note how Chesterton defends the miracles of the New Testament which constitute the central evidence for the Deity of our Lord:

"Somehow or other an extraordinary idea has arisen that the disbelievers in miracles consider them coldly and fairly, while believers in miracles accept them only in connection with some dogma. The fact is quite the other way. The believers in miracles accept them (rightly or wrongly) because they have evidence for them. The disbelievers in miracles deny them (rightly or wrongly) because they have a doctrine against them."

Chesterton's point—here and in general—is that the facts are on the side of Christian orthodoxy. If one is willing to investigate those facts, the truth of the faith will become plain. It is unbelieving dogmatism which keeps a fallen race from the gospel, not an absence of factual evidence for it.

Ronald Knox, the great translator of the New Testament, noted this essential characteristic of Chesterton's apologetic as it is reflected in the methods of Father Brown: "The real secret of Father Brown is that there is nothing of the mystic about him. When he falls into a reverie—I had almost said, a brown study—the other people in the story think that he must be having an ecstasy, because he is a Catholic priest, and will proceed to solve the mystery by some kind of heaven-sent intuition. And the reader, if he is not careful, will get carried away by the same miscalculation. ... And all the time Father Brown is doing just what Poirot does; he is using his little grey cells. He is noticing something which the reader hasn't noticed, and will kick himself later for not having noticed."

Chesterton's genuineness

It has been frequently said that "one's life speaks so loudly that it is difficult to hear what one is saying." In the case of some apologists for Christian faith, their lives have been so unattractive that their arguments have not been taken seriously.

In evangelical circles, the problem has often been one of sanctimonious pietism. The spokesperson for the gospel has been so legalistic and negative that the lifestyle represented has repelled the unbeliever. For example, by "majoring in minors" and insisting on "blue-laws," the evangelical has given the impression that to become a Christian one must first of all give up all alcohol, tobacco, theatre, etc. When faced with this personal and ecclesiastical style, the unbeliever has not infrequently found it difficult to listen to what may well constitute sound apologetic arguments for the faith.

Chesterton never fell into this trap. He had a strong doctrine of Creation and saw the beauties and pleasures of this world as gifts of God. A strong aspect of his apologetic was his criticism of pietistic legalism. He devoted, for example, an entire novel to the absurdities of Prohibition (the notion that by removing alcohol from a society one somehow makes the society more moral or more religious). In *The Flying Inn*, Chesterton supposes that a Muslim prime minister is elected in England and that all Inns and Pubs are abolished as a consequence (creating a situation paralleling Prohibition in the America of the 1920s). Then the same evils arise as on the other side of the water: bureaucracy, crime, and the general increase—not decrease—of social problems. The happy-go-lucky creators of a "flying Inn," which moves from place to place just ahead of the authorities bent on stamping it out, display the kind of relaxed openness which characterises believers confident in the world in which God has placed them.

Chesterton himself enjoyed fine cuisine and wines. He dressed idiosyncratically and sometimes eccentrically. He understood the scriptural emphasis on the unique importance of each individual before God and hated all bureaucratic and totalitarian attempts at enforced conformity. He was the polar opposite of the Pharisee; and there is little doubt that his transparent genuineness powerfully reinforced the persuasiveness of his formal apologetic arguments.

Chesterton's continuing relevance today

Fine apologists such as Dorothy Sayers do not always hold the interest of the present generation owing to the time-bound nature of their creative writing (one thinks of her Lord Peter Wimsey detective stories). Does Chesterton suffer from this problem?

To be sure, no one writes in a cultural vacuum, and Chesterton, as a professional journalist, produced much ephemera which have little interest today except for scholars of his work. But the apologetic value of his contributions remains unassailable.

One of the major reasons for this is the resurfacing of theological liberalism. Many thought that two World Wars would put paid to the modernist target of much of Chesterton's apologetic salvoes. But Karl Barth's Neo-Orthodox corrective to the old liberalism, while trying to oust one theological devil, nonetheless — by refusing to critique modernism's acceptance of radical biblical criticism — opened the doors to a number of other demons: Bultmannian existentialism and demythologising; Tillich's ontological reductionism; process theologies denying God's transcendence; and, finally, the death-of-God movement.

Now the pendulum has swung back to very much the kind of theological liberalism which Chesterton opposed with such force and effectiveness. The "Jesus Seminar" and Bishop Shelby Spong seem to be Harry Emerson Fosdick and Bishop James Pike *redivivi*; and all of them, in their rationalistic refusal to take the Gospel records seriously, their presuppositionalist denial of the miraculous, and their opposition to reliable biblical revelation, place themselves directly in the sights of Chesterton's heavy artillery.

To all such deviations from classical Christian orthodoxy, Chesterton continues to speak with the clearest of voices, and we do well to listen closely to what he says:

"On the third day the friends of Christ coming at daybreak to the place found the grave empty and the stone rolled away. In varying ways they realised the new wonder; but even they hardly realised that the world had died in the night. What they were looking at was the first day of a new creation, with a new heaven and a new earth; and in a semblance of the gardener God walked again in the garden, in the cool not of the evening but the dawn."

2. Tolkien: Lord of the Occult?

J. R. R. Tolkien's popularity and readership have grown exponentially in the years since the first publication of *Lord of the Rings*. The massive success of the film trilogy has but reinforced what was already a world-wide phenomenon.[1] Indeed, Tolkien fs impact has been like the proverbial stone thrown into water, producing wave after wave of concentric rings (*double entendre*): the trilogy is the source of a whole body of contemporary fantasy literature.

One cannot enter an occult bookshop without finding Tolkien on the shelves, together with interpretations of his work which give him an honoured place among the aficionados of the New Age.[2] Thus, in a recent French edition of Robert Kirk's *The Secret Commonwealth*—a 17th century classic of fairy literature—the editor writes:

> L'adaptation cinématographique de la trilogie du *Seigneur des anneaux* de Tolkien et sa diffusion mondiale peuvent être qualifiées d'événement exceptionnel dans la perspective de la pensée *New Age,* elle-même quelque peu mise sur la touche au cours des dernières décennies, même si celles-ci relèvent déjà de l'informelle pensée de l'ère du Verseau.
>
> Tout comme les aventures de Harry Potter, celles-ci, bien sûr d'une qualité littéraire inférieure à l'oeuvre monde de Tolkien, celles de Bilbo, s'opposent aussi bien au rationalisme, à la pensée judéo-chrétienne, au néochristianisme contemporain vaguement teinté paradoxalement d'athéisme qu'à l'agnosticisme ambiant.[3]

So there we have it: *The Lord of the Rings* is an exceptional event from the perspective of the New Age and its informal predecessor, the Age of Aquarius. Like the Harry Potter books, it stands over against not only rationalism but also Judeo-Christian thought and those neo-Christian contemporary ideologies tainted by agnosticism and atheism.

---

[1] Witness the publication in 2004 of the corrected, definitive "50th anniversary edition" by Harper Collins, issued in uniform binding with a corresponding definitive "deluxe edition" of *The Hobbit*.

[2] For a particularly breathtaking example, see Terry Donaldson, Peter Pracownik, and Mike Fitzgerald, *The Lord of the Rings: Tarot Deck & Card Game* (U.S. Games Systems, 1997)—also available in a "Deluxe Gold Edition."

[3] Jean-Pierre Deloux, "Le grand retour des fées," introduction à *La République mystérieuse* par Robert Kirk, trans. Rémy Salvator (Courbevoie, France: Durante, 2003), p. 5. For a discussion of Kirk's book, see John Warwick Montgomery, *Principalities and Powers: The World of the Occult* (3d ed.; Calgary, Alberta, Canada: Canadian Institute for Law, Theology and Public Policy, 2001), pp. 135, 240.

The constant recurrence of this kind of evaluation of Tolkien's work warrants a short but decisive analysis and reply.[4]

The Case for an Occult Tolkien

Why should one regard *The Lord of the Rings* as a New Age work rather than one infused by and in support of traditional Christianity? The most common arguments are the following:

1. God—Christian or otherwise—never appears in the work and there is no explicit Christian theology there set forth. The characters make freewill decisions and are not the pawns of any kind of divine operation. Tolkien's battle is against rationalism, not against religious unbelief; he wants a world open to the spiritual and the mythic in the widest sense. Moreover, he himself has told us not to allegorise what he has written.[5]
2. If one is looking for schema of interpretation for understanding *The Lord of the Rings*, Jung's Gnostic and non-Christian archetypal depth psychology is far more helpful than any kind of theologising.[6] "The visionary moments I have pointed to [in *The Lord of the Rings*] may be archetypal but they are not religious in any ordinary sense."[7]
3. Tolkien's literary themes are predominantly those of pagan and occult myth.[8] The "ring" itself is a powerful symbol in Norse mythology, in the Volsunga saga, and in Celtic and Saxon myths.[9] Wagner's use of such material amply demonstrates that it need not have Christian connections.

---

[4] We shall not attempt to define the amorphous New Age belief orientation (or, rather, orientations). One of the best attempts is that by sociologist Eileen Barker (London School of Economics), who, *inter alia*, characterises the New Age—over against "traditional religion"—as focussing on the immanent (not the transcendent); eternal, cyclical return (rather than the biblical stress on historical movement from creation to final judgement); "lack of attunement, balance and/or awareness" as the human problem (not objective sin/evil or the work of a personal, Satanic being); and "reincarnation/transmigation of souls" (rather than salvation and ultimate resurrection): paper presented at the conference on New Religious Movements, Authority and Democracy, Högskolan Dalarna, Sweden, 2004-05-06.
[5] Tolkien's "Foreword" to the one-volume edition (1968) of *The Lord of the Rings*.
[6] Cf. Timothy R. O'Neill, *The Individuated Hobbit: Jung, Tolkien and the Archetypes of Middle-earth* (London: Thames and Hudson, 1980).
[7] Joe R. Christopher, "The Moral Epiphanies in *The Lord of the Rings*," *Proceedings of the J. R. R. Tolkien Centenary Conference, Keble College, Oxford, 1992*, ed. Patricia Reynolds and Glen H. GoodKnight (Altadena, California: Mythopoeic Press, and Milton Keynes, England: The Tolkien Society, 1995), p. 123.
[8] See Ruth S. Noel, *The Mythology of Middle-Earth* (Boston: Houghton Mifflin, 1977). Cf. Iain Lowson, Keith Marshall and Daniel O'Brien, *World of the Rings: The Unauthorised Guide to the World of JRR Tolkien* (London: Reynolds & Hearn, 2002), pp. 88-96.
[9] David Day, *Tolkien's Ring* (London: HarperCollins, 1994).

To take a single example from ancient mythology, the One Ring is a reminder of the Egyptian occult symbol of the Ouroboros—the serpent which eternally devours its own tail. As in Zoroastrian thought, Tolkien's "Sauron is the evil alchemist who works with the destructive fires of Ahriman."[10]

Why Tolkien Must Not Be Classed As a New Ager

Answering the above arguments is not a difficult task.

1) *No God in* The Lord of the Rings? Writes Professor Clyde Kilby, who personally worked with Tolkien on *The Silmarillion*:

> It is true that the word 'God' never appears in any of Tolkien's stories, not even in *Leaf by Niggle* where some Christian implications are overwhelming, including a conversation between God and Christ. ... [Tolkien] spoke of invocations to Elbereth Gilthoniel and added, 'These and other references to religion in *The Lord of the Rings* are frequently overlooked' [*The Road Goes Ever On*, p. 65]. ...
>
> Responding to a letter from Father Robert Murray ... Tolkien wrote: "*The Lord of the Rings* is of course a fundamentally religious and Catholic work; unconsciously so at first but consciously in the revision. I ... have cut out practically all references to anything like 'religion,' to cults and practices in the imaginary world. For the religious element is absorbed into the story and the symbolism" [*The Tablet*, 15 September 1973].[11]

Is the freewill manifested by the Fellowship of the Ring an indicator of a non-theistic world-view on Tolkien's part? In Christian thought, even among hyper-Calvinists, the relationship between divine sovereignty and human decision has always been regarded as an unfathomable mystery which in no way cancels out the pragmatic operation of freewill. Did not Jesus say, "If anyone will do his [God's] will, he shall know of the doctrine, whether it be of God" (John 7:17)? And—last we heard—all Christian evangelism is based on the assumption that one can decide whether to believe or not (cf. Billy Graham's "Hour of Decision"). Moreover, behind the scenes in Tolkien's epics—behind the volitional acts at stage centre—transcendent purposes operate:

---

[10] Maria Florencia Rampoldi, *Tolkien le Seigneur des Mythes* (Barcelona, Spain: Circulo Latino, 2003), p. 58.
[11] Clyde S. Kilby, *Tolkien & The Silmarillion* (Wheaton, Illinois: Harold Shaw, 1976), pp. 55-56. For Professor Kilby's full-scale analysis, see his essay, "Mythic and Christian Elements in Tolkien," in: John Warwick Montgomery (ed.), *Myth, Allegory and Gospel* (Minneapolis: Bethany, 1974), pp. 119-43.

As ancient lore foretold, the counter melody of Melkor's rebellion was used as an unwitting instrument in the hands of a great composer. "For he that attempteth this," the words of Ilúvater echo, "shall prove but mine instrument in the devising of things more wonderful, which he himself hath not imagined.[12]

As for "rationalism," there is no doubt that Tolkien opposed it with his infinitely broader and deeper view of reality. John Howe, who has illustrated a number of Tolkien's writings and served as artistic co-director for the three *Lord of the Rings* films, was asked in a recent interview in Strasbourg, France, why it took Europe longer to appreciate Tolkien's brand of heroic fantasy than was the case in America and Britain. His reply: "The Anglo-Saxon countries, never having known the Enlightenment, didn't cut themselves off from their myths. They did not shelve them in the name of rationalism and science."[13] But opposing rationalism hardly makes Tolkien a pagan! Did not the 19th century littérateur and lay theologian Søren Kierkegaard fight Hegelian rationalism, tooth and nail, in the name of the Christian gospel?

2) *Gnostic, Jungian archetypes?* There is no doubt that one can legitimately find Jungian archetypes in *The Lord of the Rings*. But this is because Jung discovered these "archetypes of the collective unconscious" deep within the human psyche. Per se they are not incompatible with a Christian world-view; indeed, in creating modern literary fairy tales, Tolkien and C. S. Lewis consciously employed such symbolism, thereby touching the depths of the reader's inner existence. A similar literary phenomenon can be found in the work of the 17th century Lutheran theologian Johann Valentin Andreae, whose thoroughly Christian *Chymische Hochzeit* I have analysed using Jungian categories.[14] Even O'Neill, who has provided the major Jungian treatment of Tolkien, admits at the end of his book that

> Tolkien was a believer. ... God was to Jung a very real and potent force, but a force within the psyche, not outside it; this approach casts God in the role of an archetype identified with the Self, an instinct that Man *projects* from in-

---

[12] Kurt Bruner and Jim Ware, *Finding God in The Lord of the Rings* (Wheaton, Illinois: Tyndale, 2001), p. 89, quoting Tolkien, Silmarillion (1977), p. 17.

[13] John Howe, "Ancrer le merveilleux dans le réel," *Dernières Nouvelles d'Alsace*, 16 December 2006. Cf. "Le moyen âge réinventé: voyage au pays de Tolkien avec John Howe," 33 *Les Saisons d'Alsace*, December, 2006, pp. 50-81. To be sure, (1) England and America did experience an "Enlightenment" (the Deists and the so-called "Age of Reason") and (2) fantastic literature has had a respectable history in France—see Marcel Schneider, *Histoire de la littérature fantastique en France* (Paris: Fayard, 1985), 463 pp.

[14] John Warwick Montgomery (ed.), *Cross and Crucible: Johann Valentin Andreae (1586-1654)* (2 vols.; "International Archives of the History of Ideas," 55; The Hague: Martinus Nijhoff, 1973), especially Vol II.

ternal potential to external reality in religious beliefs. This would have been an unappealing concept for Tolkien, as would Jung's preoccupation with religious viewpoints of Gnosticism, with its god that combines good and evil. Tolkien's approach to the problem of evil is very Christian in its personification of evil as the rebellious Melkor and his coterie of fallen angels.[15]

3) *Pagan and occult mythology?* Tolkien had been a professor of Anglo-Saxon language and literature and considered himself a philologist. He was steeped in Norse mythology and had a superb literary background. Thus nothing could be more natural than his use of this background in *The Lord of the Rings*—as in his creation of Elvish tongues to give substance to the narrative.[16] But the fact that he employed such material offers no argument whatsoever to support a pagan interpretation of the resultant work. Indeed, to do this merely offers an illustration of the logical fallacy of *post hoc, ergo propter hoc* ("If two clocks chime at the same time, does one cause the other to chime?"). One must not confuse temporal propinquity with causation. The presence of ǥpagan h mythological elements in *The Lord of the Rings* does not mean that they are the causal source of the meaning of the work.[17] As Aristotle stressed in his Poetics, the plot is the predominant and most important element in any literary production,[18] and the plot of Tolkien's masterpiece is thoroughly theological:

> Reaching beyond Nature for the power to overcome evil indicates ... Tolkien's theism.[19]

> Like the Christian myth which underlies Tolkien's view of experience in the twentieth century, the myth of the War of the Ring gives emotional and spiritual meaning to much of what we know. It, too, affirms the grandest moral purposes of the universe, and asserts that there are ultimate values in which we may believe.[20]

Reinforcing the overarching plot of *The Lord of the Rings* (a cosmic battle between good and evil, the good ultimately triumphing by virtue of an atoning act), are the leading characters—Gandalf, Frodo, and Aragon, who, as Prophet, Priest, and King "complement one another as Christ-figures."[21] Gandalf ap-

---

[15] O'Neill, *op. cit.*, p. 162.
[16] Cf. Jim Allan, *An Introduction to Elvish ... As Set Forth in the Published Writings of Professor John Ronald Reuel Tolkien* (Frome, Somerset, England: Bran's Head Books, 1978).
[17] *Pace* Ronald Hutton, *Witches, Druids and King Arthur* (London: Hambledon & London, 2006), chap. 7 ("The Inklings and the Gods").
[18] Aristotle, *De Arte Poetica*, 1450a-1450b.
[19] U. Milo Kauffman, "Aspects of the Paradisiacal in Tolkien's Work," in: Jared Lobdell (ed.), *A Tolkien Compass* (La Salle, Illinois: Open Court, 1975), p. 152.
[20] Robley Evans, *J. R. R. Tolkien* (New York: Warner, 1972), p. 202.
[21] Gracia Fay Ellwood, *Good News from Tolkien's Middle Earth* (Grand Rapids, Michigan: Eerdmans, 1970), p. 104.

pears at critical, *kairotic* times in the story, as did the Old Testament prophets in the history of Israel; and he dies and rises again. Frodo, in his weakness, crushes the head of the serpent but suffers permanent injury (cf. the so-called "protoevangelion," Genesis 3:15): one thinks immediately of Christ's salvatory wounds, which he carried with him into eternity. Aragon is the "once and future king": the reader witnesses "the climax of the struggle between good and evil through battle between the Satanlike Dark Lord and the Christlike true king, Aragon."[22]

To be sure, any attempt to use "myth" in *The Lord of the Rings* as an argument against the Christian nature of the work fails entirely in the face of Tolkien's express understanding of deep myth, as set forth in his classic essay "On Fairy-stories."[23] There Tolkien uses the fairy story as a pointer to the Christian Gospel,[24] the difference between them being that the latter is "primarily" true, for it not only touches the depths of human need but also represents historical fact. In the Gospel story, "Art has been verified. God is the Lord, of angels, and of men—and of elves." It is clear that, even though Tolkien was admittedly not aware of the ultimate thrust of *The Lord of the Rings* early in the writing of it, and refused to have it allegorised as a modern *Pilgrim's Progress*, his trilogy ultimately took on the character of deep myth. In a real sense, *The Lord of the Rings* functions as a literary John the Baptist—it is not the Christ, but it points inexorably to him, thereby leading others to Cross, Resurrection, and a New Heaven and a New Earth.[25]

---

[22] Jane Chance Nitzsche, *Tolkien's Art* (London: Macmillan, 1980), p. 119.

[23] In *Essays Presented to Charles Williams*, ed. C. S. Lewis (London: Oxford University Press, 1947); a slightly revised version is to be found in Tolkien's *Tree and Leaf* (London: Unwin Books, 1964).

[24] "The fairy story, for Tolkien, ceases to be merely literature and becomes explicitly a vehicle for religious truth" (R. J. Reilly, "Tolkien and the Fairy Story," in: *Tolkien and the Critics*, ed. Neil D. Isaacs and Rose A. Zimbardo (Notre Dame, Indiana: University of Notre Dame Press, 1968), p. 148. Cf. Lin Carter, "Tolkien's Theory of the Fairy Story," in his *Tolkien: A Look Behind the Lord of the Rings* (New York: Ballantine Books, 1969), pp. 87-95.

[25] Cf. Stratford Caldecott, Didier Rance and Grégory Solari, *Tolkien: Faërie et Christianisme* (Geneva, Switzerland: Ad Solem, 2002); Orson Scott Card, "How Tolkien Means," in: *Meditations on Middle-Earth*, ed. Karen Haber, illus. John Howe (New York: St. Martin's Griffin, 2001), pp. 167 ff. (including Card's argument for Samwise Gamgee as servant Christ-image); and William Dowie, "The Gospel of Middle-Earth according to J. R. R. Tolkien," in: *J. R. R. Tolkien, Scholar and Storyteller: Essays In Memoriam*, ed. Mary Salu and Robert T. Farrell (Ithaca, New York: Cornell University Press, 1979), pp. 284-85.

So Why Does the Claim of an Allegedly Occult Tolkien Persist?

The arguments just presented appear so strong that one is hard put to understand why the New Age interpretation of *The Lord of the Rings* did not disappear long ago. Why has it persisted?

Tolkien's dear friend C. S. Lewis, whom he led out of atheism to Christian belief, gives us a hint by way of Screwtape—an elder devil offering advice to the less experienced tempter Wormwood. Screwtape encourages the creation of new Jesuses in the publishers' lists every thirty years or so (a humanitarian Jesus, a revolutionary Jesus, etc.). This of course directs attention away from the Jesus of the primary documents—Screwtape's object, after all.[26]

Why are such unhistorical Jesuses so readily accepted? The reason, to be sure, is that the more important and attractive the person, the more everyone wants to claim him as one's own. But to achieve this, the great man's ideology must be transmuted into that of the interpreter. This can—and generally does—require a gerrymandering on the level of the classical Procrustean bed in order to make the belief system of the object of the exercise fit the interpreter's own *Weltanschauung*.[27] We see this process very often. Luther is turned into a romantic by the German Romantic movement, into an anti-authoritarian opponent of the status quo by freethinkers, into a case study by psychoanalysts (e.g., Erik Erikson.).[28]

This is precisely what is occurring when, in the face of all the evidence, Tolkien is still held to be a crypto-New Ager and *The Lord of the Rings* a kind of Bible of occult heroic fantasy. In a sense, of course, Tolkien brought this on himself: were his literary legacy something trivial, no one would bother. But, if anyone, he was the Dante of the 20th century.[29] *Of course* then he will continue to suffer from those who, disturbed by or indifferent to his Christian faith, are compelled to make him tell their story instead of his own.

---

[26] C. S. Lewis, *The Screwtape Letters* (new ed.; London: Bles, 1961), pp. 103-104.

[27] Cf. John Warwick Montgomery, *Where Is History Going?* (Minneapolis: Bethany, 1969) and *History, Law and Christianity* (Calgary, Alberta, Canada: Canadian Institute for Law, Theology and Public Policy, 2002).

[28] See John Warwick Montgomery, *In Defense of Martin Luther* (Milwaukee: Northwestern Publishing House, 1970).

[29] On Tolkien and Dante, cf. Joseph Pearce, *Tolkien: Man and Myth* (San Francisco: Ignatius Press, 1998), pp. 100 ff.

3. Christianity and Rosicrucianism*

Why should one want to examine the relationship between Rosicrucianism and Christianity? The most influential contemporary Rosicrucian organisation, AMORC, never ceases to declare that the Rose Cross is not a religion.[1] But, if 20th-century theologian Paul Tillich was correct that there are in fact no atheists (since everyone has an "ultimate concern" which functions as his or her god), the same may be said of ideologies: they are all religious to the extent that they endeavour to make ultimate claims about the universe and about how human beings function—or ought to function—in it.[2] And the title of Max Heindel's massive and frequently cited tome surely speaks of some kind of connection between Rosicrucianism and Christian faith: *The Rosicrucian Cosmo-Conception, or Mystic Christianity*.

Properly to relate Christianity and Rosicrucianism requires a clear understanding of what these expressions mean. As the analytical philosopher Wittgenstein well put it, "anything that can be said can be said clearly."[3] What do we mean by "Christianity" and what do we mean by "Rosicrucianism"? The definition of terms may seem to pose grave difficulties in both instances, owing to the diversity of meanings attached to these belief-systems. However, the problem is not as acute as it first appears.

True, in the case of Christianity, popular parlance offers a remarkable breadth of signification. In England not too long ago, a "Christian bed for the night" was a bed free of cockroaches or other vermin. One's "Christian name" is what the French designate as one's *prénom*. And the diverse number of Christian denominations and churches would seem to militate against any single definition.

---

*Lecture presented at the Rosicrucian Conference held at Bournemouth University, U.K., 8-9 May 2010; Professor Montgomery was invited owing to his authorship of *Cross and Crucible: Johann Valentin Andreae (1586-1654), Phoenix of the Theologians* (2 vols., "International Archives of the History of Ideas," 55; The Hague: Martinus Nijhoff, 1973 [now available from Springer International]); and "The World-view of Johann Valentin Andreae," in *Das Erbe des Christian Rosenkreuz*, ed. F. A. Janssen (Amsterdam: In de Pelikaan, 1988), pp. 152-69.

[1] H. Spencer Lewis, *Rosicrucian Questions and Answers* ("Rosicrucian Library," Vol. 1; 7th ed.; San Jose, CA: AMORC, 1961), pp. 213, 261.
[2] See Montgomery, "Tillich's Philosophy of History," in his *Where Is History Going?* (Minneapolis: Bethany, 1969), pp. 118-40.
[3] Cf. Montgomery, *Tractatus Logico-Theologicus* (4th ed.; Bonn, Germany: Verlag für Kultur und Wissenschaft, 2009).

However, all orthodox Christian churches have a common doctrinal standard, exemplified by the so-called "Ecumenical Creeds": the Apostles', the Nicene, and the Athanasian symbols.[4] The shortest of these is the Apostles' Creed, which reads as follows:

> I believe in God the Father, Almighty, Maker of heaven and earth:
> And in Jesus Christ, his only begotten Son, our Lord: Who was conceived by the Holy Ghost, born of the Virgin Mary: Suffered under Pontius Pilate; was crucified, dead and buried: He descended into hell: The third day he rose again from the dead: He ascended into heaven, and sits at the right hand of God the Father Almighty: From thence he shall come to judge the quick and the dead:
> I believe in the Holy Ghost: I believe in the holy catholic [i.e. universal] church: the communion of saints: The forgiveness of sins: The resurrection of the body: And the life everlasting. Amen.

There are two common and interrelated elements in the Ecumenical Creeds—and thus in all Christian belief properly so called. First, the foundation of religious commitment lies in certain objective facts (God created the world; God redeems by the incarnation and atoning death of His Son—the historical person of Jesus Christ; a physical resurrection of mankind will occur at the end of time; etc.). Personal, existential, religious ("mystical," if you will) experience must be grounded in these objective facts.

This characteristic of all genuine Christian belief is nicely illustrated by an exchange between one Dr Couchoud, a physician, and the eminent, late French Academician Jean Guitton. Remarked Couchoud, "I believe everything in the Apostles' Creed except the phrase, 'He suffered under Pontius Pilate.'" Replied Guitton: "What you reject is the heart of Christianity: the mystery of a *real* incarnation."[5]

The second common element in all Christian belief is the notion that one cannot save oneself. Biblically, the opposite viewpoint is illustrated by the story of the Tower of Babel: the effort to build a human structure that would reach to heaven. Result: confusion of languages and the destruction of human culture. "No man hath ascended up to heaven, but he that came down from heaven, even the Son of man which is in heaven," declared Jesus (John 3:13). Granted, there have been innumerable theological discussions as to how precisely human freewill relates to the divine act of grace, but in all Christian churches and confessions it is maintained that only by relating to what God has done for mankind in Jesus Christ can one enter into the fullness of salvation. Human

---

[4] See Philip Schaff (ed.), *The Creeds of Christendom* (3 vols., 6th ed.; New York: Harper and Row, 1931).
[5] Jean Guitton, *Journal, 1952-1955* (Paris: Plon, 1959), pp. 19-21.

selfcentredness precludes a fallen race from saving itself by any kind of technique—ritualistic or ethical. "While we were yet sinners, Christ died for us," declares the Apostle (Romans 5:8). A particularly attractive formulation of this truth can be found in Luther's commentary on the Third Article of the Apostles' Creed ("I believe in the Holy Ghost"), in his Shorter Catechism:

> I believe that I cannot of my own understanding and strength believe in or come to Jesus Christ my Lord, but that the Holy Ghost has called me by the Gospel, and illuminated me with His gifts, and sanctified and preserved me in the true faith, just as He calls, gathers together, illuminates, sanctifies, and preserves in Jesus Christ all Christendom throughout the earth in the one true faith; in which Christendom He daily bestows abundantly on me and all believers forgiveness of sins; and on the last day He will awaken me and all the dead, and will give to me and all that believe in Christ eternal life. This is most certainly true.

What about Rosicrucianism? Can it be defined in equally straightforward terms? It would seem not. The diversity of materials cited in F. Leigh Gardner's bibliography of Rosicrucian literature appears to defy classification.[6] Writes Frances A. Yates in the preface to her book on *The Rosicrucian Enlightenment*, "I do not know exactly what a Rosicrucian was, nor whether there were any."[7] As a barrister member of Middle Temple and a frequent worshipper at the Temple Church, I am not encouraged by phallist Hargrove Jennings' claim that the Temple Church is replete with "Rosicrucian" symbolism[8]—though the claim is no more (and no less) fanciful than the use of that location in Dan Brown's unhistorical novel, *The Da Vinci Code*.[9]

However, it would appear that one can distinguish two fairly concrete, historical meanings of the term "Rosicrucian": its signification at the time of Rosicrucian origins in the 17th century, as reflected in the appearance of the *Fama*, the *Confessio*, and Johann Valentin Andreae's *Chymische Hochzeit*; and the meaning of the Rose Cross to those who have modernly endeavoured to establish (or, in their view, re-establish) Rosicrucian fellowships. We shall begin

---

[6] F. Leigh Gardner, *A Catalogue Raisonné of Works on the Occult Sciences. Vol. I: Rosicrucian Books* (2^d ed.; Leipzig: Muellers Druckerei/Privately Printed, 1923).
[7] Frances A. Yates, *The Rosicrucian Enlightenment* (London: Routledge & Kegan Paul, 1972), p. xiv. Cf. Ralph White (ed.), *The Rosicrucian Enlightenment Revisited* (Great Barrington, MA: Lindisfarne Books/SteinerBooks/Anthroposophic Press, 1999).
[8] Hargrave Jennings, *The Rosicrucians: Their Rites and Mysteries* (2 vols., 3^d ed.; London: John C. Nimmo, 1887), II, 76 ff.
[9] The current Master of the Temple Church, Robin Griffith-Jones, has provided a thorough refutation: *The Da Vinci Code and the Secrets of the Temple* (Grand Rapids, MI: Eerdmans, 2006).

with the latter and conclude with the former. In both instances, our aim will be to determine in what sense, if any, the Rosicrucian adept can legitimately be considered a Christian believer.

Modern and Contemporary Rosicrucianism

After the flurry of interest in identifying a mystical Order of the Rose Cross in the 17th century, Rosicrucianism became more of less moribund during the 18th century "Age of Reason." To be sure, the Freemasons introduced a Rosicrucian degree into their liturgical rites,[10] but the *esprit systématique* (vs. an *esprit de système*) of the era militated against mystical belief systems.

> The activities and aims [of the few societies which did exist], as stated in contemporary sources, were a matter of superstition and ceremonial, bearing little trace of the ideals that had inspired the early Rosicrucian manifestos. During this period occultists began to fabricate evidence of the antiquity of organized Rosicrucianism, a tendency that reached its climax during the 19th century and is still evident today.[11]

By the 19th century, on the European continent, Rosicrucian ideas had been absorbed into the French occultism of Eliphas Lévi, Stanislas de Guiata, Joseph Péladan, and Gérard Encausse ("Papus") — eventually becoming an element in the eclectic thought of Madame Blavatsky. Her disciple, Annie Besant, created in England an "Order of the Temple of the Rose Cross" in 1912, stressing reincarnational and theosophical themes.[12] A "Societas Rosicruciana in Anglia" had been founded in 1865 by Dr Wynn Westcott, who became its Supreme Magus in 1891 and went on to found the famous (but also infamous) Hermetic Order of the Golden Dawn. In America, A. E. Waite could find no earlier Order of the Rose Cross than that founded by Paschal Beverly Randolph, the author of the occult novel, *Ravalette: The Rosicrucian's Story*.[13] Randolph had been initiated in Paris, and, as Waite notes, "the mantle laid down by Randolph" was assumed

---

[10] Cf. Paul Arnold, *Histoire des Rose-Croix et les origines de la Franc-Maçonnerie* (Paris: Mercure de France, 1955) et *La Rose-Croix et ses rapports avec la Franc-Maçonnerie* (Paris: G.-P. Maisonneuve & Larose, 1970); also, Serge Hutin, *Histoire des Rose-Croix* (Paris: Librairie "Courrier du Livre," 1962).

[11] Mervyn Jones, "The Rosicrucians," in *Secret Societies*, ed. Norman MacKenzie (New York: Crescent Books/Crown Publishers, 1967), p. 144.

[12] See Arnold, *Histoire des Rose-Croix* (*op. cit.*), p. 270, and cf. Hutin, *op. cit.*, p. 57.

[13] Arthur Edward Waite, *The Brotherhood of the Rosy Cross* (reprint ed.; New Hyde Park, NY: University Books, 1961), p. 610. This work was first published in 1924.

by Dr R. Swinburne Clymer.[14] This brings us to a discussion of the beliefs of the four significant Rosicrucian groups to have graced the contemporary western hemisphere.[15]

The Rosicrucian Fraternity, Beverly Hall, Quakertown, Pennsylvania

This organisation was founded in 1902 as a result of the prolific activities, literary and otherwise, of R. Swinburne Clymer. Its special emphasis was on the doctrine of reincarnation and karma. Writes Clymer:

> No student on enrolling is requested to subscribe to the teachings relative to Reincarnation. Many who do enrol do not at first believe in it. However, as they progress in the Great Work and the mystery of life is unveiled to them, they come to see that it is the *law of justice*, in one of its variable forms, and they come to know Reincarnation as the basic principle of continuous life.[16]

Though a "Church of Illumination" is associated with the Fraternity, the non-Christian character of this Rosicrucian organisation should be patently clear. Clymer writes, in direct opposition to the biblical teaching that no-one is saved by his or her own efforts but only by the work of Jesus Christ on the cross (Eph. 2:8-9, etc.): "Man, through his own efforts, must attain spiritual enlightenment and ultimate immortality."[17] As to reincarnation, the Christian Scriptures are explicit: "It is appointed unto men once to die, but after this the judgment" (Hebrews 9:27). There is therefore only one death per person. Moreover, "justice" is achieved, in Christian understanding, not by one's living several lives in succession—lives which allegedly punish or reward past human efforts—but solely by recognising that no person can save himself or herself by the exercise of goodness (since "all have sinned and come short of the glory of God"—Romans 3:23), and by accepting Christ's free gift of salvation. Justice

---

[14] *Ibid.*, p. 616.
[15] We leave aside—since we have treated elsewhere (in *Cross and Crucible*, I, 237-38)—the views of Rudolf Steiner, founder of Anthroposophy, who, in his *The Mission of Christian Rosencreutz* (published with his *Rosicrucianism and Modern Initiation*) informs us, *inter alia*, that "Christian Rosencreutz sends Buddha, his closest pupil, to Mars" ([London: Rudolf Steiner Publishing Co., 1950], pp. 6, 88-90).
[16] R. Swinburne Clymer, Prologue to *Ravalette: The Rosicrucian's Story*, by Paschal Beverly Randolph (Quakertown, PA: Philosophical Publishing Co., 1939), p. 18 (italics Clymer's).
[17] R. Swinburne Clymer, *The Secret Schools* (Quakertown, PA: Fraternitatis Rosae Crucis, 1930), p. 19.

and salvation come about as a result of God's perfect sacrifice of Himself on the cross, thereby achieving for a fallen race what we could never do for ourselves, no matter how many lives we lived.

Societas Rosicruciana in America (S.R.I.A), New York City (now headquarted in Bayonne, New Jersey)

According to Waite, this organisation was a spin-off from the *Societas Rosicruciana in Scotia*, which, in turn, originated from the *Societas Rosicruciana in Anglia*.[18] It was founded by one Sylvester C. Gould in 1908, a year before his death. The S.R.I.A. leadership then passed to Gould's associate, George Winslow Plummer, who subsequently established the "Holy Orthodox Church in America," the membership of which has been entwined with the S.R.I.A. The Society's "principles" are set forth in the organisation's *Rosicrucian Manual*.[19] There are five affirmations required of members: "The existence of One Infinite Intelligence ... from which we emanated as unconscious spirit substance"; "The Incarnation of the Spirit ... for the purpose of Experience"; "All life is Continuous, without Beginning and without Ending, Evolutional, in a constantly ascending scale of Progression"; The Mortal may attain to the Knowledge of the Spiritual, while yet Incarnate"; and "The Truth of Re-incarnation as a factor in the Soul's Evolutionary Progress, necessary as many times as may be required for the Assimilation of the Requisite Experience."[20] Along with these affirmations, the adept is presented with a list of moral qualities, not unlike the Boy Scout Oath and Law; they include: "Be entirely unselfish"; be patient, kind, not envious, not boastful, not vain, not ambitious, not irritable.[21] There are also rules for "Rhythmic Breathing," including a formula to be repeated every morning: "First—expel all carbonic acid gases from the lungs, so thoroly [sic] that the effects will be felt in the lower lobes. Second—Inhale, Retain, and Exhale thru a given length of time, to wit: INHALE 6 Seconds, RETAIN 3 Seconds, EXHALE 6 Seconds, WAIT THREE SECONDS AND REPEAT."[22]

There is obviously nothing unchristian in the moral qualities set forth here, though they tend toward the vacuous and appear to suggest that one can attain some degree of ethical perfection by dint of concerted effort—rather like pulling oneself up by one's own bootstraps. But the five affirmations are clearly

---

[18] Waite, *op. cit.* [in note 13, *supra*], p. 615.
[19] S.R.I.A., *Rosicrucian Manual* (New York: Flame Press, 1920).
[20] *Ibid.*, p. 37.
[21] *Ibid.*, pp. 47-51. Cf. George Winslow Plummer, *Principles and Practice for Rosicrucians* (New York: Society of Rosicrucians, 1947).
[22] *Ibid.*, p. 42.

contrary to fundamental Christian doctrine. Creation, we are taught, occurs by emanation, not through the *ex nihilo* act of a transcendent God. Incarnation is not the unique, historical entrance of the Son of God into human history—"God in Christ, reconciling the world unto himself" (2 Corinthians 5:19)—but the "incarnation" of the individual soul for purposes of attaining the highest possible level of experience. Humans are regarded as capable of evolving in their own right, "in a constantly ascending scale of Progression." And reincarnation is seen as essential to the attainment of the evolutionary goal.

The Rosicrucian Fellowship, Oceanside, California

This organisation is the offspring of Max Heindel, who died in 1919. A theosophist, he claimed to have been visited in Europe by an "Elder Brother" of the Rosicrucian Order, who appointed him to teach and directed him to a Temple of the Rose Cross where he received the esoteric knowledge contained in his massive tome, *The Rosicrucian Cosmo-Conception*. As the subtitle ("Mystic Christianity") suggests, this Fellowship considers itself to be presenting an esoteric brand of Christian faith: Jesus Christ is to be one's ideal. The details of the belief system, however, belie any realistic connection with historic Christianity.

This is not because of the Fellowship's astrological emphases per se; as I have argued elsewhere, astrology is only contrary to Christian commitment when it substitutes reliance on (generally questionable) stellar interpretations for dependence on the God of the Bible.[23] The theological problems of the Rosicrucian Fellowship cut far deeper than that.

Firstly, there is a denial of the cardinal, orthodox Christian doctrine of the Holy Trinity. Heindel writes:

> It is necessary for all beings high or low in the scale of existence to possess vehicles for expression in any particular world in which they may wish to manifest. Even the Seven Spirits before the Throne must possess these necessary vehicles, which of course are differently conditioned for each of Them. Collectively, They are God, and make up the Triune Godhead.[24]

---

[23] Montgomery, *Principalities and Powers: The World of the Occult* (2d ed.; Calgary, Alberta: Canadian Institute for Law, Theology and Public Policy, 2001), chap. 4 ("The Stars and the Hermetic Tradition"), pp. 96-120.
[24] Max Heindel, *The Rosicrucian Cosmo-Conception* (Oceanside, CA: Rosicrucian Fellowship, 1937), p. 252.

> "The Father" is the highest Initiate among the humanity of the Saturn Period. ... "The Son" (Christ) is the highest Initiate of the Sun Period. ... The Holy Spirit (Jehovah) is the highest Initiate of the Moon Period.[25]

Secondly, in consequence of having blended the Persons of the Holy Trinity with the "Seven Spirits" and having reduced them to quasi-human, quasi-astrological "Initiates," Heindel turns the historical, uniquely incarnated Christ into a human ideal, indistinguishable from other religious leaders such as the Buddha:

> Jesus Himself was a spirit belonging to our human evolution, and so was Gautama Buddha. ... The Christ spirit which entered the body of Jesus when Jesus himself vacated it, was a ray from the cosmic Christ. We may follow Jesus back in his previous incarnations, and we can trace his growth to the present day.[26]

Thirdly, in what is essentially a pantheistic scheme, salvation consists of our realizing our inherent divine nature. Christ is to be imitated; he is not seen as divinely sacrificing himself to counter human depravity and provide a unique path to God.

The Ancient & Mystical Order Rosae Crucis (AMORC), San Jose, California

This Rosicrucian group is the largest in the world, representing more than 90% of all Rosicrucians. It was founded by H. Spencer Lewis in 1915 and maintains extensive advertising and distance-education programmes to spread its teachings. The emphasis, unlike that of Heindel's Rosicrucian Fellowship, is on "practice," not metaphysical theory.[27] Lewis maintained, as noted earlier, that one's religious commitment is no bar to membership, since AMORC does not deal with divisive religious issues. Though clearly believing in reincarnation, Lewis carefully states that "the doctrine of reincarnation explains many of the mysteries of life, but the doctrine itself need not be adopted by any student of the Rosicrucian teachings unless he or she has found from personal experience that the doctrine is true."[28]

---

[25] *Ibid.*, p. 376.
[26] Max Heindel, *The Rosicrucian Philosophy in Questions and Answers* (Oceanside, CA: Rosicrucian Fellowship, 1922), p. 181.
[27] Lewis (*op. cit.* [in note 1 *supra*], p. 175, and elsewhere) criticises the S.R.I.A. and Heindel's Rosicrucian Fellowship as merely "semi-Rosicrucian." Unhappily, Lewis' group has not been immune to nasty internecine warfare and litigation; see "Infighting and Lawsuits Affecting AMORC Rosicrucians," *Christian Research Journal*, Fall 1990, p. 6.
[28] Lewis, *op. cit.* p. 267.

There is, however, a specific theology lying behind AMORC "practical" life teaching, and that theology is certainly not Christian. The Order holds that God's Word to mankind is not limited to a single, biblical revelation: "The whole purpose of the Rosicrucian Order is to acquaint the seeking mind with an understandable explanation and analysis as well as a logical classification of all the Revelations that have been made to man in the past."[29] A pantheistic view of the world is maintained—which entails necessarily the belief that one does not need transcendent salvation, since one is already "part" of the universal Soul:

> The Rosicrucians believe and have always believed that there is but one soul in the universe, and that is the universal soul or the universal consciousness of God. Furthermore, the Rosicrucians have always taught that a segment, or essence, of that universal soul resides in each being that possesses soul. And this essence is never separated from the universal soul or is never an entity in such a sense as to make it independent and individual.[30]

In 2001, AMORC provided for all to read on the internet[31] a 26-page modern *Manifesto* dealing with major issues of contemporary life: politics, economics, science, technology, art, nature, morality, and religion. Much contained there, if rather idealistic and naïve, accords with common sense (e.g., opposition to pollution). But no Christian believer would agree that

> The survival of the great religions depends more than ever upon their ability to discard the most dogmatic moral and doctrinal beliefs and positions they have adopted through the centuries. . . . Nonetheless, we presume that their disappearance is inevitable and that, under the influence of a worldwide expansion of consciousness, they will give birth to a universal religion. (Page 15)

Rosicrucianism in the 17th Century

Having seen the essential incompatibility of modern and contemporary Rosicrucianisms with historic Christian faith, we now wish to look at the understandings of the Rose Cross during the earliest verifiable period of its history. We shall be raising the same question: Are those understandings compatible with Christian religion?

---

[29] *Ibid.*, p. 282.
[30] *Ibid.*, p. 237.
[31] http://www.rosicrucian.org/publications/positio.pdf

Fama fraternitatis and *Confessio* and *Chymische Hochzeit*

The *Fama* and the *Confessio*, as is well known, mark the beginning of historic Rosicrucianism. We have summarized their contents elsewhere and do not need to repeat the analysis here.[32] What is striking about these manifestos is their remarkable contrast with the documents and teachings of the modern and contemporary Rosicrucian positions we have just been describing.

The *Fama* presents a quasi-mythical account of the peregrinations of one Christian Rosencreutz ("Christian of the Rose Cross") and his founding of an Order. But the beliefs of that Order are not set forth—except for their commitment to the Bible as their "greatest treasure," to the Christocentric aphorism, *Jesus mihi omnia* ("Jesus is everything to me"), to Trinitarian theology: *Ex Deo nascimur, in Jesu morimur, per spiritum sanctum reviviscimus* ("We are born of God, we die in Jesus, we are reborn through the Holy Spirit"), and to the Protestant/Lutheran employment of no more than the two biblically justified sacraments. The only practical activity of the Fraternity set forth is "that none of them should profess any other thing, than to cure the sick, and that *gratis*." Crass alchemy is condemned, and "the Pope, Mahomet, Scribes, Artists, and Sophisters" are to be "roughly handled."

The *Confessio* gives birth and death dates for Christian Rosencreutz, but adds nothing else to the myth set out in the *Fama*. The treatise is more explicitly anti-Catholic, but no programme of the Fraternity appears there. Rather, the treatise is of an eschatological nature—predicting the end of the world and doing so on the basis of a cabalistic handling of Scripture and an astrologically supported chiliasm. The Brotherhood sees the world as "falling to decay" and holds that the Pope will soon be overthrown and the Millennium arrive.

It will be noted here that nothing in the express content of these founding documents of Rosicrucianism is anti-Christian. Arising in Germany in the wake of the Protestant Reformation, there is certainly opposition to the Roman Church, but in no sense to biblical Christianity as such. There is not a trace of reincarnation, pantheism, or a willingness to create a syncretism of diverse religions or belief systems. Cabalistic hermeneutical method is present in the *Confessio*, but not the emanationist metaphysics characteristic of cabalis-

---

[32] See Montgomery, *Cross and Crucible* (*op. cit.* [in the initial asterisked note], I, 163-71. We there point out that the *Allgemeine und General Reformation*, being no more than a German translation of an unrelated Italian satirical writing, does not in fact shed light on the positive beliefs of the first promulgators of the myth of Christian Rosencreutz.

tic occultism.³³ The aim of the manifestos appears to be to establish — or speak for — a society of committed persons who recognize the social evils of the day and would minister to them, especially in the medical field.

A positive mention of the iatrochemist Paracelsus appears in the *Fama*, and the publications of these Rosicrucian documents attracted the high interest of alchemists and nature mystics. To counter this, Johann Valentin Andreae, Lutheran pastor and littérateur, produced his *Chymische Hochzeit*, setting forth an allegory of transmutation and a "Christian alchemy" in strict accord with the orthodox Lutheran theology of the Protestant Reformation.³⁴ Andreae saw that the *Fama* and the *Confessio* left open the possibility of occult interpretation (e.g., its notions of hidden wisdom and the substitution of the mystic city of Damcar for the holy city of Jerusalem) and, in opposition to an occult, non-Christian Rosicrucianism, he wrote his utopian *Christianopolis*³⁵ and endeavoured to promote a *Societas Christiana*, whose aim was social amelioration in a thoroughly biblical context.³⁶

Subsequent 17th-century Developments

Writings pro and con "Rosicrucianism" proliferated after the dissemination of the *Fama*, the *Confessio*, and the *Chymische Hochzeit*. Some distinguished Christian believers — one thinks immediately of Lutheran chemist Andreas Libavius — fought against the whole notion. Others, such as Michael Maier, Count Palatine, author of *Themis aurea* (1618), supported the idea of the Fraternity, "convinced that its myth could be understood in Christian terms and that the Order was hospitable to the advancement of a Christian alchemy."³⁷

The claim that Maier "visited England and admitted Robert Fludd, M. A. and M. D. Oxon. to Rosicrucian Adeptship,"³⁸ is doubtless false, since Maier stated that he was not a member of the Rosicrucian Fraternity and Fludd never

---

³³ See Montgomery, *Principalities and Powers* (*op. cit.* [in note 23 *supra*]), chap. 3 ("Cabala and Christ"), pp. 74-95. The cabala tradition was in no sense limited to Jewish mysticism; see Joseph Leon Blau, *The Christian Interpretation of the Cabala in the Renaissance* (New York: Columbia University Press, 1944). The theological problem with cabala lay in its occultic emanation (*Sephiroth*) doctrine, not with its biblical numerology — though the latter leaves much to be desired hermeneutically.

³⁴ This is argued *in extenso* in my *Cross and Crucible*, and defended in my essay in *Das Erbe des Christian Rosencreutz* (*op. cit.* [in the initial asterisked note, *supra*]).

³⁵ Newly translated and edited by Edward H. Thompson ("International Archives of the History of Ideas," 162; Dordrecht, Netherlands: Kluwer Academic, 1999).

³⁶ Montgomery, *Cross and Crucible* (*op. cit.*), I, 211-23.

³⁷ *Ibid.*, I, 18-19, 236, II, 283.

³⁸ Gardner, *op. cit.* [in note 6, *supra*], p. xviii.

explicitly declared himself to be a Rosicrucian. However, Fludd staunchly defended an understanding of the Rose Cross not dissimilar to Andreae's. As demonstrated by his several publications,[39] Fludd could not have been further ideologically from the occultic Rosicrucianism of some of his contemporaries—or from the beliefs and aims of today's Rosicrucian organizations. Thus Fludd

> puts on record his personal conviction that all persons whatsoever may and shall be accounted as true Brethren of the Rosy Cross if they are (1) rooted firmly in the Christian faith, (2) confirmed in the knowledge of themselves and (3) consciously built up on that corner-stone which is Christ Spiritual. The head of all is Christ, of whose mystical body there are many members. The point has become of such importance that he returns thereon and repeats it with a slight variation of form: "I affirm that every *Theologus* of the Church Mystical is a real Brother of the Rosy Cross, wheresoever he may be and under what obedience soever of the Churches politic."[40]

Here we are very much in the *Weltanschauung* of 17th-century Anglican poet and hymn writer George Herbert, who christianised alchemy, one of the favourite Rosicrucian themes, in the following terms:

> Teach me, my God and King,
> In all things thee to see;
> And what I do in anything
> To do it as for thee ...

---

[39] Robert Fludd, *Apologia compendiaria Fraternitatem de Rosea Cruce* ... (Leyden: G. Basson, 1616); *Tractatus apologeticus, integritatem Societatis de Rosea Cruce defendens* (Leyden: G. Basson, 1617); and *Clavis philosophiae* (Frankfurt, 1633). A work titled, *Summum bonum* (1629), whose author's name is given on the title page as Joachim Fritz, has often been attributed to Fludd, though he expressly denied authorship of it. The Rosicrucian section (Part 4) of the *Summum bonum* is included, with attribution to Fludd and in English translation from a German translation (!) in Paul M. Allen's *A Christian Rosencreutz Anthology* (Blauvelt, NY: Rudolf Steiner Publications, 1968), pp. 349-79. The presentation and defense of the Rose Cross in the *Summum bonum* is consistent with Fludd's published views, but should not be regarded as equivalent to what he himself in fact wrote.

[40] Waite, *op. cit.* [in note 13, *supra*], pp. 303-304, referring to Fludd's *Clavis philosophiae*. Waite's mature discussion of Fludd's views, though coloured by his own brand of mysticism, is very valuable (chap. 10 ["English Rosicrucianism"], pp. 271-309); Waite's much earlier treatment of Fludd (in his *The Real History of the Rosicrucians*, 1887) was heavily relied upon by J. B. Craven, *Doctor Robert Fludd (Robertus de Fluctibus), the English Rosicrucian* (Kirkwall, Scotland: William Peace and Son, 1902). It is hardly the case that "we must turn to Robert Fludd for the English culmination of all the occult strains of alchemical, Paracelsian, kabbalistic, and neo-Platonic thought" (Allen G. Debus, *The English Paracelsians* [London: Oldbourne, 1965], p. 105).

> This is the famous stone
> That turneth all to gold;
> For that which God doth touch and own
> Cannot for less be told.[41]

Comments Yates: "So sang George Herbert of his Christian religious experience, and it was such spiritual gold as this that the German Rosicrucian movement sought."[42]

A "Christian Rosicrucianism"?

After discussing the history of Rosicrucianism in modern times, Mervyn Jones concludes with the following dismal evaluation: "The world has scarcely been influenced, much less reformed, by its existence. Whether its students have imbibed more knowledge or nonsense is an open question. At least it can be said that, compared with many secret societies, the Order of the Rose Cross has not done much harm."[43]

This is probably an accurate picture of modern and contemporary Rosicrucian movements. But it is imperative not to confuse these with the ideals of those who initially promoted the Rose Cross—and particularly not with the kind of Christian understanding of the Rosicrucian ideal as set forth by Johann Valentin Andreae, Michael Maier, and Robert Fludd. These thinkers longed for a transformation of society and realized that societal evils can often best be (and sometimes can only be) countered by dedicated and likeminded individu-

---

[41] Text in, *inter alia, Hymns Ancient and Modern, Revised* (London: William Clowes and Sons, n.d.), No. 337. On Herbert, see my Patrick Henry College faculty colleague Gene Edward Veith's *Reformation Spirituality: The Religion of George Herbert* (Lewisburg, PA: Bucknell University Press, 1985).

[42] Yates, *op. cit.* [in note 7, *supra*], p. 225. Unfortunately, Yates does not appreciate the great gulf that lay between the Christian alchemical and "Rosicrucian" thinking of Andreae and his *Societas Christiana* on the one hand and the occult employment of the *Fama* tradition by others. Thus she writes (p. 223): "Kepler moved in Andreae's circle, and seems to have been later associated with the Christian Unions. ... He speaks mysteriously, and apparently slightingly, of 'the brothers of the Rosy Cross' in his *Apologia* of 1622. ... Yet Kepler's association with the Rosicrucian world is so close that one might almost call him a heretic from Rosicrucianism." A heretic, hardly! Simply an opponent of non-Christian Rosicrucian ideology (cf. Montgomery, *Cross and Crucible*, I, 10-12).

[43] Jones, *op. cit.* [in note 10, *supra*], p. 151.

als banded together for a common purpose.⁴⁴ They also understood clearly the difference between a pagan nature mysticism that sees human beings as capable of self-salvation and the biblical perspective that recognizes in self-salvation the very *hubris* which brought about mankind's present misery—a misery able to be eliminated only by Christ's atoning sacrifice on the cross. In my essay, "The World-view of Johann Valentin Andreae," I presented in tabular form the difference between these two conceptions of alchemy⁴⁵; the exact same conceptualization can be applied to two contrasting approaches to the Rose Cross:

	Basis of Salvation	Mechanism of Salvation
Gnostic, Occult Alchemy/ Rose Cross	REPEATABLE MYTH	HUMAN WORKS
Andreae's Lutheran Alchemy/ Rose Cross	ONCE-FOR-ALL HISTORICAL ACTS *(HEILSGESCHICHTE)*	GRACE THROUGH FAITH

It is not enough that a philosophy of the Rose Cross "not do much harm." In its original conception, it was to do much good—for the individual and for society at large. But the only way for this to occur is for its mysticism and its ideals to be grounded in eternal verities—and that means grounded in Christian revelation. Thus Andreae advocated the creation of a *Societas Christiana* that would embody the genuinely biblical elements of the Rose Cross without commitment to its actual or potential errors.

---

⁴⁴One thinks immediately of prison reform, the elimination of the slave trade, etc., achieved in early 19ᵗʰ-century England through the efforts of the so-called "Clapham sect," chief of whose members was William Wilberforce. Cf. Montgomery, "Slavery, Human Dignity and Human Rights": *Evangelical Quarterly*, April, 2007; *Law & Justice: The Christian Law Review*, No. 158 (Hilary/Easter, 2007); *Human Rights—A Global Agenda*, ed. V. B. Malleswari (Punjagutta, Hyderabad, India: Icfai University Press/Amicus Books, 2007); and in the present volume (Part Eight, chap. 1).

⁴⁵Montgomery, in *Das Erbe des Christian Rosenkreuz* (*op. cit.* [in the initial asterisked note, *supra*]), p. 165.

As the early Christian proponents of the Rose Cross held, the only legitimate Philosopher's Stone is Christ: the Stone which the builders rejected and which has become the head of the corner" (Acts 4:10-12, etc.). "Other foundation can no man lay than that is laid, which is Jesus Christ" (1 Corinthians 3:11)—for He is the Rose of Sharon (Song of Solomon 2:1). "In him dwells all the fullness of the Godhead bodily" (Colossians 2:9). Any Rosicrucianism taking another path has always, and will always, end in futility. Like Luther's coat-of-arms, the Rosicrucian emblem needs to have the historical cross of Christ—accepted by grace alone through faith—centred on and giving meaning to the rose of personal and societal salvation.

We end with Luther's own description of this christocentric emblem:

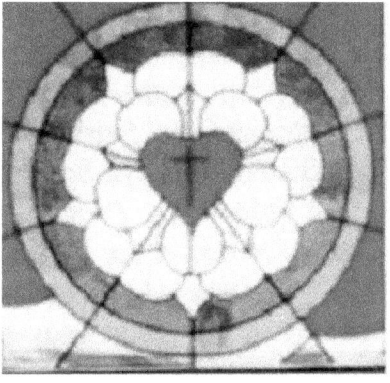

First, there is a black cross set in a heart of natural colour to remind me that the Crucified One saves us. For if one believes from the heart, one is justified. Even though it is a black cross, one that mortifies the flesh and should produce pain, it leaves the colour of the heart intact and does not destroy our nature, that is, it does not kill but preserves life. For "the just shall live by faith"—"by faith in the Crucified." This heart is mounted in the centre of a white rose to show that faith brings joy, comfort and peace. In short, faith transports us into a field of joyous roses. Since this peace and joy are unlike that of the world, the rose is white and not red, for white is the colour of spirits and all angels. The rose is set in a sky-blue field to show that such joy of the spirit and faith is the beginning of the heavenly joy to come—present, indeed, already in our joy now and embraced by hope, but not yet made manifest. And around the field is a golden ring, symbolizing that in heaven such blessedness lasts forever and has no end, and in addition is precious beyond all joy and goods, just as gold is the most valuable and precious metal.[46]

---

[46] Martin Luther, Letter of 8 July 1530 to Lazarus Spengler, town clerk of Nuremberg: *WA, Briefwechsel*, V, No. 1628; English translation in the American (partial) edition of Luther's *Works*, Vol. 49, *Letters* II, ed. Gottfried G. Krodel (Philadelphia: Fortress Press, 1972), No. 221, pp. 356 ff. See, in this connection, Montgomery, *Heraldic Aspects of the German Reformation* (Bonn, Germany: Verlag für Kultur und Wissenschaft, 2003), especially pp. 27-32.

4. Transcendental Gastronomy

The holiday season is nearly upon us: Thanksgiving, soon to be followed by Christmas. Times of merriment, good fellowship, and banqueting—and times, for many evangelicals, of guilt-ridden, conscience-striken breast-beating. How can we kill the fatted calf (even if we can still afford the inflationary beast) when others less fortunate do not have one? Should we not instead try to get by on the barest minimum, in protest against the consumer society and its values? One West Coast evangelical couple has recently written in behalf of "Christian poverty," describing the humble, sanctified growing of their own vegetables (and their own attempt at making toothpaste, which, however, proved abrasive to the teeth).

Ambivalently torn by competing values, evangelicals realize dimly that they cannot reject the season's festal board without contributing to the demise of holidays that are essentially or should be holy days; yet their Protestant work ethic and a somber strain of pietism cast a dark cloud of self-doubt over the candlelit table.

On November 13, 1974, in Paris, I had the temerity to accept the invitation of the French Gastronomical Academy to become one of its fifty living academicians, to occupy the chair named for Bertrand Guégan, the translator of Apicius and author of several classic works on cuisine. During the previous summer, I conducted two seminars on gastronomy in Strasbourg for the benefit of overflow audiences concerned with the significance of cuisine. Another sign of my hopelessly unsanctified state? Possibly, but bear with me; even Balaam's ass—an eater of straw—had something to say.

I am convinced that evangelicals (whom some clever critic has called "the monks of Protestantism") have so allowed their negative attitude toward "the world" to influence them that in the realm of eating, as in so many other realms (such as entertainment, dress, art, literature) they cut themselves off from God's creative gifts. I believe, *contra* more than one evangelical, that gastronomy is not to be classed among the materialistic "lower immediacies," at the bottom of the axiological ladder of values (to use the expression of the late Edward John Carnell of Fuller Seminary, in his *Philosophy of the Christian Religion*), but deserves transcendental status! In the words of the greatest of all writers on the subject, Brillat-Savarin (*The Physiology of Taste*), gourmandism, far from representing the deadly sin of gluttony—which arises from its *misuse*—"denotes implicit obedience to the commands of the Creator, who bade us eat that we might live."

But here we must be careful, as with all discussion of the transcendental. Metaphysical speculations apart from revelation have been trivial at best, pompous at worst—mercifully relieved only by unconscious humor. The dangers relative to gastronomical speculation are hilariously set out in Marcel Rouff's classic, *The Life and Passion of Dodin-Bouffant, Gourmet*, where the hero, on a visit to Germany, encounters "Prof. Dokt. Hugo Stumm," a philosopher who has already churned out the first 1,783 pages of his definitive Hegelian-Platonic masterpiece, "The Metaphysics of Cuisine," and who, in order practically to reflect the transcendental purity of food as an Ideal, now eats nothing but boiled potatoes and cauliflower!

In this matter, as in all others that touch eternity, only scriptural revelation can keep us from speculative absurdity. But here many evangelicals are in for a surprise, for our sociological pietism has blinded us to a powerful biblical emphasis. Throughout Scripture, eating and drinking are regularly associated with events of the highest theological and spiritual importance.

The Bible opens with man's fall—described in terms of choosing to eat not what God had provided but what he had forbidden ("Of every tree of the garden thou mayest freely eat, but of the tree of the knowledge of good and evil"); it ends with the Marriage Supper of the Lamb, eschatologically restoring Eden and ushering in the New Heaven and New Earth (Rev. 19:9). The prime representation of grace under the Old Covenant was the Passover meal, and it foreshadowed the Sacrament of Eucharist, which our Lord expressly connects with the eternal Marriage Supper when he says: "I will not drink henceforth of this fruit of the vine until that day when I drink it new with you in my Father's kingdom" (Matt. 26:29 and parallels). The centrality of feasting in the early Church is evidenced by its agapes or love feasts, and the observance of the "feasts" or "festivals" of the saints has been a vital part of Christian worship in all the historic confessional traditions.

The conclusion seems inescapable that the Lord of Scripture wants our meals—as the most basic and regular of our conscious activities—to remind us of things eternal. To be sure, our table graces are a halting recognition of this, but do we exercise our talents to prepare meals artistically and gastronomically worthy of the graces we say over them?

The Alsatian Confrérie St-Étienne uses the invitatory: *"Primo mirate, deinde gustate, tandem gaudete ad magnam Dei gloriam"* (First look with wonder, then taste, finally give praise to God's great glory). How many of our meals compel us to look with wonder and taste with praise? Could our reliance on TV dinners signify just the opposite of spirituality—a gross indifference to and ingratitude for God's culinary gifts to us? As Brillat-Savarin aphoristically and uncomfortably put it: "Tell me what you eat: I will tell you what you are."

This holiday season is it not time to apply Horatius Bonar's Communion hymn in its widest sense?

> *Feast after feast thus comes and passes by,*
> *Yet, passing, points to the glad feast above,*
> *Giving sweet foretaste of the festal joy,*
> *The Lamb's great bridal feast of bliss and love.*

Sociologist Peter Berger, in his *Rumor of Angels*, notes that certain activities, from children's games to great concerts, can link one to eternity, for as one is caught up in them time and mortality seem momentarily arrested and a window opens on another world. Banquets and feasts can be like that. If you listen very closely at your Thanksgiving or Christmas table, you may just hear the flutter of angels' wings: a cloud of witnesses rejoicing with you, waiting to welcome you to an even greater banquet.

Part Eight

The Impact of the Gospel

1. Slavery, Human Dignity and Human Rights[1]

Synopsis

Slavery continues to be practiced in many parts of the world: not only chattel slavery but also indirect varieties (enforced child labour, prostitution, debt enslavement, etc.). Secular organisations opposed to these practices seek to provide a suitable philosophical counter to those supporting or tolerating the evils.

The present paper considers natural law and neo-Kantian arguments and finds them wanting. It then looks at biblical principles and the history of the abolition of the slave trade in England and the emancipation movement in the United States (18th-19th centuries). From this ideological and historical survey, an attempt is made to discover why Enlightenment principles, as exemplified by the French philosophes, *Thomas Jefferson, and other Revolutionaries, failed to impact, whilst evangelical christians (Granville Sharp, John Newton, Wilberforece, et al.) succeeded in their hard-won crusade to outlaw slavery.*

By way of conclusion, a parallel is drawn with the contemporary right-to-life movement and jurisprudent Ronald Dworkin's position on abortion.

I. The paradox

When, a quarter century ago, I taught at the International School of Law, Washington, D.C., we lived in Falls Church, Virginia. I could always get a laugh at Commonwealth parties (Virginia must be so designated—never as a mere 'State') by observing that I was having great difficulty finding slaves to proofread my book manuscripts. In today's climate of political correctness, such attempts at humour would be regarded as offensive at best, obnoxious at worst.

In the modern world, every one, everywhere condemns slavery. The formal opposition to it is as powerful as is the universal acclaim for human rights (which are lauded both by doctrinaire liberals and by the worst of dictators). Indeed, the international legal instruments could not be more specific—from the Slavery Convention of the League of Nations, which entered into force 9

---

[1] This paper was presented by invitation at the 4th Annual Lilly Fellows Program National Research Conference ('Christianity and Human Rights'), held at Samford University, 11-14 November 2004; and at the 57th Annual National Meeting of the Evangelical Theological Society, Valley Forge, Pennsylvania, 17 November 2005.

March 1927, through Article 4 of both the Universal Declaration of Human Rights and the European Convention of Human Rights, to the Supplementary Convention on the Abolition of Slavery, the Slave Trade, and Institutions and Practices Similar to Slavery, adopted in 1956 under UN sponsorship to reinforce and augment the 1927 Slavery Convention. Not only is traditional, chattel slavery declared to be unqualifiedly illegal ('No one shall be held in slavery or servitude; slavery and the slave trade shall be prohibited in all their forms'—Universal Declaration of 1948), but the category of slavery is expanded (1956-1957 Supplementary Convention) to include:

> (a) Debt bondage, that is to say, the status or condition arising from a pledge by a debtor of his personal services or of those of a person under his control as security for a debt, if the value of those services as reasonably assessed is not applied towards the liquidation of the debt or the length and nature of those services are not respectively limited and defined;
>
> (b) Serfdom, that is to say, the condition or status of a tenant who is by law, custom or agreement bound to live and labour on land belonging to another person and to render some determinate service to such other person, whether for reward or not, and is not free to change his status;
>
> (c) Any institution or practice whereby:
>
> (i) A woman, without the right to refuse, is promised or given in marriage on payment of a consideration in money or in kind to her parents, guardian, family or any other person or group; or
>
> (ii) The husband of a woman, his family, or his clan, has the right to transfer her to another person for value received or otherwise; or
>
> (iii) A woman on the death of her husband is liable to be inherited by another person;
>
> (d) Any institution or practice whereby a child or young person under the age of 18 years, is delivered by either or both of his natural parents or by his guardian to another person, whether for reward or not, with a view to the exploitation of the child or young person or of his labour.

The countries ratifying these international treaties cover virtually the entire globe. Thus—to take but one example—the Supplementary Convention just quoted has been ratified by 119 States-parties, from Afghanistan in 1966 (!) to Zimbabwe in 1998 (!!). The *de jure* situation, then, appears entirely unambiguous: slavery, direct or indirect, anywhere and everywhere, is a legal wrong in every respect, whatever the terminology applied to it.

Paradoxically, however, things are much different *de facto*. Responsible anti-slavery organisations cite innumerable instances of the continuing enslavement of human beings by their fellows. The American Anti-Slavery Group (http://

www.iabolish.com) cites the documented prevalence of carpet slaves (especially child labourers in the weaving trade) in India[2]; debt slavery in Haiti's sugar industry; sex slaves in Southeast Asia; and even literal chattel slavery persisting in Mauritania and Sudan. From the website just given, here is a sobering list of 'slavery hotspots':

Thailand: Women and children forced to work as sex slaves for tourists

Ivory Coast: Boys forced to work on cocoa plantations

India: Children trapped in debt bondage roll beedi cigarettes 14 hours a day

Sudan: Arab militias from the North abduct black African women and children in slave raids

Dominican Republic: Haitians lured across the border are forced to cut cane on sugar plantations

Albania: Teenage girls are tricked into sex slavery and trafficked by organised crime rings

Brazil: Lured into the rainforest, families burn trees into charcoal at gunpoint

United Arab Emirates: Little Bangladeshi boys are imported to be jockeys for camel racing

United States: 50,000 trafficked in each year, as sex slaves, domestics, seamstresses, and agricultural workers

Burma: The ruling military junta exploits civilian forced labour for infrastructure projects

Ghana: Families repent for sins by giving daughters as slaves to fetish priests

Pakistan: Children with 'nimble fingers' are forced to weave carpets in dark looms

Mauritania: Arabo-Berbers buy and sell black Africans as inheritable property

---

[2] Cf. Joanna Watson, 'Modern Day Slavery,' *The christian Lawyer: The Journal of the Lawyers' christian Fellowship* [U.K.], Summer, 2004, 10-11; and Peter Hammond, "Slavery Today and the Battle Over History," 16 November 2006 (http://www.frontline.org.za). A useful popular article on the continuing problem of slavery ('21st Century Slaves'), with bibliographical references, may be found in *National Geographic* (September, 2003). For a scholarly journal devoted to studies in the field of the present paper, see *Slavery & Abolition: A Journal of Slave and Post-Slave Studies* (Routledge).

That this catalogue of inhuman activities is by no means exaggerated is illustrated by a 21 February 2004 *Times* (London) news article, 'Brazilian Slaves Are Freed in Jungle Raid':

> Forty-nine men, women and children, who had been subjected to months of enforced labour, clearing jungle vegetation from the Fazenda Macauba cattle ranch were freed after telling inspectors that they had spent at least 80 days working 10 hours a day, without pay. ...
>
> The raid on the Fazenda Macauba was triggered after [an escapee] reported the conditions to the Pastoral Earth Commission, a Roman Catholic organisation that campaigns against slavery in Brazil. ...
>
> The raid ... is the latest in a recent crackdown on modern slavery, a practice still common in Brazil, especially in the cattle ranches of the Amazon and sugar and coffee plantations in the states of Bahia and Maranhao. ...
>
> President da Silva has pledged his Government to freeing at least 25,000 people estimated to be in slavery. 'A modern Brazil cannot tolerate such an archaic practice', he said.

Slavery, in short, is by no means a dead issue. Such statistics as 'the sixty-six slaveholding societies in the Murdock world sample' and the classification of 'the large-scale slave systems' presented by sociologist Orlando Patterson, though valuable historically, do not by any means exhaust the subject.[3]

The widespread continuation of slavery practices, paradoxically combined with universal condemnation of the phenomenon, is highlighted by a passage at the end of one of the works of the most distinguished English-language historian of slavery, David Brion Davis of Yale University:

> As Conor Cruise O'Brien has pointed out, the United Nations is political theater dominated by an institutional tone of 'lofty morality' perfectly suited for the dramatic exploitation of guilt—in particular, 'Western guilt feelings toward the non-white world'. The influx of new African states enabled the nonwhite members to win hegemonic control over the 'moral conscience of mankind'. Unfortunately, condemnations of colonialism and apartheid as the twentieth-century equivalents of slavery sometimes served to shield forms of oppression for which whites bore no responsibility. In a complacent report of 1965, the Republic of Mali contended that a benign, paternalistic servitude had preceded European colonization and that national independence, accompanied by genuine social democracy, had brought the final abolition of slavery and similar institutions. Yet slave-trading continued to flourish in Mauritania, Mali, Niger, and Chad, along the drought-stricken

---

[3] Orlando Patterson, *Slavery and Social Death: A Comparative Study* (Cambridge, Mass.: Harvard University Press, 1982), 345-64.

southern fringe of the Sahara. Historical mythology minimizing or denying African and Arab involvement in the slave trade has fostered the false assumption that slavery depended for its survival on colonial regimes.[4]

The source of the paradox of continuing slavery is not 'colonialism' or any other related stereotype; its roots lie much deeper, in the conceptions of the human person and in the *Weltanschauungen* which inform those conceptions. In a syllabus for a graduate course in 'Slavery As a Critique of the Concept of Human Rights', Professor Raymond Fleming of Florida State University's Department of Modern Languages and Linguistics, put it well:

> Our attention to the various forms of slavery will enable us to focus upon what Western culture wishes to affirm or deny about the notion of a human subject. Whether it is the Scholastics in the Middle Ages affirming man as a *res sacra*, a sacredness, or Pico della Mirandola in the Renaissance asserting the dignity of man, or Thomas Jefferson proclaiming the self-evident character of specific human rights, we will note along this continuum just how society and *Realpolitik* invariably undermine such declarations. We will see how slavery provides us with an effective critique of the rhetoric of 'high culture', and also how the existence of slavery in the face of such sentiments reveals what these utterances leave out of their formulations. What are often left out, what Roland Barthes terms, 'what goes without saying', are the ideologies informing such declarations.

Though we shall certainly not engage in the deconstruction here suggested, we shall indeed focus upon the 'ideologies' which underlie both the attitudes and the declarations relating to slavery. Our purpose will be to discover what kind of foundation, if any, can put paid to the hypocrisy so often met with in treatments of the phenomenon of slavery.

II. Philosophical opposition to slavery

The chief modern philosophical arguments against slavery have been those of Enlightenment natural law theory and Kantian and neo-Kantian universalism. These, alone or in combination, have provided the underpinning for most contemporary human rights philosophies and their opposition to all forms of slavery. The question remains, however: Are these theories adequate?

---

[4] David Brion Davis, *Slavery and Human Progress* (New York: Oxford University Press, 1984), 318-19. Cf. Davis, *Challenging the Boundaries of Slavery* (Cambridge, Mass.: Harvard University Press, 2003), and Thomas Bender (ed.), *The Antislavery Debate: Capitalism and Abolitionism As a Problem in Historical Interpretation* (Berkeley, Ca.: University of California Press, 1992) [with contributions by David Brion Davis].

The jusnaturalism of the French *philosophes* and American 'founding fathers' such as Jefferson maintained that there is a built-in ethic of human dignity which all must recognise. The human person benefits from 'certain inalienable rights', including the rights to 'life, liberty, and the pursuit of happiness'. Both the French Declaration of the Rights of Man and the American Bill of Rights endeavoured to summarise the essential civil liberties of the citizen. These rights were supposed to be justified by the agreement of all rational persons. After all, did not the 18th century Enlightenment usher in an 'Age of Reason' (Thomas Paine's profoundly influential book title), elevating mankind beyond prior centuries of theological superstition?

Unhappily, this humanistic version of jusnaturalism was — and is — incapable of providing the needed bulwark against slavery. In classical Roman jurisprudence, to which the Enlightenment advocates of the viewpoint frequently turned for their main historical precedent, slavery was allowed by way of the *Ius gentium* ('law of nations/international law') even though it was directly contrary to the natural law: 'Slavery is the only case in which, in the extant sources of Roman law, a conflict is declared to exist between the *Ius Gentium* and the *Ius Naturale*. It is of course inconsistent with that universal equality of man which Roman speculations on the Law of Nature assume'.[5]

The same ambivalence was present in the thinking versus the practice of French and American Enlightenment revolutionaries. The Marquis de Condorcet, biographer of Voltaire and committed anti-christian progressive, ruefully admitted that 'only a few *philosophes* have from time to time dared raise a cry in favour of humanity [over against slaveholding]'.[6] Thomas Jefferson's views of equality did not preserve him from antisemitism[7] — much less from a quietist maintenance of the status quo where slaveholding was concerned. It appears likely that he fathered illegitimate children whose mother was one of his slaves.[8] Even a Jefferson hagiographer has to write:

> Jefferson's perception of slavery was determined by several ambivalent circumstances: he was a planter-slaveowner, a Virginian whose strongest allegiance, when the test came, was to his state and section, and withal a

---

[5] W. W. Buckland, *The Roman Law of Slavery: The Condition of the Slave in Private Law from Augustus to Justinian* (reprint ed.; Cambridge, England: Cambridge University Press, 1970), 1.

[6] M. J. A. Condorcet, *Remarques sur les Pensées de Pascal*, in Condorcet's *Oeuvres* (12 vols.; Paris: Firmin-Didot, 1847-1849), III, 649.

[7] Cf. Arthur Hertzberg, *The French Enlightenment and the Jews* (New York: Columbia University Press, 1990).

[8] Cf. Lucia Stanton, *Slavery at Monticello* (Monticello, Virginia: Thomas Jefferson Memorial Foundation, 1996), 20-22, 50 (note 21 and the literature there cited). In his Preface to this monograph, Julian Bond writes that the 'gross imbalance he [Jefferson] represents between national promise and execution remains our greatest state embarrassment today.'

man of the eighteenth century Enlightenment. This circumstance created in Jefferson's mind an ambiguity and a dissonance which he never succeeded in resolving to his own satisfaction. While Jefferson regarded slavery as a 'hideous evil', the bane of American society, and wholly irreconcilable with his ideal of 'republican virtue', he was never able wholly to cast aside the prejudices and the fears which he had absorbed from his surroundings toward people of color; he did not free himself from dependence upon slave labor; and, in the end, he made the expansion of slavery into the territories a constitutional right, and a *conditio sine qua non* of the South's adherence to the Union.[9]

I have pointed elsewhere to law professor and distinguished Federal judge John T. Noonan's demonstration that 'Jefferson and his legal mentor George Wythe aided in perpetuating a forensic vocabulary that classed blacks as transferable property, thereby permitting whites to carry on slavery while "democratically" supporting human freedom and dignity in the founding documents of the nation'.[10]

Why did these Enlightenment thinkers suffer from such a disparity between their principles and their practice? As with the Roman jurisprudents, the reason lies surely in the vagueness and ambiguity of their 'natural law' principles.[11] Nowhere is the content of the natural law set forth with sufficient explicitness to counter the indignities suffered by those in slavery. Thus rationalisation could easily enter the picture when concrete questions were raised as to the ethical treatment of slaves and the proper criteria of manumission.

Eighteenth-century secular jusnaturalism was later to suffer a devastating blow when in the 19th and 20th centuries anthropologists demonstrated the wide diversity of cultural patterns in non-Western societies. Apparently, not everyone agreed with the 'rationality' of enlightened Europeans. Slavery was practised and condoned in many cultures; was it therefore really contrary to the 'natural law'? And suppose everyone *had* been against it—would general agreement (*consensus gentium*) suddenly have become a satisfactory test of truth?

As for the ethical theories deriving from Immanuel Kant's Categorical Imperative ('act only on that maxim which you can will to be a universal law'), they have fared no better as a bulwark against slavery. When neo-Kantian John Rawls tells us that we should act under a 'veil of ignorance' as to our special

---

[9] John Chester Miller, *The Wolf by the Ears: Thomas Jefferson and Slavery* (New York: Free Press, 1977), 2-3. Cf. Matthew T. Mellon, *Early American Views on Negro Slavery* (Boston: Meador, 1934), especially 120-22.

[10] John Warwick Montgomery, *The Shaping of America* (revised ed.; Minneapolis: Bethany, 1981), 54. See Noonan's *Persons and Masks of the Law* (New York: Farrar, Straus & Giroux, 1975).

[11] John Warwick Montgomery, *The Law Above the Law* (Minneapolis: Bethany, 1975), especially 37-42.

advantages and therefore follow genuine 'principles of justice', treating our fellowmen as equal in rights and dignity, the historical response has generally been that our special advantages are precisely our ground for *not* treating others (such as potential or actual slaves) as we would want to be treated. When Alan Gewirth insists that you rationally 'act in accord with the generic rights of your recipients as well as of yourself', not because you are someone special ('Wordsworth Donisthorpe'), the slaver will invariably respond that it is precisely because he *is* 'Wordsworth Donisthorpe'—or someone else of superior power, influence, or connections—that he is in a position to function as slavetrader or slaveowner. The Ghengis Khans of this world have seldom been impressed by arguments of rationalistic universalisation.[12]

Kantian and neo-Kantian arguments suffer from the same difficulty as claims made on the basis of humanistic jusnaturalism: they do not define adequately the content of ethical action; they do not specify *which* specific actions and activities are *good* and *which* are *bad*. Recently, the international press has had a field day with the trial of one Armin Meiwes, who advertised on the net (his occupation was computer programmer) for those who would like him to eat them. After having consumed a number of willing victims, Mr Meiwes was arrested on the charge of having murdered at least one of them. However, he was not convicted of murder but was sentenced by a Kassel court to a mere eight-and-a-half year prison term on the ground that—to quote the judge—'this was an act between two … people who both wanted something from each other'.[13] Suppose that we grant that the eater would have been willing to become the eatee, or vice-versa; would such universalisation of cannibalism therefore establish the ethics of anthropophagy? Surely not; but this means that one must be able to set forth and justify solidly grounded ethical strictures against cannibalism—and slavery—in order to oppose those practices. Merely stating a formal principle of 'generic consistency' will hardly be adequate.

Moreover, even supposing that one could successfully demonstrate the correctness of a natural-law ethic or categorical imperative, would this mean that people would necessarily follow it? Must one be rational, when rationality goes against self-interest? History certainly does not support the view that just because one can show that a course of action is right, people will take that route. Quite clearly, to deal with the issue of slavery, one must *change the slavetrader's or slaveowner's value-system*. His or her motivations must undergo radical al-

---

[12] On the neo-Kantian attempts to establish a foundation for ethics, see our detailed critiques in John Warwick Montgomery, *Human Rights and Human Dignity* (rev. ed.; Calgary, Alberta, Canada: Canadian Institute for Law, Theology and Public Policy, 1995), especially 92-98, 183; and *Tractatus Logico-Theologicus* (rev. ed.; Bonn, Germany: Verlag für Kultur und Wissenschaft, 2003), 171-74 (sec. 5.5-5.6).

[13] *Washington Times*, 31 January 2004 (UPI dispatch).

teration. In traditional terminology, what is required is *conversion*. But this is precisely what—in spite of all the good will exercised—humanistic ethics has never been able to produce. Doubtless this is why the abolition of slavery, insofar as it has been accomplished, stemmed not from Roman law, naturalistic ethics, or the Enlightenment, but from the impact of christian faith.

III. Slavery and christian witness

Christianity—Orthodox, Catholic, and Protestant—has always maintained that (1) God has spoken revelationally, providing absolute standards for human conduct, and (2) through a personal relationship with Jesus Christ, the Son of God, who died on the Cross to expiate human sin and selfishness, one can be transformed ethically, receiving a 'new spirit' and a new value-system which will result in treating the neighbour as oneself. In principle, therefore, the revealed christian gospel has the needed answer to the slavery problem. Has this been the case in practice?

Jewish scholar E. E. Urbach asserts that neither 'in classical Greek literature, in the writings of the Stoics, and in the christian Scriptures … nor in the Jewish sources is there the slightest suggestion of any notions of the abolition of slavery'.[14] We would agree as to all of the above—save 'the christian Scriptures'. To be sure, no call to social revolution occurs there (and the immediate elimination of slavery in the Roman world would have produced just that). But the central teaching of Jesus as to 'treating the neighbour as oneself', coupled with the changed hearts of those who came to believe in him, meant the eventual death of a system based on treating the slave as a chattel and not as a human being worth as much as his master.

> In such an economic context [that of the Roman Empire] it was virtually impossible for anyone to conceive of abolishing slavery as a legal-economic institution. To have turned all the slaves into free day laborers would have been to create an economy in which those at the bottom would have suffered even more insecurity and potential poverty than before. To be sure, according to all known traditions, neither Jesus nor His immediate followers owned slaves; nor did Paul, Barnabas, or Timothy. So both the example of Jesus and His great concern for the poor proved to be a challenge for many early christians to conceive of themselves as living already among themselves in an alternative social-legal environment (note how Paul appeals to Philemon to release Onesimus sooner than he may have planned). For the author of

---

[14] E. E. Urbach, *The Laws Regarding Slavery: As a Source for Social History of the Period of the Second Temple, the Mishnah and Talmud* (New York: Arno Press, 1979), 93-94.

1 Clem. 55:2 Christ's love working through humble spirits has motivated some christians to sell themselves in order to have money to buy the freedom of others (see She Henn. Mand. 8:10; Sim. 1:8; Ign. Polyc. 4:3).[15]

* * * * *

Le maître devait ménager les esclaves comme ses égaux en liberté; il devait les ménager encore comme étant lui-même leur frère en servitude; c'est une autre face de la vérité chrétienne que les Pères développent à l'envi, pour mieux faire entrer dans les âmes le sentiment des devoirs de l'egalité. Nous sommes tous nés en servitude, nous sommes tous rachetés en Jesus-Christ. ...

Ainsi, du moment où le christianisme eut révélé sa doctrine, la cause de la liberté avait vaincu. Le jour du triomphe devait se faire attendre, il est vrai; et déjà le signe du salut dominait dans le monde, qu'on l'attendait encore. Mais pendant ces retards forcés l'Eglise n'oublia point les esclaves; et, en même temps qu'elle leur préparait des ressources désormais honorables après l'affranchissement, elle prétendait leur faire donner une place au foyer domestique, dans l'éducation de la famille, dans l'estime publique; elle réclamait pour eux tous les droits et les traitements de l'homme libre, sauf le droit de disposer de soi, que l'homme libre d'ailleurs cessa bientôt presque généralement d'avoir lui-même.[16]

True, professing christians have not always condemned slavery and some (for example, in the pre-Civil War South of the United States) have supported it and even attempted to justify their actions in that regard. But when they have done so, they have acted contrary to the faith they profess, not in response to the teachings of its Founder. Indeed, it is an unarguable historical fact that the abolition of slavery in modern times stems directly from christian

---

[15] S. Scott Bartchy, 'Slavery,' *International Standard Bible Encyclopedia*, ed. Geoffrey W. Bromiley (rev. ed., 4 vols.; Grand Rapids, Mich.: Eerdmans, 1979-1988), IV, 546. See also Markus Barth and Helmut Blanke, 'The Social Background: Slavery at Paul's Time,' in their *The Letter to Philemon: A New Translation with Notes and Commentary* (Grand Rapids, Mich.: Eerdmans, 2000), 1-102.

[16] Henri Wallon, *Histoire de l'esclavage dans l'Antiquité*, ed. Jean Christian Dumont (Paris: Robert Laffont, 1988), 801, 835. This magisterial 19th century work remains of immense importance on the subject of slavery in the ancient world and the christian impact upon it. On the reference in the first quoted paragraph to redemption from slavery in Jesus Christ, see an important study of the New Testament use of slavery motifs to characterise every human being's bondage to sin and the primary need to be freed from it: Dale B. Martin, *Slavery As Salvation: The Metaphor of Slavery in Pauline Christianity* (New Haven, Conn.: Yale University Press, 1990). In the second quoted paragraph, Wallon's reference in the final two lines is to the soon-to-come barbarian invasions of the Roman Empire and the establishment of feudal serfdom as a desperate attempt at economic stability in the decentralised chaos of the early Middle Ages.

influence.[17] We shall briefly review the pertinent ideological background, with special reference to the Anglo-American struggle against slavery and its worldwide repercussions.

The stage was set for the British outlawing of the slave trade and American abolition by christian theologians, pamphleteers, and preachers from Reformation times to the 19th century. The distinguished German Lutheran theologian J. F. Buddeus (1667-1729), author, *inter alia*, of *Selecta juris naturae et gentium*, argued that even if some blacks were legally captured or received criminal convictions leading to slavery, their offspring should not be subject to bondage by inheritance.[18]

Quakers were especially strong in condemning slavery per se. Benjamin Lay declared in 1736: '*As God gave his only begotten Son, that whosoever believed in him might have everlasting Life;* so the Devil gives his only begotten Child, *the Merchandize of Slaves and Souls of Men,* that whosoever believes and trades in it might have everlasting Damnation'.[19] Quaker John Woolman, in his *Journal* and his *Some Considerations on the Keeping of Negroes* (1754, second part, 1762), devastatingly set forth as a christian argument the selfishness, immorality and greed inherent in the slave trade and prophetically predicted dire consequences for the future of America if slavery was not eliminated.[20]

In England, Bishop Warburton likewise condemned slavery in the American colonies. Before the Society for the Propagation of the Gospel he declared: 'Gracious God! To talk (as in herds of Cattle) of Property in rational Creatures!'[21] christian apologist William Paley characterised slavery as an 'abominable tyranny' and 'an institution replete with human misery' which could no longer possibly be justified, even on utilitarian grounds.[22]

---

[17] Alvin J. Schmidt, *Under the Influence: How Christianity Transformed Civilization* (Grand Rapids, Mich.: Zondervan, 2001), chap. 11 ('Slavery Abolished: A christian Achievement'), 272-91; Rodney Stark, *For the Glory of God: How Monotheism Led to Reformations, Science, Witch-Hunts, and the End of Slavery* (Princeton, NJ: Princeton University Press, 2004), pp. 291 ff.
[18] See the biographical article in the *Allgemeine Deutsche Biographie*.
[19] Benjamin Lay, *All Slave-keepers that Keep the Innocent in Bondage …* (Philadelphia, 1737), 10-13.
[20] David Brion Davis concludes his magisterial study, *The Problem of Slavery in Western Culture* (Ithaca, N.Y.: Cornell University Press, 1966), with 'Epilogue: John Woolman's Prophecy' (483-93).
[21] William Warburton, *A Sermon Preached Before the Incorporated Society for the Propagation of the Gospel in Foreign Parts* (London, 1766), 25-26. The Warburton Lectures, devoted by the terms of Warburton's bequest to the defense of the christian faith, continue today at Lincoln's Inn (one of the four barristers' Inns of Court), London.
[22] William Paley, *The Principles of Moral and Political Philosophy* (London, 1785), 196-98 (cf. 'Introduction').

John Wesley, the Anglican founder of Methodism, asserted that 'the dreadful consequence of slavery is the same amongst every people and in every nation where it prevails'. To the slaveowner he declared: 'Thy hands, thy bed, thy furniture, thy house, thy lands are at present stained with blood' as a result of using slave labour, and only repentance before God and emancipation could put things right.[23]

John Newton's dramatic conversion from slave trader to clergyman had tremendous impact in changing the English climate of opinion. It was Newton who not only composed such classic hymns as 'Amazing Grace', 'How Sweet the Name of Jesus Sounds', and 'Glorious Things of Thee Are Spoken',[24] but who also spoke uncompromisingly against the unchristian activity with which he had formerly been connected.[25] Newton's autobiography was circulating in a cheap, popular edition in France in the years immediately prior to the abolition of slavery in the French colonies (1848).[26] Wesley and Newton are excellent illustrations of what David Brion Davis has termed the 'important connection between evangelical religion and antislavery'.[27]

These believers from a wide variety of confessional traditions provided the backdrop for the political action that finally succeeded in destroying slavery in England and America.[28] The chief names associated with that activity in England were Granville Sharp and William Wilberforce. Both of them were directly and centrally motivated by their christian convictions.

---

[23] John Wesley, *Thoughts upon Slavery* (Philadelphia, 1774), especially 39-55.

[24] On Newton's hymnody, see my former professor Erik Routley's *I'll Praise My Maker: Studies in English Classical Hymnody* (London: Independent Press, 1951), 145-78. The most accessible primary source on Newton's life is the contemporary biography by Richard Cecil; it has been responsibly edited and updated by Marylynn Rousse: *The Life of John Newton* (Geanies House, Fearn, Ross-shire, Great Britain: christian Focus Publications, 2000); see also Jonathan Aitken, *John Newton: From Disgrace to Amazing Grace* (London: Continuum, 2007). An in-print edition of Newton's *Works* in 6 vols. is available from Banner of Truth Trust (Edinburgh, Scotland). The Cowper and Newton Museum in Olney, Bucks, is well worth visiting; Newton was pastor in Olney 'near sixteen years' (Newton's epitaph).

[25] John Newton, *Thoughts Upon the African Slave Trade* (2d ed.; London, 1788); Newton's *Journal of a Slave Trader* (1750-54) and *Thoughts Upon the African Slave Trade* were reprinted in one volume by Epworth Press in 1962. Cf. Gail Cameron and Stan Crooke, *Liverpool—Capital of the Slave Trade* (Liverpool, England: Picton Press, 1992), and James Walvin, *Black Ivory: Slavery in the British Empire* (2d ed.; Oxford: Blackwell, 2001).

[26] *Récit authentique de la Vie de J. Newton ... écrit par lui-même dans une suite de lettres adressées au Docteur Haweis* [Toulouse: J.-M. Corne, 1835]). Copy in the author's personal library.

[27] Davis, *The Problem of Slavery in Western Culture* (*op. cit.*), 388-90. See also D. Bruce Hindmarsh, *John Newton and the English Evangelical Tradition* (Grand Rapids, Mich.; Eerdmans, 2001), and Adam Hochschild, *Bury the Chains: Prophets and Rebels in the Fight to Free an Empire's Slaves* (New York: Houghton Mifflin, 2005).

[28] Cf. Thomas Clarkson, *The History of the Rise, Progress, and Accomplishment of the Abolition of*

Granville Sharp (1735-1813) is still a household name in New Testament scholarship, for he formulated the rule bearing his name which recognises that 'when two personal nouns of the same case and connected by the copulate *kai*, if the former has the definite article and the latter has not, they both belong to the same person'. This rule is of tremendous theological importance, for it establishes, in passages such as 2 Thess. 1:12, the identity of Jesus Christ with God the Father.[29] Sharp was one of the founders of the British and Foreign Bible Society and of the Society for the Conversion of the Jews.

But Granville Sharp's undying fame rests on his success in abolishing the slave trade. As the inscription on his monument in Poets' Corner, Westminster Abbey has it:

> He took his post among the foremost of the honourable band
> Associated to deliver Africa from the rapacity of Europe,
> By the abolition of the Slave Trade.
> Nor was death permitted to interrupt his career of usefulness,
> Till he had witnessed that Act of the British Parliament
> By which the abolition was decreed.

In 1767, Sharp encountered a West Indian planter's slave named Jonathan Strong who had been brought to London and badly beaten by his master; once recovered, he was sold by the master to a third party. Sharp was so incensed by this that he examined the legal situation for himself and finally, five years later, in the *Somersett* case, succeeded in obtaining Lord Mansfield's judgment: 'The state of slavery is so odious that nothing can be suffered to support it but positive law, and there is no law'.[30] This meant, in effect, that a slave must forthwith receive freedom the moment he or she set foot on English soil.[31]

---

the African Slave-trade by the British Parliament (2 vols., reprint ed.; London: Frank Cass, 1968), especially I, 5-192 and II, 570-87. This classic work by one who devoted his life to opposing slavery internationally was originally published in 1808, immediately following the British Parliament's outlawing of the slave trade. Clarkson declares (I, 8-9): 'Among the evils, corrected or subdued, either by the general influence of Christianity on the minds of men, or by particular associations of christians, the African Slave-trade appears to me to have occupied the foremost place.' Cf. Melvin D. Kennedy, *Lafayette and Slavery: From His Letters to Thomas Clarkson and Granville Sharp* (Easton, Pa.: American Friends of Lafayette, 1950).

[29] Granville Sharp, *Remarks on the Uses of the Definitive Article in the Greek Text of the New Testament, Containing many New Proofs of the Divinity of Christ* ..., ed. William David McBrayer (reprint ed.; Atlanta/Roswell, Ga.: Original Word, 1995).

[30] Cf. Steven M. Wise, *Though the Heavens May Fall: The Landmark Trial That Led to the End of Human Slavery* (Boston: Merloyd Lawrence, 2005).

[31] See Granville Sharp, *A Tract on the Law of Nature, and Principles of Action in Man* (London: B. White; and E. and C. Dilly, 1777), and *Tracts on Slavery and Liberty: The Just Limitation of Slavery in the Laws of God... The Law of Passive Obedience... The Law of Liberty...* (reprint ed.; Westport, Conn.: Negro Universities Press, 1969). Cf. Edward C. Lascelles, *Granville Sharp and*

The forty-year long, ultimately successful struggle of William Wilberforce (1759-1833) to obtain a Parliamentary act abolishing slavery is too well known to require detailed discussion here; the literature is extensive.[32] What needs to be stressed is Wilberforce's root motivation in engaging in this formidable task: his christian conviction that slavery was an offense to almighty God and a detriment to the effective spread of Christ's gospel.[33] Wilberforce experienced evangelical conversion in his 20's and came under the influence of former slave trader John Newton. In 1787, he declared: 'God has set before me two great objects: the abolition of the slave trade and the reformation of manners'. From that point he never looked back. As one of the leaders of the so-called 'Clapham Sect'—evangelicals who promoted political, philanthropic, and ethical causes—he championed prison reform, Bible distribution, missionary endeavour, and charitable work of many kinds. In his crusade against slavery as a Member of Parliament, he first succeeded after eighteen years in seeing the slave trade outlawed (1807-1808), and then, after another twenty-six years, the passing of the Emancipation Bill (in 1833, just three days before his demise).

The efforts of Wilberforce and likeminded English opponents of slavery had an impact far beyond Great Britain. Their 'transcendent belief stirred abolitionists in the United States during the antebellum and Civil War periods, in France during the 1840s, in Cuba during the Ten Years' War (1868-78), and in Brazil during the 1880s'.[34]

In America, the English evangelical impact is clear, for example, in the writings of Thomas Branagan of Philadelphia (1774-1843), like Newton personally involved in slaving and subsequently converted to christian belief.[35] In his essay on 'Human Slavery', he refers specifically to Wilberforce's Parliamentary

---

the *Freedom of Slaves in England* (London: Oxford University Press/Humphrey Milford, 1928) [with extensive documentation and illustrations]; Oliver Ransford, *The Slave Trade: The Story of Transatlantic Slavery* (Newton Arrot, Devon, England: Readers Union, 1972), 178 ff.; and Daniel B. Wallace, 'Granville Sharp: A Model of Evangelical Scholarship and Social Activism,' *Journal of the Evangelical Theological Society*, 41 (1998), 591-613.

[32] Leonard W. Cowie, *William Wilberforce, 1759-1833: A Bibliography* (Westport, Conn.: Greenwood, 1992).

[33] See especially: John Pollock, *Wilberforce* (London: Constable, 1977); David J. Vaughan and George Grant, *Statesman and Saint: The Principled Politics of William Wilberforce* (Nashville, Tenn.: Cumberland House, 2001); Kevin Belmonte, *Hero for Humanity: A Biography of William Wilberforce* (Colorado Springs, Colo.: Navpress, 2002)—and, to be sure, Leslie Stephen's classic article on him in the *Dictionary of National Biography*.

[34] Davis, *Slavery and Human Progress* (op. cit.), 280-81.

[35] On Branagan, see Lewis Leary, 'Thomas Branagan,' in his *Soundings: Some Early American Writers* (Athens, Ga.: University of Georgia Press, 1975), 229-52; and Leary, 'Thomas Branagan,' in James A. Levernier and Douglas R. Wilmes (eds.), *American Writers Before 1800: A Biographical and Critical Dictionary* (Westport, Conn.: Greenwood Press, 1983), 195-96.

struggles and declares: 'Slavery, hateful to God and man, and the greatest evil and sum-total of all evils under the sun, and inflicted by Americans, the most favoured people, and, may I not say, the most enlightened and highest in profession of liberty and Christianity, must render us the most inexcusable, and draw down, unless expiated by sincere repentance and undoing heavy burdens, the just indignation of Him who does not even let a sparrow fall without his notice'.[36]

The American abolition movement drew its power directly from christian sources. Harriet Beecher Stowe, the author *Uncle Tom's Cabin* (1851-52), the most influential anti-slavery fiction ever written, selling on publication a half a million copies in the United States and double that number in Great Britain, was the daughter of the Revd Lyman Beecher, president of Lane Theological Seminary; wife of a Lane Seminary professor; and sister of the celebrated preacher Henry Ward Beecher. She began writing her novel following a church service in which she had a mystical experience; afterwards she said that 'The Lord himself wrote', i.e., was the real author, of her book.[37]

The impact of the Lane Theological Seminary on the abolition movement was considerable.

> In 1833 Oberlin College was founded in northern Ohio. Into some of the first classes there women were admitted on equal terms with men. In 1835 the trustees offered the presidency to Professor Asa Mahan, of Lane Seminary. He was himself an abolitionist from a slave State, and he refused to be President of Oberlin College unless negroes were admitted on equal terms with other students. Oberlin thus became the first institution in the country which extended the privileges of the higher education to both sexes of all races. It was a distinctly religious institution devoted to radical reforms of many kinds.[38]

Far less well known than Harriet Beecher Stowe were an influential number of christian writers who condemned American slavery. As early as 1816, George Bourne posed the rhetorical question, 'Can you conscientiously believe, that a slaveholder exhibits that assimilation to the meek and lowly Jesus, which is in-

---

[36] [Thomas Branagan,] *The Guardian Genius ... or, Patriotic Admonitions ... in relation to ... Human Slavery. ... By a Philanthropist* (New York, 1839), 25 ff.
[37] Ransford, *op. cit.*, 235-43.
[38] Jesse Macy, *The Anti-Slavery Crusade: A Chronicle of the Gathering Storm* (New Haven, Conn.: Yale University Press, 1920), 50-51. Fascinatingly, the radical anti-slavery activism of many Lane theological students was more than even that institution could tolerate; a considerable number of students (the so-called 'Lane Rebels') decamped to Oberlin in 1834; see Stuart C. Henry, 'Lane Theological Seminary,' in *Dictionary of Heresy Trials in American Christianity*, ed. George H. Shriver (Westport, Conn.: Greenwood Press, 1997), 214-21.

dispensable to an enjoyment of the inheritance of the Saints in light?'[39] Slavery was also to be condemned, argued Bourne, because it undermined the God-given institution of marriage.[40]

Charles Elliott (1792-1869), Methodist missionary to the Indians, abolitionist and sometime president of Iowa Wesleyan University, maintained that (1) slaves could not help but hate their oppressors and therefore slavery promoted hateful and murderous thoughts—directly contrary to Jesus' teachings (e.g., Matt. 5:21-22)[41]; (2) slaveholders break up families and necessarily maltreat little children—one of the most heinous of sins according to Jesus (Matt. 18:2-6; cf. Rev. 18:21)[42]; (3) slavery keeps the blacks in ignorance, whereas the gospel message requires christian education (Luke 11:52; John 5:39)[43]; (4) Christ—in Luke 4—effectively incorporated into his teaching and expanded upon the Old Testament special year of Jubilee (when slaves were freed), such that he 'established, in his public administrations, a foundation for the universal emancipation of slaves'[44]; and, most important of all, (5) since Jesus redeemed everyone, there can be no justification for one person's enslaving another:

> All men are redeemed by the same blood of Christ; and therefore, this common and general redemption by the blood of Christ is at variance with slavery. ...
> The same great sacrifice has been made for the slave as for the master; and therefore, the soul of the slave is worth as much as the soul of the master.[45]

The collected volumes of American slave cases also evidence the profound influence of the christian message on the institution of slavery in the years preceding the American Civil War and emancipation. For example, one Thomas Reynolds of Virginia, a Methodist believer, prepared a testamentary instrument

---

[39] George Bourne, *The Book* [i.e., the Bible] *and Slavery Irreconcilable* (Philadelphia: J. M. Sanderson, 1816), 196.

[40] Ken Glover, 'Jesus on American Slavery: What He Said, What He Did Not Say, and What He Was Said To Have Said,' Unpublished paper presented at the 55th Annual Meeting of the Evangelical Theological Society, Atlanta, Ga., 20 November 2003.

[41] Charles Elliott, *Sinfulness of American Slavery: Proved from Its Evil Sources; Its Injustice; Its Wrongs; Its Contrariety to Many Scriptural Commands, Prohibitions, and Principles, and to the christian Spirit*, ed. B. F. Tefft (2 vols.; Cincinnati, Ohio: Swormstedt & Power, 1850), II, 25. This edition was reprinted by Negro Universities Press in New York in 1968.

[42] *Ibid.*, I, 87.

[43] *Ibid.*, I, 126.

[44] *Ibid.*, II, 265-66.

[45] *Ibid.*, I, 303-305. On Charles Elliott, see the biographical article in the *Dictionary of American Biography*. Another of Elliott's works was entitled, *The Bible and Slavery: in which the Abrahamic and Mosaic Discipline is Considered in Connection with the Most Ancient Forms of Slavery, and the Pauline Code on Slavery as Related to Roman Slavery and the Discipline of the Apostolic Churches* (1857).

in which he declared that 'for certain good causes, but more especially that it is contrary to the command of Christ to keep my fellow creatures in bondage, I do hereby liberate all my slaves'. When the slaves in question ultimately sued for their freedom, the lower court refused on the ground that the instrument had not been proved and recorded in a proper court. The case then went to Virginia's Court of Appeals, and its President, the great Henry St. George Tucker (1780-1848) spoke for a unanimous court: 'It would be monstrous to say that where a testator retained, till his last breath, the anxious purpose to give effect to a previous deed of emancipation, that purpose should be defeated by his casual death before the session of the probate court'. The former slaves were granted their freedom.[46]

The historical and ideological background of such cases is clarified by Philip J. Schwarz:

> Quakers and their associates provided an even better method of escape for some slaves in 1782 when they successfully lobbied in the Old Dominion's legislature for the law that thereafter allowed white emancipators to free any slaves they wanted to by deed without having to petition the state government for a private law. As Quakers, Methodists, and others began to take advantage of this legislation, they created one more ambiguous situation for slaves. The increasing number of individual manumissions for slaves encouraged early abolitionists to put more effort into advocating a general emancipation of the state's slaves.[47]

IV. Concluding caveats

What do we learn from history for our continuing battle against contemporary forms of slavery? At least four important truths:

First, *we must oppose, root and branch, all forms of modern relativism*. For the post-modern relativist, there are, a priori, no absolutes. Therefore, there is nothing inherently wrong with slavery—though it may be evaluated and perhaps critiqued on (fluctuating) sociological grounds. This will simply not do. Was

---

[46] *Manns v. Givens*, 7 Leigh 689 at 718-19 (July 1836): *Judicial Cases concerning American Slavery and the Negro*, ed. Helen T. Catterall (5 vols.; Washington, D.C.: Carnegie Institution, 1926-1937), I, 183-85. Cf. also: Barnett Hollander, *Slavery in America: Its Legal History* (London: Bowes & Bowes, 1962); Paul Finkelman, *Slavery in the Courtroom: An Annotated Bibliography of American Cases* (Washington, D. C.: Library of Congress, 1985); and William E. Wiethoff, *A Peculiar Humanism: The Judicial Advocacy of Slavery in High Courts of the Old South, 1820-1850* (Athens, Ga.: University of Georgia Press, 1996). On Tucker, see, *inter alia*, the *Biographical Directory of the United States Congress* and the *Dictionary of American Biography*.
[47] Philip J. Schwarz, *Twice Condemned: Slaves and the Criminal Laws of Virginia, 1705-1865* (Baton Rouge, La.: Louisiana State University Press, 1988), 193.

it not the Third Reich that endeavoured to justify its enslavement (and worse) of Jews by claiming Aryan superiority and therefore sociological, Nietzschean, *Uebermensch* exemptions from proper humanitarian standards? Sobering is an argument presented by the eminent Ugaritic scholar Cyrus Gordon:

> ... that it was no crime for men to copulate with animals in Ugarit is indicated by the fact that the favorite god Baal impregnated a heifer (67: V: 17-22), a myth, which, for all we know, may have been enacted ritually by reputable priests. To the Hebrews, on the other hand, copulation with beasts was a heinous crime calling for the death penalty (Ex. 22:18; Lev. 18:23; Deut. 27:21). Moreover, the Bible tells us that the Hebrews' pagan neighbors practised beastiality (Lev. 18:24), as we now know to be literally true from the Ugaritic documents. All this implies that if we discuss Hebrew criminology, we should include beastiality, for in Hebrew society it was a crime. However, there is no basis for including beastiality in a treatment of the criminology of Ugarit, since it was not a crime there. ... The test of the significance of a social phenomenon is this: Does the group in question make an issue of it ?[48]

This may well serve as an adequate description of social phenomena; it is certainly *not* an adequate way of handling serious ethical issues. If beastiality is wrong, it is wrong under *all* conditions and in *any* society. If slavery is to be condemned, it is to be condemned wherever it occurs. Though tolerated (like divorce) 'for the hardness of hearts' under certain past circumstances (Mark 10:2-9), a moral evil does not become a moral good owing to such concessions. Wrong is wrong, and sociological considerations do not change that fact.

But, secondly, this leads us to the vital point (made earlier) that *a transcendent source of ethical principles is the only adequate bulwark against the trivialising of slavery and comparable moral evils.* Any other attempted justification of antislavery will be no more than human opinion, which, if set forth by humans, can be revoked by humans as the sociological context changes. Thus, we need a religious foundation for our opposition to slavery—and not just any religion will do. David Brion Davis notes that when, in the 1840s, British civil servants told the Turkish sultan in no uncertain terms that slavery had to be eliminated or there would be negative political consequences, Viscount Ponsonby, the ambassador to Turkey, reported that the message was heard 'with extreme astonishment accompanied with a smile at a proposition for destroying an institution closely interwoven with the frame of society in this country, and intimately connected with the Law and with the habits and even the religion of all classes, from the Sultan himself down to the lowest peasant'.[49] A current website in

---

[48] Cyrus H. Gordon, *Ugaritic Literature: A Comprehensive Translation of the Poetic and Prose Texts* (Rome: Pontificium Institutum Biblicum, 1949), 8.
[49] Quoted in Davis, *Slavery and Human Progress* (*op. cit.*), 302.

defense of Islam (http://sdsd.essortment.com/educationfrom_rfxl.htm) readily admits that 'slavery is not prohibited in Islam'. Davis puts it starkly: 'Like algebra and knowledge of the Greek classics, racial slavery appears to have been one of the Arabs' contributions to Western civilization'.[50] In a word, one must choose one's transcendental foundation very carefully.[51]

Thirdly, even if one arrives at absolute moral principles, *one must discover a way of interiorising genuine human dignity:* the heart will need to be changed, or one will not regard one's neighbour as oneself and enslavement of the neighbour will remain a live possibility. In one of the most pregnant interchanges in Jesus' ministry, the following dialogue took place:

> Then said Jesus to those Jews who believed in him, If you continue in my word, then you are my disciples indeed, and you shall know the truth, and the truth shall set you free.
>
> They answered him, We are Abraham's seed, and were never in bondage to anyone: how do you say, You shall be made free?
>
> Jesus answered them, Verily, verily, I say to you, Whosoever commits sin is the slave to sin—and the slave does not remain in the house forever; but the Son abides forever. If the Son therefore shall make you free, you will be free indeed.[52]

Jesus' hearers, ironically, were in hopeless bondage to the Romans, who had subjugated Israel and would, in A.D. 70, destroy the Temple and cause the dispersion of the Jewish people for millennia. But their immediate problem was their lack of recognition that their worse slavery followed from their own selfcentredness. They needed changed hearts—which Jesus offered to them as a entirely free gift. It is that transformation which alone can provide the essential motivation to give up slaving practices. No philosophy, ideology, or humanistic panacea can achieve this—and without it all the moralistic rhetoric in the world will achieve little, as past history has abundantly demonstrated.

Finally, *one must see the larger picture.* Slavery is but one affront to human dignity. Its basic error is not to recognise the humanity of all those who benefit from the same genetic-chromosomal nature. Slavery refuses to treat genuine human beings as such; it reduces them to things, to chattel. This is precisely what occurs in other realms, and we must see the pattern, so that we do not engage in limited crusades instead of fighting the problem at its core.

---

[50] David Brion Davis, *Religion, Moral Values, and Our Heritage of Slavery* (New Haven, Conn.: Yale University Press, 2001), 148.
[51] Cf. Alvin J. Schmidt, *The Great Divide: The Failure of Islam and the Triumph of the West* (Boston, Mass.: Regina Orthodox Press, 2004), chap. 4 ('Slavery'), 100-122.
[52] John 8:31-36.

When legal philosopher Ronald Dworkin's book, *Life's Dominion,* was published, the author gave a public lecture, followed by discussion, in London. The argument of the book is that, owing to the need for the state to allow for religious differences, the civil law should stay clear of the abortion issue, since it is a religious matter (some arguing against it on the basis of their convictions, others arguing the other way according to their value-system). I posed the question: 'Like the slave, the fetus satisfies the entire genetic-chromosomal definition of a human being, but is incapable of defending his or her rights, including the right to life. I assume, therefore, on the basis of the argument in your book, that you would have stayed clear of the fight to emancipate the slaves and would have opposed efforts to legislate against slavery—since the acceptance or rejection of slavery likewise turns on conflicting ideological values?' Dworkin would not accept the logic of the analogy—overwhelming as it is—so, needless to say, my question did not receive a satisfactory reply.[53]

Fundamental moral questions are always interlocked. We must therefore fight modern variants of slavery with the clarity which comes from a transcendental perspective—and at the same time recognise the need simultaneously to battle against the multifarious parallel affronts to human dignity which mask as 'choices' rather than what they really are: devices to reduce human persons to the status of means rather than ends.

---

[53] See John Warwick Montgomery, 'New Light on the Abortion Controversy?,' 60/7 *New Oxford Review* (September 1993), 24-26 (and reprinted below as Part Nine, chap. 11 of the present volume); *Slaughter of the Innocents: Abortion, Birth Control and Divorce in Light of Science, Law and Theology* (Westchester, Ill.: Crossway Books, 1981); and 'Human Dignity in Birth and Death: A Question of Values,' in his *Christ Our Advocate* (Bonn, Germany: Verlag für Kultur und Wissenschaft, 2002), 153 ff. Cf. John Warwick Montgomery, 'Evangelical Social Responsibility in Theological Perspective,' in Gary Collins (ed.), *Our Society in Turmoil* (Carol Stream, Ill.: Creation House, 1970), 13-23, 281-82.

2. C. T. Studd

Synopsis

Among the contributors to The Fundamentals *there was hardly a more colourful figure than C(harles) T(homas) Studd (1860-1931). One of the greatest cricketers of his day; converted to Christ through the impact of Dwight Moody; a "rich young ruler" who, rather than "going away sorrowful," gave up his vast wealth to serve his Lord; a leading member of the "Cambridge Seven" university graduates who made China their mission field; and the founder of what would become one of the most influential independent missionary organisations in the world—Studd has provided the evangelical world with a worthy counterpart to Roman Catholicism's Mother Teresa.*

Studd's Spirtual Experience As Described in The Fundamentals

C. T. Studd's contribution to Volume IV of *The Fundamentals* was autobiographical in character.[1] We can therefore appropriately let him introduce himself.

Studd informs us that he "was brought up in the Church of England and was pretty religious—so most people thought." However, in spite of being baptised and confirmed, his knowledge of Jesus Christ was roughly equivalent to his knowledge of "President Taft"—i.e., a correct formal knowledge, not a living, personal relationship. C. T.'s early religious experience was what we often term "dead orthodoxy."

Studd's father was a very wealthy businessman—a retired jute and indigo planter—who was converted at the revival meetings of Dwight Moody. (On giving away his entire £25,000+ inheritance—several million dollars today—C. T. would contribute a fifth of it to the building of the Moody Bible Institute.[2]) Studd's father, after his conversion, invited Christian believers to conduct meetings at his country house, and through one of them C. T. himself met Christ personally.

---

[1] Studd's contribution to *The Fundamentals* was also issued as an undated booklet under two titles: (1) *The Personal Testimony of C(harles) T. Studd* and (2) *The Life Story of an Eton, Cambridge and All-England Cricketer*. These were published by his wife and/or by the Worldwide Evangelization Crusade; they went through numerous editions, including some foreign language translations (e.g., an Italian edition in 1945).

[2] John T. Erskine, *Millionaire for God: The Story of C. T. Studd*, pp. 28-30.

Subsequently, Studd experienced a "second blessing"—not apparently in the Pentecostal, charismatic sense, but in terms of unqualified, total commitment to serve the Lord.³ The human agency was Hannah Whitall Smith's evangelical devotional classic, *The Christian's Secret of a Happy Life*.⁴ Here is how he describes what happened to him:

> I had known about Jesus Christ's dying for me, but I had never understood that if he had died for me, then I didn't belong to myself. Redemption means "buying back" so that if I belonged to Him, either I had to be a thief and keep what wasn't mine, or else I had to give up everything to God. When I came to see that Jesus Christ had died for me, it didn't seem hard to give up all to Him. It seemed just common, ordinary honesty. Then I read in the book: "When you have surrendered all to God, you have given him all the responsibility, as well as everything else. It is God who is responsible to look after you and all you have to do is to trust. Put your hand in His and the Lord will lead you." It seemed quite a different thing after that and in a very short time God had told me what to do and where to go. God doesn't tell a person first by his head; He tells him first by the heart. God put it in my heart and made me long to go to China.

Throughout his life—though he occasionally provided somewhat different accounts of his conversion and spiritual deepening—C. T. would consistently emphasise the principle here stated: that giving up every material advantage for Christ was merely one's "reasonable service" (Rom. 12:1-2) in light of our Lord's entire giving of himself on the Cross for our salvation.

Cricketer Extraordinaire

But it was not as a missionary that C. T. Studd obtained his initial celebrity. Whilst at Eton and later at Cambridge Studd gained undying fame as a cricketer. His two brothers (also Christians) played as well, and the three were characterised by the British humour magazine *Punch* as "the set of Studds."⁵ The

---

³ Cf. Norman P. Grubb, *Once Caught, No Escape*, pp. 82-90 ("There Is a 'Second Blessing'").
⁴ Reissued by Ballantine Books as recently as 1989.
⁵ C. T.'s eldest brother, J(ohn) E(dward) K(ynaston) Studd (1858-1944) would become a major promoter of foreign missions. His tour of twenty American college campuses in 1885 at Dwight Moody's invitation impacted John R. Mott and thus the Student Volunteer Movement. He was co-founder, with Quintin Hogg, of the Regent Street Polytechnic (Hogg's son would later serve the Queen as Lord Chancellor and his grandson, Lord Hailsham of St Marylebone, twice in that same capacity—see Ross Clifford, *Leading Lawyers Look at the Resurrection* [Sutherland, NSW, Australia: Albatross Books, 1991], pp. 70-81, and John Warwick Montgomery, *Human Rights and Human Dignity* [rev. ed.; Calgary, Alberta, Canada: Canadian Institute for Law, Theology, and Public Policy, 1995], pp. 138, 293). J. E. K. Studd was knighted in 1923 and served as Lord Mayor of London for 1928-29 (*Dictionary of National Biography*, art. "Studd, Sir (John Edward) Kynas-

report of the Eton-Harrow match of 1879 declared: "Incomparably the best cricketer was the Eton Captain, C. T. Studd. He should make a great name someday."[6]

This predication was eminently fulfilled. At Trinity College, Cambridge, C. T. was given his Cricket Blue as a freshman. The next academic year, the three brothers were on the Varsity XI. *Lillywhite's Cricket Record* commented on C. T. in the following terms: "Very few players have a finer style: brilliant leg hitting and driving, with a very hard wrist stroke in front of point, a real straight bat, and a resolute nerve make together a batsman whose back bowlers are very glad to see." The following year (C. T.'s third year at Cambridge), *Lillywhite's* would say: "Mr C. T. Studd must be given the premier position amongst the batsmen of 1882, and it would be difficult to instance three finer innings played by so young a cricketer against the best bowling of the day than his three-figure scores against Australia and the Players."[7]

Those Australia matches were historic in more ways than one. In spite of the best efforts of the English team, including not only C. T. but also Dr W. G. Grace (probably the greatest ever cricketer), Australia beat England in a Test match for the very first time. The *Sporting Times* did an obituary for English cricket, ending with the line: "The body will be cremated and the ashes taken to Australia."[8] Subsequently, the English Test Team travelled to Australia and won two matches out of three. Some Melbourne ladies thereupon presented them with some ashes in a little silver urn inscribed "When Ivo goes back with the Urn, the Urn,\ Studds, Steel, Read and Tylecote return, return!\ The welkin will ring loud,\ The great crowd will feel proud …" This gave rise to the cricket expression, "the Ashes." To this day that little urn constitutes the token trophy for the English and Australian Test matches, in perpetual memory of the 1882 events in which C. T. played a key role. The *Cricketing Annual* said of C. T.: he

---

ton, first baronet," by B. Studd; *Biographical Dictionary of Christian Missions*, pp. 649-50).

[6] Quoted in Norman P. Grubb, *C. T. Studd: Cricketer and Pioneer*, p. 22. (This excellent work was written by Studd's son-in-law, who served with him in Central Africa.) For a description of the Eton-Harrow matches of 1878 and 1879, with photographs of the teams, including the Studds, see Robert Titchener-Barrett, *Eton & Harrow at Lord's* (London: Quiller Press, 1996), pp. 152-54.

[7] Quoted in Grubb, *C. T. Studd: Cricketer and Pioneer*, pp. 23-24.

[8] Kenneth Gregory (ed.), *In Celebration of Cricket* (London: Pavilion Library, 1987), p. 32; for a detailed account of the 1882 match, see pp. 28-33 (taken from H. S. Altham's *A History of Cricket* [1926]). Neville Cardus has characterised that event as "The Greatest Test Match": Christopher Lee (ed.), *Through the Covers: An Anthology of Cricket Writing* (Oxford: Oxford University Press, 1996), pp. 340-45.

"must for the second year in succession be accorded the premier position as an all-round cricketer, and some years have elapsed since the post has been filled by a player so excellent in all the three departments of the game."[9]

Studd's extraordinary prowess as a cricketer has not been forgotten. In 1986, Tim Rice (celebrated musical co-creator with Andrew Lloyd Webber and sometime president of the Marylebone Cricket Club) chose C. T. for his ideal "World XI" team:

> At the critical position of number three, C. T. Studd (Middlesex) is chosen to remind us that even the tiniest details of the game are of crucial importance. No man in this side will slip as he turns for a quick second run. It would have been possible for me to have picked nine Studds, nearly two Boots' worth, but 1 did not want to skimp in my coverage of other departments of the game. C. T. was the most talented of the Studd family, topping the first-class averages in 1882 and playing five times for England, which is why he is the Studd I have collared.[10]

To understand C. T.'s post-conversion philosophy of cricket (and of sport in general), we need to listen to him again. Studd contributed a chapter on "Chinese Boys" to a little, now forgotten Victorian volume titled, *Boys and Boys: A Missionary Book*. The following passage—a far cry from today's "political correctness"—deserves quoting *in extenso*:

> It is to be hoped that our English boys will never become like Chinese, but that the Chinese may become like English boys. This can only be done by our taking to the Chinese what has picked us up and made us into a nation, and that the foremost in the world, viz. the Gospel of the Lord Jesus Christ.
>
> Our games and sports should make our boys truly manly and great. We deny ourselves, and train our bodies to win a silver cup for ourselves or our house, or honour for our school or university, and such ambitions are noble and good; but let us see to it that we be not weary in well-doing—that we go on to perfection; for should not these lead us up to grander, nobler, and yet more engrossing ambitions? ... To win a match is good, but surely to win even one heathen soul for Christ is better than to win a dozen matches for self or house, school or university. These, we might say of athletics, ought we to have done, and not to have left the other, the greater spiritual work, undone. ... To be a true Christian is as much above being an athlete as to be an athlete is above being a baby sucking ivory rings, or an infant playing with a humming top. To be a true Christian is to be a hero. ... Religion consisteth

---

[9] Grubb, *C. T. Studd: Cricketer and Pioneer*, p. 30.
[10] Tim Rice, *Quick Singles*, quoted in Christopher Martin-Jenkins, *The Spirit of Cricket* (London: Faber and Faber, 1994), p. 220.

not, as many vainly imagine, in wearing a black coat and white tie, reading prayers and preaching sermons in churches, more or less full of professing Christians, who have from childhood read in their Bibles or heard in their churches of the way of salvation—but in surrender to Jesus Christ as a rebel to a king, in accepting His free gift of pardon and salvation bought by His own death on the cross for you, and enlisting in His army to bring this lost world to the knowledge of salvation, vowing and giving utter obedience to a Commander who never made, nor can make, a mistake. As St. Paul says, "Making it my aim so to preach the Gospel, not where Christ was already named, that I might not build upon another man's foundation; but as it is written, They shall see to whom no tidings of Him came, and they who have not heard shall understand."

The present-day religion may be, and is too often, an effeminacy, a mere parody of the religion of Jesus Christ, and the heroic obedience, self-sacrifice and valour of His early and true disciples.[11]

But Studd's career in cricket was (and is) of tremendous importance to the long-term impact of his life in behalf of his Lord. This may appear strange to 21st century observers—and especially to those not in the British Isles or outside the Commonwealth and former Commonwealth countries. In the English tradition, cricket—even today—is a very special kind of sport. Unlike (to take but a fairly obvious example) soccer or football, cricket represents a consummate ideal of clean, ethical, gentlemanly sportsmanship.

You do well to love it [cricket], for it is more free from anything sordid, anything dishonourable, than any game in the world. To play it keenly, honourably, generously, self-sacrificingly is a moral lesson in itself, and the class-room is God's air and sunshine.[12]

In C. T.'s time, it was even more than that: cricket was a kind of living symbol of all of the best that England represented—when English ideals were the envy of the civilised world and "the sun never set on the British Empire."

If everything else in this nation of ours were lost but cricket - her Constitution and the laws of England of Lord Halsbury—it would be possible ro reconstruct from the theory and the practice of cricket all the eternal Englishness which has gone to the establishment of that Constitution and the laws aforesaid.

Where the English language is unspoken there can be no real cricket, which is to say that the Americans have never excelled at the game. In every English village a cricket field is as much part of the landscape as the old church.

---

[11] C. T. Studd, "Chinese Boys," in Eugene Stock (ed.), *Boys and Boys: A Missionary Book*, pp. 82-85.
[12] Lord Harris, Letter to *The Times*, February 3, 1931.

> Everybody born in England has some notion of what is a cricket match, even folks who have never had a cricket bat in their hands in their lives (few must be their number, since it is as natural to give a cricket bat as a present to a little boy as it is to give him a bucket and spade when he goes to the seaside).
>
> I should challenge the Englishness of any man who could walk down a country lane, come unexpectedly on a cricket match, and not lean over the fence and watch for a while. ....[13]

For a master cricketer to exchange his bat for the Bible was, then, an example par excellence to bring others to face the reality and the challenge of the gospel of Jesus Christ. On his sixtieth birthday, C. T. was to write from Africa: "I am sixty not out, keeping my end up on a fiery pitch against the Devil's fast bowling."[14]

China

C. T. tells us that after his father's death and during his cricketing days he "backslid" for some six years, but that his conviction that his brother George ("G. B.") was dying led him to a more serious life commitment.[15] Moody's preaching was instrumental at this point in his life, as it had been in his father's; Moody had returned to England to conduct revival meetings and C. T. was deeply influenced by his messages. The result was that he "determined to join another well-known Cambridge athlete, Stanley Smith the oarsman, in the then little-known China Inland Mission led by J. Hudson Taylor. Five of their friends followed their example and volunteered, making the celebrated 'Cambridge Seven,' who left for China in 1885."[16] Such an exemplification of what has been termed Victorian "muscular Christianity" was not lost on the British public: "The Cambridge Seven helped catapult the China Inland Mission from obscurity to 'embarrassing prominence,' and inspired hundreds of other recruits for CIM and other missionary societies."[17]

The China Inland Mission had been formed by Hudson Taylor in reaction to his experiences in the Chinese Evangelization Society — "a curiously incom-

---

[13] Neville Cardus, *Cricket* (1930), quoted in Martin-Jenkins, p. 5.
[14] Quoted in Thomas B. Walters, *Charles T. Studd: Cricketer and Missionary*, p. 113.
[15] G. B. recovered. C. T. recounts that when, on a world tour for his health, George later visited him on the Chinese mission field, he was able to bring him to a more consistent life of faith — and that this was proof that in giving up his personal fortune C. T. had received, according to the biblical promise, "a hundredfold for everything we give to him. A hundredfold is a wonderful percentage; it is ten thousand per cent."
[16] John C. Pollock, "Studd, Charles Thomas," *Dictionary of National Biography*. On the "Cambridge Seven," see Pollock's book of that title (1955).
[17] Peter Hammond, *The Greatest Century of Missions*, p. 111.

petent body which almost wholly failed to meet its obligations."[18] In contrast, the CIM was built on a principled philosophy with which C. T. could agree without difficulty. That philosophy entailed: (1) Commitment to a conservative, interdenominational doctrinal statement. (2) A living faith in Christ and a personal call to the mission field was required of candidates, but one did not need to be an ordained clergyman or have a formal theological education. (3) The mission was to be directed from China, not England, and the missionaries would wear Chinese dress and identify as fully as possible with the Chinese people.[19] (4) The primary aim of the mission was evangelism; educational activity and church growth were always to be subordinated to that aim.[20]

Studd served for nine years (1885-1894) as a pioneer missionary in north China until he had to return for reasons of health.[21] By 1895, the CIM "counted 641 missionaries, 462 Chinese helpers, 260 stations and out-stations, and 5,211 communicants."[22] The organisation was unable to avoid criticism; here is what probably constitutes a balanced judgment:

> Criticisms have from time to time been made that this society, in its anxiety to start new centres and occupy new provinces, has sent out men and women whose chief qualification was their intense desire to become missionaries, but who had given no evidence that they were able to act as Christian teachers under the extremely difficult conditions under which their work in China would have to be carried on. These criticisms, which have sometimes been made by those who knew China well and were anxious to promote missions to the Chinese, are to some extent justified, but the fact that enthusiasm

---

[18] Stephen Neill, *A History of Christian Missions* ("Pelican History of the Church," Vol. 6; Harmondsworth, England: Penguin, 1964), p. 333.

[19] For a photograph of Studd and the other members of the Cambridge Seven in Chinese dress (1885), see C. T. Studd, *Reminiscences of Mrs. C. T. Studd*, facing p. 29.; the same photograph is reproduced in Hammond, *loc. cit.*

[20] On the CIM in Studd's day, see Dr and Mrs Howard Taylor, *Hudson Taylor's Spiritual Secret* (London: China Inland Mission, 1950) and *Hudson Taylor and the China Inland Mission* (London: Religious Tract Society, 1940); and M. Geraldine Guinness, *The Story of the China Inland Mission* (2 vols.; London: Morgan and Scott, 1893-1894).

[21] The accomplishments of the other members of the Cambridge Seven varied considerably: Dixon Hoste eventually succeeded Hudson Taylor as director the CIM; two of the strongly Anglican members left the CIM to found a Church of England diocese in Szechwan; one left to become a wandering missionary; and the spokesman of the group, Stanley Smith, was finally forced to resign from the CIM owing to his having embraced what he regarded as "the larger hope" of universal salvation.

[22] Kenneth Scott Latourette, *The Great Century: North Africa and Asia, 1800 A.D.-1914 A.D.* ("A History of the Expansion of Christianity," 3d ed., Vol. VI; New York: Harper, 1944), pp. 330-31. Cf. also Latourette, *A History of Christian Missions in China* (New York: Macmillan, 1929).

has outrun knowledge and that the methods adopted have been proved by experience to be faulty, must not be allowed to diminish our appreciation of the great work which has been accomplished by this society.[23]

I myself have argued that missionaries to China have often short-circuited

> full theological training, relying on little more than a Sunday School or Bible School knowledge of the faith. This is always a deadly mistake, and particularly so where China is concerned. We have seen that even the nineteenth-century missionary organisations such as the Student Volunteer Movement and the China Inland Mission were "minimalists" theologically—putting questions of the sacraments, church polity, etc. aside while they concentrated on the evangelistic task. But the result was ultimately, under Maoism, a single Protestant church lacking in the kind of doctrinal precision and inerrantist view of Scripture so vital as bulwarks against the inroads of liberal theology.[24]

But C. T. Studd was always the exception: even without formal theological training, his grasp of the central Christian verities was solid—as illustrated in two of his poems, the first on the inerrancy of Scripture and the second sarcastically criticising liberal biblical criticism:

> Were we without the letters of
>   John, Peter, James and Paul,
> We'd be like some poor cricketer
>   Without a bat or ball.
>
> If Genesis is humbug,
>   We must cast into the flames,
> The Gospels, Acts and Hebrews,
>   Galatians, Romans, James. ...
>
> Be sure, in their originals,
>   Each word came straight from God;
> "Yea! Every jot and tittle's true,"
>   Said Jesus Christ the Lord.

* * * * *

---

[23] Charles Henry Robinson, *History of Christian Missions* (Edinburgh: T. & T. Clark, 1915), p. 193.

[24] John Warwick Montgomery, *Giant in Chains: China Today and Tomorrow* (Milton Keynes, England: Nelson Word, 1994), pp. 171-72. For the German edition, see Montgomery, *Wohin marschiert China?* (Neuhausen-Stuttgart: Haenssler-Verlag; Kehl: Editions Trobisch, 1991).

> I wouldn't be a Sadducee,
>   Whose faith has gone to grass,
> Cram full of self importance,
>   An intellectual ass. ...
>
> His courage is abnormal,
>   His conscience half awake,
> He's editing the Bible,
>   To free it from mistake. ...
>
> The Resurrection's nonsense,
>   That any man can tell
> (Who's learned the Devil's lesson
>   And qualified for hell). ...
>
> ... since the Apostles preached it,
>   And wrought the works of God,
> And since the saints of ages
>   Have sealed it with their blood;
>
> And since such men as Kelvin,
>   Newton, Gladstone, Gordon, Paul,
> Have all declared it to be truth,
>   And crowned Christ Lord of all;
>
> I ever shall confess it
>   Without a blush of shame,
> And preach Christ's gospel boldly,
>   And glorify His Name.[25]

Whilst in China, Studd married. The bride was also a missionary: Priscilla Livingstone (1864-1929), daughter of William Stewart, a flax merchant in Lisburn, near Belfast, Northern Ireland.[26] Priscilla's spiritual experience had been largely with the Salvation Army and she would be C. T.'s batsman and commissary sergeant for his missionary endeavours throughout life. The Studds were to have four daughters, two of whom eventually served with their husbands on C. T.'s mission field in Africa.[27]

---

[25] C. T. Studd, *Quaint Rhymes for the Battlefield*, pp. 33-35, 45-49. Alfred Buxton, in pledging, with eight others to join the work in Africa, echoed C. T.'s own position on Scripture when he wrote to him: "It seems absurd to us that any alternative regarding the Bible [than "our absolute belief in the Bible as inerrant & the Word of God"] should be worth discussion much less of acceptance. ... We would not dare undertake such a task unless we could rely on the promises pledged, the instructions given, and the facts recorded [in Scripture], as being in very truth, as they claim & as Christ asserted them to be, the Words of God" (MS letter of 9 March 1912; Studd archive at WEC headquarters, Gerrards Cross, Bucks, England).
[26] Cf. Eileen Vincent, *C. T. Studd and Priscilla: United to Fight for Jesus*.
[27] The four daughters were photographed together as children and may be seen in C. T. Studd,

India and Africa

From 1896 to 1898, C. T. toured North American universities and did all that he could to encourage the Student Volunteer Movement. During that time Dwight Moody and R. A. Torrey ordained him by the laying on of hands "in the presence of the Lord's congregation" at Northfield, Massachusetts.[28] In 1900, the Studds went to India where C. T. served as minister to the English-speaking congregation at Ootacamund; they remained there for six years. In 1906, health problems required his return to England, where he again spent his time promoting missionary endeavour.

In 1910, having been impacted by the ambiguous line in a poster, "Cannibals want missionaries," Studd determined—against the advice of physicians and family members—to go to Africa. There, in the Congo, from 1913 until his death in 1931, he laboured under the most primitive conditions to bring the gospel to the natives. His efforts resulted in the founding of the Heart of Africa mission, which eventually became the Worldwide Evangelization Crusade (WEC).[29] During this time, his wife Priscilla remained in England promoting the mission; in poor health, she was able to travel to the Congo only once, shortly before her death.

C. T.'s relations with the other missionaries working with him and with personnel connected with other missionary societies were often stormy. Thus,

> when differences arose between the strongly individualistic Studd and his colleagues in the 1920s, Buxton felt obliged to differ with his father-in-law.

Reminiscences of Mrs. C. T. Studd, facing p. 36. The two missionary daughters were Edith, who married Alfred Buxton, and Pauline, whose husband was Norman Grubb (author of the best of the existing biographies of C. T. Studd). Edith Buxton wrote her own autobiographical account: *Reluctant Missionary*, containing valuable material on her father and excellent photographs. Articles on Alfred Buxton and Norman Grubb, with bibliography, may be found in the *Biographical Dictionary of Christian Missions*.

[28] *Fool and Fanatic? Quotations from the Letters of C. T. Studd*, ed. Jean Walker, p. 114. Priscilla Studd refers to her husband's ordination in a letter to the Buxtons in 1917 (Studd archive at WEC headquarters, Gerrards Cross, Bucks, England).

[29] "In 1964 the WEC celebrated its 50th Anniversary. C. T. Studd's vision had become a reality. In 1914 there was one man and one field. In 1964 there were more than 1,000 (includes CLC) crusaders scattered throughout 40 countries; 1,300 indigenous churches; 1,000 national workers; scores of primary and secondary schools; 10 Bible institutes with a combined enrollment of approximately 500; a worldwide literature program including 4 printing presses, mobile units, Bible correspondence courses in 8 languages, Christian magazines, translation work and bookstores; a widespread medical work with approximately 50 hospitals and clinics; a worldwide radio ministry with 4 recording studios preparing gospel broadcasts in 8 or 9 languages" (*The Encyclopedia of Modern Christian Missions*, ed. Burton L. Goddard [Camden, N.J.: Thomas Nelson, 1967], p. 707). WEC's record is even more impressive today: the organisation now has over 1,800 members from 45 nationalities working in more than 60 countries.

He travelled to the United States in 1927 to try to repair relationships with their American supporters. He was then dismissed by Studd as "disloyal," although Buxton's and Studd's personal links were never broken.[30]

Dr Peter Hammond, one of the most responsible 21st century missionaries to Africa and a firm supporter of Studd's theology and accomplishments, nevertheless describes him as "incredible, bold, abrasive and controversial," "a most difficult person to work with," "stubborn and inflexible in what he required and demanded of others," "ruthless in the standards he set for himself and others", one who "interpreted leisure and recreation as idleness" — in a word, a full-fledged "eccentric" who "to many of his contemporaries … was a fanatic."[31]

The WEC, Studd's continuing organisational legacy, recognises the problem, having published in his defence a little book with the title, *Fool and Fanatic? Quotations from the Letters of C. T. Studd*; and permission to examine the extensive Studd archives and correspondence at the WEC international headquarters is contingent on signing an agreement that "no reference from this archival material to the inter-Mission problems of Central Africa pre-1932 shall be made in any published statement or other publication."[32]

Taking account of this restriction, we believe that C. T.'s personality can best be appreciated by way of his unpublished correspondence. Here are a few samples:

> *[Letter of 25 November 1910 to his wife:]*
>
> W seems to think he can dictate as he please & run the whole show like a Pope. If that's so I shall ere long clear out & run my own show with the help of God.
>
> Meanwhile [owing the health dangers in Khartoum] I have declined to take you … I simply dare not & will not. The fact is you are far too precious to me. … You are too important and necessary to me & to the girls. I will not risk you. … Well, you are more to me than all, & I gladly tho sorrowfully make the sacrifice rather than risk losing you darling. … God will see us thro this & … enable us both to do the biggest work of our lives for Christ these coming years.

---

[30] Jocelyn Murray, "Buxton, Alfred," *Biographical Dictionary of Christian Missions*, p. 104. In her autobiography, Studd's daughter Edith, who was Buxton's wife, briefly recounts this sad event: *Reluctant Missionary*, pp. 140-42, as does Norman Grubb in his biography of Buxton (*Alfred Buxton of Abyssinia and Congo*, pp. 80 ff.).

[31] Hammond, pp. 114-15.

[32] Restrictions on the use of the archive exist primarily because of Norman Grubb's reluctance to open C. T.'s surviving correspondence to those who might produce a critical picture of Studd which would lessen the impact of the portrait given in Grubb's own biography. In point of fact, Grubb's fear was unrealistic: Studd, in death as in life, is entirely capable of putting his critics to rout.

[Letter to his wife and daughters from Khartoum 15 January 1911:]
2 sermons today, & not enough gospel to save a baby spider & no Jesus mentioned this evening. ... I think these mummy hunters & temple discoverers [the clergy archeologists who took the services] get like the dead things they seek: fancy a clergyman spending his time digging up old temples when he has a living, loving Saviour to preach to millions who have never heard of the name of Jesus.

[Letter of 20 August 1930—eleven months before C. T.'s demise—to missionaries in the field:]
God is Almighty and may still have some use for His fool of a clown down here and be a bit worried at the idea of such a clown arriving in heaven, and so He may exercise His Omnipotence and extend the number of my days for the convenience of Heaven and the testing of those on earth: but otherwise my days must be few. ...

Of friends and enemies alike I would make but one request, viz., that they would all pray for me that I may ever do my very damndest for Jesus Whom I am assured did His very damndest for me. I conceive even among my severest critics who have called me "blasphemer" etc. there will be nobody who will find fault with the last sentence, viz., the description of the grace of Jesus on behalf of such a rascally sinner as myself.

Evaluation

In his article on Studd in the *Biographical Dictionary of Christian Missions*, J. J. Bonk characterises him as "obstinate" and "unreasonable"—indeed "incorrigible."[33] Clearly this negative judgement has more than a little to do with Bonk's discomfort with Studd's theology, but it raises the legitimate question of C. T.'s character. In his defence, several points can—and should—be made.

C. T. must be seen against the background of his time. He reflected the tough ideal of "muscular Christianity" so characteristic of Victorian low churchmanship: games, practical knowledge rather than theoretical learning and doctrinal technicalities, dislike of ecclesiastical vestments and sacerdotalism, plain speaking, goal-directedness, a life commitment to high ideals.[34]

---

[33] Jonathan J. Bonk, "Studd, C(harles) T(homas)," *Biographical Dictionary of Christian Missions*, p. 649.
[34] Cf. David Newsome, *Godliness & Good Learning: Four Studies on a Victorian Ideal* (London: Cassell, 1961), especially section IV ("Godliness and Manliness"), pp. 195 ff.

In some ways, C. T. was the missionary counterpart of his contemporary, Lt. General Baden-Powell, hero of Mafeking and founder of the Boy Scouts (1857-1941), who wrote from Africa to inspire the youth of England to heroism: "Remember that God has, as it were, lent you your body for your lifetime, and it is up to you to make the best use of it."[35] Baden-Powell was also regarded by many as a fanatic, and he certainly was an eccentric (happiest under the most primitive conditions and "obsessed by the vicious properties of 'suppressed perspiration'"[36]).

But C. T. never fell into the theological superficiality of muscular Christianity. Of the latter, a prominent English educational historian has written: "Christian practice seems not seldom to mean little more than being clean and physically well-developed."[37] And Baden-Powell's religious position has been described as "a bluff and hearty theism almost indistinguishable from secular morality. ... For Baden-Powell manliness had passed over into perpetual boyishness and Christianity had almost disappeared into wholesomeness."[38] The muscular Christians would have been incapable of C. T.'s oft-quoted remark—which offended even his fellow evangelicals—that he "didn't care a damn" about anything other than saving souls.[39]

That kind of statement reminds one of other great heroes of the faith such as Martin Luther whose singlemindedness was often expressed in language not exactly appropriate to the drawing room.[40] Indeed, the parallel was not lost on Priscilla Studd, who included in the Foreword to her husband's little book of poetry the following quatrain:

> Grand rough old Martin Luther
> Bloomed fables—flowers on furze;
> The better the uncouther;
> Do roses stick like burrs?[41]

---

[35] Lord Baden-Powell, *Paddle Your Own Canoe, or Tips for Boys from the Jungle and Elsewhere* (London: Macmillan, 1939), p. 108. Cf. J. A. Mangan, *The Games Ethic and Imperialism* (Harmondsworth, England: Viking, 1986), pp. 47-48 (citing Baden-Powell).
[36] Piers Brendon, *Eminent Edwardians* (London: Pimlico, 2003), p. 199 (pp. 195-255 are devoted to Baden-Powell).
[37] Edward C. Mack, *Public Schools and British Opinion, 1780-1860* (London: Methuen, 1938), p. 328.
[38] Norman Vance, *The Sinews of the Spirit: The Ideal of Christian Manliness in Victorian Literature and Religious Thought* (Cambridge: Cambridge University Press, 1985), pp. 174, 184. Cf. Michael Rosenthal, *The Character Factory: Baden-Powell and the Origins of the Boy Scout Movement* (New York: HarperCollins, 1986).
[39] Quoted in Hammond, *loc. cit.*
[40] See John Warwick Montgomery, *In Defense of Martin Luther* (Milwaukee: Northwestern Publishing House, 1970), especially pp. 159-69 ("Luther and the Missionary Challenge").
[41] *Quaint Rhymes by a Quondam Cricketer*, p. 8.

Men like Luther and Studd care little or nothing about their personal reputations; their commitment to Christ's cause gives them a kind of tunnel vision in which only the gospel is important. Individuals of this mindset can perhaps be faulted for absence of tact, but hardly for an inadequate value system.

The one point at which C. T.'s lack of sensitivity does pose a theological problem would seem to be his apparent belief that the life of faith demands of every believer the same renunciation which he himself underwent. It is that belief — seldom expressed in so many words but apparent in his writings — which underlies his harsh treatment of fellow missionaries, the unrealistic expectations he often had for others, his downgrading of leisure, etc., etc. In this he unwittingly deviated from the Scripture to which he was otherwise so committed. 1 Corinthians 12 (to mention only the most detailed of many passages on the subject) teaches plainly the "diversity of gifts" within the body of Christ: the need to recognise that one's own calling must not be made a template against which the lives of other Christians are to be evaluated.

It must also be said that C. T. focused so entirely on God's redemptive work that he paid little attention to the creation side of Trinitarian doctrine. The world which God created was of little importance to C. T., so concerned was he to save souls. He reminds the present author of an evangelical friend of college days who, like Studd, devoted his life to missionary work, and who was wont to say that a Christian should regard things gastronomical as little more than "a tanker pulling up for a refill" — since the only important thing is to do gospel work. C. T. may not have been one of those evangelicals Karl Barth criticised as "unitarians of the Second Person" — C. T., after all, placed great emphasis on the activity of the Holy Spirit as well as on the redeeming work of the Son of God — but there is little doubt that C. T.'s theology suffered from a lack of balance: an indifference (even suspicion) of those callings which seek to discover and appreciate the world in which God the Father has placed us.

But, having said all this, one cannot but see in C. T. Studd one of the very greatest heroes of the faith. How remarkably his missionary life contrasts with, for example, that of the far better known Albert Schweitzer — whose *de facto* and *de jure* Unitarian theology reduced his African labours to the level of mere humanitarianism.[42] Not so C. T., whose life was based on the principle (to quote him) that "if Jesus Christ be God and died for me, then no sacrifice can be too great for me to make for Him."

Doubtless, it was C. T.'s son-in-law who best summed up his life (the son-in-law, it will be remembered, whom at one point C. T. regarded as "disloyal"):

---

[42] Schweitzer joined the International Unitarian Association shortly before his death; see below, our article on Schweitzer in Part Ten of the present work.

C. T.'s life stands as some rugged Gibraltar—a sign to all succeeding generations that it is worth while to lose all this world can offer and stake everything on the world to come. His life will be an eternal rebuke to easy-going Christianity. He has demonstrated what it means to follow Christ without counting the cost and without looking back.[43]

Works on the life of C. T. Studd

(This listing includes only those works we have cited which provide significant material on Studd's life and work. There is, unfortunately, no comprehensive biographical treatment which takes full account of the extensive Studd correspondence preserved at the WEC International headquarters, Bulstrode, Oxford Road, Gerrard's Cross, Bucks, England.)

Biographical Dictionary of Christian Missions. Edited by Gerald H. Anderson. New York: Macmillan/Simon & Schuster, 1998. [Articles, with bibliography, on C. T. Studd, J. E. K. Studd, Alfred Buxton, and Norman Grubb. The scholarly quality of these articles varies considerably.]

Buxton, Edith. *Reluctant Missionary.* London: Lutterworth Press, 1968.

Erskine, John T. *Millionaire for God: The Story of C. T. Studd.* Guildford and London: Lutterworth Press, 1968. [Written for young people and based chiefly upon Norman Grubb's *C. T. Studd: Cricketer and Pioneer (infra).*]

Dictionary of National Biography. [The standard English collective biography. The article on C. T. Studd is written by John Pollock, the evangelical biographer and author of *The Cambridge Seven (infra).*]

Grubb, Norman P. *Alfred Buxton of Abyssinia and Congo.* London: Lutterworth, 1943.

C. T. Studd: Cricketer and Pioneer. London: Lutterworth, 1933 (and frequently reprinted). With additional postscript (1948 edition). [The best existing biography.]

Once Caught, No Escape. London: Lutterworth, 1969. [Grubb's autobiography.]

---

[43] Alfred B. Buxton, Foreword to Grubb, *C. T. Studd: Cricketer and Pioneer*, p. 5.

With C. T. Studd in Congo Forests. Grand Rapids, Michigan: Eerdmans, 1946. [This book was also published in England under the title, *Christ in Congo Forests.*]

Hammond, Peter. *The Greatest Century of Missions.* Cape Town, South Africa: Christian Liberty Books, 2002. [A fine, though brief, treatment of Studd's life is to be found on pp. 110-15.]

Polhill-Turner, Arthur. *A Story Retold: "The Cambridge Seven."* London: Morgan & Scott, 1902. [Polhill-Turner was one of the Seven.]

Pollock, John C. *The Cambridge Seven.* London: Inter-Varsity Fellowship, 1955.

Vincent, Eileen. *No Sacrifice Too Great: C. T. Studd and Priscilla.* (2nd rev. ed.; Gerrards Cross, England: WEC, 1992). [1st ed. published as *C. T. Studd and Priscilla* (Kingsway Publications, 1988). Contains a valuable bibliography of source material, pp. 255-61.]

Walters, Thomas B. *Charles T. Studd: Cricketer and Missionary.* London: Epworth Press, 1930. [Useful supplement to Grubb's biography. Contains some material derived from the personal notes of Cecil Polhill-Turner, one of the Cambridge Seven. On pp. 6 and 115 are listings of ephemera (booklets, etc.) written by Studd and those associated with him and published by the Worldwide Evangelization Crusade.]

Works by C. T. Studd

(C. T. wrote no books, apart from the little volume of poetry and the memorial to his wife cited below. He did, however, contribute to collected works, such as The Fundamentals, *and* Boys and Boys *[infra], and he wrote a number of pamphlets. [One of his pamphlet-tracts is being disseminated electronically:* The Chocolate Soldier *appears on a foreign missions website to encourage missionary commitment: http://www.wholesomewords.org/missions/msctserm.html(.)] Copies of C. T.'s pamphlets may be found, along with his extensive and essentially unpublished correspondence, at the British headquarters of the Worldwide Evangelization Crusade; J. J. Bonk [Biographical Dictionary of Christian Missions] is incorrect that Studd correspondence is also to be found at the Crusade's American headquarters in Fort Washington, Pennsylvania.)*

"Chinese Boys," in: Eugene Stock (ed.), *Boys and Boys: A Missionary Book.* London: Church Missionary Society [1896]. Pp. 78-85.

Fool and Fanatic? Quotations from the Letters of C. T. Studd. Edited by Jean Walker. Gerrards Cross, England: WEC, 1980. [Represents only a fraction of the surviving Studd correspondence, and the selections are unfortunately not dated.]

Quaint Rhymes by a Quondam Cricketer. London: James Clarke, 1914. [Foreword by Mrs. Priscilla Studd. C. T. wrote these theological poems when "delayed on his way to his destination in the heart of Africa."]

Reminiscences of Mrs. C. T. Studd. London: Worldwide Evangelization Crusade [1930]. [Written by C. T. just after her death in 1929.]

3. Life Can Be Difficult If You Are Bessarabian Orthodox

(Bessarabian Orthodox Church v Moldova
Before the European Court of Human Rights)

Background and Significance of the Case

On 13 December 2001, the First Chamber of the European Court of Human Rights in Strasbourg delivered its judgment in Case No. 45701/99, vindicating the right of a small Orthodox Church to be recognised and registered as a legitimate ecclesiastical body in Moldova. That judgment was—uncommonly—unanimous, even the Moldovan judge ruling in favour of the Applicant Church. The government of Moldova, which had refused for decades to register the Church, filed a last-ditch argument to have the decision reviewed by the full Court; that demand was rejected on 27 March 2002.

A week before the final ruling came down, Vlad Cubreacov, the leading representative of the Bessarabian Orthodox Church (and a distinguished Moldovan M.P. and member of the Council of Europe's Parliamentary Chamber) was kidnapped in front of his own home. After two months of intense pressure by the European Parliament, the European Court, the Council of Ministers, and the author of this article, Cubreacov was released by the unidentified assailants, who, however, when he had asked for a Bible during his incarceration, provided him with a version tied to the government-recognised Orthodox Church in Moldova!

At the close of his Sir Thomas More Lecture at Lincoln's Inn, delivered on 17 October 2002, Sir Nicolas Bratza, distinguished judge of the European Court of Human Rights, after describing the immense case-load problems now facing the Court, encouraged his audience by listing the five or six most significant cases which had come down since the implementation of the new structure of the Court.[1] The single example he gave under Art. 9 was the *Bessarabian Church* case.

Why should this case, involving a very small church body in a very poor and troubled country new to the European human rights system, be regarded as so significant? Its importance lies in the fact that it clearly delineates what is permissible and what is not in the state registration of religious bodies (and, by implication, of other non-governmental organisations). The *Bessarabian* deci-

---

[1] By way of Protocol 11, which came into force 1 November 1998.

sion makes crystal clear that, even though required government registration of churches is not *per se* contrary to the European Convention, a government will not be allowed to use it as a subtle or not so subtle cloak for discriminating against organisations of which the state does not approve ideologically.

In Moldova, the government was at that time—and indeed until July, 2009—still in the hands of old Marxists (names changed to protect the guilty!). The government refused to recognise the Bessarabians essentially because that church had placed itself under the Patriarchate of Bucharest. The government assumed (without any compelling evidence) that the Church was an undercover political organisation attempting to reunite Moldovans with Romania. To be sure, with their Marxist past, the leaders of the Moldovan government took the paternalistic line of preferring a single, easily controllable Orthodox Church allied with Moscow. The position of the Minister of Justice in his oral argument before the Court reduced to the simple proposition that societal chaos would engulf the country if true pluralism were allowed in the Moldovan context and that the state had a duty to protect the citizenry against such an eventuality.

The *Bessarabian Church* case goes far in delimiting permissible governmental power in the religious domain, especially where governments hide their real motives behind a facade of bureaucratic regulation. It also demonstrates the great importance of the European human rights system for upholding civil liberties, particularly in the Eastern European countries which have more recently ratified the Convention. (May we suggest that Prime Minister Blair should have been much more wary than he was when he entertained as a possible solution to the influx of asylum seekers that the U.K. might renege on its commitments under Art. 3 of the European Convention of Human Rights? If there ever were a remedy worse than the disease, that would *surely* be it—particularly when other, far less draconian, solutions are available.)

The author was counsel for the Applicants before the Court during the three years of litigation there, and since the language of the case was French and therefore inaccessible to many readers, I am here providing an account of the main issues and argument.[2] Hard-won freedom obtained by any historic, confessional church should be a matter of rejoicing for all true Christian churches, since, to quote the Apostle Paul, 'wherever Christ is preached, I do rejoice' (Philippians 1:18).[3]

---

[2] My thanks to Alex Dos Santos, barrister-at-law, my former student and junior counsel in the case, for his consistent support.

[3] Cf. John Warwick Montgomery, *Christ Our Advocate* (Bonn: Verlag für Kultur und Wissenschaft, 2002; ISBN 3-932829-40-9); and *The Repression of Evangelism in Greece* (Lanham, Md.: University Press of America, 2001; ISBN 0-7618-1956-8).

The Issues in the Case

Relevant Articles of the ECHR

These were Article 6 (right to a fair trial), Article 9 (freedom of thought, conscience and religion), Article 11 (freedom of association), Article 13 (failure to provide an effective remedy) and Article 14 (prohibition of discrimination).

Preliminary Points

The Moldovan Government raised some preliminary points, claiming, for example, a delay in filing and a failure to exhaust domestic remedies. In addition, it asserted that the Applicants did not specifically assert Article 6.1, Article 9 (conjoined with Article 14), and Article 13 claims before the national tribunals, and that their Article 11 claim was only addressed to the Moldovan Court of Appeal. The Government was apparently unaware that there is no requirement that Applicants specifically cite the ECHR in their national litigation: it is entirely sufficient that the *substance* of their claims relate to violations of the ECHR.

> The Commission has long found that an Applicant does not necessarily have to invoke directly the European Convention on Human Rights in the domestic courts, if he has invoked domestic legal provisions with an essentially similar content. In this respect, the Court has evaluated the exhaustion of remedies requirement in the light of whether the Applicant has afforded the domestic courts 'the opportunity which is in principle intended to be afforded to Contracting States by Article 26, namely the opportunity of preventing or putting right the violations alleged against them,' however the legal provisions at issue are characterised.[4]

> In *Castells v Spain* [A 236 paras 24-32 (1992)], for example, the question arose whether the Applicant had actually formulated his complaint before the Constitutional Court in terms of an interference with freedom of expression. The government claimed that in his *amparo* appeal he had referred to the relevant provision of the Spanish constitution only indirectly and had made no mention of Article 10 of the Convention. The Court was satisfied, however, after scrutiny of the pleadings before the national courts, that, both before the Supreme Court and the Constitutional Court, he had raised in substance his Convention complaint. ... See also *Endagoz v Turkey* No.

---

[4] D. Gomien, D. Harris, and L. Zwaak, *Law and Practice of the European Convention on Human Rights and the European Social Charter* (Strasbourg: Council of Europe Publishing, 1996), p. 56, citing *Hentrich v France*, judgment of 22 September 1994, Series A, No. 296-A, para. 33.

17128/90, 71 DR 275 [1991]—even in a state where the Convention is directly applicable the Applicant may raise equivalent arguments before the national authority instead of invoking a specific Convention provision.[5]

The Applicants argued that it was perfectly plain from a review of their arguments before the numerous levels of the Moldovan court system to which they took their claims, that they made crystal clear that they were not being afforded due process and natural justice (Article 6.1), that, on a discriminatory basis, their church body was being deprived of freedom to function (Article 14 taken in conjunction with Articles 9 and 6.1), that they were not being allowed to exercise their freedom of association (Article 11), and that they did not have recourse to an effective remedy for this unfortunate state of affairs (Article 13). The interlocking of all these violations with the central issue of the freedom of a church to function without State interference was entirely plain at all levels in the national litigation. The Applicants did not need to cite chapter and verse of the ECHR in order to make their case plain in the national courts, as long as the substance of their claims was set forth unambiguously.

The Application of Individual Articles of the ECHR

Article 13

The Government maintained that Article 13 was inapplicable to this case because its protections were narrower than those of Article 6.1. It should be emphasised, however, that Article 13 applies even to merely 'arguable' claims,[6] that the violation of the Article may exist even if it cannot be attached to the violation of another (substantive) Article,[7] and that an Article 13 claim can warrant separate treatment in any case.

> In a number of cases, the Commission and Court have held than an examination of an Article 13 claim is rendered moot by an examination of either Article 5(4) or Article 6. However, it is important to note that Article 13 may be the sole applicable provision in cases raising the lack of an effective remedy in regard to violations of rights that are of neither a civil nor a criminal character under the Convention. Furthermore, the Commission and Court have thus far failed to recognise that where an Applicant has raised an arguable claim that the state followed improper procedures in regard to mat-

---

[5] D. Harris, M. O'Boyle, and C. Warbrick, *Law of the European Convention on Human Rights* (London: Butterworths, 1995), p. 612.
[6] *Leander v France*, judgment of 26 March 1987, Series A, No. 116, para. 77a.
[7] *Boyle and Rice v UK*, judgment of 27 April 1988, Series A, No. 131, para. 52-55.

ters covered by Article 5(4) or Article 6 and has also argued that no means to challenge the improprieties existed at the domestic level, that a separate claim thus arises under Article 13.[8]

Currently, Moldovan Religious Law does not provide a legal mechanism for the acknowledgement of, or criteria for, the refusal to acknowledge and register religious organisations. This meant that the Applicants were effectively denied legal recourse within Moldovan law to achieve the registration of their church. Since there is in reality no way under civil or criminal law in Moldova (no equivalent of the extraordinary writ of *mandamus*, for example) to force the Government to register the Bessarabian Orthodox Church, and since, as pointed out in the original application, there were numerous procedural violations in the judicial treatment of the Applicants, for which no remedies appeared to exist, Article 13 would seem to remain relevant to Applicants' claim before this Honourable Court.

Moreover, even if the ECHR were to decide that the 'requirements [of Article 13] are less strict than, and are here absorbed by, those of Article 6 par. 1,'[9] this would merely shift the focus of the Applicants' argument to Article 6.1: it would by no means eliminate a consideration of the violations of due process and natural justice which characterised this matter at the national court level.

Article 6.1

The Government argued that this was not violated, since even though the Bessarabian Orthodox Church — not being recognised by the Government — cannot go to law, its members can themselves go to law indirectly in its behalf on the basis of their common interests.

The Applicants replied that, at minimum, this argument simply highlighted the legal disabilities forced upon the Bessarabian Orthodox Church by the Government's refusal to give it recognition. The Church has no legal personality in Moldova, and so, regardless of the unrestricted right of its members to go to law, the Church body *itself* was and is deprived of legal recourse, in violation of Article 6.1, if not of Article 13. The ECHR has recognised that deprivation of due process occurs where the interested party has no standing to litigate in the national tribunals. Thus, the *Philis* case[10] it held that 'a rule by which a claim in respect of fees for work done by a professional person cannot be brought by him, but must be subrogated to a professional organisation, which then has control

---

[8] Gomien, Harris, and Zwaak, 343.
[9] *Sporrong and Lönnroth v Sweden*, judgment of 23 September 1982, Series A, No. 52, para. 88.
[10] *Philis v Greece*, judgment of 27 August 1991, Series A, No. 209.

over its exercise, robs him of the "essence" of what is a personal right.'[11] And in its *Holy Monasteries* judgment, the court did not tolerate a situation in which certain Greek monasteries were themselves barred from bringing legal action in respect of their property—even though the Greek Orthodox denomination of which they were a part could bring such an action. The Court declared:

> By depriving them of any further possibility of bringing before the appropriate courts any complaint they might make against the Greek State, third parties or the Greek Church itself in relation to their rights of property, or even of intervening in such proceedings, section 1(1) [of the Greek statute] impairs the very essence of their 'right to a court'.[12]

It is true that, in the above case, the monasteries in question had separate legal personality, unlike the Bessarabian Orthodox Church (the latter situation due solely to the Moldovan state's refusal to allow it!); but the fundamental point remained: Article 6.1 enshrines the principle that the interested party must be able to litigate for himself, herself, or itself. That individuals can litigate on behalf of the Church is *not* an adequate alternative to the Church's right to legal personality.[13]

Denial of legal personality and therefore capacity to institute proceedings impairs the substance of the right to go to court. In its *Canea Catholic Church*[14] judgment, the ECHR held that denying the Applicant Church legal personality constituted a violation of Article 6 of the Convention and of Article 14 taken in conjunction with Article 6. That judgment reads in part:

> In holding that the Applicant Church had no capacity to take legal proceedings, the [Greek] Court of Cassation ... imposed a real restriction on the Applicant Church, preventing it on this particular occasion and for the future from having any dispute relating to its rights determined by the courts. ... Such a limitation impairs the very substance of the Applicant Church's 'right to a court' and therefore constitutes a breach of Article 6.1 of the Convention.[15]

In the above case, the ECHR recognised that where the religious nature of the body deprived of legal personality is the underlying reason for the denial of legal status, the violation of Article 6 is combined with a violation of Article 14:

---

[11] Harris, O'Boyle, and Warbrick, 200.
[12] *Holy Monasteries v Greece*, judgment of 9 December 1994, Series A, No. 301-A, para. 83.
[13] See below, paragraphs 21 and 29.
[14] *Canea Catholic Church v Greece*, judgment of 16 December 1997, to be published in R.J.D. 1997.
[15] Id. at para. 42.

The Court does no more than note that the Applicant Church, which owns its land and buildings, has been prevented from taking legal proceedings to protect them whereas the Orthodox Church or the Jewish community can do so in order to protect their own property without any formality or required procedure.

Having regard to its conclusion under Article 6.1 of the Convention, the Court considers that there has also been a breach of Article 14 taken together with Article 6.1 *as no objective and reasonable justification for such a difference of treatment has been put forward.*[16]

By analogy with the Bessarabian Church's situation: suppose that a particular business entity were in a discriminatory manner refused the legal right to incorporate; its Board of Directors and its clientele might theoretically still go to law, but the legal detriment to the entity itself, being deprived of legal personhood, would still remain. Accordingly, the Applicants contended that in its treatment of the Applicant Church, the Moldovan state had in fact violated the due process and natural justice guarantees enshrined in Article 6.1 of the ECHR. And since in the instant case the reason for the deprivation of legal personality could not be shown to be other than the religious character of the Bessarabian Orthodox Church, it was clear that there was a violation of Article 6.1 combined with Article 14 discrimination.

Article 11

The Government contended that Article 11 had not been violated, since the European Convention *'ne confère pas aux associations le droit à avoir de la personnalité juridique'.* The latter was accepted by the Applicants as being quite correct as an abstract principle, but, as the Government itself recognised, the right of free association is honoured in such cases only *'si l'association préserve sa liberté de continuer ses activités'* (*ibid.*). But it is precisely the lack of juridical personality that kept the Bessarabian Orthodox Church from being able to carry on normal church activities: it could not go to law to preserve its interests or protect its rights. The Government admitted this when it declared elsewhere in its brief: *'Comme il a été mentionné plus haut, la Métropolie de Bessarabie, puisque dépourvue de personnalité juridique, n'aurait pas d'accès à la justice et donc ne jouirait pas de protection juridictionnelle.'* A clearer evidence that the Church's right to free association has been severely curtailed could hardly be imagined. Would the Court have entertained for a moment the argument that Article 11 had not been violated if a labour union were discriminatorily refused

---

[16] Id. at para. 47 (our emphasis).

legal recognition (since, after all, its individual members could still assemble together)? Surely not; and the same must apply, *mutatis mutandis*, to the Bessarabian Church.

Freedom of association, as guaranteed by Article 11 and as construed by the ECHR, has both a positive and a negative aspect: positively, the State and its agencies must not prohibit voluntary association; negatively, they must not force individuals into associations against their will. Failure to accord legal personality to an association can constitute a violation of the ECHR.[17] By refusing to give legal personality to the Bessarabian Orthodox Church, the Moldovan Government in effect made it impossible for that association to function in a normal manner—in the manner in which registered churches in Moldova can function. Thus, functionally, they limited the association rights of those who wished to worship and carry out religious practice in that particular context. As the ECHR had already said:

> An individual does not enjoy the right to freedom of association if in reality the freedom of action or choice which remains available to him is either nonexistent or so reduced as to be of no practical value (see, *mutatis mutandis*, the Airey judgment of 9 October 1979, Series A no. 32, p. 12, par. 24).[18]

Moreover, the pattern of persecution of Bessarabian Orthodox priests and laity (*e.g.*, court-sanctioned clergy fines; prohibition of church invitations to foreign clergy to share their ministry in Bessarabian Orthodox parishes; the barring of ingress to their churches, as by the police at Ghiliceni in August 1998—acts directly imputable to the State, since carried out by agents of the State) constituted plain evidence of the State's complicity in forcing adherents of the Bessarabian Church to worship elsewhere if they wished to worship at all.

The ECHR has observed on more than one occasion that Article 11 rights are often integrally connected with Article 9 rights:

> Moreover, notwithstanding its autonomous role and particular sphere of application, Article 11 must, in the present case, also be considered in the light of Articles 9 and 10 (see, *mutatis mutandis*, the Kjeldsen, Busk Madsen and Pedersen judgment of 7 December 1976, Series A no. 23, p. 26, par. 52). …

---

[17] Application 26695/95, *Sidiropulos and Others v Greece*, (Rep.) 11 April 1997, pending before the Court.
[18] *Young, James and Webster v UK*, judgment of 13 August 1981, Series A, No. 44, para. 56.

The protection of personal opinion afforded by Articles 9 and 10 in the shape of freedom of thought, conscience and religion and of freedom of expression is also one of the purposes of freedom of association as guaranteed by Article 11.[19]

Article 9 taken alone and in conjunction with Article 14

The Applicants argued that it was insufficient that individual members of a Church be allowed to litigate on its behalf—the Church as a collective entity must be able to manage its affairs and interests, and protect them legally. The Commission has clearly stated that

> the right to manifest one's religion 'in community with others' has always been regarded as an essential part of the freedom of religion and finds that the two alternatives 'either alone or in community with others' in Article 9(1) cannot be considered as mutually exclusive, or as leaving a choice to the authorities, but only as recognising that religion may be practised in either form'[20]

The essence of the Government's argument that Article 9 had not been violated was that the Bessarabian Church was not in fact an independent church body but a schismatic part of the recognised Orthodox Church in Moldova and that to recognise it would in itself be State interference in religious matters:

> Selon la Cour [Suprême], il ne s'agissait pas là de l'enregistrement d'un nouveau culte, mais d'un conflit administratif au sein d'une église, ce que relève de la compétence des organes ecclésiastiques. ... Il a été constaté également que toute ingérence de l'Etat en la matière pouvait aggraver la situation (pp. 8-9).
>
> La Métropolie de Bessarabie n'est pas un nouveau culte. ... Le motif du refus des autorités nationales de reconnaître la Métropolie de Bessarabie est que cette Eglise ne représente pas un nouveau culte, le culte orthodoxe étant déjà reconnu (pp. 17-18).

The remarkable aspect of this argument is that it assumes that the State has the right to declare what is, and what is not, an independent church—or that it is within its rights to defer to the judgment of one church as to the status of another. But, of course, it is exactly this kind of State action that is prohibited by Article 9 of the ECHR. If a group of religionists decide that they wish to constitute a new and independent church body, that is *their* decision, not the State's or that of the church body wishing to retain them. If the desire to form

---

[19] Id. at para. 57.
[20] Application 8160/78, *X v the UK*, D&R 22 (1981), p. 27 at 33-37.

an independent church body constitutes a problem with an existing church organisation, then the two groups can resolve their differences amicably—or go to court if, for example, property disputes cannot be resolved in any other way. But it is not the State's role to decide that those within a church body cannot separate from it and start an independent church—or to favour one church over another. To do this is the most egregious interference in religious liberty, for it makes the State the definer of what in fact constitutes an independent religious commitment.

That the Moldovan State was in fact engaged in just such definition is clear from the Government's justification for recognising the Eparchie Orthodoxe de Vieux Rite de Chisinau, connected with the Russian Orthodox Church of the Ancient Rite:

> La reconnaissance de cette Eparchie s'explique par le fait qu'elle est distincte de l'Eglise Orthodoxe de Moldova. La distinction repose sur le mode de manifester la religion, de même que sa composition (les croyants et le clergé de cette église sont exclusivement de souche russe) (p. 18).

It is surely no part of the State's function to determine which religious beliefs are 'distinct' from which other religious beliefs, or to establish by fiat the criteria for the recognition of independent churches (in Moldova, apparently, ethnic origin!). Religious criteria are the province of religious believers, and if they wish to join together in churches, the State has no business withholding from them the legal recognition they seek. In *Manoussakis*[21] The Court said that 'the State is excluded from the discretion to determine whether religious beliefs or the means to express such beliefs are legitimate'. This principle carries into the present case, in that the State has no right to determine whether or not the Applicant Church is an individual entity or part of another church body.

As was successfully argued in another case before the ECHR, 'a law which made the practice of a religion subject to the prior grant of an authorisation, whose absence incurred liability to ... sanction, constituted an "impediment" to that religion.'[22] The Moldovan State's refusal to grant legal recognition to the Bessarabian Orthodox Church was, the Applicants claimed, precisely such an impediment.

If the Government could demonstrate that the Bessarabian Church were engaged in illegal or antisocial practices deleterious to the peace of the realm, that would be one thing (Article 9.2). But no such demonstration was made—or was possible on the facts.[23] State limitation of and interference with Article

---

[21] *Manoussakis* [1997] 23 EHRR 387, para. 9-10.
[22] Id. at para. 37.
[23] Indeed, even the Commission for Religious Affairs and Culture of the Moldovan Parliament could find nothing illegal in the activity of the Bessarabian Orthodox Church, declaring: 'The

9 and related rights guaranteed by the Convention are justifiable only when 'prescribed by law and are necessary in a democratic society in the interests of public safety, for the protection of public order, health or morals, or for the protection of the rights and freedoms of others—"necessary" in this context [of the Convention articles] not having the flexibility of terms such as "useful" or "appropriate."'[24]

The Government's claim that were the State to recognise the Bessarabian Church this would increase tension in the existing, recognised Orthodox Church in Moldova, even if true, was, the Applicants submitted, no legitimate, 'necessary' or proportionate ground for depriving Moldovan citizens of their religious freedom contrary to Article 9 of the ECHR. If the clergy of the recognised Orthodox Church were bothered by competition in what is supposed to be an open marketplace of religious ideas, that was their problem. The State has no business taking sides by refusing to recognise a new church body—particularly when evidence exists aplenty that in other countries several Orthodox Churches have been recognised and exist side by side.[25]

In *Sidiropulos*,[26] the Greek government contended that an association requesting legal personality had objectives that were 'against the national interest of Greece and, consequently, against the law'.[27] The Commission disagreed and found a violation of the Convention, stating:

> In the light of all the above and the domestic margin of appreciation notwithstanding, the Commission is not satisfied that the reasons adduced by the domestic authorities to justify the interference with the Applicants' freedom of association were 'relevant and sufficient'; nor was the interference 'proportionate to the legitimate aim pursued.' It follows that it has not been established that the measure complained of was 'necessary in a democratic society in the interests of national security or public safety, for the prevention of disorder ... or for the protection of the rights and freedoms of others.'[28]

The right to freedom of religion, as protected by Article 9(1), has a collective dimension. The very functioning of churches depends on respect for the right of freedom of religion, and churches are eminently placed to defend this right.

Commission finds that the actions of the Church and its petition for recognition presented before the government are not against the law. Therefore, the Church should be officially recognized.' The Moldovan Ministry of Justice came to the same conclusion: 'In our opinion, the [Church's] Statute does not violate the Constitution or any present law.'

[24] *Handyside v UK*, judgment of 7 December 1976, Series A, No. 24, para. 48.
[25] E.g. Russia, Lithuania, Latvia.
[26] Application 26695/95, *Sidiropulos and Others v Greece*, (Rep.) 11 April 1997, pending before the Court.
[27] Id. at para. 18.
[28] Id. at para. 59.

The Commission has recognised that a church has in itself a right to manifest its religion.[29] The Commission has also opined that any distinction between a church body and its members is artificial:

> When a church body lodges an application under the Convention, it does so in reality in behalf of its members. It should therefore be accepted that a church body is capable of possessing and exercising the rights contained in Article 9(1) in its own capacity as a representative of its members.[30]

That Article 14 discrimination was involved in the refusal of the Government to recognise the Bessarabian Orthodox Church is evident both from the fact that other churches (Orthodox and non-Orthodox) have been recognised whilst the Bessarabian Church has not, and from the clear evidence of the sanctioning of persecution of its clergy and members by agents of the State. In the *Belgian Linguistic Case*[31] the ECHR held that a distinction is discriminatory if it 'has no objective and reasonable justification', that is if it does not pursue a 'legitimate aim' or if there is not a 'reasonable relationship of proportionality between the means employed and the aim sought to be realised.' Furthermore:

> From the text of Article 14 which demands to secure the 'enjoyment of the rights and freedoms ...' it follows that not only an equal application of the existing law is required, but even more important, that the legislator must provide for *equal treatment* of every person. Formal equality is not sufficient; what is required is material and effective equality.[32]

On the discriminatory treatment of the Bessarabian Church as compared with other church bodies, the District Court of Buiucani, Chisinau, in giving judgment for the Bessarabian Church, stated the case succinctly:

> The Court finds that absent any violation of any present law, the Church should be granted official recognition. Further, since the Moldovan Government recognized other, non-Christian denominations, the Court finds no reason why the Government should refuse to recognize the official status of the Bessarabian Church. The laws of the Republic of Moldova declare that no one should be forced to practice or not to practice the beliefs of a religious denomination. Therefore, the membership of believers and their communities to one specific church or another is legal and constitutional as long as the decision is based solely on free choice and personal convictions.[33]

---

[29] Application 7374/76, *X v Denmark*, D&R 5 (1976), page 157, at 158.
[30] Application 7805/77, *Pastor X and Church of Scientology v Sweden*, Yearbook XXII (1979), p. 244, at 246.
[31] *Belgian Linguistic Case*, judgment of 23 July 1968, Series A, No. 6, paras. 9-10.
[32] Karl Josef Partsch, 'Discrimination,' in: *The European System for the Protection of Human Rights*, ed. R. St. J. Macdonald, F. Matscher and H. Petzold (Dordrecht, Boston, London: Martinus Nijhoff, 1993), p. 584 (emphasis added).
[33] The district Court was reversed by the Moldovan Supreme Court.

The Government rejected the long list of persecutions, many with the concurrence of or indifference on the part of agents of the Moldovan State, to which Bessarabian Orthodox priests and laity have been subjected in recent years. First, the Government noted—and they were technically correct—that such instances prior to 12 September 1997, the date when the ECHR entered into force in Moldova—could not be taken into account. Then the Government argued that a number of the subsequent instances were not officially registered at local police stations. Having begun their *Mémoire* with legal technicalities (trivial late filings as evidence of the Applicants' not having properly exhausted domestic remedies), the Government ended its case on the same level. The substance of the persecutions was never dealt with, even though this treatment says much concerning the atmosphere of hostility in which the Bessarabian Church had valiantly endeavoured to assert its legitimate existence. The Applicants submitted that these persecutions very definitely showed a 'state of mind' in which the Church, individually and collectively, has suffered the deprivation of religious liberty on the basis of discrimination.

The Applicants also pointed out that the Government, so indifferent to the legal consequences of Church *registration* that it had the effrontery to assert that the Bessarabian Orthodox believers really were not suffering from the lack of it, then turned around and argued that without the *registration* of religious persecution at local police stations, one should be able to ignore such events as if they had never happened!

Conclusion

It might well be asked, in light of the foregoing, what the real reason was for the refusal of the Moldovan Government to recognise the Bessarabian Orthodox Church. The reason, as has been identified widely by commentators inside and outside of Moldova, is in fact not religious, but political. The Bessarabian Church is Romanian-speaking, not Russian-speaking, and sees its roots in Romanian ecclesiastical culture. The State is not happy with this, particularly after generations of close association with Russia during the existence of the USSR. The Bessarabian Church is seen as a threat and its legal existence a confirmation of a Romanian focus which the State would prefer not to exist at all. To argue, as the Government did, that to recognise the Bessarabian Orthodox Church would produce civil war in Moldova was too absurd for serious consideration—as the ECHR obviously recognised. No evidence was offered to show that the Bessarabian Church, its clergy or its laity, had been or are engaged in any revolutionary political activities whatsoever. The Church wished to function as other churches function: as a body of likeminded believers, united, as was the early church, 'in the apostles' doctrine and fellowship, and in breaking of bread, and in prayers' (Acts 2:42). Politics and hostility to Romanian culture must not, the Applicants submitted, be allowed to truncate in a discriminatory way the fundamental rights to religious freedom and religious association. Indeed, in the recent *Sidiropulos* case, in which Macedonian-orientated Applicants were prohibited by the Greek government from establishing by registration a non-profit-making association, the Commission declared:

> It is true that the domestic courts, on the basis of the evidence before them, could have reached the reasonable conclusion that the real aim of the association was to promote the idea that a 'Macedonian' minority exists in Greece and that the rights of the members of such a minority are not fully respected. *However, the Commission considers that this could not have justified in itself a restriction in the Applicants' right to freedom of association.* According to the case-law of the Court, a democratic society must, in principle, tolerate the free discussion not only of ideas which are favourably received or are regarded as inoffensive or as a matter of indifference, but also of ideas that offend, shock or disturb the State or any sector of the population (Eur. Court HR, *Handyside v. United Kingdom*, judgment of 29 April 1976, Series A, no. 24, para. 49, p. 23).[34]

The closest contemporary analogy to the position taken by the Moldovan Government in this matter would appear to be that of the People's Republic of China. There, the Roman Catholic Church has been outlawed on the ground that to have a hierarchical connection with ecclesiastical authority outside the country (the Roman Pontiff) is to imperil the State; only a 'non-Roman' Catholic Church is therefore officially recognised and permitted to function. In Moldova, church registration is being employed as a device to prohibit the existence of a church because of its suspect foreign (here, Romanian) orientation. Communist China is not, sadly, subject to the standards of religious freedom enshrined in the ECHR. Moldova, however, has voluntarily taken on that commitment, and must be held to it.

---

[34] Application 26695/95, *Sidiropulos and Others v Greece*, (Rep.) 11 April 1997, para. 56 (emphasis ours); case pending before the Court.

Appendix I: Applicants' Brief Before the European Court of Human Rights[35]

Application No. 45701/99
BETWEEN

    METROPOLITAN CHURCH OF BESSARABIA   <u>Applicants</u>
    AND THE EXARCHATE OF LANDS
    - And -
    12 OTHERS
    - v -
    MOLDOVA   <u>Respondents</u>

BRIEF

SUBMITTED ON BEHALF OF THE APPLICANTS BY:
Professor Dr. John Warwick Montgomery
Barrister-at-law and Counsel for the Applicants

Introduction

1. We do not propose to repeat our complaints against the Moldovan Government; these have been set forth in full in our initial Application. Nor do we intend to review the facts of the case, since these are substantially agreed as between the parties: the Moldovan Government refuses to register the Bessarabian Orthodox Church as a distinct ecclesiastical entity. The purpose of the present brief is to speak to the Government's attempted defence of its actions as set forth in its (undated) response to the five questions posed to it by the Court on 9 November 1999—and, in the course of our rejoinder, to highlight what we believe to be the central and critical human rights issues in the instant case.

---

[35] Owing to space limitations, we have not reproduced the voluminous documentary exhibits submitted to the Court with the original Brief, and we have excised references to those exhibits from the text to follow.

The Government's Arguments

The Government's claim that Applicants did not in fact exhaust domestic remedies

2. The Government states (pp. 8, 11 and 12 of their *Mémoire*) that the Applicants did not conform to Article 238 of the Moldovan *Code of Civil Procedure*, in that on two occasions the Applicants did not timely file: they filed a month later than the one-month filing date. Our Moldovan counsel, Maître Mihai Potoroaca argued that in fact no such violation occurred or, alternatively, vitiated the effectiveness of the national proceedings.

3. Even if Maître Mihai Potoroaca's argument is disputed, the Government does not (and factually cannot) allege that the Applicants neglected to use each and every legal avenue available to them within the Moldovan legal system. Over a considerable period of time, the Applicants pursued their legal remedies right to the Moldovan Supreme Court. The Government is reduced, therefore, to minute legalism in an effort to avoid the substantive issues of the case.

4. The Government cites Article 35, para. 1 of the ECHR, not apparently observing its language: that Applicants must conform '*au moins au fond*' to the procedural requirements and limitation periods of national law. This is precisely what the jurisprudence declares: that the principle of the exhaustion of domestic remedies must be applied with 'some degree of flexibility and without excessive formalism.'[36] The trivial filing delays relied upon by the Government, even if they did occur, surely do not go to the '*fond*' so as to vitiate the Applicants' good faith endeavours to exhaust all domestic remedies before coming to Strasbourg. Moreover, the mere fact that the Moldovan Supreme Court heard the case in spite of the trivial delayed filings serves to estop the Government from employing this argument: by the very fact that the case was heard in the highest national court, the alleged defects were cured before the case even reached Strasbourg. The Government's argument here is thus unworthy of serious legal consideration.

5. The Government also asserts (p. 12) that the Applicants did not specifically assert Article 6.1, Article 9 (conjoined with Article 14), and Article 13 claims before the national tribunals, and that their Article 11 claim was only addressed to the Moldovan Court of Appeal. The Government is apparently unaware that there is no requirement that Applicants specifically cite the ECHR in their national litigation: it is entirely sufficient that the *substance* of their claims relate to violations of the ECHR.

---

[36] *Cardot v France*, judgment of 19 March 1991, Series A, No. 200, para. 34.

The Commission has long found that an Applicant does not necessarily have to invoke directly the European Convention on Human Rights in the domestic courts, if he has invoked domestic legal provisions with an essentially similar content. In this respect, the Court has evaluated the exhaustion of remedies requirement in the light of whether the applicant has afforded the domestic courts 'the opportunity which is in principle intended to be afforded to Contracting States by Article 26, namely the opportunity of preventing or putting right the violations alleged against them,' however the legal provisions at issue are characterised.[37]

In *Castells v Spain* [A 236 paras 24-32 (1992)], for example, the question arose whether the Applicant had actually formulated his complaint before the Constitutional Court in terms of an interference with freedom of expression. The government claimed that in his *amparo* appeal he had referred to the relevant provision of the Spanish constitution only indirectly and had made no mention of Article 10 of the Convention. The Court was satisfied, however, after scrutiny of the pleadings before the national courts, that, both before the Supreme Court and the Constitutional Court, he had raised in substance his Convention complaint. ... See also *Endagoz v Turkey No 17128/90*, 71 DR275 (1991)—even in a state where the Convention is directly applicable the Applicant may raise equivalent arguments before the national authority instead of invoking a specific Convention provision.[38]

6. It is perfectly plain from a review of the Applicants' arguments before the numerous levels of the Moldovan court system to which they took their claims that they made crystal clear that they were not being afforded due process and natural justice (Article 6.1), that, on a discriminatory basis, their church body was being deprived of freedom to function (Article 14 taken in conjunction with Articles 9 and 6.1), that they were not being allowed to exercise their freedom of association (Article 11), and that they did not have recourse to an effective remedy for this unfortunate state of affairs (Article 13). The interlocking of all these violations with the central issue of the freedom of a church to function without State interference was entirely plain at all levels in the national litigation. The Applicants did not need to cite chapter and verse of the ECHR in order to make their case plain in the national courts, as long as the substance of their claims was set forth unambiguously. No reading of the record below can escape the conclusion that the Moldovan Supreme Court was fully aware of the issues before it in this case. Now that Applicants are forced to take the violation

---

[37] D. Gomien, D. Harris, and L. Zwaak, *Law and Practice of the European Convention on Human Rights and the European Social Charter* (Strasbourg: Council of Europe Publishing, 1996), p. 56, citing *Hentrich v France*, judgment of 22 September 1994, Series A, No. 296-A, para. 33.
[38] D. Harris, M. O'Boyle, and C. Warbrick, *Law of the European Convention on Human Rights* (London: Butterworths, 1995), p. 612.

of their rights to Strasbourg, specific citation of the ECHR is appropriate and necessary. The absence, in whole or in part, of such citation on the national level in no sense signifies that the Applicants did not exhaust their domestic remedies before having to assert their rights in Strasbourg.

Article 13

7. The Government maintains that Article 13 is inapplicable to the instant case because its protections are narrower than those of Article 6.1. It should be emphasised, however, that Article 13 applies even to merely 'arguable' claims,[39] that the violation of the Article may exist even if it cannot be attached to the violation of another (substantive) Article,[40] and that an Article 13 claim can warrant separate treatment in any case.

> In a number of cases, the Commission and Court have held than an examination of an Article 13 claim is rendered moot by an examination of either Article 5(4) or Article 6. However, it is important to note that Article 13 may be the sole applicable provision in cases raising the lack of an effective remedy in regard to violations of rights that are of neither a civil nor a criminal character under the Convention. Furthermore, the Commission and Court have thus far failed to recognise that where an Applicant has raised an arguable claim that the state followed improper procedures in regard to matters covered by Article 5(4) or Article 6 and has also argued that no means to challenge the improprieties existed at the domestic level, then a separate claim thus arises under Article 13.[41]

8. It will be observed from the current Moldovan Religious Law that there is no legal mechanism set forth for the acknowledgement of or criteria for the refusal to acknowledge and register religious organisations. This means that the Applicants are effectively denied legal recourse within Moldovan law to achieve the registration of their church. Since there is in reality no way under civil or criminal law in Moldova (no equivalent of the extraordinary writ of *Mandamus*, for example) to force the Government to register the Bessarabian Orthodox Church, and since, as pointed out in our original Application, there have been numerous procedural violations in the judicial treatment of the Applicants, for which no remedies appear to exist, Article 13 would seem to remain relevant to Applicants' claim before this Honourable Court.

---

[39] *Leander v France*, judgment of 26 March 1987, Series A, No. 116, para. 77a.
[40] *Boyle and Rice v UK*, judgment of 27 April 1988, Series A, No. 131, para. 52-55.
[41] D. Gomien, D. Harris, and L. Zwaak, *Law and Practice of the European Convention on Human Rights and the European Social Charter* (Strasbourg: Council of Europe Publishing, 1996), p. 343.

9. Moreover, even if this Honourable Court were to decide that the 'requirements [of Article 13] are less strict than, and are here absorbed by, those of Article 6 par. 1,'[42] this merely shifts the focus of our argument to Article 6.1: it by no means eliminates a consideration of the violations of due process and natural justice which have characterised this matter at the national court level.

Article 6.1

10. As for the claimed violation of Article 6.1, the Government holds that it has not been violated, since even though the Bessarabian Orthodox Church—not being recognised by the Government—cannot go to law, its members can themselves go to law indirectly in its behalf on the basis of their common interests.

11. At minimum, this argument simply highlights the legal disabilities forced upon the Bessarabian Orthodox Church by the Government's refusal to give it recognition. The Church has no legal personality in Moldova, and so, regardless of the unrestricted right of its members to go to law, the Church body *itself* is deprived of legal recourse, in violation of Article 6.1, if not of Article 13. This Honourable Court has recognised that deprivation of due process occurs where the interested party has no standing to litigate in the national tribunals. Thus, the *Philis* case[43] held that 'a rule by which a claim in respect of fees for work done by a professional person cannot be brought by him, but must be subrogated to a professional organisation, which then has control over its exercise, robs him of the "essence" of what is a personal right.'[44] And in its *Holy Monasteries* judgment, this Honourable Court did not tolerate a situation in which certain Greek monasteries were themselves barred from bringing legal action in respect of their property—even though the Greek Orthodox denomination of which they were a part could bring such an action. This Court declared:

> By depriving them of any further possibility of bringing before the appropriate courts any complaint they might make against the Greek State, third parties or the Greek Church itself in relation to their rights of property, or even of intervening in such proceedings, section 1(1) [of the Greek statute] impairs the very essence of their 'right to a court.'[45]

12. Granted that, in the case just cited, the monasteries in question had separate legal personality, unlike the Bessarabian Orthodox Church (the latter

---

[42] *Sporrong and Lönnroth v Sweden*, judgment of 23 September 1982, Series A, No. 52, para. 88.
[43] *Philis v Greece*, judgment of 27 August 1991, Series A, No. 209.
[44] D. Harris, M. O'Boyle, and C. Warbrick, *Law of the European Convention on Human Rights* (London: Butterworths, 1995), p. 200.
[45] *Holy Monasteries v Greece*, judgment of 9 December 1994, Series A, No. 301-A, para. 83.

situation due solely to the Moldovan state's refusal to allow it!); but the fundamental point remains: Article 6.1 enshrines the principle that the interested party must be able to litigate for himself, herself, or itself. That individuals can litigate on behalf of the Church is *not* an adequate alternative to the Church's right to legal personality.[46]

13. Denial of legal personality and therefore capacity to institute proceedings impairs the substance of the right to go to court. In its *Canea Catholic Church*[47] judgment, this Honourable Court held that denying the Applicant Church legal personality constituted a violation of Article 6 of the Convention and of Article 14 taken in conjunction with Article 6. That judgment reads in part:

> In holding that the Applicant Church had no capacity to take legal proceedings, the [Greek] Court of Cassation ... imposed a real restriction on the Applicant Church, preventing it on this particular occasion and for the future from having any dispute relating to its rights determined by the courts. ... Such a limitation impairs the very substance of the Applicant Church's 'right to a court' and therefore constitutes a breach of Article 6.1 of the Convention.[48]

14. In the just cited case, this Honourable Court recognised that where the religious nature of the body deprived of legal personality is the underlying reason for the denial of legal status, the violation of Article 6 is combined with a violation of Article 14:

> The Court does no more than note that the Applicant Church, which owns its land and buildings, has been prevented from taking legal proceedings to protect them whereas the Orthodox Church or the Jewish community can do so in order to protect their own property without any formality or required procedure.

> Having regard to its conclusion under Article 6.1 of the Convention, the Court considers that there has also been a breach of Article 14 taken together with Article 6.1 *as no objective and reasonable justification for such a difference of treatment has been put forward.*[49]

15. By analogy with the Bessarabian Church's situation: suppose that a particular business entity were in a discriminatory manner refused the legal right to incorporate; its Board of Directors and its clientele might theoretically still go to law, but the legal detriment to the entity itself, being deprived of legal

---

[46] See below, paragraphs 21 and 29.
[47] *Canea Catholic Church v Greece*, judgment of 16 December 1997, to be published in R.J.D. 1997.
[48] Id, at para. 42.
[49] Id, at para. 47 (our emphasis).

personhood, would still remain. We contend, therefore, that in its treatment of the Applicant Church, the Moldovan state has in fact violated the due process and natural justice guarantees enshrined in Article 6.1 of the ECHR. And since, in the instant case, the reason for the deprivation of legal personality cannot be shown to be other than the religious character of the Bessarabian Orthodox Church, we see the violation of Article 6.1 as combined with Article 14 discrimination.

Article 11

16. The Government contends that Article 11 has not been violated, since the European Convention *'ne confère pas aux associations le droit à avoir de la personnalité juridique'* (p. 15). The latter is quite correct as an abstract principle, but, as the Government itself recognises, the right of free association will be honoured in such cases only *'si l'association préserve sa liberté de continuer ses activités' (ibid.)*. But it is precisely the lack of juridical personality that keeps the Bessarabian Orthodox Church from being able to carry on normal church activities: it cannot go to law to preserve its interests or protect its rights. The Government admits this when it declares elsewhere in its brief (p. 18): *'Comme il a été mentionné plus haut, la Métropolie de Bessarabie, puisque dépourvue de personnalité juridique, n'aurait pas d'accès à la justice et donc ne jouirait pas de protection juridictionnelle.'* A clearer evidence that the Church's right to free association has been severely curtailed could hardly be imagined. Would the Court entertain for a moment the argument that Article 11 had not been violated if a labour union were discriminatorily refused legal recognition (since, after all, its individual members could still assemble together)? Surely not; and the same must apply, *mutatis mutandis,* to the Bessarabian Church.

17. Freedom of association, as guaranteed by Article 11 (and as construed by this Honourable Court), has both a positive and a negative aspect: positively, the State and its agencies must not prohibit voluntary association; negatively, they must not force individuals into associations against their will. Failure to accord legal personality to an association can constitute a violation of the ECHR.[50] By refusing to give legal personality to the Bessarabian Orthodox Church, the Moldovan Government in effect made it impossible for that association to function in a normal manner—in the manner in which registered churches in Moldova can function. Thus, functionally, they limited the association rights of those who wished to worship and carry out religious practice in that particular context. As this Honourable Court has said elsewhere:

---

[50] Application 26695/95, *Sidiropulos and Others v Greece*, (Rep.) 11 April 1997, pending before the Court.

An individual does not enjoy the right to freedom of association if in reality the freedom of action or choice which remains available to him is either non-existent or so reduced as to be of no practical value (see, *mutatis mutandis*, the Airey judgment of 9 October 1979, Series A no. 32, p. 12, par. 24).[51]

18. Moreover, the pattern of persecution of Bessarabian Orthodox priests and laity (*e.g.,* court-sanctioned clergy fines; prohibition of church invitations to foreign clergy to share their ministry in Bessarabian Orthodox parishes; the barring of ingress to their churches, as by the police at Ghiliceni in the month of August 1998—acts directly imputable to the State, since carried out by agents of the State) evidence the State's complicity in forcing adherents of the Bessarabian Church to worship elsewhere if they wish to worship at all.

19. All of which points to what has been observed in more than one Article 11 case before this Court: that Article 11 rights are often integrally connected with Article 9 rights:

> Moreover, notwithstanding its autonomous role and particular sphere of application, Article 11 must, in the present case, also be considered in the light of Articles 9 and 10 (see, *mutatis mutandis*, the Kjeldsen, Busk Madsen and Pedersen judgment of 7 December 1976, Series A no. 23, p. 26, par. 52). ...
>
> The protection of personal opinion afforded by Articles 9 and 10 in the shape of freedom of thought, conscience and religion and of freedom of expression is also one of the purposes of freedom of association as guaranteed by Article 11.[52]

20. We therefore proceed to a consideration of the central issue of the Moldovan state's violation of the Bessarabian Orthodox Church's Article 9 rights—which violation necessarily impacts Article 11 as just discussed.

Article 9 taken alone and in conjunction with Article 14

21. It is insufficient that individual members of a Church be allowed to litigate on its behalf—the Church as a collective entity must be able to manage its affairs and interests, and protect them legally. The Commission has clearly stated that

> the right to manifest one's religion 'in community with others' has always been regarded as an essential part of the freedom of religion and finds that the two alternatives 'either alone or in community with others' in Article

---

[51] *Young, James and Webster v UK*, judgment of 13 August 1981, Series A, No. 44, para 56.
[52] Id. at para. 57.

9(1) cannot be considered as mutually exclusive, or as leaving a choice to the authorities, but only as recognising that religion may be practised in either form.[53]

22. The essence of the Government's argument that Article 9 had not been violated is that the Bessarabian Church is not in fact an independent church body but a schismatic part of the recognised Orthodox Church in Moldova and that to recognise it would in itself be State interference in religious matters:

> Selon la Cour [Suprême], il ne s'agissait pas là de l'enregistrement d'un nouveau culte, mais d'un conflit administratif au sein d'une église, ce que relève de la compétence des organes ecclésiastiques. ... Il a été constaté également que toute ingérence de l'Etat en la matière pouvait aggraver la situation (pp. 8-9).
>
> La Métropolie de Bessarabie n'est pas un nouveau culte. ... Le motif du refus des autorités nationales de reconnaître la Métropolie de Bessarabie est que cette Eglise ne représente pas un nouveau culte, le culte orthodoxe étant déjà reconnu (pp. 17-18).

23. The remarkable aspect of this argument is that it assumes that the State has the right to declare what is, and what is not, an independent church — or that it is within its rights to defer to the judgment of one church as to the status of another. But, of course, it is exactly this kind of State action that is prohibited by Article 9 of the ECHR. If a group of religionists decide that they wish to constitute a new and independent church body, that is *their* decision, not the State's or that of the church body wishing to retain them. If the desire to form an independent church body constitutes a problem with an existing church organisation, then the two groups can resolve their differences amicably — or go to court if, for example, property disputes cannot be resolved in any other way. But it is not the State's role to decide that those within a church body cannot separate from it and start an independent church — or to favour one church over another. To do this is the most egregious interference in religious liberty, for it makes the State the definer of what in fact constitutes an independent religious commitment.

24. That the Moldovan State was in fact engaged in just such definition is clear from the Government's justification for recognising the Eparchie Orthodoxe de Vieux Rite de Chisinau, connected with the Russian Orthodox Church of the Ancient Rite:

---

[53] Application 8160/78, *X v the UK*, D&R 22 (1981), p. 27 at 33-37.

La reconnaissance de cette Eparchie s'explique par le fait qu'elle est distincte de l'Eglise Orthodoxe de Moldova. La distinction repose sur le mode de manifester la religion, de même que sa composition (les croyants et le clergé de cette église sont exclusivement de souche russe) (p. 18).

25. It is surely no part of the State's function to determine which religious beliefs are 'distinct' from which other religious beliefs, or to establish by fiat the criteria for the recognition of independent churches (in Moldova, apparently, ethnic origin!). Religious criteria are the province of religious believers, and if they wish to join together in churches, the State has no business withholding from them the legal recognition they seek. In *Manoussakis*[54] The Court said that 'the State is excluded from the discretion to determine whether religious beliefs or the means to express such beliefs are legitimate'. This principle carries into the present case, in that the State has no right to determine whether or not the Applicant Church is an individual entity or part of another church body.

26. As was successfully argued in *Manoussakis*, 'a law which made the practice of a religion subject to the prior grant of an authorisation, whose absence incurred liability to ... sanction, constituted an "impediment" to that religion.'[55] The Moldovan State's refusal to grant legal recognition to the Bessarabian Orthodox Church is precisely such an impediment.

27. To be sure, if the Government could demonstrate that the Bessarabian Church were engaged in illegal or antisocial practices deleterious to the peace of the realm, that would be one thing (Article 9.2). But no such demonstration has been made—or is possible on the facts.[56] State limitation of and interference with Article 9 and related rights guaranteed by the Convention are justifiable only when 'prescribed by law and are necessary in a democratic society in the interests of public safety, for the protection of public order, health or morals, or for the protection of the rights and freedoms of others'—"necessary" in this context [of the Convention articles] not having the flexibility of terms such as "useful" or "appropriate".'[57]

28. The Government's claim that were the State to recognise the Bessarabian Church, this would increase tension in the existing, recognised Orthodox Church in Moldova, even if true, is no legitimate, 'necessary' or proportionate

---

[54] *Manoussakis* [1997] 23 EHRR 387, para. 9-10.
[55] Id. at para. 37.
[56] Indeed, even the Commission for Religious Affairs and Culture of the Moldovan Parliament could find nothing illegal in the activity of the Bessarabian Orthodox Church, declaring: 'The Commission finds that the actions of the Church and its petition for recognition presented before the government are not against the law. Therefore, the Church should be officially recognized.' The Moldovan Ministry of Justice came to the same conclusion: 'In our opinion, the [Church's] Statute does not violate the Constitution or any present law.'
[57] *Handyside v UK*, judgment of 7 December 1976, Series A, No. 24, para. 48.

ground for depriving Moldovan citizens of their religious freedom contrary to Article 9 of the ECHR. If the clergy of the recognised Orthodox Church are bothered by competition in what is supposed to be an open marketplace of religious ideas, that is their problem. The State has no business taking sides by refusing to recognise a new church body—particularly when evidence exists aplenty that in other countries several Orthodox Churches have been recognised and exist side by side.[58]

29. In *Sidiropulos*,[59] the Greek government contended that an association requesting legal personality had objectives that were 'against the national interest of Greece and, consequently, against the law.'[60] The Commission disagreed and found a violation of the Convention, stating:

> In the light of all the above and the domestic margin of appreciation notwithstanding, the Commission is not satisfied that the reasons adduced by the domestic authorities to justify the interference with the Applicants' freedom of association were 'relevant and sufficient'; nor was the interference 'proportionate to the legitimate aim pursued.' It follows that it has not been established that the measure complained of was 'necessary in a democratic society in the interests of national security or public safety, for the prevention of disorder ... or for the protection of the rights and freedoms of others.'[61]

30. The right to freedom of religion, as protected by Article 9(1), has a collective dimension. The very functioning of churches depends on respect for the right of freedom of religion, and churches are eminently placed to defend this right. The Commission has recognised that a church has in itself a right to manifest its religion.[62] The Commission has also opined that any distinction between a church body and its members is artificial:

> When a church body lodges an application under the Convention, it does so in reality in behalf of its members. It should therefore be accepted that a church body is capable of possessing and exercising the rights contained in Article 9(1) in its own capacity as a representative of its members.[63]

31. That Article 14 discrimination is involved in the refusal of the Government to recognise the Bessarabian Orthodox Church is evident both from the fact that other churches (Orthodox and non-Orthodox) have been recognised

---

[58] E.g. Russia, Lithuania, Latvia.
[59] Application 26695/95, *Sidiropulos and Others v Greece*, (Rep.) 11 April 1997, pending before the Court.
[60] Id. at para. 18.
[61] Id. at para. 59.
[62] Application 7374/76, *X v Denmark*, D&R 5 (1976), page 157, at 158.
[63] Application 7805/77, *Pastor X and Church of Scientology v Sweden*, Yearbook XXII (1979), p. 244, at 246.

whilst the Bessarabian Church has not, and from the clear evidence of the sanctioning of persecution of its clergy and members by agents of the State. In the *Belgian Linguistic Case*[64] this Honourable Court held that a distinction is discriminatory if it 'has no objective and reasonable justification', that is if it does not pursue a 'legitimate aim' or if there is not a 'reasonable relationship of proportionality between the means employed and the aim sought to be realised.' Furthermore:

> From the text of Article 14 which demands to secure the 'enjoyment of the rights and freedoms …' it follows that not only an equal application of the existing law is required, but even more important, that the legislator must provide for *equal treatment* of every person. Formal equality is not sufficient; what is required is material and effective equality.[65]

32. On the discriminatory treatment of the Bessarabian Church as compared with other church bodies, the District Court of Buiucani, Chisinau, in giving judgment for the Bessarabian Church, stated the case succinctly:

> The Court finds that absent any violation of any present law, the Church should be granted official recognition. Further, since the Moldovan Government recognized other, non-Christian denominations, the Court finds no reason why the Government should refuse to recognize the official status of the Bessarabian Church. The laws of the Republic of Moldova declare that no one should be forced to practice or not to practice the beliefs of a religious denomination. Therefore, the membership of believers and their communities to one specific church or another is legal and constitutional as long as the decision is based solely on free choice and personal convictions.[66]

33. The Government rejects the long list of persecutions, many with the concurrence of or indifference on the part of agents of the Moldovan State, to which Bessarabian Orthodox priests and laity have been subjected in recent years.[67] First, the Government notes—and they are technically correct—that such instances prior to 12 September 1997, the date when the ECHR entered into force in Moldova—cannot here be taken into account. Then they argue that a number of the subsequent instances were not officially registered at local police stations. Having begun their *Mémoire* with legal technicalities (trivial late filings as evidence of the Applicants' not having properly exhausted domestic remedies), the Government ends its case on the same level. The substance of the

---

[64] *Belgian Linguistic Case*, judgment of 23 July 1968, Series A, No. 6, paras. 9-10.
[65] Karl Josef Partsch, 'Discrimination,' in: *The European System for the Protection of Human Rights*, ed. R. St. J. Macdonald, F. Matscher and H. Petzold (Dordrecht, Boston, London: Martinus Nijhoff, 1993), p. 584 (emphasis added).
[66] The District Court was reversed by the Moldovan Supreme Court.
[67] See the documentation submitted with our initial Application and the supplementary documents thereafter filed with this Court.

persecutions is never dealt with, even though this treatment says much concerning the atmosphere of hostility in which the Bessarabian Church has valiantly endeavoured to assert its legitimate existence. These persecutions very definitely show a 'state of mind' in which the Church, individually and collectively, has suffered the deprivation of religious liberty owing to rank discrimination.

34. And it is perhaps worth noting that the Government, so indifferent to the legal consequences of Church *registration* that it has the effrontery to assert that the Bessarabian Orthodox believers really are not suffering from the lack of it, then turns around and argues that without the *registration* of religious persecution at local police stations, one should be able to ignore such events as if they had never happened!

Conclusion

35. It might well be asked, in light of the foregoing, what the real reason was for the refusal of the Moldovan government to recognise the Bessarabian Orthodox Church. The reason, as has been identified widely by commentators inside and outside of Moldova, is in fact not religious, but political. The Bessarabian Church is Romanian-speaking, not Russian-speaking, and sees its roots in Romanian ecclesiastical culture. The State is not happy with this, particularly after generations of close association with Russia during the existence of the USSR. The Bessarabian Church is seen as a threat and its legal existence a confirmation of a Romanian focus which the State would prefer not to exist at all. To argue, as the Government did, that to recognise the Bessarabian Orthodox Church would produce civil war in Moldova was too absurd for serious consideration.

36. It goes without saying that no evidence was offered to show that the Bessarabian Church, its clergy or its laity, had been or are engaged in any revolutionary political activities whatsoever. The Church wished to function as other churches function: as a body of likeminded believers, united, as was the early church, 'in the apostles' doctrine and fellowship, and in breaking of bread, and in prayers' (Acts 2:42). Politics and hostility to Romanian culture must not, the Applicants submitted, be allowed to truncate in a discriminatory way the fundamental rights to religious freedom and religious association. Indeed, in the recent *Sidiropulos* case, in which Macedonian-orientated Applicants were prohibited by the Greek government from establishing by registration a non-profit-making association, the Commission declared:

> It is true that the domestic courts, on the basis of the evidence before them, could have reached the reasonable conclusion that the real aim of the association was to promote the idea that a 'Macedonian' minority exists in

Greece and that the rights of the members of such a minority are not fully respected. *However, the Commission considers that this could not have justified in itself a restriction in the Applicants' right to freedom of association.* According to the case-law of the Court, a democratic society must, in principle, tolerate the free discussion not only of ideas which are favourably received or are regarded as inoffensive or as a matter of indifference, but also of ideas that offend, shock or disturb the State or any sector of the population (Eur. Court HR, *Handyside v. United Kingdom* judgment of 29 April 1976, Series A no. 24, para. 49, p. 23).[68]

37. The closest contemporary analogy to the position taken by the Moldovan Government in this matter would appear to be that of the People's Republic of China. There, the Roman Catholic Church has been outlawed on the ground that to have a hierarchical connection with ecclesiastical authority outside the country (the Roman Pontiff) is to imperil the State; only a 'non-Roman' Catholic Church is therefore officially recognised and permitted to function. In Moldova, church registration is being employed as a device to prohibit the existence of a church because of its suspect foreign (here, Romanian) orientation. Communist China is not, sadly, subject to the standards of religious freedom enshrined in the ECHR. Moldova, however, has voluntarily taken on that commitment, and must be held to it.

38. We trust that this Honourable Court will recognise the casuistry and speciousness of reasoning employed by the Moldovan Government to justify its treatment of the Bessarabian Church and accede to the Applicants' prayer for the immediate legal recognition of that Church in Moldova, together with appropriate damages for the time and legal costs entailed in obtaining what would be regarded among other Member States of the European Human Rights system as an obvious human right, guaranteed under Article 9 of the European Convention on Human Rights.[69]

---

[68] Application 26695/95, *Sidiropulos and Others v Greece*, (Rep.) 11 April 1997, para. 56 (emphasis ours); case pending before the Court.

[69] Even the Procurator General of Moldova has recognised that the Moldovan Government has violated the ECHR in its treatment of the Bessarabian Church.

Appendix II: Oral Argument Before the European Court of Human Rights, Strasbourg, France (2 October 2001)

Part One

Mme la Présidente and Members of the Court, our remarks in the instant case will differ considerably from those we made in the case of *Larissis et al. v Greece*. There, the facts were in dispute and considerable time had to be devoted to establishing the legal basis for vindicating Applicants' religious activity. Here, there is no essential divergence of opinion on the facts: the Moldovan government has refused, and continues to refuse, the lawful registration of the Bessarabian Orthodox Church, and the Applicants claim that such refusal constitutes an egregious violation of the European Convention of Human Rights, Arts. 6(1) and 9 (these articles taken alone and in conjunction with Art. 14), together with Arts. 11 and 13.

We begin by speaking to the questions received yesterday from the Court. We are asked, first of all, to specify any acts of intimidation against the Bessarabian Orthodox Church and/or its members after 12 September 1997 (the date when Moldova ratified the ECHR). In our Brief submitted to this Court 16 March 2000, we supplied as documentation an egregious instance among many of such intimidation (Appendixes C[4] and C[6]): the police having locked believers out of their own church in Cucioaia during the month of August 1998. We also refer the Court to several communications previously addressed to this Court, for example, a Helsinki Human Rights Commission report documenting acts of vandalism and persecution exerted upon the Bessarabian Orthodox Church and its members since 1997 (letters of 14 and 16 January 1999); and communications from the Metropolitanate of Bessarabia documenting insults and threats recently directed to the Church and its members (letters of 9, 12, 15 and 19 January 1999). The Moldovan Government and its agents have done nothing concrete to protect Bessarabian Church interests in these and other similar instances.

As to the Court's second question of yesterday, namely, what internal legal protections exist in such areas as property rights from which the Applicant can benefit, and in regard to the violation of which it can complain under Article 6, we respond in terms of Appendix A of our submitted Brief of 16 March 2000 (the sections «Le manque de personnalité juridique» and «La transgression du droit de propriété» (para. 6-9): Without legal personality, the Bessarabian Church cannot employ the national court system to enforce its rights in regard to property ownership or in any other respect. As a result of the Government's intransigence in refusing to recognise and register it, it has no legal status whatsoever. Were that not the case, it would be able to rely on property and other civil statutes and remedies available, for example, to the Metropolitanate of Moldova owing to the latter's registered status.

In its written submission, the Moldovan government has provided a number of convoluted arguments to support its claim that the Applicants did not exhaust domestic remedies. These have properly been rejected by the Court in granting admissibility to the present Application, and require no further discussion here. On the single, central substantive issue—the Government's refusal to register the Bessarabian Orthodox Church as a religious organisation—what does the Government say to justify its actions?

The Government's claims reduce to three. First, we are told that the Bessarabian Church is not really a separate ecclesiastical entity at all: it is a mere schismatic group, and its members, being Eastern Orthodox in belief, do not suffer in the least from non-recognition, since they can happily worship in the Metropolitanate of Moldova—the chief Orthodox body recognised by the state and in communion with the Moscow Patriarchate. Second, the Government maintains that since, after 1940, there has been no Moldovan administrative unit called "Bessarabia," the use of such terminology can only produce bad cultural and national effects. Thirdly, the Government claims that the Bessarabian Orthodox Church is but superficially a religious entity: in reality, it is a political movement, insisting on relating itself to the Romanian (Bucharest) rather than the Russian (Moscow) Patriarchate because its true objective is to destabilise—indeed, destroy—the Moldovan Republic.

Such claims are almost too far-fetched to warrant serious response. On the first point, need it be pointed out that it is not the function of government to establish by fiat the defining boundaries of a religious body? If religious believers do not consider themselves members of Church A and wish instead to establish Church B, it is for *them*, not for the political authorities, to make such a decision. In the 19th century, Bismarck engaged in just such totalitarian decision-making when he forced German Lutherans and Calvinists to unite in the so-called Prussian Union (after all, said the government, the two beliefs are *really* the same!); the result was the emigration of thousands of Lutherans from Germany who insisted on maintaining their own independent church body. Suppose, in the United States, the government were to assert that Southern Baptists could not function as a recognised church body, since their beliefs are really no different from those of the Northern Baptists—and that Southern Baptists should be satisfied to worship in Northern Baptist churches? Would anyone today in a civilised nation benefiting from the common or civil law traditions regard this as a legitimate governmental act?

The argument that the Bessarabian Orthodox Church does not deserve recognition because no "Bessarabian" administrative unit currently exists appears to confuse *semantics* on the one hand with law, religious freedom, and human rights on the other. Should the British government refuse to allow Imperial Oil to incorporate because the sun has now set on the British Empire? Should the French government refuse to allow a church with the name *Eglise de la Gaule*, on the ground that "Gaul" as an administrative entity has not existed for centuries? To quote Humpty Dumpty in Lewis Carroll'a *Through the Looking-Glass:*

> "When *I use* a word . . . it means just what I choose it to mean — neither more nor less."
> "The question is," said Alice, "whether you *can* make words mean so many different things."
> "The question is, said Humpty Dumpty, "which is to be master — that's all."

Here, the issue is simply whether a government can legitimately be the master of religious vocabulary, arrogating to itself the right to recognise only those groups with whose terminology it feels comfortable.

Thirdly, the Moldovan government claims that the Bessarabian Church is nothing more than an underground Romanian political movement. What evidence does it offer for this extraordinary claim? Nothing beyond the fact that individuals connected with the Church (such as Mr Cubreacov, member of the Parliamentary Assembly of the Council of Europe, who sits beside me as one of the Applicants in this case) have systematically criticised in the media and before international bodies the Moldovan government's refusal to recognise their Church! Last we heard, the expression of dissent in a state which has ratified the European Convention on Human Rights does not constitute illegal revolutionary activity.

What legal principles should be brought to bear on this issue? Why is the Moldovan's government's refusal to register the Bessarabian Church in violation of the European Convention?

International human rights law recognises the right of a state to set forth procedures for the registration of religious bodies — *as long as registration does not become a cloak for the denial of fundamental rights to religious believers and their churches*. Thus, the Dutch Advisory Council on International Affairs, in its report (No. 21, June 2001) titled, *Registration of Communities Based on Religion or Belief,* after having analysed the existing law, concludes:

> Governments have a positive duty to make freedom of thought, conscience and religion or belief possible. They must not interfere with the development of new communities centred around a new belief or adhering to a different interpretation of an existing belief. If such new communities do not wish to

be part of an existing community, they should not be denied registration on the grounds that either the number of institutions based on religion or belief must be kept within reasonable limits or that such institutions must remain unified. In this regard, it should also be noted that although the idea of an established or official religion or belief is not in itself a violation of international law, such a system should be non-discriminatory: this means that the state may not withhold registration from religious and belief communities because it wants to protect an established or official religion or belief. Nor may a state withhold registration because it does not approve of the religion or belief concerned. Such communities should be able to obtain legal status according to the same criteria as other associations.

This is precisely the position reached by this Honourable Court in recent cases that have come before it. Besides those cited in our submitted brief, we refer the Court to the reasoning and the decisions reached in *Serif v Greece* (No. 38178/97; ECHR 1999-) and *Hasan and Chaush v Bulgaria* (No. 30985/96; ECHR 26 Oct. 2000); cf. *Stankovitnd the United Macedonian Organisation Ilinden v Bulgaria* (No. 29221/95 and 29225/95; deliberation in private 17 October 2000).

In *Serif* (para. 51-54), this Court refused to justify the criminal conviction of a Moslem religious leader because he conducted religious activities outside of the framework of a recognised Moslem body:

> 51. The domestic courts convicted the applicant on the following established facts: issuing a message about the religious significance of a feast, delivering a speech at a religious gathering, issuing another message on the occasion of a religious holiday and appearing in the clothes of a religious leader. Moreover, it has not been disputed that the applicant had the support of at least a part of the Moslem community in Rodopi. However, in the Court's view, punishing a person for the mere fact that he acted as the religious leader of a group that willingly followed him can hardly be considered compatible with the demands of religious pluralism in a democratic society.
>
> 52. The Court is not oblivious of the fact that in Rodopi there existed, in addition to the applicant, an officially appointed Mufti. Moreover, the Government argued that the applicant's conviction was necessary in a democratic society because his actions undermined the system put in place by the State for the organisation of the religious life of the Moslem community in the region. However, the Court recalls that there is no indication that the applicant attempted at any time to exercise the judicial and administrative functions for which the legislation on the Muftis and other ministers of "known religions" makes provision. As for the rest, the Court does not consider that, in democratic societies, the State needs to take measures to ensure that religious communities remain or are brought under a unified leadership.

53. It is true that the Government argued that, in the particular circumstances of the case, the authorities had to intervene in order to avoid the creation of tension among the Moslems in Rodopi and between the Moslems and the Christians of the area as well as Greece and Turkey. Although the Court recognises that it is possible that tension is created in situations where a religious or any other community becomes divided, it considers that this is one of the unavoidable consequences of pluralism. The role of the authorities in such circumstances is not to remove the cause of tension by eliminating pluralism, but to ensure that the competing groups tolerate each other (see, *mutatis mutandis*, Eur. Court HR, *Plattform "Ärzte für das Leben"* v. *Austria* judgment of 21 June 1988, Series A no. 139, p. 13, § 32). In this connection, the Court notes that, apart from a general reference to the creation of tension, the Government did not make any allusion to disturbances among the Moslems in Rodopi that had actually been or could have been caused by the existence of two religious leaders. Moreover, the Court considers that nothing was adduced that could warrant qualifying the risk of tension between the Moslems and Christians or between Greece and Turkey as anything more than a very remote possibility.

54. In the light of all the above, the Court considers that it has not been shown that the applicant's conviction under Articles 175 and 176 of the Criminal Code was justified in the circumstances of the case by "a pressing social need". As a result, the interference with the applicant's right, in community with others and in public, to manifest his religion in worship and teaching was not "necessary in a democratic society for the protection of public order" under Article 9 § 2 of the Convention. There has, therefore, been a violation of Article 9 of the Convention.

In the *Hasan* case, this Court reached precisely the same conclusions as to the illegitimacy of state interference in the religious activities of believers. The Bulgarian government, which had substituted another Muslim leader for a leader validly elected by the faithful, was found to have violated the rights of the Muslim community to choose its own leadership. In paras. 67, 78, 81, and 82 of its Judgment this Court declared:

67. The applicants further maintained that State interference with the internal affairs of the religious community had not been based on clear legal rules. They considered that the law in Bulgaria in matters concerning religious communities did not provide clarity and guarantees against abuse of administrative discretion. In their view the relations between the State and religious communities in Bulgaria were governed not by law, but by politics. Indeed, the replacement of the leadership of the Muslim religion had curiously coincided with the change of government in Bulgaria.

78. Nevertheless, the Court considers, like the Commission, that facts demonstrating a failure by the authorities to remain neutral in the exercise of

their powers in this domain must lead to the conclusion that the State interfered with the believers' freedom to manifest their religion within the meaning of Article 9 of the Convention. It recalls that, but for very exceptional cases, the right to freedom of religion as guaranteed under the Convention excludes any discretion on the part of the State to determine whether religious beliefs or the means used to express such beliefs are legitimate. State action favouring one leader of a divided religious community or undertaken with the purpose of forcing the community to come together under a single leadership against its own wishes would likewise constitute an interference with freedom of religion. In democratic societies the State does not need to take measures to ensure that religious communities are brought under a unified leadership (*Serif v. Greece*, no. 38178/97, § 52, ECHR 1999-).

81. The Government's argument that nothing prevented the first applicant and those supporting him from organising meetings is not an answer to the applicants' grievances. It cannot be seriously maintained that any State action short of restricting the freedom of assembly could not amount to an interference with the rights protected by Article 9 of the Convention even though it adversely affected the internal life of the religious community.

82. The Court therefore finds, like the Commission, that Decree R-12, the decision of the Directorate of Religious Denominations of 23 February 1995, and the subsequent refusal of the Council of Ministers to recognise the existence of the organisation led by Mr Hasan were more than acts of routine registration or of correcting past irregularities. Their effect was to favour one faction of the Muslim community, granting it the status of the single official leadership, to the complete exclusion of the hitherto recognised leadership. The acts of the authorities operated, in law and in practice, to deprive the excluded leadership of any possibility of continuing to represent at least part of the Muslim community and of managing its affairs according to the will of that part of the community. There was therefore an interference with the internal organisation of the Muslim religious community and with the applicants' right to freedom of religion as protected by Article 9 of the Convention.

One would be hard put to find cases more on all fours with the instant case: here, the Moldovan government, operating with a religious registration procedure open to great abuse through political influence, decides what constitutes and what does not constitute legitimate religious connections and endeavours to force believers, against their will, into a denominational arrangement (the Metropolitinate of Moldova) when they wish to worship within the framework of Bessarabian Orthodoxy.

Granted, there are limitations on Article 9 freedoms of religious activity and on Article 11 freedoms of association: governments may indeed legitimately limit such freedoms in the interests of public safety, public order, health, morals, and the protection of the rights and freedoms of others; national security may also legitimate restrictions on assembly and association. However, these limitations are allowable *only* where "necessary in a democratic society." What kind of restrictions on religious activity are therefore permissible, and can the Moldovan government justify its treatment of the Bessarabian Orthodox Church along those lines?

The very recent decision of this Court upholding Turkey's banning of the fundamentalist Prosperity Party (*Refah Partisi and Others v Turkey* [Nos. 41340/98, 41342-41344/98, decision of 31 July 2001]) indicates clearly that a religious position which is inherently anti-democratic and anti-pluralistic can be banned from the political arena in the interests of preserving the open societies which the European Convention on Human Rights endeavours to guarantee. At para. 50 of that decision, a further illustration is provided:

> La Cour a également estimé que le fait d'empêcher un opposant islamique algérien de se livrer à des activités de propagande sur le territoire suisse était nécessaire, dans une société démocratique à la protection de la sécurité nationale et de la sûreté publique (*Zaoui c. Suisse* (déc.), no. 41615/98, 18 janvier 2001, non publiée).

One can easily imagine other examples: an Aztec Church advocating and engaging in human sacrifice, or an Anthropophagous Church (not "loving your neighbour" but "digesting your neighbour") being legitimately denied religious recognition and registration in Member States of the European human rights system.

But to suggest that the Bessarabian Orthodox Church is an affront to national security or public morals is an utter absurdity. The Moldovan government has in no way demonstrated such, and the burden to do so—a heavy legal and human rights burden indeed—rests squarely with the state.

As fully demonstrated in our written, documented submissions, the Bessarabian Church has suffered much from lack of recognition by the Moldovan government. Its clergy and laity have been subjected to physical abuse and persecution either directly from government agents or indirectly through lack of police protection. Its pastors have been denied social insurance benefits such as pensions on the ground that they have not served a recognised religious body. The Church cannot own property. And, in the most general terms, it cannot benefit from the legal system, since it has no juridical personality whatsoever.

Adding insult to injury, on 19 September 2001—whilst the instant case was in the bosom of this Honourable Court—the Moldovan Cabinet of Ministers, chaired by Premier Vasile Tarlev, approved a decision declaring the state-registered Metropolitanate of Moldova, under the Moscow Patriarchate, to be the successor in legal interest of the unregistered Bessarabian Metropolitanate!

Such a decision, if implemented, would short-circuit this Court's judgment by eliminating, by state action, Applicant's right to exist as a separate, registrable, ecclesiastical entity. How many times must we reiterate that Article 9 of the ECHR vests in believers, not in government, the determination of their religious commitment, and that Article 11 definitively guarantees religious believers the right to choose their organisational associations?

Simultaneously with the above-described Cabinet decision, President Vladimir Voronin addressed a letter to this Honourable Court in an effort politically to influence its judgment in the instant case. He incredibly argues that since the state has recognised the Metropolitanate of Moldova, to recognise the Bessarabian Metropolitanate would be "l'intervention de l'état dans les affaires intérieures de l'Eglise, ce que constituterait une violation flagrante de la Constitution de la République de Moldova (art. 31)"! The convoluted logic here seems to be that once the state recognises one church, to allow another to operate legally is state interference with religious affairs. The President needs to rethink what interference in religious matters *actually* means: it occurs, as here, where the state substitutes itself for believers in deciding which churches deserve recognition and which deserve only to be cast into outer legal darkness.

The latest act in this unfortunate drama consists of the intervention of the state-registered Metropolitanate of Moldova in the instant case. Its nine-page, self-serving argument by undated letter (accepted by this Court 25 September 2001 for submission by the Government in the name of the church) consists of (1) the claim that the Bessarabian Orthodox Church is schismatic and represents, at most, but 10% of the practising Orthodox believers in the country; (2) the assertion that to recognise and register it is to encourage "destabilisation of Moldovan religious life" and the deterioration of the country's "social-political" framework; (3) an attempt to discount as "disinformation" the independently demonstrated instances of persecution suffered by clergy and members of the Bessarabian Church at the hands of the dominant church body and with the concurrence of the Government; and (4) the argument that a single Orthodox church body is the only thing left which can hold all Moldovans together.

To these arguments, we can only point out the obvious. In the open, democratic societies of Europe, sustained by the legal machinery of the ECHR, even "schismatics" have the right to exist and to be recognised by the state. (Would this Court tolerate for a moment a State Party's refusal to recognise and register the Methodist Church because the Anglican Church could well argue historically that Methodists are schismatic Anglicans?) And numbers of adherents have nothing at all to do with the matter. (Does a church deserve the protections of the ECHR only when its numbers reach a certain percentage?) Article 9 gives those with religious convictions the right to believe, practice, and associate with other likeminded believers—and specifically opposes state interference in such matters. A state has no business making religious decisions for its people—by registering a single church so as to "stabilise" the country. If there are religious conflicts, even with political overtones, they must be resolved on a level playing field where all churches and religious organisations are afforded the same rights as guaranteed by the ECHR. The issue before this Honourable Court is neither schism nor stabilisation: it is *religious freedom*—freedom for the Bessarabian Orthodox Church no longer to suffer as a second-class organisation persecuted by those irrationally fearful of it.

Surely, the current situation must not be allowed to continue. We respectfully call upon this Honourable Court to rectify this sad state of affairs by finding for the Applicants on all counts.

Part Two

This Honourable Court will have noted that the Government's arguments just presented do little more than reiterate what they have said in their written submission. Rather than wasting the Court's valuable time with further repetitions, we shall conclude with three related considerations that we believe should influence the final judgment and the need for a serious implementation of it.

First, *the root argument of the Moldovan government.* In its unsuccessful attempt to postpone this hearing *sine die,* the Government offered a two-year old "Communiqué" (15 January 1999) to show that it was making serious efforts to obtain better relations between the Applicant (the unrecognised Bessarabian Metropolitanate) and the Government-recognised Metropolitanate of Moldova. Needless to say, this Honourable Court did not regard such diplomatic activity on the part of the State as providing a friendly settlement within the terms of Convention jurisprudence or as advancing the legal situation in any way. But the very fact that the Government would present such an argument points to the underlying fallacy in its entire reasoning. To quote the Government's letter of request for a postponement (1 September 2001): the instant case "est un conflit purement intraconfessionel et non un litige entre l'Etat et la religion."

The Government continues to hold that no violation of the ECHR occurs if a State chooses to recognise one religious body whilst refusing to register another—as long as the object is to reduce disagreements between the two churches! It should be painfully obvious that the State is, at best, taking sides in a religious controversy and, at worst, interfering with the religious practices of its citizenry. Article 9 makes such government interference an egregious human rights violation—pure and simple. The state is obliged by the Convention to take a *neutral and non-discriminatory position vis-à-vis religions desiring recognition.* If it does not, it must justify its interference by discharging the heavy evidential burden of showing that the rejected religion is the source of serious social ills, as defined in Article 9, para. 2. The Government engages in nothing more than a feeble rationalisation when it characterises its foray into church affairs as a mere attempt to arbitrate and mitigate "a purely interconfessional conflict." Interference is interference. Pigs is pigs. The inter-church relations of two Orthodox bodies and their patriarchs have *no bearing whatsoever* on the issue in this case; that issue is the *Moldovan government's* refusal to recognise and register one of these church bodies but not the other.

Secondly, *the root motivation on the part of the Moldovan Government*. Why is the Government reduced to such patently illogical arguments? The reason, sad to say, lies in its underlying value-system. The Government, doubtless from its double heritage of Caesaropapism and Marxist totalitarianism, hates the idea of too much religious diversity. The 17th century aphorism of *Cuius regio, eius religio* again rears its ugly head. An open marketplace of ideas, where religions not necessarily agreeing with each other coexist, seems incomprehensible to the Moldovan authorities—even though their official commitment to the ECHR compels such.

One thinks of the attitude of Roman imperial government towards the early Christians. Legal philosopher Adam Gearey has recently described it thus: "Roman disdain for Christianity is hostility towards a belief in personal salvation that can put the individual in opposition to the political community. The violence with which the Romans persecuted the early Christians is thus the physical reflex of a system of ideas and beliefs that felt challenged by something that seemed to move beyond it. ... A new interpretation performs a kind of violence on any opposed view" (*Law and Aesthetics* [Oxford: Hart, 2001], p. 62). For the *Roman state*, read the *Moldovan state*; for the *early Christians*, read the *Bessarabian Orthodox believers*.

Thirdly and finally, *the strength of the Government's conviction*. As we have seen, the Moldovan government operates with an underlying philosophy of paternalism—of benevolent despotism—whereby it must keep its citizenry from hurting themselves by joining churches supposedly bad for them. The state sees the marginalisation, and, indeed, the elimination of the Bessarabian Orthodox Church as a positive duty. To achieve this is vital to the country and to its people: the existence of a single, dominant Orthodox body (the Metropolitanate of Moldova) makes political and cultural life immensely easier for everyone.

This Honourable Court must not overlook the strength of this conviction. In an interview of 8 February 2000 with Ion Rabacu, a chief counsellor in the Moldovan government and an official of the Directorate for Social Affairs that oversees the State Service for the Affairs of Cults, the distinguished Keston

Institute asked Rabacu whether his Government would register the Bessarabian Metropolitanate if Moldova lost the instant case in Strasbourg. "He responded categorically: 'No, it will not register it.'" On 19 September 2001—less than two weeks ago—the Moldovan Premier Vasile Tarlev declared to the press: "The Government will not fulfil the decision of the European Court of Human Rights with its eyes closed, because the Republic of Moldova is an independent country and has its own national interests. We will fulfil the ECHR decision in case it is a well thought and balanced decision on the international level."

Now, we appreciate that only the Council of Ministers can enforce the judgments of this Honourable Court. However, the intransigence of the Moldovan government—as fully demonstrated throughout the long history of this matter both in Moldova and in Strasbourg—warrants, we submit, a resounding judgment in favour of the Applicants and the full damages prayed for. A clear message needs to be sent that, within the ambit of the European human rights system, governments have no legal choice but to treat all religious convictions and religious organisations with equal respect.

Part Nine
Letters from Europe

1. The Strange Decline of American Evangelicalism

The evangelical—representing by far the majority of American Protestants—stands for an experiential relationship with Christ, a strong view of the Bible, personal holiness of life, and eschatological confidence in the return of the Lord to judge the world. He or she is also generally opposed to evolutionary theory. Recent evidence suggests that Evangelicalism is now illustrating its opposition to evolution by its own activities: by regressing rather than going forward.

According to a recent report by the Princeton Religion Research Center, based on a nationwide Gallup poll, the average American's belief in the reliability of Scripture has declined by half in the last 30 years (from 65 percent in 1963 to 32 percent today), and 69 percent of U.S. adults now identify with moral relativism. The conclusion seems inescapable: On two of its most important agenda items, the promotion of biblical authority and moral absolutes, Evangelicalism has been a conspicuous failure in our generation.

This sad state of affairs is particularly surprising when one recalls that in the late 1950s and early 1960s the success of Evangelicalism seemed assured. A Gallup poll at the time revealed that a significant majority of American Protestant clergymen, irrespective of denomination, preferred to designate their theology and churchmanship as "evangelical." *Christianity Today*, whose premier issue appeared on October 15, 1956, soon overwhelmingly out-distanced the modernist *Christian Century* in readership. Billy Graham was consistently regarded as the most respected living American, according to the polls. Theological seminaries of evangelical persuasion, such as Fuller in California and Trinity in Illinois, attracted many of the best college graduates, while enrollments at more-or-less modernist, mainline denominational seminaries steadily declined. The biennial International Missionary Conventions of the Inter-Varsity Christian Fellowship and the activities of Campus Crusade for Christ on secular university and college campuses touched many with the evangelical message and resulted in significant missionary activity at home and abroad. The "death of God" movement of the 1960s epitomized the vacuity of liberal theology, and the former's death seemed to confirm the inevitable success of all that Evangelicalism stood for.

And today? When one thinks of evangelists, one's first thought is not of Billy Graham, now in his 70s, but of such media figures as Jerry Falwell and his now defunct Moral Majority; Oral Roberts, who, because of financial problems, had to sell his City of Faith medical complex which a 900-foot Jesus was supposed to have told him in a vision to build; Jimmy Swaggart and his steamy sexual recreations; and Jim Bakker with his grandiose, fraudulent schemes and lachrymose, eyelashed ex-wife.

Christianity Today began as a journal of opinion under the editorship of theologian Carl F. H. Henry, who located it in the nation's capital so as maximally to influence the secular climate of opinion. Partly for financial reasons, the operation was moved to the Wheaton, Illinois area: roughly, Evangelicalism's capital city. Henry left in disgust. The mantle fell on Harold Lindsell, also no mean theologian, who did all he could to maintain the journal's standards. But the pressure was on to increase circulation. Lindsell's successor virtually turned the magazine over to breezy journalists. The "Current Religious Thought" page, which had been written by such luminaries as G. C. Berkouwer of Amsterdam, was eliminated. What had been a journal of ideas soon descended to the level of a slick, evangelically-oriented family magazine. Here (read them and weep!) are typical major articles in the February through April 1992 issues: "Getting the Small Picture: Recovery from our Love Affair with Bigness"; "Withering Flowers in the Garden of Hope"; "Laughing with Sarah"; and "Secret Sins [i.e., incest] in the Church Closet." Once upon a time, *CT* made news by impacting the world of ideas; today, at best, it merely reports news, with substantive content almost solely limited to so-called in-depth interviews.

Evangelical book publishers have followed a similar route. From the 1940s through the 1970s, some very serious theological works were issued by the evangelical houses in Grand Rapids, Michigan, and by evangelical publishing firms elsewhere in the country. (One thinks, for example, of the works of Wilbur Smith and Edward John Carnell.) But when Hal Lindsey's *Late, Great Planet Earth* became a national bestseller, evangelical publishers realized the possibility of mass sales of popular titles. The result has been to turn the annual Christian Booksellers Convention trade fair into a cheap carnival of trivia and the average local Christian bookshop into a place to purchase audiocassettes of evangelical country and western music and pencils inscribed with Bible verses. I take at random the 24 new titles reviewed in the latest issue of a respectable U.S. evangelical church paper: 13 of the 24 deal with sex and marriage, daily living, and personal crises, or are fiction, including children's books. Only one title (on science and religion) attempts to break new ground or reach the thinking unbeliever. The evangelical publisher of my *Suicide of Christian Theology* (1970) now features Christian romance novels. That publisher prides itself on having sold 970,000 copies of *Free To Be Thin*, an evangelical weight-loss plan.

Many evangelical seminaries and colleges have made significant—and devastating—theological shifts. Fuller Seminary has altered its doctrinal statement, dropping the word "inerrant" in reference to the Scriptures. Westmont College has refused to discipline a professor who proclaims an "evangelical" redaction criticism which sees such events in the Gospel of Matthew as the coming of the Magi as nonhistorical sermon illustrations paralleling the Jewish midrash. Other evangelical seminaries have experienced hideous internecine warfare; one thinks of Concordia Seminary in Fort Wayne, Indiana, where distinguished scholar and president Robert Preus was forcibly retired, took legal action, and was then defrocked for seeking due process.

On the other hand, evangelicals still manifest toward each other an appalling moralism and legalism, thereby frightening off the unbeliever who might otherwise be attracted by the message. For example, at a distinguished Bible college, a professor was discharged not so long ago because his *wife* wrote a "feminist" book.

Why these sad phenomena? What explains Evangelicalism's inability to fulfill its promise of a generation ago? At least four factors contribute to the problem.

1. *Evangelicalism's deep-seated anti-intellectualism.* In spite of the herculean efforts made by many fine evangelical scholars and institutions of higher learning, Evangelicalism's invidious contrasting of heart and head, to the detriment of the latter, cripples its cause. Whenever pragmatics and emotion can be chosen in preference to ratiocination, the evangelical will do so. Thus money and emotional ties to the womb-like security of the Midwestern Bible Belt determined the retreat of *Christianity Today* from Washington, D.C.

2. *Evangelicalism's confused social behavior.* The modernist criticizes the evangelical for "biblicism," but in reality the evangelical is not biblical enough: He does not allow the Scriptures to criticize his own societal behavior. Thus the evangelical seldom subjects the salesmanship of the television evangelist or the popularity craze in evangelical publishing to biblical standards. If he did, he would see how he constantly attempts—unsuccessfully—to serve two masters.

3. *Evangelicalism's overstress on inner experience.* C. S. Lewis well noted in *The Screwtape Letters* that the devil encourages us to push our strengths until they become major weaknesses. In the face of dead churchmanship, evangelicals have historically insisted on a living, personal Christ-experience, and quite correctly. But this personal emphasis has readily and often imperceptibly been transformed into something quite different: a religious experientialism in which general principle and even biblical principle are ignored. The charismatic side of Evangelicalism displays this weakness in particular, but the same phenomenon lies at the root of the overall evangelical impatience with theological formulations, church organization, and stable ministry.

4. *Evangelicalism's poor priorities.* Ever since Wesley made sanctification rather than justification the focus of the 18th-century evangelical revival, evangelicals have looked upon holiness as their central concern (public morality; private conformity to evangelical blue-laws). But Luther was far more biblical than Wesley when he declared that you do not need to preach to a good tree to bear good fruit. When sanctification is separated from justification, as often occurs in Evangelicalism, the result is pharisaic moralism. This is probably Evangelicalism's most obnoxious characteristic. It was classically lampooned in Sir Henry Bashford's *Augustus Carp, Esq., Being the Autobiography of a Really Good Man* (1924), but it is rampant throughout the evangelical scene. Here is a personal illustration. When Jerry Falwell and I were both members of a small delegation invited by the late President Sadat of Egypt to discuss the Middle East conflict, Falwell attempted to prevent the Egyptians from serving wine at a state dinner: He cared far less about the impact of our Gospel message than about his notion of improving our hosts' morals. And I recently ran across a passage in John Hillaby's *London* (1987) in which the author speaks briefly of the central church of London's Anglican Evangelicalism, All Souls, Langham Place: "To me there seemed no awe in the Presence especially in the vicinity of the altar." Perhaps this suggests that moralism can be a far cry from true holiness.

To return to our *point de départ:* The evangelical, in attempting to refute evolutionary theory, argues that entropy, by way of the second law of thermodynamics, is more basic than biological development: Everything ultimately runs down, not up. Unhappily, this argument may also apply to Evangelicalism itself. But if the evangelical wishes to postpone that eventuality, he should seriously consider seeking his roots much further back than 18th-century revivalism—journeying, one might hope, to the early church and to the Reformation for a creedal Christianity and the genuine holiness of classical church worship.

2. Eugen Drewermann's Trivialization of Theology

We thought we'd heard it all. The 1960s gave us Episcopal Bishop James Pike in America ("I've jettisoned the Trinity, the Virgin Birth, and the Incarnation"), Anglican Bishop J. A. T. "Honest-to-God" Robinson in England, and the post-Bultmannians on the European continent. The 1970s and 1980s spawned process theologians and liberation theologians aplenty. On the Roman Catholic front, each successive book by Hans Küng has cut away more material from what was regarded as a seamless garment, so that infallibility is no longer found anywhere—not even in Holy Scripture.

Now along comes Eugen Drewermann, a 51-year-old priest and psychotherapist, who, until removed from his position in September 1991, was professor on the Faculty of Theology at Paderborn. Although now under discipline so that he cannot officially preach, he is still carrying on "spiritual conversations" after Mass and is the most popular Roman Catholic theological author in German-speaking Europe. His 38 books, many of them bestsellers, have sold more than a million copies. *Der Spiegel* featured Drewermann in its pre-Christmas (December 23, 1991) issue, and the interview became a cover story this year in *L'Autre Journal*, a major magazine of opinion in the French-speaking world.

What does Drewermann believe? As is common in such cases, it is easier to state what he does *not* believe. He is against clerical celibacy, an all-male priesthood, and the Roman Catholic Church's position on the remarriage of divorced persons. To be sure, such views could derive—and have been derived by some classical Protestant divines—from serious (though perhaps erroneous) biblical exegesis. Exegesis, however, is not Drewermann's forte.

For him, the Scriptures are to be understood in a symbolic, humanistic fashion. He agrees with Bultmann that the historical portrait of Jesus in the New Testament is thoroughly impregnated with nonhistorical, mythological elements, but he disagrees with Bultmann that the Bible should therefore be demythologized—for myth is vital psychologically. Thus, of the Ascension, Drewermann says: "We can only understand the Ascension as a symbol of elevation above human anguish ... Those who look at it any other way are professing not the faith but superstition." At the same time, in a spirit of liberal tolerance, he declares: "Each person ought to have the right to believe in a manner that helps him or her remove anxieties. I am the last person to label a belief heretical."

Miracles, according to Drewermann, do not fit the divine character.

> The thesis according to which God abrogated natural laws in Jesus' time and for him so as to do miracles is, in my view, false and dangerous ... The significance of miracle stories is not that one must wait for God to do miracles but that we must apply these symbols ourselves—by giving without counting the cost (the feeding of the 5,000) and by surmounting our own anxieties (walking on water).

And the death of Christ? According to Drewermann, "The religious theory of sacrifice as related to sin has no connection with Jesus. ... Jesus never subordinated the remission of sins to a redemptive act or to any kind of sacrifice." Indeed, "Jesus didn't attach any meaning to his own death."

If such be the case, how does Christianity differ from non-Christian religions? For Drewermann, all religions "are in a sense medicines, destined for specific illnesses." The differences among religions are not that important. After all, "the Aztec religion believed in immaculate conception, the rising again of the dead, and the accomplishments of a son of God." Indeed, following Jung and Eliade, Drewermann holds that "all men have in their unconscious a common and comprehensible language—the language of images. ... We need to reflect on these images to understand the Christic message."

Faced with Drewermann's psychological reductionisms, one could, to be sure, point up his appalling disregard of both biblical and extrabiblical fact: Was Jesus not so concerned to set forth the sacrificial meaning of his death that he declared—in the earliest of the Gospels—"I come to give my life a ransom for many" (Mk. 10:45; Mt. 20:28)? Is it not the grossest insensitivity to fact not to see a diametrical opposition on this point between Christianity and, say, the Aztecs, who engaged in forced human sacrifice?

What Drewermann teaches us is that the tree of 19th-century radical biblical criticism continues to bear poisoned fruit. In spite of the advent of Einstein's open universe, liberal theologians still try to eliminate the miraculous in Jesus' ministry, and with it the eyewitness reliability of the records concerning him. Thus the historical *inruption* of God to save a fallen race is trivialized to the level of personal, psychological imagery.

To those Athenian readers drawn to "some new thing" (in this case, Drewermann), we provide, free of charge, the motto on the Montgomery coat-of-arms: *Gardez bien!* (freely translated, "For heaven's sake, watch out!").

3. The Bishop and the Muslims

Those interested in the more bizarre side of contemporary church history will recall that, in 1984, the roof of the Durham Cathedral was struck by lightning near to the time its new Anglican bishop was to be consecrated. Public opinion in certain quarters—as displayed by some remarkable letters to the London *Times*—suggested a direct causal connection between the two events. It was said that the Lord God had put up with enough from David Jenkins, a former academic theologian, and that his elevation to the see of Durham had pushed the Deity to an act of dramatic temporal judgement.

Since Dr Jenkins became Bishop of Durham, he has not in any way toned down his radical theological views. To the contrary, he has lost no media opportunity to expand upon them. In doing so, he has become the Elisha to Bishop John A. T. ('Honest To God') Robinson's Elijah, and the English successor to America's Bishop James Pike.

Just before his consecration, Jenkins—on the London Weekend Television's religion show 'Credo'—had in effect shouted, 'Non credo!': he had informed the public that he did not consider the Virgin Birth or the Resurrection of Christ to be historical events. Now, eight years later, Jenkins continues to reaffirm and extend these non-beliefs.

In an interview published this year in *Alpha*, an English evangelical periodical, Clive Calver, director of the Evangelical Alliance, asked the Bishop about his current theological views. Jenkins responded that, though he is not absolutely certain on the point, he thinks that the body of Christ might still be rediscovered in a Middle Eastern tomb. "I think the more I am involved in this, the less likely I think that anything that might be called physical reconstruction or resurrection took place."

The Bishop also claimed that the language of the Fourth Gospel is not literally true, but should be considered "powerfully descriptive of what the literal truth was about." Thus, according to Jenkins, it was John who put the words, "I am the way, the truth, and the life," into Jesus' mouth (John 14:6): Jesus himself never uttered those words.

Christologically, the Bishop stated that he is now approaching an adoptionist position. It seems more and more likely to him that God adopted the man Jesus to be his son. After all, there was no Virgin Birth!

What is the general effect of Jenkins' position? One might suppose that it would be powerfully influential in the Anglican community, where the bishop is the locus of church authority. However, Jenkins' views have had little impact in Anglican circles, in spite of his being a darling of the media. At least three factors provide an explanation: first, the serious Anglican skeptics (they are very few in number) consider Jenkins a mere pop-theologian and continue to rally around the even more radical Don Cupitt; second, the 'comprehensiveness' of the 16th-century Anglican settlement has always made room for theological eccentrics, and the Bishop fills the bill most adequately; and, most importantly, the broad church element in the C of E is being swallowed up by its far more powerful rival, evangelicalism—often reinforced by charismatic and anglo-catholic beliefs. A generation ago, conservative biblical scholarship of the F. F. Bruce variety began its takeover of Anglican theological colleges; today the statistics suggest that by the year 2000 the evangelical wing will be the dominating element in the Church of England. (See, in Mowbray's Lambeth Series 'The Anglican Church Today,' Michael Saward, *Evangelicals on the Move* [London, 1987].) Thus David Jenkins' radical views are far less influential within the church than one might otherwise suppose.

But outside the Christian fold, the picture is different. England, like most modern nations, is becoming more and more a pluralistic society, in which many religious and philosophical positions clamour for a hearing, Islam is a steadily growing influence, and many English cities (one thinks especially of Luton, home of Vauxhall motors) now have minarets as well as church steeples.

The value of the Bishop of Durham to Islam has not been lost on The Islamic Propagation Centre. With headquarters in Birmingham and an extensive publication program of books, pamphlets, and tracts, the Centre has made much of Jenkins' beliefs. In a leaflet featuring an attractive picture of 'The Rev. Professor,' and titled 'Jesus—As Only a Messenger,' the Centre waxes eloquent on the theme that Jenkins' "rejection of Jesus' divinity … is indeed a flicker of light at the end of the long, dark tunnel of Christianity in which the Christians have been sadly groping for over 2,000 years." The Bishop's position is, we are told, "the endorsement of the Muslim viewpoint … as regards the REAL STATUS of Jesus Christ (on whom be peace)."

And here one sees the true tragedy of the churchman (whatever his denominational connection) who sits on a theological limb while cutting it off beneath him. His ignominious fall may be of little consequence (indeed, may even seem amusing) to his fellow members, but to those outside the fold he provides powerful ammunition to support false religion as well as irreligion. With friends like the Bishop of Durham, Christians don't need enemies.

The annual general meeting of the Sherlock Holmes Society of London (on which be peace) will take place at the House of Commons in January. David Jenkins is the invited speaker and I am the Society member chosen to reply. My theme will be Holmes' rule that "it is a capital mistake to theorize in advance of the facts." Christianity depends on the facts—and, in particular, the eye-witness fact of a physically resurrected Christ. The 'many infallible proofs' (Acts 1:3) of that fact will survive the Bishop of Durham—and, indeed, all else—until the Resurrected One physically returns to judge the quick and the dead, whose Kingdom shall have no end.

4. A New Archbishop of Canterbury

Many Anglicans breathed a deep sigh of relief when Archbishop Robert Runcie arrived at the mandatory retirement age. During World War II Runcie had been a tank commander, and it was said that his last resolute decisions were made in that capacity. Certainly, as Archbishop of Canterbury he was the archetypal "good ol' wishy-washy Charlie Brown."

Now the mantle has fallen on George Carey. What is *his* theological perspective? He is generally identified as evangelical-cum-charismatic, and as such—on the lesser of evils principle—he can only be an improvement on his predecessor. But evaluating him requires an examination of his views.

Just before his elevation to Canterbury, Carey declared that opposition to the ordination of women priests is a "heresy." This produced a veritable uproar. Many pointed out that the new Archbishop was—*de minimis*—rusty on his theological terminology. The strong definition of "heresy" involves "the formal denial or doubt of any defined doctrine of the Catholic faith," and quite obviously the Church Catholic has never defined a pro-women's ordination doctrine. The weaker definition of heresy entails denial of a cardinal or salvatory teaching of Christian faith; but a refusal to ordain women hardly reaches the level of imperiling the Gospel. As the hubbub increased, Carey retracted his statement, nonetheless leaving doubt as to his theological, and indeed also his political, skills.

If that were not enough, the Archbishop-elect also suggested that liturgically "a language 300 or 400 years old" is used "for sentiment's sake." The Prayer Book Society responded in no uncertain terms:

> Canon A5 makes the Book of Common Prayer a yardstick by which the doctrine of the Church is defined. Since many modern services represent inadequately the doctrine of the Church, we would ask what sort of faith will the Church pass on to future generations if they are kept in ignorance of the Book of Common Prayer.

In other words, the issue is not guitars versus Palestrina and Bach. Again, the depth of Carey's theological commitment was left in doubt.

In March of 1992 the Archbishop broke a 150-year-old precedent by turning down an invitation to become patron of the CMJ—the Anglican Church's Ministry among the Jews. His reason? As he stated it, had he accepted the patronage (held by Archbishops of Canterbury since 1841), it would have been unhelpful in his efforts to "encourage trust and friendship between the different faith communities in our land." Of this very surprising decision, one distinguished clergyman wrote to *The Times*: "For many it will be seen ... as detracting from our Lord's commission to evangelise the whole world, including his own people, the Jews." Otherwise stated, the new evangelical Archbishop was not proving to be truly evangelical.

Archbishop Carey has a minor reputation as a writer of rather serious religious books. One can glean from these writings a fairly specific picture of his position on key theological issues, and the vista is not always what one might expect of an evangelical. Thus, in his *I Believe* (1991), he tells us that as a theological student he "could not square up 1 Kings with 1 Chronicles." For Carey,

Old Testament history must be seen as "sometimes romanticized, sometimes idealized, and in which past and present are sometimes confusingly mixed"; higher criticism must be accepted. Quite remarkably, he demonstrates no acquaintance with the contemporary archeological reconciliation of the Kings/Chronicles dating problem (see Edwin R. Thiele, *The Mysterious Numbers of the Hebrew Kings,* rev. ed., 1984). Indeed, he capitulates without a fight to the higher critics, showing little awareness of the devastating effect an unreliable Old Testament can have on the larger issue of historical revelation.

In sum, it would appear that the new Archbishop is less theologically astute, less faithful to Scripture and church tradition, and less evangelical than was expected of him. Certainly his emphasis on a personal, living relationship with Jesus Christ is something to be thankful for, and in a sinful, broken world we should always be grateful for such favors. Carey is not as bad as he could be; but neither is he as good as he should be.

5. Trust Me?

The October 5, 1992, issue of *The Times* carried a troubling, but not atypical, news article by the paper's religion correspondent. It announced that fundamental changes were in the offing for one of England's most prestigious public (i.e., in American terms, private) religious schools: Roman Catholic St. Philip's sixth form college in Birmingham, founded by Cardinal Newman and including among its alumni J. R. R. Tolkien, author of *The Hobbit* and *The Lord of the Rings*. The plan is to turn the college into a non-sectarian boys' secondary school. Senior priests at Birmingham Oratory defended this move on the ground that more than two-thirds of the pupils are now non-Catholic; indeed, as a result of the presence of many Asian and non-Christian students on the campus, even the Lord's Prayer and the sign of the Cross have already been "deemed inappropriate" at the college.

The sticking point, however, as raised by the Governors (the Board of Trustees) and dissenting parents is the college trust deed. According to its terms, the Fathers provide buildings for "the performance of public worship according to the rites and ceremonies of the Roman Catholic religion"; the deed declares that the college is to be maintained "in accordance with the principles of the Roman Catholic faith."

On the surface, it would appear that the proposed changes would be legally out of the question. The trust deed says what it says: how can it be disregarded? The answer, these days, is to argue that a trust deed is subject to modification by way of the equitable doctrine of *cy-près* (Old French for "the nearest equivalent"). When changed circumstances militate against the continued performance of the grantor's original intention, then (it is said) one may redirect the purposes of the trust. Here, allegedly, our late 20th-century secular and multiracial society makes a strictly Catholic education, as envisaged by the original grantors, unrealistic. Thus the modification of the trust purpose can be legitimated. And since the grantors have long gone to their heavenly rewards, they are not around to dispute the case before the chancery judge who rules on such questions.

May we point out that such argumentation is both legally specious and morally repugnant? Juridically, the *cy-près* doctrine ought to be applied only in cases where it is now impossible to carry out the original purpose of the trust (see L. A. Sheridan and V. T. H. Delany, *The Cy-Près Doctrine* [1959]). Impossibility may occur, for example, because the trust corpus is no longer sufficient to carry out its original purpose (a trust for nuclear research which, through bad investment, now consists of only $500); or because the original trust purpose has become meaningless (a trust for superannuated dray horses after they have all been replaced by transit vans, or a trust for the conquest of infantile paralysis in Ohio, when no more infants suffer from the disease in that jurisdiction). Under such circumstances, a court of equity will agree to modify the trust purpose—but only to the extent strictly demanded by the changed circumstances and in a manner as closely in accord with the grantor's original intent as can be found. Thus, in the case of the grant for conquering the now conquered infantile paralysis, the court may allow the trustees to use the investment interest from the trust corpus to combat another and still existent, equally virulent childhood disease.

The moral issue here—clearly reflected in the law's reticence to modify a trust purpose—is that a grantor or benefactor who explicitly gives his property for a defined purpose has a sacred right to have his wherewithal used for that purpose and for that purpose alone, if there is any realistic way in which this can still be done. Since the grantor is usually no longer present to defend his interests, any violation of them is an especially cowardly and obnoxious act.

And now back to Birmingham. Can the original St. Philip's trust no longer be performed? Does an Asian or multiracial student body prevent the college masters from teaching their students—who, after all, attend the college voluntarily—the Holy Catholic faith? Even the posing of the question reveals its absurdity.

The disregard and modification of religiously-orientated trusts is endemic today on both sides of the Atlantic, and is by no means restricted to Roman Catholic circles. A Protestant example is provided by the Warburton Lecture, held at Lincoln's Inn, London, since 1768, when it was founded by a testamentary bequest of £500 from Anglican Bishop William Warburton. The preacher or lecturer is "to prove the truth of revealed religion in general and of the Christian in particular from the prophecies of the Old and New Testament which relate to the Christian church, especially to the apostacy of papal Rome." Alfred Edersheim's great work, *Prophecy and History in Relation to the Messiah*, originated as a Warburton Lecture. And today? A year ago the preacher was a Roman Catholic archbishop—who, incidentally, did not so much as mention biblical apologetics in his address!

What can be done about such egregious by-passing of law and morals? The answer is to sensitize the general public (after all, when such actions become endemic, trusts for the care and feeding of puppies can end up being used for vivisection), and to be willing to litigate in behalf of the original trust purposes. The grantor is no longer in a position to help himself; we, his beneficiaries, must step into his shoes. As in so many areas of life, here also Pericles' aphorism is directly applicable: the secret of freedom is courage.

6. Anglican Priestesses

On November 11, 1992, the General Synod of the Church of England, by a majority of five votes, determined to ordain women priests. Since nearly everyone and his brother (or sister?) has offered an opinion on this subject, I can see no good reason why I should not do the same.

But am I not biased? Do I not have my axe to grind? Certainly. From a psychological standpoint, I look at the matter much as did Dr Johnson, when a female Quaker was mentioned to him in conversation. "Sir," said Johnson, "a woman's preaching is like a dog's walking on his hinder legs. It is not done well; but you are surprized to find it done at all." My wife agrees. In the States she felt as uncomfortable as I in the presence of female Episcopalian vicars.

To be sure, the issue runs far deeper than psychological prejudice. The most jarring aspect of the recent Anglican decision, in my judgment, was not the result but the reasoning by which that result was reached. Let us look briefly at the logic involved, the procedure employed, and the ecumenical repercussions—and finally glance at the Scriptural perspective. (In modern churchmanship, the Bible usually comes last, so we are merely following the crowd in our order of discussion.)

As one listened to the arguments pro and con the ordination of women, there was the distinct feeling that the ground had given way and one had dropped down the rabbit hole into wonderland. On the Sunday preceding the General Synod's vote, BBC 1's prestigious, prime-time *Everyman* program dealt with the "Hidden Tradition"—the allegedly concealed fact that the early church had in fact ordained women! Opinions were presented by such obvious authorities as Mary Ann Rossi of the Women's Research Center of the University of Wisconsin and the Rev. Frances Young, a Methodist clergyman and professor of theology in Birmingham. Evidence adduced consisted of (1) a passage in a tract on virginity ascribed to Athanasius (4th century) to the effect that holy virgins could legitimately celebrate the breaking of bread together without the presence of a male priest, and (2) a eucharistic fresco in the Greek chapel of the Priscilla catacomb in Rome showing seven women presumably concelebrating with Priscilla's husband. To be sure, Athanasius could have been referring to an agape feast, and Priscilla's husband is clearly officiating as celebrant! But even if there were isolated instances of female ordination in early Christian history, would that make it right as a general practice? No one apparently had heard of G. E. Moore's naturalistic fallacy: that the "is" must not be confused with the "ought."

Those opposing the ordination of women did not win any prizes in logic either. The most frequent argument was that the priest must represent Jesus, and Jesus was male. Would it also follow that the priest must be of Jewish extraction? wear first-century garb? not drive an automobile to church? One thinks of the Amish—or of some fundamentalists—who believe that to be truly Christian requires a one hundred per cent "imitation of Christ." (Cf. the line: "*Jesus* didn't smoke. If He had wanted *you* to smoke, he would have put a smokestack on your head.")

Turning to the manner in which the Church of England made its decision, I was reminded of the truth lawyers are perhaps more aware of than others: that good procedure can contribute more to fairness and justice than the substantive law itself, and bad procedure can have a correspondingly horrendous effect. Wholly apart from the substantive illogic of much of the Church's argumentation, the process by which the decision was reached appears fatally flawed. A two-thirds majority was needed in all three houses of bishops, clergy, and laity, to approve women's ordination. Why two-thirds? What is the magic of such a formula? In point of fact, if but two lay members had voted the other way, the Priests (Ordination of Women) Measure would have been lost.

The bishops voted 75% to 25% to ordain women; the clergy, 70% to 30%; and the laity 67% to 33%. In the church at large, it is believed that the measure would have been roundly defeated had a referendum been held. Of course, it wasn't. Archbishop Carey favoured female ordination and put much pressure on the Synod to pass the controverted measure: the last thing he wanted was a church-wide vote. Like John Major on Maastricht, the idea was to downgrade grass-roots opinion in comparison with the glories of "representative" government (i. e., don't be democratic if it means you lose!).

Sadly, the result is that Anglicans are now saddled with a decision which by no means represents a consensus. The Church is split wide open, and it is estimated that a thousand priests may well now demit their ministry.

Ecumenically, the decision creates incredible problems for Anglican-Roman Catholic and Anglican-Orthodox relations. One London *Times* writer opined that this is for the best, since now the Anglican Church had finally stood up for truth rather than ecumenical compromise! (It would indeed be refreshing to see the Church of England subordinate politics to theology, but what we have here is hardly such an example: the case for women's ordination, as we have observed, was not exactly argued with theological sophistication.)

Last we heard, Christian doctrine is supposed to have its source—its fons et origo—in revelation. What does Scripture have to say on the subject? It states unequivocally (1 Tim. 2:12) that women are not to assume authority in the church. In the Anglican Church, the locus of authority resides in the episcopal office, so, strictly speaking, violence has not been done to Scripture unless and until a woman is ordained a bishop (one of the marks of apostasy in the American Episcopal Church is the fact that this has now occurred there). But some may not be blamed for thinking that with the camel's head in the church door, it will not be long before the entire beast sits on the communion table. Indeed, that eventuality is now a *fait accompli* as a result of the Anglican national assembly's vote on 12 July 2010 to ordain woman bishops.

Perhaps the most sobering lesson to learn from the Anglican female-ordination circus is that as a church's confidence in Scriptural revelation declines, its ability to think theologically declines with it. Thus the bizarre and grotesque reasoning, procedural insensitivity, and ecumenical blindness characteristic of the General Synod's November vote. To paraphrase the Litany: "From all such error, pestilence, and calamity: Good Lord, deliver us!"

7. Can a Scientist Pray?

The term "apologetics" classically designated one of the three main branches of systematic theology, the others being dogmatics and ethics. Today, however, there is not a theological seminary in the world (to my knowledge) that gives the same stress to apologetics as it does to dogmatics or ethics—unless one thinks of certain liberal schools of theology where the three fields are equalized by placing no significant stress on any of them. One is hard put to think of Christian writers of the caliber of C. S. Lewis who are currently defending the faith with both an ability to communicate to a non-specialized audience and the respect of their peers for the quality of their scholarship. The dearth of serious Christian apologists is particularly unfortunate in our era of increasing secularism: Where are the apologists, we might well ask, just when we need them most?

A ray of hope is provided by the work of Dr. John Polkinghorne, FRS. Formerly a professor of mathematical physics at Cambridge University, he took Anglican orders and spent a number of years as priest of a little, out-of-the-way parish. During that time he wrote several highly significant books dealing with the interrelations of science and Christian faith. Recently he was appointed President of Queens' College, Cambridge—attesting to the respect in which he is held by his academic peers. His books include *The Way the World Is* (1983), *One World* (1986), *Science and Creation* (1988), *Science and Providence* (1989), and *Reason and Reality* (1991)—all published by S.P.C.K. in England—and he regularly fulfils prestigious lecture commitments in the British Isles. Since Polkinghorne is not yet well known on the other side of the Atlantic, it is worthwhile to give a taste of his approach—if only to whet one's appetite for more.

On October 20, 1992, Polkinghorne addressed the Royal Society of Arts on the subject "Can a Scientist Pray?" As a Fellow of the Society, I attended. Particularly illuminating was the reaction of the audience, which, drawn together by purely secular interest in arts, science, and technology, hung on his every word—an atypical response, if there ever was one, for a Society whose historical luminaries are not theologians but secular saints like Benjamin Franklin.

Polkinghorne began by blasting the mechanical universe of 18th-century deism, observing that its "clockmaker" image of God and its deterministic model of the world are hopelessly outmoded. Both quantum physics and Einsteinian relativity contradict the mechanistic universe. Today's field of "chaotic dynamics" has shown that "almost all of the everyday physical world is so exquisitely sensitive that the smallest disturbance produces quite uncontrollable and unpredictable consequences." The result, of course, is an open rather than a closed (Newtonian) universe—and an open universe is one which has room for answered prayer.

Christian theology has always set itself against not only the deistic idea of God as an indifferent spectator but also the notion of God as a cosmic puppet-master: Christian faith holds that the God of love gave his creatures genuine free will. But prayers for specifics and answers to prayers for specifics do not consist of reminding God of what He has forgotten, or of getting Him to do what He wouldn't have done otherwise. The dynamics of prayer lie elsewhere. In the nondeterministic universe God has set out a pattern of general laws, but

He has "left Himself and us room to maneuver." When we pray we give our own room to maneuver to Him so that He can use it with *His* room to maneuver. This can align human and divine will—make them operate coherently—and things can happen that wouldn't occur otherwise. Science and Christian faith agree that the universe has overall structure but an open future, and prayer is a prime factor in fine-tuning that future.

As might be expected, Polkinghorne is stronger in scientific than in historical or biblical apologetics. In the discussion period following his lecture, I asked for his response to the notorious Flew-Wisdom parable (to the effect that one can never find clean evidence of a caring God—of a loving Gardener who takes care of the garden of this world). He cited examples from Peter Berger's *A Rumor of Angels*, and referred to the beauty of mathematical equations in physics as evidence of a rationally governed universe, but at the same time he insisted that God is "always hidden." Another member of the audience then pointed to God's revelatory non-hiddenness in 1 Kings 18 (Elijah's empirical test on Mount Carmel, proving the falsity of Baal and the truth of the God of Israel) and the "many infallible proofs" (Acts 1:3) of the resurrection of Christ. Polkinghorne's rather lame answer was that he had always found 1 Kings 18 to be one of his most difficult passages and that even in science one can only see if one first believes.

Though Polkinghorne may tend to misapply Augustine's *credo ut intelligam* to the apologetic task, his forthright endeavor to relate hard science to Christian truth on the cutting edge of contemporary physics and cosmology is most refreshing.

8. Did Jesus Exist?

An absurd question, you may well respond. Why, the longest biographical article in the *Encyclopaedia Britannica* is devoted to Jesus! But this query is the title of one of four scholarly books by G. A. Wells, emeritus professor of German at Birbeck College, London, critiquing Jesus' historicity, and they have had considerable influence on both sides of the Atlantic.

First came *The Jesus of the Early Christians* (1971) then *Did Jesus Exist?* (1975; rev. ed., 1986), then *The Historical Evidence for Jesus* (1982), and finally *Who Was Jesus? A Critique of the New Testament Record* (1989). In the United States, Professor Wells' publications are distributed by Prometheus Books, the major rationalist publishing house (which, by what I have always regarded as strong evidence of temporal judgment, has the misfortune to be located in Buffalo,

New York). Wells' ideas have had popular impact in the British Isles through his appearance on a national television broadcast having the same title as his latest blast at Jesus' historicity.

It was therefore with considerable glee that I accepted the invitation of the Lawyers' Christian Fellowship to debate the good professor at the Inns of Court School of Law (the graduate training college for barristers) on 10 February 1993.

Wells' argument in the debate predictably tracked the case he endeavours to make in his books. As he wrote in the preface to *The Historical Evidence for Jesus*: "My fundamental theses remain the same: namely, the earliest references to the historical Jesus are so vague that it is not necessary to hold that he ever existed; the rise of Christianity can, from the undoubtedly historical antecedents, be explained quite well without him; and reasons can be given to show why, from about A. D. 80 or 90, Christians began to suppose that he had lived in Palestine about fifty years earlier." Specifically, according to Wells, it was Paul who in effect created Jesus—but as a divine figure, not as a historical personage. After all, Paul's writings preceded the Gospel accounts, and the Pauline letters are utterly indifferent as to biographical detail on Jesus' life and ministry. The Gospels themselves, as modern theological scholarship agrees, are hopeless as historical accounts and really display, not historical facts about Jesus, but a record of the faith experiences of the early believing communities of Christians.

What had fascinated me about Wells' approach in his books, and what became the *point de départ* for my response to him in the debate, was the fundamental source of his ideas. As a professor of German, emphasizing the history of ideas from the Enlightenment to the present, Wells has immersed himself in German biblical criticism. He has gorged himself on an indigestible diet of radical German critical scholarship and its English-language counterparts. (In the latter category, he especially enjoys liberal Roman Catholic New Testament scholars Raymond E. Brown and Joseph A. Fitzmyer.) Instead of attempting to look at the primary records of Jesus in their own right, he gazes at them through the coloured glasses of the documentary, form, and redaction critics—and the Bultmannian and post-Bultmannian efforts to baptize and apply existential anti-objectivism to the study of Christian origins.

In the debate, therefore, I insisted upon (1) a strict reliance on the primary sources—the 1st and early 2nd century historical materials themselves, and (2) a moratorium on the use of any and all modern theologians, whether liberal or conservative. If modern scholarship were to be cited, let it be neutral, non-theological scholarship (secular historians, legal scholars, literary specialists), so as to give the biblical materials the benefit of the scholarly criteria applicable to historical testimony in general.

I then proceeded to deal with the New Testament records by way of military historian Chauncey Sanders' three criteria: the documentary, internal, and external tests (*Introduction to Research in English Literary History* [1952]). Citing the late principal director of the British Museum and classical archeologist Sir Frederic Kenyon, I argued that, from a documentary standpoint, "both the *authenticity* and the *general integrity* of the books of the New Testament may be regarded as finally established" (*The Bible and Archaeology* [1940], Kenyon's italics). I referred to the more than 5,000 Greek manuscripts of the New Testament (J. K. Elliott, *A Bibliography of Greek New Testament MSS* [1989]). I cited the internal claims of the Gospels to be written by eyewitnesses or close associates of eyewitnesses, and the external confirmation of these claims (Polycarp and Papias), together with recent archeological support for the historicity of the Gospel accounts (e.g., the 1961 discovery at Caesarea of the Pilate inscription independently confirming his procuratorship). I noted that when Wells dismisses such testimony as Papias offers, he does so, typically, not on the basis of the testimony itself, but because post-Bultmannian German theological scholarship—in this case Conzelmann—questions it. But in history, literature, and law, persons and documents are supposed to be innocent until proven guilty, not the other way around!

To be sure, the primary-source value of the Gospel records would not per se establish the truth of Jesus' claims in those documents. There we find that Jesus forgives sin, declares that "he who has seen me has seen the Father," and is crucified on the charge of blasphemy. But was he in fact the Divine Saviour he claimed to be?

At which point, we went into the case for Jesus' resurrection. Using legal argumentation, I noted that if Jesus did not rise (as the primary-source accounts say he did), then his body had to have been stolen. But the three interest-groups in the situation would not have stolen it: it was against the interest of the Romans or of the Jewish religious leaders to do so, and the disciples surely would not have made off with the body and then knowingly died for their own preaching of the resurrection!

As for alleged errors and contradictions in the Gospel accounts, they simply point to the non-collusive nature of the testimony: Dean Bennett of the Boston University School of Law observed as long ago as 1899 (*The Four Gospels from a Lawyer's Standpoint*) that the Gospel writers testify from their own unique viewpoints, as veridical witnesses to an accident will see the same event from different angles.

All in all, it was not a good evening for Professor Wells. But when one argues the flat-earth theory, one should expect problems. I could not resist quoting Dr Johnson in the *Rambler* on the value of retirement (Professor Wells having just accepted emeritus status): it affords the opportunity to deliberate on eternity—"forming the only plan in which miscarriage cannot be repaired, and examining the only question in which mistake cannot be rectified."

9. When Is a Jew Not a Jew?

Answer: when he is a Messianic Jew. According to Israeli law, a Jew ceases to be a Jew for purposes of immigration to Israel when he or she embraces another religion, in particular Christianity. At first glance, such an approach may not appear surprising, but in fact it produces a host of anomalous consequences and raises some exceedingly fundamental human rights issues.

The occasion for treating the question here is an Israeli Supreme Court judgment of 2 July 1992, consolidating several appeals by Messianic Jews in Israel to remain in the country after having been informed that they could no longer do so. As an international human rights specialist, I was recently asked by those representing the appellants to advise on the case, and its wider ramifications make it a fascinating subject for theological reflection.

Three Jewish families were involved in the long-term legal hassle that eventuated in the July Supreme Court decision. The Beresfords, husband and wife, arrived in Israel from Zimbabwe on tourist visas in December of 1986. On petitioning for immigrant status pursuant to the Law of Return—which automatically provides residency for ethnic Jews or Jewish converts—they were informed that, even though they were indeed Jews by birth, they could not immigrate under the Law of Return because they believed Jesus to be the Messiah. In maintaining such a belief, the Beresfords had adopted "another religion," and had fallen under the axe of section 4B of the Law of Return, which defines who is entitled to benefit from that Law, specifically, "whoever was born to a Jewish mother or has been converted to Judaism, and who does not belong to another religion."

Sidney and Linda Speakman and their minor daughter Dawn came to Israel in September, 1988, from Portland, Oregon, where they had opposed the right-wing, neo-Nazi, anti-Semitic activities of the Pike organisation and had been subjected to threats of physical harm as a consequence. Like the Beresfords, they entered Israel as tourists and later attempted to obtain permanent residency under the Law of Return. As Messianic Jews, the parents were informed that their petition could not be granted, but that their daughter could receive Israeli citizenship, since when she was born her mother had not yet regarded herself as a Messianic Jew, i.e., the daughter had been a minor when her parents became Messianic Jews (sec. 4A[a] of the Law of Return). The Speakmans argued that it was unthinkable for the family to be split up in this manner; that they had established a productive building construction business in Israel; and that "we came only to live in Israel and to help build up this land": all to no avail; appeal denied.

The story of the Kendall family was depressingly similar. Only the four Kendall children may remain in Israel. The parents, because of their Messianic convictions, must leave—with or without them.

To be sure, the Law of Return is not the only legal route to Israeli citizenship. Those who do not qualify under that Law may make application under the Entry into Israel Law, designed for non-Jews, and containing no religious restriction. All of the petitioners, once they had been denied the benefits of the Law of Return, then sought to remain in the country by way of this second route—and promptly had this door slammed in their face by the Ministry of the Interior. In point of fact, as the Supreme Court stated, the Interior Minister "is given broad discretion in this matter," "is not obligated to give reasons for his decision," and his policy, "applied for many years, is not to grant Permanent Residence Visas to foreigners, except in exceptional cases wherein exist special considerations. This policy has withstood the review of this Court."

Much could of course be said on the legal aspects of this sad situation (for example, the lack of responsible judicial review of the Interior Ministry's administrative action, which appears prima facie to be arbitrary, discriminatory, and lacking in natural justice, and which clearly evacuates the Entry into Israel Law of virtually all significance). But our interest here is principally on the theological side, in reference to the Law of Return.

Quoting a High Court judgment in an earlier case, the Israeli Supreme Court approvingly wrote: "We have not yet heard about Jesuits who are considered and accepted as Jews. The thing is simply unacceptable. ... Please ask a Jew in the street if such a thing is possible and his definitive answer will be: 'No.'" Fascinatingly enough, this attempt to take judicial notice of Israeli public opinion was in fact entirely misdirected; a scientific survey by the Dahaf Research Institute in Tel Aviv in 1988 revealed that 78% of the interview sample ("Jews in the street") would give immigrant status under the Law of Return to anyone who believes in Jesus as the Messiah as long as he is "born to a Jewish mother, faithful to the State of Israel, pays his taxes to the State, serves in the army, celebrates the Jewish holidays, keeps the commandments of Israel's tradition, [and] feels that he is a Jew." Indeed: almost all first-generation Christians were Jews, and they never considered their belief in Christ to detract one iota from their Jewishness!

The supreme irony of the present situation is that whereas an ethnic Jew who is an atheist can readily obtain permanent residence under the Law of Return (the only practical route to residency, as we have seen, since the Entry into Israel Law is an impossibly narrow conduit), a Jew who sees Jesus as the fulfilment of Israel's hope and wishes to worship in a Messianic synagogue can only visit Israel as a temporary tourist.

Israel is in fact a highly intolerant, repressive state. In 1986, at the Greek Court of Appeals in Athens, I successfully defended Christian missionaries convicted under the Greek anti-proselytising law (the "Athens 3" case). A similar enactment exists in Israel: the 1977 Penal Law Amendment (Enticement to Change Religion) Law. In discussing this with the Director of the Israeli government's Division for Relations with the Churches, I pointed out that such laws strangle the tender plant of freedom, have a chilling effect on the search for religious truth, and serve as a particularly unfortunate commentary on a nation which came into existence as a refuge for a people that itself suffered terribly from ideological discrimination and the removal of civil liberties. As Amnesty International has shown, the State of Israel has one of the most negative human rights records of any developed nation. Perhaps she is the very country which would benefit most from one Jeshua who declared, "If the Son shall make you free, you shall be free indeed."

10. Feminism and Theology

In March, 1993, I flew across the pond to deliver a guest lecture in the 24th annual Philosophy Symposium at the California State University, Fullerton. Other participants included theologian Ninian Smart, philosopher of religion D. Z. Phillips, and feminist Emily Culpepper. The subject was "Rationality and Spirituality," and I was particularly interested in hearing what contemporary feminism had to do with either or both.

Past experiences with feminists had not offered much encouragement. After a public lecture on Right-to-Life at the School of Law of the University of Missouri at Kansas City some years ago, a feminist opened the discussion with the apodictic assertion: "Dr Montgomery, you have no right to speak on the subject of abortion: you are not a woman." (I replied in the words of my old Cornell philosophy mentor and Wittgenstein interpreter Max Black: "True as to my sex, Madam, but epistemologically irrelevant.")

Emily Culpepper, a Harvard Th.D., appeared without make-up, wearing a tee-shirt emblazoned with the feminist double-axe logo, and spoke for an hour without once quoting a male theologian. Her sources were such standard feminist writers as Mary Daly (also on the CSUF program) and "Starhawk." Before we look at the specifics of Culpepper's paper, it may be useful to get on the wave-length of these thinkers. A convenient source of their ideas is the anthology, *Womanspirit Rising: A Feminist Reader in Religion,* edited by Carol Christ and Judith Plaskow (Harper).

Mary Daly, in her well-known essay, "After the Death of God the Father: Woman's Liberation and the Transformation of Christian Consciousness," sets forth the themes of theological feminism: "The Judaic-Christian tradition has served to legitimate sexually imbalanced patriarchal society." How, precisely? "The image of the Father God, spawned in the human imagination and sustained as plausible by patriarchy, has in turn rendered service to this type of society by making its mechanisms for the oppression of women appear right and fitting." Christology falls under the same critical axe; "The imbalance in Christian ideology resulting from sexual hierarchy is manifested not only in the doctrine of God but also in the notion of Jesus as the unique God-man." A feminist theological revolution will mean an ethical revolution: "The becoming of women implies also a transvaluation of values in Christian morality ... which will go far beyond Nietzsche's merely reactionary rejection of Christian values." But, as a matter of fact, subsequent to writing this passage, Daly herself opted for rejection of those same values; her editor comments: "She has repudiated the Christian symbol system since writing this essay."

"Starhawk" (Miriam Simos, priestess and first national president of the pagan Covenant of the Goddess church) typifies the occult dimension of contemporary feminist theology. In her paper, "Witchcraft and Women's Culture," presented to the American Academy of Religion in 1977, she argued that witchcraft is a positive force for the attainment of feminist ideals. "Witchcraft, 'the craft of the wise,' is the last remnant in the west of the time of women's strength and power." Of what does true witchcraft consist? "The old religion of witchcraft before the advent of Christianity, was an earth-centered, nature-oriented worship that venerated the Goddess, the source of life, as well as her son-lover-consort, who was seen as the Horned God of the hunt and animal life." In practice this means a "basic orientation to the earth," "no dichotomy between spirit and flesh, no split between Godhead and the world," and "spiritual union found in life, within nature, passion, sensuality."

Emily Culpepper took up these themes in her CSUF presentation. By overturning the traditional patriarchal society, she declared, the modern woman can make a new leap in consciousness, arriving at a higher level of holistic understanding. Achieving this goal entails the employment of new metaphors, in line with the concept of "presentational symbolism" in the work of semanticist Suzanne K. Langer. Thus the common use of the "Amazon" symbol by feminists: as the modern woman develops an Amazon sense of self, she absorbs internal strength and a "non-victim identity." But even this is not enough.

The new symbol introduced by Culpepper via her essay was the "Gorgon." In classical mythology, to be sure, Gorgon referred to one of three snaky-haired sisters (the most well-known being Medusa), whose terrifying aspect turned the beholder to stone. Emphasizing that a symbol is only good if it "works for you," Culpepper recommended Gorgon symbolism by means of a personal example. When she was potentially attacked at the door of her Cambridge flat by an unknown male, she made such a horrible face that he ran off. Immediately afterward, she went to her mirror and did it again—subjectively to reinforce this "enormous event." How far she had moved from her Southern white gentility and Christian origins! Christianity had become for her "compost in her life"—a source of fecundity still but no longer a model of faith or of behavior.

In the discussion following this paper, I restrained myself (with difficulty) from drawing a comparison between the Gorgon and feminist ugliness, and I refrained from pointing out that in my beloved France the women, too intelligent to be confrontational, have for centuries run the country by their sheer beauty and elegance. But I did offer the following theological observation, which no one attempted to challenge: When the Christian gospel ceases to be a living faith—when it becomes mere "compost" or the like—its doctrine of original and universal sin invariably loses out to the notion that evil can be located in one segment of mankind (and it's never one's *own* segment). Thus Marxism saw the capitalists as the locus of evil, while the proletariat—and the Party allegedly representing it—could do no wrong. Pagan, immanentist, and occultic feminism finds all the problems of humankind focussed in "patriarchy," thus effectively blinding itself to the sin resident also in the heart of woman. Lord Acton is still correct: "Power corrupts, and absolute power corrupts absolutely"—and this includes feminist, Gorgon power. And, last we heard, in Christ there is neither male nor female (Gal. 3:28), for all of us—men *and* women—are equally and desperately in need of His saving grace.

11. New Light on the Abortion Controversy?

Considering the quantity of literature on abortion that has poured from the academic and popular press since 1973, when *Roe* v *Wade* effectively legitimated abortion on demand in the United States, one looks with amazement on any claim to offer a new solution to the pro-life/pro-choice controversy. But just such a claim has now been presented—and by the immensely influential philosopher of law Ronald Dworkin, H. L. A. Hart's successor in the chair of jurisprudence at Oxford.

Dworkin's latest book, *Life's Dominion*, came off the press on May 20, 1993, and is available both in England and in the United States (HarperCollins). Its inevitable impact warrants our closest attention to the author's views, particularly since Dworkin, as a classic political liberal (and American citizen), could someday be implementing his approach as a Supreme Court justice. As the London *Times* put it on April 27: "With a Democrat back in the White House, Oxford's favourite lawyer is a hot tip to join the Supreme Court."

The argument of *Life's Dominion* was presented in summary by its author over a year ago, in a lecture at the University of London which I was privileged to attend (March, 1992). On May 18 of this year, Dworkin participated in a public debate on the subject, "How Much Is Life Worth?" at the London Institute of Education, and again offered a straightforward précis of his position. What is his viewpoint and why does he regard it as unique?

For Dworkin, the abortion controversy is unnecessarily polarized and excessively confrontational. One side (the pro-lifers) are supposed to believe in the sanctity of life, while the other side (pro-choice) presumably does not. However, argues Dworkin, the pro-choice advocate does *not* say that abortion is a good: that it can properly be used to eliminate girl babies if one prefers to have a boy, or that it can without moral impunity be carried out simply because otherwise one might miss a desired theatrical performance. The pro-choicer, *like* the pro-lifer, sees life as sacred, but focuses not so much on the *biological* aspect of sanctity (the genetically human nature of the fetus) but on the *personal* dimension of life's sanctity (the human goals, plans, aspirations, and ideals of the pregnant woman). In the philosophy of pro-choice, the latter must be taken into account and not be legalistically frustrated. In the pro-life perspective, it is the biological growth of the fetus that must not be frustrated. Both sides in the controversy believe in the unique value of human life; each is concentrating on a legitimate, but different, aspect of human worth.

But which of the two is the more *important* defining element of human value? The original creation of life (the pro-life view) or the human contribution to life (the pro-choice position)? One's answer will determine, for example, whether one will permit a pregnant teenager to have an abortion. But a close examination of the question shows that this kind of choice is really based on one's conception of what is truly ultimate, i.e., it is in reality a *religious* decision. And thus such decisions, according to Dworkin, must be left entirely to the individual. The state must not interfere in an area where personal freedom of religious conviction lies at the very heart. Here, in an area of such religious sensitivity, no group is wise or numerous enough to impose its views on others. By recognizing this to be the case, we can deal with "the bitterness in our national soul. Freedom of choice can be accepted by all sides with no sense of moral compromise, just as all religious groups and sects can accept with no sense of compromise, freedom for other versions of spiritual truth."

Two fundamental questions need to be raised about Dworkin's viewpoint, and I raised them in the public discussion following the Institute of Education debate and with Dworkin himself personally. First: does his approach in fact constitute something new — a breakthrough capable of depolarizing the abortion controversy? Second: is his position correct?

I contend that Dworkin's approach is not in fact unique at all, but is no more than a sophisticated restatement of pro-choice. He maintains that the abortion controversy needs to be seen as a religious issue: two value-systems, both committed to human worth, oppose each other as to the best approach to human dignity, and they must therefore be left politically alone to follow the light of personal, individual conscience.

But even in the most libertarian societies, religious views do not escape regulation when they cause harm to others or to the body politic. In England, where there is a state church, there are enforceable anti-blasphemy laws. In America, Mormon polygamy was prohibited as a result of such 19th century Supreme Court cases as *Reynolds* v *United States*; Native Americans have been legally restrained from using peyote as a sacrament; and Christian Scientists and Jehovah's Witnesses have not been allowed to cause the death of others by withholding medical treatment from them. How far would I get if I were to argue that my personal, individual Aztec religious beliefs ought to prevail over all state interference so as to permit me to engage in human sacrifice?

Or take a historical example. At the time of the American Civil War, the emancipation issue certainly had a powerful religious dimension. Honourable Southerners truly believed in the institution of slavery and argued — often eloquently — that the good of the Blacks was being enhanced by that paternalistic social arrangement. Would the religious aspect of this conflict have justified leaving the slavery question to personal conscience and doing nothing about it politically or constitutionally?

Dworkin countered that in all these instances we are dealing with developed *persons*, whereas in the case of the unborn we are not. By such an admission, Dworkin of course blows his cover: his underlying commitment to the non-personhood of the fetus justifies him in not attributing the right to life to the unborn. But the moment one follows overwhelming genetic-chromosomal evidence to the conclusion that personhood begins at conception, one cannot leave the fate of the fetus, any more than the fate of a slave, to the vagaries of individual conscience or religious opinion. (See, further, the present author's articles in the *Journal of the American Medical Association*, Dec. 7, 1970, and in the *Simon Greenleaf Law Review*, Vol. 5 [1985-86], and his book, *Slaughter of the Innocents* [1981].) But this puts the abortion controversy right back where it has always been at the unavoidable crossroads issue of the personhood of the unborn.

Finally, is Dworkin right that pro-choicers as well as pro-lifers respect the sanctity of life, the pro-choice advocates merely looking at it from a different angle, that of adult contributions to life rather than biological point of origin?

In the discussion following the London debate on May 18, a young and attractive representative of Planned Parenthood embarrassed Professor Dworkin by saying: "Sex is now almost universally regarded as recreational. We women enjoy it and we see no reason to forego it or put up with nine months of suffering and unwanted children. As for contraception, it is notoriously unreliable."

It would appear that sanctity (whether sanctity of life or sanctity in general) is not at a high premium in pro-choice circles, *pace* the views of a possible future American Supreme Court justice.

12. Fido in Heaven?

Readers of this column will perhaps recall that exactly a year ago we followed the tortuous path of influential German priest and psychotherapist Eugen Drewermann's theological meanderings ("Drewermann's Trivialization of Theology," October, 1992). The present article demonstrates that we are capable of firing the other barrel of the shotgun at the same target, given a sufficient incentive.

The incentive? The recent publication, in French translation, by the distinguished house Les Editions du Cerf, Paris, of Drewermann's essay, "On the Immortality of Animals: Hope for the Suffering Creation." Although only some thirty-seven pages long (but made into a respectable paperback by the addition of a long preface by novelist Luise Rinser and an equally long theological postface), the essay offers valuable insight as to where modern theologians end up once they have jettisoned any serious belief in special revelation.

Drewermann commences with a broadside against the traditional biblical and theological view of animals. Man is regarded as "infinite distinct from other creatures and in a privileged position over against all other living beings." Thus Thomas Aquinas declares that "the soul of animals does not participate in eternal being"; as species, they may be regarded as eternal, since they have a desire to reproduce, but they have no individual desire for eternity (*Summa contra gentiles*, II, 82). Such a viewpoint, we are reminded, derives from Plato's notion of the immortality of the rational soul and from Aristotelian philosophy.

However, according to Drewermann, at least three considerations militate against retaining such a position. (1) Environmentalism today focuses, quite rightly, upon population and birth control. But the traditional Christian position, as just described, *must* seek maximum human births, since only humans are fit for eternity. This means irresponsible reproduction among Christians and a lack of concern for the problems and the suffering of animals. (2) The worsening global economy pushes us to use animals as means to our ends (forced feeding, industrial breeding, experimentation, etc.), and the Christian will justify all this by the idea that animals exist only to serve human ends. (3) Scientific evolution has permanently destroyed the notion that man is a unique creation of God. Medieval, "static" theology, deriving from Aristotle's static philosophy of being, cannot accommodate the fact of changes in substantial being: yet this is just what evolution displays. Christianity cannot honestly look into either the microscope or the telescope; what they reveal leads to "the complete refutation of Christian anthropocentrism."

Moreover, why do we assume that evolution has ceased with man as a supposed pinnacle of creation? Better the view of Konrad Lorenz: "The missing link between ape and the true human being is *ourselves*." Instead of justifying our uniqueness and immortality by virtue of Christ's incarnation and resurrection as one of us, we should consider the representation of Vishnu, the second person of the Hindu trinity: he never ceases to return to earth, at each stage of life's development, to be manifested in ever new forms.

But what justifies Drewermann's belief in the immortality of all evolutionary forms? First, he offers a philosophical argument. Kant, it will be remembered, reasoned that even though there could be no formal proof of eternity or of the human soul, they had to be presupposed as a foundation for morals. But animals *also* exhort us to justice, moderation, and ethical values. Ergo, we should presuppose *their* immortality.

Secondly, we need to expand our religious symbol-systems. Here, the ancient Egyptians—"to which Christian theology owes its imagery of resurrection and of immortality" (*sic!*)—is of utmost value. The Egyptians not only saw the immense value of animals as moral beacon-lights, but also "considered the animals as inseparable from the sphere of the gods and naturally interconnected with man." As an ancient Mexican poet rightly said: "Whoever dies is transformed into God." Or as Rinser puts it in the preface to Drewermann's essay, "Weep not, your [recently deceased] dog is now in the presence of the Great Dog."

One must not be cavalier in evaluating such a viewpoint. C. S. Lewis, in *The Last Battle*, has the child-heroes of his Narnian chronicles meet their animals in the apocalyptic kingdom—for "no good thing is forever lost." But Lewis based his view, not on secular philosophy, general religiosity, non-Christian mythology, or contemporary environmentalisms, but on the character of the God of Scripture, as revealed to us in its pages. And, to be sure, Lewis was not formulating doctrine. On such a difficult question, a standard scholastic school text of the 18th century, after discussing the question at length, says simply: "The condition of the souls of animals after death is unknown" (Florian Dalham, *De ratione recte cogitandi* ... [Venice, 1770], II, 482).

Drewermann, in contrast, reaches his conclusions by conscious departure from the sources of special revelation. He substitutes for them other symbol-systems, and in particular the Egyptian. But why the latter rather than the former? Clearly because the Bible and the great theologians of the church are not saying what Drewermann wants to hear. Observe: the criterion of truth has become (inevitably in such a case) the modern theologian's *own ideas*—which, if they aren't supported biblically, result in a jettisoning or downplaying or "radical reinterpreting" of Scripture, together with the all-too-frequent substitution of other "authorities" that do in fact agree with him.

G. K. Chesterton's priest-detective Father Brown often solved purely "natural" crimes which so baffled the police that they were convinced there had to be supernatural or occult explanations for them. Why? Because Father Brown had a stable theology—a solid understanding of the nature of the supernatural, derived from his commitment to revelational sources. Thus he could see the difference between theological truth and mere speculation. The Drewermanns of our time are like Chesterton's secular detectives: having no rock of special revelation to build upon, they are swept away by every wind of contemporary ideology.

13. Lessons from the Amish

West of Strasbourg, my home city on the French-German border, lie the Vosges mountains. Unlike the Alps or the Rockies, but like the Appalachians, they present no towering peaks: the centuries have worn them down into a magical landscape of undulating hills and valleys. In the Middle Ages—indeed, to the end of the Thirty Years War—they were the epitome of political decentralisation, dotted with hundreds of castles and dependent villages under the aegis of petty and competing territorial lords. The fairytale villages and the castle ruins contribute mightily today to the charm of the area for locals and tourists alike.

Ideologically and religiously, the Vosges have also been characterised by decentralisation: a region of the out-of-the-ordinary, the mystical, the unique. The area is particularly rich in folklore, centering on semi-transcendent beings (giants, ogres, fairies, and their ilk). The medieval monastery of Sainte Odile is a kind of local Lourdes, with emphasis upon miraculous healings. In the obscure village of Waldersbach in the late 18th century, Lutheran pastor Jean Frederic Oberlin set forth his remarkable educational techniques for the religious (later, secular) instruction of children. And in those same mountains the Amish sect developed one of their most important centres of influence prior to resettlement in America.

On the occasion of the 300th anniversary of the Amish schism from mainline Anabaptism, a major international symposium on the Amish contribution has just taken place in the Alsatian village of Sainte-Marie-aux-Mines (19-22 August, 1993). Speakers included Thomas Keyer from the United States; J.-L. Eichenlaub of Colmar, a local historian, who spoke on the economic, political, and religious character of the area at the end of the 17th century, when the Amish schism occurred; Jean Séguy, who dealt with Anabaptist origins in the Alsace; and Robert Baecher, who analyzed the fascinating question as to how and why the Amish split from the general Anabaptist-Mennonite stream of the radical Reformation. This International Amish Colloquium gives us an opportunity to observe the Amish phenomenon and to draw some theological lessons from a fascinating byway in the history of Christian thought.

The roots of Alsatian Anabaptism lay in the Swiss radical pacifists of Zurich at the beginning of the 16th century. Ejected by the Swiss political authorities, these Anabaptists (so-called, of course, because they rejected infant baptism in favour of adult conversion) spread up the Rhine as far as the Netherlands. Their settlements were invariably rural, so as to avoid the temptations, pressures, and persecutions of city life. The Alsace was an especially hospitable location, owing to the fact that Strasbourg was a free city of the Holy Roman Empire; its dependencies were therefore less subject to hierarchial political and ecclesiastical control. Many of the dissidents settled in the valley of Lièpvre and eventually took over land abandoned during the Thirty Years War. The result was a thriving agricultural community, characterised by industry, thrift, and the development of advanced farming techniques.

The worldly success of the brethren was not, however, to the liking of the more radical members of the sect. One Jacob Amann denounced mixed marriages and extra-community contacts. He insisted on the use of the Berne (Swiss-German) dialect, refused all military service and the holding of public office, and required the wearing of austere clothing and (for men only!) beards. In 1693 came the schism. The Rhenish Anabaptists split roughly into eastern and western groups: those east of the Rhine, in the German Palatinate, continuing as mainline Mennonites; those west of the Rhine, in the Alsace, becoming Amish (followers of Amann). In 1712, Louis XIV expelled most of them from the Vosges; those who remained immigrated to the United States (especially Pennsylvania) in the 19th century, to avoid new conscription laws. Today, no Amish remain in the Alsace. As for the Mennonites, they now total only some 3,000 in all of France.

What lessons can be drawn from the Amish phenomenon? Here are a few miscellaneous (but, hopefully, pregnant) suggestions.

First: Conservatism theologically can be combined with the spirit of innovation in everyday affairs. The Amish were hopelessly reactionary in their religious lifestyle, but forward-looking and thoroughly innovative in their agricultural operations. For example, while the non-Amish peasant was still using the sickle or reaping-hook, the Amish adopted the scythe. We are continually told today that religious conservatism necessarily produces stagnation in all areas of life. This is nonsense, as the Amish demonstrate. Indeed, it may be just the opposite: unwavering belief in divine verities may give the freedom and incentive to serve the Lord with greater zeal and openness to new techniques and methods.

Second: Religious history tends to repeat itself. The Anabaptists became rich because of their singleminded, spiritual focus on quality in their agricultural endeavours; this led to a reforming movement (the Amish) in reaction to the wealth that had been acquired. The parallel is very close with the medieval monastic Orders, which received legacies from secular princes in proportion to their reputation for self-denial and piety; but as they became wealthy, they "lost their first love" (or were perceived-to have done so) and reforming Orders split from them to restore primitive simplicity and spirituality. We must always ask ourselves: what stage have *we* reached in our personal or collective ministries, and how can we guard against counter-productive schisms?

Thirdly: The Amish force us to consider anew Charles Williams' distinction between the Way of Negation ("Neither is this Thou") and the Way of Affirmation ("This also is Thou"): those two fundamental themes running through all of church history. The Amish chose—in spades—the Way of Negation. Separation was their byword: literally, by settling in out-of-the-way, rural areas, far removed from urban centres of influence; symbolically, by their archaic language, dress, and lifestyle. For them personal "holiness" (as they defined it) took precedence over witness to an unbelieving world. In every church body, there are those who think Amish: to them, reaching the lost is less consequential, in the ultimate scheme of things, than the sanctification of the believer. Ought one not, however, remind oneself from time to time of the biblical value-system? Our Lord's final word to the church was not, *nota bene*, "Be thou sanctified and seek personal holiness," but "Go and preach the gospel to every creature." In a fallen world, the Amish can teach us a great deal both by example and by counter-example.

14. The Virgin Birth: A Problem?

England is the pre-eminent country for the celebration of Christmas. Blessed with Dickens and no separation of church and state (and therefore no killjoy ACLU or anti-Christian political correctness), London's Trafalgar Square each December sports not only a magnificent Christmas tree but also a life-size Nativity scene — at public expense, to be sure. So christmasy are the English that by August hotels throughout the country have printed Christmas brochures to entice the populace to celebrate Noel before their respective hearths.

A Sheffield University astronomer, one David Hughes, has, however, just dropped a bombshell (or, rather, a starshell). He argues that an unusual conjunction of Jupiter and Saturn on September 15, 7 B.C., marks the true date of Our Lord's birth, so Christmas ought properly to be celebrated three months early. So much for Christina Rossetti's "In the Bleak Mid-Winter"!

To which three responses at least are possible: (1) What's the big deal? The merchants have almost reached the point of commencing their Christmas promotions that early anyway. (2) Dr Hughes has his stars confused: surely a planetary conjunction is not going to guide Magi to a particular stable/cave and then stand over it. (3) Quoting the London *Times*'s third leader on the subject: "The birthday of Jesus is a date for mystery not precision."

But if the date isn't important, why is the *manner* of that birth? Could we not equally claim, as do so many liberal theologians of both Catholic and Protestant persuasion today, that the precise manner of Jesus' birth is as unimportant as its date?

Space forbids a comprehensive defence of the Virgin Birth, and readers interested in such are referred to J. Gresham Machen's classic of that title; of it, skeptic and cynic H. L. Mencken said that the liberals had never answered it, chiefly because they were incapable of understanding its scholarship. But we do wish to speak to several of the egregious errors of logic made by those who think Christian theology (and Christmas) could easily do without a Virgin Birth.

One of the recurrent arguments against the facticity of the Virgin Birth is its appearance in only two Gospels, Matthew and Luke, and no reference to it at all in the earliest Gospel, Mark, or in John, or in the Pauline Epistles. One may legitimately reply that the case is by no means airtight for Marcan priority: New Testament scholars of considerable repute (one thinks, for example, of Basil Butler and E. J. Goodspeed) have made a powerful case for Matthew as the earliest Gospel.

But even if Matthew did not precede Mark, its primary-source value cannot readily be dismissed. Papias declares unambiguously that the First Gospel was written originally by the Apostle and former tax collector. Apostolic authorship means direct contact with Mary and therefore the highest possible reliability in regard to the details of Jesus' birth. As for Luke, he claims, in his Thucydidian preface (1:1-4), to have checked out his data thoroughly; as a physician, he would have been particularly careful to record obstetrical/gynecological information accurately.

Mark was doing a kind of shorter catechism for new believers, and so omits a considerable amount of detail. John and Paul are interested in the theological implications of what Jesus did, not biographical detail. Paul states explicitly that he resolved "not to know any thing among you save Jesus Christ and him crucified" (1 Cor. 2:2): since salvation depends not on Jesus' teachings or the particulars of his life but solely on his death on the Cross and Resurrection (i.e., on the gospel message itself — 1 Cor. 15:1-3), Paul concentrates in a single-minded fashion on those final events of Jesus' earthly ministry, omitting virtually everything else.

It is amusing that religious liberals much prefer the teachings of the Sermon on the Mount to the miraculous aspects of the Gospel record, but never seem to realize that the Sermon on the Mount, like the Virgin Birth, appears only in Matthew and Luke. I have never known a religious liberal to question the Sermon on the Mount because it does not appear in Mark, John, or Paul. Does this not perhaps suggest that the real reason the Virgin Birth is rejected in these circles has little to do with textual questions? Such theological inconsistency among religious liberals reminds one of Chesterton's remark concerning them: "The man who does not believe in original sin believes in the immaculate conception of everybody."

Then it is argued that mythologies and other religious traditions have claimed virgin births also (the *Golden Bough*/Joseph Campbell syndrome). But: (1) As we have seen, the Gospel accounts are primary-source narratives, based on first-hand contact with the principals — a far cry from timeless, ahistorical mythologies. (2) The extra-biblical tales can equally be regarded as precursors of Christ's birth, the latter constituting the ultimate, historical fulfilment of mankind's mythological longings: Vergil's Fourth Eclogue as an example of common grace, Simone Weil's "intimations of Christianity among the ancients." (3) If pagan stories of parthenogenesis are factually untrue, does it follow that the Gospel writers were *also* mistaken? If two clocks strike the hour at the same time, did one cause the other to strike? Here we have a classic instance of the logical fallacy of *post hoc, ergo propter hoc*.

The same fallacy, to be sure, underlies the argument that since contemporary Jewish Midrash literature used miracle stories as sermon illustrations to reinforce spiritual truths, so Matthew must have invented the Virgin Birth to give more credence to the Incarnation. But why, pray tell, should the latter follow from the former? Must we always do what our contemporaries do?

We are also told that the very idea of a Virgin Birth denegrates a proper view of sexuality, for it says that a normal birth did not meet divine standards. To this (fairly bizarre, rather feminist) argument, one need only observe that the Incarnation, in its uniqueness, was hardly intended as a model for birth in general, and the clear biblical analogy between husband/wife and Christ/the church (Eph. 5) and the prohibition against married couples avoiding normal sexual relations (1 Cor. 7:5) demonstrate beyond question the high view Scripture takes of legitimate sexuality.

But, in the final analysis, was the Virgin Birth necessary? Couldn't God have become man otherwise? Not being privy to the infinite range of divine possibilities, we cannot rule out another method of Incarnation. But one thing is sure: *This* is how he *did* do it, and it stands as a test of whether we are willing to accept his methods over our speculations. When Jesus healed the blind man with clay and spittle (John 9) he was not normalizing a new medical technique: he was testing the man's faith. With Luther, we need to pass the crèche like a peasant, doffing our cap and going our way. Christmas is a time, not for pushing our own clever solutions to cosmic problems, but for wonder and awe at the way God chose to save us, unworthy as we are.

15. Je*sus in the Dic*tion*ar*y

Can dictionaries engender controversy? They certainly can in England—from Dr Johnson's definition of oats ("a grain, which in England is generally given to horses, but in Scotland supports the people") to the just published *New Shorter Oxford English Dictionary*'s entry for Jesus, who is defined as "the central figure of the Christian faith, a Jewish preacher (c 5B.C.—c 30A.D.) regarded by his followers as the Son of God and God incarnate." In providing examples of usage, the new edition eschews quotations from the classic hymnology of Charles Wesley and instead cites "Jesus freak" and "Jesus! he cried, I'm glad to be here."

The result has been a flap of major proportions. For example, Tony Higton, a senior evangelical and clerical member of the Anglican General Synod, was not pleased with the dictionary's definition of "Jesus freak." Also, he declared: "They have used almost as many words to define the blasphemous use of it ['Jesus! he cried, I'm glad ...'] as the theological, historical definition. I also find the idea of Jesus as a 'Jewish preacher' to be a rather derogatory term." A Lambeth Palace spokesman was no less disturbed; said he: "It is deeply regrettable that the examples given emphasise the negative use of the word, and that there are no positive ones such as 'Jesus Lives' or 'Through Jesus Christ our Lord.'" To which the General Editor of the £3 million, 13-year project, Alan M. Hughes, replied in a letter to The *Times* (Oct. 15, 1993): "Since many speakers of English are not Christians, we aimed at a wording that does not assume a Christian faith on the part of a reader, and is equally valid for a Muslim, a Jew, or an atheist."

How significant *is* this matter of definition? Ought the whole business to be regarded as a proverbial tempest-in-a-teapot? After all, as John Chipman Gray once wrote, "A mistake by Sir Isaac [Newton] in calculating the orbit of the earth would not send it spinning round the sun with an increased velocity." Likewise, a lexicographer's mistake or inaccuracy or infelicity of definition hardly alters the reality or true nature of the definiendum.

At the same time, we have Humpty Dumpty's observation in *Through the Looking-Glass:* "When I use a word, it means just what I choose it to mean ... When I make a word do a lot of work ... I always pay it extra." Definitions can in principle be of any sort, but they can exact a payment, and the cost may not be worth the definition. How much "extra" must be paid for *The New Shorter OED*'s definition of Jesus, and is it worth it?

To answer this question, one must first be clear as to the purpose of a dictionary. In describing the world, is the lexicographer to tell us what reality is *in fact* or what reality is *perceived* to be by the literate public? Jesus is *in reality* God incarnate, but since he is not so perceived by a significant number of English speakers and writers, is the dictionary not justified in employing the expression, "*regarded by his followers as* God incarnate"? And in providing examples of usage, should these be limited to "reality-reflecting" illustrations or also include current, popular examples which may or may not do justice to the real character of the definiendum? Would *The New Shorter OED* be wrong to give as an example of usage for Napoleon, Sherlock Holmes's reference to "the Napoleon of crime"?

As one ponders these matters of lexicological philosophy, one discovers a nonlexicological issue embedded deeply therein: the relationship between Christians and the secular society in which they necessarily function today.

How fully can believers expect non-Christians to accept and reflect a Christian world view? If the contemporary secularist does not consider the name of Jesus any more important or sacral than any other name, can we expect a general dictionary of modem usage to present a theologically sound definition of his nature and character as objectively true, as the only proper definition?

Perhaps the critics of *The New Shorter OED* are betraying a kind of linguistic triumphalism that reveals an obtuseness to the nature of the modern world. One is reminded of the fundamentalist Moral Majority, a movement which simply expected non-Christians to agree with biblical morality whatever their theology (or lack of it). The advocates of Sunday closing laws and prayers in American public schools operate with much the same mentality. And if the secularists do not agree to such Christian agendas, they will be forced by believers' pressure groups to conform anyway. (Should Christians boycott bookstores selling *The New Shorter OED*?)

Unquestionably, a dictionary will have to pay far too much "extra" in loss of permanent value if it drops historically well-established usages for the sake of popular fashion. After all, the distinction needs to be maintained between standard dictionaries and lexica of slang and argot (such as those by Eric Partridge). But, having said that, dictionaries come and go and are continually revised, and few users of them are converted or rendered apostate by way of the religious entries therein. A pluralistic definition of Jesus, however it may personally irritate us, can have the salutary effect of reminding believers of the reality of the pluralistic societies in which the gospel must be preached today.

Lobbying to improve a definition in *The New Shorter OED* — or in any other dictionary — will not save souls, and it might well reinforce the secularist's (not entirely unfounded) belief that Christians are in the business of ramming their convictions down everyone's throat whether the victim likes it or not. Salvation still requires personal decision, last we heard, and thus the way to christianize remains that of sensitively and forthrightly preaching and defending the gospel: solid evangelism and a persuasive apologetic. Definitions do not convert. Recognizing the milieu we live in might, in God's grace, serve as a genuine impetus to evangelization.

16. So Much for Hell and the Second Coming

David Jenkins, Bishop of Durham, is at it again. Readers of this column will recall (November, 1992) that the Bishop has long denied the historicity of the Virgin Birth and the Resurrection of Christ and that his adoptionist christology has so delighted Muslims in the United Kingdom that they have used his public comments to bolster their own position.

Now—just in time for Advent and the Christmas season—Jenkins provided further edification for the flock. At a December conference for Anglican lay readers, the Bishop informed his audience that there was no such thing as everlasting torment in hell and that there would be no Second Coming.

On hell, he declared that the teaching of the Book of Revelation concerning torment "day and night for ever and ever" was "pretty pathological," and that "if there is such a god, he is a small, cultic deity who is so bad tempered that the sooner we forget him the better." Indeed, "I am clear that there can be no hell for eternity—our God could not be so cruel." As for the return of Our Lord at the end of time to judge the quick and the dead, the Bishop expressed himself no less apodictically: "I do not think it possible to believe any longer in a literal Second Coming at the end of the world."

One could, of course, dismiss such comments *ad hominem*. For a number of years, Jenkins has had the obnoxious habit of swiping at historic Christian doctrine just before major church holidays, especially Christmas and Easter. It would appear that he loves public controversy and the limelight—indeed, that he is attracted to the media like a moth is drawn to a flame. Perhaps, in the immortal words of the old vaudeville number, the Bishop is "more to be pitied than censured": after all, what will become of him once he has run the gamut of all the teachings of the Nicene Creed? The thought of media indifference is too awful (hellish?) to contemplate.

But, to be sure, more is at stake by far than a publicity-seeking Bishop. A *Times* leader on the subject, appropriately titled "To Hell from Durham" (December 15, 1993), sagely observed: "The usefulness of the Bishop of Durham's pronouncements is precisely that they do provoke those with a firmer faith to debate the mysteries of the Christian Church." What, then, can be said concerning the eschatological issues the Bishop raises?

First, as to hell and everlasting punishment. No one in his right mind *likes* the idea of permanent alienation from God, but surely the question is not whether we like it but whether it in fact exists. Does not the essence of maturity consist of our being willing to adjust our desires to the nature of reality, instead of insisting that reality conform to our wishes? Contrary to Jiminy Cricket, wishing *doesn't* make it so.

Hell is plainly taught in Scripture, and it is not a product of the so-called "wrathful deity of the Old Testament." The Old Testament, in fact, says virtually nothing about hell. It is Jesus himself who provides the fullest picture in the Bible concerning the horrors of the lost. Indeed, Our Lord's references to hell and its torments are far more frequent than his references to heaven. If heaven is a reality, why should not hell be equally real?

The Bishop's answer is that hell offends his moral sensibilities. But, apart from the revelation of a transcendent God as to the nature of absolute moral standards, how would the Bishop (or anyone else) *justify* his particular ethical sensibilities? In a contingent universe, one cannot declare as inherently immoral the notion that the worst possible *lèse-majesté* will result in the worst possible punishment. By cutting himself off from a reliable scriptural revelation, the Bishop has radically reduced his chances of justifying any ethical absolutes. In consequence, his personal morality becomes no more than that: an expression of personal opinion. And if one avoids the Bishop's error by standing on the high ground of biblical authority, one can hardly use it to criticize the ethics of the very Deity who provided the biblical revelation in the first place!

If there is genuine freewill, and if God respects his creatures' decisions, even when they are terribly mistaken and perverse, hell is inevitable. Wrote W. H. Auden of Christian littérateur Charles Williams: "The popular notion of hell is morally revolting and intellectually incredible because it is conceived of in terms of human criminal law, as a torture imposed upon the sinner against his will by an all-powerful God. Charles Williams succeeds, where even Dante, I think, fails, in showing us that nobody is ever *sent* to hell; he, or she, insists on going there." Williams' description of the damnation of a woman who insisted on being her own god captures the essence of biblical teaching on the subject and ought to give us all pause: "She cried out, 'You thought you'd got me, didn't you?' They saw the immortal fixity of her constricted face, gleeful in her supposed triumph, lunatic in her escape, as it had at once a subdued lunatic glee in its cruel indulgence; and then she broke through the window again and was gone into that other City, there to wait and wander and mutter till she found what companions she could."

As for the Bishop's views on the Second Coming, Martin Ivens, in a trenchant *Times* article ("A Brief History of Hell," December 15), poses the key questions: "Does Dr Jenkins acknowledge the eschatological nature of the Christian Gospel? Long ago Albert Schweitzer pointed out that the expectation of the immanent end of the world was a central aspect of the gospel accounts of the teaching of Jesus. If he denies a literal Second Coming, in what sort of metaphorical end does Dr Jenkins believe?"

The earliest texts on the Second Coming purport to be asserting literal, not metaphorical, truth—e.g., Acts 1:11: "This same Jesus, who is taken up from you into heaven, shall so come in like manner as you have seen him go into heaven." Why, then, impose metaphor upon such passages? We suspect that, for the Bishop, nothing is more uncomfortable than when God literally, factually intervenes in history, whether by a genuine incarnation or by a literal reappearance—or, even worse, by an actual separation of sheep and goats in final judgment.

Perhaps the very reality, the givenness, of Christian revelation is what at root most offends the Bishop. Metaphor can always be manipulated at the hands of the interpreting theologian, who thereby becomes the focal center (as he is when he appears before the television cameras). To take God at his Word has the great disadvantage of placing God in the center and shutting the mouths of his creatures—including the mouths of theologians and even bishops.

17. Dracula or Jesus?

What do most of us know of Romania? Practically nothing, I should imagine. The best known "Romanian" (he would actually have been Hungarian, for in his day Romanian Transylvania was a part of Hungary) is doubtless Bram Stoker's fictionalized Count Dracula, based on the bloodthirsty 15th-century Prince Vlad "the Impaler."

But I learned considerably more than that about one of the poorest and most troubled countries of Eastern Europe during an invitational lectureship at the University of Cluj (Romania's second largest university, after Bucharest) the first week of January, 1994. While many of my colleagues were vacationing in sun-drenched Tenerife or Bermuda, I was proceeding, at a snail's pace, across the snow-covered landscape between Budapest and Cluj, and was subjected to border crossings in the tradition of the old East Germany—with uniformed guards even removing the train seats to make sure that no Romanians were illegally concealed there in order to flee the country.

Romania as a national state is a surprisingly recent phenomenon. Prior to 1862, Romania was a geographical, not a political conception. After the Russian defeat in the Crimean War (1853-1856), Romanian nationalism grew, the state came into existence, and in 1877 it declared its independence from the Ottoman Empire. When Austria-Hungary was defeated in the First World War, Transylvania, with a large Hungarian-speaking population, became part of Romania. A fascist dictatorship took over during World War II and the Nazis were invited in. As the Soviet army approached Romania's borders, the country changed sides, declaring war on Germany. The losses were staggering: half a million Romanian soldiers died fighting for the Axis, and another 170,000 died after joining the Allies.

After the War, Romania became Communist, but its Communism was unique and fiercely nationalistic. Soviet troops were entirely removed as early as 1958 and Romania condemned the Soviet invasion of Prague in 1968. The Romanian President Ceausescu established an absolutism which lasted for twenty-five years. Though he paid off the national debt (no mean feat), Ceausescu raised nepotism to a new level: his wife was made first deputy prime minister, his son served as political boss of Transylvania, and three brothers held key posts in Bucharest.

On 15 December 1989, Reformed pastor László Tökés publicly spoke out against the dictator from his small Hungarian church in Timisoara. What he said touched a chord in a population thoroughly dissatisfied with the Ceausescu regime, and on 23 December the President and his wife were executed. It is now known that the dictator's enemies had in fact been preparing a coup for some time, and they took immediate advantage of the popular uprising. Their National Salvation Front (FSN) quickly replaced the former government. Its leaders are former Party members, and the new bureaucracy is in many respects indistinguishable from the old—except for the replacement of Marxist ideology by rampant nationalism (or, rather, regionalism, since Hungarians among the Romanian population are now being treated as second-class citizens) and by the removal of thought-control and the consequent reopening of places of worship (Ceausescu had closed down all churches and mosques).

What hope is there for this troubled land, whose native genius is reflected in such distinguished 20th-century émigrés as playwright Eugene Ionesco and religious phenomenologist Mircea Eliade? In my judgment, the sources of life for Romania are its *universities* and *Christian churches.*

I was invited to the University of Cluj to lecture on "The Ethical Foundations of Human Rights" by its Rector, the eminent philosopher Andrei Marga—a scholar equally at home in English, French, and German, who has done important work on pragmatism at the Woodrow Wilson Center. In his essay on the "University and Politics," Marga calls for the ratification by the Romanian universities of the Lima Declaration on Academic Freedom and Autonomy of Institutions of Higher Education (1989), and asserts: "The de-politicizing of the University is comprehensible only on condition that one fully realizes the devastating effects of the Communist politicizing of the University." The University, in Marga's judgment, only fulfills its purpose when it commits itself to "the priority of truth, the guarantee of the fundamental individual liberties and rights, equality of chances in argumentation, the right to criticize, political pluralism" (A. Marga, *Philosophy in the Eastern Transition* [Cluj: Biblioteca Apostrof, 1993], pp. 185, 189). It is this kind of thinking that can, in principle at least, transform the country by educating a new generation of leaders unafraid of critical thinking.

My other co-host was Cluj psychology professor Dr Mihaly Tapolyai, a psychiatrist who also holds an earned Doctor of the Ministry degree from the United States and who has strong connections with the Reformed Church in Hungary and in Romania. (Romania is the only Romance-language country that is predominately Eastern Orthodox; the Reformed Church is its strongest Protestant denomination; Roman Catholics account for six percent of the population.) I lectured or preached — for some reason, in my case, the one always seems to blend with the other! — on the meaning of the Christian gospel, the historical evidences in support of it, and its application to personal and to national life, to rapt audiences of students, faculty, and non-U laymen who had heard very little along these lines for more than a generation.

Why is Christianity so important to the national salvation (and I do not refer to the FSN) of Romania? Because it stands squarely for freedom of thought and against rabid, discriminatory nationalism. Declared Jesus: "If any one wills to do his [God's] will, he shall know of the doctrine, whether it be of God" (John 7:17). Christianity insists upon the right to make free decisions, in time and for eternity. And St. Paul asserts without qualification: "There is neither Jew nor Greek, there is neither bond nor free, there is neither male nor female: for you are all one in Christ Jesus" (Gal. 3:28). Nationalistic and regionalistic discriminations are simply incompatible with true Christian faith.

New creaturehood is indeed available to Romanians, individually and collectively. And since, in its post-Marxist, regionalist disarray, Romania is a true microcosm of the former Soviet Eastern bloc in general, should we not pray fervently that the political Draculas who suck a people's blood be replaced there and everywhere by living faith in the One who gave His blood as the medicine of immortality to a broken world?

18. On the Reliability of the Four Gospels

Debate time again in London! A year ago, your humble servant engaged in public dialogue with Professor G. A. Wells, who denies Jesus' existence (*New Oxford Review*, May, 1993). The sponsor of that confrontation, the Lawyers' Christian Fellowship — an organisation with immensely more teeth in it than novelist John Mortimer's crusty barrister Horace Rumpole would lead one to believe—has just provided a second opportunity for classic Christianity and secularism to battle it out in the marketplace of ideas.

On February 17, 1994, at the Inns of Court School of Law, where future barristers receive their year of professional training, Richard Cunningham, a Christian apologist, took on Darren Newman of the Central London Humanist Society. The subject: What basis for truth? Good debates, though they seldom settle issues, can assist greatly in sharpening them. That was certainly the case in this instance.

Newman commenced with the admission (seldom as clearly recognised by the modern theologian!) that the truth of Christianity depends squarely on the historical veracity of the resurrection of Jesus Christ: if it happened, Christianity is true; if not, not. Thus all depends on the reliability of the Gospel accounts—and, according to Newman, when they are weighed in the balance they are found wanting. Consider: (1) The four Gospels are all anonymous; from the books themselves we cannot tell who their authors were. (2) A forty year gap separates the events they recount, including the alleged resurrection of Jesus, from the writing down of them. And we need only remind ourselves that in less time than that after the assassination of President Kennedy myths developed concerning that event and its true explanation. (3) "Matthew," "Luke," and "John" could not possibly have been eyewitnesses, for they rely on source materials by others—and the same is probably true of "Mark" as well; an eyewitness has no need to consult accounts of the events he has himself observed. (4) The Gospel accounts contain doublets (for example, the feeding of the 4,000 and the feeding of the 5,000: obviously two confused treatments of the same alleged event) and sheer contradictions (the Roman guard at the tomb appears in only one account and is totally ignored in the others, whereas he would surely have been mentioned by all had he really been there). (5) Detailed narratives, such as Jesus' prayer in the Garden of Gethsemane, are set forth which no one could have known (the disciples were asleep!). It therefore follows that the Evangelists' accounts are not historical descriptions but literary creations. (6) A Gospel writer such as "Matthew" romanticises by elaboration; thus, to the more simple accounts of Jesus' crucifixion set forth by the other writers, he adds the earthquake and the saints coming forth from their graves. In light of such mythologising, Newman has no choice but to opt (says he) for reality—the reality of humanness, as exemplified by the Humanist credo.

Richard Cunningham, who has debated widely in behalf of classical Christianity in the United Kingdom, chose not to speak to these particular points, leaving them, in effect, for the question period. For him, it was dangerous to lose sight of the forest for the trees. Cunningham preferred to turn his guns on Humanism itself.

He pointed out, especially by way of the writings of the eminent French historian of ideas Paul Hazard, that the replacement of supernatural revelation by humanistic immanentism in the last two centuries has been an unmitigated catastrophe. Humanism has been incapable of sustaining human value because it is entirely lacking in an absolute ethic. As a result, the sensitive modern man has been brought to the point of utter despair, as witnessed by the rise of atheistic existentialism (Camus, *et. al.*). Indeed, Humanism cannot even take credit, as it constantly tries to do, for the rise of science by way of the 18th century Enlightenment: modern science was in full swing by the 17th century (Kepler, the Royal Society) because of pre-Enlightenment man's revelationally grounded confidence that God had created all things in an ordered way, capable of rational discovery and interpretation by His creatures. Unlike Humanism, Christianity has *explanatory power*; it does not stop with the Big Bang and an irrational universe, but moves on to a personal, loving Creator and to a human story which is anything but the tale told by an idiot signifying nothing. Contemporary English novelist Fay Weldon is quite right to ask why secular science never seems to answer the *fundamental* questions we humans continue to ask. Only Christianity offers sound answers to *those* questions.

The discussion time provided an opportunity to return to Newman's attempted decimation of the New Testament. After all, even if Humanism is superficial and inadequate (as it surely is; was it not Malcolm Muggeridge who said that he had yet to find a Unitarian leper colony?), its debility would hardly prove Christianity to be true! Professor Wells and I both happened to be present at this year's debate, so the occasion was propitious for answering criticisms of the biblical material which Newman had in fact largely derived from Wells' own writings.

We take them up in Newman's order: (1) Papias, a disciple of the Apostle John himself, informs us of the primary-source authorship of all four Gospels, as told to him personally by John. (2) Remembering crucial events after forty years is no problem, especially among first-century Jews who were taught to rely on memory to a far greater extent than we do today. And does anyone really doubt the *fact* of Kennedy's assassination? (3) Eyewitnesses do indeed often use supplementary sources by others when they write up what they have seen. My celebrated relation Field Marshal Montgomery of Alamein did so when he published his own history of the North Africa campaign. (4) The Gospel writers, like witnesses in court, are not obliged to tell everything every other witness tells: they are only required to be truthful as to what they do narrate. It is no "contradiction" if one writer omits something another has included. Logically, if 5,000 were fed, it follows that 4,000 were fed! (And how do we know that there were not *two* miraculous picnics anyway?) (5) The resurrected Jesus spent forty days with his disciples before returning to heaven. Did this not afford enough time to fill them in on what he had prayed in Gethsemene? There are equally painless explanations for the other instances of the Evangelists' accounts of "private" happenings. (6) Each Evangelist wrote with his own special purposes in mind, and included or did not include information accordingly. Just because Matthew gives more detail than Mark, it hardly follows that Matthew is romantically embroidering the facts with mythical additions. Is *Time* magazine in the myth business when it gives a news story in considerably more detail than the daily newspaper report of the same event?

I learned not too long ago from a student of mine, now retired as pastor of the American Church in Paris, that Albert Camus was to have been baptised there within the month of his tragic death in a car accident. Camus had seen the bankruptcy of humanistic existentialism, and, like intelligent souls across the centuries, had found the Gospel narratives no obstacle to belief. To the contrary, they remain, as Luther put it, the cradle in which the Christ child is offered to us all.

19. Philosophy Revisited

Don't tell *me* that intellectual standards are declining in England. Where, in the United States, could you find a major newspaper that would devote both a lead editorial and a substantial article to the publication of a new philosophy textbook? But this is precisely what happens in England. The *Times* has just provided its readers with a lengthy review and a "first leader" concerning Roger Scruton's *Modern Philosophy: An Introduction and Survey*, published (March, 1994) by Sinclair-Stevenson in London. And, just a few days later, the *Times* followed up these articles with an in-depth interview with the author.

How can this be accounted for? Is Scruton also a rock star or a closet gay? *Au contraire*. Educated at Jesus College, Cambridge, he has taught for twenty years at Birkbeck College of the University of London, and also holds a professorship in philosophy at Boston University. He is editor of the *Salisbury Review* and a forthright spokesman for political conservativism, known for his learned polemic, *The Meaning of Conservatism*. On sex, he has declared, in his book-length treatise, *Sexual Desire*: "Homosexual love is metaphysically impossible."

Is his new book therefore disguised politics or special pleading? Not at all. As the *Times* leader put it (23 March): "Those expecting a proselytising right-wing version of Russell's *History of Western Philosophy* will be disappointed. *Modern Philosophy* is precisely what its subtitle declares: 'an introduction and survey,' designed to provide the student and general reader with opportunity to understand and interact with the great ideas and issues that have characterised the Western philosophical tradition and have especially concerned thinkers of the 20th century Anglo-American analytical school."

The university lectures which formed the basis of the volume are organised thematically: Scruton deals with some thirty-one topics, including Truth, Appearance and Reality, Space and Time, Being, Paradox, Meaning, the Self, Cause, Freedom, God, the Devil, the Soul, and Morality. Instead of cluttering his text with footnotes, the author has appended a 100-page, chapter-by-chapter "Study Guide," providing citations to the essential primary and secondary sources and suggestions for further reading. Detailed subject and name indexes conclude the volume.

The value of such a book should be obvious: providing the general public with the means and incentive to consider fundamental ideas seriously in the age of the sound-bite is an accomplishment in itself. But let us examine Scruton's treatment of some theologically related themes to see if his conservatism has made him sensitive to problems touching what C. S. Lewis termed "the case for Christianity."

The nature of truth. Scruton has little patience with relativism: "Vulgar relativism has no hope of surviving outside the minds of ignorant rascals; sophisticated relativism has to be so sophisticated as barely to deserve the name." But, in company with so many metaphysicians, he gives short shrift to verification, repeating the old saw, "How, after all, would you verify the [verification] principle?" The answer, of course, is that verification, like the inferential processes of deduction, induction, and abduction/retroduction, required to carry it out, are *necessitarian*: without it *no* meaningful investigation of the world is possible at all, and the academic enterprise (including philosophy) comes to a grinding halt. To answer Pilate's query, "What is truth?," one must be able to distinguish meaningful assertions concerning reality from technical nonsense, and nowhere is this more important than in the religious realm, where unverifiable truth-claims abound (especially in California).

God's existence. We expected Scruton to provide us with a sophisticated account of the contingency argument (viz., the contingent universe forces us to go beyond it—to a non-contingent Absolute—to explain it) and its superb scientific illustration, the Second Law of Thermodynamics (energy in a closed system will reach heat-death in a finite time, so the universe cannot be infinite; it must have been created, or it would already have reached heat-death). But, instead, we encounter little more than Kant's refutation of the Aristotelian proofs for God's existence, and Scruton appears to accept Kant's reasoning. Why are we not at least introduced to Frederick C. Copleston's magnificent defence of the traditional theistic arguments, as he battered Bertrand Russell with them in their celebrated debate on the BBC in 1948?

The problem of evil. Scruton devotes but a page to this overarching unbelievers' argument. Plotinus, Leibniz, and Rilke are quoted; why is there no mention of C. S. Lewis' *Problem of Pain,* Alvin Plantinga's *God and Other Minds* (though Plantinga is cited elsewhere on other topics), or John S. Feinberg's recently published *Many Faces of Evil?*

The Devil, however, turns up twice: "first, as the source of Descartes's doubt, secondly as the 'deconstructor' [in Derrida's sense] of the social world." Scruton describes the latter form of the demonic in striking—but hardly ontological—terms: "The devil has one message, which is that there is no first-person plural. ... All institutions and communities, all culture and law, are objects of a sublime mockery. ... By promising to 'liberate' the self, the devil establishes a world where nothing *but* the self exists."

The immortality of the soul. This vital topic is touched on only obliquely, in terms of "physicalism," the "unity" of the soul, personal identity, and "the mystery of death." It seems remarkable that there is no reference whatsoever to the dialogue between Karl Popper and John Eccles (*The Self and Its Brain,* Springer-Verlag, 1977), demonstrating that the Self cannot be regarded as just another name for the brain, but in fact exists independently of and indeed "uses" its brain. That being the case, there is no reason in principle why the death of the latter should entail the death of the former.

Divine revelation. Considering the inability of classical or contemporary philosophy to answer the profound questions with which it wrestles, one would think that Scruton would examine in depth the claim that God in His grace has given mankind solutions which man himself could never arrive at by unaided reason. The author does make mention of "what Chateaubriand called the 'genius' of Christianity, that it gives flesh to God's abstract personality ... The incarnation of God in Christ has therefore been a fruitful source for the understanding of God's personality, and of the special features of our relationship with him." But nowhere is the confirmatory argument from miracle dealt with, or refutations provided for Hume's widely touted objection to all miracle arguments or for Lessing's claim that one cannot move from the probabilities of history to the certainties of metaphysical truth as claimed by Christian revelation.

In sum, as valuable as it is to benefit from a fresh introduction to the classic themes of philosophy, one deserves more, viz., a serious interaction between philosophical questions and religious solutions. Conservative Scruton may be, but he needs to do much more to conserve the classic interplay of philosophy and theology. There is a *philosophia perennis* which must not be forgotten.

20. Back to the Sixties

England at the moment is in the throes of nostalgia: a 1960's revival is in progress. The precipitating factor seems to be the realisation that a full generation has now passed since that decade of flower-power, Carnaby Street sidewalk artists, and belief that a new era of "love not war" was just around the corner. On a deeper level, current criticism of national institutions (the monarchy, the criminal justice system, the established church) has left in its wake a longing to recover a time of (supposed) innocence, freedom, and idealism.

For two nights—April 15 and 16, 1994—the Royal Albert Hall was packed to the rafters (or, rather, the dome) for the anniversary concerts of The Seekers, an Australian singing group who at one point in the Sixties outsold the Beatles with their spirited and moving renditions of such songs of love and hope as "Morningtown Ride" (a lullaby of safety and security), "A World of Our Own" (the dream of a couple's love rendering everything else unreal), "Turn, Turn, Turn" (the lyrics consisting entirely of the text of Ecclesiastes 3:1-8). The Albert Hall reunion concerts attracted both the man on the Clapham omnibus and such show-business luminaries as Sir John Mills and his daughter Hayley. Alan Jackson concluded his review in the *Times*: "The resultant whole whipped a delirious audience into a frenzy of community singing and unbridled nostalgia. Niceness with knobs on, and absolutely nothing wrong with that." I couldn't agree more: the evening brought tears to the eyes of this hard-bitten barrister.

But, to be sure, there was far more to the Sixties than The Beatles and The Seekers. In 1963, the Profumo scandal rocked England to the core. John Profumo, the then Minister of War in the Macmillan government, became involved in an adulterous affair with party girl Christine Keeler, whom he had met through Stephen Ward, a licentious and dissolute London osteopath and sycophant to those in positions of power. Miss Keeler later declared that she was also sleeping with a Captain Ivanov, the Russian Naval Attaché. When the sordid mess became public, Ward was prosecuted for living off immoral earnings, and committed suicide; Profumo resigned in disgrace; and the affair was one of the chief factors that led to the fall of Macmillan's Tory government, in spite of a sober Report by the eminent judge Lord Denning which showed that national security had not been imperiled (the Report sold 4,000 copies the first hour of its publication!). The nation was both attracted and repelled by the easy morals and hedonism of those involved. The 30th anniversary of the trial of Stephen Ward has brought forth a photolithographic reprint of the Denning Report, a full-length, meticulously researched movie on the scandal (with distinguished actor John Hurt, who played *The Elephant Man*, now playing Stephen Ward)—and even a *Times* obituary of Captain Ivanov, who recently died of alcoholism in Moscow.

One of the classic scholarly evaluations of the Sixties has also been reprinted: Christopher Booker's *The Neophiliacs: The Revolution in English Life in the Fifties and Sixties* (Pimlico edition, with a new introduction by the author). This careful ideological analysis of the period, when originally published, was hailed by Malcolm Muggeridge as "a remarkable book ... enormously stimulating, readable and perceptive." Booker's thesis is that in essence the Sixties replaced reality by fantasy: the spirit of the times was to give up belief in a settled order of things—what Lovejoy called "the great chain of being"—and to think seriously that everything (morals, values, society) could be built *de novo*. Thus the characteristic idealism, naiveté, and experimentation with alternative life styles (the LSD culture, etc.) that typified the decade.

What can we say of the Sixties? Are we still too close to those years to be able to judge them? Perhaps, but some clear lessons do seem to have emerged.

Christian clergy and theologians during the Sixties tended either to condemn everything going on or to identify uncritically with it. I recall one of my colleagues in a distinguished graduate theological seminary seriously asserting in a faculty meeting that one of our students who was leading a (peaceful) anti-Vietnam War protest was "demon-possessed." I also well remember my public encounters with the late Bishop James Pike and death-of-God theologian Thomas Altizer, who typified the opposite extreme: jettisoning the theological baby (historic Christian truth) with the conservative bathwater (opposition to rock music, long hair, and short skirts). Why is it so difficult for the church to comprehend that God's Word stands in judgment equally over past fustiness *and* present change-for-change's sake?

The Sixties illustrated in another way Luther's observation that the history of our fallen race is the story of a drunk reeling from one wall to the other. Because the decade offered no solid criteria for judging values, but only an emotional blind faith in one's ability to make immediate, existential commitments (Woodstock; Fletcher's "situation ethics"), the flower-folk of the Sixties easily became the ruthless entrepreneurs of the Seventies and Eighties. (Think of John Updike's archetypical "Rabbit" in the epic novels about his sad progress—or regress?—through life.) "The times they are a changin'": profoundly true. Modern man cannot do without the compass of revelational truth as guide through the rapids of accelerating cultural change.

The Sixties' passion for Utopia—for a perfect world of love, not war—was certainly its most endearing characteristic. Unhappily, that dream was combined with an utterly unrealistic view of human nature; the Fall did not have a place in the theology, popular or mainline, of the decade. The Seekers (note carefully the name of the group!) were almost unique in employing Negro spirituals to convey—perhaps unwittingly—the truth that such hope, if it is not inevitably to collapse into discouragement and cynicism, must be apocalyptic. There *is* "a new world somewhere"; "someday, one day" all will be made right. The Lord of history will himself transform this sorry world, but this will happen only at the Last Day, "when the stars begin to fall."

21. The Religion of Doctor Johnson

It is one of the myths of modernity that the truly great intellectuals of history must have been skeptics. To be sure, we are told, in the prescientific "age of faith" before modern Enlightenment, thinkers necessarily suffered from superstitious religious commitments, but they were in this respect children of their time.

In England, this utterly fallacious mythology is much more difficult to maintain than in America, where history is so easily swallowed up in progress and change. Example: my barrister's chambers and London flat are situated just five minutes from Samuel Johnson's Gough Square house, where he produced his *Dictionary* and *The Rambler*; down the Strand is a statue of Johnson, so prominently placed as to be unavoidable, right next to the Church of St. Dunstan-in-the-West; and when I frequent the historic Cheshire Cheese chop house off Fleet Street, I see the chair Johnson sat in while regaling the likes of Sir Joshua Reynolds and displaying skills that made him unquestionably the greatest conversationalist and raconteur of all time. And what was the religious position of this 18th-century intellectual, living smack in the center of the so-called Age of Reason?

Biographer Peter Quennell, in his *Samuel Johnson: His Friends and Enemies*, leaves no room for ambiguity: "Johnson was a Christian Fundamentalist, who admitted no compromise, but asserted the unshakable truth of every major point of Christian doctrine."

That this is no exaggeration can be seen both from the intimate details of Johnson's spiritual life and from his numerous conversational declarations on religion. As a student at Oxford, he was deeply touched by William Law's *Serious Call to a Holy Life*; Johnson himself would later compose an informal diary of prayers (published only posthumously). These *Prayers and Meditations* show us that Johnson placed all aspects of his existence *sub specie aeternitatis*. On beginning the second volume of his *Dictionary*, he prayed, for example: "O God, Who hast hitherto supported me, enable me to proceed in this labour, and in the whole task of my present state; that when I shall render up at the last day an account of the talent committed to me, I may receive pardon for the sake of Jesus Christ." When he began *The Rambler* he prayed: "Grant, I beseech Thee, that in this my undertaking, Thy Holy Spirit may not be withheld from me, but that I may promote Thy glory, and the salvation both of myself and others."

Though temperamentally aligned with 17th-century orthodoxy rather than with 18th-century pietism, Johnson had a "wonderful" religious experience in February, 1784, during the last year of his life; this experience was what we would today term an entry into the "deeper life" or perhaps even a "second blessing," and Chester Chapin, in his work, *The Religious Thought of Samuel Johnson* (1968), comments on it that "in the last months of his life Johnson adopted a view of conversion not unlike that held by many Evangelicals."

Conversationally, Johnson's thoroughgoing Christian orthodoxy was so plain and forthright that it was a constant embarrassment to mediating friends who had absorbed the 18th-century *Zeitgeist*.

"What do you mean by damned?" the amiable Dr Adams once asked him. Johnson answered (passionately and loudly), "Sent to Hell, Sir, and punished everlastingly." Mrs. Adams replied, "You seem, Sir, to forget the merits of our Redeemer." Johnson said, "Madam, I do not forget the merits of my Redeemer; but my Redeemer has said that He will set some on His right hand and some on His left."

Johnson had absolutely no patience with the deists or skeptics of his day. He unmercifully criticized Boswell for having visited Rousseau: "Rousseau, Sir, is a very bad man. I would sooner sign a sentence for his transportation, than that of any felon who has gone from the Old Bailey these many years. Yes, I should like to have him work in the plantations." Boswell asked, "Sir, do you think him as bad a man as Voltaire?" Johnson replied, "Why, Sir, it is difficult to settle the proportions of iniquity between them."

But Johnson not only affirmed an uncompromising biblical orthodoxy; he vigorously defended it in an age when such thinkers as David Hume were eroding confidence in the veracity of Christian faith. Here is a typical example of Johnson's apologetic method:

"For revealed religion (Johnson said), there was such historical evidence, as, upon any subject not religious, would have left no doubt. Had the facts recorded in the New Testament been mere civil occurrences, no one would have called in question the testimony by which they are established; but the importance annexed to them, amounting to nothing less than the salvation of mankind, raised a cloud in their minds, and created doubts unknown upon any other subject. Of proofs to be derived from history, one of the most cogent, he seemed to think, was the opinion so well authenticated, and so long entertained, of a Deliverer that was to appear about that time. ..."

"For the immediate life and miracles of Christ, such attestation as that of the apostles, who all, except St. John, confirmed their testimony with their blood; such belief as their witness procured from a people best furnished with the means of judging, and least disposed to judge favourably; such an extension afterwards of that belief over all the nations of the earth, though originating from a nation of all others most despised, would leave no doubt that the things witnessed were true, and were of a nature more than human. With respect to evidence, Dr Johnson observed that we had not such evidence that Caesar died in the Capitol, as that Christ died in the manner related."

A *Times* editorial, commemorating the 200th anniversary of Johnson's death, opined: "Samuel would have regarded as blasphemous any proposal for his canonization: he had a highly developed and neurotic sense of his own worthlessness." But what do you do with a man who on his deathbed refused sedatives because he was not going to "meet God in a state of idiocy" and was chiefly worried about his black friend and servant whom he was leaving: "Attend, Francis, to the salvation of your soul, which is the object of greatest importance"? If not a saint, Johnson at least reminds us that the greatest minds are still those who agree with the Psalmist that the fear of the Lord is the beginning of wisdom.

22. The Famous in France: Why They Believe

Briskly selling in France at the moment is a collection of 137 testimonies (3 of them cartoons) under the title, *Pourquoi croyez-vous en Dieu?*—"*Why Do You Believe in God?*" The publisher is Criterion (Paris) and the editor, François Bluche, a distinguished writer and historian whose biography of Louis XIV has been translated into English and Russian.

Normally, books of testimonies elicit about as much public interest as sermon collections (just below works on the building of bird baths). What makes this anthology different is the surprising list of its contributors—including famous names few would have associated with Christian faith. In effect, a number of very famous French have blown their cover and can now be identified as serious, committed Christian believers. The list includes the exceedingly popular cartoonists Jacques Faizant and Pierre de Montvallon (who draws under his acronym "Piem"), prolific writer Jean Raspail, Sorbonne professor and academic historian François-Georges Dreyfus, and several members of the Institute such as historian of ideas Professor Francis Rapp—and Louis Pauwels, whose entire career has been associated with mysticism, the occult, and New Age vagaries.

And, to be sure, the volume also gives the reader familiar Christian spokesmen: theologian Oscar Cullmann; conservative retired Bishop of Strasbourg Mgr Léon Elchinger; the great lay Catholic theologian and polymath Jean Guitton; and heroic scientific defender of the rights of the unborn Professor Jérôme Lejeune, who died at about the time his testimony was published. The editor casts his net widely: most of the contributors are Roman Catholics (as one would expect in a French anthology), but Lutherans such as Cullmann and Dreyfus, and my friend Professor Henri Blocher, dean of the Free Faculty of Evangelical Theology at Vaux-sur-Seine, are also represented.

Let us examine some of the most striking of these testimonies, and then try to draw some lessons with the assistance of the book's editor.

First, the professional theologians and clerics. The difficulties with which they wrestle are fairly predictable. Oscar Cullmann speaks of "two crucial problems": the "sad fact that God is hidden and His existence is not evident *a priori*" and "the fact—and often the triumph—of evil." He concludes that, in light of these considerations, we cannot "prove" God's existence, but we *can* believe in Him and in fact we *must*. "Faith is thus the most precious gift and an absolute duty." For Henri Blocher, the key is Christ's resurrection. "If the skeptics abound, even among my brother theologians, I cannot but see this as an intellectual fad or, alas, as a secret concession to rampant unbelief." Mgr Elchinger analogizes belief in God to an engagement: "To say to one's fiancée, 'I believe in you', does not just mean, 'I believe that you exist'; it expresses a commitment to the future—a profound giving up of oneself."

Among the laity, we find Professor Lejeune contrasting Christian belief in God with the philosophies of Darwin and of Marxism. "For the strict Darwinian, human intelligence is only … a product of chance." "For the serious disciples of Engels, mind is a mere dialectic necessity. Thus, if one rejects the Creator, nothing any longer has significance or the least ultimate reason for existence. A scientist *must* therefore believe in God! Jean Guitton gives us but a short paragraph, informing the reader that he has taught the proofs for God's existence and holds to them. "But, at the close of my life, if you ask me as to the roots of my belief, my answer will be: the *absolute* evidence of the absurdity of denying God's existence."

The historians speak in considerably more personal terms, and their testimonies are perhaps the most telling in the book. Professor Dreyfus informs us that it was through believing scoutmasters that he came, as a boy, to discover God and trust in Christ. He was baptized in the Reformed Church of France after the war, and during the 50's discovered Luther and Lutheranism in the Alsace, and with it the truth that "faith alone" and the "Scriptures alone" are indissolubly connected. What especially troubles him today is theological liberalism: "How can churches derived from the Reformation remain faithful to the Bible while tolerating the ordination of women, homosexuality, abortion?" "'Soft theology' [he uses the English expression] naturally creates new clients for the psychiatrists and the sects." "Don't forget that Troeltsch's liberal modernism ... became the foundation for the racist neo-Protestantism of the Nazi era."

Francis Rapp touchingly speaks of his faith as that of the hod carrier (*charbonnier*): "I never had a vision or special illumination; yet, as far back as I can remember, God has been present in my life. I am comfortable in His presence, in His churches, and I know that one day I shall be with Him forever. ... At the end of the road, I know very well that my Father's house is there and that He awaits me at the threshold." "My profession of historian has shown me the history of those who have followed Christ—heroes innumerable, soldiers often known only to God." "The Lisbon earthquake, which gave Voltaire the opportunity to condemn naive optimism and the 'best of all possible worlds' ... simply invites me to reaffirm the choice which my parents made for me on the day of my baptism." "To sin is to refuse love. May we not be paralyzed by our faults or judge ourselves. 'If our hearts condemn us, God is greater than our hearts.' It was the thief on the cross whom Christ said he would see in paradise."

As for the former "New Ager" Louis Pauwels, he recounts a veritable Damascus Road experience: he had a violent fall—pushed to the ground by an invisible hand. "God, by His love, was the one who threw me against the concrete—to *save* me—and I then had to be a different person. And I do not mean the *idea* of God, represented by some kind of religious sentiment ... but the God of the Church, our Father who knows our inmost hearts."

Testimonies fascinate, as William James demonstrated by way of his classic, *Varieties of Religious Experience*. What do we learn from Bluche's collection? First, that it is a modern myth that the movers and shakers of our time are necessarily pagans. Today, as throughout history, a remarkable number of those who impact civilization for good are motivated by the love of Christ. Second, whatever their church connection, Christian believers invariably point to Christ and His grace, not to themselves and their accomplishments, as the source of their belief: *sola gratia*—"Amazing Grace"—is a defining mark of Christian experience. Thirdly, theologians do not necessarily make the most moving witnesses to a non-Christian world—perhaps because they tend to professionalize their faith, but more because they seem always to be speaking to other theologians. The layman may not be as theologically sophisticated, but he has not lost touch with the world desperate to hear a word of grace. Lastly, as Francois Bluche remarks in his editorial introduction, it is remarkable how many testimonies of learned intellectuals and members of the Academy are of the nature of the hod carrier's simple faith—reminding us that, after all, God chose Jacob—"that rude cowboy"—and that the Incarnation was announced to simple shepherds.

No better illustration of this point can be offered than two of the shortest testimonies in Bluche's volume. Jean Raspail: "I must believe in God. Period. Without Him, existence has no sense at all." And cartoonist Piem, who draws a typical French bourgeois standing in front of a tombstone, looking upward at a dove flying heavenward. On the gravestone, surmounted by a Cross, are the words from the Nicene Creed: "And His Kingdom shall have no end."

23. The Idea of Empire and a Christian Renaissance

A battle is currently raging in Europe which will ultimately influence the course of history to a far greater extent than Eastern European ethnic wars. I refer to the battle between those who wish to create a European political union (a "United States of Europe") and those who do not.

On the side of the Eurocentrists one meets the outgoing head of the European Commission, Jacques Delors, whose efforts to reduplicate himself in the choice of his successor came to grief through United Kingdom veto. On the anti-Maastricht side one encounters ex-Prime Minister Maggie Thatcher and her counterparts in most European countries, who roundly condemn the centralizing tendencies in Brussels and the top-heavy Eurocracy which would erode national sovereignty and dictate (*inter alia*) a uniform color for telephone booths throughout the continent.

Those who favor European political union argue, following Servan-Schreiber's seminal critique a generation ago (*Le Défi américain*—"The American Challenge") that only a united Europe can hope to succeed against the incredible economic pressure exerted by the United States. American goods and services—and the ideological impact of American films, pop music, and teen idioms—are fully capable of swallowing up European culture. The individual European countries are simply not capable of marshalling effective resistance—as illustrated by the recent puerile attempt by the French National Assembly to limit by law the use of foreign words in French advertising without French translations in the same type-size. Only a united Europe, say the Europaphiles, can fight the americanization of the continent and its ancient culture with the strength essential for success.

The Europaphobes, however, see a bureaucratic United States of Europe as an even greater evil. In their view, so much diversity of national tradition exists in Europe that to try on any level to homogenize it is to throw out the baby with the bathwater. The stronger the national spirit, the more such an argument is persuasive. Thus, almost 50% of French voters were opposed to ratifying the Maastricht Treaty, and the Tory party in England would not even permit a corresponding U.K. referendum, knowing full well that the majority of the populace would have rejected the unifying Treaty. The so-called "special relationship" between the U.K. and the U.S. undoubtedly has had a powerful influence over English thinking in this area.

Christians have aligned themselves on both sides of the battle, but more appear to oppose a united Europe than to favor it. Thus Graham Wood, in a widely distributed pamphlet titled, *Maastricht: A Christian Dilemma*, published by the Campaign for an Independent Britain, declares: "Vast areas of national policy are to be determined by the EC with an ever increasing flow of mandatory and often very costly bureaucratic 'directives' that are socially and commercially punitive." Wood opposes monetary union, arguing that "if the love of money is the root of all (kinds) of evil, then the control of it also has a high potential for evil."

Over this minefield of conflicting viewpoints a healthy wind has been blowing, in the person of a elderly (81 year old) Euro-MP, Dr Otto von Habsburg, once Crown Prince of the Austro-Hungarian Empire. In a recent interview (the *Times*, 24 May, 1994), von Habsburg opts for the Austro-Hungarian empire's experiment with flexible federalism. "In Bosnia under Austria-Hungary we had peace. Now, you see, they kill each other. Liberalism and honesty were very characteristic of Austria-Hungary. Liberalism in the sense of rights for small language groups."

Von Habsburg's general political philosophy is set out in his magisterial book, published originally in German and now available in French translation with an introduction by Pierre Chaunu of the Institute (*L'idée impériale*—"The Imperial Idea"—published by the Presses Universitaires de Nancy). Its subtitle reads: "The history and future of a supranational order." Chaunu notes that von Habsburg is "not one of those Eurocrats who can dream only of a Superstate, peopled with dead souls, but one whose dream is of a great community made up of all our differences put together to form a fragrant and sparkling bouquet. ... Pushed to its logical extreme, in contrast, the ideology of [Rousseau's] Social Contract leads to the atomization of society and then, surely, by reaction, to tyranny and to civil and foreign war."

What ideology, then, underlies von Habsburg's dream? A thoroughly Christian perspective. In his chapter entitled, "The Christian Renaissance of Europe," he declares: "The European idea has profound Christian roots. It follows with certainty that the future of Europe is unimaginable without the revival of religion." Admittedly, "our opponents point out that the churches are empty and that immanence is triumphing"; but in point of fact they are confusing the future with the past. "We are living today not with the signs of a new era of materialism but with the evidence of the last convulsions of a period of materialistic agony."

The French Revolution's cult of Reason led directly to historical materialism and totalitarianism. "Even Einstein, an agnostic throughout his life, came to recognize shortly before his death that above the visible world there has to be an invisible Orchestra Conductor." And so it has been with the fathers of European unification: "Schuman, Adenauer, and De Gaspari were believing Catholics, and their Christianity was the inspiration for their lofty ideals."

What does this mean in practice? "Christians do not have the right, like the Pharisee and the Levite on the road to Jericho, to pass by on the other side: we must come to the aid of the peoples in need on our continent … They are our brothers (Genesis 4:8-9) and we are responsible for them before God."

As an indefatigable optimist, von Habsburg looks forward to a new Europe. "Those who built the cathedrals of Europe were not buffoons. Our ancestors trusted in God, hammered away, and created our incomparable civilization." "I believe in the younger generation … With God's help, they will reach the goal." Whether they do or not, von Habsburg is right about one thing: without a vision, the people perish; and the only proper and lasting vision for individual or corporate life is that of the Christ of Scripture.

24. Jesus and the Bell Curve

On my birthday I received a card from my sister Mary in America, enclosing the *New York Times* obituary of Harvard psychologist Richard J. Herrnstein, whose widow, Sue Gouinlock, attended our high school and is a close friend of my sister. The next day (October 19, 1994), the London *Times* ran a column-length article on *The Bell Curve*, Herrnstein and Murray's just published study of the connections between I.Q., race, and social class.

This book is causing what may mildly be termed an uproar on both sides of the Atlantic. An essay on the subject of their book by the two authors appeared in the October 31 issue of *The New Republic*, followed by some 19 rejoinders by staff members at the magazine, furious over the editor's decision to include the piece at all. Alan Ryan, who teaches politics at Princeton, concluded his analysis of Herrnstein and Murray's book in *The New York Review of Books* (November 17) with the line: "In short, *The Bell Curve* is not only sleazy; it is, intellectually, a mess."

No doubt the book is an oddity. Its over 600 pages are stuffed with graphs, bar charts, and tables in the manner of a scientific monograph for specialists, yet at the same time the book contains italicized summaries for the general reader and not a little tendentious, even soap-box ideology. The perspectives and concerns of the two authors are not identical, producing awkward unevenness of presentation. But having said all of this, *The Bell Curve* is an exceedingly important work, worthy of much reflection.

Why is this, and why the furor over it? The answer, of course, lies in the authors' theses. The book endeavors to make three overarching points. First, intelligence is more-or-less a constant, virtually unalterable by training, education, or other forms of social manipulation. Dr Herrnstein began his career as a disciple of behaviorist B. F. Skinner, but moved away from Skinner's environmentalism through the influence of Charles Spearman, an early 20th-century British statistician who held that each person has a given, hereditary quantity of general intelligence. In *The Bell Curve* it is pointed out, as Nobel prizewinner William Shockley did fifteen years ago, that group differences in I.Q. are considerable: African Americans are one standard deviation (15%) inferior to white Americans on analytical and spatial intelligence tests—while East Asians can be 15% superior to American whites on the same tests! Such conclusions (indeed, the very *idea* of such studies) have called down the wrath of the liberal establishment.

Second, Herrnstein and Murray maintain, on the basis of the I.Q. evidence, that the welfare-state efforts to bring some minorities and socially disadvantaged groups up to the level of the white majority are simply unrealistic. Head Start and similar affirmative action programmes may well be, on this interpretation, a colossal waste of taxpayers' money and a country's resources.

Thirdly, the authors look pessimistically at the future. Those with low intelligence (which correlates with crime and social deviancy) breed faster and younger than those with higher I.Q.s. The less bright produce three generations of their own while the more intelligent, who have their children later, produce only two. Result, as Sir Keith Joseph, education minister to Mrs. Thatcher, noted with alarm: our modern Western societies are in real danger of descending into mediocrity and lawlessness, perhaps requiring the police state even to survive.

What can be said to all this? Attempts are of course being made to argue that the scientific and statistical sides of *The Bell Curve* are fatally flawed. This seems most unlikely, since the underlying data employed are taken from the exceedingly reputable NLSY (the "National Longitudinal Survey of Labor Market Experience of Youth"), surveying 12,500 Americans age 14 to 22 in 1979 and carefully monitoring them from that year to the present. But even if intelligence does correlate with race or social class, and even if I.Q. were in fact shown to be hereditary and unalterable, would it necessarily follow that affirmative action programmes could not be justified? Ryan perceptively notes that "Herrnstein's views on intelligence are in principle consistent with the politics of almost any persuasion. ... Socialists might think that ineradicable differences in I.Q. should be met by making sure that the less clever were compensated with more education than the gifted, and with income supplements to make up for their difficulties in the competitive marketplace."

From the Christian viewpoint, several points cry out to be made. (1) Truth, even if it is not what we would like it to be, must be discovered and faced. There must be no suppression of research such as Herrnstein and Murray's or refusal to allow investigations into sensitive and politically incorrect areas. Finite creatures in a contingent universe cannot ever legitimately impose their political or social dogmas on reality, declaring what must be the case and substituting mythology for the facts as they are. If intelligence is essentially or significantly hereditary, better that we should know it even if it goes against our fondest wishes. A fallen world is not likely to be a place of perfect rationality or equity. (2) At the same time, our Lord informs us, in the Parable of the Talents, that the important thing is not how much we have been given relative to others, but what we do with what we have been given: the servant with five talents who doubled them received exactly the same praise from his master as the servant with ten talents who doubled his. All of us use but a fraction of our mental abilities, and we all have known those who have sadly dissipated great talents, in contrast with others with far less who have accomplished far more. (3) The test of acceptance before God and moral living has never been intelligence or social standing. Quite the contrary: "Not many wise men after the flesh, not many mighty, not many noble, are called." The receptive child is the symbol of the Kingdom, and he or she is given no intelligence test. By the foolishness of preaching God saves those who believe. The answer to crime is not the I.Q.: it is the Spirit of God changing hearts and wills and motivations.

Pessimism for the future? Not on the ground of declining intelligence; rather on the grounds of declining evangelism and declining faith. "When the Son of man comes, shall he find faith on the earth?"

25. Will the True Biblical Scholar Please Stand Up?

Two days after St. Valentine's Day, 1995, anything but a love-feast took place at the University of Hull. Before an audience of roughly one-quarter of the student population and a smattering of the instructional staff, your humble servant debated the University's Dean of the Theology Department on the subject of the historicity of the Resurrection of Jesus Christ. My protagonist, Dr Lester Grabbe, an American and former Pentecostal Bible-believer, was converted to theological liberalism whilst taking his doctorate at the Claremont Graduate School of Theology in California. I shall not rehash the debate here but rather look closely at one of Dr Grabbe's most fervently held convictions: that belief in the full authority of the Bible precludes one from practicing true biblical scholarship.

In a local *Festschrift* for retiring professor A. T. Hanson (Hull University Press, 1987), Grabbe contributed an essay entitled, "Fundamentalism and Scholarship." The article sets itself to answer the question, "Can one be a fundamentalist and still claim the label 'biblical scholar'?" "Fundamentalism" is defined for the purpose of the essay as "a certain attitude and approach to the Bible, generally formalised as a belief that the biblical text is 'inerrant in the autographs'"—as the doctrinal statement of the Evangelical Theological Society, for example, expresses it.

Grabbe's answer to his own question is, predictably, a resounding negative: "Fundamentalism is incompatible with scholarship." Why is this? because "Fundamentalism has already determined its conclusions. ... Fundamentalism can never conclude that the Bible is wrong." The Bible-believer is really engaged in an analytically meaningless endeavour, where no evidence can ever count against the invincible ignorance of his presupposition. "His model is really circular, in that he begins and ends with 'truth,' while the data do not ultimately affect the conclusion." In reality, what passes as Bible-believing scholarship is "an apologetic under the guise of scholarship." Grabbe thus explicitly casts into outer scholarly darkness such distinguished Old Testament specialists as R. K. Harrison, Bruce Waltke, D. J. Wiseman, Kenneth Kitchen, Gleason Archer, and Edwin Yamauchi.

What can be said of this argument? Does commitment really preclude scholarly objectivity? Are theological liberals in fact the open and unbiased ones, whilst the biblical conservatives possess minds so narrow that (as one wag put it) they can see through a keyhole with both eyes simultaneously? I must say that for me this thesis fell apart when, many years ago, I served as Librarian of the University of Chicago Divinity School: I discovered that my "liberal" colleagues never selected conservative material for the library, whereas, at neighboring Trinity Evangelical Divinity School, all the liberal authors were represented along with the conservative ones. But let us formally examine the Grabbe thesis and then see how Grabbe himself does biblical scholarship.

Are convinced Christians "invincibly ignorant"? Would nothing count against their faith? I have never met a serious Bible believer who (contrast Paul Tillich or Bishop Pike) was indifferent to the historical facticity of the physical Resurrection of Christ. *All* conservative Christians hold with St. Paul (1 Cor. 15) that "if Christ be not risen" the Christian faith is *false* and should be given up. Thus it is orthodox, not liberal, theology which is in principle disconfirmable and, for that reason, analytically meaningful. Only the liberal will continue to play the role of Christian while giving up serious belief in its most central historic doctrines.

Moreover, why does Grabbe assume that objective evidence has nothing to do with the Bible-believer's having arrived at his position in the first place? C. S. Lewis (and yours truly) were "dragged kicking and screaming" into the Kingdom by the sheer force of the case for the Resurrection of our Lord. There is nothing wrong (and everything right) in offering scholarly support for a conviction that one has reached by legitimately weighing the evidence for competing religious options. And if Jesus Christ did rise from the dead, he is the Divine Being he said he was, and his view of biblical authority will outweigh contrary human views on the subject. There will then always be some satisfactory explanation for scriptural difficulties, and we have the best of all scholarly reasons for seeking them out.

The model of advocacy may also help. In our common law courts, an advocate provides the best case for his client, and the neutral trier of fact (judge or jury) makes the ultimate decision. Is law therefore not scholarship but mere apologetics? Hardly. The truth is often best revealed when convinced and conscientious advocates do their very best to present their side of the case.

But do liberal, critical biblical scholars in fact offer positive examples of objective scholarship? Let us take Grabbe himself as illustrative.

The dating of the New Testament documents. In his two-volume textbook, *Judaism from Cyrus to Hadrian*, Grabbe blandly asserts that the four Gospels are all "post-70," "the 80s or 90s for Luke, the same or later for Acts." Not a word is said about the powerful trend toward early dating of these New Testament materials (W. F. Albright and even J. A. T. Robinson asserting that the Synoptic Gospels all preceded the fall of Jerusalem in A.D. 70). Nor, in dealing with Acts, is there any reference to Harnack's impressive argument that Acts (and therefore the Synoptics) had to have been written before Paul's death (no later than 65) — an argument recently employed with great effectiveness by New Testament scholar Robert Gundry.

Luke's historical inaccuracies. Grabbe says that Luke "shows shocking ignorance of some fairly basic details of history (e.g. the census of Quirinius; and he refers to Agrippa I as 'Herod')." But such distinguished historians as Sir William Ramsay, A. N. Sherwin-White, and Ethelbert Stauffer have offered entirely reasonable hypotheses to explain Luke's reference to a general census authorised by Augustus and carried out in the days of Herod. As for Luke's designation of Agrippa as "Herod" in Acts 12 when this was not his proper name, Daniel Schwartz, in the latest (1990) monograph devoted to Agrippa I (published in Tübingen by Mohr in the prestigious monograph series, "Texte und Studien zum antiken Judentum") observes simply that the reference "testifies that the king is being viewed typologically, as another persecutor in the Church's Judaean history, following Herod, Herod Antipas, Herodias and the Herodians, who figure as persecutors in the Gospel stories." Grabbe mentions none of these possible explanations.

Mark's historical blundering. Mark 6, Grabbe tells us, "states that Herodias was the wife of Philip, whereas her daughter Salome was Philip's wife." However, William Lane, in his highly regarded 1974 commentary on Mark, following Lenski a generation earlier, noted that "the full name of Herodias' first husband is unknown, but no evidence exists that it was not Herod Philip," and, as for Salome, "she was later married to the tetrarch Herod Philip" (her own half-uncle). Vincent Taylor points out in his classic commentary on Mark that the problem reading "of Philip" does not even appear in the 3^d century Chester Beatty papyrus (**p**^{45}) of the Marcan text. Why does Grabbe tell us none of this?

Answer: because he has no desire to give the biblical text the benefit of the doubt. He ignores Aristotle's dictum in the *Poetics* that a text (even a poetic text such as Homer) should be treated as innocent until proven guilty, and should therefore benefit from scholarly harmonisation wherever possible. It is Grabbe and his ilk who prove themselves deficient in scholarship, not the "fundamentalists." In most fields of human endeavour the irony is that the professed liberal turns out so often to be far more illiberal than the conservative he pillories.

26. On Becoming a French *Avocat*

It is a commonplace that the French legal system is code based, in contrast with the case-law approach of the Anglo-American common law. True, common-law jurisdictions depend more and more on codifications, and there are important areas of French law (for example, administrative law) in which case law—*jurisprudence* is the French term—predominates. But overall the generalisation holds. This is true for the rules of admission as an *avocat*: they are expressly set forth in a series of laws and decrees collected in the *Nouveau Code de Procédure Civile*—the Law of 31 December 1971, art. 11 ff.; the Decree of 27 November 1991, art. 42 ff., 99 and 100; and the "RIN" (the *Décision* of the National Council of the Bars of France, 2005, which has normative legal force). Since there is no single national French bar (the bars are regional, half of all French lawyers belonging to the Paris bar), the individual bars can and do supplement the RIN regulations with their own *règlements intérieurs*—permitted as long as these do not conflict with the national rules.

So how does one become an *avocat*? The answer is a bit like the answer to the question, "How do nudists dance?": *Carefully, very carefully*. In point of fact, there are several answers to the question, depending on one's particular status. If one is a French citizen or a foreigner wanting to obtain his or her legal training in France, the standard route consists of obtaining a master's degree in law (the former *licence en droit*), followed by an 18-month programme at a regional centre of professional training; the latter has both an entrance and a final examination, and the programme consists of courses, a major project, and an apprenticeship. Successful completion leads to the "CAPA"—the aptitude certificate allowing one to apply to become a member of a French bar. It is noteworthy that exceptions of various kinds to these requirements exist for members of related professions; thus, a law professor at a French university will automatically be admitted to the bar simply by virtue of his professorial rank.

But if one is a foreign lawyer—i.e., not a French citizen but a legal practitioner in another country—all will depend on whether one is or is not a citizen of one of the EU countries or of a member state of the European Economic Community (Switzerland being expressly included as well).

For the non-EU lawyer wishing to become a French *avocat*, the key issue is whether his or her country has bar admissions rules reciprocal to those of France; if so, those rules will of course apply. If not—which is the usual situation—an examination (the celebrated "Article 100" test) is the only route available. This examination consists of two 3-hour written papers, one in civil law, the other—at the candidate's choice—in administrative law, commercial law, employment law, or criminal law. These are followed by two oral examinations—one chosen by lot among two subjects ([1] civil, criminal or administrative procedure; [2] the French judicial system and its organisation), and the other, *déontologie*, i.e., the nature, professional standards, and ethics of French legal practice. One must obtain an overall passing average (10 out of 20 points) and the examination can be taken only three times. If one passes, one has the right to be enrolled in any of the French regional bars as an *avocat* in full standing.

For the non-French EU lawyer, the regime is different. If, say, a German or a U.K. lawyer simply wishes to plead a single case, he will be allowed to do so with the aid of French practitioner (much like the *pro hac vice* rule in American jurisdictions, though that rule applies to a lawyer from one state wishing to plead a single case in an American state where he/she is not a member of the bar). Should the non-French EU lawyer wish to set up an office (primary or secondary) in France, this is possible—but only if he or she joins a French bar under one's legal title of origin; practice will be limited to that lawyer's foreign law and will not extend to giving advice on French law or to pleading in French tribunals.

Interestingly, this EU-directed arrangement was fought tooth and nail by French bars, which did not want competition from other EU lawyers. And even more restrictive jurisdictions—Luxembourg being the archetypal example—tried all sorts of underhanded ruses to prevent foreign EU lawyers from even this limited bar membership. When the Luxembourg bar tried to augment the European directive with a local language requirement (French, German, and Luxembourgish!), the European Court of Justice ruled that this was contrary to the spirit of the free establishment of European workers and against the clear intent of the directive (decision of 19 September 2006).

But a non-French EU lawyer, even when he or she successfully enters into such an arrangement, is very obviously a second-class citizen. He or she must pay the full fees to the bar that a French *avocat* pays and must fulfil the same annual continuing legal education requirements that apply to the French *avocat*—but one's name appears in small letters in a separate section of the *Tableau des Avocats* (the official regional listing) or in minuscule type in the Paris bar directory.

And if the non-French lawyer wishes to become a full-fledged *avocat*? Here, two paths exist. The one appears simple and non-threatening: three years of practice in France, and no examinations! This possibility, to be sure, came about not through any French efforts (quite to the contrary) but by way of a European directive of 16 February 1998—which did not get transposed into French law until 11 February 2004! (It now comprises Articles 89 and 90 of the revised Law of 31 December 1971.) The problem with this alternative is that the three years of required full-time practice need to be in "French law." But, being a foreign attorney, the non-French lawyer is not supposed to be practicing French law! The text goes on to say that if there is insufficient evidence of such practice, the bar to which he or she applies has the right to "evaluate the regular and effective character of the activity exercised, as well as the capacity of the candidate to pursue such." This, of course, leaves open a wide area of discretion to the local bar—even though, technically, the burden of proof in rejecting the candidate falls on the bar, not on the applicant.

The second route for the non-French EU lawyer to become an *avocat* is to pass "Article 99" examinations. These are set individually for each applicant, and can consist of up to four tests, depending on how closely the candidate's legal education and experience parallel the French model. One examination is always on the practice and ethics of the profession (*déontologie*). The others are specified from a list derived from the CAPA requirements; civil law is a standard—plus commercial law, administrative law, criminal law, and employment law. If four subjects are assigned, one of them (chosen by the National Council of the Bar, which sets the list for each candidate) must consist of a four-hour written examination. The other subjects are tested by oral examination before juries. Two examination periods maximum are now set each year, one in Paris, the other in Versailles; in Paris, the jury consists of three examiners (a law professor who is a specialist in the given subject, a former member of the Bar Council, and a practitioner), whereas Versailles employs five-member juries.

If the European lawyer comes from a Napoleonic Code jurisdiction (say, Italy) or from a strongly French-speaking area (say, Belgium), he/she may be required only to do an oral in one or two subjects (*déontologie* is always mandatory). But all U.K. lawyers (solicitors, barristers, Scottish advocates), being from common-law backgrounds—after all, even the civil-law Scots end up before the common-law Judicial Committee of the House of Lords—are required to do the maximum of four subjects, and this means at least the one 4-hour written examination, plus three oral examinations. What is expected of the candidate is not the "practical, problem-solving" style of the Art. 100 examinations, but the academic, essay style of the French university curriculum, where, for example, in the legal area, one always divides one's answer into two major subsections! To pass, one must average 10 out of 20 *in toto*, and one can only sit for the examination three times.

And now, a personal word. After two years as a member of the Strasbourg bar and three years a member of the Paris bar—both under my foreign practicing title of barrister-at-law (England and Wales)—I applied to take the oath as a French *avocat*. My dossier was replete with evidence of my legal activity in France, chiefly in the area of my specialty, religious liberty litigation before the European Court of Human Rights in Strasbourg. I was informed that this was inadequate. Why? Because I could not show that my income derived principally from this practice. *Of course it did not*: I am a university professor and my legal work has been largely *pro bono*. I pointed out, using an article on the Paris bar's own website, that historically the French bar has valued unremunerated service in behalf of the poor and downtrodden. Indeed, the French bar grew out of eleemosynary service by lawyers who were clergy. "Would a physician be less good a doctor if he treated patients for free?" I asked. I also reminded the powers-that-be that one of the differences between French lawyers and Anglo-

American lawyers is that the French *avocat* must not engage in any form of commercial activity. Indeed, an *avocat* cannot simultaneously be a member of any other profession (medicine, accountancy, etc.)—with the exception of university teaching or a religious ministry. (A few years ago, in 2003, a young *avocate* was suspended for having played an accordion for money on a public street—though this was reversed on appeal.) My arguments were to no avail. I withdrew my application and determined to take the tougher route.

I was therefore left with the Article 99 examinations. In spite of my possessing four earned law degrees, including the LLD—the higher doctorate in law—from Cardiff University, the National Council of French Bars required me to pass the maximum of four examinations. Their only concession, on the basis of my practice in France, was to substitute criminal law for civil law as the four-hour written examination. The oral examinations required of me were in commercial law (with its independent *Code de Commerce* and separate commercial courts), administrative law (again, independent of the *Code Civil*, and having its own "supreme court," the Conseil d'Etat), plus, of course, *déontologie*. The subject of my four-hour paper in criminal law turned out not to be any of the traditional, classical areas (crimes against the person, against property, against the state or against humanity), but "the criminal liability risks of corporations"!

I passed. Then, in completing the paper work for admission as an *avocat à la cour* (Paris), I was told that my *contrat de collaboration* with my colleagues in chambers had to be revised to state a minimum monthly salary! (This may be justified to prevent young associates from falling into slavery, but it again smacked of an unrecognized commercialism in a profession officially opposing filthy lucre as having anything to do with its nature.) But, all of this having been finally resolved, I took the oath to become an *avocat* in an impressive ceremony in the First Chamber of the Palais de Justice's Court of Appeal—where the trial of Pétain had been held following the liberation of Paris and the defeat of the Nazis.

Was it worth it? Of course. But never think that lawyers are lacking in old fashioned territorialism—even when it goes against there own principles. The oath of the *avocat* pledges him or her not only to "dignity," "conscientiousness," "independence," and "honesty"—but also to "humanity." Surely "humanity" should embrace greater appreciation of the high legal standards of our European states in general, as well as (why not?) the recognition that a lawyer can be a fine practitioner even if he is not well remunerated for it.

27. Passion Play Problems[1]

The 2010 decennial Passion Play season at Oberammergau is now history. Of course this author attended: he is a Passion Play groupie, having been present at no less than six productions (1970, 1980, the special anniversary season in 1984, 1990, 2000, and 2010), and having shepherded Christian groups to three of those productions. In 2000 and 2010, my wife and I attended with International Academy of Apologetics colleague Craig Parton and his spouse; readers of the *Global Journal of Classical Theology* (www.phc.edu) will recall Professor Parton's article, "Why Liberals Didn't Understand Passion Play 2000" (Vol. 4, No. 1, February 2004). I myself commented on the 2000 production in my Editor's Introduction to Vol. 2, No. 3 (August 2001). My personal library contains the text of the 1900 Passion Play, together with all the versions from 1930 to the present (there was no Play in 1940, owing to the Second World War). *But I shall probably not attend again—and not because I am getting on in years.*

On the positive side, the Play sends a clear message (hard to find these days) that Jesus was indeed God's Son, the fulfilment of numerous Old Testament types and prophecies, and that his death was a divine atonement for the sins of all mankind. Christ's trial before the Sanhedrin is shown to be a ghastly travesty of justice. The text is based chiefly on the Gospel of John and its message is taken with complete seriousness. The music is deeply moving and occasionally (for example, during the tableaux of Daniel in the lions' den and the mocking of Job, and accompanying the Way of the Cross) rises to truly remarkable heights. So what is the problem?

The actors have a tendency toward histrionics, but that may be inevitable considering the nature of the production. The English translation of the German text leaves something to be desired. *Judas to Jesus*: "How are you so peculiar!"; *Annas*: "How much longer will you be reluctant to set limits to this stream of corruption? It has already broken through all the dams and like an all-consuming, wildly foaming flood is pouring across Judea." But the real difficulty comes through the modifications introduced in 2010 into the standard text of the Play—by way of both additions and omissions.

True, there has always been a minor degree of tinkering with the text; in 2000, for example, efforts (largely unsuccessful) were made to pre-empt criticism of the Play for anti-Semitism by toning down some very strong dialog. But in 2010 the changes have been far more extreme. Thus:

1) Judas Iscariot is given a far more prominent place than ever before ("Judas before the High Council"—Act III, Scene 4; "Judas Wanders About Aim-

---

[1] See also, *infra*, Part Ten, chap. 14.

lessly" and "Judas Demands the Release of Jesus"—Act VII, Scenes 1 and 4). The object is clearly to make Judas a tragic, sympathetic figure; his acceptance of the thirty pieces of silver is seen as essentially an agreement to force Jesus into a meeting with the High Council, not a traitorous bargain with Jesus' enemies. Merely from an aesthetic point of view, Judas' monologues are an agonizing distraction from the overall thrust of the drama.

2) The Lord's Supper scene is made more narrowly Jewish than before, with Jesus' uttering the Verba in Hebrew—doubtless to assuage criticisms from Jewish anti-defamation leagues. However, our Lord spoke Aramaic, not Hebrew; and the 2010 text gives, if anything, a far more condemnatory picture of the Jewish religious leadership of the time than in previous texts (thus, the excessively colourful and impressive costumes of the High Council, and the overlong and boring discussions amongst the Jewish religious leadership).

3) Most troubling, however, is the truncated treatment of the Resurrection, constituting the final scene of the Play. In previous versions, there was significant dialog between the Roman soldiers guarding the tomb and the women arriving there on Easter morning. This included (2000) lines such as:

Pedius: I'd prefer any other kind of assignment to this deathwatch the priests have saddled us with.

Sabinus: Ridiculous, they are even afraid of the dead!

Titus: Not the dead—they are afraid of his disciples, that they will steal his corpse and then start the rumour that he has risen from the dead.

Earlier versions of the Play were even stronger; thus, in 1930, the line just above reads:

"This Man of Nazareth, so the rumour goes, has said that on the third day He would return from the dead; hence the fear."

The 1930 text has the soldiers encountering the earthquake, discovering the stone rolled away, and declaring: "He must have risen. No man came here. So, what the priests most feared has happened! He has fulfilled His word!"

A précis of the 1900 Play describes the scene thus: "A great noise is heard. The stone at the door of the sepulchre is overturned, the watchmen fall to the ground, and out of the sepulchre appears the Saviour, who has overcome death."[2]

---

[2] Hermine Diemer, *Oberammergau and Its Passion Play*, trans. Walter S. Manning (Munich and Oberammergau: Carl Aug. Seyfried, 1900), p. 250.

In the 2010 text, the soldiers have been entirely eliminated and there is no earthquake or appearance of Jesus from the tomb. A glowing light is introduced to symbolise the Resurrection, and Jesus simply stands there, saying nothing. The scene is still entitled "The Encounter with the Risen One," but it is a minimal encounter to say the least.

So how has this come about? Clearly, over the years—and particularly in 2010—less and less stress has been placed on the factual aspects of the Resurrection. And in the most recent version, there is much attention directed to the existential agonies of Judas and dialogistic interplay among the Jewish religious leaders.

Answer, then, to our question: modern German theology raises its ugly head. Dialog, *Existenz*, and subjective impact rather than biblical historicity.

How do we know this? The 2010 playbook, supplied to attendees, contains a Preface3 by "theological advisor of the Oberammergau Passion Play 2010," one Prof. Dr Ludwig Moedl, "Spiritual [!] at the Herzoglichen Georgianum Munich and Universitaetsprediger at St. Ludwig." He says of the changes in the text: "For the last two seasons passages had already been revised, and the current staging includes entirely new parts of the text, which essentially were written by Christian Stueckl (director) and Otto Huber (playwright)." (Incidentally, we learned from a master woodcarver in the village that it was Stueckl who insisted, against the will of the community, to schedule the Play in the afternoons and evenings, instead of the mornings and afternoons—thus making it impossible to follow the text after the sun sets and forcing the audience to pass into the dark night after leaving the theatre following the closing Resurrection scene! Our woodcarver also informed us that Stueckl the director would have entirely eliminated the Resurrection scene had not the village folk virulently protested removing it.)[4]

Declares the "theological advisor": "Today's audience differs from that of twenty and even ten years ago. ... Thus, in the representation of the suffering and death of Christ the questions of the meaning and future of human existence are illuminated in a dramatic way." Last we heard, though audiences change, the eternal message of the gospel remains the same: "yesterday, today and forever."

---

[3] *Passionsspiele 2010 Oberammergau: Textbuch*, trans. Ingrid Shafer (Oberammergau, 2010), pp. 5-7.
[4] Particularly troubling was Stueckl's personal comment in an interview included in a book on the Play available for purchase in Oberammergau: "For me, Jesus is not a suffering servant of God, not a sacrificial lamb. For me, Jesus is an argumentative young Jew who was nailed to the cross for proclaiming a message that is still valid today."

Concerning the climactic Resurrection scene, Moedl writes most revealingly: "The final scene is also staged in a new way. Jesus is laid to rest, but the tomb is not visible. This eliminates having to show the guards at the tomb. The Risen Lord appears only briefly. ... The character of the numinous is conveyed through the glowing light, the music, and the restrained visual presentation. It is, as theology teaches, a mystery of faith."

Nonsense. Classical theology has always taught that the Resurrection was as historical, factual and visible as the crucifixion. It was the liberal theology of Martin Kaehler and the neo-orthodoxy of Karl Barth that drove a wedge between ordinary historical events (*Historie*) and the supernatural events of Christ's life such as the Resurrection, which had to be relegated to a realm of "supra-history" (*Geschichte*)—a realm not subject to historical investigation and therefore immune to criticism. The real "mystery of faith" is the mystery as to how modern theologians think that they are helping Christianity by converting it from historical reality into analytically meaningless subjectivity.

Two lessons from the Oberammergau Passion Play 2010: (1) "If it ain't broke, don't fix it." (2) Keep liberal theologians—and unbelieving directors—entirely away from fine artistic representations of revelational truth.

28. Religious "Irrationality" and Civil Liberties

The theme of the Ecclesiastical Law Society's 2010 Day Conference, held on 13 March in London, was "Freedom of Religion: Protection or Equality." One of the speakers, Lucy Vickers, professor of law at Oxford Brookes University and specialist on religious discrimination in the workplace, declared that in her opinion the fundamental ground for legally protecting religious belief and practice is the essential irrationality of religious positions: since their truth cannot, unlike scientific views, be demonstrated, they need the protection of the law even more than do other ideas. Another speaker, Christopher McCrudden, professor of human rights law at the University of Oxford, indicated that he felt very uncomfortable with this argument, though there was no time at the conference to go into the issue in depth.

Then, a little over a month later (29 April), Lord Justice Laws issued his opinion in the case of *McFarlane v Relate Avon Ltd* [2010] EWCA Civ B1, on appeal from the Employment Appeal Tribunal. Gary McFarlane, a relationships counselor in Bristol, with strong evangelical Christian beliefs, had refused to provide sexual counseling to homosexual couples; as a result, he was dismissed by the Relate Avon organization, whose position was upheld by the Employment Tribunal. Lord Justice Laws denied McFarlane's subsequent application to have his case heard by the Court of Appeal. The Lord Justice gave his *ratio* as follows: "[I]n the eye of everyone save the believer religious faith is necessarily subjective, being incommunicable by any kind of proof or evidence. ... [I]t lies only in the heart of the believer, who is alone bound by it. No one else is or can be so bound, unless by his own free choice he accepts its claims. The promulgation of law for the protection of a position held purely on religious grounds cannot therefore be justified. It is irrational, as preferring the subjective over the objective" (paras. 23-24).

These remarks created a considerable flap in the press, and former Archbishop George Carey took sharp issue with Lord Justice Laws' refusal to allow McFarlane's appeal. Some critics reasoned *ad hominem,* condemning the Lord Justice on the basis of his reputation as a "legal activist."

But the especially interesting aspect of the Laws' decision is that, whilst agreeing entirely with Professor Vickers' view that religion is essentially subjective, and therefore unprovable and irrational, the Lord Justice concludes that, instead of particularly deserving the protection of the law, religious claims must not be upheld legally against the (non-religious) views of others. In other words, from the premise of religious irrationality, Vickers and Laws draw precisely opposite conclusions!

In the present essayist's view, neither Vickers nor Laws is correct, and for three compelling reasons: (1) It is incorrect to suppose that ideological conflicts in society pit "religious" beliefs against "non-religious" positions. (2) Religious beliefs are not necessarily irrational. (3) A proper basis for the protection—and the limitation—of religious practices must be found in an entirely different realm from that of supposed "religious irrationality." Let us briefly speak to each of these points.

(1) The 20th-century theologian Paul Tillich stressed that there are in fact no atheists, since everyone has an "ultimate concern"—a value system determining his or her actions individually and societally. Thus, in *McFarlane*, Relate Avon, no less than McFarlane himself, held religious convictions—for Relate Avon, that homosexual relationships are ethically proper and as such deserve the benefits of sexual counseling no less than heterosexual relationships. Lord Justice Laws himself therefore acted irrationally in rejecting on grounds of religious irrationality McFarlane's overt religiosity in favour of Relate Avon's unstated, but no less religious, value system.

(2) As for the claim by Vickers and Laws that religions are *per se* irrational, we might paraphrase George Orwell: all religions are equal, but some are more equal than others. There are indeed religions such as Buddhism that rely 100% on personal, subjective experience as verification for their beliefs, as well as cultic movements such as Scientology having no way of objectively

demonstrating the factuality of their doctrines (e.g., that "body thetans" are the product of Xenu of the Galactic Confederacy and need to be treated through therapeutic "auditing" processes). But this is hardly a description of all religious phenomena. An obvious counter-example is classic Christian faith, which centres on the historical facts of Jesus' life, death, and resurrection. The centuries-old discipline of Christian apologetics has offered powerful objective evidences for the truth of the Christian worldview; one thinks of the work of Pascal, William Paley, John Henry Newman, C. S. Lewis, Richard Swinburne—and lawyers such as Hugo Grotius (*De veritate religionis Christianae*), Simon Greenleaf (*The Testimony of the Evangelists*)—and Sir Norman Anderson, late director of the University of London's Institute of Advanced Legal Studies (*The Evidence for the Resurrection*). In recent years, the arguments for cosmic, universal "intelligent design" as presented by scientists such as William Dembski and Francis Collins have brought even distinguished atheistic philosophers (e.g., Antony Flew) to belief in God.

(3) Where, then, should one go to find an adequate basis for the protection of religious beliefs and practices—and proper grounds for limiting them? The answer is not to label religion as "irrational" and then to draw positive or negative conclusions from that characterization, but rather to consider far more carefully the proper function of law in general in an open society. As political philosopher John Rawls emphasized by way of his First Principle of Justice (that dealing with civil liberties), "Each person is to have an equal right to the most extensive scheme of equal basic liberties compatible with a similar scheme of liberties for others." This means that unless one's belief or desired activity—including religious belief and activity—hurts others, it should be allowed. It also means that if the courts can find a way for a belief or activity to function without significant hurt to others, that belief or activity should be legitimated. In the *McFarlane* matter, therefore, since other relationship counselors holding worldviews other than McFarlane's could readily treat the homosexual couples, McFarlane should have been allowed to retain his position—respect being shown to his personal beliefs by allowing him to give sex therapy only to heterosexual couples. (This is in line with medical practice in many civilized countries, where physicians and nurses opposing abortion do not have their public hospital privileges taken away, but are exempted from performing abortions and instead are assigned to perform other medical procedures.)

There is a further consideration of the greatest consequence to the judicial evaluation of religious belief and practice. That principle is encapsulated in a celebrated remark attributed to Voltaire: "I may not agree with what you say but I will defend to the death your right to say it." In an open society, even beliefs regarded by some as "irrational" need to be tolerated. Why? Because of the inherent dignity of the human persons holding those ideas. We need a free marketplace of ideas, not a society where some ideas (religious ones, for example) are given such second-class status that actions dependent on them are per se removed from legal protection—even when their alleged harm to the society cannot be demonstrated. Today, in certain European states, one can be jailed for unpopular ideas (holocaust revisionism, for example); such obnoxious notions ought to be refuted in the public marketplace of ideas, not repressed by law. Religious beliefs, even those we disagree with, need to expressed—and practiced—in an open society. And, surely, those religious positions with solid, objective evidence in their behalf must not suffer ostracism simply because of their religious label! Otherwise, political correctness will prevail, and political correctness is no less a religion because it does not use that terminology. Indeed, in many ways it is far more dangerous to the public weal than are the religious ideas and practices it endeavours to repress.

29. Christianity's Unique Intellectual Opportunity

There is now an opportunity available to Christians to have an impact on secular society which has been virtually impossible during three centuries of modern secularism.

The 18th century marked the death of special revelation (deistic representatives of the misnamed Age of Reason threw out the Bible's supernatural content, substituted a "God of Nature" for the trinitarian God, and reduced Jesus to an ethical model); the 19th century was characterized by the death of God—including the deists' God of Nature—as evolutionary naturalism replaced divine teleology; and the 20th century has displayed the consequential death of Man (slaughtered by his fellows in numbers exceeding the total of all the fallen in all the prior wars of recorded history).

Why has modern man nonetheless remained committed to secularism? Roger Garaudy helps us toward an answer with his aphorism, "*Nous tous, nous sommes nés vieux*": All of us are born old (i.e., we enter life already weighed down by a heavy load of cultural baggage). For the last century that baggage has consisted especially of the ideas of those Paul Ricoeur has termed the "three modern masters of suspicion": Nietzsche, Marx, and Sigmund Freud, each of whom is now a fallen idol.

Nietzsche gave literary form to the death of God and the possibility (indeed, necessity, in light of His death) of transcending all values. If God is dead, all is permitted. The *Übermensch* ("Superman"), whether a Hitler, a Stalin, or an Amin Dada, can create whatever world he is capable of imposing on others. The results of such a loss of absolute value have been so traumatic that ever since the Nuremberg War Crimes Trials the human rights movement has been searching desperately for a solid basis for inalienable rights. Few today display the naïveté of a recent dating ad from the Washington, D. C., area: "Democrat & Atheist [seeks companion] with comparable values." Nietzsche fell from his pedestal because atheism offers *no* values.

Only six years ago, Marx's ideas dominated half the globe. In November, 1989, that house of cards began to collapse. Ironically, the great strength of Marxism was supposed to be economics, yet it was incipient economic catastrophe, more than any other factor, that led Gorbachev to move away from the planned economy and intervention in other Communist countries, with the consequent disappearance of the Berlin Wall and the Eastern Marxist bloc.

Marx's world view suffered from crippling flaws. The greatest of these was his misreading of human nature: his atheistic materialism led him to believe that by solving man's economic ills a millennial society could be created, and his lack of recognition of original sin resulted in his conviction that man is basically good and needs only to have unjust economic restraints removed to attain perfection. Marxist societies themselves proved both these notions utterly fallacious.

Freud has also lost hieratic status. Our century has been termed the Age of Analysis, owing chiefly to the psychoanalytic dogma that the unconscious (however understood) determines human action: we are motivated other than by factors that we know about, and we require expert therapeutic assistance to understand ourselves, our beliefs, and our actions. God is but a projection of the father-image; salvation lies not in supernatural grace but in psychological technique. To be sure, criticisms of psychoanalytic theory have never been absent (e. g., one thinks of Andrew Salter's *Case Against Psychoanalysis* [1952]), but until very recently these have been seen as little dogs yapping at the feet of a giant.

No longer. Freud's own admission that the most he could do with his patients was to turn neurosis into "common unhappiness" has been confirmed: his own therapeutic labors accomplished little. Frederick Crews has recently pointed up the fundamental unverifiability of the whole Freudian edifice: it is in the final analysis "secure from the menace of rigorous testing." And, logically, if the unconscious is the key to the conscious, requiring expert assistance to reveal the meaning of conscious beliefs and acts, how was the first psychoanalyst (Freud?) ever able to unlock *his* unconscious? This infinite regress can only be broken by assuming that, ultimately, the conscious is capable of making sense of its own thoughts and actions. The *Times Higher Education Supplement*'s psychology and psychiatry number (May 20, 1994) had every reason to declare: "After the ... humbling of Marx, we now have the defenestration of Freud."

And the consequences of all of this? Like the great image in the Book of Daniel, modern secularist thought has been revealed as an idol with clay feet. The crushing burden of modem secular ideology is being lifted from us, like the weight of sin on the back of Bunyan's Pilgrim. The immediate result is an ideological vacuum, and nature abhors all vacuums. If Christians do not fill this one as century 21 comes on, the seven devils of Jesus' parable may well replace the devil who has been cast out. But here lies the challenge and the opportunity: for three centuries no more wondrous door to impact minds and hearts with Christ's message has been opened to God's people.

Part Ten
A Mini-Encyclopedia

1. Law

*Grammar**

What is "law"? You have certainly heard of the law of gravity and are acquainted with the law the policeman enforces when he stops the motorist (you?) for speeding. How do these different kinds of law connect with each other? And is there a deeper meaning to the notion of law in general?

All law—whether physical law or societal law—involves two elements: order and compulsion. We can see this if we consider the major varieties of law: scientific law, custom, moral law, and juridical law.

Scientific law involves finding regularities in nature. We observe the world, see patterns, and then attempt to describe them in general terms. Our first attempts are often called "hypotheses." We then test those hypotheses by examining more and perhaps better data; this results, perhaps, in a rejection of our initial explanation, or, if we are on the right track, in a refining of our hypothesis. Such refinements raise our hypotheses to the level of a "theory." Finally, if our theory holds up under even more and better investigations of the physical world, and there appears to be no evidence contradicting it, we may be able to present the result as a scientific law.

Scientific laws describe regularities in the physical universe. They also—and inevitably—entail sanctions, that is to say, negative consequences if we disregard or violate them. The law of gravity, for example, tells us that on this planet all physical objects fall toward the center of the earth and that they do this in accord with a strict mathematical formula. If you try to defy the law of gravity—by attempting to fly from the roof of your house without benefit of aircraft, for example—the sanction is that you will break a leg (if not worse).

Customs are part of every society. They are regular, widely accepted social patterns, and disregarding them can result in ostracism. For example, if you insist on wearing a swimsuit to a wedding, you will not be invited to other weddings—and maybe people will hesitate to invite you out at all!

Moral law is often confused with custom (Latin, *mores*). But moral law cuts much deeper. To treat shabbily a person weaker than oneself or to take advantage of someone who cannot protect himself or herself will be considered far more serious than not wearing the right clothes at a social occasion. The

---

*This article on the nature of Law is organised in three sections, corresponding to the classical school curriculum, which was divided into three progressive levels: Grammar, Logic (or Dialectic), and Rhetoric.

treatment of Jews by the Nazis during the Second World War is regarded almost universally today as heinous—as deserving ethical condemnation and the severest of societal punishments. When immoral acts are committed and someone "gets away with it," people often say, "There ought to be a law!" But often there are no laws to cover such acts, and many immoral actions (such as lying, unkindness, selfish use of family property, hurtful treatment of friends) cannot be effectively treated by the state. One comes to see that moral law has a transcendent dimension—that is, it touches matters so fundamental that without a Last Judgment to punish the disregard of it, the universe would be inherently immoral and irrational.

Finally, we come to the law of the land—juridical law. This is the law that is enforced not by social ostracism (as is custom) or by moral opprobrium (as is the moral law), but by state sanctions. Most modern nations have legal systems that distinguish civil law and criminal law. Civil law attaches penalties (generally money payments or injunctions forcing people to do what they should) to acts which cause quantifiable or objectively provable harm to others. Criminal law deals with those far more serious acts which are inherently harmful to the society as a whole (homicide, physical attacks, stealing, corruption, etc.), and attaches much more serious penalties to their commission (incarceration and sometimes even the death penalty).

Juridical law comes about through the passing of general laws and regulations by legislatures, reinforced by the decisions of judges in particular cases. Constitutions set forth fundamental law, thereby restraining legislators from passing laws which would go against the general will of the people.

Like the moral law, juridical law has a transcendent dimension. This is reflected in the building of courthouses (often, as in the case of the Royal Courts of Justice in London, England, they are styled like cathedrals), in the robes worn by judges, and in the formal, often majestic style of courtroom proceedings. When the death penalty was still imposed in England, the judge would don a black cap in pronouncing the fateful sentence. Again, one inevitably thinks in terms of Last Judgment. People often say that a murderer who has not been found guilty—who has "gotten off" because of a legal technicality—won't get away with it when he stands before the bar of God's justice on the Last Day.

If we focus our attention on juridical law, what are the major issues we should consider? Three very important problem areas are the connection between law and morality, legal reasoning, and how law can be justified.

1) How does morality relate to juridical law? As we have seen, they are certainly not the same thing. There are laws having a very minor moral element—for example, the rule that one must drive on the right-hand side of the road (in the British Isles and former British colonies, one drives on the left-hand

side of the road). There are also many immoral acts that cannot effectively be punished by the juridical law—especially subjective immoralities such as envy and covetousness, but also instances where a greater evil would be produced by legal action, such as allowing forced confessions or tainted evidence to be used against the accused.

But clearly law and morality are interrelated. One of the major purposes of the law is to make sure that a decent society is maintained. This immediately raises the issue for the Christian believer of the extent to which Christians should "enforce morality" through legislation. This was the subject of an important controversy in England some years ago—the so-called Hart-Devlin debate. H. L. A. Hart, an eminent philosopher of law at Oxford, argued that one should not attempt to enforce morals, whilst Lord Devlin maintained that doing so is quite legitimate, indeed, inevitable. The concrete issue in that debate was homosexuality—should it be criminalized?

Here is a suggested approach; think about it and come to your own conclusion. The moral laws of the Bible are absolute, since they come from the God of the universe who has created mankind. But we live in a fallen world, where everyone desperately needs to receive the gospel of Jesus Christ for eternal salvation. Therefore, we should do all that we can to promote biblical morality through the law—as long as by doing so we don't so alienate the unbeliever that he or she will no longer listen to the gospel. In practice, this will mean that we will not create "Christian coalitions" to force Sunday closing laws on the community where this would drive the non-Christian to the view that we are trying to ram our Christian beliefs down the throats of those who are not themselves believers.

The sole exception to this approach might well be in the area of right-to-life. We would not want to hold the unborn hostage to the possibility of successfully evangelizing the pro-choicer—any more than during the Third Reich Christians would have been right not to oppose the death camps on the ground that to do so might have been to offend Nazis and reduce the effectiveness of evangelism to them! But short of right-to-life, evangelism should trump efforts at moral improvement. After all, our Lord's "Great Commission" to the church, was "Go and preach the gospel to every creature"—not "Be sure to raise the moral tone of society"!

2) How do lawyers and judges reason? Answer: just like scientists or historians—or anyone else who uses one's head. That is to say, the lawyer or judge collects facts (the facts bearing on the case and the record of similar and relevant past cases), creates the best theory or argument to account for those facts and their legal implications, and then sets forth a reasoned conclusion. Analytical philosophers Ludwig Wittgenstein and Karl Popper employed a very effective

analogy for this process: the shoe and the foot. The "foot" is the factual situation; what we try to do in science, history, law, or ordinary life is to develop an explanation which, like a good shoe, will exactly "fit" that situation. We don't want explanations that so pinch the facts that they distort them; nor do we want explanations so general and vague that they would fit any facts.

To be sure, the law has special reasoning techniques appropriate to the nature of legal procedure. Thus, evidence will be excluded if it is so prejudicial that it would inflame the jury and keep them from coming to a balanced, reasonable conclusion. Precise "standards of proof" are set forth—a "preponderance" of evidence (51%) to win in a civil case, but "proof to a moral certainty, beyond reasonable doubt" to convict in a criminal case, where the consequences are so much more severe.

Fascinatingly, these high standards of legal evidence have been employed by legally trained Christian apologists to show the soundness of the case for the reliability of the gospel records and the facticity of the resurrection of Jesus Christ; we shall have more to say about this below.

3) How can law—legal rules—be justified? The problem here is that if laws are merely relative—like customs—then why should one obey them if one can get away with not doing so? To be effective and enforceable, laws must have an authority beyond the changing mores of society. And where constitutional principles are involved, we must somehow reach the level of what the Declaration of Independence termed "inalienable rights"—legal standards so immutable that no one has the right to change them.

Secular philosophers of law have tried very hard to find and justify such standards. Probably the most influential attempts have been the natural law and the neo-Kantian approaches. Let's look at both of these very briefly.

Natural law thinkers have argued that everyone has built-in moral standards—therefore we naturally know what should be legally accepted and what should be rejected. In consequence, we are told that law can appeal to undeniable universal standards.

Modern secular philosophy of law has been deeply influenced by the ethical thought of 18th-century rationalist philosopher Immanuel Kant. Kant did not believe that one could prove God's existence but he did believe an absolute ethical principle could be set forth. He called it the "categorical imperative": so act that your action can become a universal rule. In the 20th century, a major political philosopher (John Rawls) and a major philosopher of law (Alan Gewirth) have used this Kantian approach to try to justify law.

Rawls suggests that if, hypothetically, people were placed under a "veil of ignorance"—so that they did not know anything about their particular advantages over against other people—they would logically and inevitably arrive at a society built upon two "principles of justice" entailing civil liberties and an economic and social life which would benefit the least advantaged. Gewirth claims that since every human being is a "purposive agent," each of us must make "freedom and well-being" available to others, not just to oneself. We must not base our personal freedom (civil liberties) and well-being (social and economic rights) on any special characteristic we may possess—our race, our wealth, our social position, our family background—but only on the humanity we share with everyone else, i.e., our common characteristic of being "purposive agents." For Rawls and Gewirth, then, fundamental civil and social rights can be justified on a purely secular, humanistic basis.

Let us analyze these philosophies in our next section.

Dialectic

What is the problem with secular attempts to provide a basis for law? The fundamental difficulty is illustrated by the two positions we have just been describing.

Secular natural law. Natural law thinking may seem like a viewpoint consistent with biblical revelation. After all, does not the Apostle Paul say in Romans 1 that God's law is "written on our hearts"? Yes, he does, but he follows this with the condemnation of the entire human race—Jew and Gentile alike—for having consistently violated that law: "All have sinned and come short of the glory of God" (Romans 3:23).

The problem with secular natural law theory in a fallen world is threefold: (1) It assumes that everyone will agree on moral and legal standards, but, obviously, people don't: there are great differences in moral standards and legal rules across the globe. (2) Even if everyone agreed, that would not necessarily mean that what was agreed upon was right. *Consensus gentium*—the agreement of the peoples—is not a sufficient test of truth (and, indeed constitutes a logical fallacy when so used—"Fifty million Frenchmen can be wrong"). (3) To arrive at any kind of commonality of standards, the natural law rules have to be stated in so general a way that they can mean almost anything and are capable of being applied in almost any direction—including frightening ones. Example: the great principle of classical natural law (in the *Digest* of the 6th-century Justinian's Code) that "each person should get what he deserves" was placed in German translation *(Jedem das Seine)* by the Nazis on the gate leading into the Buchenwald death camp.

The great Christian legal thinkers, such as Sir William Blackstone, have stressed that a special revelation (Holy Scripture) is absolutely essential to show a sinful and fallen humanity which "writing on the human heart" comes from God and which from self-interest. Jiminy Cricket's philosophy of "let your conscience be your guide" is naïve at best, highly dangerous at worst.

Neo-Kantian approaches. Kant's categorical imperative sounds a bit like the Golden Rule. But Jesus never used it as a rationalistic principle — as an argument to explain societal action. Rather, Jesus employs the principle of "doing unto others as you would have them do unto you" to show us how far our actions deviate from God's standard as to the way we should be treating others. (Like everything in the Sermon on the Mount — summed up in the command, "Be ye therefore perfect, even as your heavenly Father is perfect" — the object is to show us how desperately we need Jesus' sacrifice on the cross for our sins.)

Rawls and Gewirth hypothesize a situation in which people act rationally without any regard for their own advantages. This, however, is hopelessly unrealistic. In fact, people always take into account their own strengths — and the weaknesses of others — in their actions. Rawls and Gewirth, like their mentor Kant, have no serious awareness of sin — of the radical self-centeredness of a fallen race.

Suppose we were to try to convince, let us say, Ghengis Khan, to institute a proper legal system — one involving civil liberties and socio-economic equality. We might say to Ghengis: "Ghengis, have you been out raping and pillaging again?" Reply: "Well, yes. Frankly, I enjoy raping and pillaging." "But Ghengis, you should be acting so that your action could become a universal rule! You should be thinking in terms of just legality — civil and social rights — for everyone, not just your own interests. How would you like it if others treated you as you are treating them? You should be thinking in terms of a universal rule of law!" Ghengis: "GRRRHH! Listen up! I happen to be bigger and stronger than they are. There is no chance that they could get away with raping or pillaging me."

The point here is that in a fallen world, even if people will admit a rational principle (such as the categorical imperative), this in no way ensures that they will follow it.

Fallen creatures are perfectly happy with a rule of law for their own protection; but they invariably balk when attempts are made to apply legal standards to their personal disadvantage. Think of the popular legal area of human rights: everyone favors them — including the worst dictators — but human rights are invariably interpreted to protect the political interest group or dictator, and disregarded when to do so is to the advantage of that state or individual.

The problem with all secular efforts to justify law is that, arising from human sources — and sinful, self-centered sources at that — they cannot possibly arrive at the absolute ethical principles needed to ground legal systems.

Water doesn't rise above its own level. Remember Archimedes? Said he, "Give me a lever long enough and a fulcrum outside the world, and I shall move it." This is sound physics—and an equally sound ethical and legal principle. The necessary condition for moving the world is that the fulcrum lie outside it; otherwise, one is trying to pull oneself up by one's own bootstraps—and a painful fall is inevitable! To arrive at the needed absolute principles to ground a legal system, one needs a source outside the world—a source uncontaminated by the sinful and finite human condition.

Two thinkers have seen this clearly, though they were not themselves believers. Jean-Jacques Rousseau, in his *Social Contract*, wrote: "It would take gods to give men laws." And Ludwig Wittgenstein asserted: "The sense of the world must lie outside the world. ... Ethics is transcendental"—explaining this by saying, "I can only describe my feeling by the metaphor, that, if a man could write a book on Ethics which really was a book on Ethics, this book would, with an explosion, destroy all the other books in the world."

That book, of course, is the Holy Scriptures. In the inerrant word of God, one finds the absolute principles capable of providing a sound foundation for human legal systems. These principles are absolute—inalienable—because they have been revealed by a God who is the only source of the absolute and the inalienable. Moreover, the Bible gives a fallen race not only the legal principles it so desperately needs as the criterion for identifying the proper content of the law written on the heart, but also the solution to fallen mankind's self-centeredness: the cross of Christ as the way of redemption and a new life in which one will indeed "love one's neighbor as oneself" and seek to establish and implement legal systems reflecting God's standards.

One might, of course, raise the question as to the effectiveness and the application of such biblical standards in our modern secular, pluralistic world. We have already noted that morality (including biblical standards) must not be forced on a non-Christian society so as to reduce the effectiveness of evangelism to that society. But in our culture, impregnated as it has been with the western Christian tradition, the unbeliever is "living off the inherited capital" of biblical morality. He or she can then be appealed to on the basis of that morality and legal perspective. "Surely," we can argue, "you want your children not to be impacted by internet porn—or suffer the psychological miseries of abortion—or lose the opportunity for a decent marriage as a result of a redefinition of it to include homosexual unions?" Common ground arguments of this kind can persuade the unbeliever to move in the direction of biblical morality and biblically based legislation without imperiling evangelism.

Rhetorical Response

How can one personally respond to the issues in this vital area of legal thinking? Let us consider a number of possibilities.

The biblical aspect. We have argued that only Holy Scripture can serve as a proper foundation for law, since only the Bible is a transcendent book capable of providing absolute principles — principles uncontaminated by the sinful and limited human perspective.

Fine. But this will hardly work if you yourself do not know the Scriptures. Are you well enough acquainted with the actual content of biblical revelation to know what its fundamental principles are? This, of course, is a lifetime task. But why not start now? Plan to read the Bible through, say, every three years. Take good courses on particular books of the Bible. There are fine correspondence courses available (for example, from the Moody Bible Institute in Chicago). Consider the possibility of going to a Bible school for a year after high school — especially if you are planning to attend a secular university.

And there is the problem of "rightly dividing" the word of God, that is to say, properly interpreting it. In the history of the church, even those who have been convinced of the total truth of the Bible have sometimes interpreted it in a manner that has badly hurt its message and impact.

For example, there is the viewpoint that all proper law is given in Scripture and that we should not be allowed to do anything that is not expressly commanded in the Bible. On this basis, during the Commonwealth period in England (17th century), people were fined for celebrating Christmas — since nowhere in the Bible is it commanded to keep that holiday! To be sure, the proper approach is that we are allowed by God to do whatever is not condemned in Scripture. The Bible is not an "Encyclopedia Britannica," giving all possible information and specific rules for all particular actions. We are expected to use the heads God has placed on our shoulders to handle particular issues. Just as the Bible does not provide rules for television repair, so it does not set out statutes for promissory notes or traffic safety. We are to employ sanctified common sense, through the guidance of the Holy Spirit, in drafting our laws and choosing our actions in a manner that will maximally glorify the Christ who has died for us.

Moreover, one must face the question of the relationship between the Old Testament and the New. There are Christians who have thought that the entire Old Testament law is (or should be) applied today. These folk have wanted to legislate the levitical law — much as orthodox Jews try to do. One of them has actually said that it would be desirable today to stone prostitutes and kill children who will not obey their parents. You need to understand that whilst the moral law of the Old Testament is permanently applicable, the civil and ceremonial law of ancient Israel definitely is not. That law, unique to the preservation of the nation Israel as the cradle for Messiah's coming, was abrogated by its fulfillment in our Lord's advent, as is plain from the Apostles' refusal in the New Testament to require circumcision of gentile converts. Occasionally it may be difficult to draw the line between Old Testament moral law on the one hand and the civil and ceremonial law on the other, but the critical importance of the distinction remains nonetheless.

Going further, one needs to understand what Luther termed "the proper distinction between law and gospel." He declared that "the true doctor of theology is the person who can properly distinguish law from gospel." What did he mean? Luther was referring to the two great doctrinal themes that run through the entire Bible. He was not suggesting, as some have thought, that one can divide the Bible into law, equivalent to the Old Testament, and gospel, equivalent to the New Testament! In point of fact, law and gospel are inherent to both Testaments. Law, in the theological sense, refers to what we do in response to God's commands; gospel, on the other hand, describes what God does for us to save us. Grave problems arise whenever law and gospel are confused. When gospel is turned into law, people try to save themselves by their own moral and law-abiding efforts. (Haven't you heard a non-Christian say, "I don't need salvation—I've led a good moral life—never been in jail"?) When law is turned into gospel, people and societies become unaware of their sin and think that God is a Santa Claus who saves them—maybe everybody—without there being any moral or legal standards at all. Theologian Dietrich Bonhoeffer called this the notion of "cheap grace."

The Reformers distinguished three main "uses" of the law—meaning the functions of the revealed law in the Bible as well as the functions of human legislation. The first use of all law is *political*—the law which structures sinful society and keeps us from eating each other! The second use is the *pedagogical* use—the "law as a schoolmaster [Greek, *paidagogos*] to bring us to Christ" (Galatians 3:24). This is—for Luther—the most important of the three uses, for it points up the fact that all law, biblical and juridical, if taken seriously, demonstrates that our fallen race does not conform to God's standards—or even to the human ideals it sets for itself—and therefore needs the salvation provided by Christ alone. (Incidentally, in classical times the *paidagogos* was not the teacher, but the mere slave who brought the child to the teacher! This is what the law properly does: it drives us to the cross by showing us how far short we fall from divine standards.) Christ interiorized the Old Testament law, making it even more stringent—leaving no one without excuse: "Has it been said of old time, thou shalt not kill? I say unto you, he who hates his brother has already committed murder in his heart"; etc., etc. The third use of the law—unlike the first two—applies only to believers: it is the *sanctifying* use. Only the believer can come to "love God's law" as the expression of his character and will. The unbeliever will always and ever see God's law as a threat—and rightly so—since, as the Reformers put it, *lex semper accusat* ("the law always accuses"). Only at the cross is the law seen as reflecting God's own loving nature, since he was willing to take the hideous violations of it by a fallen race on himself, expiating our sin by the blood of his cross.

These kinds of theological and biblical understandings are essential if one wishes to apply law in the fullest sense to one's personal situation and to the society of which one is a part.

The political aspect. More than a few evangelical Christians have beliefs which reduce the effectiveness of their witness in the political and legal world of our time. You need to engage in self-examination to make sure that you are not unknowingly hurting the cause in this way.

There are evangelicals who hopelessly confuse biblical religion with conservative politics. They may not believe that no Democrats go to heaven, but they would be surprised if the number was very great! As for socialists—*well*, they are surely in outer darkness with gnashing of teeth ...

Now, I have almost always voted Republican, and I certainly believe that "the best government is the government that governs least" (I'm for less government, rather than more). But this is a far cry from being an anarchist (no government at all) or a libertarian (who may not even want the state to license doctors or lawyers). The facts are that Holy Scripture does not mandate any single form of government and, since original sin is universal, there is no assurance that either Democrats or Republicans will always be right! In some situations, government should stay out of things; in others, government intervention and an increase in legislation can be badly needed. The point is that each policy and each piece of proposed legislation and each legal case needs to be evaluated as such—by biblical standards. Sometimes the "conservatives" will be right; sometimes the political "liberals" will be right. We must not become doctrinaire, lock-step rightists who refuse to "test the spirits" on an issue-by-issue, case-by-case basis.

The same point needs to be made in regard to "Americanism." There are Bible believers among us who give the impression that the American constitutional documents are a kind of infallible extension of Holy Scripture, and that the founding fathers of our country were all saints. Theologically and historically, this is simply not correct. We are blessed with a constitutional and legal system deeply impregnated with biblical ideals, but this is not to say that ours is in fact a Christian nation. No country is. The kingdoms of this world will all pass away one day and will be replaced by "the kingdom of our God and of his Christ." Just as in the case of conservative vs. liberal, so in our beliefs concerning our own nation, we need to place everything under the authority of the Holy Scriptures—meaning that we need to judge our country's actions (not just the actions of other nations) by God's eternal standards as set forth in his holy word. Often our nation will show itself a beacon light in a dark world; at other times we may need to speak prophetically to its leaders, its legislators, and its judges.

This brings us the matter of international law. Some evangelicals seem to think that there is sometimes inherently demonic about things international. Is international law always bad—always worse than our national law? True, there is often less direct accountability to legislatures in the case of international law. But here's a sobering example: The American Convention (=Treaty) on Human Rights, ratified by most of the countries on the American continent—but not by the United States—protects the right to life "from the moment of conception." Why has the U.S. Senate not ratified this treaty? Because, were it to do so, the U.S. would immediately be brought before the Inter-American Court of Human Rights for violating the treaty owing to our federal law (*Roe v Wade*), which allows abortion on demand during the first trimester of pregnancy. Here, again, the issue is not whether something is national (supposedly always good) or international (supposedly always bad). National law as well as international law needs to be evaluated by biblical criteria, and there is no guarantee that the one will always be right or the other always wrong.

Only God's word "lasts forever."

The professional aspect. Do you really want to move your country and your world in a more biblical direction? Here are some suggestions.

First, analyze why things are a mess (or, at least, why they aren't better than they are). The reason will not be because your favorite candidate didn't get elected or your favorite law did not get enacted—or because someone on the U.S. Supreme Court didn't get a fatal heart attack.

The fundamental problem will turn out to be much more profound than that, involving such considerations as the perspective of the citizenry (in the recent national election, wasn't economics more important—right across the country—than right-to-life?). How could such a perspective be changed for the better?

Answer: by influencing the climate of opinion. And how is this done? Let's begin by noting how it won't be done. It will not be accomplished by the typical evangelical style of separating oneself from the society. We have tended to take the approach, "if we can't beat 'em, we'll separate from 'em." We go to isolated, non-denominational churches; we build our Bible schools and Christian colleges in the middle of nowhere (so that we won't be contaminated by secular society); we avoid the social atmosphere and recreational activities of "the world"; etc., etc. Result: though we have the eternal gospel in our hearts (and, hopefully, also in our heads), the non-Christian never hears it—for we are simply not on his or her planet. We need to be like our Lord and like his Apostles: "in the world, but not of it."

The Apostles, it is seldom noted, focused their evangelism in the cities—at the centers of political and cultural influence in their day. They expected, quite rightly, that the gospel would spread from there into the hinterlands. We, however, often do the very opposite: we go out into the bush, as far as possible from the "pagan" centers of our society, and hope that the gospel will somehow trickle to the points of power. Sadly, it seldom works that way. One might think that we are more concerned with our own spiritual health—our personal sanctification—rather than the needs of a dying world.

Practically speaking, why not think of going to a Christian college having the goal of impacting the political and legal climate for Christ? They are rarer than the proverbial hen's teeth, but they exist. Or why not go to a fine secular university—one with a strong Christian student work on campus so that you can maintain solid Christian fellowship whilst presenting the eternal gospel of salvation to those who might never hear it otherwise?

Of course, to do the latter, you need to know how to defend the faith—how to present the powerful evidence in its behalf and show the fallacies of the views that contradict it. This means doing what the Apostle Paul clearly did: learning the views of the non-Christian so as to be able to speak intelligently to them. (In Athens, Paul quoted the Stoic poet-philosophers to move the Stoics away from their "unknown god" to Jesus Christ; Paul hadn't studied Stoicism in his rabbinic education—he'd gone to the trouble of learning it because he wanted to reach the Stoics for Christ.) Start, therefore, studying apologetics now. In a secular society, wherever you go to college, you'll need to follow the Apostle Peter's instruction to "be ready always to give an answer [Greek, *apologia*] for the hope within you."

Fascinatingly, as we alluded to earlier, many great lawyers have examined the case for Christianity using the rigorous standards of legal evidence—and have ended up as Christian believers. Here are but three examples: Theophilus Parsons, 19th-century chief justice of the Massachusetts Supreme Court, who declared: "I examined the proofs and weighed the objections to Christianity many years ago, with the accuracy of a lawyer; and the result was so entire a conviction of its truth, that I have only to regret that my belief has not more completely influenced my conduct." Professor Simon Greenleaf of Harvard, the greatest 19th-century authority on the law of evidence, and author of *The Testimony of the Evangelists*, showing that the four Gospels would be accepted in any common law court as solid evidence for the life and divine claims of Jesus Christ. Sir Norman Anderson, late head of the School of Advanced Legal Studies at the University of London, and the greatest non-Muslim specialist of his generation on Muslim law—who wrote several books defending Christian truth, including a treatise entitled, *The Evidence for the Resurrection*.

Here apologetics and law come together—and this is highly significant, since the law deals with the most serious evidential issues in society, those on which life and death depend. The "ancient documents rule" will allow the New Testament books to be admitted into evidence. Examining the witnesses to Jesus Christ in those sound historical documents will show them to be reliable. Thus, if one subjects them to "internal" and "external" juridical examination, one can say that the witnesses had no reason to present anything other than the truth about Jesus' life and ministry; and if one looks, again "internally" and "externally," at what they wrote, one finds the four Gospels to present what one would expect of four witnesses to the same event describing it from their own personal angles—in harmony but not collusively; and the archeological confirmations of the New Testament during the last century and a half have supported again and again the veracity of the documentary material. And it is well worth emphasizing that if the disciples had tried to introduce a false or skewed picture of Jesus' ministry, or of the Old Testament prophecies he fulfilled, they could hardly have gotten away with it: the Jewish religious leaders had "the means, the motive, and the opportunity" (as lawyers put it) to refute any such false claims, since the events of Jesus' life took place in full public view. The great New Testament scholar F. F. Bruce has observed that the presence of these hostile witnesses is the functional equivalent of cross-examination in a court of law.

As for the central attestation of the truth of Jesus' claims, his resurrection from the dead, we have the powerful legal argument of Frank Morison, in his book, *Who Moved the Stone?*, that if one doesn't accept the miraculous resurrection, one has to explain the missing body: the Romans and the Jewish religious leaders would hardly have stolen it (it was, to use the technical legal term, "against their interest") and the disciples would certainly not have stolen it and then died for what they knew to be untrue. As the juridical phrase has it, *res ipsa loquitur* ("the thing speaks for itself"). And when unbelievers claim that one can't prove a unique event like the resurrection, we have the devastating rebuttal of Thomas Sherlock, master (chief pastor) of the barristers' Temple Church in London, who noted that a resurrection is simply a person dead at point A and alive again at point B; granted that in our experience, people are alive at point A and dead at point B—but the evidential problem is identical in both instances: we certainly know the difference between a dead man and a live one (eating fish, for example, means the person is alive—as Jesus was when, after Easter morning, he ate fish with his disciples on the road to Emmaus).

So the answer is to learn to present and defend the gospel effectively. This is not just an option; it is a spiritual duty in the secular world in which we live. Legal skills can offer much assistance in this regard. And getting our own legal philosophy straightened out is equally vital. After all, when we witness to unbelievers, we must be able to point them to the proper distinction between law and gospel—which will occur only if we have reached the point of making that vital distinction ourselves!

Luther noted that the way to change society is to "become a little Christ to your neighbor." What we really need is more Christians per cubic inch. Can you imagine the effect of just one more solid Christian believer teaching a critical course at Harvard? Serving in the Senate? Having the role of American ambassador to the United Nations? Sitting as a U.S. Supreme Court justice—or acting in the capacity of judge or lawyer in your community?

Why not aim high? Maybe the way you can impact the law is by making a career of it. Law school isn't easy, but there is no reason why you can't handle it. And if the Lord is leading you in some other direction, aim high there too. Scripture tells us that "he who is within you is more powerful than he who is against you." If you believe that, act on it.

Bibliography. C. J. Friedrich, *The Philosophy of Law in Historical Perspective* (2^d ed.; Chicago: University of Chicago Press, 1963); I. H. Linton, *A Lawyer Examines the Bible* (Boston: W. A. Wilde, 1943); J. W. Montgomery, *The Law Above the Law* (Minneapolis: Bethany, 1975) [includes Simon Greenleaf's *Testimony of the Evangelists*]; J. W. Montgomery, *Human Rights and Human Dignity* (2^d ed.; Calgary, Alberta, Canada: Canadian Institute for Law, Theology and Public Policy, 1995); J. W. Montgomery, *The Shaping of America* (Minneapolis: Bethany, 1976); C. F. W. Walther, *The Proper Distinction between Law and Gospel* (Saint Louis, MO: Concordia Publishing House, 1986).

2. Human Rights

The modern human rights movement is generally considered to have arisen following the Nuremberg war crimes trials at the end of World War II. The horrors of the Nazi atrocities led to the United Nations' Universal Declaration of Human Rights and the creation of the European Court of Human Rights in Strasbourg, France, to implement the European Declaration of Human Rights;

the latter became the model for the American Declaration on Human Rights and the corresponding American system of human rights protection with its Inter-American Court sitting in Costa Rica.

But modern human rights did not arise *ex nihilo*. The concept of fundamental civil liberties can be found in the revolutionary instruments of the 18th century: the American Declaration of Independence and the French Declaration of the Rights of Man. These, in turn, were directly influenced by biblical values imparted to Western civilisation by the Judeo-Christian tradition. In a very real sense, the modern—and generally secular—human rights movement is living off the inherited capital of biblical faith.

We shall briefly consider (1) the nature of human rights, (2) philosophical attempts to justify human rights, (3) human rights in non-Christian religions, (4) Christianity and human rights.

(1) The Nature of Human Rights. Rights must be distinguished from *wants* and from *needs*. The fact that I want something (a vacation in Tahiti) does not mean that I have a right to it. And my needing something (a higher salary) does not *per se* indicate that I have a right to receive it.

Such considerations lead inevitably to the question of the source and justification of rights. Are they universal and inalienable—or are they culture-bound and changeable? Human rights theorists in non-Western nations have argued that the emphasis on civil liberties in the West should not be applied to societies such as theirs where social and economic inequalities need to trump civil liberties at least until those parts of the world attain the quality of life represented by Western nations. The problem with such a relativistic view of human rights is that it allows each nation, region, or culture to justify its treatment of people according to its own standards. But wasn't this exactly the argument of the Nazi leaders at Nuremberg—that their philosophy of Aryan supremacy should not be criticised by the victors, whose view of human dignity (including the dignity of Jews) was different from their own?

The American Declaration of Independence was therefore quite right in calling for "inalienable rights"—rights which are inherent to the human person and which no one (including the individual himself or herself) has the right to remove or curtail. The question then becomes: where can such rights be found and how can they be justified?

(2) Philosophical Justifications of Human Rights. The most influential philosophical attempts to justify human rights have come from (a) the *natural law* tradition and, in modern times, from (b) *Marxist theory* (the communist East) and from (c) *thinkers influenced by the ethical views of Immanuel Kant* (the capitalist West).

(a) Natural law.

Natural law theory, which can be traced back to Greco-Roman times, maintains that there is a higher law, a standard, which is built into human nature and which defines the content of human rights. The 6th century Justinian Code gives the following classic formulation: "to live honestly, harm no one, and make sure that each person gets what he properly deserves." The difficulties with this view are manifold. First, its vagueness: The third element in the Justinian definition (in German, *Jedem das Seine*) was posted at the entrance of the death camp at Buchenwald! And what, exactly, does living honestly mean? What constitutes genuine harm to others? Who should determine this—the actor or the one influenced by his/her action? What is properly "one's own," such that he/she should receive it and not be deprived of it? Secondly, natural law theory suffers from a serious dose of what ethicist G. E. Moore termed "the naturalistic fallacy"—the notion that one can automatically move from the *is* to the *ought*—from description to valuation. The mere fact that many (or even all) people claim a particular right hardly justifies it: fifty million Frenchmen can be wrong. Thirdly, human nature (the alleged fount of natural law values) is not necessarily a positive moral source. Thomas Hobbes (*Leviathan*) described it as "nasty and brutish." The fact is that human beings have a dark side and their affirmations of "natural" human rights are often just a reflection of their personal or corporate self-interest. The worst of modern dictators have given lip service to human rights—but for them this has meant the protection of *their own* rights, not those of others. Christian faith, interestingly enough, recognises that human beings are created in the image of God—but are fallen—and thus that their viewpoints do not necessarily represent God's will. The problem for the natural law advocate is to identify when one is reflecting the image of God and when one is merely acting out of sinful selfishness. In other words, the natural law advocate, before declaring the nature of human rights, must ask: will the *real* human nature please stand up?

(b) Marxist theory.

For the Marxist, human rights depend on social and economic factors: the ultimate source of all violations of human dignity lies in the bad economic conditions to which mankind is subject, and the sole answer to the problem lies in the creation of a society where there is equal ownership of the means of production and the inequities of the capitalist system have been eliminated. The unrealistic nature of this viewpoint became very evident during the existence of the U.S.S.R. and its Marxist satellite states of Eastern Europe: in point of fact, violations of human dignity were endemic in that part of the world. The argument that those states were still at the stage of the dictatorship of the proletariat and had not yet reached the condition of the millennial classless society did not help much—since the classless society had never come about anywhere (doubtless because of the truth of Christian believer Lord Acton's aphorism, "Power tends to corrupt; absolute power corrupts absolutely"). More fundamentally, if economic and social conditions are the source of violations of human dignity, what is the root source of those deadly conditions? They have not been imposed by Martians on the human race; human beings are *themselves* clearly responsible. It follows that Marxism refused to face the fact that human beings—from within themselves—are the cause of rights violations, and that, logically, only a change in human nature could in principle purify the human rights landscape. Absent a doctrine of personal redemption (to which atheistic Marxism could hardly subscribe), Marxist human rights theory was left with no assurance whatever that manipulations or revolutionary alterations in man's external economic environment could ever bring in a perfect society mirroring true human rights.

(c) Kantianisms.

The 18th century German philosopher Immanuel Kant believed that ethics (including what we today term human rights) could be justified on a purely humanistic basis. An absolute ethic followed inexorably from his "categorical imperative": "Act only on that maxim which you can will to be a universal law." This principle of "universalisability" was believed by Kant to be rationally necessary: no action can be justified unless the actor is willing to be subject to the same action carried out toward him by others. Three overarching problems with this philosophy render it impossible as a justification of inalienable rights. First, the actions permitted by the rule remain undefined, so a perverse individual (a sado-masochist, for example) could well be more than happy to have his activities extended to the world's population and be directed back upon himself. Secondly, Ghengis Khan (as representative of the tyrants of this world) would not be persuaded by the categorical imperative to stop raping and pillaging, for he would not agree that he and others are equal members of a common humanity; *they* do not have the strength to rape and pillage *him*, whereas *he* does have the power to treat *them* in such a fashion. Thirdly, Kant's ethical philosophy collapses due to its rationalistic character: he assumes that human beings will view others as the rational equivalent of themselves and will therefore treat them as they would want to be treated. But, apart from a transformation of the selfish nature of man, such an expectation is entirely unrealistic—even if human beings were equal in strength, intelligence, and abilities (which they are not).

John Rawls, the influential political philosopher, has offered by way of 17th-18th century contract theories (Hobbes, Locke, Rousseau) a variant on Kant's ethical approach and applied it to human rights questions. For Rawls, human beings placed under a "veil of ignorance" as to their special advantages will, by rationalistic necessity, arrive at his two fundamental Principles of Justice (embracing civil and social rights) and thus establish a rationally-sound political and legal order. This approach is generalisable on the international human rights scene if *nations* place themselves under a similar veil of ignorance: they will necessarily arrive at the fundamental human rights principles embodied in international instruments such as the Universal Declaration and the European Convention on Human Rights. *However*, the last thing members of a fallen race are going to do is to give up—even theoretically, to say nothing of practically—their special advantages, since it is their personal strengths (over against others) which give them the opportunity to exercise their selfishness. And "even if Rawls's theorem can be established, the self-interested moral skeptic may still decline to make a once-and-for-all commitment, even to a principle chosen from self-interest. Fidelity to principle is not, after all, deducible from bare formal rationality" (Robert Paul Wolff). The root problem with Rawls' rationalism is thus the same as that of his mentor Kant: he assumes that "formal rationality" will yield "fidelity to principle" and other ethical virtues. Sinners have a nasty habit of disregarding virtue, even when it would constitute the rational course of action—and even when it would, in the long run, be in their own best interest.

Alan Gewirth, the legal philosopher, applies Kantian universalisation to ethics and concludes that it provides a solid basis for human rights. He offers the following syllogistic argument:

1. Human beings always act purposively.
2. To act purposively, human beings must have freedom (embracing civil and political rights) and well-being (entailing social and economic rights).
3. They must therefore object to the removal of or the interference with their freedom and well-being by others.
4. The ground of one's freedom and well-being is the mere fact that one is a "prospective personal agent"; that ground does not lie in any special strengths or characteristics one may possess.
5. All prospective personal agents have rights to freedom and well-being; and
6. One ought to act in accord with the generic rights of one's recipients as well as of oneself—thereby establishing the general moral principle:
7. Act in accord with the generic rights of your recipients as well as of yourself.

In respect to crucial consideration (4), Gewirth argues that, were one to reject it and "to insist, instead, that the only reason he has the generic rights is that he has some more restrictive characteristic R [such as] being an American, being a professor, being an *Uebermensch*, being male, being a capitalist or a proletarian, being white, being named 'Wordsworth Donisthorpe,' ... he would then be in the position of saying that if he did not have R, he would not have the generic rights." *Precisely!* This is what a fallen human race always maintains: that one's special advantages, not one's common humanity, justifies one's actions and special treatment. Hegel, for example, asserted that the great men of history are not subject to ordinary moral standards. Our favourite ethical example, Ghengis Khan, will be delighted to point out that his right to do whatever he wishes (raping and pillaging) derives from his personal strength and power, not from any quality of prospective personal agent which he shares with others; and that, had he not such strength and power, he would of course become the object, not the subject, of raping and pillaging. It follows that attempts to justify and strengthen Gewirth's position (e.g., by D. Beyleveld) have not been able successfully to rehabilitate it.

(3) Human Rights in Non-Christian Religions. The failure of philosophical justifications of human rights leads to a consideration of religious answers. Worth examining briefly are (a) Eastern religions and (b) Islam.

(a) The Religions of the East.

Professor Peter Woo ("A Metaphysical Approach to Human Rights from a Chinese Point of View," in Rosenbaum) maintains that the Chinese "were, for a long time, ... strangers to the concepts of human rights. ... In view of the acceptance of universal unity and harmony, the issue of individual rights among men did not take the shape of a problem. ... [Confucianism] was to inculcate the acceptance of fate or of any living conditions, since all forms of revolt were ruled out." After a decade-long frustration with Marxism, novelist Arthur Koestler drank deeply at the founts of Eastern wisdom; his rejection of the Buddhist path (*The Lotus and the Robot*) was due principally to its lack of any clear moral direction, as exemplified by Zen monks who had no difficulty in becoming kamikaze pilots. Francis Schaeffer writes that Christianity stands "in clear distinction, for example, from the Hindu or the Buddhist concept of God. To these gods, everything is the same, so that there is no distinction between good and evil, cruelty and non-cruelty, between tyranny and non-tyranny. In such a setting, speaking of inalienable rights or human rights would be meaningless, because to the Hindu or Buddhist the final reality—their concept of God as the all, the everything—would give no voice, no word, as to why anything is bad; why anything is humanness or anything is lack of humanness. The proof of this is very easy to ascertain. All one has to do is to look at the Hindu situation in India itself with its caste systems. There are no intrinsic human rights" ("Christian Faith and Human Rights," 2 *Simon Greenleaf Law Review* 5 [1982-1983]). Though not a Christian, Ghandi acknowledged that it was the Christian missionaries and not his co-religionists who awakened in him a revulsion for the caste system and for the maltreatment of outcastes. And not a few observers have argued that the Tantristic sacralizing of animal life has been one of the roots of the denigration of human values in the contemporary Western animal rights movement.

(b) Islam.

Muslim scholars have stressed that the Qur'an teaches the right to life, the right to education, the right to work and to form trade unions, and the right to possess property (though only as a steward or life tenant, since Allah alone holds property in fee simple absolute). However, after all that can be said is said along these lines, it is apparent that Islam has some very serious human rights defects. Sir Norman Anderson, late director of the Institute of Advanced Legal Studies at the University of London, notes (in his *The World's Religions*, pp. 82-94) the following doctrinal deficiencies of Islam in the human rights sphere: (1) The "cast-iron view of Predestination," leading to a "fatalism [which] plays a large part in the daily lives of millions of Muslims. To this the lethargy and lack of progress which, until recently at least, has for centuries characterized Muslim countries can be partially attributed." (2) "Islam sanctions slavery and the slave-trade, and the unlimited right of concubinage which a Muslim enjoys with his female slaves.... This extends even to married women captured in war, and opened the door to terrible abuse during the early wars of expansion, when almost any woman in a conquered land could be considered a slave by capture.... The would-be reformer of the position of women finds that polygamy, slave-concubinage, unilateral divorce and the beating of refractory wives is permitted by divine authority." (3) "The last section of the Shari'a deals with 'Punishments' or criminal sanctions. These provide, *inter alia*, for the murderer to be executed by the family of his victim; for one who causes physical ijury to another to be submitted to the like; for the thief to have his right hand cut off; and for the adulterer to be stoned and the fornicator beaten." (4) Though the UN Universal Declaration of Human Rights has been "approved by all Muslim states, except Sa'udi Arabia and the Yemen, which are members of the United Nations Organization, yet the clause which affirms a man's right to change his religion if he so wishes runs directly counter both to the Islamic law of apostasy and to the practice of most of the Muslim states concerned."

Of course, the most serious problem with such religious human rights positions as those just described is their epistemological failing, namely the impossibility of verifying the revelational truth-claims they make. Why should one regard Confucian, Hindu, Buddhist, or Muslim assertions—in the human rights area or, indeed, in any other sphere—as representing the divinely-approved? In the case of Eastern religions, they claim to be self-validating experientially, but, as philosopher Kai Nielsen has shown, "faith" is incapable of "validating God-talk." Islam declares that Muhammed is the unique and final prophet of God and that the Qur'an is in every respect God's revelation of divine truth; but a claim is surely not equivalent to a proof. But without a solid basis for accepting these religions as veridical, there is no reason to take their human rights positions (or lack of them) as compelling.

(4) Christianity and Human Rights. Historic Christianity has two overarching advantages over its philosophical and religious rivals where human rights are concerned. The first has to do with the matter just alluded to: (a) proving one's absolute claims (and the need for a revelation to supply them); the second concerns (b) the essentiality of changing hearts to achieve human rights ends.

(a) The need for and proof of absolute claims.

Why have the various philosophical endeavours to provide a basis for human rights not been successful? Wittgenstein, in his *Tractatus Logico-Philosophicus* (6.421) and his posthumously published "Lecture on Ethics" (74 *Philosophical Review* [1965]) made this very clear. Said he: "Ethics is transcendental." That is to say, a genuine ethic would have to be an absolute (an inalienable) ethic—true for all times and all places. But no finite person is capable of providing such absolutes, since we are all conditioned and limited by our finitude—by our time and place in history and by our personal and societal deficiencies in the moral realm. It follows that the only possible source of true ethics would be a transcendent, absolute source, i.e., an ethic deriving from an absolute God himself. And to know what that ethic was, there would need to be a verifiable revelation from the God who is the source of ethical absolutes and inalienable rights.

The philosophical positions offering human rights theories do not see that, just as water cannot rise above its own level, so human speculation concerning human rights will never attain inalienable values when its source lies in finite human opinion. And whereas non-Christian religions expect to have their human rights views accepted simply because they assert them, Christianity offers in behalf of its claim that the Bible is indeed God's revelation the historical case for Jesus' as God incarnate by virtue of fulfilled prophecy and his resurrection from the dead.

If this claim holds, then the Bible becomes the source of the absolute ethical principles essential for human rights. These principles, which go far beyond the vagueness of natural law offerings, embrace (1) the Ten Commandments and other permanent moral guidelines in the Old Testament (but not the civil or ceremonial laws of Israel contained therein, since their force ended with the coming of Messiah), and (2) the refinement and interiorisation of the Old Testament moral law as provided by Jesus himself and by the New Testament writers. In Holy Scripture can be found the justification not only for so-called "first generation" human rights (civil and political freedoms) but also for the major "second generation" guarantees (social and economic rights) and even some of the newer rights of the "third generation" (e.g., environmental rights).

(b) Changed hearts.

The philosophical approaches to human rights—as well as the non-Christian religious solutions—never get beyond an attempt to provide prescriptive human rights principles. They do not realise that, even if such inalienable rights were identified (and they have been entirely incapable of providing them), this would in no way guarantee that individuals or societies would follow them. Because of self-interest, deriving from the fallen condition of the human race, people will invariably sacrifice rational, moral conduct and the interests of others in favour of what they believe will benefit themselves. This is the fundamental source of the human rights problem. Biblical revelation declares (and great literature and psychoanalytic study of the human personality confirm) that the fallen creature's fundamental problem is a lack of motivation to do what is right (indeed, a penchant to do what is wrong), even when he or she rationally knows the truth and the difference between right and wrong. In Christianity, uniquely, the right principles are accompanied by a mechanism to change hearts so that one will indeed "love the neighbour as oneself." Christian faith offers not merely the finest moral example—Jesus Christ himself as God incarnate—but also the possibility of redemption and a genuine change of motivation ("conversion") so that Jesus' example and biblical precept can be followed in practice (1 Peter 2:21; John 8:34-36; 2 Corinthians 5:17). The result of this is the potentiality to become, as Luther put it, a "little Christ to one's neighbour." God's grace in Christ thus touches the world at the point of the redeemed sinner and spreads out from him or her to those whose wounds need binding up.

Even after recognising the presence of "hypocrites in the church" and the extent to which self-styled believers and religious "fellow-travellers" have acted inconsistently with the message and principles of Christ (the Inquisition, etc.), there is no doubt whatever that Christianity has been the single most impactive force for human rights the world has ever seen. As Kenneth Scott Latourette rightly argued, in his *History of the Expansion of Christianity*, the empirical evidence shows that Christians have been more responsible for ameliorating social evils than has any other group in human history. Christians have motivated, *inter alia*, the first orphans' homes and hospices, the Red Cross, the abolition of slavery, the elevation of women, charity in general, literacy and public education, the common and civil law traditions, and the modern university—and such a list is by no means exclusive (A. J. Schmidt; R. Stark). Malcolm Muggeridge had every right to make the rhetorical comment, "I have yet to find a Unitarian leper colony."

Christian thinkers have been at the forefront of the human rights debates focusing on medical issues (abortion, euthanasia, genetic manipulation). Because Holy Scripture values life from the moment of conception and places the end of life in the hands of the God who gave it, the historic churches have insisted on applying the most fundamental of all human rights, the Right to Life, to the protection of the unborn and those at the end of their earthly existence who are incapable of protecting themselves. And Christian thought has not tolerated the Marxist and situationist notion that the end justifies the means as it has been employed to justify embryonic stem-cell cloning which requires the sacrifice of unborn human life. Just as in the first centuries of the Christian church's existence, Christian faith prefers to err on the side of life rather than death and to refuse the sacrifice of individual creatures of God to utilitarian social planning.

In short, whether one considers the matter theoretically or practically, transcendent, historic Christian revelation has offered the most attractive (and apparently the only justifiable) case for inalienable human rights and the protection of human beings from the predatory actions of their fellows.

Bibliography. (1) *General:* J. W. Montgomery, *Human Rights and Human Dignity* (2[d] ed.; Alberta, Canada: Canadian Institute for Law, Theology and Public Policy, 1995) [with annotated bibliography and extensive references]; J. W. Montgomery, *The Law Above the Law* (Minneapolis: Bethany, 1975); J. Witte, Jr., and J. D. van der Vyver, eds., *Religious Human Rights in Global Perspective* (2 vols.; The Hague: Martinus Nijhoff, 1996); (2) *Philosophical:* A. S. Rosenbaum, ed., *The Philosophy of Human Rights: International Perspectives* (Westport, CT: Greenwood, 1980); J. W. Montgomery, *Tractatus Logico-Theologicus* (Bonn, Germany: Verlag für Kultur und Wissenschaft, 2004), especially sec. 5; J. W. Montgomery, *The Marxist Approach to Human Rights: Analysis and Critique* (Simon Greenleaf Law Review, 3 [1983-1984]); (3) *Non-Christian Religions:* N. Anderson, *The World's Religions* (3[d] ed.; London: InterVarsity Press,

1955]); J. W. Montgomery, *Giant in Chains: China Today and Tomorrow* (Milton Keynes, England: Nelson Word, 1994); (4) *Christianity:* R. Ruston, *Human Rights and the Image of God* (London: SCM Press, 2004) [strongly influenced by the Roman Catholic natural law tradition]; K. Cronin, *Rights and Christian Ethics* (Cambridge, England: Cambridge University Press, 1992); A. J. Schmidt, *How Christianity Changed the World* (Grand Rapids, MI: Zondervan, 2004); R. Stark, *The Victory of Reason* (New York: Random House, 2006); G. A. Haugen, *Good News About Injustice* (Leicester, England: InterVarsity Press, 1999); J. W. Montgomery, "Slavery, Human Dignity and Human Rights," 79/2 *Evangelical Quarterly* 113-31 (2007) [above, in this volume, Chapter 7:1]; J. W. Montgomery, *Christ Our Advocate* (Bonn: Verlag für Kultur und Wissenschaft, 2002).

3. Blasphemy

Exodus 20:7 declares: "Thou shalt not take the name of the Lord thy God in vain; for the Lord will not hold him guiltless that taketh his name in vain." Blasphemy consists, not in employing crude or scatological language—what the French refer to as *gros mots*—but in violating this biblical Commandment in a particularly egregious manner.

In the 1917 Roman Catholic *Corpus Iuris Canonici,* blasphemy is to be punished according to the decision of the Ordinary (can. 2323). The corresponding section of the 1983 Code consists of canons 1368-1369. Canon 1369 declares: "A person is to be punished with a just penalty, who, at a public event or assembly, or in a published writing, or by otherwise using the means of social communication, utters blasphemy, or gravely harms public morals, or rails at or excites hatred of or contempt for religion or the Church."

Should blasphemy be subject to civil law sanctions? In early American law, this was the case (e.g. by a Virginia statute in 1699), but modernly only English law has continued to criminalize blasphemous words and acts; and on 9 May 2008 this prohibition was abolished when royal assent was given to the new Criminal Justice and Immigration Bill. The most famous successful contemporary prosecution was that in the 1978 *Gay News* case, where that periodical had published a poem of breathtaking offensiveness concerning Jesus (*inter alia*, ascribing to him homosexual practices with the Apostles).

The only contemporary attempts to promote blasphemy regulations in the American context come from the Calvinist Theonomists (also known as Reconstructionists), who would re-establish the civil and criminal laws of Old

Testament Israel. Such a programme falls foul of the Constitutional separation of church and state (the 1st Amendment) and reminds one of countries where Muslim *Shari'a* law is in force, making blasphemy and apostasy capital offenses.

In countries where there is no state church, anti-blasphemy regulations seem to be justifiable only where the speech or acts in question are such as to produce riot and affray; but general criminal laws prohibiting any conduct leading to a breach of the peace would seem to cover such situations in any case. Moreover, proscribing forms of religious speech as such can well pose grave dangers to free expression and therefore to civil liberties in general.

Bibliography. L. W. Levy, *Blasphemy: Verbal Offense Against the Sacred, from Moses to Salman Rushdie* (2d ed.; Chapel Hill: University of North Carolina Press, 1995); D. Nash, *Blasphemy in Modern Britain, 1789 to the Present* (Aldershot: Ashgate, 1999); R. J. Rushdoony, *The Institutes of Biblical Law* (Nutley, N. J.: Presbyterian and Reformed Publishing Co., 1973) [Theonomist]; J. W. Montgomery, "Can Blasphemy Law Be Justified?," in his *Christ Our Advocate* (Bonn: Verlag für Kultur und Wissenschaft, 2002), pp. 133-52.

4. Canon Law

Ecclesiastical or church law, the Greek word "kanôn" signifying a "rule." The development of Canon law in the High Middle Ages (12th through 14th centuries) had tremendous impact on the subsequent history of the Western secular legal tradition. It impacted in particular the spheres of family law (separation and divorce), succession (wills and estates), contract law (the sale of goods), and the criminal law (theft). Indeed, in studies of comparative law today, Canon law is classed, alongside of Roman law, the Anglo-American common law, the European civil law, Jewish law, Muslim law, and Marxist law as one of the most influential legal systems of all time.

Though the Apostles clearly taught that "one is justified by faith without the deeds of the law" (Romans 3:28; cf. Galatians 2:16), the Christian church has never existed without rules. The Acts of the Apostles contains a record of the first church Council (that at Jerusalem, dealing with the circumcision issue—Acts 15). This was followed by others such as Nicaea (325) which condemned the Arian heresy, and Chalcedon (451) which dealt with the two natures of Christ but also legislated on such matters as the necessity for clergy not to take their disputes to the secular courts. Charlemagne, the first of the Holy Roman Emperors, insisted on the circulation of a collection of conciliar decrees.

The most well-developed Canon law system in the West is surely that of the Roman Catholic church, and its character was formed during what historian Charles Homer Haskins well termed "the Renaissance of the 12th century." Beginning with Gratian's *Decretum,* emphasis came to be placed on the interpretation and reconciliation of papal decrees. At that time Canon law gained tremendously in geographical influence and academic importance, especially through the labours of the canonists at the prestigious law faculty of the University at Bologna — Canon law being taught as a discipline separate from Roman law. From the Middle Ages to modern times, editions of the *Corpus iuris canonici* have been produced within the Roman Catholic church, binding the faithful in doctrine and ecclesiastical practice.

The 12th century marked a considerable change in the Church's legal style. The eminent Roman Catholic canonist Stephan Kuttner, in his *Studies in the History of Medieval Canon Law* (Aldershot, U.K.: Variorum, 1990), 9:207-208), speaks disapprovingly of "the transformation from 'sacramental' law": "An unhealthy *imitatio imperii* crept over the conduct of the papal office; an often callous routine turned the delicate instrument of dispensations into a marketable tool for flouting just law. Canon law was ripe for reform on all levels; but the answer of the Church to the challenge of the Reformation remained fragmentary." Peter Shannon, evaluating the Roman Catholic Code of Canon Law in force from 1918 to 1967 (prior to the new Code which grew out of the Second Vatican Council), characterised even that modern formulation as suffering from "a seeming unawareness of basic theology," "an emphasis on centralization rather than subsidiarity," and "an unevangelical over-emphasis on the letter of the law" (8/3 *Concilium* 26-30 [1967]).

It was not strange, therefore, that the Reformation categorically refused to recognise the *Corpus iuris canonici.* Luther symbolically burned a copy of it along with the papal bull excommunicating him, writing in the same year (1520): "Today Canon law is not what is in the books but what is in the sweet will of the pope and his flatterers. ... In the Bible more than enough directions have been penned for our guidance in life. The study of the Canon law only stands in the way of the study of Holy Scripture." Henry VIII abolished the study of Canon law at Oxford and at Cambridge — its not appearing on the English university scene again until the establishment of an LL.M. programme in Canon law at the University of Cardiff in Wales in 1991.

But the Reformers' objection to a traditionalist, papal church government did not mean that mainline Protestant churches jettisoned ecclesiastical law as such: their object was to purify the church's legal structures from structural elements and accretions which, in their view, deviated from biblical teaching. The great 17th-18th century Lutheran legal scholar J. H. Boehmer, for example, produced a 6-volume *Jus ecclesiasticum Protestantium* (1714) which had wide influence. Anglican Canon law, based on the state-church principle, has had an impressive history, reinforced by the fact that the decisions of English ecclesiastical tribunals have the force of civil law.

To be sure, on the contemporary ecclesiastical scene, influenced as it is by invidious situationist oppositions between "love" and "law," there have been some efforts to eliminate legal protections within communities of believers. The Lutheran Church-Missouri Synod, a biblically conservative American church body with considerable international influence, recently abolished its excellent adjudicatory system of church courts, substitutiing a "mediation" approach which leaves local churches, clergy, and laity with little legal protection.

No organisation can exist without principles and structure of some kind—even if they are implicit rather than being embodied in creed or statute. The pietistic "No creed but Christ" hides the fact that even in churches where there are no written standards, there is always a measure of agreement as to who Christ is and what he taught, i.e., an implicit creedal understanding. The same is true in regard to the administrative operations of every church body: even without express rules, some actions are allowable and some are not. Canon law, then, is a way of making what is in any case necessary both sufficiently clear and explicit that it can be understood, appreciated, and corrected when inadequate. As in the secular sphere, the Rule of Law is vital, and the adage that "one is presumed to know the law" has meaning only when the law is clear and accessible. The issue, then, is not whether a church body should have a Canon law; it is, rather, what criteria are proper for establishing and critiquing it. Here, classical Protestantism divides from the rest of Christendom. In the words of the Lutheran *Formula of Concord* (Solid Declaration, Summary Formulation, 9): "God's Word alone is and should remain the only standard and norm of all teachings, and no human being's writings dare be put on a par with it, but everything must be subjected to it."

Bibliography: R. H. Helmholz, *The Spirit of Classical Canon Law* (Athens: University of Georgia Press, 1996); J. W. Montgomery, *Christ Our Advocate* (Bonn: Verlag für Kultur und Wissenschaft, 2002); *Ecclesiastical Law Journal,* Vol. I (1990 to date); R. Jones, *The Canon Law of the Roman Catholic Church and the Church of England* (Edinburgh: T & T Clark, 2000) [a dictionary of terms]; E. Caparros, M. Theriault, J. Thorn, and H. Aube, eds., *Code of Canon Law Annotated* (2^d ed.; Woodridge, IL: Midwest Theological Forum, 2004) [Roman Catholic]; N. Doe, *The Legal Framework of the Church of England* (Oxford: Clarendon Press, 1996); W. J. Henry and W. L. Harris, eds., *Ecclesiastical Law and Rules of Evidence* (Cincinnati, OH: Walden and Stowe, 1881) [Methodist Episcopal]; J. W. Montgomery, "An Invitation to Injustice," *Christian News,* January 18, 1993 and August 27, 2007 [Lutheran].

5. Capital Punishment

Today, this form of punishment is rare in the Western world. The European Convention of Human Rights, to which all States-members of the European Union must subscribe, bans it unqualifiedly, and extradition of criminals to the United States is made contingent on American authorities' covenanting that they will not seek the death penalty for the accused. The U.S. Supreme Court's position today is that the Constitutional prohibition against "cruel and unusual punishment" does not apply to capital punishment *per se*, but only to painful and degrading methods of carrying it out. Considerable pressure, however, is continually being exercised by American opponents of the death penalty, especially in light of the high proportion of executions involving members of minority races and the significant number of miscarriages of justice revealed by DNA testing.

Theologically, conservatives have generally backed the death penalty, whilst liberals have opposed it. The principal arguments in favour of capital punishment are its biblical warrant in the Old Testament and its alleged deterrent effect. However: (1) The death penalty is intimately connected with the internal legislation of Israel under the Old Covenant and, as with the civil and ceremonial laws of the Old Testament in general (created to preserve God's chosen people for the coming of Messiah), it can be regarded as no longer binding under Christ's new dispensation. (2) Capital punishment of course deters the criminal himself from recidivism, but there is no hard evidence that it deters anyone else. When criminals were publicly hanged at Tyburn, cut-pursing (pickpocketing) was a capital offense, but the pickpockets regularly worked the crowds watching the executions. Apparently, owing to the egoism of original sin, the criminal never thinks that he or she will end up caught and executed. Strange to say, conservatives seldom draw the further corollary from the doctrine of human depravity that fallibility and incompetence inevitably result in judicial errors which can hardly be rectified after the death penalty has been carried out.

To be sure, where capital punishment is abolished, it needs to be accompanied by sentences of life imprisonment, often without possibility of parole. Since the cost of execution in the United States is roughly the equivalent of keeping a prisoner in gaol for forty years, there would seem to be no effective economic argument for the exercise of the death penalty.

A further theological point for reflection is based on the general agreement that the church's *raison d'être* is the saving of souls. A live prisoner is at least in principle capable of conversion; a dead one is not.

Bibliography. L. R. Bailey, *Capital Punishment: What the Bible Says* (Nashville, Tenn: Abingdon, 1987); J. J. Megivern, *The Death Penalty: An Historical and Theological Survey* (Mahwah, New Jersey: Paulist Press, 1997); G. C. Hanks, *Against the Death Penalty: Christian and Secular Arguments Against Capital Punishment* (Scottdale, Penn.: Herald Press, 1997). F. E. Zimring, *The Contradictions of American Capital Punishment* (New York: Oxford University Press, 2004); J. D. Carlson, ed., *Religion and the Death Penalty* (Grand Rapids, Mich.: Eerdmans, 2004).

6. Divorce

A contested issue theologically, even though all branches of the Christian church hold high the value of marriage and of the traditional family.

The Roman Catholic approach to the issue stems from its doctrine, first set forth officially by Pope Alexander II in 1159, that marriage between consenting persons (*sponsalis per verba de praesenti*) constitutes a sacramental union — even though the marriage were never in fact consummated. "Impediments" of two kinds came, however, to be recognised: prohibiting impediments, which imposed legal penalties but did not dissolve the marriage; and invalidating impediments, which gave grounds for canonically declaring that the marriage never took place at all. The former made possible legal separation (divorce *a mensa et thoro*), which did not permit remarriage; the latter allowed the parties subsequently to marry, but did not condone remarriage, since *de jure* they had never been married before. By a far wider application of the concept of annulment than exists in most secular legal systems, the canon law of the Roman Church permits a severing of marital relationships without compromising its theoretical position that marriage is indissoluble except by death. But because of the procedural complexity in obtaining an annulment, that avenue, though open to all Roman Catholics in theory, may be available in practice largely to those with the financial resources to pursue the torturous process to its end.

At the opposite end of the spectrum are the broad-church, liberal Protestant and the charismatic approaches to divorce. The Church of England's recent Working Party Report on "Marriage in Church After Divorce" employs higher critical and redactive approaches to the New Testament teaching on the subject, arguing that "what matters is what the Spirit is now saying to the churches." In this view, the Spirit, working the the context of the individual heart and/or the believing community, dictates an attitude of forgiveness and acceptance, such that no barriers should be raised to church marriage of previous divorced persons. Though charismatics are often associated with the conservative wing of contemporary Christianity, they in fact have much in common with religious liberals: for both, Scripture is not determinative; what *is* decisive is the experiential "leading of the Spirit." Thus Ken Crispin titles his book on the subject, *Divorce—The Forgivable Sin?* and deals with it in terms of his "covenant principle" of marriage (genuine marriage exists only as long as the covenant between the parties is maintained).

The classic Protestant position on the matter falls between the two views just discussed. Luther, whilst holding to a very high view of marriage, could not accept its sacramental character. Luther scholar Paul Althaus correctly states that "for Luther, a sacrament consists in the combination of the word of promise with a sign, that is, it is a promise accompanied by a sign instituted by God and a sign accompanied by a promise. This means, first, that a sign or a symbol by itself is not yet a sacrament. Luther explains that every visible act can naturally mean something and be understood as a picture or an analogy of invisible realities. This is not enough, however, to make a symbolic act into a sacrament. The symbolic act must be instituted by God and combined with a promise. Sacramental character ultimately depends on the presence of a divine word of promise. Where this is missing, as in marriage or confirmation, one cannot speak of a sacrament. On the other hand, however, there are realties and deeds in the Christian life such as prayer, hearing and meditating on the word, and the cross, to which God has attached a promise. But they lack the characteristic of a sign or a symbol. This is the case, for example, in the so-called sacrament of penance. Strictly speaking therefore there are only two sacraments in the church of God: baptism and the Lord's Supper. For only in these is there both a sign instituted by God and the promise of the forgiveness of sins." If marriage is not a sacrament (and it is noteworthy that even in the Roman theology marriage is regarded as a sacrament created by the mutual promises of the couple, not by the act of the priest), then its human extent and the conditions for its lawful termination need to be sought in God's word, the Holy Scriptures. As early as 1522, Luther concluded that divorce and remarriage could scripturally be allowed, but only when adultery or abandonment had occurred.

Based therefore upon the two key biblical texts (Matthew 19:9 and 1 Corinthians 7:15), Luther and the Reformation theology which developed from his thinking came to a viewpoint which may be described as follows: (1) Marriage is ideally for life and any marital break-up is the result of sin. (2) Only one legitimate "cause" of divorce is recognised in Scripture: that of adultery. Here the innocent party has the option of staying in the relationship or of divorcing the guilty partner. (3) Malicious desertion by an unbelieving spouse constitutes divorce per se; here, the innocent spouse is freed from the marital bond by the desertion, but may choose to wait for the return of the deserting spouse and to re-establish a marriage with that person. (4) In the case of desertion, "unbelief" does not mean that an innocent spouse is freed from the marriage only if the deserting spouse is a professed non-Christian; conduct utterly inconsistent with Christian profession may properly relegate the deserter to the functional status of unbeliever for purposes of terminating the marriage. (5) Desertion may be actual or constructive, the latter consisting, for example, of physical abuse or antisocial conduct of such seriousness that it forces the couple apart, or irrational refusal to enter into sexual relations (thus separating the couple on a fundamental level). (6) Even when neither adultery nor malicious desertion has occurred, it is conceivable (but rare) that a divorce can be ecclesiastically recognised on the ground that, though an evil, it is a lesser of evils. (7) Whenever the divorce is theologically legitimate, remarriage is likewise legitimate and may be performed in the church and according to church rites.

Bibliography. Code of Canon Law, ed. E. Caparros, *et al.* (Montréal: Wilson and Lafleur, 1993), can. 1141-1155; W. J. S. Wamboldt, "Canon Law on Indissolubility of Marriage in the Roman Catholic Church," 21 *Studia canonica* 265-70 (1987); A. Clarkson, *et al.*, "Marriage in [the Anglican] Church After Divorce," 2 *Ecclesiastical Law Journal* 359; K. Crispin, *Divorce — The Forgivable Sin?* (London: Hodder & Stoughton, 1989); W. H. Lazareth, *Luther on the Christian Home* (Philadelphia: Muhlenberg/Fortress Press, 1960); J. W. Montgomery, "Church Remarriage After Divorce," in his *Christ Our Advocate* (Bonn: Verlag für Kultur und Wissenschaft, 2002), pp, 117-31.

7. Euthanasia

The Christian church in all its branches has been opposed to suicide and assisted suicide. Every instance of suicide in Holy Scripture is related to spiritual collapse, from Saul to Judas (1 Samuel 31:4; 2 Samuel 17:23; 1 Kings 16:18-20; Matthew 27:5; Acts 1:18).

The contrast with secular thought could hardly be greater. Voltaire regarded the suicides of Brutus, Cassius, and Marc Antony as victories over nature. Montesquieu admired the Roman practice of suicide which allegedly "gave every one the liberty of finishing his part on the stage of the world in what scene he pleased." David Hume concluded in his *Essays on Suicide* (1783) that "the life of a man is of no greater importance to the universe than that of an oyster" — a position contrasting markedly with that of Jesus, who declared that "you are of more value than many sparrows."

The Christian opposition to suicide and assisted suicide is grounded in a realistic view of fallen human nature. Owing to original sin, the human race is subject to fallibility, laziness, and perversity. Where voluntary euthanasia is allowed, the patient and/or the physician may err in diagnosis of the true medical condition and the chances of survival; indeed, not a few instances have been recorded of patients waking up even after years in a comatose state. The patient and/or his loved ones may simply tire of life and of the care needed to sustain it. Those who will survive the patient may even be motivated by greed or by the potential benefits accruing to them from the patient's early demise. Where euthanasia has been legalised (as in the Netherlands) studies have shown that these sad consequences are by no means rare.

To be sure, pain and suffering can become virtually intolerable, and in limiting cases there may be a lesser of evils argument for helping to terminate life. However, a lesser evil does not become a good. And, as St. John-Stevas has rightly stressed: "Once a concession about the disposability of innocent life is made in one sphere, it will inevitably spread to others."

Today, when suicide has been almost universally decriminalised and where assisting suicide has come under greater and greater approbation, the Christian who opposes the practice is faced with difficult questions: (1) Should not the matter be left in the realm of private morality? (2) Is euthanasia not a victimless act? To the first, one notes the deleterious consequences of leaving issues of human worth to private decision-making (should slavery have been left to the consciences of the slave-owners?). To the second, one remembers John Donne's admonition: "Never send to know for whom the bell tolls: it tolls for thee." Lord Chancellor Hailsham put it touchingly in his first autobiography where he refers to the suicide of his brother: "If only Edward had known the pain he was inflicting on us all who were left behind ... he would have never done what he did. ... Suicide is wrong, wrong, wrong, and Christians were amongst the first to recognise the fact. Their spiritual insight is to be recognised as among the proofs, as well as the consolations, of Christianity."

Bibliography. J. Keown, ed., *Euthanasia Examined: Ethical, Clinical and Legal Perspectives* (reprint ed.; Cambridge: Cambridge University Press, 2004); D. Humphry, *Final Exit: The Practicalities of Self-Deliverance and Assisted Suicide* (3^d ed.; New York: Delta Books, 2002); N. St. John-Stevas, *Life, Death and the Law* (Frederick, MD: BeardBooks, 2002); J. W. Montgomery, "Do We Have the Right to Die?," *Christianity Today* 469-79 (January 21, 1977); J. W. Montgomery, "Whose Life Anyway?," in his *Christ Our Advocate* (Bonn: Verlag für Kultur und Wissenschaft, 2002), pp. 169-95.

8. Existentialist Theology

Existentialism is generally regarded as having as its modern origins in the thought of Danish Lutheran lay theologian Søren Kierkegaard (1813-1855). In reaction both to "dead orthodoxy" in the state church and even more to Hegelian "essentialism" (one can rationally come to understand the cosmos), Kierkegaard argued that it is in fact impossible to get beyond one's own finite and sinful "existence." In Kierkegaard's celebrated aphorism, "truth is subjectivity." To think that one is capable of setting forth a necessarily true universal metaphysic is to misunderstand the human condition of estrangement and Angst and to fall into egoistic *hubris*. The only hope for fallen mankind is to recognise one's fall from essence to existence and to seek personal, existential salvation through Jesus Christ.

Kierkegaard wrote in Danish and it was not until the second half of the 19th century that he began to impact German thought and the early decades of the 20th century before he became accessible to English readers. By then, increasing secularism made inevitable his appropriation by non-Christian philosophers such as Martin Heidegger in Germany and Jean-Paul Sartre in France. These thinkers looked into their Existenz and found only brokenness—not the Christ. For the secular 20th-century existentialists, the only way to find value in an atheistic universe was to create it by the act of decision. In a famous exchange with a young Frenchman, torn between supporting his mother in Vichy-occupied France or escaping to serve with the Free French, Sartre declared, "There are no omens in the world, and, if there were, we would give them their meaning. Decide!"

Some few 20th-century theologians stayed with Kierkegaard's Christian roots (e.g., Gabriel Marcel), but in general the result was a de-objectifying of theology, particularly in the realm of New Testament studies. Rudolf Bultmann (1884-1976), who had contact with Heidegger at Marburg in 1926 and spent his career at that University, maintained that the *dass* (the "thatness") of the historical Jesus was sufficient: the details of his life, as presented in the New Testament documents, were thoroughly impregnated by mythological elements and needed to be "demythologized." The believer could only find the saving Christ in existential encounter.

The so-called "Post-Bultmannians" (mostly disciples of Bultmann himself)—Conzelmann, Günther Bornkamm, Käsemann, Fuchs, Ebeling, James M. Robinson, *et al.*—felt uncomfortable with this historical minimalism and tried in a number of ways to engage in a "New Quest" of the historical Jesus (i.e., one which would flesh out to a greater extent his historicity) whilst at the same time maintaining the centrality of existential experience in understanding

Jesus' place in the origins of Christianity and in personal faith. None of these efforts have been particularly successful, owing to the firm commitment of all the Post-Bultmannians to radical literary and redaction criticism of the New Testament.

It may be suggested that in a very real sense Kierkegaard "threw out the baby with the bath water." In properly criticising Hegelianism and the German idealistic philosophical tradition for their unrealistic pride in thinking that they could rationally explain the universe, he went to the opposite extreme of subjective scepticism as to the possibility of arriving at objectively sound theological knowledge at all. In point of fact, biblical revelation can be well supported as historically sound and the picture of Jesus there presented has higher credibility than that of most of the universally accepted figures of the classical world. Christian dogmatics has consistently maintained that *fides* (public affirmation of faith) and *fiducia* (personal—existential—commitment to the truth of the faith) must be grounded in *notitia* (objective knowledge and the factual soundness of the faith). Theological existentialism has—often without meaning to do so—relegated historic Christianity to the status of an a-historical Eastern religion or cultic phenomenon dependent solely on inner experience for its *raison d'être*.

Bibliography. S. Kierkegaard, *Writings,* ed. H. V. and E. H. Hong (26 vols.; Princeton, NJ: Princeton University Press, 1978-2000); J.-P. Sartre, *Existentialism and Human Emotions*, trans. H. E. Barnes (New York: Philosophical Library, 1957); C. W. Kegley, ed., *The Theology of Rudolf Bultmann* (New York: Harper, 1966); R. Bauckham, *Jesus and the Eyewitnesses: The Gospels As Eyewitness Testimony* (Grand Rapids, MI: Eerdmans, 2006; J. W. Montgomery, *Where Is History Going?* (Minneapolis: Bethany, 1969); J. W. Montgomery, *The Suicide of Christian Theology* (Minneapolis: Bethany, 1970); J. W. Montgomery, *Tractatus Logico-Theologicus* (Bonn, Germany: Verlag für Kultur und Wissenschaft, 2004), especially sec. 2.5.

9. Inerrancy of the Bible

A doctrine maintained historically by all branches of the Christian church but today maintained chiefly by evangelical Protestants and by conservative American denominations (the largest being the Lutheran Church-Missouri Synod and the Southern Baptist Convention, both of which underwent intense internal struggles over the issue). Among American evangelicals are institutions, such as the Fuller Theological Seminary, which have removed biblical inerrancy from their doctrinal stance. On the English ecclesiastical scene, the general spiritual authority of Scripture is stressed, but there is considerable reticence toward the use of the terminology of scriptural inerrancy.

Opponents of biblical inerrancy, such as James Barr, argue, *inter alia*: (1) the word is not employed in the Bible itself; (2) the concept directs attention away from the authority of Jesus, the living Word, substituting a "paper pope" for a living faith; (3) the Bible in fact contains internal contradictions; (4) it is hopeless today to defend the Bible against scientific and historical errors. In Roman Catholic circles, Hans Küng (*Infallible?*) has questioned the whole idea of perfection here on earth—whether represented by an infallible Pope or an infallible Bible.

Proponents of an inerrant Scripture counter: (1) many central doctrinal teachings, such as the Trinity, are part and parcel of biblical teaching, though the modern terminology for them is not found in the Scriptures; (2) if the Bible is unreliable, it cannot be trusted in what it says about Jesus, so the authority of the living Word is compromised when one denies scriptural reliability; (3) what are often superficially regarded as biblical contradictions are in fact cases of different biblical accounts complementing each other; (4) conflicts between the Bible and "modern knowledge" are generally conflicts between inadequate biblical *interpretations* and unproven contemporary secular *theories*—and, where the issues are indeed factual, responsible harmonisations have been the order of the day throughout Christian history.

The inerrantist position is especially strengthened by its historical roots: it was maintained by Augustine in the 5th century, by Luther and Calvin at the time of the Reformation, and by the Roman Church in the *Canans and Decrees* of the Council of Trent. To those arguing that one can accept the "spiritual and moral" in the Bible without accepting its factual reliability, the response is simply that the Bible centres on God's revelation in history; if that history is unreliable, why should its spirituality and morality be any better? As Jesus said, "If I have told you earthly things and you do not believe, how shall you believe if I tell you of heavenly things?" (John 3:12). A particularly telling point, frequently made by those holding to this view, is that if the Bible contains both truth and error, what criterion can be used to distinguish the wheat from the chaff? This would presumably require a Bible-to-the-second-power—which would itself need to be inerrant.

Bibliography. J. Barr, *Fundamentalism* (Philadelphia: Westminster, 1978); B. B. Warfield, *The Inspiration and Authority of the Bible,* ed. S. G. Craig (Phillipsburg, New Jersey: Presbyterian and Reformed, 1948); W. F. Arndt, *Does the Bible Contradict Itself?* (5th ed.; Saint Louis, Mo.: Concordia, 1955); G. L. Archer, Jr., *New International Encyclopedia of Bible Difficulties* (Grand Rapids,

Mich.: Zondervan, 2001); J. W. Montgomery, *Crisis in Lutheran Theology* (2 vols., 2ᵈ ed.; Minneapolis: Bethany, 1973); J. W. Montgomery, ed., *God's Inerrant Word* (Minneapolis: Bethany, 1974).

10. Kenosis

Kenotic theory takes its name from the Greek word for "emptying" in Philippians 2:6-8. Though the passage says nothing concerning fallibility on Jesus' part, the idea of incarnational limitation has been employed in modern critical theology and by some liberal evangelicals to support a belief in Jesus' authority in the face of supposed errors in his teaching (especially his clear belief in the entire trustworthiness of the Old Testament). The Kenotic position holds that Jesus' views could well have been coloured by the very fact of his becoming a human being limited to the knowledge of his time. Accordingly, Jesus either unknowingly was limited, or knowingly limited himself, to the thought-forms of his day.

In support of this view, Kenotic proponents cite Jesus' admission that he did not know the day or hour of his (second) coming (Mark 13:32). However, (1) This was a unique item of eschatological knowledge withheld by divine fiat, and (2) Jesus' disclaimer of knowledge on this point shows that in his incarnate state he was nonetheless fully aware of the boundaries of his knowledge.

The problems with Kenotic reasoning are considerable. Had Jesus purposely given incorrect teaching in order to accommodate to the views of his time, he would have committed the basic moral fault of letting the end justify the means. Moreover, he appears to have been quite willing to present teachings, especially as to his own nature as pre-existent Son of God, which flew directly in the face of contemporary religious opinion.

If Jesus could not help giving false information (owing to the exigencies of incarnation), then it would appear that the very concept of incarnation loses all meaningfulness, since not a single word of what he taught could necessarily be regarded as more than a product of human fallibility.

Finally, if Jesus' teaching in fact consisted of a combination of genuine revelation and mere human, fallible opinion (to which he accommodated himself or could not help but accept, owing to his taking on human flesh), we would never be able to identify which portion was which in the absence of a higher (absolute) criterion—which would logically have to come from an unqualified, non-Kenotic revelation (precisely what Kenotic theory excludes).

Bibliography. A. Oepke, "Kenóō," *Theological Dictionary of the New Testament,* ed. G. Kittel, trans. G. W. Bromiley, III (Grand Rapids, Mich.: Eerdmans, 1965), 661-62; F. Pieper, *Christian Dogmatics* (4 vols.; Saint Louis, Mo.: Concordia, 1950-1957), IV, 453-54; J. W. Montgomery, *Tractatus Logico-Theologicus* (Bonn, Germany: Verlag für Kultur und Wissenschaft, 2004), sec. 3.78.

11. Llull, Ramon

L(l)ull — or Lullius (the Latin form of his name), *ca.* 1235-1315 — was a contemporary of Thomas Aquinas. Like Aquinas, he was a theologian in what James Walsh, one of the Roman Church's eulogists, has termed the "greatest of centuries," since it was then that the Church's enduring systematic theological formulations were developed.

But Lull was very different from Aquinas. The latter devoted his life to the systematising of the Church's teaching, based on the philosophical principles of the Aristotelian revival in his time. He wrote for those within the framework of western Christendom. One interpreter has observed, not unjustly, that when Thomas wrote his *Summa contra gentiles* ("Summation Against the Pagans") he had probably never met a pagan!

Lull, on the other hand, was a polymath who believed that theology could only be properly pursued in the context of missionary endeavour — and that new methods had to be developed to achieve results in contexts where western approaches would not carry the weight they did at home. Lull was ultimately to die a martyr for his beliefs whilst preaching the gospel to that most difficult audience, the followers of Islam. The great 19th century missionary statesman Samuel M. Zwemer characterised Lull as, quite simply, the "first missionary to the Moslems." And, like C. S. Lewis in the 20th century, Lull's apologetic was not just a tough-minded one; he produced (in his own, Catalan tongue) a remarkable missionary novel, *Blanquerna,* which has been compared to Bunyan's *Pilgrim's Progress.*

Lull's theological "Art" or method was scholastic but not Aristotelian — and its unique character has given it a place in the history of logic. Martin Gardner, in his well-received work on *Logic Machines and Diagrams,* begins with Lull and devotes to him an entire chapter of the nine comprising his book. Gardner offers the following illustration of the Lullian method for resolving theological problems by exhaustively interrelating combinations of divine qualities:

For example, we realize that predestination and free will must be combined in some mysterious way beyond our ken; for God is both infinitely wise and infinitely just; therefore He must know every detail of the future, yet at the same time be incapable of withholding from any sinner the privilege of choosing the way of salvation. Lull considered this a demonstration *"per aequiparantium,"* or by means of equivalent relations. Instead of connecting ideas in a cause-and-effect chain, we trace them back to a common origin. Free will and predestination sprout from equally necessary attributes of God, like two twigs growing on branches attached to the trunk of a single tree.

Indeed, as Pring-Mill well puts it:

> The most distinctive characteristic of Lull's Art is clearly its combinatory nature, which led to both the use of complex semimechanical techniques that sometimes required figures with separately revolving concentric wheels — "volvelles," in bibliographical parlance ... — and to the symbolic notation of its alphabet. These features justify its classification among the forerunners of both modern symbolic logic and computer science.

Bibliography. Anthony Bonner (ed. and trans.), *Selected Works of Ramon Llull (1232-1316)*, (2 vols.; Princeton, N.J.: Princeton University Press, 1985); Samuel M. Zwemer, *Raymund Lull: First Missionary to the Moslems* (New York and London: Funk & Wagnalls, 1902); R. D. F. Pring-Mill, "Lull, Ramon," *Dictionary of Scientific Biography,* ed. C. C. Gillispie (16 vols.; New York: Scribner's, 1970-1980), VIII, 548-49; J. W. Montgomery, "Computer Origins and the Defense of the Faith," 56/3 *Perspectives on Science and Christian Faith* 189-203 (2004) [in this volume, Part Two, chap. 2].

12. Natural Theology

So-called "natural" theology differs from "revealed" theology in that it endeavours to provide evidence for God's existence and for divine truths without reference to a special revelation from God (as claimed for the Bible or, outside the Christian tradition, for such writings as the Qur'an). The most influential exponent of natural theology in western Christendom has been Thomas Aquinas, who held that a foundation for accepting special revelation can be found in Aristotle's classic arguments for God's existence. Natural and revealed theology operated largely in tandem until the advent of 18th century Deism — which endeavoured to base ultimate principles upon Nature alone (as in Thomas Paine's *Age of Reason*) — and Immanuel Kant — who claimed that an ethical "categorical imperative" could be justified without recourse to a revelatory Deity.

In spite of Kantian and Humean arguments against the traditional Aristotelian-Thomist proofs of God's existence from nature alone, those proofs stand in their underlying essence: (1) Nothing in the world can explain itself; (2) The world is the sum total of everything in it; (3) The world as a whole is thus a contingent entity, requiring an explanation beyond itself, i.e., a transcendent God; (4) If that Deity were non-transcendent, a higher-level God would be needed to explain the lesser God, resulting in potential infinite regress, which would leave the universe itself without explanation; (5) Ergo, an absolute, non-contingent God is required as the final explanation of the contingent world. This "contingency argument" is supported scientifically by the Second Law of Thermodynamics, by Olbers' Paradox, by evidences of Intelligent Design, etc.

The limitations of such reasoning from natural theology are, however, considerable. One can doubtless assert the personhood and intelligence of the Deity on naturalistic grounds (otherwise, there is no accounting for human personality and intelligence), but the all-important issues of God's moral character and his will for mankind remain obscure. Thus, in spite of the herculean efforts of Bishop Butler in his *Analogy* to argue for the truth of specific Christian doctrines on naturalistic grounds and the attempts of Roman Catholic and Anglican moral theologians and secular human rights theorists to establish a universal ethic without the need of special revelation, it appears that St Paul knew what he was talking about when on the Areopagus he insisted that without Jesus Christ one is left with little more than "an unknown god" (Acts 17).

Bibliography: N. Kretzmann, *The Metaphysics of Theism: Aquinas's Natural Theology* (new ed.; New York: Oxford University Press, 2002); J. Sennett and D. Groothuis, eds., *In Defense of Natural Theology: A Post-Humean Assessment* (Downers Grove, IL: InterVarsity Press, 2005); S. L. Jaki, *The Paradox of Olbers' Paradox* (New York: Herder and Herder, 1969); J. W. Montgomery, *Tractatus Logico-Theologicus* (Bonn, Germany: Verlag für Kultur und Wissenschaft, 2004), sec. 3.8.

13. Neo-Orthodox Theology

A hugely influential Protestant school of thought between the 1st and 2nd World Wars and associated particularly with the names of Karl Barth (1886-1968) and Emil Brunner (1889-1966). The viewpoint, also known as "Crisis theology," has continuing (though considerably less) impact at the present day, its disciples being found especially in Scottish and Swiss Protestant theological faculties.

Barth's theology developed as a reaction to the humanistic-liberal philosophical theologies of the 19th and early 20th centuries. His wartime experiences made clear to him that the denial of sin in progressivistic liberal theology was utterly unrealistic and contrary to biblical teaching. In his commentary on the Book of Romans (1919), Barth took such naïve progressivisms to task and endeavoured to rehabilitate the Pauline understanding of God's transcendence, human sin and divine grace. Barth's aim was no less than to restore a biblical and Reformation theology to the Protestantism of his time. Thus the *Orthodox* in "Neo-Orthodoxy."

What about the *Neo-*? Whilst denying the immanentism and "every-day-in-every-way-I-am-becoming-better-and-better" thinking of his predecessors, Barth accepted as valid the critical biblical scholarship which had originated in the 18th century Enlightenment and moved from dehistoricising the Old Testament to reducing the New Testament narratives to little more than expressions of the faith experiences of the early Church. Thus, whereas Rudolf Bultmann, the most influential of the 20th century higher critics of the New Testament, simply denied that the physical resurrection of Jesus Christ from the dead was more than a myth, Barth claimed that Jesus had indeed risen—but in the realm of *Heilsgeschichte* ("salvation history"), unprovable in ordinary history (*Historie*). The consequence was that Neo-Orthodoxy tried desperately to maintain the biblical gospel without attempting to defend—or, indeed, being capable of defending—the objective historical foundations of the biblical text setting forth that gospel.

Barth, as a Calvinist, fell back on divine election and inner faith (cf. his *Anselm: Fides Quaerens Intellectum* and *Church Dogmatics*) to justify what surely appeared to those outside the Church as an irrational effort to have one's cake and eat it too. And the inherent instability of this so-called "dialectic theology" of *Yes* (to the Gospel) but *No* (to the reliability of Scripture) led to Neo-Orthodoxy's rapid replacement by more left-wing options—such as Tillichian ontological theology and ultimately the death-of-God movement.

The major difference in viewpoint between Barth and Brunner relates to natural theology. Barth, reacting against the neglect of revealed theology by the 19th century liberal theologians, denied any place to arguments for the truth of the faith from outside Scripture, extra-biblical arguments for God's existence, or natural morality. Brunner, however, on the basis of Romans 1, maintained that the natural world does indeed point to a Creator and that God's law is written on the human heart—but that, as a result of sin, the fallen race needs special revelation to show God's nature and to define the content of his moral requirements. As for the social dimension of Neo-Orthodoxy, it can best be seen in the work of H. Richard Niebuhr (*Christ and Culture*, etc.).

Bibliography; Natural Theology: Comprising "Nature and Grace" by Prof. Dr. Emil Brunner and the Reply "No!" by Dr. Karl Barth, trans. P. Fraenkel (London: Bles, 1946); C. Van Til, *Christianity and Barthianism* (Grand Rapids, MI: Baker, 1962); J. W. Montgomery, "Karl Barth and Contemporary Theology of History," in his *Where Is History Going?* (Minneapolis: Bethany, 1969), pp. 100-117; J. W. Montgomery, *The Suicide of Christian Theology* (Minneapolis: Bethany, 1970).

14. Oberammergau

A small village in Bavaria, not far from Munich, where, since 1634, the most famous of all Passion Plays takes place every ten years, with occasional (as in 1984) special anniversary performances.

This dramatic production, common in the Middle Ages but rare today, sets forth in words, tableaux, and music the biblical account of Our Lord's crucifixion and resurrection. In 1633, the area had been decimated by the plague, and the villagers promised that if they were spared they would perform such a play in perpetuity. Today, a child of the village will appear as one of the Palm Sunday crowd; later, he or she will take an adult part, and finally, perhaps, in old age play the role of Simeon or Anna.

In our era of political correctness, the most recent seasons of the Play have been subject to strident criticism. In particular, Jewish anti-defamation organisations have claimed that the Play is anti-semitic. Their argument rests essentially on the text references to "the Jews" having rejected Jesus as the Messiah. The problem here is that the Play text follows, almost slavishly, the Gospel of John, where such phraseology is employed. It does not seem to occur to the critics that the expression, "the Jews", can hardly mean all those of Jewish race, since Jesus and His followers were *themselves* Jews.

Some editorial concessions and expansions were made in the 2000 text to deflect such criticisms. For example, the number of Old Testament references has been increased and Gamaliel is introduced as a believing member of the Jewish High Council, making such declarations as: "But I confess: According to his own way, the one whom you condemn serves the God of our fathers. He believes everything written in the Law and the Prophets, and has the same hopeful faith in God that many among us here share as well." Fortunately, the recent editors of the late-19th century Daisenberger script did not dilute the Johannine message for the sake of avoiding criticism. As for the music, it is of concert quality, employing not only locals but a number of professionals; the original score, a product of an Oberammergau composer, Rochus Dedler (1820), is still largely intact; a bit romantic, to be sure, but so was Mendelssohn!

Some have been concerned that Passion Play takes place in a strongly Roman Catholic and conservative part of Germany (Bavaria — the home of the Hapsburg emperors and eccentric baroque prince Duke Ludwig of Neuschwanstein fame). But aside from one or two lines gratuitously spoken by Mary which the biblical authors give to others (e.g., "He was like a lamb led to the slaughter and djd not open his mouth" — and John 3:16!), the Play is certainly in no sense a special pleading for Romanism. It is simply what C. S. Lewis in another context termed "mere Christianity."

Bibliography. S. S. Friedman, T*he Oberammergau Passion Play: A Lance Against Civilization* (Carbondale: Southern Illinois University Press, 1984) [polemic against]; H. Diemer, *Oberammergau and Its Passion Play*, trans. W. S. Manning (Munich: Seyfried, 1900); J. Bentley, *Oberammergau and the Passion Play* (Harmondsworth, Middlesex: Penguin Books, 1984); C. Stueckl, *et al., The Passion Play of the Community of Oberammergau* (Oberammergau, 1990); *Oberammergau Passion Play 2000: Textbook*, trans. I. Shafer (Oberammergau, 2000). [Concerning the 2010 performance season and text, see above, Part Nine, chap. 27.]

15. Process Theology

A 20th-century theological position deriving from process philosophy. The process philosophers Whitehead and Hartshorne concluded from relativity theory and the Heisenberg indeterminacy principle that one must regard Becoming rather than Being — process rather than substance — as fundamental and therefore that sharing and involvement are basic to a proper understanding of reality. For Hartshorne, God is to be understood "panentheistically" — as embracing the world — in contrast with traditional Theism (which sees the world as an independent creation of God) or with Pantheism (which regards God and the world as coterminous). Hartshorne's God is greater than the world but contains it, such that world experience occurs within God and is part of God's own experience.

Some would place Roman Catholic Teilhard de Chardin within the ambit of process theology in that he saw evolutionary change and development as primary—the world evolving to a christic "Omega Point." God waits "up ahead" for the eschatological fulfilment of the cosmic process, whose motor is divine love.

Process theology in the strict sense, however, relates to the thinking of a small number of liberal Protestant theologians, in particular John B. Cobb, Jr. and Schubert Ogden. Whitehead's natural theology is here taken over, virtually *en bloc*. The world—including the human sphere—operates within the Deity. This leaves no appreciable room for sin (since human depravity would make God a sinner) or for redemption. There are no index references whatever to Jesus Christ in Cobb's magnum opus, *A Christian Natural Theology*; and the process theologians present the religious response in terms of worship, adventure, meaning, companionship, and peace. The Bible is viewed, not as a propositionally true revelation but as an organic growth and a dynamic source of insights. The church is a place of interaction and ethical development.

Harry K. Wells, in evaluating process thinking, has argued that such a position needs to be justified, not by classic Aristotelian logic (which is static and depends on the law of non-contradiction) but by Hegel's so-called "dialectic logic" (involving the dynamic interplay of thesis, antithesis, and synthesis). The problem here, of course, is that Hegel's system necessarily presupposes a non-contradictory understanding of basic Hegelian concepts such as thesis, antithesis, and synthesis, i.e., it must itself start from a non-relativistic point. The same is true of relativity theory (which has to employ a constant—"c," the velocity of light) and indeterminacy (initial observations cannot dispense with the subject-object distinction). Hence Bertrand Russell's comment on the Hegelian system (equally applicable to process thinking): "This illustrates an important truth, namely, that the worse your logic, the more interesting the consequences to which it gives rise."

Bibliography, E. R. Baltazar, "Teilhard de Chardin: A Philosophy of Procession," in M. E. Marty and D. G. Peerman, eds., *New Theology No. 2* (New York: Macmillan, 1965), pp. 134-50; A. N. Whitehead, *The Philosophy of Alfred North Whitehead* ("Library of Living Philosophers"; 2^d ed.; Chicago: Open Court, 1989); A. N. Whitehead, *Process and Reality* (New York: Free Press, 1985); W. A. Christian, *An Interpretation of Whitehead's Metaphysics* (New Haven, CT: Yale University Press, 1967); H. K. Wells, *Process and Unreality: A Criticism of Method in Whitehead's Philosophy* (New York: King's Crown Press, 1950); C. Hartshorne and L. E. Hahn, eds., *The Philosophy of Charles Hartshorne* ("Library of Living Philosophers"; Chicago: Open Court, 1991); N. Pittenger, *Process Thought and Christian Faith* (New York: Macmillan, 1968); J. B. Cobb, Jr., *A Christian Natural Theology: Based on the Thought of Alfred North Whitehead* (2^d ed.; Philadelphia: Westminster John Knox Press, 2007); S. M. Ogden, *The Re-*

ality of God and Other Essays (Dallas, TX: Southern Methodist University Press, 1992); B. Russell, *A History of Western Philosophy* (New York: Simon and Schuster, 1945), pp. 730-46; J. W. Montgomery, *Tractatus Logico-Theologicus* (Bonn, Germany: Verlag für Kultur und Wissenschaft, 2004), sec. 2.2 and 2.4.

16. Prophecy

The early Christian church employed two major styles of apologetic: miracle and prophecy, the first directed especially to the Gentiles, the second particularly to the Jewish community. A remarkable feature of the Christian apologetic was the inherent interconnection of the two approaches, owing to the fact that miracles central to the faith (such as the Virgin Birth of Our Lord) had often been the object of specific Old Testament prophecies. Today, three forms of prophetic attestation are offered to support the truth of Christian faith: *charismatic* (experiential) prophecy, *end-time* (futuristic) prophecy, and *fulfilled* (historical) prophecy.

Charismatic Prophecy. It is frequently maintained in charismatic and Pentecostal circles that, in line with 1 Corinthians 14 and other related references in the New Testament, miraculous tongue-speaking occurs with fair regularity among believers today. Indeed, it is an article of faith with Pentecostals that a "Second Blessing" is properly to be sought by all Christians and that with this empowering will normally come the miraculous gift of tongues. When the Christian speaks in tongues and another, possessing the gift of interpretation, makes known the meaning in an ordinary language, the miraculous truth of the faith is allegedly demonstrated.

William Samarin, however, argues persuasively: "We know more about language than the glossolalist does. We know enough to declare what is and what is not language. We know as much as a mathematician, who can tell the difference between a real formula and a pseudo-formula—one that *looks* like mathematical language but does not *say* anything. ... A charismatist's religious experience can be real, revolutionary, reconstitutive. A glossolalist accepts this transformation as supernatural, that is, *caused* by God. If it is a dramatic change—taking place where one did not expect it or more quickly than one expected—it takes on all the more appearance of the supernatural. But none of this proves that glossolalia is supernatural. No number of 'miraculous' transformations will make of glossolalia what it is not."

End-Time Prophecy. Through Christian history attempts have been made to predict the future, based on scriptural data, especially the mysterious passages in the Old Testament Book of Daniel and the New Testament Book of Revelation. In our day, the Dispensational theology of the Scofield Reference Bible has been the basis of the phenomenally successful *Left Behind* series of prophetic novels by Tim LaHaye and Jerry Jenkins.

The problem with such prophetic attempts is clearly that we do not have the perspective on our own time sufficient to be able to predict the future accurately or confidently relate biblical prophecy to what is happening at the moment. Sadly, examples abound: the widely held medieval belief that the year 1,000 would usher in the end of the world; the 19th century Adventists' conviction that our Lord's Second Coming would occur in the year 1844; the Revd M. Baxter's attempt to show that Emperor Louis Napoleon of France was the Antichrist (1866); Pastor Oswald J. Smith's identification of the Antichrist with Mussolini (1927).

As early as the 5th century, St Augustine pointed up the dangers of biblical speculation: "Now it is an unseemly and mischievous thing, and greatly to be avoided, that a Christian man ... should talk so foolishly that the unbeliever on hearing him, and observing the extravagance of his error, should hardly be able to refrain from laughing. And the great mischief is, not so much that the man himself is laughed at for his errors, but that our authors are believed, by people without the Church, to have taught such things, and are so condemned as unlearned, and cast aside, to the great loss of those for whose salvation we are so much concerned. For when they find one belonging to the Christian body, falling into error ... and when they see him moreover enforcing his groundless opinion by the authority of our Sacred Books, how are they likely to put trust in these Books about the resurrection of the dead, and the hope of eternal life, and the kingdom of heaven ... ?" It is no doubt sage to note that Jesus himself declared that "sufficient unto the day is the evil thereof" and that it was not given even to him to know the day and hour of his Second Coming.

Historically Fulfilled Prophecy. The Christian church in all its branches has regularly appealed to the prophecies of the Old Testament which have already been fulfilled—principally the prophecies of Christ's First Coming. Though there are significant Old Testament prophecies of which secular history demonstrates the fulfilment (the destruction of Tyre and Sidon, etc.), the most commonly cited are those concerning the First Advent of our Lord. Genuine fulfilment in the New Testament of Old Testament prophecies concerning our Lord adds considerable weight to the Christian claim that the entire Bible is the product of divine revelation, since the fulfilled Old Testament prophecies come from a wide variety of Old Testament books, written at widely different times.

Fascinatingly enough, the value of such fulfilled prophecy can be specified mathematically. One can, by using the statistician's well-known "product rule," calculate the probabilities against mere chance accounting for a given number of such prophecies. If one arbitrarily sets the probability of the occurrence of a single valid Old Testament prophecy of Christ at 50-50 (1/2), then the probabilities against 25 of them happening by chance is $1/2^{25}$, or 1 in 33 million. But since the likelihood of any one of these prophecies succeeding is considerably less than 50-50 ("Behold a virgin shall conceive and bear a son", etc.), one can legitimately lower the probability of one occurrence to 25% (1/4). The probability against 25 similar events transpiring by mere chance would then be $1/4^{25}$, or 1 in a thousand trillion.

To discount the force of this argument, one would have to show that the New Testament writers unhistorically conformed the life of Christ to the Old Testament prophecies of the coming of Messiah. But it is clear that their religious opponents were well schooled in the Old Testament and also well acquainted with the actual events of Jesus' life and earthly career; thus the writers of the New Testament books could hardly have gotten away with such fabrication even if they had had no ethical scruples about doing so (which they clearly did, since their Master had taught them that lying was of the devil—John 8:44).

The kind of prophetic success here described is unparalleled when compared with the claims of even the most highly regarded secular prophets (Nostradamus, for example), and explains why biblical prophecy remains a potent weapon in the hands of the Christian apologist.

Bibliography. J. Urquhart, *The Wonders of Prophecy* (Camp Hill, Pa.: Christian Publications, n.d.); J. B. Payne, *Encyclopedia of Biblical Prophecy* (New York: Harper & Row, 1973); R. Anderson, *The Coming Prince* (reprint ed.; Grand Rapids, MI: Kregel, 1957); H. O. Taylor, "Mathematics and Prophecy," in *Modern Science and Christian Faith,* ed. American Scientific Affiliation (Wheaton, Ill.: Van Kampen Press, 1948); J. W. Montgomery, ed., *Evidence for Faith: Deciding the God Question* (Dallas, TX: Probe, 1991), pp. 173-214 (essays by J. A. Bloom and R. C. Newman); J. W. Montgomery, "Prophecy, Eschatology and Apologetics," in D. W. Baker, ed., *Looking Into the Future* (Grand Rapids, MI: Baker Academic, 2001), pp. 362-70.

17. Schweitzer, Albert

Recipient of the Nobel Peace Prize, Albert Schweitzer (1875-1965) is regarded as one of the great humanitarians of modern times. He made his mark in three very different fields: theology, music, and eleemosynary medicine.

His great work, *The Quest of the Historical Jesus* (1906) put paid to the grandiose "life and times" biographies of Jesus typical of the 19th century. Those works presented Jesus essentially as an evolutionary model for humanity. Schweitzer, however, insisted that one go back to the New Testament documents to discover Jesus' own conception of himself—which, according to Schweitzer, was that of an apocalyptic figure destined to break himself on the wheel of the world and bring in the eschatological kingdom of God.

Though technically a Lutheran Protestant, taking his theological doctorate at the University of Strasbourg during the time the Alsace was incorporated by force into the Second German Reich, Schweitzer was never an orthodox believer. Growing up in the fairy-tale village of Kaysersberg, he imbibed the spirit of Rhenish mysticism (Ruysbroeck, Thomas à Kempis) in which Jesus was a mystical figure to be venerated and imitated (cf. *The Imitation of Christ*) much more than a Saviour expiating our sins through his substitutionary sacrifice on the Cross.

Characteristically, then, though Schweitzer was one of the great modern interpreters of Johann Sebastian Bach on the organ and author of a standard work on that great Lutheran composer, he had great difficulty appreciating the central impact on Bach's life and work of Luther's thoroughly biblical theology.

At the midpoint of his life (age 38), Schweitzer determined to serve humanity not with words or with music, but with deeds. He therefore returned to the University of Strasbourg for a third doctorate, this one in medicine, and subsequently settled in Africa, creating a hospital at Lambaréné (now in Gabon) and returning to western Europe and America only when he needed to raise funds for his humanitarian work.

At Lambaréné he taught the natives "Jesus loves me, this I know, for the Bible tells me so," but he himself did not believe in its literal truth or in the claims Jesus made about himself. Schweitzer joined the Church of the Larger Fellowship, an arm of the Unitarian Universalist Association, thereby making clear that he did not believe in Jesus' deity or in Trinitarian Christianity. Oddly enough, he is still regarded as a Protestant saint in the Alsace and among many church people worldwide. He should, however, be classified as a humanitarian, not as a missionary in the sense of one whose object is to save souls.

Fascinatingly, Schweitzer's medical dissertation at Strasbourg had as its subject, *The Psychiatric Study of Jesus*. In this short work, Schweitzer endeavoured to vindicate Jesus from a charge of mental illness—for how could someone be sane and think that he was the Divine Messiah, come to earth to save it? In the Preface to the English translation, Dr. Winfred Overholser, past president of the American Psychiatric Association, expresses doubt as to the success of Schweitzer's endeavour, since not understanding one's own real character is generally considered a mark of autism.

More important in many ways to Schweitzer than traditional Christian belief was his commitment to "reverence for life." Though this connects well with current environmentalist emphases both within the church and without, it also has its dark side. Medical and lay visitors to Lambaréné reported their concerns over Schweitzer's reticence to kill even insects within the hospital.

Bibliography. A. Schweitzer, *Out of My Life and Thought* (Baltimore: Johns Hopkins University Press, 1998); A. Schweitzer, *Reverence for Life,* trans. R. H. Fuller (New York: Harper & Row, 1969); A. Schweitzer, *The Psychiatric Study of Jesus* (Boston: Beacon Press, 1958); J. Brabazon, *Albert Schweitzer: A Biography* (2^d ed.; Syracuse: Syracuse University Press, 2000) [hagiographical, but comprehensive].

18. Trinity

One of the key defining doctrines of historic Christianity, held by all branches of the Christian church, Eastern Orthodox, Roman Catholic, and Protestant. Trinitarian doctrine asserts that God is one in nature and essence and exists in three equally powerful, equally eternal persons, Father, Son, and Holy Spirit. This conception of God is taught, implicitly or explicitly, in all three of the "Ecumenical Creeds" of the church: the Apostles' Creed, the Nicene-Constantinopolitan Creed, and the Athanasian Creed.

Today's critics of Trinitarianism, such as Elaine Pagels and other advocates of early Gnosticism, argue that the doctrine appeared late on the scene, was a product largely of Greek philosophical speculation, and was impressed on the church by the Council of Nicaea (4th century) after the ruthless suppression of Gnostic and other heretical views which allegedly went back to the time of the Gospels. This conspiracy theory has little to commend it and there is no significant difficulty in showing Trinitarian doctrine to be central to Jesus' own teachings in the Synoptic Gospels and the Gospel of John.

Jesus' so-called Great Commission, given to his disciples after his resurrection and prior to his ascension into heaven is thoroughly Trinitarian: "Go and baptise in the name [one name—singular noun] of the Father, and of the Son, and of the Holy Spirit" (Matthew 28:19). Jesus declares that "I and the Father are one" and "he who has seen me has seen the Father" (John 10:30; 14:9). Jesus also promises (John 14:16) that he will send the Holy Spirit—"another Comforter," the original text referring to "another of the same kind qualitatively (*allos*)" as himself, not "another of a different kind (*heteros*)." True, Jesus spoke Aramaic, not Greek; but there is no basis for arguing that the earliest records of his words do not accurately represent what he in fact said. Since Jesus identifies the Holy Spirit with himself and also identifies himself with the Father, it follows that the Holy Spirit is also to be identified with the Father. Together with these identities, the Gospel records present the Father, the Son, and the Holy Spirit as having distinct personalities and being engaged in the performance of separate, though often simultaneous, acts (as at Jesus' baptism). In Jesus' own teaching, therefore, Father, Son, and Holy Spirit must be considered separate Persons united in one Godhead.

Since the rise of modern biblical criticism, the argument has frequently been heard that the Gospel records do not represent the actual words of Jesus but only teaching placed in his mouth by the "faith experience" of the early Christian communities (and thus that those words are an insufficient basis for establishing Trinitarian doctrine). But the difficulty with making this case is twofold. First, we have no documents earlier than the Gospels themselves to tell us what Jesus said, so all "higher critical" or "redactionist" attempts to get behind those records to something more representative of Jesus' actual beliefs inevitably fall into subjectivism—or into literary analyses which say little more than that the Gospel writers did not employ the stylistic criteria of the critic. Secondly, if this position were correct, one would need to find a source or sources other than Jesus himself to account for the early church's Trinitarian "faith experiences"; no such sources, however, have been successfully identified.

Unquestionably, the church's final acceptance of Trinitarianism as being essential to salvation—explicitly stated in the Athanasian Creed—was preceded by doctrinal struggles during the Patristic period. By the end of the 3rd century, the two forms of Monarchianism—Modalism and Adoptionism—had come and gone (these positions held that the Christ was but a "mode" of Divine activity or had been "adopted" by the Father for his saving role). Fourth-century Arianism constituted the most influential deviant view; it was based on the teachings of Lucian of Antioch and his more famous disciple, Arius of Alexandria. The Arian view maintained that since a son had to be younger than his father, Christ must have been the first created being and could not be co-eternal with God the Father. But Jesus' own teachings ultimately prevailed through the labours of theologians such as Athanasius, and at the Council of Nicaea Arianism was declared incompatible with orthodox Christianity.

In modern times, the Arian denial of Trinitarian teaching has been revived by the Jehovah's Witness sect. They argue that, owing to the absence of the definite article before the Greek word for God in John 1:1 ("The Word was God

... and the Word was made flesh"), the text asserts only that Jesus was "divine," not the incarnation of the God of the Old Testament. The problem with this exegesis is that it disregards not only "Colwell's rule" (reversal of word order, as here, establishes definiteness without the use of the definite article) but also the clear testimony later in the same Gospel that the resurrected Christ himself accepted the attribution of Deity (Thomas: "My Lord and my God [definite article present]" (John 20:28).

Unitarians, successors of the left-wing Socinians of the Reformation period, have claimed that Trinitarian teaching is irrational ("three does not equal one"). However, if Jesus did in fact present that teaching as true, and if he demonstrated his Deity by rising from the dead, then to suppress a part of what he taught is to fly in the face of the facts. The competent scientist takes into account all relevant data, even if he or she cannot put it into a satisfactory rational scheme. Thus, physical light is regarded as both corpuscular and undulatory even though particles and waves are rationally incompatible; the "photon" (a wave-particle, the unit of light) is required by the full range of the physical data. In like manner, "Trinity" functions theologically as a description of God's nature, revealed by God himself in Christ—not as an explanation but as an effort to embrace the totality of revelational data.

Moreover, adherents of unitarian theologies or religious positions which deny the Trinity (e.g., Islam) face real difficulty in proclaiming the inherently loving character of God. If God is indeed love, and has always been so (even before he created other persons), he would have to be more than monopersonal, since love by definition requires both a personal subject and a personal object.

Bibliography. A. C. McGiffert, *A History of Christian Thought,* Vol. I (New York: Charles Scribner's Sons, 1932), pp. 246-57; J. L. Neve, *A History of Christian Thought,* Vol. I (Philadelphia: Muhlenberg Press, 1946), pp. 106-124; J. Thompson, *Modern Trinitarian Perspectives* (New York: Oxford University Press, 1994); T. F. Torrance, *The Christian Doctrine of God: One Being Three Persons* (Edinburgh: T. & T. Clark, 2002); J. S. Feinberg, *No One Like Him: The Doctrine of God* (Wheaton, IL: Crossway Books, 2006); J. W. Montgomery, *Tractatus Logico-Theologicus* (Bonn, Germany: Verlag für Kultur und Wissenschaft, 2004), sec. 2.8; 3.5; 3.74.

19. Truth

Pontius Pilate's ironic question, "What is truth?" poses the central epistemological question for both philosophy and theology.

Philosophically, the fundamental issue is between those who hold truth to be absolute and those who maintain relativistic views of the nature of truth. Absolutists have generally maintained a *correspondence* understanding (truth is what corresponds to external reality), whilst relativists commonly hold to a *coherence* view (truth is found in internal consistency). Boston University philosopher Edgar Sheffield Brightman endeavoured to combine these insights by defining truth as *systematic consistency* (a true statement fits the facts of the external world and is internally consistent), and that approach was echoed theologically by Edward John Carnell (*An Introduction to Christian Apologetics*). More recently, the so-called Post-modernists have embraced a scepticism lying somewhere between solipsism (there is no external reality) and existentialism (one's personal existence determines the character of things): "My world is not necessarily your world, nor my story your story."

Theologically, a Post-modernist approach is generally regarded as incompatible with the thrust of Christian revelation, which asserts that the world is God's objective creation and the de facto object of his redemptive love in Christ. Moreover, where consistency appears to conflict with factuality (as in the case of Trinitarian doctrine or the tension between divine election and human freewill), theology chooses *fact*—for "God's ways are not our ways, nor his thoughts our thoughts."

Among contemporary theologians, ideological conflict is often seen between truth as *objective event* (the factual reliability of the written Word, the Scriptures, and the events of the human life of Christ, the living Word) and truth as *personal commitment* (Jesus' affirmation that he personally is "the way, *the truth, and the life*"). But the two are surely not incompatible, since, in the final analysis, it is the truth of God's objective revelation which justifies commitment to its personal centre: Jesus Christ as Saviour and Lord.

Bibliography. G. Pitcher, ed., *Truth* ("Contemporary Perspectives in Philosophy"; Englewood Cliffs, N.J.: Prentice Hall, 1964); *Encyclopedia of Philosophy*, ed. Paul Edwards (8 vols. and Supplement; New York: Macmillan 1967-1996), arts. "Truth," "Coherence Theory," "Correspondence Theory"; J. W. Montgomery, "The Theologian's Craft," in his *The Suicide of Christian Theology* (Minneapolis: Bethany, 1970) [in this volume, Part Two, chap. 1]; J. W. Montgomery, *Tractatus Logico-Theologicus* (Bonn, Germany: Verlag für Kultur und Wissenschaft, 2004).

20. Vaughan Williams, Ralph

Vaughan Williams (1872-1958) is often interpreted from the standpoint of his quintessential Englishness, as manifested in the clear influence of Tudor music and the English folk song and dance on his work. Simon Heffer says of him that he challenges "Elgar's hitherto unquestioned supremacy as the leading composer of the English musical renaissance."

However, Vaughan Williams' lasting impact may well lie far more in his contributions to church music than in any other realm. He contributed significantly (1904-1906) to the *English Hymnal* and co-edited *Songs of Praise* (1925; enlarged edition, 1931). These contain six original tunes composed by him, plus no less than thirty arrangements from his hand. Michael Kennedy observes that "several hymn service-books were based on *Songs of Praise* and the BBC's religious broadcasts, when they began, used it regularly." Vaughan Williams also co-edited the *Oxford Book of Carols*. His quasi-opera, *The Pilgrim's Progress*, which he himself described as a "Morality in a prologue, four acts and an epilogue founded on Bunyan's allegory of the same name," contains a new tune for the classic hymn, "Who Would True Valour See"—Vaughan Williams' earlier version, "*Monk's Gate*," having passed into most of the standard Protestant hymnals.

What was Vaughan Williams' own religious position? His second wife, Ursula, herself not a Christian believer, writes in a discursive biography of her husband: "He was an atheist during his later years at Charterhouse and at Cambridge, though he later drifted into a cheerful agnosticism: he was never a professing Christian." But this is very hard to accept in terms of the depth of biblical and theological feeling expressed in his compositions—to say nothing of his appreciation of Johann Sebastian Bach. One need only consider "*Sine Nomine*," Vaughan Williams' magnificent setting of "For All the Saints." Though he left no personal testimony, one of his letters may well provide a most helpful light on his religious perspective. In 1952, he wrote to one of the organisers of the Leith Hill Festival: "I am amazed to hear that some members of your choir have taken exception to the beautiful words of Holst's *Tomorrow shall be my Dancing Day,* apparently on the grounds firstly that dancing and religion are something apart and consequently that it is wrong to use the words 'This have I done for my true love' in connection with a statement of the central doctrines of Christianity. ... What about the 150th Psalm, 'Praise Him with the timbrel and dances'? Surely Bunyan's *Pilgrim's Progress* is full of the highest religious fervour and he makes Mr. Ready-to-Halt celebrate his deliverance by dancing. ... As regards my other point, human love has always been taken as a symbol of man's relationship to divine things. *The Song of Solomon* has been treated in all the churches as a symbol of the relationship of God to man. And what about Isaiah and his 'beloved's vineyard'? And is not the Church in the Book of Revelation always symbolized as the bride?"

To be sure, in Anglicanism, where doctrinal subscription is *quatenus* rather than *quia,* and where contemporary secular composers (the Lloyd Webbers, *et al.*) received their early training in church choirs, there is no guarantee that church musicians are necessarily believers. But in the case of Vaughan Williams, the burden of proof surely is not on those who hold that he deeply believed in the truth of what he set to enduring music.

Bibliography. R. Vaughan Williams, *National Music and Other Essays* (2^d ed.; Oxford: Oxford University Press, 1987); M. Kennedy, *The Works of Ralph Vaughan Williams* (London: Oxford University Press, 1964 [a comprehensive biography]; U. Vaughan Williams, *R. V. W.: A Biography* (corrected ed.; Oxford: Clarendon Press, 1984); F. Howes, *The Music of Ralph Vaughan Williams* (London: Oxford University Press, 1954); W. Mellers, *Vaughan Williams and the Vision of Albion* (revised ed.; Ilminster, Somerset: Albion Music, 1997); additional perspectives from Lanalee de Kant Montgomery, harpist under Ralph Vaughan Williams' direction at Cornell University, 21 November 1954.

Index of Names

Index of Names

A

Abu Qurra, Theodore 116
Acton, Lord 520, 588
Adam, Melchior 123, 156, 160, 168, 247, 252, 282, 283, 314, 315
Adams, C. 246
Adams, Charles Kendall 357
Adler, Mortimer 182
Agassi, Joseph 47
Aiken, Howard 92, 93
Aitken, Jonathan 431
Albert, Charles S. 328, 350, 353, 619
Albrecht, W. W. F. 59
Aldrich, Virgil C. 67
Alexander, Archibald 34
Allan, Jim 397
Allbeck, W. D. 148
Allen, Woody 20
Althamer, Andreas 118
Althaus, Paul 601
Alt, Heinrich 374
Altizer, Thomas 26
Amann, Jacob 526, 527
Andersen, Hans Christian 389
Anderson, R. 84, 454, 584, 591, 594, 617
Andrada, Diego 362, 363, 364
Andreae, J. V. 68, 82, 83, 150, 396, 402, 410, 411, 412, 413
Andreson, Terence 184
Applebaum, Wilbur 84
Aquinas, Thomas 77, 78, 79, 117, 125, 147, 174, 199, 245, 523, 608, 609, 610
Archer, Gleason L. 555, 606
Archer, Harry G. 378, 380
Arminius, Jacob 272
Arndt, W. F. 332, 333, 334, 341, 350, 606
Arnold, Paul 403
Astruc, Jean 24
Aube, H. 598
Auden, W. H. 18, 534
Augustine 34, 35, 116, 118, 128, 168, 170, 174, 199, 244, 276, 281, 282, 364, 513, 606, 616
Aulén, Gustaf 64, 145, 256
Austin, John 196
Ayer, A. J. 20

B

Baalen, J. K. 55, 58
Babbage, Charles 78, 91, 92, 93, 94, 95, 96, 97, 98, 99, 100, 101, 102, 103, 254
Bach, Johann Sebastian 7, 118, 506, 618, 623
Bacon, Francis 29, 47, 290, 294
Badehorn, Leonard 359
Baden-Powell 452
Badham, Leslie 129, 130
Baecher, Robert 526
Bahnsen, Greg 122
Bailey, L. R. 546, 600
Baillet, A. 314
Baker, D. W. 38, 84, 114, 294, 313, 612, 617
Bakker, Jim 499
Ball, V. C. 175
Baltazar, E. R. 614
Barraclough, G. 350
Barrett, C. K. 309
Barr, James 606
Bartchy, S. Scott 429

Index of Names

Barth, Karl 25, 26, 51, 52, 55, 117, 118, 144, 250, 312, 392, 429, 453, 565, 610, 611, 612
Bastible, James 63, 251
Batiffol, Pierre 373
Battles, Ford Lewis 138, 252
Bauckham, R. 605
Baum 301, 302, 303, 312
Bauman, Michael 29
Baxter, M. 316, 616
Baylay, Atwell M. Y. 373
Beattie, James 260
Beauregard, Mario 107
Beckett, Samuel 104
Beecher, Lyman 434
Beecher Stowe, Harriet 434
Bell, M. N. M. 215, 217, 218, 290, 291, 350, 552
Belmonte, Kevin 433
Benchetrit, Samuel 172
Benchley, Robert 23
Bender, Thomas 424
Bennett, Dean 515
Bennion, Francis 240
Bentham, Jeremy 184, 196
Bentley, J. 613
Berbig, George 328, 329, 333, 337, 339, 340
Berg 29
Berger, Peter 148, 162, 276, 277, 417, 513
Berkouwer, G. C. 298, 312, 499
Bernanos, Georges 29
Besant, Annie 403
Besse, Clément 89
Beumer, Johannes 73
Beyleveld, D. 203, 590
Bickerton, L. M. 195
Biermann, Kurt R. 254
Birks, Thomas Rawson 249, 254
Black, Jonathan 229, 231
Black, Max 44, 45, 47
Blackmun, Harry A. 220
Blackstone, William 194, 212, 219, 229, 230, 231, 576
Blanke, Helmut 429
Blau, Joseph Leon 410
Blocher, Henri 548
Bloom, J. A. 617
Bluche, Francois 547, 549, 550
Boehmer, J. H. 597
Bohr, Niels 23
Bonar, Horatius 416
Bond, John J. 350
Bond, Julian 425
Bonhoeffer, Dietrich 580
Bonk, J. J. 451
Bonner, Anthony 80, 82, 609
Bora, Catherine 321
Borchert, Donald M. 188
Bork, Robert 32, 33, 292
Bornkamm, Günther 311, 604
Boswell, James 546
Bouillard, Henri 52
Bourne, George 435
Bouwsma, O. K. 43, 69, 70
Bowles, T. G. A. 215, 217
Bowman, Robert M. 118, 119
Boxsel, Matthijs 164
Brabazon, J. 619
Bracewell, Ronald N. 245
Bradley, F. H. 20
Braithwaite, R. B. 46, 47
Branagan, Thomas 433, 434
Bratza, Nicolas 457
Breen, Quirinus 311, 312
Brendon, Piers 452
Brian, Denis 271

Brightman, E. S.   122, 166, 167, 622
Brilioth, Y.   299, 300, 301, 302, 303, 305, 306, 312
Brion, Marcel   261
Brock, G. S.   74
Brohi, A. K.   207
Bromiley, G. W.   259, 274, 429, 608
Bronner, Ethan   33, 292
Broom, Herbert   289
Broughton, William   124
Brown, Harold   233
Brown, Raymond E.   514
Bruce F. F.   51, 133, 176, 180, 286, 312, 504, 584
Brully, Pierre   302, 303
Bruner, Kurt   396
Brunner, Emil   36, 610, 611, 612
Brüsz, Theodore   302
Bucer, Martin   302, 306
Buckland, W. W.   425
Buddeus, J. F.   430
Bulloch, Penelope   197
Bultmann, Rudolf   25, 26, 54, 55, 56, 61, 144, 287, 502, 604, 605, 611
Bungener, L. F.   355, 371
Bunyan   79, 570, 608, 623
Burckhardt, Jakob   67
Burque, Francois Xavier   255
Burrows, Roland   290, 291
Buswell, J. Oliver, Jr.   60, 252
Butler   120, 529, 610
Buxton, Alfred   449, 450, 454
Buxton, Edith   454
Byrne, J.   290

C

Cailliet, Emile   87
Caldecott, Stratford   398
Calver, Clive   504
Calvin, John   55, 138, 139, 140, 141, 142, 143, 252, 273, 298, 299, 300, 301, 302, 303, 304, 305, 306, 307, 308, 309, 310, 311, 312, 313, 350, 354, 368, 371, 606
Cameron, Gail   431
Campanella, Tommaso   247
Campbell-Kelly, Martin   92, 94, 97
Camus, Albert   539, 540
Caparros, E.   598, 602
Carey, George   506, 507, 510
Carles, Jules   237
Carlson, J. D.   600
Carnegie, Dale   31
Carnell, Edward   60, 116, 122, 124, 128, 415, 499, 622
Carroll, Sean M.   21, 104, 105, 106, 108
Cass, Frank   432
Cassirer, Ernst   67, 364
Catterall, Helen T.   436
Chandler, H. P.   175
Chardin, Teilhard   249
Charon, Jean E.   76
Chaunu, Pierre   551
Chemnitz, Martin   15, 65, 149, 251, 350, 352, 353, 354, 355, 356, 357, 361, 362, 363, 364, 365, 366, 367, 368, 369, 370, 371
Chenu, M. D.   79
Chesterton, G. K.   15, 124, 248, 388, 389, 390, 391, 392, 525, 529
Chkhikvadze, V. M.   229
Chomsky, Noam   104
Christian W. A.   614
Christopher, Joe R.   394
Chytraeus, David   149, 153, 256, 283
Ciardi, John   66

Index of Names

Cicero, Marcus Tullius 199
Clarke, W. N. 55
Clark, Gordon 52, 122, 144, 151, 598, 621
Clarkson, A. 602
Clarkson, Thomas 431, 432
Clifford, Ross 124, 441
Closen, M. L. 224
Clymer, R. Swinburne 404
Cobb, John B. 54, 55, 614
Coke, Edward 212, 229, 281
Collingwood, R. G. 67
Collins, Francis 567
Collins, Gary 439
Comrie, John D. 326
Condorcet, M. J. A. 425
Contarini, Giulio 367
Conzelmann, H. 515, 604
Cook, Rebecca J. 218, 238, 239
Copernicus 50, 53, 254
Copleston, Frederick C. 77, 542
Corkill, M. M. 326
Cotta, John Frederick 333, 335, 351
Couchoud 401
Coulson, N. J. 179
Cowan, Steven B. 193
Cowie, Leonard W. 433
Craig, William 101, 123, 124, 606
Craven, J. B. 411
Crews, Frederick C. 26, 27, 28, 569
Cricket, Jiminy 442, 443, 445, 533, 577
Crick, Francis 37, 45, 46, 49, 52
Crispin, Ken 601, 602
Croce, Benedetto 67
Cronhelm, Frederick William 255
Cronin, K. 595
Crooke, Stan 431
Cross, Rupert 290
Crowe 73, 245, 247, 255, 261
Cubreacov, Vlad 457
Cullmann, Oscar 548
Culpepper, Emily 518, 519, 520
Cunitz 302
Cunningham, Richard 538

D

Daiches, David 122
Daisenberger 612
Dalham, Florian 525
Daly, C. B. 44
Daly, Mary 519
Dankbaar, Willem Prederik 308, 312
D'Arcy, M. C. 79
Darwin 96, 120, 287, 288, 548
Daube, D. 177
Dau, W. H. T. 293
Davis, Charles 255
Davis, David Brion 423, 424, 430, 431, 437, 438
Dawkins, Richard 14, 22, 110, 111, 112, 119
Day, David 394
Debus, Allen G. 411
De Concilio, J. 246
Dedler, Rochus 613
Dejob, Charles 371
Delany, V. T. H. 508
Delors, Jacques 550
Deloux, Jean-Pierre 393
Dembski, William 123, 567
Derrida, Jacques 26, 130, 542
Descartes 246, 542
Desmond, Adrian 287
Destro, R. A. 240
Devlin, Lord 574

Dickens, Bernard 66, 171, 212, 214, 218, 238, 239, 385, 528
Dick, Steven J. 245, 246
Diemer, H. 613
Diemer, Hermine 563
Digby, K. E. 231, 232
Dilly, C. 432
Dilly, E. 432
Doe, N. 220, 221, 226, 598
Döllinger, Johann 371
Donaldson, Terry 393
Donne, John 170, 603
Donnelly, Jack 205
Dostoyevsky 37, 105
Doumergue, E. 138, 140, 141, 143, 299, 300, 301, 302, 303, 305, 313
Dowie, William 398
Doyle, Conan 64, 388
Dresser, Matthew 314, 315, 315, 321
Drewermann, Eugen 501, 502, 503, 523, 524, 525
Dreyfus, F.-G. 548
Duchamp, Marcel 37
Dugdale, Anthony M. 210
Dulles, Avery 114
Dumont, Jean Christian 429
Duquaire, Henri 249
Dworkin, Ronald 196, 197, 198, 211, 291, 292, 420, 439, 521, 522, 523

E

Earman, John 19, 98, 108, 122, 188
Easton, Susan 279
Ebeling, Gerhard 54, 604
Eccles, John 107, 271, 542
Edersheim, Alfred 509
Edgar, William 114
Edmonds, David 33
Edwards, Paul 622
Edwords, Fred 104, 105
Eekelaar, John 291
Ehrenreich, Barbara 31
Eidinow, John 33
Einstein, Albert 23, 48, 105, 188, 271, 276, 503, 552
Elchinger, Léon 548
Eler 382
Elert, Werner 36, 69, 283
Eliot, T. S. 21, 388
Elliott, Charles 435
Elliott, J. K. 515
Ellwood, Gracia Fay 397
Elton, G. R. 36
Encausse, Gérard 403
Engelder, T. 59
Engle, George 290
Erikson, Erik 399
Ernst, M. L. 220
Erskine, John 454
Erskine, John T. 440
Esher, Lord 29
Evans, Jim 292
Evans, Robley 397

F

Faizant, Jacques 547
Falwell, Jerry 498, 501
Farrar, John H. 210
Farrell, Robert T. 398
Feinberg, J. S. 166, 168, 542, 621
Ferré, Frederick 45, 57
Finch, John 224
Finkelman, Paul 436
Finney, Charles 114
Finnis, John 199, 200, 201, 222, 238
Fischer, Robert H. 310, 313

Index of Names

Fitzgerald, Mike 393
Fitzmyer, Joseph A. 514
Fitzpatrick, Peter 291
Flaherty, D. H. 230
Fleischacker, Samuel 278, 279
Fletcher, Joseph 282
Flew, Antony 22, 106, 108, 165, 513, 567
Fludd, Robert 410, 411, 412
Foelsch 381
Fosdick, Harry Emerson 56, 392
Foster, Michael 70, 77
Fraenkel, P. 612
Frame, John 122
Frankena, W. K. 238
Frederick, John 318, 322
French, David P. 246, 260
Freud, Sigmund 27, 32, 134, 568, 569, 570
Friedman, S. S. 194, 613
Friedrich, C. J. 352, 585
Frossard, André 109
Froude, James Anthony 357, 358, 371
Fuchs, Ernst 54, 604
Fuller 122, 197, 383, 498, 499, 605, 619
Funk, Robert W. 25

G

Gaine, Simon Francis 276
Galileo 50, 53, 247
Galpin, Brian 290
Gardner, Martin 80, 402, 410, 608
Garnett, A. C. 43
Geisler, Norman 14, 123, 125, 193
Gerblich, Walter 84
Gerecht, Reuel Marc 126
Gerhard, Johann 15, 54, 60, 65, 328, 329, 330, 331, 332, 334, 335, 336, 337, 338, 339, 340, 344, 345, 349, 350
Gewirth, Alan 202, 203, 427, 575, 576, 577, 589, 590
Ghandi 591
Gillispie, C. C. 81
Gilson, Etienne 41, 79
Gingerich, Owen 108
Gish, Duane T. 46
Glenn, G. D. 220
Glover, Ken 435
Gluckman, Max 177
Goddard, Burton L. 449
Gomien, D. 459, 461, 473, 474
Goodspeed, E. J. 529
Gorby, John D. 233
Gordon, Cyrus H. 437
Gould, C. 405
Gould, Rupert T. 74
Grabbe, Lester 555, 556, 557
Grace, W. G. 442
Gradgrind, Thomas 66
Graf 24
Graham, Billy 122, 286, 395, 498, 551
Grant, George 433
Grass, Hans 311, 313
Gray, John Chipman 201
Greenleaf, Simon 15, 124, 133, 176, 181, 183, 201, 220, 523, 523, 567, 583, 585, 591, 594
Gribbin, John 256
Groothuis, D. 610
Grotius, Hugo 110, 118, 567
Grubb, Norman 441, 443, 450, 454
Grynaeus, Simon 341, 343
Guégan, Bertrand 415

Guiata, Stanislas	403	Hay, William	255
Guitton, Jean	401, 548	Hazard, Paul	539
Gundry, Robert	556	Heffer, Simon	41, 623
Gundry, S. N.	130, 294	Hegel	19, 20, 21, 120, 201, 202, 287, 590, 614

H

		Heidegger, M.	20, 43, 55, 120, 604
Haber, Karen	398	Heim, Karl	67
Habermas, Gary	123, 203	Heindel, Max	400, 406, 407
Hacker	292	Heisenberg	23, 24, 26, 27, 613
Hägglund, Bengt	351	Helmholz, R. H.	598
Hahn, L. E.	614	Henry, Carl F. H.	160, 104, 31, 120, 183, 283, 312, 350, 412, 434, 436, 499, 501, 597, 598
Hailsham of St Marylebone, Lord Chancellor	441, 603		
Hall, Albert	543	Herbert, George	412
Hall, David	29	Herrnstein, R. J.	552, 553, 554
Hammond, Peter	422, 450, 455	Hertzberg, Arthur	425
Hanks, G. C.	600	Herzog	373
Hanson, N. R.	48, 49, 50, 76, 555	Hick, John	57, 62
Harding, E. F.	91	Higton, Tony	531
Harding, Rosamond	41	Hilbert, David	106
Harnack, Adolf	135, 556	Hill, John	326
Harris, D.	460, 461, 462	Hindle, Brooke	249
Harrison, R. K.	555	Hindmarsh, Bruce	431
Harris, W. L.	211, 221, 291, 444, 459, 473, 474, 475, 598	Hirschl, S. D.	175
		Hitler, Adolf	569
Hart, H. L. A.	196, 197, 291, 292, 293, 521, 574	Hobbes, Thomas	203, 587, 589
		Hochschild, Adam	431
Hartshorne, Charles	48, 166, 613, 614	Hodge, Charles	34, 252
		Hoefer	314, 326
Haskins, Charles Homer	597	Hogg, Quintin	441
Hassold, Henry	354	Holdsworth, W.	229
Hastie, William	278	Hollander, Barnett	436
Hastings, James	351	Holmes, Sherlock	18, 64
Hauck	373	Honeycomb, P. R.	27
Haugen, G. A.	595	Hong, E. H.	605
Hawking, Stephen	21, 22, 276	Hong, H. V.	605
Hay, Charles A.	372	Hooper, Walter	25, 284
Hayes, Carlton J. H.	351	Hoover, Roy W.	25
Haynes, Stephen R.	287	Hordern, William	43, 44, 72

Horn	379
Horn, Edward	374
Horn, Edward T.	374
Howard, Roy J.	287
Howe, John	67, 396, 398
Howes, F.	624
Huber, Otto	564
Hughes, Alan M.	528, 531
Huizinga, Johan	67
Humboldt, Alexander	254
Hume, David	19, 98, 99, 100, 101, 108, 122, 165, 174, 188, 260, 542, 546, 602
Humphry, D.	603
Hunt, Alan	291
Hurt, John	544
Huss, John	358
Hutchison, John A.	50
Hutin, Serge	403
Hutter, Leonhard	148
Hutton, Ronald	397
Huxley	22

I

Ifrah, George	91, 94, 96, 101, 103
Ionesco, Eugene	536
Isaacs, Neil D.	398
Ivens, Martin	534

J

Jackson, Robert H.	208, 543
Jacobs, Henry E.	69, 353, 354, 356, 361, 362, 370, 372, 375, 376, 377
Jaki, S. L.	610
Janik, Allan	183
Janssen, F. A.	82, 400
Japrisot, Sébastien	45, 67
Jarque, J. E.	261
Jedin, Hubert	371
Jefferson, Thomas	425
Jenkins, Jerry	445, 503, 504, 505, 533, 534, 616
Jennings, Hargrave	402
Johnson, Samuel	509, 515, 516, 530, 545, 546, 547
Johnston, O. R.	273
Jolowicz, H. F.	178
Jonas, Robert E.	233
Jones, R.	237, 315, 402, 403, 412, 598
Jordan, Jeff	89, 90
Jovanovich, Harcourt Brace	248
Jowett, Benjamin	119
Joyce, James	104
Jung, Carl Gustav	27, 47, 132, 394, 396, 397, 503
Junghans, Helmar	326

K

Kadish, Sanford H.	238
Kaehler, Martin	565
Kähler, Martin	26
Kane, Robert	270
Kant, Immanuel	21, 119, 174, 202, 203, 204, 245, 278, 279, 336, 365, 366, 426, 524, 541, 575, 577, 586, 588, 589, 609
Kantzer, Kenneth S.	130, 294
Käsemann	604
Kauffman, U. Milo	397
Kaufmann, Walter	41, 42, 60, 72
Keeler, Christine	543
Kegley, C. W.	605
Keil, Richard	351
Keil, Robert	351
Kelman, Mark	291
Kelsen, Hans	196

Kennedy, Duncan	30, 204, 239, 291, 432, 538, 539, 623, 624	Kurian, G. T.	16
Kent, J.	230	Kuttner, Stephan	597
Kenyon, Frederick	108, 515	Kuyper, Abraham	144
Keown, J.	603		

L

Kepler	47, 49, 50, 53, 83, 84, 85, 87, 412, 539	Lacan, Jacques	132, 133
		Lacerous, Simon	27
Keyer, Thomas	526	Lafuma, Louis	91
Khan, Ghengis	204, 385, 577, 588, 590	LaHaye, Tim	616
		Lane, William	193, 557
Kierkegaard, Sören	20, 104, 118, 120, 336, 351, 353, 354, 365, 384, 396, 604, 605	Langer, Suzanne K.	520
		Langer, William L.	351
		LaRue, Janet	220
Kilby, Clyde	395	Lascelles, Edward C.	432
Kilgour, David	130	Latourette, Kenneth Scott	334, 351, 446, 594
Kirk, Robert	393		
Kiss, Alexandre	235	Lau, Franz	326
Kitchen, Kenneth	555	Lay, Benjamin	430
Kittel, G.	259, 274, 608	Leary, Lewis	433
Klibansky, Raymond	50	Leitch, William	254, 255
Klug, Eugene F. A.	286, 287	Leith, Thomas H.	45
Knight, Robert	196, 261, 313	Lejeune, J.	548
Knox, John	301, 302, 306	Lennon, John	38
Knox, Ronald	390	Lenzen, Victor F.	23
Koertge, Noretta	131	Lessing, Gotthold	119, 174, 542
Koestler, Arthur	590	Levernier, James A.	433
Kolb, Robert	273, 274	Lévi, Eliphas	403
Kommers, D. P.	233	Levy, L. W.	596
Kooiman	311	Lewis, C. S.	25, 56, 79, 104, 110, 116, 122, 124, 164, 166, 169, 181, 195, 248, 249, 255, 258, 259, 260, 284, 315, 370, 371, 388, 389, 396, 398, 399, 400, 407, 500, 511, 512, 524, 525, 541, 541, 542, 556, 567, 608, 613
Körner, Theodor	84	
Kramer, Matthew H.	30	
Krauth, C. P.	326, 353, 371, 376, 382	
Kretzmann, N.	610	
Krodel, Gottfried G.	414	
Kuenen	24	Libavius, Andreas	410
Kuhn, Thomas	23	Liddell-Scott	326
Küng, Hans	55, 501, 606	Lindsell, Harold	499
Kunze, Johannes	352	Linton, I. H.	585

Index of Names

Lipsius, Justus 315
Livingstone, David 288
Livingstone, Priscilla 448
Llinarès, A. 81
Llull, Ramon *see:* Lull, Ramon
Locke, John 203, 589
Lohe, Wilhelm 374
Lonergan, Bernard 53, 72, 73
Longman, Oyez 240
Lorenz, Konrad 524
Löringhoff, Freytag 84, 86
Lossius, Lukas 378, 379, 382
Louis, Roger 46, 59, 63
Lovejoy, Arthur 36
Lowson, Iain 394
Ludwig II, Duke of Bavaria 613
Lull Ramon 9, 78, 79, 80, 81, 82, 83, 92, 101, 102, 103, 117, 608, 609
Luther, Anna 323
Luther, Martin 18, 19, 36, 37, 47, 55, 65, 68, 71, 76, 118, 128, 148, 149, 150, 151, 152, 169, 245, 246, 273, 274, 275, 276, 293, 298, 307, 308, 310, 311, 313, 314, 315, 316, 317, 320, 321, 336, 351, 353, 354, 358, 359, 360, 365, 367, 369, 370, 375, 378, 379, 380, 381, 382, 383, 384, 402, 414, 401, 453, 413, 414, 452, 501, 530, 544, 548, 549, 580, 160, 585, 593, 597, 601, 617, 618
Luther, Paul 15, 314, 315, 316, 317, 318, 319, 320, 321, 322, 323, 325, 326
Lynch, P. 251

M

MacCormick, Neil 240
Macdonald, J. 468, 482
Machen, J. Gresham 528
Mack, Edward C. 452
MacKenzie, Norman 403
Macquarrie, John 43
Macy, Jesse 434
Mahan, Asa 434
Maier, Michael 410, 412
Maistre de, Joseph 260
Maitland, Frederic William 281, 289
Malleswari, V. B. 413
Mangan, J. A. 452
Manning, W. S. 613
Manschreck, Clyde L. 246
Mansfield, Lord 432
Marcel, Gabriel 37, 416, 604
Marga, A. 536, 537
Marie, Jean-Bernard 235
Maritain, Jacques 77
Marschalck, Nicolas 320
Marshall, John 32
Marshall, Keith 394
Martin-Jenkins, Christopher 443
Martin, Walter 71, 80, 247, 289, 313, 314, 385, 429, 445
Marty, M. E. 614
Marx, Karl 27, 568, 569, 570
Masterson, Myron 27
Matscher, F. 468, 482
Maurice, F. D. 46, 57
Maximillian, Duke 340
Maxwell, W. D. 290, 299, 300, 301, 302, 303, 305, 306, 313
Mayer, Thomas 126
McBrayer, William David 432
McCaffray 362
McCloskey 179, 180
McColley, Grant 247
McCormick, C. T. 175
McDowell, Josh 124

McFarlane	565, 566, 567
McGiffert, A. C.	621
McGrath, G. J.	15
McKenzie, Steven L.	287
M'Clintock	357
McLuhan, Marshall	126
McNeill	138, 252, 298, 313, 356
Meadows, A. J.	246
Megivern, J. J.	600
Meister, Chad V.	125
Meiwes, Armin	427
Melanchthon, Philip	149, 157, 160, 246, 315, 321, 351, 353, 358
Melden, A. I.	240
Mellers, W.	624
Mellon, Matthew T.	426
Melville, R. D.	231
Mencken, H. L.	528
Mendelsohn, S.	178, 613
Mendham, J.	356, 357, 367, 371
Menuge, Angus	104, 105
Meynell, Alice	253, 254
Michaud	314, 315, 321, 327
Miles, Sara	288
Milichius, Jacob	317, 321
Millar, James	379
Miller, John Chester	426
Miller, William Ian	282
Milne, A. A.	26
Miodinow, Leonard	22
Mitchell, Mark T.	24
Moedl, Ludwig	564, 565
Mohr, James C.	219
Montvallon, Pierre	547
Moody, Dwight	449
Moore, G. E.	200, 226, 287, 288, 510, 587
More, Thomas	117
Morgan, Edmund	183, 216, 247, 446, 455
Morison, Frank	584
Mortimer, John	104, 165, 538
Mott, John R.	441
Mountfield, Helen	194
Mousnier, Roland	36
Mueller, J. T.	59
Mueller-Vollmer, Kurt	287
Muggeridge, Malcolm	539, 544, 594
Mumma, Howard	132
Mumm, Reinhard	362, 371
Murray, Robert	312, 395, 450, 552, 553, 554

N

Napoleon, Louis	101, 107, 108, 531, 616
Nash, D.	44, 45, 47, 151, 596
Nash, Leonard	44, 45, 47, 151
Neill, Stephen	446
Nelson, Thomas	193
Neve, J. L.	621
Newman, J. H.	104, 109, 110, 120, 124, 507, 538, 539, 567, 617
Newsome, David	451
Newton	50, 53, 271, 420, 431, 433, 448, 531
Nicoll, W. Robertson	259
Niebuhr, H. Richard	611
Nielsen, Kai	592
Niesel, Wilhelm	307, 308, 313
Nietzsche, F.	27, 120, 519, 568, 569
Nigrinus, Georg	354
Nijhoff, Martinus	69, 400, 482
Nisbet, James	42
Nischan, Bodo	327
Nitzsche, Jane	398

Index of Names

Noble, Alistair	104, 105
Noel, Ruth S.	394
Noll, Mark	288
Noonan, John T.	219, 222, 426
Norton, W.	276

O

Oberlin, Jean Frederic	526
O'Boyle, M.	460, 462, 473, 475
O'Brien, Daniel	394
Odgers, Charles E.	290
Oepke, A.	608
Oettingen, Alexander	139
Ogden, S. M.	290, 614
Olander	382
Olbers	105, 165, 610
Oliphint, K. Scott	114, 123
Olson, Elder	28
O'Neill, Timothy R.	394, 397
Orr, James	121
Orwell, George	566
Otten, Herman	385, 386
Ott, Heinrich	54, 61, 63, 250, 251
Otto, Rudolf	69, 230, 551
Overholser, Winfred	618

P

Packer, J. I.	273
Padovano, Anthony T.	250
Pagels, Elaine	619
Paine, Thomas	19, 56, 114, 254, 255, 425, 609
Paley, William	119, 430, 567
Palin, Sarah	105
Pallavicini, Sforza	356, 372
Parsons, Talcott	66
Parton, Craig	562
Partsch, Karl Josef	468, 482
Pascal, Blaise	7, 78, 87, 88, 89, 90, 91, 92, 101, 102, 103, 109, 110, 118, 119, 339, 425
Patterson, Orlando	423
Pauli, W.	47
Pauli, Wolfgang	22
Pauwels, Louis	548, 549
Payne, J. B.	617
Peake, A. S.	259
Peale, Norman Vincent	31
Pearce, Joseph	399
Peerman, D. G.	614
Peirce, C. S.	48, 49
Péladan, Joseph	403
Pelagius	364
Pelikan, Jaroslav	61, 336, 351, 353, 354, 365, 372, 384
Pensées, Pascal	7
Perkins, Mary	372
Perry, Michael J.	205, 206
Perutz, Max	46
Peterson, Luther D.	327
Petzold, H.	468, 482
Philippi, Ferdinand	139
Philippi, Friedrich Adolph	138, 139
Phillips, J. B.	109, 180, 518
Pieper, Franz	58, 59, 65, 251, 252, 608
Pike, James	295, 392, 501, 503, 516, 544, 556
Piper, Christine	279
Pitcher, G.	622
Pittenger, N.	614
Plantinga, Alvin	123, 167, 168, 542
Plaskow, Judith	519
Pliny the Younger	379
Plummer, George Winslow	405
Pohle, Joseph	249, 258
Polack, W. G.	373

Index of Names

Polanyi, Michael 24
Pole, Cardinal 367
Polhill-Turner, Arthur 455
Polkinghorne, John 512, 513
Pollock, Frederick 281
Pollock, John C. 433, 445, 455
Pomet 324, 327
Popper, Karl 33, 34, 44, 45, 107, 271, 292, 293, 542, 574
Pracownik, Peter 393
Preus, Robert 15, 60, 153, 251, 383, 384, 386, 500
Preus J. A. O. 352
Preuss Eduard 352
Prévost, R. 81
Pring-Mill, R. D. F. 81, 609
Proust, Marcel 18
Putnam, Hilary 104

Q

Quenstedt, Johann Andreas 65
Quilliet, Bernard 271

R

Racette, Jean 53
Rahner, Karl 55
Ralph, Stephen 325
Ramm, Bernard 114, 143, 144
Rampoldi, Maria Florencia 395
Ramsay, William 557
Ramsey, Ian 52, 53, 57, 67, 68, 70, 71, 76
Rance, Didier 398
Randall, John Henry, Jr. 372
Ranke, L. von 356, 357, 367, 368
Ransford, Oliver 433
Rapids, Grand 248, 252, 259
Rapp, Francis 548, 549
Raspail, Jean 547, 550

Rast, Lawrence R. 377
Ratke, David 374
Ravasi, Monseignor 272
Rawls, John 202, 203, 204, 426, 567, 575, 576, 577, 589
Raymond, Guy 235
Raz, Joseph 197, 292
Reed, Luther D. 301, 313, 340, 351, 369, 372, 373, 374, 375, 378, 379, 380, 381
Rees, Martin J. 106
Rehtmeyer, P. J. 352
Reid, J. K. S. 312
Reid, Thomas 34, 260
Reilly, R. J. 398
Reuss 302, 303, 312
Reymond, Robert 161
Reynolds, Patricia 394
Richter, David 323
Rieke, Richard 183
Riemann, Bernhard 106
Rietschel, Georg 379
Rinser, Luise 523, 524
Rittenhouse, David 248, 249, 258
Robertson, A. H. 234
Robertson, W. 312
Robin, Christopher 27
Robinson, James M. 44, 54, 55, 176, 447, 501, 503, 556, 604
Rorem, Paul 36
Rosenbaum, A. S. 590, 594
Rosenthal, Michael 452
Rosin, Hanna 31
Rossetti, Christina 528
Rossi, Mary Ann 510
Rousseau, Jean-Jacques 203, 546, 551, 578, 589
Rousse, Marylinn 431
Rowling, J. K. 104

Rumpole, Horace 538
Rushdoony, R. J. 596
Russell, Bertrand 56, 102, 110, 540, 542, 614, 615
Ruston, R. 595

S

Sacco 27
Salu, Mary 398
Samarin, William 615
Sammons, Martha C. 248
Sanderson, J. M. 435
Santos, Alex 458
Sarpi, Fra Paolo 356, 372
Sartre, J.-P. 120, 132, 604, 605
Sasse, Hermann 18, 143, 148, 307, 308, 313
Saylor, C. L. 245
Schaeffer, Francis 590
Schaff, Philip 352, 355, 356, 360, 363, 365, 368, 372, 373, 401
Scheible, Heinz 327
Schelling 26
Schiaparelli 23
Schickard, Wilhelm 78, 82, 83, 84, 85, 86, 87, 90, 92, 101, 102, 103
Schiff, Richard 277
Schirrmacher, Thomas 126
Schlink, Edmund 150, 151, 152, 155, 156, 157
Schmauk, Theodore E. 377, 378
Schmid, Heinrich 353, 354, 372
Schmidt, A. J. 158, 430, 438, 594, 595
Schmucker, Beale 376, 377
Schneider, Marcel 396
Schoeberlein 382
Schoenberg 29, 179, 180
Scholz, Heinrich 52

Schroeder, H. J. 363, 369
Schum, David 182, 184
Schwartz, A. U. 220
Schwartz, Daniel 557
Schwarz, Diebold 306
Schwarz, Philip J. 436
Schweitzer, Albert 453, 534, 617, 618, 619
Scruton, Roger 540, 541, 542, 543
Sealy, T. R. 234
Searle, John 22
Séguy, Jean 526
Sehling 374
Seiss, Joseph Augustus 376, 377, 378, 381, 382
Selby-Bigge, L. A. 19
Sennett, J. 610
Sententiae, Menander 164
Sertillanges, A. D. 79
Shain, M. 176
Shannon, Peter 597
Sharp, Granville 290, 432, 433
Sheridan, L. A. 508
Sherlock, Thomas 18, 119, 120, 124, 186, 388, 505, 531, 584
Shockley, William 553
Shriver, George H. 434
Silva, Moises 288
Simeon, Charles 97, 612
Simons, Geoff 78, 100, 101
Simos, Miriam 519
Simpson, W. B. 183, 229, 238
Sim, Stuart 130
Skinner, B. F. 553
Slade, Michael 225
Smith, Wilbur 23, 67, 121, 122, 164, 241, 247, 250, 374, 441, 445, 446, 499, 616
Smits, Edmund 251

Snowden, Robert 239
Solari, Grégory 398
Solotareff, G. 168
Somerville, Margaret A. 224
Spangenberg, Johann 378, 382
Speakman, Linda 516
Spener, P. J. 334
Spengler, Lazarus 414
Sperry, Willard 101, 121
Spielberg, Steven 249
Spitzer, W. O. 245
Spong, Shelby 392
Sproul, R. C. 15, 102, 123, 149, 193, 251
Stackhouse, John 124
Stanton, Lucia 425
Stark, R. 430, 594, 595
Stauffer, Ethelbert 557
Stewart, H. F. 88, 89
Stock, Eugene 455
Strodach, Paul 374, 380, 382
Studd, C. T. 440, 441, 442, 443, 444, 446, 447, 448, 449, 450, 451, 453, 454, 455
Studd, Priscilla 456
Stueckl, Christian 564, 613
Stumm, Hugo 416
Sundem, Garth 29
Swade, Doron 93
Swaggart, Jimmy 499
Swedenborg, Emanuel 244, 247
Swinburne, Richard 104, 123, 167, 188, 567

T

Tannery, P. 246
Tapolyai, Mihaly 537
Taton, René 84
Tavard, George H. 55

Taylor, H. O. 445, 446, 557, 617
Tefft, B. F. 435
Temkin, O. 238
Terry, Richard R. 283, 286, 304, 313
Thatcher, Maggie 550, 553
Theriault, M. 598
Thiele, Edwin R. 507
Tholuck, F. A. G. 299, 313
Thompson, J. 410, 621
Thomson, William A. R. 326
Thorne, Kip S. 276
Thorn, J. 598
Thro, Ellen 112
Tietjen, John 383
Tillich, Paul 25, 26, 42, 54, 57, 61, 62, 250, 400, 556,
Timmins, Nicholas 215
Tökés, László 536
Tolkien, J. R. R. 15, 109, 124, 248, 253, 388, 393, 394, 395, 396, 397, 398, 399, 507
Tooley, Michael 210, 211, 228, 237, 240
Torrance, T. F. 621
Torrey, R. A. 127, 449
Toulmin, Stephen 45, 46, 52, 174, 182, 183
Traina, Robert 60
Trintignant, Jean-Louis 172
Troeltsch, Ernst 351
Tuttle, Kate 31
Twining, William 184
Twining, William L. 183

U

Ukert, G. H. U. 327
Unger, Roberto 30, 204, 291
Urbach, E. E. 428

Index of Names

Urquhart, J. 617

V

Van Til, Cornelius 121, 122, 123, 127, 151, 161, 612
Valla, Lorenzo 364
Vance, Norman 452
Vanhoozer, Kevin J. 131
Vanzetti 27
Varghese, R. A. 22
Vaughan, David J. 433
Veatch, Henry B. 200
Veith, Gene 16, 124, 412
Vere, Aubrey 253, 254
Vickers, Lucy 565, 566
Vincent, Eileen 448, 455
Vitz, Paul 107
Vyver, J. D. 594

W

Wackernagel, Philipp 379
Wade, Roe 30, 214, 220, 221, 222, 233, 236, 238, 241, 520, 582
Wadham, John 194
Waite, A. E. 403, 405
Walker, Jean 456
Wallace, Ronald S. 307, 309, 313, 433
Wallon, Henri 429
Walls, Jerry 275
Walsh, James 79, 608
Walters, Thomas B. 445, 455
Walther, C. F. W. 293, 585
Waltke, Bruce 555
Walvin, James 431
Wamboldt, W. J. S. 602
Warbrick, C. 460, 462, 473, 475
Warburton, William 430, 509
Ward, Stephen 543, 544
Ware, Jim 396
Warfield, B. B. 34, 121, 127, 312, 606
Watson, James 45, 46, 49, 52, 71
Watson, Joanna 422
Webber, Andrew Lloyd 443, 624
Weber, Max 66
Webern 29
Wecker, John Jacob 327
Weil, Simone 529
Weiss, Paul 48, 55, 56
Weizsäcker, Carl von 379
Weldon, Fay 539
Wellhausen 24
Wells, Harry K. 108, 513, 514, 515, 516, 537, 539, 614
Wendel, Francois 307, 313
Wesley, John 431
Westcott, Wynn 403
Whately, Richard 101
Whewell, William 97, 249, 254
White, Andrew Dickson 78
White, B. 432
Whitehead, A. N. 56, 67, 613, 614
White, Ralph 402
Wiethoff, William E. 436
Wigmore, John Henry 182, 183, 184, 188
Wilberforce, William 413, 431, 433
Wilkins, Maurice 46
William, Frederick 320, 323, 326
Williams, Charles 84, 217, 623, 624, 534, 624, 622, 623
Will, Robert 273
Wilmes, Douglas R. 433
Wimsey, Peter 392
Winch, Peter 66, 287
Window, Harvey C. 27

Winfrey, Oprah 31
Winsheimius, Vitus-Ortelius 321
Winston, Morton E. 204, 205
Wirth, Niklaus 91
Wiseberg, Laurie S. 194
Wiseman, D. J. 555
Wise, Steven M. 432
Witte, J. 594
Wittenberg, J. D. 224
Wittgenstein, Ludwig 33, 34, 43, 44, 46, 49, 66, 72, 76, 77, 105, 121, 159, 167, 206, 292, 293, 388, 400, 518, 574, 578
Witt, John 140
Wolff, Robert Paul 204, 589
Wolpert 104, 105, 106, 107
Wolterstorff, Nicholas 34
Woods, G. F. 42, 72
Woolman, John 430
Worrall, John 184
Wright, G. H. 47, 214, 287
Wythe, George 426

Y

Yates, Frances A. 402
Yeats, W. B. 104
Yellen, Sherman 64
Young, Frances 510

Z

Zagzebski, Linda T. 275
Zahar, Elia 184
Zahn, Theodor 135
Zander, Michael 241
Zeiser, Samuel R. 377
Zimbardo, Rose A. 398
Zimring, F. E. 600
Zizek, Slavoj 164
Zuse, Konrad 92
Zuurdeeg, Willem 70, 72
Zwaak, L. 461, 473, 474
Zweerink, Jeff 21
Zwemer, Samuel 79, 608, 609
Zwingli 18, 148, 150, 157, 298, 300, 302, 307

Endorsements

What makes J. W. Montgomery tick? What has driven him over a massively productive career to such wide-ranging interests as computers and Chemnitz, legal theory and apologetics, human rights and Christology, Dawkins and Duchamp? The answer is clear: The gospel of Jesus Christ and its defense, articulation, and application to the real world in which the Word became flesh, died, and rose again as the Savior. Many of our best confessional-era theologians, both Lutheran and Reformed, were "Renaissance men," but that's rarely the case today. Dr. Montgomery is a glaring exception and this book is a wonderful display of that full scope of his remarkable insights. While being an ardent defender of the Lutheran confession, he is far from parochial. Even in places where one might disagree, the clarity, logic, and relentless rigor of his arguments will kindle fires in hearths that we didn't even know we had and make us better advocates for the gospel.

Dr. Michael Horton, J. Gresham Machen Professor of Systematic Theology and Apologetics, Westminster Seminary California

Arguing brilliantly for Christ as the centre of all reality, this book takes the reader on an amazing journey through law, theology, art, apologetics and human rights. In so doing, it is a much needed corrective to the theological confusion and compromise that is often published today. Montgomery, as with all his writings, shows an extraordinary command of the history of ideas and cultural developments which impact us all. The author has the rare ability of wearing his sophisticated scholarship lightly and the book is therefore a wonderful aid to all those who take seriously the biblical injunction to be prepared to give a reason for the hope that is within them (1 Peter 3:15). Montgomery's case for Christ is grounded in a faithfulness to the Bible. Theological liberals and sceptics beware—this book will not only encourage and motivate, it will inspire a new generation of Christian apologists for all areas of life. A must read!

Rev. Dr. Ross Clifford, AM, Principal of Morling Theological College, author of John Warwick Montgomery's Legal Apologetic and Leading Lawyers' Case for the Resurrection, Vice President Baptist World Alliance

A blockbuster from the pen of the polymath Lutheran apologist/lawyer. For anyone interested in the Christian's apologetic call (1 Peter 3:15) but who sees it as an arcane enterprise for "pointy-heads" only, Dr. Montgomery applies the defense of Gospel truth to a breathtaking range of subjects, showing how the

Biblical Christ supplies the only answer for today's secularized people. Regardless of your interest, there is an essay in this volume that will pique that interest (not just apologetics per se, but science, law, philosophy, Reformation studies, systematic theology, literature—even computer science!). And, unlike most tomes on the subject, Dr. Montgomery's can be recommended to non-Christians as a possible "way in."

Dr. Rosenbladt, Professor of Theology & Christian Apologetics: Concordia University Irvine, co-host: the White Horse Inn

John Warwick Montgomery is widely recognized as one of the top evangelical intellectuals during the last half-century. For all those who love his academic writings, this collection of publications is a real treat. Consisting of several dozen essays on a wide variety of topics, one-third of these papers are new publications, while the remainder include items that are not always easy to obtain. The total anthology is sure to interest apologetic students as well as others. I recommend it highly.

Dr. Gary R. Habermas, Distinguished Research Professor, Liberty University & Theological Seminary

W. B. Yeats observed that modernity is flying apart because its center cannot hold. In this scintillating apologetic feast—encompassing everything from legal and literary theory to cosmology and philosophy, and from computer science to gastronomy—Montgomery not only shows how secularism flounders in evasive speculation, but also provides the hard evidence that all things hold together in Christ.

Angus Menuge, Ph.D., D.C.A., Professor of Philosophy, Concordia University Wisconsin, USA

Dr. Montgomery's latest book is one that every serious reader interested in clear Christian thinking should have on a table near her most comfortable reading chair. It is filled with a wide variety of bite-sized essays that are absolutely delightful—knowledgeable, fun, witty, and unexpected. If you have never read the work of J.W. Montgomery before, you are in for a treat. This is a book that brings together his best writing from the past with his latest essays. It's a Christian feast of ideas that celebrates our Lord and His unfailing Word.

Craig J. Hazen, Ph.D., Director, MA Program in Christian Apologetics, Biola University

Once you begin to think about it, you begin to realize that the central convictions of the Christian faith lead us to think differently about almost everything in life, and then we are led to doing things differently. The result is different not only from secularism and atheism but also from other world religions. Professor Montgomery has invested a lifetime in learning how to think in the light of Christ. This means he is a very good person from whom others can learn. Read, think, and learn.

Prof. Dr. Thomas K. Johnson, The Comenius Institute

duct-compliance